The red line drawn on this
to follow the follow

A—B.— The frontier defined by the Treaty of Berlin of 13th July 1878 and by the Treaty of San Stefano of 3rd March 1878.

B—C.— The frontier demarcated by the Turco-Persian Frontier Commission in 1913-14 on the basis of the Protocol signed at Constantinople on the 4(17) November 1913 excepting in sectors *a—b* and *c—d* where the red line is intended to follow the line of the previous *de facto* frontier described on page 139 and 140 of the Minutes of the Frontier Commission in a note dated the 1/14th October 1914 by the Russian and British Commissioners.

C—D—E.— The limit of territorial waters of the Arabian peninsula excepting the Sultanate of Koweit and the Farsan Archipelago.

E—F.— The frontier defined by the Anglo-Turkish convention of 1st October 1906.

F—G.— The red line is intended to follow the decision of the Conference of London on the 13th February 1914 in execution of Article 5 of the Treaty of London of 17/30th May 1913 and Article 15 of the Treaty of Athens of the 1/14th November 1913.

G—H.— The frontier defined by the Treaty of Constantinople on the 16/29th September 1913.

H—A.— The limit of the territorial waters of Turkey in the Black Sea.

BANKING ON BAGHDAD

Also by Edwin Black

WAR AGAINST THE WEAK
Eugenics and America's Campaign to Create a Master Race

IBM AND THE HOLOCAUST
*The Strategic Alliance Between Nazi Germany
and America's Most Powerful Corporation*

THE TRANSFER AGREEMENT
*The Dramatic Story of the Pact
Between the Third Reich and Jewish Palestine*

FORMAT C:
A Novel

BANKING ON BAGHDAD

Inside Iraq's 7,000-Year History
of War, Profit, and Conflict

EDWIN BLACK

WILEY

John Wiley & Sons, Inc.

Published by John Wiley & Sons, Inc., Hoboken, New Jersey.
Published simultaneously in Canada.

Part and Chapter Openers are details of the gates and doorways of the Madrasa al-Mustansiriya in Baghdad built 1227–1234. Photos by Kevin O'Hara/age fotostock america, inc. Reproduced with permission of age fotostock america, inc.

For general information on our other products and services please contact our Customer Care Department within the United States at (800) 762-2974, outside the United States at (317) 572-3993 or fax (317) 572-4002.

Wiley also publishes its books in a variety of electronic formats. Some content that appears in print may not be available in electronic books. For more information about Wiley products, visit our web site at www.Wiley.com

Library of Congress Cataloging-in-Publication Data:
Black, Edwin.
    Banking on Baghdad : inside Iraq's 7,000-year history of war, profit, and conflict / Edwin Black.
        p.   cm.
    Includes bibliographical references.
    ISBN 0-471-67186-X (cloth)
    1. Iraq.   I. Title.
    DS70.6.B58 2004
    956.7044'3—dc22

2004018008

Printed in the United States of America

10 9 8 7 6 5 4 3 2 1

BANKING ON BAGHDAD

Inside Iraq's 7,000-Year History of War, Profit, and Conflict

EDWIN BLACK

WILEY

John Wiley & Sons, Inc.

Library of Congress Cataloging-in-Publication Data:
Black, Edwin.
    Banking on Baghdad : inside Iraq's 7,000-year history of war, profit, and conflict / Edwin Black.
        p. cm.
    Includes bibliographical references.
    ISBN 0-471-67186-X (cloth)
    1. Iraq. I. Title.
    DS70.6.B58 2004
    956.7044'3—dc22
                                                                    2004018008

To my father, Harry,
who fought and survived in the forests of Europe
and taught me to question the hidden histories.

CONTENTS

ACKNOWLEDGMENTS

Banking on Baghdad was physically and intellectually exhausting. This project would have been impossible without an elaborate network of assistance. Epic thanks are in order for the many institutions, companies, and individuals who bent over backward to facilitate my work, and the many researchers who devoted themselves to this work. Space does not permit me to list everyone, and I apologize to those omitted.

In my Washington, D.C., office, a tenacious team managed my own private archives and hour-to-hour research needs as we assembled facts from the ancient epochs of prehistory to the latest throes of contemporary times. Hard-driving and intellectually voracious Eve Jones headed up all research and documentation; she employed a hairsplitting sense of accuracy as she helped verify thousands of facts across the millennia, and coordinated researchers across numerous time zones. John Corrado helped Eve in the triple-checking process, ensuring that the physical documentation within more than a thousand footnote folders supported the text; John's rapier-like fact-finding talents helped make our information bulletproof. Paul Dwyer maintained a standby vigil at Washington's best university libraries, digging out rare and obscure limited editions, often appearing just in time with a brimming box of forgotten memoirs or impossible-to-locate academic studies. Paul and Eve also mined important documents at the National Archives in Washington. Eve, John, and Paul are all veterans of the *War Against the Weak* research project, and are all precious intellectual assets.

Some 50,000 documents were filed in my office according to their original archival record group order. Each of these documents was then reviewed for relevant dates and chronologically cross-filed in hundreds of monthly folders. Barb Jewell doggedly organized this painstaking process, with assistance from Rachel Black, Maital Dahan, Shari Fierman, and Eric Moore among others.

Elizabeth Black tirelessly headed up research and documentation for the second half of the twentieth century, and dug through unprocessed files at the New Jersey–based Urman Collection at Justice for Jews from Arab Countries.

Among those outside Washington, of supreme importance was Phyllis Bailey of Montreal, who accompanied me to London and Coventry where we examined thousands of records at the Public Record Office, the British Library, and private oil company archives. Phyllis returned to London and Coventry for follow-up research, and also endured eyestrain at Harvard, scrutinizing thousands of micro-formed League of Nations files.

Several other key researchers in the United States were simply invaluable. Jamie Awamleh in California spearheaded our Islamic research and also spent many sleepless nights delving through the electronic files of the Securities and Exchange Commission as we probed contemporary corporate involvement in Iraq. David Arnold in St. Louis performed spot research on numerous topics, especially diplomatic papers. Deborah Cohn undertook detailed research at the American Jewish Archives in Cincinnati,where she reviewed thousands of documents on Iraqi Jews. Other American researchers include Rachel Shindelman in Chicago, Sveta Zlatareva at Columbia University in New York, and Lorraine Ramsey in Chico, California, who surveyed thousands of pages of American diplomatic papers; Geoff Price in Miami who worked on early twentieth century topics; and Hank Albarelli in the Tampa area, who worked on contemporary corporate structures.

In London, Nick Charles was a researcher's researcher, laboring day after day at the Public Record Office and the British Library; typically we would e-mail or phone in information requests to Nick at night and by the next day the documents had been located, verified, copied, and then mailed across the pond. Other London volunteers, too numerous to mention, helped Nick from time to time, and of them I am appreciative. In addition, Karl Lampl, who worked from Canada, Brazil, and Austria, provided key German translations. French translations were provided by Richard Marcus in Toronto, plus Phyllis Bailey, Eva Bild, and Fred Bild in Montreal.

All of my efforts were contingent on several remarkable archivists. First among them was Peter Housego, BP Archive and Records manager, in Coventry, England. The cooperation of Housego, and indeed that of corporate BP, was nothing short of spectacular, as they provided thousands of pages of documents, often on a punishing schedule. In this effort, Housego was assisted by an energetic staff including Rachel Sampson, Vanna Skelley, Joanna Wong, Bethan Thomas, and Amandeep Birk. BP and the archival profession should rightly be proud of these skilled and dedicated individuals.

Thanks are due to the staff at the Public Record Office, the world's best archive and one that puts many other national archival collections to shame. I have researched at the PRO for decades. Through computerization and a highly skilled staff, every year it becomes easier and easier to identify, retrieve, and reproduce documents. It would be a disservice to laud specific individuals at the PRO because all members of the staff that I have encountered are equally delightful to work with. The PRO is literally a gift to the world.

At the British Library, undoubtedly the world's finest and most inspiring repository of books, we thank key staff, especially Beryl Blair, for being as helpful as humanly possible in locating records and working around the institution's photocopying protocol. The Imperial War Museum photo archivists also provided assistance.

In Coventry, England, I must also thank the staff of the Modern Records Centre at the University of Warwick. The university made every effort to accommodate me. Special thanks are due to Matthew Scott of the housing unit and Peter Dunn of university relations, who responded with alacrity to every request.

Elsewhere in Europe, the Gulbenkian Foundation in Lisbon was profoundly helpful in locating rare photographic and textual materials, and enabling their usage. Thanks are due to Isabel Moura and Gulbenkian Foundation director Jorge Wemans. In Poland, Auschwitz archivist Piotr Setkiewicz extracted, scanned, and transmitted obscure documents, and I thank him for the help. I must also thank certain individuals connected to British and Persian Gulf oil companies, who cannot be named but who made their corporate documents available, thus allowing me to complete the puzzle.

In Israel, we were dazzled by swift and gracious assistance from several archives. At the Central Zionist Archives, Rochelle Rubenstein rushed my requests, as did photo archivist Reuven Koffler and his colleague Reuven Milon. At Hagana Archives, wonderful staffers, including Orly Levi and Ilan Shtayer, dug through their files to verify details and provide copies. At Israel State Archives, Moshe Mosseck, assisted by Michal Saft, was a pleasure to work with, upholding the proud tradition of the ISA. At the Government Press Office Photo Archives, Elana Dayan worked furiously with no notice to locate vital photographic evidence and help make my deadline.

In the United States, the National Archives in Washington extended very special cooperation; here I thank first and foremost Marie Carpenti, and thanks also go to project manager Anne Cummings and State Department archivist Sally Kusiel. At the American Jewish Archives in Cincinnati, Devhra Bennett Jones made it possible to pore through hundreds of files from the post–World War I period. Significant thanks are due to Stanley Urman for opening up his private collection from Justice for Jews from Arab Countries. In addition, we thank Amy Fitch at the Rockefeller Archives outside New York City for facilitating research, and Hassan Mneimneh at the Iraq Foundation in Washington for opening their newly assembled security files. At Harvard's repository for League of Nations files, Vida Margaitis extended technical assistance and hospitality; we were among the first to exploit this newly available collection.

Along with the distinguished archivists, many librarians made all the difference, as they found key passages in rare books and faxed them to my office or extended very special borrowing privileges. These include, first and foremost, Ann Flower, reference librarian at Monterey Institute of International Studies (MIIS); Molly Molloy, reference librarian, Hoover Institute Library, Stanford University; and the Western Washington University Library reference team.

Plus, we thank librarians Sarah Barnhard and Daniel Rettberg at the Klau Library of Hebrew Union College in Cincinnati; Gerald Schwab at the Columbus Public Library; the staff of the Meriam Library at California State University, Chico; the staff at Asher Library of Spertus Institute in Chicago; the staff at the Warwick University Library in Coventry; Kelley Sallade at Rock Hill Public Library in St. Louis; Cyma Horowitz at the American Jewish Committee's

Blaustein Library; Phoebe Acheson, at Duke University's Perkins Library; David Zubatsky at Millersville University Library; Pam Beegle from Miami's NOVA Southeastern University Public Library; Kat Hubschmann at Weiner Library in London; and many others too numerous to mention.

Only two organizations denied me access to their archives. The first was IBM, which repeatedly refused my request to examine World War I–era files relating to Turkey and the Armenians. The second was Halliburton, which repeatedly refused permission to check its historical archives and repeatedly denied such archives even existed. Despite this obstruction, I was able to persevere and locate Halliburton's company archives in Houston, where thousands of files are maintained. It is a trove of well-organized, easily retrievable information.

Special mention is needed for certain individuals who made a difference. These include Rick Shenkman of History News Network, who provided critical access to certain materials. Mitchell Bard of Jewish Virtual Library, Arthur Berger of the United States Holocaust Memorial Museum, Aaron Breitbart of the Simon Wiesenthal Center, Stephen Feinstein of the Center for Holocaust and Genocide Studies at University of Minnesota, and Moshe Gat at Bar Ilan University, all of whom assisted with expedited information from time to time.

Particular thanks must be extended to EDGAR Online Pro, the most effective means of searching Securities and Exchange Commission records; EDGAR Online Pro facilitated use of its powerful retrieval system. Similarly, I thank JSTOR and Proquest for their excellent retrieval systems.

A debt is also owed to numerous experts who carefully and repeatedly read the early pre-nineteenth-century chapters and made numerous suggestions, all of which were incorporated to their satisfaction. For the opening chapter set in Najaf, I thank Lt. Col. Chris Hughes, U. S. Army. In the archaeological section, these include six of the most respected in their field: Hans J. Nissen of the Free University of Berlin, J. Nicholas Postgate of Cambridge University, Robert Englund of UCLA, Abraham Winitzer of Harvard, Martha Roth of Chicago's Oriental Institute, and Denise Schmandt-Besserat of the University of Texas. In the Islamic history and Mongol sections, these include two of the most accomplished Mideast, Islamic, and Mongol experts: David

Morgan of the University of Wisconsin and David Nicolle in England, as well as anthropologist Jack Weatherford of Macalester College. In the Ottoman section, Colin Imber of the University of Manchester was most helpful.

A special thank-you is extended to Sir Martin Gilbert in London, among the world's most prolific and respected historians, for providing some key documentation on Winston Churchill, and for reading my entire manuscript.

As expected, it takes more than historical expertise to bring to fruition a complicated project like *Banking on Baghdad*. I received strategic support from Tom Fogle at Dell Computers. Web work was performed by Les Weber in Minnesota, John Roth in Utah, Kieren Simon in New Zealand, and others. I am grateful for their skills.

Creative inspiration was continually derived from the soundtracks of the incomparable and recently deceased Jerry Goldsmith, as well as Hans Zimmer, John Barry, Danny Elfman, James Newton Howard, Graeme Revell, David Arnold, James Horner, Moby, BT, Paul Van Dyk, Tangerine Dream, Kansas, and Asia. The staff always knew when chapters were being finished. Zimmer or Goldsmith came on, and the volume roared, driving many out of the office.

During the publication of my previous three books, I have been blessed with caring publishers and editors, all of whom were profoundly committed to the projects. However, in John Wiley & Sons, I may have met some of the most supportive and reassuring professionals any author could hope to work with. Here I speak of my editor Matt Holt and marketing manager Michelle Patterson, both of whom continuously—and I mean, daily—put all their efforts behind this project and me as an author. During the many consuming days and sleepless nights, that knowledge steeled me to type yet another page and make the deadline. Holt and Patterson were just the leading edge of an extraordinary, high-energy publication team at Wiley that included publisher Larry Alexander, publicists Mike Onorato and Jessica Church, as well as Helene Godin, plus the many in production who supported them with gymnastics during the compressed schedule, such as senior production editor Micheline Frederick and the team at North Market Street Graphics. Special praise goes to the book cover designer, Michael J. Freeland, who created so many versions and finally settled on one that could speak to 7,000 years of Iraqi history.

In addition, a project like this one required the continuous support and encouragement of my agent Lynne Rabinoff of the Lynne Rabinoff Agency. She marshaled the *Banking on Baghdad* project through every moment of every phase, from inception to publication. Lynne Rabinoff has made my several books available in 13 languages in 60 countries, and thereby helped deliver the fruits of these labors around the world. Nothing sharpens the senses like knowing the audience is everywhere.

As always, I must apologize to my family, friends, and loved ones who thought I could finally reappear after my last book, only to see me disappear again into the tall stacks and towering dramas of history. For authors like everyone else, history repeats itself.

Edwin Black
Washington, D.C.
www.edwinblack.com
August 15, 2004

INTRODUCTION

When you chase the winds of Mideast history the view is often obstructed by sandstorms and mirages. Within that obscurity we find Iraq, whose history swirls around all who enter. In the twenty-first century, the world once again finds itself buffeted by those ancient winds, blinded by future promise, and oblivious to its past. But unless we thoroughly understand Iraq's past, we will never find the answers to the recurring tragedies and conflicts of that all-important region. We won't even know what questions to ask.

We are of course confronted by one dominant question above all others. Iraq—Mesopotamia—was the Cradle of Civilization. The region enjoyed a several-thousand-year head start on the rest of humanity. What happened? How did that society become so victimized and so victimizing, so oppressed and so oppressive, so impervious to its own potential and so entangled with the rest of an exploitative world? No one will understand Iraq, or this question, unless they start at the beginning—the very beginning. That is what I did, probing 7,000 years of Iraqi and Mesopotamian history, from the dawn of civilization to the moonless nights of the Gulf wars, thus allowing me to assemble a tragic epic as sweeping as the story of mankind itself.

Hence, I begin with an apology. I wish I could have written more. But it was not possible to write or publish a book that rightly should be 10 times bigger. Therefore, my work first and foremost became a task of filtering the facts of this monumental history. Indeed, every one of my 18 chapters could have yielded its own thick volume. Every chapter is, in fact, an invitation to read more about these compelling eras, from the rise of civilization, to the conquest of Islam, to the destruction by the Mongols, to the neglect of the Ottomans, and finally to the discovery by the West that Iraq was the indispensable key to its commercial success. What was the basis for that commercial success? Answer: The region's inherent geography and geology gave rise to a crossroads for conflict, conquest, and commerce that has endured through the ages—not because of the people but because of the land they walked on.

In consequence, our story cannot be confined to Iraq—that is, the three provinces between the two rivers that the ancients called "Mesopotamia." What happened in the boardrooms and war rooms of London, Paris, Washington, Constantinople, Bombay, Berlin, Jerusalem, Cairo, Teheran, and even in rural Pennsylvania dictated the realities for the people of Iraq and those who ambitiously intersected with them. Therefore, my investigation encompassed not just the annals of the territories of Iraq, but also the tumultuous inside stories of colonial, political, religious, and commercial upheaval that caused nearly every action and reaction in that country.

To assemble this challenging story, I recruited a team of some 30 researchers (see Acknowledgments) working in the United States, Canada, England, and Israel accessing original documents and obscure materials in some 20 archives and other repositories, as well as nearly 50 libraries in five nations. This includes the private files of British Petroleum, Turkish Petroleum, Anglo-Persian Oil Company, Anglo-Iranian Oil Company, and Iraqi Petroleum, all of which are organically connected entities. The result was a trove of some 50,000 documents, plus hundreds of scholarly books and journal articles that ultimately yielded the dots that connected into a recognizable line. Ironically, in many cases, that line runs in circles. In Iraq, history not only repeats itself; the unstoppable repetition constitutes the very nature of its history—and likely its future.

Although we probed back to antiquity, my team used the most advanced twenty-first-century technology I have yet seen. At any given time, up to a dozen researchers were working in various archives and libraries in such cities as Coventry, London, Washington, or New York. Telephone calls in archives and libraries are strictly prohibited. Instead, we used cell phone text messaging, laptop computers, and wireless PDA to share real-time discoveries about corporations, officials, and themes. For example, we might trip across an obscure executive's name while reviewing documents in an oil company archive; that name was text-messaged out to others standing by at the Public Record Office and the British Library or other repositories where the lead was pursued, with new information coming back to track down further information in the oil company files. Sometimes this international exchange could be accomplished in just moments.

To bridge the gap between cities, we created a private password-protected intranet site where files and information were posted so researchers in various cities could view them just moments after they were discovered. In many cases, we used books so rare that only one copy might be available in London's library system, or only a few copies anywhere in the United States. For example, an obscure volume of published diplomatic papers of Iraq from the 1950s was found in St. Louis. Needed pages of this book and others were scanned by researchers and posted on their private web sites. We could then print them in my Washington office.

In addition, modern databases and digital collections allowed us to instantly search the actual page images for keywords in diplomatic correspondence, newspapers, and journal articles hailing back more than a century. This new digital capability is startling and has redefined historical research. Moreover, because researchers were located in various time zones, research could be done in the Pacific evening or European morning and be ready for us in Washington when we woke up.

As is usual in my works, a hairsplitting, triple-checking documentation team labored with me to footnote nearly every paragraph. Behind every footnote is a folder. Within every folder sit the documents supporting every fact.

The scale of my research is important not because of its technology but because it demonstrates how difficult it is to mine the true facts about Iraq's history, going beyond legends and superficial explanations. Indeed, we often found that the most accepted story or scholarly account was incorrect or could not be verified, especially when traced back to documents and sources. This was important because so much of Iraq's turbulent story is shrouded in shifting mysteries and "almost facts." In fact, there are so many "almost facts" in Iraq's history that the arguments over who actually owns Iraq's oil, where the Iraqi borders lie, and even who the Iraqi people are, create their own saga. This saga of conflicting efforts by outsiders and insiders alike to impose facts on the people and the land is the saga of *Banking on Baghdad*. The clash of cultures, corporations, religions, and governments, each fortified with its self-endowed primacy, fuels the fires that never stop burning in Iraq. The quality of mercilessness in Iraq's history is limitless in all its dimensions. In a country defined by corporate monopoly, cruelty was a commodity freely traded.

To be sure, this book is not politically correct, but it is as historically accurate as humanly possible. In that respect, a few words are needed about some of the companies, ethnic groups, and religions depicted in the book. First, a word about Moslems, Christians, and Jews. We delve into the formative centuries of each religion—the first 200 to 300 years. Islam clearly emerges as violent, conquering, and intolerant in its formative years. I never quoted from the Koran, the Torah, or the Holy Scriptures because all those books can be quoted at will to support any violent or pacific intention desired. Instead, I relied solely upon historical facts—in other words, what the founding fathers and mothers of the religions actually did at the time. If anyone wants to transfer those events to modern-day communities and draw conclusions, they are more than wrong—don't use this book as an excuse.

A word is needed about the Turks. The society created by the Ottoman sultans and then the Young Turks is no longer part of the modern Turkish mind-set. Turkey today stands as a beacon of democracy at the doorstep to the Moslem Middle East.

A word is also needed about British Petroleum, formerly Anglo-Persian Oil Company and Anglo-Iranian, as well as a partner in Turkish Petroleum. BP literally shaped the commercial, political, and military consequences in the modern Middle East. But that imperialist oil company no longer exists, the British government no longer owns part of the firm, and BP's outlook is now one of openness. BP cooperated in every aspect of my investigation, granting me unrestricted access to the sensitive papers I sought in their archives, and went above and beyond in providing documents. Do not judge the company today by their founders of 5 to 10 decades ago. BP's model of openness is one for other former colonial corporations to emulate.

Indeed, with few exceptions (see Acknowledgments), I was granted unfailing cooperation by all the governments, corporations, organizations, and individuals contacted. There is now an understanding that the continuity of Iraq's history must overtake the misleading fragments our world has been given over time.

In each of my books, I have stated that if you cannot read my entire book, do not read it at all. I am not interested in partial stories. Such fragments have plagued Iraq for centuries. Indeed, the value of this book is not in the specific chapters but in how they link together, the continuity and sad repetition they document. Therefore, once again I ask readers to read it all or not at all.

Whether driven by a belief in one all-powerful God or one almighty dollar, those who have been banking on Baghdad have invested their blood and tears in a single region, and we need to understand how and why.

Edwin Black
Washington, DC
www.edwinblack.com
September 1, 2004

NOTES ON USAGE

Much of the source material on Mesopotamia, Iraq, Islam, Mongols, Ottomans, and all the attendant topics derives from English transliterations. Hence, one encounters numerous and confusing spellings of the same name, city, or religious precept. These names are so divergent that the uninitiated might think different individuals, locations, or principles are being referenced.

For example, the name of the holy book of Islam is officially written as Koran, Quran, Qur'n, and other variants. Its author: Mohammed, Muhammad, and so on. The great Mongol conqueror is frequently written as Genghis, Chingis, and other variants. The Hashemite ruler who rode with Lawrence of Arabia is written as Hussein, Husayn, and other variants. Baghdad is sometimes—especially in German—written without the *h*. Basra is sometimes Basrah, and in old British documents, Bussorah. Constantinople and Istanbul are frequently used interchangeably.

What's more, numerous British, British Indian, and other source documents use British spellings for such words as *labor, color,* and *center.*

To avoid confusion, we have standardized, to the best of our ability, all spellings in the text, except where a change would interfere with a title or context. In addition, original spellings of any nature are retained in the bibiliography (see "Major Sources").

PART ONE

From Cradle to Crossroads

CHAPTER ONE

Have a Nice Day

"In city—yes. In city—okay.

"Mosque—*No!*" argued an animated, bearded Shi'a Moslem at the very front of a gathering mob.

April 3, 2003, 6 A.M. The Shi'a city of Najaf in southern Iraq.

"In city—yes. In city—okay. Mosque—*No!*" From everywhere, Moslems in Najaf, Iraq, raced into the narrow, bannered street leading to their historic gold-domed Ali Mosque. Boasting tall twin minarets, reaching for the heavens, this structure is among the holiest Islamic sites for all Shi'a Moslems. Ali was the son-in-law and cousin of the Prophet Mohammed. The mosque holds his tomb in a massive gold-emblazoned cube. By Shi'a tradition, this is also the burial place of Adam and Noah. The crowd menacingly pumped their right arms in defiance, with the anger of centuries in their eyes, pressing forward against a too-thin cordon of Shi'a clerics, arms barely linked, trying to calm them down.[1]

Facing the frenzied mob, eyeball-to-eyeball, was Lt. Col. Chris Hughes, a simple-spoken Red Oak, Iowa, man, 42 years old and an elite war fighter. Hughes was battalion commander of the lethal and legendary Second Battalion, 327th Infantry of the 101st Airborne,

3

which had thrust through the desert to secure Najaf, spearheading away from the main columns pouring into Iraq.

"In city—yes. In city—okay. Mosque—*No!*" By now the crowd had multiplied to several hundred chanting zealots, egged on by Saddam Hussein's Ba'ath loyalists secreted in the crowd. "They are coming to invade the mosque!" screamed the Ba'athist instigators in the throng. "They will invade the mosque!"[2] That was false.

"No mosque! No mosque!" railed the angry group with vehemence as they edged closer and closer toward Hughes, even as spread-armed clerics were losing the battle to hold them back. Hughes tried to reason with the mob, explaining he was not there to invade the mosque or infringe on any holy ground, just to provide protection to their leader, Grand Ayatollah Sayyed Sistani. For years, Ayatollah Sistani had been under house arrest, just down the street some yards toward the revered Ali Mosque. In those first chaotic hours between flight and occupation in the Second Gulf War, the Ayatollah Sistani had, through intermediaries, requested American military protection. But now, no one in the street understood that. They feared the worst—American defilement of their sacred mosque.[3]

Mustered behind Hughes was Bravo Company, about 130 strong, plus a platoon of a dozen troops armed with deadly vehicle-mounted antiarmor missiles, plus a Special Forces "A Team" of 12 commandos, psy ops advisors, a linguistic team, and some intel operatives amorphously described as "other government organizations"—about 200 men in all. American snipers peering through their high-magnification scopes searched for *fedayeen* snipers—rooftops, windows, rooftops, balcony, rooftops. Hughes himself was armed in full desert combat array: Kevlar vest, contoured Kevlar battle helmet, in his hand an M-4 rifle capable of firing 700 to 1,000 rounds per minute, and a 9-mm Beretta strapped tight, gunfighter-style, to his right thigh. A wooden crucifix blessed by his sister-in-law's church in Dubuque was still wedged inside Hughes's front breastplate.[4]

Fired up by the Ba'athist agitators, the screaming crowd, now squeezed into the width of a narrow street, roiled out of control. Rocks were thrown. Bravo Company, armed and ready, watched sharply. The tense scene was a candidate for a bloodbath.[5]

Hughes stayed calm. "I didn't have time to get nervous. I figured I had just a few minutes to make a decision," he remembers. "Do I fire a warning shot in the air? Do I negotiate? Do I explain?"[6]

Now the clerics could barely restrain the mob.[7]

Days previously, the Second Battalion had stormed out of its Camp Pennsylvania staging area in Kuwait, 880 warriors, traveling unarmored for speed, but heavily armed for ultimate firepower. They headed straight for Najaf through the rippling heat along what the charts called a jeep track, but what seemed to Hughes like nothing more than a goat trail. The Second is one of America's most deadly units—dubbed "No Slack."[8]

Originally formed during World War I, the unit went on the heroic offense at Meuse-Argonne. In World War II, the Second fought valiantly at Normandy, then pushed on to Bastogne, where they earned the name "Bastogne Bulldogs" for their dogged defense of the city. During the Battle of the Bulge, they gained immortality when they held out against a relentless Nazi siege. The German general offered them an ultimatum: surrender or death. The divisional commander sent back a famous one-word answer: "Nuts." The German general never understood. "Nuts?"[9]

In 1967, in Vietnam, one of their finest was slain just before rotating home. His favorite adage was "cut the enemy no slack." Since that day and in his honor, the unit has been known as "No Slack." Hughes explains, "Our mission is simple. We are the guys who knock the door down and kill the enemy. We get around the battlefield in Blackhawk helicopters, make contact with the enemy, and kill them. We're the ones." That was Hughes's assignment as he sped toward Najaf at the end of March 2003.[10]

The drive across Iraq's hostile desert was a long one—54 hours. Riding in Hughes's Humvee was Kadhim al-Waeli, an Iraq-American dual-national hailing from St. Louis. "The drive gave me an opportunity to listen for 54 hours," remembers Hughes. "I had already studied the Koran when I was on the investigating commission following the bombing of the USS *Cole*. Before 9/11, I was in the joint anti-terrorism task force, and I traveled around the world making vulnerability assessments. I had read several books on Mohammed the Prophet and understood the concept of *jihad*. But I was heading to Najaf and now I had to carefully listen to Kadhim, to understand much more about the Shi'as and Islam."[11]

Four days before the incident at Ali Mosque, Hughes and company had conducted deliberate attacks against the western outskirts of Najaf. In one intense three-and-half-hour battle, Abrams tanks were firing rounds in front. Above him, every form of aircraft, including merciless F-16s, B-52s, and British Tornados, were hailing hellfire down on enemy positions, and his troops were shooting intense volleys. Saddam snipers on rooftops, seemingly in every direction, threw a torrent of bullets and rocket-propelled grenades at Hughes's men. Three Iraqi artillery pieces, ensconced on the high ridge, lobbed one shell after another. With bullets whizzing, grenades exploding, and shells arcing overhead past his position, Hughes ordered some 56 tube-launched missiles to be fired against windows to take out snipers and against the ridge to kill artillery. Helicopter guns took out the third artillery piece.[12]

Suddenly, in the middle of the fierce fighting, through the smoke of war, the stunning gold mosque gleamed. "I had seen a lot of mosques," remembers Hughes, "but this was the first one with a gold dome." At one point in the campaign, Hughes heard a thud. It was Kadhim, right next to him, prostrate in the dirt at the very sight of the Ali Mosque. "Kadhim told me I had brought him closer to God, just to see the mosque, visually, just to see it," recounted Hughes. Emotional and almost overcome, Kadhim blessed Hughes and his children for generations. "Now, when I die, I will go heaven," cried Kadhim.[13]

"I'm a Catholic," recollects Hughes. "I had to relate it to Catholics coming upon Vatican Square, or Jews at the Wailing Wall. Kadhim couldn't stop thanking me. Okay, I get it. This mosque is important—very important."[14]

As the firefight continued, Kadhim tugged on Hughes's elbow to announce it was 30 minutes until the call to prayer. But the battle was still raging. Nonetheless, Hughes called for the speaker trucks to advance from the rear. Through Kadhim, Hughes announced to the enemy, "We will not fight you during your prayer and we will not hurt your mosque. We are not here to steal your religion. We are here to get rid of Saddam Hussein."

White flags began appearing on the ridge as Iraqi men started filing right through the field of fire and into the mosque for their prayers. Hughes's men, as ordered, did not fire. "I did not want to attack in a way that would threaten the mosque," recounts Hughes. "I was going to keep that mosque safe. Special Forces told me that the Shi'a Ayatollah Sistani was there as well. He is like their pope. I wanted to make sure his residence and the mosque were not in my surface danger zones."[15]

The city's Ba'ath Party headquarters had been pulverized into rubble with a 2,000-pound laser-guided bomb from a B-1 targeted so precisely that a nearby hospital was untouched. Helicopter gunships chased or blasted away pockets of resistance. An elderly man pointed out a swath of 69 antitank mines; 20 of those were neutralized with pop-and-drop C-4 charges until demolition experts could detect the planting pattern and defuse the rest. Saddam's great statue, this one as a charging horseman, was detonated into twisted wreckage by another unit. Soon, the Iraqi forces disappeared altogether. They fled, except for entrenched Saddam supporters, especially fedayeen and local Ba'athists, who oozed back into the city.[16]

With Saddam forces routed, Najaf was jubilant. Rejoicing villagers filled the streets, cheering for the cameras. "Bushgood, Bushgood," they extolled. Children everywhere smiled brightly as they accepted candy bars and handshakes, and threw thumbs-up gestures. Thousands of Shi'as danced, clapped in cadence, and ebulliently congratulated Hughes for liberating their city. "It was like the liberation of Paris," he said.[17]

Among the Saddam forces that ran were those guarding Ayatollah Sistani, until then still under house arrest. Suddenly, the ayatollah was free—and unguarded. The ayatollah wanted protection in case Saddam loyalists returned. At the same time, Hughes wanted a *fatwa,* that is, a religious decree, instructing all Shi'a people not to interfere with American forces "so we could continue to move to Baghdad," explains Hughes.[18]

But who could approach the ayatollah? "We did not think he wanted to meet with infidels," remembers Hughes. Three candidate Moslem intermediaries were transported in to undergo vetting, that is, investigated to see if they were as credible as purported. The first was rejected as an exaggerator who falsely portrayed himself as an acquaintance of the ayatollah; he was quickly exposed. But the second was the son of Ayatollah Sistani's predecessor and a man the army believed could approach the holy man. Through other intermediaries, the esteemed son of a predecessor was cleared to carry a message to the ayatollah from Hughes.[19]

Ayatollah Sistani is a profound abstract thinker and mystic. He believes that *time* itself has a name, but that its elusive name varies with the concept of *place*. Moreover, he embraces very clear ideas about the nature of *requests,* believing each could be divided into three components, *ordering, begging,* and *asking.* Through Kadhim, Hughes became familiar with the ayatollah's teachings. Hughes and senior commanders selected their words very carefully, in line with their study of Islamic tradition and an understanding of the ayatollah's philosophy. "My message was," recollects Hughes, "we are here to seek your guidance so we don't harm your people, your mosque, or your religion. We hope you can take leadership in helping us."[20]

Ayatollah Sistani was impressed with Hughes. He had heard that the American soldier ordered a cessation of fighting during prayers. In addition, Ayatollah Sistani admired the respectful tone of Hughes's entreaty. He agreed to meet with Hughes, both to arrange for protection and to consider a helpful fatwa.[21]

But Hughes would have to get to the ayatollah's home, located just yards from the Ali Mosque. "I thought, how do I go to his house and secure him without making it look like I'm putting him under arrest?" Hughes recounts. "I was afraid his people and the world would misunderstand. I needed to take off my weapons for the meeting. Not even a sidearm, to show absolute respect, because he deserved absolute respect as the Shi'as' supreme religious leader."[22]

But first Hughes needed to get to the house. Hughes checked with his emissaries, and they repeated that he was welcome to proceed. "I told my men—200 guys—'Let's move.' " Slowly, columns of heavily armed No Slack soldiers walked through the alleys of Najaf, their neoprene-soled desert boots pressing diagonal chevrons into the sandy streets, toward the intersection leading to the Ali Mosque. Until this instant the crowds had been congratulatory.[23]

But as they advanced, a crowd naturally gathered, wondering why cadres of heavily armed American soldiers were heading toward the mosque. They weren't. They were heading for the ayatollah's home near the mosque, and Hughes intended to disarm before any meeting. "Through intermediaries, I offered a speaker truck for Sistani to advise the crowd," recalls Hughes. "That took another hour. But then our intermediaries said Ayatollah Sistani was too afraid to come out of his home. However, he would send his students to fan out and tell everybody it was okay for me to proceed."

"So now everyone was happy and cheering because we were going to help Sistani," he continues. But as the column took a few paces forward, the bystanders suddenly became angry and rocks began flying. Saddam loyalists screamed, "They are coming to invade the mosque!" Hughes remembers, "It all changed in 13 or 14 seconds."

Agitated men poured into the street to confront Hughes. Someone who spoke English blared, "In city—yes. In city—okay. Mosque—*No!*" Others joined him. "This is a misunderstanding," Hughes tried to reason. His words, like sand in the wind, simply blew past. Ayatollah Sistani's students were struggling to restrain the irate mob, but their interlocked arms soon gave way.[24] The smallest provocation could now ignite the street into a deadly scene, with numerous embedded TV crews, radio reporters, and print journalists recording every moment.

Hughes led one of the army's best-trained warfare machines. For days, he and his men had been shot at with artillery rounds, RPGs, and machine gun volleys. They had never flinched, liquidating all opponents. Elsewhere, in the newer part of Najaf, they had kicked down doors without hesitation during search missions, fearlessly burst into hidden weapons caches, and overwhelmed any adversary that stood in their way. The Second Battalion and Bravo Company would never cut the enemy any slack.[25]

But Hughes's men were disciplined, quick-thinking warriors. This was not a time for confrontation. If successful, a fatwa would mean mandated noninterference and pave the way for a speedier victory in Iraq. If a bloodbath ensued, every Shi'a in the country would consider Americans his mortal enemy. In vain, Hughes tried to show his non-hostile intent. He turned his M-4 rifle vertical and upside down, holding it by the barrel.[26]

No matter. The fiery crowd would not yield, and they pushed threateningly closer to Hughes and his men.

That morning, Hughes and his men found themselves trapped not only at an intersection in Najaf, but at an intersection in history. Just an hour north were the ruins of ancient Babylon, which to him was almost unbelievable. Hughes was intensely aware and awed that he was in the cradle of civilization.[27]

But somehow civilization in Iraq had been stopped in its infancy. It had never matured. Instead, it became a mere cradle fit for robbery and abuse by the greatest forces in history: by the most murderous barbarians, by the most powerful nations, by the greediest corporations, by the onslaught of progress that sprang from its midst and took root elsewhere, continents away, and by the ravages of cultural self-wounding that ensured Iraq would remain a prisoner of its own heritage. Indeed, for nearly 7,000 years, Iraq has been shackled to unspeakable violence, toppled pride, cruel despotic authorities, and an utter lack of self-governance. The unbreachable continuum of its legacy inculcated bitter alienation as a birthright. Rather than becoming an intersection of the most splendid and accomplished, as European civilizations ultimately became, Iraq has become a crossroads of conquest and conflict.

Then Hughes did something that had never been done in Iraq in 7,000 years. He decided, "It made no sense to hurt people just to talk to a guy. I wasn't going to do it. It was obviously a misunderstanding. So I just defused the confused."[28]

Suddenly, Hughes called out to his men, "Take a knee, everybody take a knee." He continued, "I have taught my men, 'I will always tell you the *why* in every order—so when I don't have time—you'll trust me.'" Hughes had no time. In a split second, the seething mob could erupt. "My men were nervous and some of them looked at me," recalled Hughes. "But I held my weapon upside down, so they all took a knee." Taking a knee is the traditional resting position or low profile for an infantryman on patrol. With little pause, all of No Slack dropped to one knee as ordered.[29]

Members of the suspicious crowd abruptly did likewise, suddenly squatting and sitting, legs folded, on the ground. What next? Hughes then issued a tactical order his men had never heard. "Smile. Everybody smile. Relax, everybody smile!" His men did not speak Arabic. The Iraqis by and large spoke no English. So dozens of heavily armed warriors began communicating by smiling. Now others in the jammed intersection were smiling as well.[30]

"Point your weapons down," shouted Hughes. His men on bended knee, smiling hard, now pointed their weapons at the dirt.[31]

In response, the crowd became slightly calmer. Hughes noticed that the Ba'athist provocateurs in the street were unhappy. They had tried to trigger a bloodbath. Hughes pulled aside his intel and Special Forces people and told them, "Pull out your digital cameras and take the picture of the face of everyone who is not happy" about the non-violent resolution. Those people would be located and dealt with that night.[32]

Although the throng's angst had receded, they were still highly flammable. Hughes could not advance to the ayatollah's house. He needed to withdraw. He told his men, "All No Slack, just turn around. Let's go." Slowly his men rose from their knees and began stepping backward away from the crowd. The crowd did not pursue. Farther back, now farther.[33]

Fomenters continued their efforts to move the mob to attack. "Just turn around," Hughes repeated. No longer facing the crowd, his men simply turned and walked away. As he departed in a sweeping flourish, Hughes demonstratively swung his right arm and placed his hand flat against his heart in the traditional Islamic gesture, "Peace be with you." He added, "Have a nice day." Then the warrior peaceably walked off.[34]

That night, the provocateurs were found and eliminated. Ayatollah Sistani issued his fatwa ordering all Shi'as to not interfere with American forces.[35] Armed with that and an unstoppable coalition, Baghdad fell within a week. Iraq was taken. Again.

Hughes's words still echo: "Have a nice day." Iraq has been waiting for 7,000 years.

CHAPTER TWO

The Cradle of Commerce

When the last Ice Age receded, some 10,000 years ago, some peoples migrated to the marshy plain between the Tigris and the Euphrates. This land, later known as Mesopotamia—or "the land between the two rivers"—is now modern Iraq. It became precious to the world as the "cradle of civilization."[1]

Of course, the very term *cradle of civilization* is imbued with the values of an advanced society determined to categorize primitive and ancient people in its own image. But what qualifies ancient Iraq as the cradle of civilization may speak volumes about its enduring relationship to the larger world and how our society still views that nation.

Disagreeing archaeologists incessantly push back their dates, resculpt their assessments and guesswork, and acrimoniously debate the facts depending on the latest dig and carbon dating. But this much seems settled: Other groups and societies, predating ancient Mesopotamia by thousands of years, have displayed the ingredients of civilization.

Cave dwellers in South Africa, 70,000 years ago, recorded symbolic concepts with geometric designs engraved on ochre stones, revealing organized expression and abstract thinking.[2]

The sensitive artisans of Lascaux, France, who 15,000 years ago painted some 600 sacred animal sketches on grotto walls and engraved nearly 1,500 more, are classed as "prehistoric." Traveling deep into remote chambers of their grotto, the people of Lascaux carried inventive contrivances for illumination. By the flicker of torches and Stone Age lamps, these people created enduring works of exquisite cave art. Their complex works feature background hues of red, yellow, black, and brown, probably mouth-sprayed or blown through a hollowed bone. Delicately brushed and painted atop the backgrounds, animals are depicted in kinetic perspective and are anatomically correct. The artistry of the Lascaux people has become a gift for all time. Their message, although undecipherable, has survived as long as any that followed. Similar cave art groups in the region date back 30,000 years. Little is known about the culture of French cave dwellers.[3] But these societies do not qualify as civilizations, as the world sees it.

Beginning more than 9,000 years ago, the first known permanently inhabited settlements appeared, such as the one at the Tell es–Sultan oasis, later known as Jericho. Its inhabitants cultivated wheat, probably employed irrigation, and ate a diverse diet of game and domesticated animals. They plastered the walls of their rectangular-shaped homes and walked on polished yellow- or red-hued floors cushioned by rush mats. Beneath at least one of those floors, residents buried skulls, carefully coated with limey clay, and then molded the clay to preserve facial features, creating realistic busts. More precisely, the preserved images of those deceased relatives live forever. Jericho grew to be approximately 10 acres in size and was home to an estimated 2,000 persons. Between the eighth and seventh millennia BCE, a defensive wall was erected, supplemented by a protective ditch. A tower was raised. Public buildings, perhaps temples, were constructed. Over thousands of years, those thick mud-baked fortifications were destroyed and rebuilt an estimated 17 times following earthquakes and invasions.[4] Each time, Jericho rallied to overcome the challenge to its existence. But the town of Jericho does not qualify as a cradle of civilization, as the world sees it.

About 7,000 years ago, the so-called Halaf culture stretched across northern Mesopotamia, reaching the Anatolian coast in what is modern Turkey and western Iran. A swath of small agrarian Halaf settlements existed across the region, known for their archetypal domed mud or limestone buildings. They exchanged distinctive ornate pottery goods, amulets, and stamping seals, as well as ritualized figurines with exaggerated female sexual features.[5] But Halaf societies do not qualify as civilizations, as the world sees it.

Despite a veritable nursery of sites worldwide where civilized and social behavior emerged, reaching back scores of millennia, it is not until the simple Halaf village culture melded into the more complex Ubaid culture of alluvial Mesopotamia, around the late fifth millennium BCE, that the world dubbed any realm the "cradle of civilization."[6]

No one is quite sure when the term was first coined. Perhaps one of the first to express it was Sir Henry Rawlinson on April 8, 1867, during a discussion at the Royal Geographical Society in London. Following a paper on Mesopotamia by surveyor J. B. Bewsher, the president of the society invited comment from other fellows. Rawlinson rose to declare enthusiastically, "The country to which Lt. Bewsher's paper referred, was the cradle of civilization. In it were first cultivated . . . the natural sciences and that study of art which afterwards spread through the world."[7] His notion, and the cliché, took root.

Certainly, during the fifth millennium BCE, numerous small villages in what is now modern Iraq had advanced into a set of more organized central societies.[8] Survival demanded it.

In the marshy realm between the Tigris and the Euphrates, the ancient Mesopotamian people were compelled to cooperate extensively between phases of ruinous havoc and hopeful cultivation. When the waters were tame enough to nourish agriculture and bestow plenty, society thrived. Canals and irrigation were required. The inhospitable marshlands of alluvial Mesopotamia offered an abundance of reeds, but were devoid of stone, metals, and to some extent, the wood needed to create shelter, storage, and the infrastructure of an advanced society. Intense labor cooperation was vital to overcoming the harsh environment. Survival and prosperity accrued to those who could work together, store grain and commodities, trade, and plan between those unpredictable river cycles. Success at some point pushed beyond subsistence to surplus.[9] The surplus made all the difference to economic development.

Resilient and innovative, the Sumerians in about 3500 BCE invented the wheel, which led to the cart, which, in tandem with boats, could move heavy loads for added productivity and thus promoted commerce. Later, people in the region developed the chariot for efficient transportation and for war.[10]

By around 3500 BCE, the region also yielded mankind's first genuine city, Uruk, located just northwest of modern Nasiriyah. Uruk developed into a complex, cohesive urban setting, rich in personal dwellings, public buildings, and structures, as well as a hierarchical administrative character and a highly developed temple-based economy. Sacred temples warehoused and dispensed the food and oversaw the labors. By 3000 to 2500 BCE, at least one of the temples was distributing rations of beer and bread.[11] Thus, from the beginning, true commerce and economics became a sanctified institution associated with the gods.

More villages and even greater cities followed throughout Mesopotamia. A pivotal quality in the development of Sumer's cities was an early sense of commerce. More than mere barter, trade, or plunder, it was the organization and regulation of transactions, trade, and surplus commodities that constituted true *commerce*.

Clay tokens were employed to record counts and, to a lesser extent, commodities. Rudimentary tokens to signify economic information had existed throughout the Near East from the ninth millennium BCE. In earliest times, some argue, an elongated cone might have designated the number "1," while a small spheroid might connote the number "6" or "10," (i.e., the next level of numerical value).[12]

Eventually, along with Uruk's rise, tokens became more complex, signifying not just numbers but commodities, such as wheat and sheep, as well as goods finished in workshops, such as rope, bread, clothing, and perfume. These tokens appear in nonresidential structures and several temples throughout the region. The vast majority of the economic tokens of Uruk, for example, were discovered in temples or other sacred structures. Tokens were almost always recovered from the sites of wealthy or powerful Sumerians, that is, priests and royalty, and are identified with power and economic control.[13] In ancient Sumer, commerce, economic strength, and religious primacy developed symbiotically.

Initially, one token represented one item, that is, one token would represent one basket of goods, four tokens signified four baskets, and so forth. By the fourth millennium BCE, by the time of Uruk, tokens could represent such specific information as the age, sex, and type of a sheep.[14] As the world sees it, the transition of simple tokens to complex tokens tracks the very history of man's ascent to civilization.

As this system developed, tokens, both simple and complex, were inserted into hollow clay "envelopes," and later the contents were marked on the outsides of these envelopes, creating a more recognizable and readily accessible ledgerlike record.[15] This was a major step toward a complex system of accounting.

The shapes and markings of accounting tokens led to two-dimensional pictographs engraved on clay tablets and numerical systems to count them, which, in turn, evolved into the famous wedge-based script known as *cuneiform*. Sumerian culture progressed from token to script in a relatively short period of time—some suggest 400 years. Originally, flanged reed implements were used to engrave signs. In the beginning, those cuneiform signs represented accounting shorthand, but they gradually developed into representations of spoken language and thence a stepping-stone en route to modern alphabets.[16] Hence, our very written language emerged not from the need to worship a god, sing praise, honor a family, immortalize sagas, or express love—but from the need for commercial accounting, that is, to certify who controlled, owned, and owed what.

Grain and other valuables in Uruk and other Sumerian cities were stored in temples. Some argue that these temples, reposing on the safest shores of the Tigris and Euphrates, became the first institutions to issue inscribed tablets, or tokens, as "receipts" for valuable deposits or trade purposes. It has been said that those secure and trusted institutions of safekeeping in ancient Mesopotamia were in fact the precursors of modern depository "banks."[17]

For centuries, Mesopotamian exchanges yielded transaction receipts and other commercial laws, such as those found at Eshnunna, dating from about 1770 BCE. Some two generations after Eshnunna, the exalted Hammurabi, the sixth king of the first Babylonian dynasty, proclaimed a collection of laws to "provide just ways for the people of the land . . . [to] establish truth and justice as the declaration to the land . . . [and to] enhance the well-being of the people." Carved onto an eight-foot black stele, topped by an image of Hammurabi receiving encouragement from the enthroned and crowned deity Shamash,

the laws were prominently displayed to be a guiding light to his subjects. Copies likely were erected in other Babylonian cities.[18]

In 282 highly specific laws, of which 271 survive, Hammurabi set
forth precepts of conduct—and the consequences for their violation—
governing such moral and personal matters as false accusation, soldier-
ing, theft, conspiracy, sexual relations, marriage, and divorce. The
consequence for transgression was generally some fixed financial compensation, but not infrequently the penalty was death.[19]

> *Law 141.* If the wife of a man who is residing in the man's
> house should decide to leave, and she appropriates goods,
> squanders her household possessions, or disparages her hus-
> band, they shall charge and convict her; and if her husband
> should declare his intention to divorce her, then he shall divorce
> her; neither her travel expenses, nor her divorce settlement, nor
> anything else shall be given to her. If her husband should not
> declare his intention to divorce her, then her husband may
> marry another woman and that [first] woman shall reside in her
> husband's house as a slave woman.

> *Law 142.* If a woman repudiates her husband, and declares,
> "You will not have marital relations with me"—her circum-
> stances shall be investigated by the authorities of her city quar-
> ter, and if she is circumspect and without fault, but her husband
> is wayward and disparages her greatly, that woman will not be
> subject to any penalty; she shall take her dowry and she shall
> depart for her father's house.[20]

Yet the majority of the 271 readable laws constitute a detailed
commercial code legislating personal and real property rights, regulations for slave property, transaction rules, wage and compensation
scales, rental procedures, and the principles of inheritance, as well as
the financial values and damages for interpersonal problems.[21]

> *Law 35.* If a man should purchase from a soldier either the cat-
> tle or the sheep and goats, which the king gave to the soldier,
> he shall forfeit his silver.

> *Law 36.* The field, orchard, and house of a soldier, fisherman,
> or a state tenant will not be sold.

Law 37. If a man should purchase a field, orchard, and house of a soldier, fisherman, or a state tenant, his deed shall be invalidated and he shall forfeit his silver; the field, orchard, or house shall revert to its owner.

Law 38. A soldier, fisherman, or a state tenant will not assign in writing to his wife or daughter any part of a field, orchard, or house attached to his service obligation, nor shall he give it to meet any outstanding obligation.[22]

Contracts, warehousing expenses, and lending were codified as well.[23]

Law 121. If a man stores grain in another man's house, he shall give 5 *silas* of grain per *kur* (i.e., per 300 *silas*) as annual rent of the granary.

Law 122. If a man intends to give silver, gold, or anything else to another man for safekeeping, he shall exhibit before witnesses anything which he intends to give, he shall draw up a written contract, and (in this manner) he shall give goods for safekeeping.[24]

Law 268. If a man rents an ox for threshing, 20 *silas* of grain is its hire.

Law 269. If he rents a donkey for threshing, 10 *silas* of grain is its hire.

Law 270. If he rents a goat for threshing, 1 *sila* of grain is its hire.

Law 271. If a man rents cattle, a wagon and its driver, he shall give 180 *silas* of grain per day.

Law 272. If a man rents only the wagon, he shall give 40 *silas* of grain per day.[25]

The principles of Hammurabi's ancient laws, together with many other Mesopotamian commercial regulations, formed the basis for later, and thus for modern, commercial law and custom. Babylonians also developed a system of loans and interest that seems to resemble the 30-year mortgages of modern times. Even compound interest is explained. One school tablet poses the following problem: "1 mina of silver was lent at a rate of 12 shekels of interest per mina per year [i.e., 20 percent]; when the money was returned, capital plus compound interest amounted to 64 minas of silver," and asks the student to determine the length of the loan period—which, based on the rules of interest, was 30 years.[26]

The world's view of the cradle of civilization emerged not from organized communal hunting societies in Siberia that learned to share food and nurture clans, or from the spiritual painters of cave art in France, or from thousands of years of continuous township at Jericho. It was the quality of economic life and commerce and its invigoration of all around it that signaled the emergence of that most valued social order—*civilization*.

More urbanized centers arose in Mesopotamia. One of them, Babylon, about 50 miles south of modern Baghdad, grew to be a magnificent city-state and the capital of the region. Babylon's canals, statuary, thoroughfares, temples, and public buildings were nothing less than spectacular.

More than simple trade and barter, *commerce* as we know it began five millennia ago in Mesopotamia. Sanctified in temples, the attribute of kings, and the enabler of dynasties, the true propulsion behind writing and the law itself, commerce was the driver of urbanization and the catalyst of civilization. Certainly, even if ancient Iraq was not the cradle of civilization according to any who would debate the precedents, it seems to have been the "cradle of commerce." Perhaps there is no distinction.

Thus ancient Mesopotamia sprang upon the consciousness of the world. It was where commerce and civilization cohabitated to create a new world social order—one that would return time and again from whence it arose.

CHAPTER THREE

Robbing the Cradle

Mesopotamia enjoyed a 2,000-year head start on Western civilization. What happened?

A single ancient people did not monopolize the historic territory between the Tigris and the Euphrates to create one cohesive, shining civilization as a beacon to others. Mesopotamia was in fact a diverse, often contentious, network of competing city-states. At different times, in different centuries BCE, cities such as Uruk, Lagash, and Eridu in the south, and Kish, Nippur, and Sippar in the midsection, as well as Assur, Nineveh, and Nimrud in the north, each flourished and made their mark. These city-states were ruled by their own kings, developed their own gods and cults, spoke their own languages and dialects, and manifested their own distinctive cultures.[1]

A succession of disparate groups came from near and far to conquer the developing prize of Mesopotamia, and each conqueror was in turn conquered. The Semitic Akkadians arose among the original Sumerians, for whom Sumer was named. In the third millennium BCE, the Akkadian king Sargon created history's first "empire," extending his political reign, military dominance, and commercial primacy from western Persia, through Syria, to what is now eastern Turkey. But Sargon's almost 150-year dynasty was overrun by the

Guti mountain people. The Guti ruled until the Sumerians regained supremacy, only to be succeeded by Amorites from the west, and then the Elamites from the Zagros Mountains. Other invaders included the Indo-European Hittites from Anatolia and the obscure Hurrians and Kassites.[2]

These invading and pervading groups destroyed and built up the city-states between the two rivers, as well as those in surrounding lands. During Mesopotamia's golden millennia, each of these dynasties and empires, no matter how transient, purloined or planted something valuable, advancing the ever more complex culture growing atop the ancient Sumerian foundation. Over 3,000 years—perhaps 120 generations—the region became not a cradle but a veritable engine of civilization, energizing the entire Fertile Crescent, that is, the lands from the Nile Valley up through Palestine and Syria into the Tigris-Euphrates valley and beyond.

The result was—for better or worse—a complex landscape of advanced societies that produced great war and peace, profound knowledge and eternal art, highly developed religious orders, and expansive trade, commerce, and prosperity.

Mesopotamia fashioned mathematical systems and even divided existence itself into equal parts. Using multiples and divisions of 60, the Mesopotamians created a sexagesimal world. The number 60 was associated with Anu, the greatest sky god. The Sumerian year comprised 360 days, that is, 60 multiplied by 6. Each hour comprised 60 minutes and each minute 60 seconds—although the ancient Sumerians, in fact, initially used only a 12-hour day, with each of their minutes equaling two of ours. A circle could be divided into 360 degrees. The governing number 60 could be squared, cubed, and fractioned to yield endless calculations.[3] In magical measures of 60 did the peoples of Mesopotamia seek to master time and space.

Perhaps most important, they created writing systems that vastly exceeded the mute imperative of mere numbers and measurements. Writing captured the verbal sounds of spoken language and conveyed them beyond one individual, and beyond one individual's lifetime, to unseen individuals and lifetimes. Surely, the immortality of the spoken word and thought, more than anything else, cross-pollinated and bequeathed the ideas and culture of one Mesopotamian generation to the next, and the next, and the next—and to distant generations in adjacent lands. Millions of cuneiform tablets were created to record trades, labors, mortgages, slave sales, commands and decrees, stories and wisdoms, epics, maps, and histories, as well as academic instruction. Some 500,000 such tablets have already been unearthed. More than 50,000 were discovered at Nippur alone.[4] Surely, knowledge and communication were the most powerful forces arising from Mesopotamia. More than bronze swords and swift chariots, it was the careful cuts and grooves sequenced into clay that made Mesopotamia the powerhouse of humanity.

Great science and turning-point inventions sprang from the civilizations of Mesopotamia. Astronomy, cartography, medicine, metallurgy, and architecture all advanced into organized disciplines. The wheel, bronze, chariots, military tactics—all were either invented or flourished in the hands of those who dwelled in or ruled these lands.[5]

But it was not enough to try to master the material and intellectual world. Mesopotamians sought to touch the gods. They developed intricate belief systems to identify, define, and even lay hands upon the all-powerful. Elaborate cults trace as far back as Eridu in 5000 BCE. By imbuing commerce with the imprimatur of the temples—and hence the gods—the sanctity of everyday transactions became a cultural ethic, thereby magnifying the essence of economic life. Religion became more than mere ritual; it was a way of living. From about 3500 BCE, at the White Temple of Uruk and then elsewhere, great stepped ziggurat temples ascended 70 feet and higher. Such ziggurats, boldly aspiring toward the sky, formed the basis for a later biblical story in which men, wracked with pride and arrogance, too eager to touch the heavens, erected a great tower; God foiled their lofty desires by confounding their language into babble so they could not communicate.[6]

In biblical tradition, Ancient Ur in southern Mesopotamia, also yielded Abraham, whose descendants and adherents spread a concept of monotheism, of an aloof God that could not be seen, touched, or even approximated. Abraham's legendary faith in an unseen but omnipresent and omnipotent Almighty revolutionized Western civilization forever.[7]

Among all the bronzed, gilded, and engraved wonders Mesopotamia had to offer, Babylon emerged as its most magnificent treasure. *Babylon!* The name itself means "gateway to god." It thrived as a mighty city-state for millennia. By the eighteenth century BCE, Babylon emerged as the all-important capital of Hammurabi's empire that burgeoned north to Assyria, east toward Elam in southwest Persia, and west toward the Mediterranean. Soaring temples, ornate shrines and gateways, well-constructed boulevards and canals—all part of a renowned, cosmopolitan center.[8]

During the centuries of greatness, decline, and resurgence, Babylon's influence stretched a thousand miles in either direction to the nations of Egypt, Persia, and Greece. By then, these other nations had developed their own advanced civilizations, inspiring the need for international law. Among history's first known bilateral agreements were peace treaties between the Hittite king Hattusilis and Egyptian pharaoh Ramses II in the thirteenth century BCE. Rather than one tablet signed by both kings, each side received a copy ratified by the other.[9]

More than mere cessation of belligerence between previously warring empires, the treaty outlined an alliance, as well as international order and respect among nations: "And if another enemy come [against] the land Hatti, and Hattusili," declared the treaty, ". . . the great king, king of Egypt shall send his troops and his chariots and shall slay [his enemy and] he shall restore confidence to the land."[10]

Despite differences in the text of each tablet, both clearly predicate their agreement on a desire for "peace and brotherhood between nations." Hittite and Egyptian emissaries, under the treaty, were given safe passage in each other's empires. Bilateral extradition of fugitives and criminals was a central feature of the agreement, further cementing the international recognition of law.[11]

Of course, the Hittite-Egyptian peace treaty did not mean that the great nations of the ancient Near East were now devoted to a respect for neighbors. The march toward international peace is a slippery ascent. Babylonia quickly slid back.

As the pendulum swung in the late 600s BCE, the Assyrians utterly destroyed Babylon, piling corpses by the thousands high along the thoroughfares. Babylon's riches were looted and carried off to the far-off Assyrian capital, Nineveh. When the pendulum swung back, the next Assyrian king arduously rebuilt Babylon to its former splendor.[12]

Assyrian kings in the eighth to sixth centuries BCE razed about 90 cities and hundreds of villages, plundering thousands of horses, sheep, and oxen and capturing more than 200,000 prisoners. The contending city-states invented new and unending cruelties to inflict upon their neighbors. The Assyrians, for example, engaged in unspeakable atrocities. During the conquest of the nearby Elamites, the king's head was raised on a pike at Nineveh and allowed to slowly decompose. The king's general was whipped bloody, his throat slashed and his carcass sliced into pieces and distributed throughout Mesopotamia as a warning.[13]

Nebuchadnezzar II was installed as king of the neo-Babylonian dynasty of Chaldea. He fortified Babylon and transformed it into a majestic metropolis as never before, erecting great palaces and public works. The crest of the city's grandiose outer walls was broad enough for chariots to patrol. The Hanging Gardens of Babylon, created by Nebuchadnezzar for his wife, were famed as one of the seven wonders of the ancient world. Nebuchadnezzar's cities were nothing less than fabulous. But Nebuchadnezzar also ruthlessly conquered other lands and displaced whole peoples. In the early sixth century BCE, for example, he sacked Jerusalem and deported some 10,000 Hebrews to Babylonia.[14]

However, when the Persian king, Cyrus the Great, conquered Babylon in about 539 BCE, Mesopotamia finally entered a new era of civilization and enlightenment. Cyrus's armies liberated the inhabitants, restored exiled peoples to their homes, helped Babylonians and all others live in dignity, and established respect for all individuals as the law of his lands. He issued the first international human rights declaration, inscribed in cuneiform onto a large elliptical cylinder.[15]

On the day of his coronation, he announced to all, "I am Cyrus, king of the world, great king, mighty king, king of Babylon. . . . When I, well disposed, entered Babylon, I established the seat of government in the royal palace amidst jubilation and rejoicing. . . . My numerous troops moved about undisturbed in the midst of Babylon. I did not allow any to terrorize the land. . . . I kept in view the needs of Babylon and all its sanctuaries to promote their well-being. The citizens of Babylon. . . . I lifted their unbecoming yoke. Their dilapidated dwellings I restored. I put an end to their misfortunes. . . . I gathered together all their inhabitants and restored to them their dwellings."[16]

As part of his human rights regime, Cyrus returned the Hebrews to Jerusalem to rebuild their temple. The Old Testament records: "In the first year of Cyrus king of Persia . . . the Lord moved the heart of Cyrus, king of Persia, to make a proclamation throughout his realm and to put in writing: '. . . The Lord, the God of Heaven, has given me all the kingdoms of the earth and he has appointed me to build a temple for him at Jerusalem in Judah. Anyone of his people among you—may his God be with him, and let him go up to Jerusalem in Judah and build the temple of the Lord, the God of Israel, the God who is in Jerusalem. And the people of any place where survivors may now be living are to provide him with silver and gold, with goods and livestock, and with freewill offerings for the temple of God in Jerusalem.' "[17]

But Mesopotamia's peace did not last long. Persian successors to Cyrus did not rule benevolently. As a crossroads between the empires of southern Europe, Asia, and Asia Minor, Babylon was too opulent and prized for coexistence. For a thousand years after Cyrus, and well into the Common Era, Mesopotamia was incessantly catapulted to heights of splendor only to career back to depths of slaughter as it passed from the alternating clutches of Alexander the Great of Greece, the Seleucid Greeks, the Parthian Empire, the Romans, and the Persians.[18]

By the Common Era, that is, after the birth of Christ, Mesopotamia was millennia removed from any cradle of civilization. The cradle had been expropriated, subjugated, rehabilitated, and liberated so many times that Mesopotamia's history had become an endless catalog of conflict between its competing conquerors.

Despite the rule of violent contending empires, various forms of monotheism survived in Mesopotamia and its surrounding region since Abraham is said to have left Ur. Originally known as Abram, the son of an idolater, he left the south of Mesopotamia following a mystical revelation from an unidentified supernatural voice commanding, "Leave your country, your people and your father's household and go to the land I will show you. . . . I will make you into a great nation."[19]

According to the writings, the Almighty later told Abram, "Look at the heavens and count the stars . . . so shall be your offspring." In a later covenant, the Almighty is said to have pledged, "You will be the father of many nations. No longer will you be called Abram; your name will be called Abraham, for I have made you a father of many nations." The name *Abraham* is thought to mean "father of many."[20]

Among Abraham's many descendants were the Arabs, who came from his son Ishmael, born of a surrogate wife, Hagar, according to Biblical tradition. Mother and son were both cast out in the wilderness, according to the verses, with the promise from God: "I will make the son of the maidservant into a nation also, because he is your offspring."[21]

While Abraham was strictly obedient to one divine voice, there is nothing explicit in the Bible regarding Abraham's monotheism.[22]

However, Abraham's descendents and adherents, beginning with Moses, were explicit, enraptured, and self-defined by the monotheistic idea: one god before all other gods. Three great religions emerged from Abraham's descendents and adherents during a turbulent but spiritual 2,000-year period in the Mideast. First came Judaism, then Christianity, and finally Islam some two millennia after the Israelites, according to tradition, received the Ten Commandments. In the initial centuries of these monotheistic faiths, the injunction of a relationship with one and only one God inspired some to private and exclusionary devotion, servitude, and obedience. For others, it was a calling to evangelize the world and share. For still others, it was a summons to destroy the unbelievers and infidels because, in some minds, monotheism leaves little room for coexistence with other gods and other forms of belief. Judaism and Christianity both found fertile ground in Mesopotamia. In Mesopotamia, however, monotheism as conqueror came from Arabs and Islam.

Just who were the Arabs? Mesopotamia's original peoples were an indistinct amalgam of Sumerian, Semitic, Indo-European, and other groups. The Arabs as a group were generally thought to be the scattered people who spoke a similar Semitic language and who, with few exceptions, dwelled stateless in the nearly empty desert far to the south that came to be known as the Arabian Peninsula. By legend and tradition, the Arabs were the descendants of Ishmael, the son of Abraham, who roamed the wilderness.[23]

One of the earliest references to Arabs is found in the Old Testament, dating to about 900 BCE, when Chronicles II records that "the Arabs" offered tribute to Israel's King Solomon. In 853 BCE, King

Ahab of Israel sealed an alliance with "Gindibu the Arab," who provided 1,000 camels, according to an Assyrian inscription. Two very different but related Arab groups arose. The first were the nomadic and colorful Bedouins, roving with their extended families and tending flocks in tow. The second group settled in oases on the western coast of the Arabian Peninsula and along the northern fringes of the Arabian Desert. Bedouins were especially known for adventurous caravans that fearlessly plied the deserts across the Mideast and northern Africa. Everywhere, they established formidable reputations as both traders and raiders. Bedouin travelers interacted with the Hebrews in Israel, the Babylonians in Mesopotamia, the Egyptians, and the Greeks. In fact, the Greeks were among the first to refer in written records to the desert peninsula as "Arabia."[24]

Proud and passionately independent, even the earliest recorded Arabs despised any attempt to dominate them. One poet wrote, "The worst evil that can befall a people . . . is that their necks are bent." As a warning against any attempt to infringe their freedom, Bedouins were fond of *ghazu,* that is, audacious marauding, killing the men in other settlements, kidnapping their wives, and stealing their animals. A Moslem poet commemorated a typical scene: "We came home with their women captive behind us on our camel saddles, and with the booty of camels." Midianite Bedouins found Joseph, according to biblical tradition, and sold him into slavery in Egypt. *Ghazu* was also a de facto means of Bedouin survival in the parched Arabian climes, where the possessions of others were capriciously—almost routinely—pilfered and plundered as a lifestyle. Of plundering Bedouins, the Mesopotamian king Sargon II wrote in the eighth century BCE, "all alike are warriors of equal rank, half nude . . . ranging widely with the help of swift horses and slender camels."[25]

Wandering in a desert that with very few exceptions defied the organization of government due to its barren environment, the dominant identification of Arabs was not any form of nationhood but rather the closely knit tribe. Tribalism defined everything: the family, friends, and foes.[26] Any group or settlement outside the tribe was fair game.

The Arabs worshipped many of the deities they encountered on their travels and raids and lived side by side with groups of Christians and Jews in Arabia. That all changed after Mohammed was born in

Mecca in 570 CE. Mecca was a prosperous town in central western Arabia, near the Red Sea. The town, popular with merchants along the north-south "spice road," was so rich in idol worship that many made pagan pilgrimages there. A few tribal clans ruled the center. Mohammed himself thrived as a Meccan merchant until, in 610, the one true God, Allah, was revealed to him in a mystic moment. Mohammed believed he was the last messenger or prophet in a long line of some 124,000 such prophets—that is, an infinite number— beginning with Adam, reaching past Noah, later Abraham, and con- tinuing through Moses and Jesus. All these prophets were seen as gifts not to just one people but to all mankind. Mohammed saw his per- sonal revelation not as canceling, but rather as completing all earlier revelations. He was determined to convert his fellow Arabs to the faith.[27]

Mohammed's five pillars—faith, daily prayer, fasting, contributions to the poor, and a pilgrimage—defined the religion known as *Islam,* that is, "surrender to God." Devotees were called *Moslems,* that is, "those who surrender to God." Mohammed's teachings and revela- tions from Allah were to form the primary moral, legal, and govern- mental underpinnings of the Arab peoples.[28]

Islam believed in the sword. Within a dozen years, Mohammed and his persecuted, boycotted, and often physically tortured follow- ers fought back against the pagan establishment throughout Arabia with armed campaigns of conversion. Opponents were massacred if necessary—polytheists or monotheists. One such was a tribe of 700 resistant Jews from the Qurayzah tribe slaughtered near Medina; the Qurayzah men were mercilessly put to the sword and their women and children abducted into slavery. Bedouin tribe after tribe elected to convert rather than to fight and see their clans decimated. Ulti- mately, Mohammed and an army of 10,000 soldiers marched on Mecca, which submitted without a fight.[29] Arabia had been won for Islam.

When Mohammed died in 632, no successor had been anointed and no succession process existed. The Koran—Mohammed's teach- ings, that is, the unaltered word of God—had not yet been tran- scribed. Moreover, with Mohammed gone and with no Islamic structure, many Bedouin tribes simply abandoned their brief adher- ence to Islam and refused to pay the *zakat,* the Moslem tax intended to assist the poor. This early phase of rejection is known in Islam as the Apostasy. Mohammed's father-in-law in Mecca assumed the succession as *caliph,* or supreme leader of the Islamic community. To restore the faith—and some order—the caliph and his forces waged fierce battles across Arabia with one tribe after another. Their technique: Attack attack attack, with waves of javelin-throwing camel riders and horsemen, supported by archers. Once the enemy fell back, Moslem fighters would leap from their animals, pursue, seize, and kill or be killed in hand-to-hand combat using knives, swords, and their bare hands. Either way—live as a blessed victor, or ascend to paradise as a soldier in the army of Allah—Islamic warriors fought fiercely and to the finish. Within two years, the desert tribes had all been won back for Allah.[30]

With the Arabian Peninsula subdued and returned to Islam, the caliph's eyes turned north and west toward all of the Mideast and northern Africa, and east toward Asia. Now would come a new empire, of both Arabs and non-Arabs, where territorial victory and political hegemony were intrinsic to religious doctrine. This was not an inadvertent result, but the original mission: to indivisibly fuse sovereign government and Islam.[31]

In 634, the Arab Conquest began in earnest. When completed decades later, the vast Islamic Empire would span continents, from the highlands of Asia to the deserts of the Arabian Peninsula to Africa's Atlantic coast. They called it *jihad,* or holy war, or personal struggle— military campaigns consecrated as sacred crusades to convert or subjugate infidels and nonbelievers. The conquered could survive only by conversion or by becoming a special separate class of citizen, known as *dhimmis,* and paying a protection tribute called the *jizya.* Those who did not convert or pay would be slaughtered.[32]

The war for Islamization began by attacks on the weakened, aging Roman Empire in Syria and Palestine and the predominantly Persian Sassanid Empire in Mesopotamia. The Arabs were determined to dislodge the Christians in Syria and the Persian monotheistic state religion, Zoroastrianism, in Mesopotamia.[33]

In 634, an army of 18,000 Moslem warriors swarmed into Mesopotamia's Euphrates Delta to launch their crusade commanded by General Khalid ibn al Walid, known as "the Sword of Islam." At the Euphrates, Khalid issued an ultimatum to the Sassanid Persians, words that would resonate in the Arab consciousness again and again for centuries: "Become Moslem and be saved. If not, accept protection from us and pay the *jizya*. If not, I shall come against you with men who love death as you love to drink wine."[34]

In Mesopotamia, sometimes the Persians enormously outnumbered the fanatical jihadist armies. It did not matter. Moslem warriors fought to the death or until their opponents surrendered—whichever came first. The Arabs wanted Mesopotamia intact and economically strong so that Islam could flourish as a true empire. Hence, theirs was not a traditional war of plunder, but an imperialistic jihad.[35]

During the next two years the Sassanid Persians surrendered to the Arabs, that is, they surrendered to Allah. Damascus surrendered. Palestine also surrendered. One by one, the nations surrendered to the superior forces of Islam.[36] *Islam* means "surrender to God."

The surrenders were relished. "O men, do you not see how Persia has been ruined and its inhabitants humiliated," an Arab poet glorified, adding, "They have become slaves who pasture your sheep. . . . God gave us victory over them, allowing us to take their countries and settle in their lands, their homes and their property."[37]

Once surrendered, the conquered lands were completely rewoven. During the decade from 634 to about 644, Islam's Caliph Omar permanently transformed Mesopotamia into an Arab Islamic nation. The ancient language of Aramaic was almost obliterated, except for some religious purposes. Christian, Jewish, Zoroastrian, and polytheistic communities were largely, but not completely, wiped out in favor of Islam. They could live by paying the *jizya* protection tax. Nomadic Arabs accustomed to desert tents now found themselves reveling in the palatial riches and baths of Babylonia's fallen cities. Two new garrison cities were built in the south, Kufa and Basra, to acquire control of a port. Both were populated with waves of soldiers from Arabia who were continuously schooled in the tenets of militant Islam. Mesopotamians freely intermarried with Arab Bedouins, creating a new people, a new nation, and a new identity.[38]

The Arabs were now more than just Arabia. Soon the Arabs controlled vast regions of land on the three adjacent continents that intersected at Mesopotamia. Moslems now dominated the fabulous Silk Road that meandered across Eurasia transporting goods between Rome and China. Key segments of the route converged on Mesopotamia, elevating the region's importance. Although Mecca remained a spiritual epicenter, Mesopotamia now emerged as an influential stronghold of Islam. It would help shape the vast Moslem Empire that eventually swelled from Mecca to Persia, Syria, and Asia Minor, to North Africa and across the straits into Spain.[39]

In 644, everything changed after a Christian slave from Persia, kidnapped to Mecca, seized an unguarded moment and repeatedly stabbed the great Omar, the second caliph, in the back. Omar died slowly. Before he expired, he organized a six-man council of generals and others to oversee an election for his successor, the third caliph.[40]

Uthman ibn Affan was elected third caliph in a contentious decision that would soon split the religion in a fashion that would reverberate for centuries and literally define the Islamic nature of Mesopotamia and the subsequent nations that would emerge in that land.[41]

Who was Uthman? He was a close companion of the Prophet Mohammed, a wealthy merchant who had financed Moslem armies and built up Islam and the Moslem Empire. During his 12-year reign, he created a Moslem navy to extend its trade and political might across the Mediterranean, instituted a vast administrative bureaucracy, and undertook enormous public works. Most important, Uthman compiled the first authoritative version of Mohammed's teachings into the Koran and distributed copies to Moslems throughout the empire.[42]

But Uthman appointed many family members from his powerful Umayyad clan as governors, and they ruled Mesopotamia harshly and for personal aggrandizement. This provoked local bitterness from the people, who felt exploited and humiliated from afar. Southern Mesopotamian Moslems became fiery dissidents against Uthman. Egyptian rebels from the southern two garrison cities of Kufa and Basra finally rose up against the oppression, waging an unstoppable insurgency right to Caliph Uthman's front door in Mecca.[43]

On Friday, June 17, 656, the rebels staged a long siege around Uthman's home. At first, Uthman negotiated reforms to his corrupt government. But when the caliph apparently withdrew those promises, irate soldiers scrambled over the roof and entered the house. They found Uthman praying over a Koran. Nonetheless, they brutally stabbed the 84-year-old holy man to death. When his wife intervened, her fingers were sliced off as well. As a further act of desecration, it has been said, the killers did not allow Uthman's disfigured body to be moved for a full day, thus violating the Islamic mandate for a speedy interment. Finally, on Saturday night, Uthman was found next to his blood-drenched Koran. The furious Umayyad governors buried Uthman as a martyr, using his original blood-soaked clothing as a shroud.[44]

An irreparable rupture would now split the faithful into two camps. On one side was the majority, those allied with the entrenched Umayyads, fortified by one of the Prophet Mohammed's widows, Aisha. In the second camp was the Mesopotamian minority, the followers of the charismatic figure Ali, and believers in leadership by blood descent.[45]

Ali was the Prophet Mohammed's son-in-law and heir apparent to the leadership of the Islamic government. The Prophet Mohammed is even said to have verbally commanded Ali's succession. Within five days, as expected, Ali was designated the new caliph and the insurgent forces retreated from Mecca to their garrisons at Kufa and Basra. But, clearly, Ali was the hero of the rebels who killed Uthman. They knew that if Uthman were deposed, Ali would inherit the caliphate. Ali was actually present in Mecca during the siege and openly negotiated with the crowds. Moreover, Ali declined to execute those of his supporters who killed Uthman, thereby tacitly endorsing their coup. Hence, the ruling Umayyads accused Ali of having blood on his hands—as either a silent or an active conspirator in the assassination. They refused to recognize him as fourth caliph.[46]

The war was on. Everywhere, Mohammed's widow Aisha vociferously rabble-roused revenge for Uthman's killing. Ultimately, the third caliph's bloody shirt, as well as his wife's dismembered fingers, were spirited out of Mecca to the Umayyad stronghold in Damascus. There, in the Damascus mosque, the gruesome shirt and fingers were hung from the pulpit to fire up the crowd. Blood was demanded of Ali.[47]

Quickly, battles erupted between the forces of the entrenched Umayyad establishment and the followers of Ali. Ali had shifted his headquarters to Kufa in defiance of the wealthy Umayyad clans. The struggle would now be nothing less than Mesopotamia against Syria, Mecca, and the empire—the disenfranchised of Islam versus the privileged of Islam.[48]

Aisha demanded a fight to the death. In December 656, according to tradition, Aisha mounted her large, magnificent camel, known as al-Askar, and led a corps of armed avengers. At first they numbered only 3,000. But as she rode from town to town, Aisha gained thousands of additional zealots, who joined her demand for vengeance. At Basra, the governor rushed out of the city with an army of defenders to stop Aisha, according to the writings. Aisha, from atop al-Askar, passionately cried out to the governor's troops, asking who would cross to her side, the side of justice and revenge. In a dramatic climax to the confrontation, half the governor's army reportedly crossed the line and stood with Aisha. Now her forces totaled 30,000.[49]

Ali's forces were fewer, only 20,000, but better trained, being seasoned soldiers from the Mesopotamian garrisons. When the two sides met near Basra, the clash was bloody, unrelenting, and tactically focused around Aisha's camel, according to tradition. Ali's troops cut down Aisha's forces, contingent by contingent. Loyal to Mohammed's widow, her men fought to the death, surrounding her, protecting her at all costs. Aisha, atop her camel, moved from place to place on the battlefield. As she did, her troops moved with her, and came under the blade. Defending and attacking bodies piled up in the camel's wake, bodies on both sides. Thousands of bodies. Finally, Ali ordered his men to chop the legs off the camel so the combat could be hastened to a close. The beast dropped to the ground and Aisha was captured. As Mohammed's widow, however, Aisha was afforded ineffable respect. She was ceremoniously ushered back to one of Islam's holy cities— some say Medina, some say Mecca—where she remained quiet.[50]

That day in 656 CE, 10,000 fell at Basra in mutual slaughter over the right to vengeance, and the event was commemorated forevermore on the Moslem calendar as the Battle of the Camel.[51]

The Battle of the Camel did not end Islam's first civil war. For years, Umayyad forces in Syria and elsewhere kept the conflict alive through combat, disobedience to Ali, and disregard of arbitrations. Increasingly, Ali's loyal forces thinned as rebels throughout the realm defied his Islamic authority, preferring that of the ruling Umayyads. Finally, in 661, one morning in Ramadan, Ali was caught on his way to a Kufa mosque and stabbed to death with a poison-tipped sword.[52]

With Ali gone, the Umayyads assumed total control and ruled from Damascus for almost a century. But Basra and other areas remained mutinous and troublesome to all who tried to rule. None in the established government were considered legitimate. An ethic of defiance was inculcated.[53]

At one point, the rejectionist movement believed that Hussein, the last surviving son of Ali and hence of the family of the Prophet Mohammed, would reclaim the caliphate. On October 10, 680, Hussein was traveling to Kufa, probably for that reason. To stop him, the Umayyad governor in Syria ordered an army of 4,000 to take action. All Hussein's supporters in the town were murdered en masse. Then the Umayyad forces surrounded Hussein's band of 100, which included a number of Hussein's family. An onslaught of arrows felled the outer guard until the swordsmen moved in. Family members and loyal followers surrounded Hussein. Umayyad swordsmen downed them one by one—two brothers, six sons, and a nephew who died in his arms. Finally, it was only Hussein standing among the bodies. Then he, too, was killed. Only his young son escaped. Hussein and most of his group were then decapitated and their heads carried back as Umayyad war trophies.[54]

With the last descendent of Ali believed to have been killed, the Umayyads regained the caliphate and ruling control over the Moslem Empire. But a fierce minority in Mesopotamia never accepted the authority or legitimacy of the vast Moslem majority, which they saw as a government not of the people but over the people. The Umayyad dynasty began to crumble from incessant uprisings, assassinations, coups, invasions, and foreign attacks. In about 750, after nearly a century of strife and bloodshed, the last Umayyad caliph was murdered. Finally, Kufa was fully regained by its stalwart dissident community.[55]

To enshrine the place where the revered Ali was killed, the fervent Moslem believers of Kufa and Basra built a holy city named Najaf around the fateful mosque. Situated just beyond the western shore of the Euphrates, Najaf, named for "the high land where water cannot reach," was safe from river flooding. Najaf's cemetery was thought to be a gateway to paradise.[56]

Forevermore, centered in Najaf and extending through the rest of southern Mesopotamia to Basra, the followers of Ali would consider themselves as downtrodden, dispossessed, defeated, desperate to avenge, determined to seek true justice, and distrustful of power and authority. Eventually, this southern Mesopotamian movement formed a dissident political party that constituted at various times about 10 percent of Islam. They would revere their patriarch, Ali, as the first imam, the leader of their community. Each succeeding imam was deemed to be of direct lineage to Ali and considered the infallible, true supreme leader of their faith. This intensely doctrinaire movement, welded to its history, would forevermore call itself "the Partisans of Ali." In Arabic: *Shi'at Ali*—or *Shi'a,* for short. The outside world would call them *Shiites.* The majority of the remaining 90 percent of Islam would become known as *Sunnis.*[57] The differences would last forever.

Words cannot adequately describe the almost perpetual tragedy inflicted upon, and inflicted by, the Moslems and Mesopotamia during the five centuries following the ouster of the Umayyads. The land and the people were subjected to an unending river of conquests, revolts, sieges, and civil wars. Unspeakable carnage was exchanged between neighboring empires, between Islamic factions and allies, and frequently between brothers eyeing and vying for the throne. Treachery and extermination, rape and plunder, mass enslavement, and a penchant for outdoing previous cruelty and humiliations regularly plagued the realm between the two rivers. Perpetrators became victims and victims became perpetrators. Many volumes would be needed to chronicle the long list of accounts.

Replacing the ruling Umayyads were the Shi'a-supported Abbasids who hailed from the clan of Abdul Abbas, the uncle of the Prophet Mohammed. Quickly, the Abbasids relocated the seat of Islamic governance from Damascus to a new Shi'a city named Najaf, near Kufa. But then, the Abbasid rulers turned on the populace, launching a bloody series of mass murders against all who posed a political threat.[58]

The first Abbasid caliph reigned as al-Saffah, that is, "Shedder of Blood." He systematically killed all the remaining Sunni Umayyads. After four years, he died, only to be succeeded by his brother, known as al-Mansur, who killed any Shi'a groups who might contest Abbasid authority.[59]

At the same time, Mansur decided he needed a new city to glorify the new Abbasid dynasty. Mansur became intrigued by the site of an ancient Persian village on the Tigris, just north of the long-destroyed Babylon. He felt the conjunction of arable land and navigable river created the perfect site for a military-religious capital. So, at that neglected ancient spot, in 762, Mansur erected a bold new metropolis encased in concentric walled rings extending some two miles in diameter. The innermost ring, more than a mile wide, seated the caliphate, the Grand Green Mosque, and a magnificent domed palace topped by a figure of a horseman that spun like a weather vane as the wind shifted. The middle ring housed the garrison soldiers, many of whom had been transferred from the Shi'a city of Kufa. The general population lived in the outer ring. Each ring was accessible by four gates named for the four corners of the Abbasid Empire. Mansur referred to his impressive circular metropolis, four years in the building, along the western bank of the Tigris as "the Round City."[60]

Because the Round City was confined within its circles, growth necessitated suburbs built to its south and on the eastern bank of the Tigris. A series of boats created a pontoon bridge across the river to link the two sides. An Islamic House of Peace was later added, thus bestowing the expanding polis with the name City of Peace. But as more suburbs, markets, palaces, and public buildings mushroomed on both sides of the river, the sprawl became collectively known by the original name of the ancient Persian village: *Baghdad.*[61]

Baghdad developed into a jeweled center of great learning, science, and urban organization. An immense library and academies were established. Civilization soared as dozens of scientists, physicians, mathematicians, philosophers, scholars, and artisans converged to advance human knowledge and achievement. Boasting more than peace, scholarship, and governance, Baghdad arguably became the world's most exotic city, spawning such stories as *A Thousand and One Arabian Nights.* Tales of Aladdin and his wondrous lamp, the seven voyages of Sinbad, and Ali Baba and the 40 thieves all sprang from the spiced realm of Baghdad.[62] For many, Baghdad sat at the cultural apex of the Arab world.

However, no amount of civil and intellectual progress stemmed the depravity and brutality of the region's history. As the Tigris and Euphrates flooded and receded, so did the unspeakable inhumanities suffered by all of Mesopotamia. For example, in 837, the Byzantine Roman emperor invaded the town Zebetra, kidnapped about a thousand women and children, and mutilated the men by cutting off their ears and noses and then gouging out their eyes. In revenge, Abbasid generals launched a force of 200,000 warriors against the Byzantine Empire and kidnapped their women and children.[63] Such incidents simply never stopped.

As the grandeur of Baghdad grew, so did the self-esteem of the Abbasid caliphs, who became aristocratic and self-deifying. Suitors were made to kiss the ground when approaching the court. A royal executioner stood behind the caliph at all times, reminding all comers that swift death could be meted out for any reason. The caliphs even arrogantly crowned themselves "the Shadow of God on Earth."[64]

Eventually, the Abbasids, like all Mesopotamian dynasties before them, were murdered and deposed from power. The last genuinely potent Abbasid caliph abdicated authority to a Persian tribal chief in 945. Abdication was not enough. By January the next year, the caliph was dragged from his palace, paraded and scorned through the streets, and later his eyes gouged out with burning irons.[65]

About a hundred years later, the weakened caliphate formed a secret alliance with the predatory Seljuks, a confederation of unschooled, marauding Sunni Moslem tribes from the Eurasian steppes. Seljuks warred, pillaged, and raped as a way of life. The caliphate's object was to blunt the growing power of the Shi'a in Baghdad by any means. The Seljuks swarmed into the city, brutishly purged Shi'as from their government positions, unleashed a merciless reign of rape and murder throughout the city and surrounding lands, and then just stayed. The Seljuks assumed power and created a new dynasty in Baghdad. They installed Persian as the official language of the realm; hence Arabs could no longer conduct business in Arabic.[66] The alienation and sense of disconnection that Mesopotamians had continuously experienced from the central authority ruling them remained unabated as Moslems entered the second millennium CE.

But Mesopotamia and Baghdad never relinquished the resiliency of their spirit and the treasure of their civilization. No one chose to fight over Baghdad or Mesopotamia because it was worthless—but because it was precious. Indeed, the inherent prize of greater Mesopotamia essentially powered all the death and destruction that wracked the land.

Baghdad, through all the terrors and tyrants, remained a center of great knowledge for centuries. A public hospital was opened. Arabs innovated medical advances. An observatory was erected to chart the stars. The circumference of the globe was estimated in Baghdad centuries before Europe finally conceded that the earth was not flat. Alchemy, arithmetic, astronomy, optics, physics, zoology, and arts and letters of all kinds flourished there. Moreover, Mesopotamia became a vital nexus for world knowledge. Great Greek works of science, mathematics, and medicine found their way to Europe and Asia via translations compiled in Baghdad. The Arab world's first college of Islamic law, Mustanseriya College, was established in 1232, along with an 80,000-volume library.[67]

Baghdad and Mesopotamia never ceased commanding the heights over the intersection of intellectual and commercial exchange between the continents and across the declining Moslem Empire. As the world entered its second millennium of the Common Era, Baghdad and Mesopotamia fought the Crusaders, the Turks, and various European powers, experiencing great bloody triumphs and desperate defeats.[68] But through it all, the composite civilization in Mesopotamia grew and flourished.

Prosperity, however, rarely proliferated down to the masses that had always believed in the union of mosque and state. A fractious Arab elite prevailed, willing to conquer for and defend its opulence and power, even as bitter anger from the dispossessed masses roiled all the days of their magnificence.

Arrogance was never exiled from Mesopotamia. For all its learning and wisdom and spiritualism, the Arab establishment continued to denigrate Christians, and Europeans in general, as *kafirs,* that is, "infidels." Frequently, all Europeans were lumped together as "Franks," so named for the Germanic Franks that Islam battled from time to time. Arabs easily parried the ad hominem denigrations Europe heaped on them with their own countercurses. One aristocratic Moslem writer expressed a typical condescension, when he wrote of Europeans, "They do not cleanse or bathe themselves more than twice, and then in cold water . . . and they do not wash their garments from the time they put them on until they fall to pieces."[69]

But one day, imperial arrogance by a high-and-mighty caliph flung a special insult. It led to a protracted nightmare from which there was no recovery for greater Mesopotamia and indeed much of the Arab world.

It began in about 1218 in the Khwarazm Empire, which occupied the originally Persian territories now known as modern Uzbekistan. The land had been Islamic since the Arab Conquest, but as the Moslem Empire became fragmented, the Khwarazm shah, himself of Turkish roots, created his own empire and functioned as a self-appointed rival caliph. He expanded his dominion eastward toward Persia and beyond. When a foreign trade mission of several hundred merchants laden with valuables reached the Khwarazm city of Otrar, the governor, Inaljuk, with the caliph's sanction, humiliated them as spies, seized their wares, and executed them all.[70] In its day, such regal fiat must have seemed trifling.

But that trade mission personally represented Genghis Khan, the most feared man on earth, the head of a mighty empire of horsemen warriors that terrorized all of Eurasia. The khan had sent those merchants to Otrar to establish mutual commercial relations. Instead, they were robbed and executed. Therefore, the khan—the battle-tested instrument of the one pantheistic god—was spurned. Therefore, his god was spurned. The khan, this man who had literally ordered the killing of hundreds of thousands, who had caused so much hardship and inhumanity, was now uncharacteristically overcome with grief and insult. According to the writings, Genghis Khan withdrew to a mountaintop where he prostrated himself for some three days and beseeched the heavens for guidance.[71]

What followed was, quite simply, the wrath of Khan.

Who were the Mongols? The Mongols were of a race of fierce warriors from the scrubby Asian Steppe who employed revolutionary war tactics, clever espionage, and divisive politics to conquer all. At the time of the trade mission to Otrar, the Mongol Empire stretched from China to the frontier of the Crusade-weakened Islamic Empire. Whereas the mighty Eurasian armies before them had won or lost battles on their bravery and superior numbers, Mongols used trickery, feigned retreat, and small attack groups to confuse their adversaries and bait them into traps—and then annihilate them. The Mongols sometimes put women and boys on horseback or strapped dummies to spare horses to create the appearance of larger cavalries. Deployed in quickly multipliable squads of 10 men, when a force totaled 10,000 soldiers, it was led by a military commander carrying the rank of *Tumen*.[72]

The Mongols were nomads who lived on their horses and cherished the natural world. They despised walled cities. They also despised any who did not submit. Resistance was futile, they believed. The Mongols waged organized terror as a war tactic to inspire surrender. When they approached, they often did so in a great tumult. Sometimes they simply beat drums outside a walled city for days before an onslaught. Or they hurled incendiary missiles, or bombarded the city walls in a perfection of siegecraft. Even as terrified inhabitants did not sleep, the Mongol warriors rested and dined on the stores they had carefully pre-positioned.[73]

Unlike other invaders, their goal was not conquest and domination but utter destruction. Typically, an overrun city would be completely dismembered and rendered useless. Every living thing had to die—men and women, children, even cats and dogs. Death to opponents was a cruel, painful exercise—the more gruesome the murder, the greater the Mongol vindication. The Mongol custom was to report body counts by chopping off the ears of their victims. Bag after bag was filled and delivered to ranking officers as proof. This was more than warfare, more than plunder and subjugation, more than mere triumph—this was extermination.[74]

The end of Khwarazm began when the khan couriered to the shah a succinct message: Deliver for punishment the insolent governor Inaljuk, who had humiliated his trade mission. Naturally, the shah refused.[75] So the khan assaulted the cities—one by one. They were all laid waste.

By April 1219, after months of siege against Otrar, the scene of the original insult, the walls were finally breached.[76] But Otrar's governor Inaljuk escaped to a distant fortress with a force of defenders. The Mongols pursued him, and after a siege of two months, swarmed into the fortress, slaying hundreds of defenders. Finally, they broke into his heavily blockaded sanctum. His last two bodyguards were slain. But simple execution was to be denied Inaljuk. Instead, he was dragged back, struggling, kicking, and screaming for his life to Genghis Khan's camp near Samarkand. As a lesson about commerce, the khan reportedly ordered molten silver poured into Inaljuk's eyes and ears.[77]

But the khan was not finished. He swore, "All [Persian] cities must be razed, so that the world may once again become a great steppe, in which Mongol mothers will suckle free and happy children."[78]

The Mongols rode from city to city, leveling the walls and ravaging the mosques and public buildings The great mosque of Bukhara was gutted and converted to a stable. All the books were burned, except a chosen few relics, and the wealth looted. Finally, they commonly destroyed the irrigation canals to flood the fields and erase the viability of the area. With equal thoroughness, they murdered nearly all the people. Their means of massacre was intensely calculated. Mongol emissaries would politely order all the inhabitants out of the city into the fields for what they called "a census." Once assembled, the selections began. To the left, to the right. Those who could provide usable craft skills or who were sexually desirable were removed into bondage and worked, often to death. The rest were brutally killed.[79]

At Nessa, 70,000 people were ordered to bind each other's hands behind their backs. Then each one was systematically slaughtered as the masses awaited their turn. At Herat, about 60,000 were killed.[80]

At Merv, a major commercial hub in northeastern Persia, the populace was cunningly convinced they could safely exit the city in an orderly fashion, taking their most valued goods. It took four days for thousands of families to frantically gather their possessions and then nervously pass through the gate. They expected the promised safe passage. Instead, the 200 wealthiest men were identified and heinously tortured until they betrayed all their commercial agents and revealed their hidden troves of wealth. Then all the families were brutally torn from one another and hideously butchered. The continuous screams and shrieks of family members were so haunting that the scene burned itself into the accounts written at the time. A second wave sought out survivors and killed them. Several hundred who hid in underground refuges were detected and killed as well during a four-day rampage of death. Still later, intent on eradicating any who might somehow have escaped, the Mongols forced muezzins to call from the minarets. Thousands more came out from hiding, believing it a call of safety—they were mercilessly cut down.[81]

At Nishapur, everything was burned, crushed, and pillaged, and all who lived were savagely murdered. The city disappeared. It was leveled to rubble, reduced to a space—except for three pyramids. To prevent any survivors from hiding among the heaps of corpses, orders went out to decapitate everyone. Those heads were towered into three ghastly monuments of extermination: one pyramid of male heads, one female, and one comprised of children.[82] They stood as grotesque beacons and warnings.

After devastating the eastern flank of Islam, the Mongols paused, declining to enter Mesopotamia proper. Spread thin, they had other business far to the east in China. For nearly three decades, the Mongols were content to consolidate their domination, creating a vast empire that all Eurasia fearfully kowtowed to. Protection tribute was regularly and punctually paid. Silks, gold, silver, cattle, horses, ornate gifts, and everything else of value were showered upon the barbarians to keep them at bay and demonstrate awe. A far-flung administration and governance system was established to keep peace throughout the Mongol Empire. At its core was the Mongol imperative—no one and no one's god rivals the khanate. All who approached and paid tribute, be they kings, popes, or caliphs, were tolerated as vassals.[83]

When the great Genghis Khan died, the Mongol Empire divided itself into four hordes—one for each of his sons—stretching from China to the Mideast. The remnant of those who had decimated Khwarazm buffeted up against the ill-defined Persian border and greater Mesopotamia. Likewise, that part of the Moslem world was now becoming increasingly fragmented and autonomous. The Baghdad caliph and other Moslem potentates secretly promoted a constant guerrilla war against the Mongols. Roaming bands had fled to the mountains around Nishapur before the Mongol slaughters. Now these bands killed local fellow Moslems, especially Sunnis, who cooperated with the Mongol occupying administration.[84]

A vanguard of the guerrilla insurrection was a years-old sect of Shi'a devoted to the art of swift, secret, political murder, generally by a sudden, fatal stab wound. Ensconced in formidable mountaintop castles, the group indoctrinated young murderers-in-training with doses of Islam and rigorous political doctrine. It was rumored, probably wildly, that to heighten their fanaticism and make them tools of death, the order regularly smoked hashish. Hence, they were called the "Hashashin." They seized several castles and created their own defiant realm from Syria to Egypt to Persia. They became so dreaded a force that Sunni officials began wearing armor under their robes to blunt an unexpected knife attack. The sect of killers reached legendary proportions; in Europe, the traditional transliteration of "Hashashin," changing the *sh* to a simple *s*, permanently created a new word: *assassin*.[85]

The Assassins, according to accounts, sent 400 of their best to kill the ruling khan in the name of Islam. The khan's many bodyguards and spies foiled the conspiracy and blamed the entire Islamic establishment. In 1251, Grand Khan Mongke made the decision. Baghdad was to be demolished.[86]

The assignment was given to Hulagu Khan, the grandson of Genghis, who launched his forces two years later, after immense preparation. The spies, the conspirators, the astrologers, the livestock, the cavalry horses, the routes, the siege machines, a thousand Chinese engineers, agents to construct bridges and clear roads, the pre-positioned resupply of wine and flour—all was made ready. In 1253, he left Mongolia and swarmed west.[87]

Hulagu did not hate Islam. He just refused to bow to it or to any belief system other than his own. Himself a pagan, intrigued by Buddhist precepts, and married to a Christian princess, Hulagu felt that Islam was an affront to monotheistic Mongol beliefs about an omnipotent god of nature that was present in all things. What's more, Hulagu believed that the Mongols were the designated overlords of the earth and its inhabitants. Therefore, any organized religion that attempted to portray itself as supreme, including Islam, was anathema.[88]

Ironically, Hulagu's resentment of preeminent religion did not prevent him from creating uneasy alliances with crusading Christian Europe, which was eager to roll back the hegemony of Islam and oust it from Jerusalem. Hulagu related to Christian European countries not so much as an army of Christ but merely as geopolitical entities. His army was gladly reinforced with Christian contingents. At the same time, the Mongols conspired with the Shi'a to eliminate their Sunni dominators in Baghdad and found internecine support among Sunnis for ending their plague—the Assassins.[89]

By early January 1256, the long-awaited invasion was ready. The mighty Mongol military machine crossed the rivers into Persia. One by one, Hulagu confronted the supposedly impenetrable Assassin castles, relentlessly killing the masters, the soldiers, the recruits, and even infants reposing in cradles. The grand master himself was allowed to beg for mercy. It was denied. Various accounts are given of how the grand master was killed, but the Mongols themselves recorded that his escorts kicked him mercilessly and then completed his dispatch with a blade.[90]

Hulagu drove toward Baghdad. From his forward encampment at nearby Hamadan, Hulagu couriered a letter to Caliph Mostassim offering a chance to surrender and warning: Resistance is futile. "Strike not the point of an awl with your fist," wrote Hulagu, adding, "Mistake not the sun for the glowing wick of a flameless taper. Level the walls of Baghdad at once, fill its moats, leave government . . . and come to us. . . . If we march against Baghdad, you will not escape us even if you hide in the deepest earth or rise to the highest heaven."[91]

Caliph Mostassim, secure in his opulent surroundings in mighty, well-defended Baghdad, provocatively sent back a snide letter. "Young man, seduced by ten days of favoring fortune, you see yourself as High Lord of the universe and think you command the decisions of destiny. . . . Know you that from the West to the East, all who worship God and hold the true faith are my servitors. . . . Walk in the ways of peace and return."[92]

Hulagu gave the caliph's envoys a return message: "War is all that remains."[93]

Quickly, Mongol forces mustered at all the roads from Baghdad. A left flank then scaled the snow-covered mountains above Baghdad. There they found a fortress under the control of a disgruntled commandant, Ake. In exchange for favors, he agreed to betray the caliph and incite other commandants in Baghdad to join a rebellion. Once at the caliphate, Ake regretted his decision and swore loyalty anew to the Mostassim. En route back to his mountain fortress, Ake was grabbed and forced to call to the people within, "We are taking a census," oversee their exit, and then supervise the self-demolition of the fortress walls. He and his household were then murdered as well.[94]

Hulagu summoned an astrologer and asked what would happen next. The astrologer assured him, "The city of the Caliph will be taken by Hulagu." The Mongols attacked.[95]

As one flank approached suburbs along the southern bank of the Tigris, a horrified throng fled across the river to the Round City of Baghdad. Some offered any available boatmen jewels and gold just for the brief transport. Others in their panic simply jumped into the water to swim. The caliph's army rushed out to meet the horde and appeared at first to defeat the first division. But when they went farther toward the main Mongol forces, behind them they discovered the Tigris canals had been breached, flooding any route of retreat. The Mongols killed them all.[96]

A few days later, the Mongols staged at the west bank of the Tigris while other forces advanced from the east. Caliph Mostassim, trapped and desperate, finally offered to surrender. He dispatched an envoy with a message: "I have yielded to Hulagu's wishes, and hope that the prince will remember his promise [to spare my life]." Hulagu retorted, "I made my demand while in Hamadan," adding, "Now I am at the gates of the city, and my wish may be different."[97]

On February 5, 1258, after a six-day siege, the eastern fortifications were won. Entourage after entourage tried to reason with Hulagu, who would not lift his siege or the invasion. Escape was impossible. The rivers were blocked. The roads choked off. The mountain passes occupied. Finally, the people of Baghdad obeyed an invitation to peaceably file out of the city gates. They were promised safe passage to Syria. But first, a census. Normally, Baghdad's population was hundreds of thousands, but with the swell of terrified refugees from the surrounding suburbs and villages, it may have exceeded a million. Soldiers, clerics, civilians, merchants, children grappled, the high and mighty of Baghdad, as well as the low and obedient, filed out to the field, defenseless, their weapons left behind as instructed.[98]

Then, one by one, family by family, thousand by thousand, the Mongols did what they always did. Only the caliph was spared—and only for a time.[99]

For seven days, the barbarians burned every mosque, dismantled every major building, gutted every vestige of authority, and utterly brought Baghdad to destruction. "They swept through the city like hungry falcons," wrote a Persian historian, "or like raging wolves attacking sheep, with loose reins and shameless faces, murdering and spreading fear. . . . Bed and cushions made of gold and encrusted with jewels were cut to pieces with knives and torn to shreds. Those hidden veils of the great harem were dragged . . . through the streets and alleys, each of them becoming a plaything in the hands of a Tatar [Mongol] master."[100]

The caliph himself, spared only to be taunted in his own palace, was finally executed. The method is recorded variously, but the most reliable accounts indicate he was wrapped in a carpet or sack and trampled to death by stampeding horses.[101]

To drive home the message to Islam, Hulagu deliberately spared the Christian churches that had existed under Islamic protection payment. Nor were any of the church's members harmed. Indeed, one of the caliph's palaces was handed over to the Christian patriarch. The relieved Christian patriarch's chronicler penned these words: "During the time of Baghdad's supremacy, like an insatiable bloodsucker, she swallowed up the whole world. Now she has been punished for all the blood she has spilled and the evil she has wrought, the measure of her iniquity being filled."[102]

Shi'a conspirators were appointed to govern what little was left of Baghdad. The stench of rotting corpses was so strong, even the mighty Hulagu was driven from the city. As he left, he ordered the unkilled to reopen the bazaars and dispose of the mountains of bodies.[103]

No one will ever know how many were slaughtered at Baghdad. An Arab historian wrote, "If anyone were to say that at no time since the creation of man by the great God had the world experienced anything like it, he would only be telling the truth. . . . It may well be that the world from now until its end . . . will not experience the like again." It is thought that Hulagu himself later bragged to King Louis IX of France that more than 2 million were killed. A Persian historian of the period stated the number was closer to 800,000. Others have estimated much more. The city's normal bustling population of nearly a million was swelled by multitudes of fleeing Moslems from the suburbs and surrounding villages.[104] The higher death tolls are probably more accurate.

Elsewhere in Mesopotamia, Hulagu continued his extirpation of the Islamic hierarchy, especially Sunnis. Shi'a strongholds at Basra and Najaf were left unharmed; in fact, a Mongol guard was left to protect the shrine of Ali. But in the northern Jazirah province, in the former Christian town of Martyropolis, they sought out the fanatic Sunni Moslem Kamil Mohammed for an unspeakable death. Kamil Mohammed had crucified a Jacobite priest from Syria who had been traveling under a Mongol passport. Georgian and Armenian Christians helped surround the city until the population had been starved into submission. Once Kamil Mohammed was seized, bits of flesh were sliced from his body and forced into his mouth.[105]

Finally, Hulagu took Damascus, smashing the final vestiges of the caliphate. Kamil Mohammed's decapitated head was displayed on a lance throughout Syria.[106]

Mesopotamia began as the cradle of civilization. It flowered greatly into a majestic and vibrant empire where unstoppable knowledge, passionate thought, urbane sophistication, and the noblest aspirations of mankind coexisted with the violence, the inhumanity, and the bloodlust of all-corrupting theocratic power. Thousands of years in the making, the fruit of dynasties and divinities, the struggle of an entire people, hewn from throughout the Middle East, mighty Mesopotamia had been reduced to scorch and rubble. Public buildings were demolished. Its irrigation systems were undone, decimating agriculture. Books were turned to ash. An intricate political structure was dismantled.

Mesopotamia never recovered from the Mongols. Never. Its civilization had been robbed for the last time. This time it was permanent.[107]

CHAPTER FOUR

The Three Ottoman Provinces

After Hulagu, Mesopotamia descended into an age of desolation. The resilient Mesopotamian remnant tried to rebuild. Even Baghdad, which had been so mercilessly decimated, was not completely lifeless—just in shambles. Survivors, those chosen by the Mongols to continue, such as the Christians and those Moslems fortunate enough to escape before the slaughter, repopulated the city. Commerce, learning, and science resumed in various forms.[1]

After 1258, Mesopotamia was administered as a mere vassal nation by Hulagu's Il-khanate, that is, the Mongol subempire designated to rule the Middle East. The khans created their own pan-Mongolian civilization, a brutish order that, ironically, facilitated intercontinental commerce, diplomacy, and learning from China to Europe. Much of this enduring progress in civilization threaded through Mesopotamia and the surrounding lands. Still, genuine revival in Mesopotamia itself was intensely stunted. Baghdad and Mesopotamia had once been the center of the Islamic world. Now the region would develop neither as its own epicenter nor as East or West, but rather as a "Mideast," a mere crossroads under the Mongol thumb.[2]

What's more, 200 years of Crusades, beginning in 1095, heinously mass-murdered thousands of Moslems, along with Jews and other

49

non-Christians, throughout the Mideast. True, the waves of Christian knights and holy European pillagers did not drive as far as the Mesopotamian heartland. But their devastating impact on the Islamic world was felt in Mesopotamia, because mutual relations with its traditional Moslem neighbors stagnated.[3]

Moreover, Mesopotamia—and the Mideast in general during the fourteenth century—suffered the ravages of the same Black Death that decimated Europe. The continent lost a third of its people, perhaps 25 million persons. It has been said that Europe's total population was set back as many as three or four centuries by the high-velocity fatal combination of bubonic and pneumonic forms of the plague. In Mesopotamia and the Mideast, the loss of life was proportionally far worse than in Europe. Undoubtedly, the plagues smote millions in Mesopotamia—some report a third of its inhabitants; no one will ever know how many. After all, while the world-changing disease began in China, it is thought to have migrated to Europe via Mongol trade and military routes, especially through Mesopotamia and the Middle East.[4]

Whole Mesopotamian villages and sections of cities ceased to exist. The more congested the city, the more rapidly the flea- and rat-borne epidemic spread, and the higher were the heaps of swollen, rotting corpses awaiting cremation or mass burial. No sword-swinging conqueror had ever killed so many so swiftly over so large an area so suddenly. Even the best Islamic thinkers thought the world was coming to an end. The great Moslem historian, Ibn Khaldun, wrote in the 1370s of "a destructive plague, which devastated nations and caused populations to vanish." He continued with dread, "Civilization decreased with the decrease of mankind. Cities and buildings were laid waste, roads and way signs were obliterated, settlements and mansions became empty, dynasties and tribes fell weak. The entire inhabited world changed."[5]

Under Mongol control, the once-great civilizations of Mesopotamia continued as mere shadows of their illustrious past selves. During this time, however, the vast Mongol Empire itself was beleaguered by its own internecine feuds across Eurasia. The Mongol peoples, dominating so many lands, naturally became more ethnically diverse. Several Mongol leaders superficially, almost theatrically, adopted Islam, and even considered themselves pious Moslems.[6]

Nonetheless, Hulagu was hardly the last Mongol to sweep incalculable horror and scorch over Mesopotamia. The wrath of the Mongols was no mere fleeting campaign. Theirs was, literally, a recurring ruination—something handed down from generation to generation, almost as a Mongol birthright.

One fierce group of emerging fourteenth-century Mongols was made up of ancestral Turkics, a rugged brand of Central Steppe horsemen and raiders from the region now known as Turkmenistan. The man who rose to lead them was Timur the Lame. A pock-faced and scarred barbarian, Timur's high cheekbones tapered to a pointy beard, creating the visage of a craggy spear tip. Because he walked with a noticeable limp from an early battle wound, his epithet in Europe was "Tamer the Lame" or Tamerlane. Lame or not, he was an intrepid warrior who killed with complete dispassion and unparalleled sadism. In the hierarchy of Mongol savagery, Timur distinguished himself as more barbarous and bloodthirsty than all his predecessors.[7]

Timur assumed power among his own horde. To bolster his leadership, he claimed common ancestry with Genghis Khan. In the years after 1370, Timur, himself raised a Moslem, ruled with legendary violence, often killing for nothing more than perceived insolence.[8]

As thinning Mongol administrative control broke down, persistent rebellions and strikes by secret pockets of vestigial Assassins provoked Timur to action. In 1383, he marched on windswept Sistan, in southeastern Persia. To terrorize all in Sistan who opposed him, Timur encased 2,000 living people in a sand and water mix, which was then used to make construction blocks. Using these ghastly megaliths, he erected a tall tower of screaming souls. Then the irrigation and dam system, so indispensable to the area, was wrecked, undoing centuries of agricultural development. Sistan was permanently returned to a parched desert.[9]

In his drive to destroy all resistance, Timur turned toward Mesopotamia. He swarmed in from southern Persia with a murderous Turco-Mongolian horde described as "ants and locusts covering the whole countryside, plundering and ravaging." In 1393, Timor terrorized Baghdad with three months of pure spoliation and slaughter. From Baghdad, his army proceeded north to Tikrit, where it liquidated the garrison and piled the hacked-off heads into grim minarets atop the demolished walls.[10]

Timur continued his conquests in various directions, almost always dispensing with either hegemony or tribute, preferring instead the incessant delivery of unrestrained torment and death. Only select artisans survived, and these were returned to his camp at the majestic garden city at Samarkand in Persia. There they constructed a magnificent city attesting to Timur's glory. However, those deemed useless were never spared. When he encountered Christian Armenians in the Anatolia region of modern Turkey, the garrison sent children out to sing a song of peace; Timur's cavalry simply galloped over them. Later, he buried the soldiers alive in the city's moat. In Damascus, he massacred the men relentlessly; the mothers were abducted as slaves, leaving their infants to die unattended.[11]

At Isfahan, in Persia, he ordered the entire city depopulated. When the citizens fought back and massacred his garrison, Timur retaliated with awesome wrath. Unlike his predecessors, content to stack dozens of heads, or even hundreds, into frightful pyramids or minarets, Timur built soaring twin towers in Isfahan. He used 70,000 beheaded beings. So many decapitated heads littered hellish Isfahan that the excess not arrayed atop ramparts was simply piled in the streets.[12]

On July 1, 1401, Timur returned to Baghdad for his second and final sacking. He launched a six-week siege at the height of an intolerable Mesopotamian heat wave that broiled and suffocated men inside their armor. At noon, when the heat was its most intense, he stormed the ramparts, knowing its defenders would have pulled off their stifling helmets. Some said he slew 20,000. Some said the dead were simply too numerous to count. This time, Baghdad was thoroughly vandalized and its complex irrigation system systematically wrecked. So complete was the devastation that its prior recoveries were utterly negated. Nearly four decades later, an Egyptian historian observed that Baghdad could no longer be recognized as a true city.[13]

Within 50 years, Europe's Age of Exploration would ensure that Mesopotamia never really recovered. Portugal was determined to explore both the interior and periphery of the nearby African Continent and to find a sea route to India and China. Bartolomeu Dias's historic voyage in 1488 from Portugal past the southern tip of Africa, later named the Cape of Good Hope, was only the beginning. In 1492, Columbus sailed across the Atlantic, also searching for a route to India and the East, only to discover a new world in the opposite direction. A half decade later, in 1498, Portuguese navigator Vasco da Gama finally rounded the Cape of Good Hope, reached the Indian harbor of Calicut, and then in 1499 returned safely to Portugal.[14]

The world changed. A modern trade route to India and the East was now open. Christianity, not Islam, now controlled the commercial byways. The centuries-old caravans and coastal seafarers so dependent on Mesopotamia, the Middle East, and the Mongol Empire, as well as all the principalities and despots attached to them, would become outmoded. Basra, once a thriving, almost irreplaceable port, was no longer Mesopotamia's precious gateway to the Persian Gulf and from there to India.[15] Mesopotamia dwindled in wealth, value, and geographic significance to little more than a frontier character.

Indeed, gone except for rubble and recollection was any semblance of Baghdad as a great civilization of a great nation. For centuries ahead, Mesopotamia would be a mere grouping of outpost provinces, once again ruled from afar by a foreign people—this time the Ottomans. As before, devoid of national identity or cohesion, Mesopotamian society distilled down to its basic units—the clan and the tribe against everyone and anyone.

For decades before Timur twice vanquished Baghdad, the Mongol presence in Mesopotamia and the Middle East had become increasingly Turkic. Not only had the disparate tribal Turks of the Central Steppe become deeply integrated into the Mongol dominions, soon Turkic Mongols became so numerous, they subsumed the very ethnic and cultural character of the western Mongols. Mongol leaders were minting coins bearing Turkish inscriptions instead of Mongolian as early as the latter thirteenth century. Timur himself was Turkic, born in the Persian border region Samarkand, an area now in modern Uzbekistan. Timur's warriors were so Turkic by nature that they rode against their adversaries waving banners and shrieking the Turkish battle cry, "*surun!*"[16]

About a year after Baghdad fell to Timur for the last time, he turned northwest toward the Ottoman Empire. On July 20, 1402, Timur defeated the Ottoman forces at Ankara in the Anatolia region.

His plunder there lasted well into the next year. In the process, Timur extended his Turco-Mongolian political influence to previously Ottoman-controlled lands.[17]

However, even before Timur stormed against the Ottomans, the Mongol Empire had already lessened to a political veneer, stretching from China's shore to eastern Europe. The khanates began collapsing of their own breadth and weight, as well as interminable succession squabbles.[18]

On February 18, 1405, as Timur was preparing to surge against China to resurrect a single unified Mongol Empire, he died, perhaps of a disease—no one is sure. A slave named Ahmad ibn Arabshah, captured as a boy by Timur, lived to write a biography of the psychopathic killer. He commemorated Timur's funeral in the following sentence: "Then they brought garments of hair from Hell and drew forth his soul . . . to the cursing and punishment of God, remaining in torment and God's infernal punishment."[19]

Soon after Timur's death, the Mongol presence in Mesopotamia dimmed into oblivion.

In the early 1500s, the sea-lanes around Africa became waves of gold. Portuguese cartographers made massive and increasingly precise maps of the coastline. Maps charting waters around Africa were so valuable, they became state secrets. The open ocean became Mesopotamia's final commercial undoing. Starting in 1507, Portuguese conquerors seized the island of Hormuz, which controlled the strategic hump-shaped Strait of Hormuz, thus choking off the Persian Gulf and the way east toward India to any rivals. Despite repeated attempts from Basra to break the blockade, and one temporary ouster, the Portuguese ruled the strait as a linchpin in their burgeoning maritime empire.[20]

Meanwhile, during the post-Timur doldrums, the irrepressible Shi'as rose once again, this time as the Safavid regime of Persia. The ornate, red-capped Safavids exhumed militant Shiism, again using the sword to convert. They looked upon Mesopotamia's Shi'a holy places, such as Najaf, as too important not to safeguard. Beginning in 1508, the Safavids conquered and annexed the three main sectors of the country: the Mosul region in the north, the central area surrounding Baghdad, and the southern district of Basra.[21]

The young Safavid strongman, Ismail I, crowned himself shah of Persia, and heretically claimed to be the representative of the final Hidden Imam—in Shi'a belief, the Deliverer who will never have a human representative. But the desperate Shi'as overlooked this heresy and welcomed a new source of political power. Ismail demanded that the predominantly Sunni population of Persia convert to Shiism, and even required a ritual cursing of the first three Sunni caliphs. In Mesopotamia, Shah Ismail embarked on a similar rampage against Sunnis, ousting them from schools and defiling graves. This pitted the resurgence of Shiism, entrenched in dilapidated Mesopotamia, against the new seat of Sunni authority—the powerful Turkish Ottomans. The Turks marched on Baghdad in 1534. Local Sunnis revolted and massacred Shi'as in anticipation of the invasion. Once in control, the Ottomans expelled the Safavids and annexed the three Mesopotamian regions as official *vilayets,* or provinces, of the Ottoman Empire.[22]

With few interruptions, the Ottomans ruled Mesopotamia from just after 1535 until the end of the first decades of the twentieth century. Their sixteenth-century postbarbarian medievalism defined the Middle East forevermore. The Turks ensured that all the foreign domination, material exploitation, irrelevant governmental authority, economic stagnation, ethnic strife, and cultural alienation of the previous five centuries would become a seemingly immutable legacy.

Who were the Ottomans? Who are the Turks?

Originally, the Turks were not one homogeneous people or even practitioners of one religion. The first Turkic tribes of the Central Steppe, such as the Kipchaks, Uzbeks, and Karluqs, were fierce, unwashed fighters and horsemen raiders. In the first millennium, most were pagan, but many gradually converted to Islam. One group of Turkics, the Seljuks, had captured Baghdad in 1055 and established a dynasty that ruled until the Mongol slaughters.[23]

Large groups of Turkic clans either assimilated into the Mongol hordes or fled west toward Anatolia, which is now in modern Turkey. The transplanted masses were broadly Eurasian, melding the physical features of the Chinese, steppe tribes, Persians, Mesopotamians, and Armenians, among others. These clans became known as *ghazis,* that is, lionized attackers of the infidels. How these Turkish raiders coalesced into the Ottoman nation is a blend of ethnic fact and dynastic myth. But it is said that in about the 1320s, the migrated Turks formed an Anatolian principality, almost completely pastoral, under their leader Osman. Osman's followers were termed *Osmanlis,* that is, "associates or followers of Osman." From the Turkish Osmanli, a series of rough permutations and transliterations yielded the European appellation, *Ottoman.*[24]

True, the Ottomans began as an Anatolian principality in a region crowded with such realms. However, from this small home territory, the Ottomans conquered one neighboring city, emirate, and kingdom after another, creating the borders of a new world power, the Ottoman Empire. Indeed, the early Ottomans waged almost perpetual war. For more than a century, the new empire pushed west into the Balkans, Greece, and elsewhere in Europe, as well as east into the Fertile Crescent and south into North Africa and Arabia, creating a truly Eurasian dominion for Islam. In fact, the Ottomans' sphere was geographically more European than Asian.[25]

In 1453, the Ottomans finally overwhelmed the fortifications of Constantinople, the seat of the Christian Byzantine Empire, also known as New Rome. Heroes in the Islamic world, the Ottomans now shifted their capitol to Constantinople. It is said that they popularly renamed it "Istinpolin" from the overheard Byzantine Greek phrase, *eis ten polin,* or "in the city." This moniker evolved into "Istanbul." Both names—Istanbul and Constantinople—survived, attesting to the city's unique status, where East meets West.[26] From here, the Ottoman sultan became a major factor in European politics and trade, and was able to conclude genuine treaties with the continent's Christian nations.

In many cases, after the Ottomans conquered a territory, they did more than just rule over the land; they formally annexed it as an official province. The Ottoman battles against east European Christian territories were deemed Holy Wars, and therefore all those lands were annexed and eventually recognized as such by subsequent treaties.

Ironically, all the battles against Moslem territories were considered equally justified by the Ottomans, and although these lands belonged to other Moslems, they were also annexed and internationally recognized as such. To justify such hegemony against fellow Moslems, the Ottoman sultan obtained specious religious rulings, such as those against the Safavid Shi'as, declaring waging war against them to be "more important than fighting the infidels."[27]

With so much conquest, the Ottomans were constantly adding provinces. In 1527, an Ottoman roster named only 12 provinces stretching from Asia Minor to Egypt. By 1609, the sultan's chancery clerk, Ayn Ali, listed 32 provinces, from Bosnia to Tripoli, from Tunis to Syria. Hence, after the sultan's military overran Mesopotamia, its three main regions routinely became three separate provinces of the empire. Beginning in 1535, those three provinces were named for their largest cities: Mosul in the north, Baghdad in the middle, and Basra in the south.[28]

But not all provinces were equal members of the Ottoman Empire.

Ottoman provinces were highly organized and administered, whether they were central to the empire's existence or merely maintained as a remote source of taxes and tribute. For many years, the sultan exercised absolute control over everyone and every place. But he greatly delegated his authority to governors-general, one for each province. The more important the province, the more prestigious and valued was the appointment.[29]

Each governor-general was administratively all-powerful in his own territory. He was expected to raise and finance territorial armies for the sultan. In exchange, the governor-general was empowered to grant and revoke patronage, impose and waive the death penalty on individuals, decide law cases, and collect fines—the proceeds of which he kept personally. Governors-general could extract a wealth of taxes, tribute, and other emolument from the far-off regions they oversaw. Hence, a governor-general could accrue great personal fortune at the expense of his province. These positions were generally, but not always, appointive, rather than hereditary. Thus, each governor-general was constantly subservient and dependent upon the pleasure of the sultan for his personal fortune.[30]

Administratively, nearly all provinces were sectioned into districts known as *sanjuks,* again generally organized around the largest town or city. The Ottomans were intensely bureaucratic. Sanjuk registrars periodically swept through their districts compiling detailed censuses of all peasant possessions, farm goods, marriages and deaths, and household members. Ideally, everyone was to be registered. Everything was to be taxed.[31]

The governor-general's relation to his province was generally one of dispassionate financial exploitation. To help him ensure the regular flow of tax and tribute and to maintain order, the governor personally designated fiefs and sanjuk governors throughout his province. These subordinates would not only rule their fiefdom and sanjuk, they would organize the army units needed to defend the borders. The term *sanjuk* means "flag," and each fief would assemble for battle under its own flag. Moreover, the fiefs were subdivided into subfiefs, ruled by a local cavalryman controlling small areas of just a few villages.[32] In many ways, the Ottoman structure was merely an Islamic variant on the military and nobility systems of feudalism, seignorialism, and serfdom that so thoroughly exploited the Christian masses of Europe.

A mixture of local and imported fiefs and sanjuk governors maintained a certain tension between local strongmen and imposed overseers. It was all designed to avert insurrection and promote the uninterrupted flow of wealth out of every corner of the province and into the sultan's coffers through these governmental and political middlemen. In fact, each fief and subfief was assigned an appraised value in silver coins, dependent on the revenues that could be reliably drained from the peasants and city dwellers.[33]

Commerce and wealth became so important to the Ottomans that thousands of families were coercively moved to help develop the capital city's economy. For example, some 30,000 individuals from the Balkans were forcibly transplanted to several dozen empty villages near Istanbul for commercial development. The *ghazi* days were over. Jewish merchants and traders, as well as other non-Moslems, were welcomed and allowed to thrive as *dhimmis,* a protected class within an Islamic society. As long as Jews, Christians, and other infidels acknowledged the primacy of the Islamic state, they could prosper unmolested. In 1477, a census of Istanbul and the nearby commercial quarter of Galata listed 16,324 families, but only 9,486 were Moslem. Greek Orthodox Christians totaled 3,743 families and Jews made up 1,647 families, with the balance composed of Armenians, Gypsies, and others.[34]

Greater Istanbul became a true metropolis, thriving on and tolerant of diverse ethnic groups. By the late 1500s, some 40 percent of its citizens were non-Moslem. The city's population may have neared 800,000, ranking it the second largest in Europe. Commerce became the lifeblood, bread, and salt of the empire. Every precious aspect of trade was highly regulated, from production to price, from purity to point of purchase. Weights and measures were elevated to a strict state function. Government-licensed brokers, and indeed government monopolies, were mandated for certain stuffs. Many goods were so intensely controlled, they could enter Istanbul only at certain gates; from there, they were tracked by trade patrols until they reached the retailers. Smuggling and profiteering were severely punished—from fines and seizures to flogging, and worse. Professional and trade guilds formed, and these crossed religious lines, emphasizing commercial caste, not mosque or church. Indeed, the sultan decreed that specific professions, in addition to social groups, were required to wear apparel that clearly identified their trades.[35]

By the late 1600s, some 2,000 ships docked annually at Istanbul, transiting everything from wine to livestock to all corners of the earth. Anything that made life sensual and spiced, durable and desired, transited through the empire. The Ottomans introduced coffee to the world. The first two coffeehouses opened in Istanbul and soon after, coffee became a major export to Europe and even to the colonies in America. The great Ottoman commercial engine—goods in, goods out—made it possible to exchange raw materials and manufactured goods worldwide on a level previously unknown, spurring industrialization in Europe, especially in Great Britain.[36]

Commercial wealth was the Ottoman way. By the mid-seventeenth century, Istanbul—the new center of the Islamic world—not only boasted 152 mosques, but also a magnificent multidomed marketplace hosting about 1,000 shops, plus an additional 800 shops spread throughout the city, along with 54 mills, 13 bathhouses, and an entire network of warehouses, bakeries, and workshops. Riches beyond belief inured to the new caliphs of commerce. About a thousand magnificent mansions and palaces for the sultan, his families, his court, and his ennobled pashas exalted Istanbul and its patterned skyline.[37]

But did the almost surreal affluence of Istanbul ever trickle down to the outer provinces? All magnificent empires and nations possess destitute corners. In the far-flung Ottoman Empire, Mesopotamia inhabited the neglected frontier.

Sanjuk governors and fief holders embraced no allegiance to their subjects and freely moved through the political hierarchy, as any other detached politico would, jockeying for better appointments and greater proximity to the sultan. Provincial officials were often replaced more than once per year. With the generation of tribute and taxes being a salient feature of any province, the three Mesopotamian provinces ranked low in the realm. In fact, in 1528, a third of the empire's income arose from just two wealthy provinces: Syria and Egypt. The chief value of Mesopotamia to the empire was not in heightening the sultan's tower of material wealth, but in creating a strategic, perhaps even desolate, Sunni buffer against the still-viable Shi'a threat residing in Safavid Persia.[38]

Nor were the Ottomans capable of governing Mesopotamia. By the late 1500s, they could barely govern themselves. They were descended from rugged steppe horsemen, but once they embraced the limitless riches of imperial commerce and tribute, they found regal life appealing. Sultans and their pashas lavished troves of money on themselves in ways unimaginable to the impoverished subjects in Mosul, Basra, or Baghdad. Rivaling the most ostentatious excesses of the czars and European monarchs, the Ottomans constructed a complex servant pecking order comprised of numerous imperial door holders, food tasters, coachmen, and even pickle holders. Each was dressed in elaborate, turbaned vestments. With iron regimentation, they reported to a hierarchy of servitor captains and other martial-style superiors, clept with such honorifics as Chief Turban Folder, Chief Attendant of the Napkin, and Senior of the Dishes.[39]

The sultan's extravagant kitchen demands taxed an entire empire. One order alone requisitioned about 113,000 kilograms of clarified butter from the Crimean port of Caffa. Whole colonies of Russian prisoners were resettled to help produce cereals. One festival banquet called for 118 kilograms of pepper to season lamb and soup, plus more than 12,000 kilograms of honey to smother the baklava. Even though they functioned as a Sunni caliphate, the Turkish appetite for culinary extravagance rivaled even their devotion to Islamic holy sites. For example, in 1532, the palace allotted 14,000 gold ducats to Mecca and

Medina; during that same year, it spent 13,866 ducats on sugar, spices, and similar items, plus 12,053 ducats on jewelry and finery.[40]

The Islamic injunction of cleanliness was the inspiration to update the old Roman and Byzantine bath into a whole new lifestyle, the Turkish bath. It became not only a place to wash, but also a rendezvous for the important to see and be seen. Long trains of attendants—men and women—helped as pashas and viziers came into royal contact with water. Rubdowns, scrubs, and skin treatments, as well as ointments, special ornate slippers, a rack full of exquisite bathing wraps, and coteries of servants created an elite atmosphere that elevated the Turkish bathhouse from religious ritual to social club. Eventually, a community of such bathhouses served not only the ruling class, but pretenders and imitators as well.[41]

Then there were the harems. Within the sultan's magnificent palaces were accommodations for hundreds of concubines, ladies in waiting, and slave girls, white and black, maintained for sexual pleasure, day and night. The term *harem* comes from the Arabic and Semitic *haram,* that is, "forbidden" or "untouchable." Confined to special windowless, sunless, and blandly walled quarters within the palace's inner sanctum, the harem was accessible only through the fabled Gate of Bliss. Entry was restricted to a favored few in the palace. Harem women, even though confined, were tutored and attended to by a hierarchy of several hundred white and black eunuchs. No man could gaze upon a woman in the sultan's harem. However, with his penis and testicles surgically removed, a eunuch was deemed to be "less than a man." The Chief Black Eunuch functioned as the supreme overseer and caretaker of the entire harem and its thousands of occupants.[42]

At times, the harem's population approached 4,000. Its women were constantly in demand. For instance, as a young man of 24 years of age, Sultan Ibrahim the Debauched was renowned for having sex with 24 women in a single day—one per hour. For such occasions, he wore a special "orgy robe," decorated with priceless gems. At one point, the irrepressible Ibrahim thought size mattered. He dispatched couriers far and wide to locate the fattest woman in the realm. They brought back a massive Armenian who became Ibrahim's special paramour. But a jealous rival strangled her, thus ending the special arrangement. When harem women were discarded or no longer useful, some were set free, but many were simply sewn into bags and thrown into the Bosporus Strait. Sultan Ibrahim alone ordered eunuchs to cast hundreds of bound consorts into the strait to drown.[43]

Harems became more than just prurient pleasure palaces within the palaces. The female members of the royal family also took up sheltered residence there, just as they would in the separate women's quarters of most Islamic homes—albeit on a massively more gilded basis. Because the sultan and his circle spent so much time enveloped in the ecstasy and familial harmony of the harem, the women's abode took on political significance as well. It was from the harem that top echelons of the Sublime Porte—the European name for the Ottoman government—could be more subtly influenced. Harem women came to wield genuine political power. Moreover, the stories of wild debauchery, perversion, and unbridled sexual indulgence in the harem led European capitals to believe that on occasion more could be accomplished in the chambers beyond the Gate of Bliss than through traditional diplomatic channels. Consequently, foreign ambassadors to the Sublime Porte were clever enough to cultivate contacts within the harem establishment to augment their regular representations and démarches.[44]

Eventually, the Ottoman harem became one of several central factors precipitating the decay and fall of the empire itself, as well as its ability to rule Mesopotamia.[45]

First, harems were massively expensive, requiring the devotion of whole fortunes. The humblest slave girl cost 400 to 500 German talers, each taler valued at 25.98 grams of silver. Whatever her station, every female was dressed in the finest robes, shawls, slippers, and accessories, generally jewel-emblazoned, one more posh than the next, in a circular competition among concubines and their armies of servants to achieve preeminence. If freed, slave women departed with their opulent possessions. Hence the investment was never-ending. One late seventeenth-century French diplomat observed in a report that the imperial treasurer's chief task was "to look for new slave girls and to dress them."[46]

The financial excesses of the harem were only symptomatic of the irrational fiscal policies that gripped every aspect of the Ottoman

Empire. More important was the issue of succession and governance itself. Here the harem played a pivotal role.

Under Ottoman practice, a sultan could sire legitimate children with any of the four wives allowed by Islam and any of hundreds of slave concubines. The sultan's sons by slave women stood equal to those of regular wives, as long as the monarch acknowledged them. Such acknowledgment automatically conferred special status upon the concubine, since she now became the mother of an heir to the throne. Incessant procreation—nine or more simultaneous concubine pregnancies were not unusual—created a plethora of potential heirs, born of either the sultan's slaves or his four wives. Indeed, the distinction blurred, since many Ottoman sultans were in fact the offspring of slave mothers. Therefore, the harem was not just a center for sexual gratification. Swirling overhead and rumbling beneath the sheets were the dynamics of who would be the next sultan—and who would not.[47]

In the first generations, when a sultan died, his many contending sons would launch horrific civil wars, which by their violence threatened the very existence of the empire. The solution? Murder the family. To save the realm, when sultans approached death, they systematically murdered their sons, save one—the designate. Or the newly ascended son would kill his brothers. Fratricide became an institutional Ottoman tradition, endorsed by the empire's Islamic scholars. In the 1400s, Sultan Mehmed formally wrote such killings into law: "For the welfare of the state, the one of my sons to whom God grants the sultanate, may lawfully put his brothers to death. A majority of the *ulema* [body of Koranic sages] considers this permissible."[48]

Fratricide continued unabated throughout most of the 1500s. Selim murdered his brothers in 1511. Suleiman killed his son in 1553 and his brother in 1561. Most heirs were strangled, but other methods were employed. Murad V's five brothers were assassinated by bow and arrow—all on a single day in December 1574. A few decades later, Mehmed III commanded a full palace massacre: the simultaneous execution of his 19 brothers and more than 20 sisters.[49]

The same day Murad was crowned sultan in 1574, his father's coffin, with the coffins of five princes behind it, was paraded through the streets of Istanbul as an outward sign of accession. On Mehmed III's accession in 1595, the sight of 19 coffins wending through the city was apparently too much for the weeping residents and palace. Thereafter, young princes were exiled not to provinces where they could function as governors and learn something of the affairs of state, but to the harems—where they could do virtually nothing.[50]

From the 1600s, with a few exceptions, those who would become Ottoman rulers spent nearly their entire lives from boyhood in the claustrophobic confines of the harem. Their small suites, isolated from the rest of the palace, were termed *kafes,* or "cages," where they were spoiled, surfeited, sexed, and schooled. But when the time came to assume the throne, they knew nothing of government, finance, militaries, statecraft, or the real world.[51] These were the people who ruled the Ottoman Empire.

True power in the realm devolved to others, such as well-placed harem women and various segments of the military establishment. Among the soldier classes rising in importance were the elite Janissary guards. The Janissaries, in particular, were a volatile and unpredictable group. When the empire began running out of Moslem warriors, it formed the Janissaries, drawn in large measure from Christian boys "levied" from their eastern European villages. In an Ottoman protocol called "the Collection," children were selected pro rata, systematically taken from their families, and raised as a special standing army. The abducted ones were nicknamed "New Troops," *Yen Ceri* in Turkish, transliterated "Janissary." From time to time, they would stage their own revolts.[52]

The empire slowly began disintegrating. Shortly after Sultan Suleiman I died in 1566, the Ottomans started losing battles and were not infrequently forced into land-ceding treaties. Bands of unpaid soldiers roamed the countryside as bandits and raiders. Local insurgencies erupted throughout the dominion, including in Basra, which was constantly beset by Bedouin pillagers. Governance of the remote provinces became even more arbitrary, centering on tax, tribute, and suppressing rebels. It rarely related to the inhabitants or their welfare. In Mesopotamia, this meant a continuation of irrelevant, exploitative authority, characterized by conspiracy, betrayal, assassination, and chaos both in the capital and in the provinces.[53]

For example, in 1622, the Janissaries stationed in Baghdad rebelled and took possession of the city. When the sultan sent a regular force to confront the rebel contingents, the Janissaries made an alliance with the empire's Shi'a rivals in Persia, paving the way for an invasion from the east. So the sultan bribed the captain of the Janissaries, Bakr Subashi, offering to make him governor of Baghdad if only he remained loyal. Bakr agreed, reneging on his promise to the Persians. But that quid pro quo was thwarted because Bakr's son then secretly allied with Shah Abbas of Persia against his father. Bakr's counter-treachery facilitated the Persian entry into Baghdad. When Abbas finally took the city on January 12, 1624, he massacred all the Sunnis. Then, for good measure, he turned on his Janissary allies, boiling them in oil on mere principle. During this period, other Janissary units in Istanbul deposed the sultan for his military blunders, and finally assassinated his mentally retarded successor. This was stunning proof that Istanbul could hardly control its provinces, east or west.[54]

Nor was there economic incentive. Basra, once a teeming port, now stagnated under the Portuguese blockade, making it even less valuable to the Sublime Porte. At one point in the mid-1600s, one caravan, made up of hundreds of camels, each laden with valuable goods, arrived in Istanbul every eight days from the Turkish port of Izmir, whereas Basra could dispatch only two per year. Moreover, the administrative structure and financial value of the southern half of Mesopotamia was so paltry that the payment system needed to maintain local cavalrymen, which was so entrenched in other provinces, simply did not exist in either Baghdad or Basra.[55]

Ottoman armies, whether loyal to the Sublime Porte or to their own selfish pecuniary interests, recaptured Baghdad for the last time in 1638. In retribution for Abbas's persecution of Sunnis, Turkish forces promptly countermassacred most of the city's Shi'as. To reduce further insurrections, Ottoman contingents then sought out Shi'as throughout the three Mesopotamian provinces and systematically slaughtered them as well. The next year, in 1639, the weakened empire finally sued for peace with Persia, signing a treaty that established a formal border, recognized internationally. That border agreement, with several bloody interruptions, has lasted to modern times.[56]

The slow-motion collapse of the empire continued as Suleiman II assumed power in November 1687. Suleiman II had been confined to his *kafe* from age six. After four decades, he was abruptly pulled from the harem, sobbing and unwilling to leave, but nonetheless instructed by palace officials to accept the sultanate. Gaunt and petrified, the middle-aged pasha, who had virtually never roamed beyond the outer courtyard of the palace, pleaded for execution rather than ascent to the throne. "If my death has been commanded," begged Suleiman II, "say so. Let me perform my prayers, then carry out your orders. Since my childhood, I have suffered forty years of imprisonment [in the *kafe*]." Emphasizing that he was totally unequipped to run an empire, Suleiman II added, "It is better to die at once than to die a little every day." His request to be murdered was ignored and he was installed as the new sultan. During his reign, he quelled another rebellion and enacted modest reforms, and he died in 1691.[57]

During the 1700s, the empire slumped further and further into paralysis. It had been careening toward bankruptcy for nearly a century. The harems, the military units, the grandiose architectural projects, the palace's largesse, and callow management frittered away their fabulous fisc. As early as 1623, Sultan Murad IV informed the Janissaries that his treasury was incapable of paying them. The unpredictable soldiers agreed to remain in cohesive units, but demanded that gold and silver from the palace be melted down, converted to coins, and distributed among their ranks.[58]

Despite the towering outward extravagance of the Turkish lifestyle, the financial realities manifested in telling ways. Hoarding became commonplace. In 1863, Turkish vizier Kara Mustafa was beheaded for the military defeats at Vienna. Mustafa's head was brought to the sultan on a silver plate. When Mustafa's home was searched for loot, 3,000 gold purses were discovered buried beneath his cemented bath. Earlier that same year, when an Austrian soldier in Venice impaled and disemboweled an Ottoman officer, he discovered six gold ducats secreted in the Turk's stomach.[59]

Yet the pasha class, like many compulsive bankrupts, was incapable of reducing its outlandish wastefulness. Sultan Mustafa, retarded but still all-powerful, threw coins into the sea so fish could have "spending money." Sultan Ahmet I embarked on a seven-year construction project to erect the wondrous Blue Mosque, designed by the greatest Ottoman architect of the day. To finish the edifice, Ahmed plundered monies and materials from across the empire and even pulled tiles off other buildings to complete the 21,000 needed just to decorate the gallery. Expensive and unprofitable warring with neighboring empires, from the Hapsburgs to Russia, continuously squandered men and money.[60]

In 1695, the Sublime Porte was so anxious to generate cash, it introduced the concept of "tax farming," that is, granting notable provincial families the right to collect farm taxes in their area in exchange for advance payment of the estimated revenue. Within a few years, this concept was rooted throughout the empire, from the Balkans in the west to the Arab territories in the east. By making the lucrative tax farm grants a matter of imperial fiat, renewable from time to time, Istanbul hoped to maintain a semblance of loyalty at the extremities of its receding dominion. Central allocations for provincial administration ceased because the funds did not exist. So governors were appointed to run their provinces and sanjuks as potentates, ravishing whatever tax, tribute, penalty, and baksheesh they could wring from the local people. Using such money lures to maintain order was preferable to Istanbul, because military efforts to project authority were no longer reliable.[61]

In 1690, just before tax farming was introduced, Bedouin tribes attempted to overrun Basra, weakened by a fresh outbreak of plague. The defense was left to the local authorities, who successfully mustered the citizenry. In the early 1700s, Baghdad was consigned to the descendants and extended family of Suleiman, which maintained the province as Ottoman at least in name. Hasan Pasha Mustafa, who became governor of Baghdad in 1704, tried to suppress continuing Bedouin marauders, but the skirmishes continued without resolution for nearly two decades. Then in 1723 when the shah of Persia was ousted, Istanbul asked Mustafa to invade, hoping to take advantage of the instability in the Shi'a nation. The four-year campaign was fruitless, resulting in many deaths and nothing more than a flimsy peace accord.[62]

Then it was Persia's turn once more. Nadir Shah, sometimes called "the Persian Napoleon," renewed the old campaign against the Sunnis. For years, Shi'a clerics had been migrating back from Persia to Najaf and Karbala, the spiritual and historic homes of Shiism. They successfully established not only an epicenter of Islamic conversion, but also a growing business for the Shi'a pilgrims and students, as well as corpses shipped in for glorious Shi'a burial. Eventually, so many

Persian Shiites came and went through Najaf and Karbala, Nadir looked upon the towns as a sphere of influence. Originally, the Sunnis tolerated the Shi'as because they could tax everything Persian that passed through the towns, from the pilgrims to the interments. But as Shi'a numbers and Persia grew, the Sunni establishment in Baghdad again found them a threat.[63]

In January 1733, to counteract the Sunni provincial establishment, Nadir subjected Baghdad to an ironclad starvation siege. People in the beleaguered city soon began dropping for lack of food and water. Indeed, the entire Mesopotamian realm was threatened, since Nadir had designs on the whole of the Persian Gulf, including Basra. Istanbul managed to assemble an expeditionary force to free Baghdad and its Sunni community. But the force was commanded by the old and crippled pasha, Othman the Lame. Othman was so unprepared for the rigors of battle that he was toted for almost six months flat on his back all the way to Mesopotamia.[64]

En route, in Kirkuk, Othman received a message from Nadir asking him to hurry so the destruction could be hastened. On July 19, 1733, at 8 A.M., Othman finally attacked, along with thousands of Kurds who had been rallied through Mosul's ruling Jalili family. But 2,000 of those Kurdish allies turned and ran as the conflict intensified. Nonetheless, later that month, Othman was able to slay 30,000 Persian fighters and break through to the city. He discovered that approximately 100,000 of Baghdad's citizens had literally starved to death. Thousands had been thrown into the river, but many more were rotting away in piles.[65]

When Baghdad was liberated, Nadir returned to his side of the frontier. But he later mustered fresh troops and swarmed back en masse to crush the Turkish defenders. Othman pleaded with Istanbul for more soldiers to fight off the next waves. But the sultan could not provide them. When the Persian onslaught came on October 26, 1733, they massacred Othman and nearly all his forces. Disarray in the Persian capital suddenly required Nadir to again retreat, so he did not reoccupy Baghdad. Ultimately, the borders defined by the prior peace treaty were reinstated, and the empire held on to its three provinces.[66]

However, the Ottoman grip on Baghdad, and indeed on all of Mesopotamia, was by now so tenuous that Istanbul had relinquished genuine authority to its local rulers. In the case of Baghdad, the city commander's son-in-law was appointed governor. He was a Mamluk, that is, a member of the Turkish slave army. The Mamluks then ruled Baghdad for decades, into the early 1800s, without interference, weathering a variety of insurrections and declining to send more than token tribute to Istanbul.[67] It meant that once again, the people of Baghdad were governed by—and neglected by—yet another alien regime.

In fact, so disconnected was governance by either the Mamluks locally or the sultan in Istanbul that when parched Najaf received a water system, it was financed not by the Ottomans, but by the government of the Shi'a state of Awadh, in north India. The massive half-million-rupee Hindiyyah Canal, begun in the 1780s and completed in 1803, finally transformed the Shi'a holy city into a more viable center by redirecting the flow of the Euphrates past Najaf. Shi'as in that city thanked not their sultan or their governor, but their brethren in India.[68]

As the 1800s dawned, the Ottoman Empire, and especially its three eastern frontier provinces, was still hypnotized by its archaic, feudal, postbarbarian culture and mind-set. The sheltered sultans continued to gorge and sex themselves to distraction, squandering the wealth of an entire empire, as they continuously battled neighbors east, north, west, and south. Meanwhile, in Mesopotamia, the dispossession, fatwa-sanctified mass murders, economic exploitation, neglect, and culture of alienation and defiance remained as irrepressible as sandstorms.

Yet the Western world had been moving forward for centuries.

England's Magna Carta was signed in 1215. Personal liberties were now a birthright for British citizens, and private land ownership broadened. Representative government manifested in the British parliament from 1265. The Renaissance began in Italy in the 1400s and swept across Europe. Named for civilization's "rebirth" from its intellectual retreat during the Middle Ages, the Renaissance once again humanized thinking men as both individuals and a collective. Feudalism was becoming outmoded. Dynastic, ecclesiastical, and imperial institutions were ported into publicly accountable structures for the national and common good. In 1517, the German scholar Martin Luther nailed his 95 theses to a door, thereby challenging the Roman Catholic Church and launching the Reformation. In 1601, England passed its Poor Laws, mandating public care of the indigent. In 1619, a representative assembly arose in a new colony called Virginia in a new world called America. In 1690, British philosopher John Locke promulgated the concept of a "social contract" with government. The Age of Enlightenment opened the door to a new era of democratic thought. In 1776, America established a revolutionary form of nationhood, enshrining the long-percolated concepts of a government for the people, of the people, and by the people. In 1792, France followed the American example, overthrowing its despots and raising up a republic based on liberty, equality, and fraternity. Nationalism based on individual liberties and freedoms and the termination of the nobility, as well as separation of church and state, spread like a new gospel across the breadth of Europe.

Civilization was once Mesopotamia's greatest export. But the balance of payments was tragic. Little came back. The land between the two rivers entered the nineteenth century so far behind, so bereft of the gifts it had bestowed upon the world that the advanced nations to the west would not respect it as anything more than a domain ripe for domination.

Enter the British.

CHAPTER FIVE

The Sick Man

By the time the East India Company arrived in Basra in 1763, English commercial interests had been allies of the Shiites against the Sunnis for more than a century. Ironically, it was nothing in Mesopotamia proper that attracted the British. It was actually India. In fact, for more than 200 years, Britain maneuvered among the factions in Mesopotamia because it was a convenient way station en route to India—that and little more.

Silks, pepper, cotton, broadcloth, and the ability to transport them from Asia to Great Britain and western Europe were, in the British mind-set, worth fighting for in far-off places. Since Vasco da Gama's voyage more than a century earlier, the Portuguese had dominated the trade routes between Europe and India. England wanted that trade.

The East India Company was invented on the last day of 1600 as a specially chartered British corporation, vested by Queen Elizabeth I with a royal monopoly to develop commerce with India, and therefore rival the Portuguese. The company functioned as a private and incorporated, but nonetheless militarized and quasi-governmental, business entity. As such, it was authorized not only to export and import ordinary goods, but also to project British imperialist policy across the seas.[1]

In pursuit of its mandate, the company sometimes shrewdly exploited ethnic conflicts. Sometimes it simply paid bribes to local potentates, who were easily bought or easily impressed. When cunning and baksheesh were insufficient, the company sealed opportunistic military alliances with anyone or against anyone who could further Britain's commercial agenda. The firm, which maintained its own navy and fighting forces, was equally prepared to unilaterally launch warfare to achieve its ends. Eventually, the East India Company became the wealthiest enterprise in Great Britain.[2] What's more, the model of the militarized corporate government surrogate embodied by the East India Company would be duplicated by other nations for centuries, and in fact still exists.

Company traders first landed ships in India in 1608, and, by 1612, defeated the Portuguese fleet there. Through a subsequent alliance with the reigning Indian Moghul, the company secured the right to establish a thriving outpost in Surat. Later, the Moghul ceded all of Bombay to Britain, which turned it over to the company as its own corporate colony. In fact, the East India Company initially functioned as the governing administration in Bombay.[3]

The Portuguese were dislodged from India by 1615. But that was not enough. Permanently denying the Portuguese the Asian trade routes also meant expelling them from their midpoint bastion at the Strait of Hormuz, which guarded the Persian Gulf access to Basra. The Portuguese actually administered their Persian Gulf base from their headquarters in India. Hence, the waterway leading to Basra and Mesopotamia were as much a part of Indian commerce as the subcontinent itself. As an underlying crosscurrent, the Indian Moghul was married to a beautiful Persian woman and was an ardent supporter of the Shi'a cause. Therefore, Britain's trade with India was inevitably tied to the Shiites in Persia and their conflict with Mesopotamia's Sunnis.[4]

Once the East India Company acquired its Bombay concession in 1615, the firm formed a broad alliance with the Persian shah, Abbas I. The treaty included the British right to trade from its domain without restriction, pay no more customs than Istanbul would demand, maintain an army to guard its ships and goods, and even exercise sole

authority to punish Christians accused of thieving or other crimes. By
1619, the British had constructed a commercial outpost at the Persian
settlement of Jask. Later, the installation was moved to Gambroon
(named for da Gama), directly challenging the nearby Portuguese fort
at Hormuz.[5]

In 1622, the East India Company fleet joined the shah's successful
invasion of the Portuguese stronghold. The secret invasion protocol
called for Shah Abbas to pay the full cost of the British vessels. The
English and the Persians were to split the booty fifty-fifty, whether
"money, goods, etc. shall be taken in city, castle, ships, [or] houses." In
the secret protocol, each side swore by their respective religions,
Christianity and Islam, to honestly divide the conquest—no holding
back.[6]

The ousted Portuguese relocated to the nearby Mesopotamian
port of Basra, but the British soon followed and established a presence
there as well. Britain did not want to risk war with the Ottomans. So,
for years, the company's position in Basra was informal and mainly
commercial. To keep a low profile, the firm relied on Armenian
traders as middlemen to transact business with the Ottoman Empire.
A separate enterprise, the much older and more limited Levant Company, organized the cloth business with the Turks between London
and Aleppo.[7]

However, when Persian Shiite conqueror Nadir Shah came to
power in the early 1730s, the company became more active and
overtly supported Shi'a military efforts against the Sunnis. The company's representatives tacitly backed Nadir's unsuccessful effort to
invade Basra in 1735 and concluded that Nadir needed a swift fleet to
do better. The company helped him get one. Nadir's flagship, *Fath-i-
Shah* was actually the renamed British vessel, the *Cowan*. The *North-
umberland* and other advanced ships were also provided. In many cases,
British captains were at the helm, assisted by Moslem crews. With a
fleet of modern, British-built vessels that vastly outperformed the
flimsy Arab ships commonly in use, the Shiites of Persia were able to
extend their conquest to other Gulf sheikhdoms, such as Bahrain and
Oman.[8]

By the mid-1700s, Britain had become a world imperial and
industrial power and even more protective of its lucrative exports and
imports with India. That meant Mesopotamia escalated in impor-

tance. The overland trek from Paris to Istanbul was roughly equidistant to the voyage from Basra to Bombay.[9] England needed to protect its precious pivot between the continents.

A watershed for England came on February 10, 1763, when Britain and Europe's other warring colonial powers finally signed the Treaty of Paris, ending the Seven Years' War. This far-flung war was fought over spheres of trade among commercial rivals, such as England, Spain, and Prussia. Perhaps the first genuine "world war," the conflict stretched from North America to the Prussian provinces, from North Africa to India, and swept across numerous islands along the way. The Paris treaty created a new world order, redrawing maps and parceling out colonial and commercial territories on four continents, from the banks of the Mississippi River and New Orleans to eastern Europe, from the island of Cuba to Senegal to the Bengal coast of India.[10]

That same year, 1763, the East India Company transferred its main Gulf outpost from Gambroon in Persia to Basra, installing a permanent resident agent. Resident agents were the company's local managers, but they acted as governors, wielding a potent arsenal of specified and unspecified prerogatives. Chief among the company's duties in Basra was supervising the mail from England to India as it transited overland from Aleppo in Syria to Basra and then via ship to Bombay.[11]

The trip was perilous. The many Arab raiders still roaming Mesopotamia frequently pillaged mailbags. At least half the inhabitants of the three provinces were still nomads with a cultural legacy of thievery and raiding. What's more, the incessant skirmishes between Persian and Ottoman forces endangered all trading in their path. Shipping mail via Baghdad was thought to be even more treacherous. Consequently, the East India Company was not interested in Baghdad and had previously rejected the notion of opening an office there. Instead, the company merely continued employing Armenian go-betweens to handle its affairs in Mesopotamia.[12]

As England increased her trade with India, it was at the expense of the Turkish routes. For example, England imported some £219,000 in silk products from the Turkish Empire from 1699 to 1701. By mid-century, that number had dwindled by more than 60 percent. From 1761 to 1765, the amount diminished to about £51,000—more than a 75 percent decline. England accounted for about a quarter of all trade with Istanbul, so the decreases were noticeable. Nor was the damage limited to trade with Britain. For the better part of the eighteenth century, French imports of Turkish silk products soared, but then declined by about two-thirds during the 12-year period from 1777 to 1789. France represented more than 40 percent of all trade with Istanbul.[13]

Because Basra was considered a mere satellite of India, the company's first resident agent was its relocated Bombay Resident, who effectively made Mesopotamia a valued alternative nexus between East and West. He was replaced in 1784 by a disreputable opportunist, Samuel Manesty, a man who had two-timed the company as well as the local tax collectors. His temporary undoing was a war against the Jewish merchants in Basra. Manesty hated Jews and was happy to bully them whenever possible. When the Jews, valuable to the sultan's treasury, complained to Istanbul, the palace pressured the British ambassador to have Manesty removed. Since the East India Company was technically independent of the British government, the ambassador's only recourse was protracted and circuitous. First he complained to the Foreign Office in London, which conveyed the message to the government's Board of Control, which under the recently passed India Act of 1784 gave the government a veto power over company operations. Senior management was lobbied, and it finally removed Manesty.[14]

But then Manesty secured a special privilege of passage to Aleppo that made him too important to overlook. He was reinstated in 1796. Upon his return to Basra, retribution was swift. Twenty-two of the wealthiest Jewish merchants in the area were delivered into his custody. He terrorized them overnight, writing at the time, "My enemies were now in my power." He thrilled at what he called, "Revenge, the darling passion of our imperfect nature."[15]

In 1798, just as Napoleon Bonaparte sailed from France for Egypt—either to conquer the Pyramids or to set the stage for an invasion of India, or both, the East India Company and the British government took countermeasures. The Sublime Porte, as Europe called the Ottoman Empire, was equally nervous. A greater alliance between the Turks and the British emerged. The company opened a Baghdad office in September, appointing Harford Jones as resident agent. Jones was a recalcitrant man, known as a quibbler, a conniver, and a seeker of personal glory. Manesty was overlooked for the position and resented it. The feud would last a long time.[16]

Jones's mission was to intercept intelligence about any of Napoleon's movements and to continually incite the pasha of Baghdad regarding supposed French designs against the empire. In essence, Jones was to ensure that the pasha felt completely obliged to the British for information and protection. Jones, a loose cannon, eschewed coordination and quickly came into conflict with Britain's true ambassadors, who did not want to speak to the Porte with two voices.[17]

When the threat from Napoleon vanished following Britain's defeat of the French naval forces in 1800, Jones was unwilling to relinquish his office. He quarreled with British associates in the government and the company, as well as with the pasha himself, about exactly what his purpose was. When challenged by fellow Britons, he tried to appoint himself "Consul-General" in Baghdad, or perhaps to a diplomatic post in Persia or in Afghanistan. When challenged by the Baghdad pasha for not supporting the pashalik with naval forces against Shiite rivals in the Gulf, an irked Jones sealed a secret pact with a Janissary military man from Basra to "replace" the pasha. The move was thwarted, and the Janissary ally killed, although Jones's involvement remained undetected.[18]

Turning his attentions to Sunni Afghanistan, Jones favored agitating or possibly even dividing that country to create a further bulwark against Napoleon's drive to India—even though the French threat no longer existed. This caused the British governor in Bombay to write with angst in 1799, "The zeal of Mr. H. Jones may possibly lead him to take steps at the Court of Kabul entirely inconsistent with those I deem essentially necessary to the security of the objects which I have in view in Oudh."[19]

"Oudh" was the British name for the wealthy Indian Shi'a state of Awadh, which, through Britain's good offices, was exercising its own sphere of governance in Najaf and the rest of Shi'a Mesopotamia. Awadh, or Oudh, had already invested a half million rupees in Najaf's Hindiyya canal, bringing needed water to the region. Persia had also assumed a paternalistic and indeed warlike role from time to time in southern Mesopotamia because of the holy cities and their Shiite brethren. In reality, as Britain engineered more Shi'a assistance from

India and deepened its strategic relationship with Shi'a Persia, London was actually extending its own influence over the Shi'a areas of Mesopotamia.[20]

Hence, while Mesopotamia was now Ottoman in name, the fringe provinces were so neglected and autonomous that the tribes—both allied and unallied—were caught in a four-way primacy struggle between the local ruling pasha of Baghdad, the Persian Shi'a, the Awadhi Indians, and the Britons, who were angling from all sides.

Jones was angling for himself. As the three provinces were pillaged, taxed, and exploited from every direction, Jones ramped up his intrigues. He saw himself as the very embodiment of London's imperial gentry. Jones even organized his own fife and drum corps to play loudly and offensively during the call to holy prayer. To countercheck Jones's uncontrollable diplomatic maneuvers and imperial ostentation, Manesty arranged for surface mail to be passed not through Jones's Baghdad office, but through a rival Armenian agent.[21] That marginalized Jones—but not for long.

The Baghdad mail route proved to be safer, less expensive, and more reliable than the traditional caravans that plied the desert to Aleppo. Out of 138 pouches dispatched via Baghdad over the previous several years, only two had been vandalized—vastly fewer than those transited directly from Basra to Aleppo. So the company's Istanbul agent ordered pouches eastbound for India to pass through Baghdad, while Bombay government officials decided to do the same for westbound correspondence.[22]

But the pasha of Baghdad was still at odds with Jones, who missed few opportunities to confront authority. The fractious Briton tried to discredit the pasha's regular doctor in favor of Jones's personal physician, James Short. Jones was accused of sex with a Moslem woman who was later killed by her family for the dishonor. His antics involved more than just one woman. The pasha complained that Jones "made it a common practice to" consort with "lewd Moslem women . . . for the purpose of prostitution in a manner so open and incautious as to be rather generally observed."[23]

A measure of how far the provinces had succumbed to economic pressures was the fact that Jones could even be allowed to live to pursue an argument with the pasha. Decades earlier, a defiant infidel would have been quickly beheaded. Now, the pasha was reduced to writing letters of complaint to Jones's perceived bosses in the British establishment and asking the sultan to intervene. No one could rein Jones in—not British government diplomats or company managers—especially since he was the master of the mails in Mesopotamia. In fact, the pasha was never able to oust Jones from Baghdad. Jones outlasted him. The pasha died in August 1802.[24]

The Mamluk pasha who replaced him fared little better—at first. Jones became emboldened, arrogant, and unrestrained. When, in 1803, an Armenian merchant under Austrian protection died in Baghdad, Jones appointed himself the widow's representative, allowing his private interpreter to receive a 5 percent commission on the estate. When the decedent's brother, a beneficiary, objected, Jones ignored him. The brother secured a formal ruling from the Porte commanding Jones to relinquish the paperwork. Jones ignored that as well.[25]

Manesty, the company man in Basra, literally competed with Jones for outlandishness. In late 1803, rioters abducted a mistress of Manesty's ship captain, claiming she was a Moslem woman. Manesty, angry and threatening his hosts, demanded reparation from the pasha. Without shrinking, he added that if "his Excellency the Pasha will not grant reparation, the King of England will compel the Ottoman Emperor to do so." In an earlier Turkish age, such words would have gruesomely cost Manesty his life. Manesty went further and tried to orchestrate the demise of the pasha, employing mercenaries from India.[26]

Eventually, the mistress was handed back, again demonstrating the growing power and position of the British citizens and their overbearing presence in Mesopotamia. But Manesty would not forget the matter. Moreover, he suspected that his rival Jones had incited the affair. Jones did not like that accusation one iota. One night late that year, he summoned the leading merchants of Baghdad to announce that Manesty, who had been wracking up expensive bills for his pomp-and-circumstance travel, could never pay his debts. That was it for Jones. Manesty revealed to the pasha that Jones had conspired against the previous pasha in 1802.[27]

For good measure, the pasha and Manesty colluded to appoint yet another Armenian to function in Baghdad as Manesty's personal assistant. Then they steered all eastbound mail to the new Armenian appointee—cutting out Jones. After all, the mail could not proceed to Bombay without passing through Basra, the seat of Manesty's authority. Jones hung on. Finally, after incessant protest from the pasha, who emphasized that Jones's life would soon be forfeit—good relations with England or not—the British ambassador intervened. In February 1806, Jones permanently departed Mesopotamia for Syria. The pressure was too much for Manesty as well; he sailed for Calcutta about a year earlier, never to return.[28]

Torn between the Ottoman Empire, local pashas, Persia, India, and Britain, the tribes of Iraq were forced in the early 1800s to confront yet another usurper: the Wahhabis. Periodically sweeping in from the Arabian Peninsula, Wahhabi armies typically boasted hundreds of festooned camel- and horse-riding fighters sporting prominent religious emblems. Wahhabi religious fanatics were part reformer, part strict constructionist, and part Bedouin raider. Founded in the eighteenth century by Mohammed ibn Abd al-Wahab, followers declared that all forms of Islam organized after 950 were blasphemous. This included both the Sunni and Shi'a establishments. Forbidding the use of tobacco and alcohol, they vehemently demanded a simple life, from featureless dress to austere personal conduct. Wahhabis condemned the sultan's gluttonous and ostentatious version of piety as an outrage against God. They were equally reviled by the ornate shrines and mosques bedizened by elaborate minarets and aureate archways. To the Wahhabis, the Blue Mosque of the Sunnis in Istanbul and the Ali Mosque of the Shi'as in Najaf were equally loathsome. For themselves, the Wahhabis built unadorned mosques. They demanded a puritanical code for all. Violators would be afflicted mercilessly.[29]

Eventually, the Wahhabis converted the desert Saud tribe, which then waged a fervent jihad against any Moslem who would not follow their ways. During the later half of the 1700s and early 1800s, the Saudis and their Wahhabi brand of strict reform conquered the entire Arabian Peninsula, establishing a capital in Riyadh. Neither the Sunnis nor the Shiites, however, were receptive to righteous conversion. Determined nonetheless, the Wahhabis from time to time raided into Mesopotamia to plunder and punish the blaspheming Moslems there.[30]

In April 1801, the Wahhabis attacked the Shi'a shrine city of Karbala. Waiting for much of the city's populace to be away on pilgrimage to Najaf, an estimated 6,000 to 12,000 camel-riding Wahhabis augmented by 400 horsemen split into three waves and then swarmed against the city. The panicky inhabitants, surrounded, could run only so far before the sword-swinging Wahhabis cut them down. At the holy shrine of Hussein, the Prophet Mohammed's last grandson, the raiders broke in and dismantled every ornate object they could pull or pick up. Gem-laden doors, exquisite carpets, the decorative railings, valued candlesticks, even the gold-covered walls and archways—all of it was ripped and torn away. Within the tomb proper, they murdered 50 who could not escape. Five hundred more were massacred just outside in the courtyard. Then the zealots systematically went from home to home, robbing, pillaging, and destroying every abode and having their brutal way with every occupant—man, woman, or child, young or old. The final death count that day exceeded 1,000.[31]

Satisfied with their doctrinaire murder and mayhem, the Wahhabis returned to their staging areas in the desert, carting all the loot they condemned as unholy. They would return time and again. Finally, in 1811, a Mamluk army from Egypt defeated the intruders.[32]

But for years after the Wahhabi defeat, Karbala remained yet another devastated Iraqi town. In fact, by the 1820s, Karbala had descended into utter lawlessness—this time from within. With no real authority, brutal criminal gangs roamed the city to steal, pillage, and enforce their will over the tradesmen, peddlers, bazaar sellers, and other defenseless townspeople struggling to survive. The mainstay of the gangs was extorting protection. During their reign of terror, gang members did anything for money, power, or whim, from exacting revenge to committing murder. If they chose to rape a woman, she was raped with impunity. Gang members looted what they chose whenever it suited them, whether from a market stall or a man's home.[33] As the Bedouin tribes were desert raiders, the Karbala gangs were street raiders.

Karbala's gangs were highly organized. There were 14 major groups. Some numbered as few as several dozen members. Larger gangs counted as many as 400 in their band. Altogether, the 14 gangs wielded about 2,500 toughs, impudently looting—and murdering those who chose not to be looted. The citizenry derisively called them *luti,* which loosely translated to "good-for-nothing."[34]

Recruitment of *luti* was easy. Devoid of authority, Karbala had become a haven for fugitives, scoundrels, killers, strong-arm artists, and numberless deserters from the military ranks. The 14 *luti* gangs operated in the style of classic European postfeudal gangsters, with a strongman, "godfather," or "patron" at the apex of a family-like tribe of criminals. As the exploitative Turks and corrupt pashas exacted tax, tribute, and baksheesh from Karbala, so the *lutis* demanded their equivalent.[35] From the *lutis'* point of view, the authorities just took the residents' money, whereas the gangs, when paid, at least provided protection. To the people of Karbala, life must have seemed like a gauntlet of confiscations.

Less fortunate than the people of Karbala were those less than 50 miles northeast in Baghdad. During the 1820s, Daoud Pasha of Baghdad presided over his own city sultanate. Ceremonially dressed Janissary guards and Georgian attendants patrolled his elaborate palace grounds. Three horsetails hung audaciously beside a great imperial Islamic crescent and star at the door to his main receiving chambers. Inside, the garish and opulent furnishings impressed foreign dignitaries as rivaling the best palaces of Istanbul. The staff was enormous. Daoud maintained his own Master of Ceremonies, Chief Chamberlain, and a coterie of officers of the Coffee, of the Sweetmeats, and of so many household appliances and edibles—even officers of the Drinking Water.[36]

Daoud's corrupt associates, extracting any price the market would bear, capriciously assessed special taxes on Jews and Christians, all collected in the name of the sultan. A superior Baghdad army was being developed. In 1824, Daoud petitioned Bombay for military equipment to arm 1,000 soldiers. Later, he asked for three fully armed warships for his personal fleet. The British denied both requests.[37]

By no means was Baghdad a city made completely destitute beneath the extravagance of its pasha. Baghdad had outwardly recovered under Daoud and his predecessor Mamluk governors. Radiant mosques, a great triple-arched, covered bazaar, schools, and a community of prosperous commercial establishments had grown up since the most recent devastation. Exquisite imported glassware, satins, fine velvets, and cloth, as well as commodities such as sugar and metals, sailed up the river regularly from Basra. The presence of British, French, and other European commercial agents was making an impact on Baghdad. The city's wealth, however, was not to the advantage of the sultan. It was the pasha's financial district.[38]

At the same time, a new sultan arose in Istanbul: Mahmud II, also known as "Mahmud the Reformer." Mahmud wanted to drag the Ottoman Empire into the rest of Europe from its aloof and decaying position at the eastern margin. He wanted everything to change: science, industry, commerce, government, diplomacy, and even personal dress. Soon, the first modern steamboat, the *Swift,* chugged through Istanbul to the amazement of the crowd along the banks. Mahmud purchased the *Swift* and a second vessel and arranged for British naval men to train his crews.[39]

Printing exploded. It had been previously disallowed by Moslem tradition as an "infidel craft." Calligraphy was king throughout the empire, with some 90,000 calligraphers and copyists providing the principal means of written communication in Istanbul. Now printing presses were imported from Europe along with the craftsman to train Turks to press raised plates against ink to create a dry, readable page. Europe had been doing it since Gutenberg's first Bible in 1455.[40]

To Mahmud, European customs became more valued and forward-looking than Islam's traditions. He favored the Austrian-made fez, not the towering turban, as everyday wear. Medical students should be required to study medicine in French, he declared, not so they could learn a foreign language but so they could adopt the latest medical developments. Mahmud wanted his military to join the new century, forsaking baggy pantaloons and war costumes for the tight-fitting britches and heavy cannon tactics of Napoleonic and British soldiers. In addition, Mahmud envisioned many sweeping political reforms to convert his feudal Ottoman dominion into a modern cohesive nation. To accomplish this, the Turkish Empire, indolent for centuries, would have to regain control of its three autonomous Mesopotamian provinces. Mahmud was determined to reconquer them.[41]

But no unification could be accomplished as long as the periodically mutinous and always bribable Janissaries existed. The special Turkish military forces, comprised largely of kidnapped Christian boys raised in captivity to be ruthless soldiers, had evolved into autonomous units and become a threat to Istanbul's authority. In the summer 1826, the sultan carefully plotted their obliteration. A commanding general, later nicknamed "Black Hell," organized the massacres. A royal decree of supervisory oversight was issued, calculated to inspire their rebellion. As expected, the furious Janissary battalions mustered through the narrow streets of Istanbul and later in the stadium. Strategically placed artillery mowed them down, unit by unit, using the latest techniques of European cannon warfare. The sword-savvy Janissaries kept waiting for the hand-to-hand combat they knew so well. Black Hell gave them only cannon shot, and only from afar. So fierce, continuous, and well planned was the bloody barrage, that within 30 to 60 minutes, the concentrated Janissary troops were all dead, some 4,000 that day.[42]

With the Janissaries decimated, Mahmud turned his face toward the provinces, including Daoud's Baghdad. Daoud had failed to forward tax and tribute. He had failed to defend nearby Karbala from the Wahhabis, forcing the Porte to import a Mamluk army from Egypt. Moreover, Daoud was accruing a wealth and power base to rival the sultan's.[43]

In late 1830, Mahmud made his determined move. He dispatched a trusted envoy, Sadiq Effendi, to demand that the Janissaries dissolve and a crippling tribute be forfeited. Daoud Pasha could not understand this challenge—and refused his sultan.[44]

"Sadiq came here from the Sultan with orders that I should pay 6,800 purses of piastres in aid of the Porte," a nervous Daoud confided to his subordinate functionary. "I answered, I am merely a slave of the Sultan and whatever I have is his. But the sum required by the Sultan is too great for my means. Yet I will exert myself and pay as much as I can. I then collected from various quarters, and sent him 1,000 purses, and the same a second time, which amounts to 2,000 purses. This, however, I heard, had displeased the Sultan."[45]

Sultan Mahmud, through Sadiq, was in fact quite displeased. Sadiq returned to his guesthouse, where he made plans to decapitate Daoud and replace him with a more trusted governor. Daoud claimed he tried to reason with Sadiq, assuring him, "I would do everything in my power to satisfy my master and himself. . . . He being more enraged at this message, abused me. . . . I waited a couple of hours to see what he would do, when I heard that he was busy writing letters to the Chiefs of the Tribes around Baghdad [announcing the removal]. I was then obliged . . . to send people into his house and kill him there, previous to the news getting out of the town."[46]

When news of Sadiq's murder reached Mahmud, the sultan was enraged. He sentenced Daoud to a death sentence—but did not know how to enforce the punishment. "The military resources of the Grand Signor [the sultan] do not permit an army being marched from Constantinople for this purpose," a British diplomat stationed in Istanbul reported to London, "but it is probable that forces will be collected in the adjoining Pashalicks to act against the Pasha of Baghdad, should he offer resistance."[47]

Daoud was not crowded into a hippodrome as the shredded Istanbul Janissaries were. Taking Baghdad would require a full cavalry assault and hand-to-hand fighting. It would be expensive for the palace to raise such an army—and it simply did not have the money. Finally, the sultan rallied the wealthy pasha of Aleppo to proceed against Baghdad. The pasha's reward would be to rule Aleppo and Baghdad—and thereby become the richest and most powerful governor in the empire. The assignment was accepted. On February 21, 1831, the sultan announced widely that Daoud Pasha was a bandit governor who must be removed. Three days later, the pasha of Aleppo marched his army toward Baghdad.[48]

British diplomats reported the outcome was by no means certain. Waging war cost money. Daoud's "treasury is overflowing," wrote the diplomat, "while that of their opponents [the sultan] is penniless." Even still, Daoud was nervous. It was now him against the empire. Just days after the Aleppo armies began advancing, Daoud asked the British envoy to intercede with the sultan in exchange for unlimited powers in the territory. London's February 10, 1831, report from its Baghdad mission stated, Daoud "threw himself upon me, and gave me full powers to act in his behalf." Daoud vowed, "By the Great God! I promise that if, through the Almighty's aid and your friendly assistance, I pass this crisis, the management of the Pashalick shall be confided to you alone . . . Save me now, and my future measures shall be guided only by your advice."[49]

London commanded its agent not to get involved and made no effort "to avert from his head the vengeance which awaits him." As good as relations were with the pasha of Baghdad, a London foreign ministry official reasoned, "I see no cause why you should not be on an equally good footing with his successor." By late March 1831, the pasha's armies were arrayed within striking distance of Baghdad.[50]

But then came the plague. The killing cholera that had for years engulfed a swath of civilization from Tabriz to Kirkuk finally entered Baghdad as a firestorm. Many thought the trade caravans and pilgrims to Mecca continuously transmitted the disease from one destination to another. Thus despite quarantines, cities such as Baghdad were reinfected time and again. By April 4, the first 150 died. Within another week, some 7,000 thousand fell dead to the swift killer. Many thousands more died over the next few weeks; sometimes 1,500 per day, sometimes twice that number. Some estimated that as few as 5 percent recovered.[51]

Daoud tried to escape, summoning his boatmen. But they were all dead. When he himself took ill, only a haggard old woman attended in place of a retinue of gaudy servitors. The pasha's loosened stallions stampeded out of the palace grounds as madness itself galloped across Baghdad.[52]

Eventually, the gravediggers died. Alleys and thoroughfares, once teeming with life, now filled with decomposing cadavers. Parentless children sought food from anywhere, but there was no food—the supplies and the suppliers were gone. Robbers vanquished undefended properties—there was no other way to get whatever foodstuffs remained. The weak perished from the epidemic, and the strong dropped soon thereafter.[53]

Finally, by April 21, the pestilence seemed to subside. Baghdad's latest surviving remnant might now survey the death. But before they could look to the heavens for an answer, all eyes instead turned upstream to the menacing Tigris.[54]

The spring floods had been merciless, and as the hours passed, the water level swelled higher and higher toward the levy brim. On April 26, the night turned to water. Dikes crumbled at the north end of Baghdad, sweeping away the first 200 houses within hours. By the next evening, the unstoppable torrents immersed unburied corpses, survivors, and their households into a ravaging cesspool. That was not enough. Then it rained, bringing a second inundation.[55]

Once more, Hell hath returned to its vestibule in Baghdad.

On June 2, 1831, the pasha of Aleppo entered a broken Baghdad to arrest or execute Daoud. The best homes were on high ground, and those survivors counted themselves in Daoud's council. Fearing the next wave of terror from the sultan's invaders, the soaked and scorched city nonetheless refused to yield Daoud without a fight to the finish. With the city surrounded, with its food depleted, and with Europe's capitals watching, Istanbul ordered the pasha of Aleppo to retreat. But the pasha could not, since his army had been promised the residuum of riches that were Baghdad until just days earlier.[56]

Daoud relinquished his sundered city, and on June 14, the pasha of Aleppo occupied it on behalf of the Sublime Porte. At the momentous meeting between the dethroned pasha of Baghdad and the triumphant pasha of Aleppo, the two men simply faced each, stared, muttered a few words, and drank coffee. Daoud was not beheaded. Instead, he was allowed to retire to another province under strict control of the sultan. Baghdad belonged to the Ottoman Empire once again.[57]

Karbala was next for reunification with the empire. This time it was not an autonomous pasha, but the city's 14 rapacious gangs that would need to succumb. For about three years, the Porte tried to reassert its authority, without success. In 1835, the sultan's pasha in Baghdad had amassed some 3,000 soldiers for an invasion. But 3,000 troops were insufficient to overwhelm 2,500 street-hardened gangsters. A stalemate resulted in the cooption of one of the leading crime bosses as the chief of the city.[58]

The deal called for the elevated gang boss to pay the Baghdad pasha a large sum of money. Thefts from the two shrines and municipal fees and taxes would be split. Protection would be jointly assured against rival gangs. Arab tribal raiders could store their loot in Karbala for convenience. Karbala now passed from being simply lawless to being a bandit state, which attracted more bandits from across Mesopotamia and Persia.[59]

Mahmud the Reformer died in 1839. His successor would do things differently. In September 1842, the new sultan installed Najib Pasha in Baghdad. Najib was a fiery Turkish chauvinist who rejected accommodation to the empire's many minorities, including the Shi'as of southern Mesopotamia. He saw Karbala as a virtually independent city, controlled in part by Persians and in part by its ruthless *luti* gangs.[60]

When Najib tried to visit a shrine, Karbala's gang bosses rebuffed him and his party. Moreover, Persian government intermediaries attempted to negotiate on behalf of Karbala. That was proof enough that the Arabs of Shiite Karbala must be subdued and Turkified. By the end of that year, Najib openly promised to oust the *lutis*. The gangs easily rallied the local Shiite masses, who resented the existing authority, to join in common cause against Najib.[61]

A succession of skirmishes and standoffs culminated in an assault during the morning darkness of January 13, 1843. While the city slept, Turkish artillery blasted a breach in the main wall. Troops poured in, opened the main gate, positioned big guns at the ramparts and circulated a reward: 150 piastres for every decapitated head of a *luti*. When Turkish soldiers began firing wildly into the crowds, hundreds of gang family members fled from the city. Throngs of regular Shiite residents tried to hide—in the recesses of alleyways, in courtyards, behind walls, anywhere—to no avail. Cornered residents merely trampled each other as Turkish gunfire sprayed into their midst. Turkish soldiers brutally secured the city. Quickly, the death toll reached hundreds, most shot or crushed by the frantic citizenry.[62]

Then the Turks exacted their revenge. Najib's soldiers raced through Karbala streets, plundering homes, killing families, raping women. Jewelry was torn from women's limbs—and if the item did not come freely, the limb was severed by blade. So much loot was taken, residents were conscripted to cart the stolen property beyond the walls to Najib's encampment. More Arabs were slaughtered, by sword and by musket fire. The killing was indiscriminate.[63]

The ghastly carnage at Karbala produced some 5,000 killed, perhaps 15 percent of its population. Dead bodies littered every lane and passageway. One captured survivor wrote, "The dead were lying on top of one another to the extent that I could not cross the street except by walking over the corpses." Dozens of bodies were heaped into streets near the shrines, doused with oil, covered with blankets, and torched.[64]

So apocalyptic was the holy city's massacre that several Shi'a sages wondered whether the Hidden Imam was finally readying his return to Earth. One merchant was so convinced the heavens had acted decisively that within months of the Karbala massacre he began a new religious faction called Baha'i, which asked for an end to all clerics, a unity of the several monotheistic religions, and utterly peaceful relations with all. But his ideals were rejected as heretical and his followers mass-murdered.[65]

In the end, the Porte proved it could assert itself. Law and order was restored to Karbala. At least briefly.

The Ottoman Empire was doomed. The world knew it.

The empire's cycle of self-inflicted barbarism and religious warfare seemed incurable. Turkey had missed both the Age of Enlightenment and the Industrial Revolution of the latter 1700s. The Ottoman Empire continued to massacre its own citizens. Turkish sultans, who doubled as the caliphs—that is, the supreme religious authorities of the majority Moslem world—were eating, drinking, sexing, and splurging themselves and their empire into decay and destruction. The only question was not *if*, but *when* the empire would break apart, either from internal disintegration or external conquest, or both.

Mesopotamia was hardly the only desolate fringe in the empire. With an estimated population of barely 1.3 million dwelling in three barren provinces, Mosul, Baghdad, and Basra were mainly of interest to western Europe for the quaint antiquity and their geographical imperative as the midpoint to India.[66]

More pressing to London, Moscow, Vienna, and Paris were the empire's western fringes, including the Balkans, Greece, and other provinces of eastern Europe, many of which were subjected to despotic helotry by their pashas or atrocities by rampaging Janissaries. France, Austria, Russia, England, and others worried about who would take over—and how many new states would suddenly emerge—once the empire imploded. Indeed, from the early 1800s, the so-called Eastern Question was hotly debated in all of Europe's capitals and in newspaper columns.[67]

During the 1830s, Europe almost erupted into a war over who would decide the Eastern Question. Certainly, numerous international alliances and treaties—secret and public—were sealed to stabilize the threat. Moreover, the Ottomans were continually either propped up or subjected to extraterritorial hegemony by neighbors hoping to postpone the inevitable.[68]

But it seemed to be a lost cause. True, the Turks dabbled in reform. Mahmud the Reformer had tried to modernize. But he died in 1839 before his best ideas took root. Efforts were made to join the industrial age and leave the hand-made age, howsoever belatedly. In the 1820s and 1830s, during Mahmud's reign, a modern spinning mill, a leather tannery and boot works, a copper-rolling facility, and weaving mills were constructed. But these small efforts were all wrong. They failed for lack of the industrial expertise that neighboring nations had accrued over centuries, as well as the simple inability to sensibly handle the logistics of materials, their transportation, manufacture, and then distribution.[69]

In 1842, an ambitious new effort was made. A forward-thinking industrial park, some nine miles long, was planned west of Istanbul. Metal foundries and cloth mills were imported lock, stock, and smelter. Materials and supply lines were arranged. Worker barracks with nearby training schools were constructed. A model agricultural enterprise was established. The Porte attempted a degree of autarky by purchasing 15,000 merino sheep for a ranch, calling in American farm specialists to help cultivate crops, and deploying a squadron of expert foreign geologists and engineers to search its mountains and plains for raw materials. The industrial park was envisioned as the prototype of the Turkish industrial revolution.[70]

But the campaign was quickly crippled by the colossal mismanagement of central state authorities. Incompetence, bad luck, and shortsightedness were never in short supply. In 1848, the powder works exploded. About that same time, the American-supervised cotton crops died off for lack of irrigation, and too few cotton gins were available to handle the amount grown. Many of the 15,000 sheep perished from malnourishment and exposure to heat; many were just stolen. The silk mills were demolished during an earthquake. Without service roads, heavy equipment such as mining drills and diggers could not be delivered to the ore fields.[71]

What's more, the projects were not a true industrialization of the nation, but merely manufacturing appendages of the palace and the military. These were all government enterprises by the state and for the state, to the virtual exclusion of civilians. The Porte could not afford to operate them or patronize them. It all constituted a tower so narrow, so tall, and so poorly built, the edifice simply toppled. Foreign infidel workers either were unwilling to stay under the frustrating conditions or were dismissed for economic reasons. By the century's halfway mark, the industrial experiment had collapsed.[72]

The Ottoman Empire was sick and dying.

East India manager Thomas Roe may have been the first to say it. In 1621, while ambassador to the Porte, Roe observed that the empire was "irrevocably sick." The description became common usage, however, beginning January 9, 1853. During a brief, conspiratorial conversation about the Eastern Question between Czar Nicholas and British ambassador Hamilton Seymour, the czar remarked in the diplomatic language of the day: "*Tenez, nous avons sur le bras un homme malade, un homme gravement malade; ce sera, je vous le dire franchement, un grand malheur, si, un de ces jours, il devait nous échapper, surtout avant que toutes les dispositions nécessaires fussent prises.*"[73]

"Look," said the czar, "we have on our hands a sick man, a man seriously ill; it will be, I wish to tell you frankly, a great misfortune if he escapes us one of these days before all the necessary arrangements are made."[74]

Seymour replied, "Your Majesty is so gracious; perhaps he will permit me to make another observation. Your Majesty will deign to excuse me if I point out that it is the strong and generous man who spares the sick and weak man."[75]

In the days to follow, Seymour injected the "sick man" reference into more dispatches to London, and pointedly repeated the epithet in further discussions with the czar as they jointly pondered whether the Ottoman Empire should be dismantled territory by territory, resuscitated, or something in between. Once the catchphrase was leaked to the newspapers, it spread across Europe as the vogue expression of the day. Turkey became the "Sick Man of Europe" in the parlance of international affairs. The world not only had to answer the Eastern Question, now it had to minister to the "Sick Man." Endless wordplays were propounded: Who would give the Sick Man his pills without the patient knowing, and who would withhold them? Who would come to the Sick Man's rescue, and who would euthanize him prematurely?[76]

By the 1850s and for the rest of the century, the "Sick Man of Europe," straddling three continents, was the world's looming problem. Its frontier provinces in Mesopotamia were simply the Sick Man's precious shortcut to someplace else. Even that international commercial attraction was about to be outmoded. In late April of 1859, digging began on the Suez Canal, which would link the Mediterranean and the Red Sea and from there to the Indian Ocean.[77]

But six months later, everything changed for Mesopotamia. Indeed, the world changed forever that hot afternoon of August 27, 1859. A revolutionary development occurred that would make Mesopotamia among the most valued places on earth, valuable enough to die for, indispensable to every advanced society East or West. This volcanic event occurred not in London, Paris, Moscow, or Istanbul, but in a dusty backwater on the other side of the globe: Titusville, Pennsylvania.

PART TWO

Fumes

CHAPTER SIX

Oil

M an knew oil long before man knew civilization.
Many millennia before Mesopotamia organized the city of Uruk, cavemen understood the usefulness of a thick black tar, later called *bitumen*. As far back as 60,000 years ago, bitumen had already become a magical substance for prehistoric society, used as an adherent on spear points and tool blades, a salve on wounds, a lubricant for heavy objects, a sealant for construction, and a decoration on surfaces. Eventually, its flammable qualities were discovered, providing heat and light for even the most primitive cave dwellers and nomads.[1]

Bitumen was easily obtainable because it oozed up from the rocks, hence its eventual name, *petroleum,* which means "rock oil." Petroleum's usefulness is amply documented throughout the inscriptions of the first civilizations, the Bible, and other ancient writings. Babylon's ziggurats, its towers of Babel, were built of bricks coated in bitumen. According to tradition, Sargon the Great and Moses the Prince, as infants, were both sent floating down the river in cradles sealed with bitumen.[2]

In the ancient Mesopotamian region, pressure beneath vast deposits of bitumen sometimes forced jets of the flammable substance high into the air. Broiling summer heat regularly ignited the spray into awesome flaming towers equal to any a dragon could exhale. No wonder angry fire gods inhabited the mind of ancient man.[3]

As civilization advanced, new and better industrial and medicinal uses were found for bitumen. The thick residue from evaporated bitumen, called *asphalt,* could be used to pave roads. Gaseous, liquefied, and distilled forms of petroleum, such as naphtha, could be set aflame to light the darkness and scorch the enemy. Cyrus the Great, in the sixth century BCE, planned to use such flammables to burn out street resistance during his famous invasion of Babylon. A thousand years later, terrifying flamethrowers from Byzantine warships at Constantinople sprayed an almost inextinguishable naphtha-based mixture called "Greek Fire."[4]

In 1846, a Canadian geologist working in the United States created a new flammable he named *kerosene,* distilled from asphalt and other hydrocarbons. A wonderful new illuminant, kerosene efficiently brought light into the shadows and darkness of city streets and their great buildings. Within a few years, thousands of gallons per day were being distilled for commercial use in major American cities. Everything changed when a safe, smokeless kerosene lamp with a glass chimney vent was invented, allowing kerosene to become a household necessity—rural and urban—both in Europe and America.[5]

Most of the slow seepages and great sprays of "rock oil," from the Americas to Asia Minor, were never efficiently captured. Oil-gathering operations included wringing oil from soaked rags, hauling buckets of the slimy crude, and simply siphoning the runoff into containers lashed to donkeys. Ultimately, oil gatherers could only watch most of their precious product simply flow away, blackening the nearby environment and constantly spurring commercial explorers to devise the technologies for oil conquest. Natural wells had been excavated, deep holes had been bored, taps had been injected into the surface flows, but no one had yet drilled into an oil pool hidden beneath strata of earth and then industrially mastered its contents.[6]

In the 1850s, medicinal oil entrepreneurs began drilling for rock oil at Oil Creek in rural Pennsylvania, where petroleum was migrating into salt layers. Travelers had noted seepages in the area for more than a hundred years. Although the main drillers at Oil Creek sought a new source of medicinal oil, others craved an abundant supply of commercially exploitable illuminant.[7]

On the afternoon of August 29, 1859, in the woodlands of northwestern Pennsylvania, at Oil Creek, just south of tiny Titusville, at a depth of 69.5 feet, an exploratory drill finally struck oil. Oil Creek spawned "Oil City," which overnight became one of several wild and rambunctious Pennsylvania drilling towns where fortunes were furiously made and lost as fast as oil could spill.[8]

Once struck, oil could be efficiently managed—controlled with pumps and caps, stored in tanks or other holding areas, and then transported by truck, pipeline, and ship. An industry waiting to be born was finally brought to life. The oil business—like its product—became the most useful undertaking on earth, and also the most explosive, both chemically and politically.

The oil business was far more complicated than just exploiting endlessly gushing streams of black gold. Finding oil, determining its grade, selling it, relying on the source, transporting it, and profiting from the enterprise required a volatile and perilous chain of events. Supply and demand is the mischievous devil of commercial oil—as it is in all commerce. At first, demand soared. America's Civil War and the country's increasingly mechanized and industrial society powered an immediate, monumental need for kerosene, lubricants, sealants, and numerous other petroleum products. Titusville and the surrounding so-called oil regions experienced a frantic "gold rush." Endless wooden-sided drilling towers, waiting teams of mules and horses, wagon-clogged service roads, as well as the omnipresent pipes, barrels, tanks, and pumping gear transfigured Pennsylvania's pastoral northwestern woodlands into a grimy, black-soaked industrial oilscape.[9]

In 1860, within a year of the Titusville strike, western Pennsylvania was producing 450,000 barrels of oil. Two years later, production had multiplied to seven times that level. The market gladly gulped every barrel. Oil barges and other hauling ships floated down the Allegheny River in packs of 150 to 200 at a time. Drilling and distribution ran around the clock.[10]

But quickly, demand, compared to uncoordinated supply, became erratic and maddening. In January 1860, a barrel of oil fetched $10. By

June, due to oversupply, the price had dropped to 50 cents per barrel, and at year's end a barrel sold for a mere dime. A year later, once supply was controlled, the price zoomed back up to $4 per barrel, and during 1863 a barrel sold for as much as $7.25.[11]

Manipulating supply and stimulating demand emerged as the fulcrum of success in the wild world of oil. Creating strategic shortages to keep prices high and occasional oversupplies to drive out competition, as well as everything in between, became the special craft of oil's robber barons. That challenge became all the more complicated as oil became a worldwide commodity. By 1878, oil production in Pennsylvania and other states, such as Ohio and West Virginia, reached 15.5 million barrels annually, of which about half was exported. The volume about tripled by 1890. Indeed, oil became America's number one nonagricultural industrial export. Distribution became all-important. Crude had to be pumped, transported, and refined in a series of steps from oil wellhead to end user, whether in the neighboring county or across the oceans.[12]

Timing was everything. Nobody wanted to drown in unused oil—but rather float on the lucrative flow. Massive pipelines traversing hundreds of miles, as well as tanker trucks and oil-hauling ships, were constructed to bring the crude to refineries and the refined oil to users—from the subterranean depths of Pennsylvania to the kitchen stoves, bedroom nightstands, and industrial cogwheels a world away. It was a logistical miracle.[13]

Moreover, the pool of oil beneath a wellhead was hardly perpetual. One Titusville-area boomtown, at Pithole Creek, was just a lush tract of Allegheny forest when, on January 7, 1865, an oil speculator brought in a gusher. Within a few months, a nearby farm was transformed into bustling "Pithole City," roiling with 15,000 excited oil zealots. The overnight population attracted more than 50 hotels and boardinghouses. The Astor House hotel was built in a day. A daily newspaper sprang up. Telegraph lines were strung. The town's brand-new post office, processing some 10,000 letters and packages per day, ranked just behind those in Philadelphia and Pittsburgh. Pithole farmland rocketed in value. One parcel sold for $1.3 million during the summer of 1865, and by the time the financing closed in September, the cost was $2 million. Pithole was for millionaires—for a while.

But by January 1866, the tempestuous gusher had been pumped dry. Most people left as suddenly as they had rushed in. Vacant buildings were mercilessly dismantled for firewood. A typical tract of that $2 million farmland was snatched up for a mere $4.37. The Danforth House hotel, which had cost $30,000 to build, was sold for firewood for just $16. Pithole, an instant urban success, just as instantly became an abandoned city.[14] That was the power of oil—from greatness to ghost town in the blink of a barrel.

In those first heady years, Pennsylvania catapulted to become the world's prime supplier of cheap, commercially extracted oil. Near-monopolistic control made Titusville and western Pennsylvania legendary across the financial and governmental centers of the world. As the geologic know-how, drilling acumen, and refining technology streamed into neighboring American states possessing oil reserves, cheap commercial oil became an almost uniquely American commodity, generating gargantuan fortunes for oil barons such as John D. Rockefeller.[15] But quickly, the lure of petrodollars brought others to the well.

Nature placed oil beneath the ground in many regions around the world and on every continent. One of the richest oil fields was in Baku, a much-contested trans-Caucasian realm on the Caspian Sea, considered Persian by some, Georgian by others, and Azerbaijani by its inhabitants, but since 1813 ceded by the shah to czarist Russia. Baku had always been renowned for oil—seeping up from crevices and sometimes exploding into untapped gushers, hundreds of feet tall, which easily ignited into fountains of fire. The city's very air was permeated with the sting of petroleum. Overhanging clouds of naphtha fumes constantly inebriated those who worked in or dwelled near the fields, creating a surreal oleic enclave.[16]

Baku's petroleum, though abundant, had always been a manual and hand-wrought industry. For centuries, petroleum effluent was carted off in buckets and baskets and channeled into holding tanks for transport to rudimentary still-like refineries located nearby. One primitive Persian well, 100 feet deep, dates back to 1594. In the early 1800s, production was merely several thousand tons per year. The first primitive oil drilling efforts are said to have occurred in 1844. In 1858, organized kerosene distillation began in Baku. But when Pennsylvania struck oil in 1859, it became cheaper to import high-grade American kerosene into Russia from across the ocean than to truck in the smelly product from Baku.[17]

In 1872, the czar broke with economic custom, releasing Baku from state control and allowing private entrepreneurs to drill using American techniques. Land was leased. Scores of wells were sunk around the perimeter of those land lots on the theory that a well would not only draw petroleum from beneath one man's acreage, but from his neighbor's as well. In truth, every well drew from the common stratum underlying everyone's plots.[18]

Baku boomed. The Nobel brothers, famous for torpedo boats and dynamite, brought in modern oil techniques. What's more, they created an efficient distribution network that included pipelines, railroad tank cars, and storage bunkers, plus they commissioned the first oil tanker, named the *Zoroaster*, to transport their commodity across the Black Sea. Baku's population increased from 12,000 in 1870 to 100,000 in 1890, while production zoomed from 10,000 tons annually to 2.7 million tons by 1890. The intoxicating flammable was openly "cooked" in dozens of open refineries. Russian oil was challenging Pennsylvania's supremacy.[19]

The euphoric fumes of Baku attracted a young Turkish man late in 1890. The 22-year-old had been traveling for several weeks, first by ship from London to Istanbul and from there by a long, arduous train trip to the trans-Caucasian region of Baku. Frequent stops along the way to discover local ethnic groups and their customs made the journey more exciting and tolerable. But the last 400 miles of mountainous terrain from the Black Sea seaport of Batum required a grueling 24-hour segment. Late in the day, the young man finally disembarked at Baku. When he arrived in the refinery district, he beheld a stark oilscape he called hideous. "Everything is black," he wrote in his journal, "the walls, the earth, the atmosphere, the sky. One feels the oil, breathes the vapors, the acrid smell seizes you by the throat. . . . You walk among clouds of smoke that obscure the atmosphere." Indeed, that refining district was known as "the Black City." He called it "the kingdom of oil."[20]

Not long after the young man arrived, he experienced Baku's mythic temperament. The earth rumbled and shook, and then suddenly a giant atomized jet of black oil exploded high into the air, expelling dirt and rocks that fell into a berm around its portal. Even from a distance, the soaring oil reached him, bathing him from head to toe with a fine mist that trickled between his fingers and soaked into his shoes.[21]

Oil was now in his nostrils and lungs, streaming over his skin, and saturating his clothes. Soon oil would be in his blood. Oil would dominate the rest of his life, and he in turn, during the next six decades, would dominate the life of oil. The young man's name was Calouste Sarkis Gulbenkian. Ultimately, the mightiest oil conglomerates and the world's greatest nations would bow to his demands. All the oil in Mesopotamia, and nearly in the entire Mideast, would be controlled by him—not by virtue of any monopoly or majority, but by virtue of his powerful fraction and his tenacious personality. Called "incredibly cruel" by some of those closest to him and a "mystery man" by many who later discovered his pivotal role, in the end Gulbenkian was one thing above all: the legendary Mr. Five Percent.

Who was Gulbenkian?

The Gulbenkians were descended from Armenian nobility, tracing their roots back to the fourth century, to the feudal princes of Rechduni, who dwelled in the disputed Asia Minor land of Vaspurkan. Once Hittite, later Persian, and eventually the Roman province named Cappadocia, the region of Vaspurkan became one of the earliest realms of Christianity—even before Constantine declared it Rome's state religion. During the Christian Byzantine centuries, the family was known as "Vart Badrik." When the Ottomans conquered Cappadocia in the 1600s, the family name was Turkified to *Gulbenkian*. The Gulbenkians continuously intermarried among their own, creating a distinct Armenian clan.[22]

In the 1800s, the family business was typical of Armenian traders in the Ottoman Empire: The Gulbenkians bought and sold, operating as commercial functionaries and go-betweens. Calouste's uncle sold fine Oriental rugs. His father, Sarkis, became wealthy as a leading importer of Russian kerosene and as a collector of revenues in Mesopotamia for the sultan's private treasury called the "Privy Purse" or the *Civile Liste.* The *Civile Liste,* as the sultan's personal fortune, was distinct from the state treasury, although in the feudal Ottoman Empire, the two often intersected. For his service, the sultan rewarded Sarkis with the governorship of Trabzon, the Black Sea capital that dominated the Eurasian trade bridge between Asia, the Caspian Sea, the Black Sea, and Asia Minor. Indeed, Gulbenkian's father controlled the kerosene markets of Baku and their provisioning to the sultan— hence the Gulbenkian petroleum fortune.[23]

Calouste Sarkis Gulbenkian himself was born near Istanbul, in March 1869, almost 10 years after the modern oil industry was born in Titusville. As a boy, Gulbenkian was tutored in English and French, which he reasonably mastered. Of course, he was equally at ease speaking Turkish to the Ottoman society at large and Armenian to his family at home.[24]

Young Gulbenkian did not live an easy life. Schoolmates tormented him, calling him "spotty face," since the Turkified surname of Gulbenkian translated to "rose pimple." Sickly and unathletic, the withdrawn lad was thought by some to be a hypochondriac because he went to extremes to remain healthy. Gulbenkian took refuge in the bazaars, where he was surrounded by and took a liking to the art of sly deal making.[25]

At age 16, he was shipped off to Kings College in London, where in 1887 he earned a degree in civil engineering. Of course, Gulbenkian displayed a fascination for oil, coming from a kerosene-importing family. So his graduation thesis focused on petroleum engineering. His predictions about the future of oil exploration struck reviewers as nothing less than prophetic—not for any technological insight, which they lacked, but for their astute economic forecasts.[26]

Early on, it became clear, Gulbenkian was destined to be an oil baron. He would not become a technocrat, that is, not a geologist, discoverer, or driller, but a magnificent go-between who would connect the wealth beneath the ground to needy consumers worldwide. In exchange, all he asked was to become fabulously wealthy.

To help him understand the family petroleum business, Gulbenkian's father sent him in 1890 on a long trip from his Kings College campus in London to the exotic oil fields of Baku. As he traveled, competing with Pennsylvania was certainly on young Gulbenkian's mind. He noted that the small Apcheron Peninsula, the seat of Baku, "consists of scarcely 2,000 square kilometers, yet annually produces almost half the quantity in all of America." But, he wrote in his journal, in spite of the progress made by the numerous wells managed by the Nobel brothers, most of the oil was still being wasted. Primitive methods, lack of management technology, and simple sabotage among rivals squandered too much oil. He contrasted Baku's situation to that of the United States, where "the American exploitation is admirably organized. There, not a drop of oil is lost."[27]

He concluded, "Let us hope that, in time, all these clouds will be dispelled and soon the oil of the Caucasus will triumph, as it deserves, over all its competitors in Asia and Pennsylvania."[28]

Gulbenkian was so enthusiastic about the prospects for Russian oil, he produced a series of articles on the subject for the eminent French magazine, *Revue des Deux Mondes.* Some months later, he organized his journal notes into a book, also written in French, detailing his colorful travels to Baku and his estimates for its great economic promise. His well-circulated writings included revealing geological findings assembled not by him but by others, since he had spent only a few days in Baku, with no time to conduct surveys. No matter, young Gulbenkian, barely 23 years of age, quickly became the foremost published expert on Russian and Eurasian oil.[29] Suddenly, Gulbenkian was in demand.

Among the first to call was Hagop Pasha, the minister of the *Civile Liste,* a close Armenian friend of Gulbenkian's father, and Selim Effendi, the Turkish state minister of mines. They jointly asked Gulbenkian to produce a comprehensive survey of the oil prospects for Mesopotamia. In 1892, Gulbenkian quickly cobbled together a highly polished report filled with geological specifics, engineering suggestions, and enticing economic projections—all based not on his own expertise but on morsels picked up from the unverified writings, observations, and conversation points of others. Later, Gulbenkian even bragged, "I elaborated a comprehensive report, which was nothing else than a compilation of various travelers's books . . . and particularly what I had heard from different engineers of the Anatolia Railway who had been in Mesopotamia." Ironically, Gulbenkian himself never set foot in Mesopotamia before his report—or after.[30]

Sultan Abdulhamid II, later known as "Abdul the Damned," enthusiastically received Gulbenkian's news that Mesopotamia might proffer great oil deposits. Anticipating that his land might hold petro-leum riches, Abdulhamid had already begun quietly transferring masses of Mesopotamian land into his private treasury, that is, the *Civile Liste,* hoping to sell oil concessions. The first was on April 8, 1889, in preparation for a railway proposal. It covered "the whole province of Mosul." After Gulbenkian's promising report, Abdul-hamid transferred vast additional sections of Mesopotamian land to the *Civile Liste.* Palace officials sent telegrams to the provincial gover-nors advising that the sultan wanted the lands. In many cases, the gov-ernors filed *tapous,* that is, cadastral or land registry certificates, which formalize land ownership. No payment was required. The *tapous* were easy enough to file when done correctly. The mere filing of the paperwork created legal property rights—this in a region where land laws were obscure and known to very few. Peasants and most of the others who lived on Mesopotamian lands understood them the least. One day the lands were simply unregistered; the next day, Abdul-hamid owned them by virtue of the *tapous.* Where others owned the lands that Abdulhamid desired, the palace requested a prompt sale. Their owners formally ceded such properties to Abdulhamid's royal estates for just a token fee.[31] Those secret land transfers created pow-erful billion-dollar factors in the subsequent disposition of the prodi-gious Mesopotamian petroleum rights and the determination of who actually owned the oil fields.

Like their other efforts to join advancing societies, the Ottomans were quite late in approaching the potential of modern oil explo-ration. For a full generation before Gulbenkian's report to the sultan, the petroleum business had been thriving. Indeed, the formative late-nineteenth-century decades of oil exploitation—and the industrial power and opportunity for wealth it conveyed—simply bypassed the Turkish regime and the Mideast lands it controlled.

The mighty industry created by the 1859 Titusville strike quickly spread to other American states, spawning a venous network of pipelines, railroad spurs, and horse-drawn wagon routes across Amer-ica. Within about a decade, John D. Rockefeller became the richest man in the world by creating a conspiratorial trust made up of numerous secret corporations and fronts calculated to drive all competitors out of business. By the 1870s, his maze of Standard Oil enterprises controlled nearly all the refineries, pipelines, and other channels of distribution in the United States, as well as in several foreign lands. So immense was this one man's power that Congress took action to craft antitrust legislation. The courts would later dismantle Rockefeller's empire into 22 smaller companies, although each was a giant commercial presence in its own right.[32]

Modern industrial oil operations soon appeared across the world. For example, in the Indian Ocean, the islands of Sumatra, Borneo, and Java were long known for medicinal oil seepages and hand-dug wells dating back a thousand years. A decade after Titusville, geologists counted no fewer than 44 seepages in Java alone, and by 1872, commercial drilling began. By 1890, with the blessing of the king of Holland, the Royal Dutch Oil Company had been founded as an international company to refine and sell Indonesian products, mainly kerosene.[33]

That same year, 1890, a British city alderman and exporter named Marcus Samuel, accustomed to shipping cheap knickknacks between Japan and Europe, stepped up to transporting a more lucrative commodity: petroleum. He built the world's first true oceangoing oil tanker to shuttle Baku crude from its outlet on the Black Sea, through Turkey's Bosporus straits, into the Mediterranean and then through the Suez Canal to ready markets in Singapore. Samuel was fascinated with the seashell-encrusted jewel boxes and trinkets he exported. So his first tanker was aptly named the *Murex,* after the murex seashell. The next three ships were named *Conch, Turbo,* and *Clam.* Soon he established a newly organized oil shipping company named Shell Transport and Trading. Shell began transporting Royal Dutch oil from Sumatra to destinations everywhere. The production-distribution partnership became so important that the two companies merged to become Royal Dutch Shell.[34]

In Poland, oil from the Carpathian Mountains had been used extensively since the 1500s, when the foul-smelling crevice seepage was scooped up and used to light streetlamps in the town of Krosno. In 1852, pharmacist and oil pioneer Ignacy Lukasiewicz began refining the seepage to create illuminants safe enough to light the interior of an entire Lvov hospital. In fact, it was the Polish petroleum guru Lukasiewicz who invented the cheap kerosene lantern that became a worldwide household appliance from the American prairies to the castles of Vienna. Soon, primitive Polish wells replaced hand-scooping. Lukasiewicz's first rudimentary refinery for seepage opened in 1859, the same year Titusville reinvented the oil industry with modern deep drilling. Poland quickly began using improved methods to exploit a large number of oil fields throughout Polish Galicia. By 1873, the fabulous oil district of Drohobycz alone was using enough American, Canadian, and native drilling technology to support 12,000 oil derricks. That year, some 900 companies and 12,000 individuals were engaged in Poland's oil industry.[35]

By 1857, the Carpathian oil that made Poland a famous petroleum center was also creating an industry in Romania that would be developed into the most bountiful oil deposits in Europe, centered in Ploieşti. In Australia, rich oil shale deposits were being mined and refined from the 1860s. Canada's thriving oil center in Petrolia, near Ontario, was engaged in commercial excavation of abundant seepages as early as 1858 and moved into advanced drilling about the time of Titusville's strike. By 1861, some 400 wells were operating in Petrolia. The next year, more than 100 powerful gushers had coated everything in town with oil. For the next decades, Canada derived some 90 percent of its household and industrial oil from this one center. Petrolia engineers then fanned out to develop similar finds in other distant parts of the world, such as the Gobi desert in China and regions of South America.[36]

The advent of Thomas Edison's electric lightbulb in the early 1880s, immediately adopted in North America and throughout Europe, did nothing to slow petroleum's expanding market. True, by 1886, nearly 200,000 incandescent lightbulbs were in use worldwide, and millions more soon after. This certainly reduced the need for illumination kerosene. But at that very time, horseless carriages, which had operated on steam for decades, were being outfitted with exciting new German-designed internal combustion machines. Those engines required fuel oil. The automobile industry was born.[37]

By 1890, when Gulbenkian arrived in Baku, the oil business was indeed a worldwide phenomenon—but not in the Middle East. Doing business in the region just seemed a barrier too high to hurdle.

Systemic corruption and graft meant that business suitors approaching the authorities were compelled to grease a long line of outstretched palms, from the lowliest doorman to the aides and assistants of key advisors to ministers and finally to the monarchs themselves. Moreover, the lack of roads, railroad tracks, and other modern conveniences made every industrial endeavor trebly more expensive and daunting.[38]

It isn't that some did not dabble in the potential. By the 1870s, Russia's oil fields, including those in Baku, were challenging Standard Oil's supremacy in Europe. Russia's ascendancy in natural resources disrupted the strategic balance of power in Europe and troubled Britain. Preliminary British Geological Society observations, as early as 1855, suggested the vast Baku oil field might extend to neighboring Persia, located just to the south. Of course, Persian bitumen seepages had been famous since antiquity.[39]

The first to try to establish a Middle East oil industry was Baron Julius de Reuter, founder of Reuters News Service. He approached the shah of Iran in 1872. Reuter secured a notorious "exclusive concession" to develop a railroad, plus all riparian mining and mineral rights in the country, including oil, for the next 70 years. This was a virtual takeover of the main commercial future of the country. The price: a mere down payment of £40,000 plus a 20 percent cut for the shah of the so-called profits. The shah took Reuter's money, but then almost laughingly frustrated all further efforts to acquire the development permits.[40]

Reuter's company protested: "It is obvious that in a country like Persia, with an autocratic government and all authority directly emanating from the Shah, no commercial enterprise of a new and strange [unusual] character can be profitably carried on." Instead of assistance to carry out the concession, "the Corporation meets with direct hostility," executives railed. Calling the whole endeavor "fruitless," Reuter demanded his money back, but the shah was giving nothing back. Soon, Reuter dissolved his concern, embittered, and the London investment market quickly dismissed Persia as a completely unreliable kingdom for investment. Even the Foreign Office rebuked Reuter for wasting his time and money on Persia.[41]

In Turkish Mesopotamia, throughout the first half of the 1800s, the Ottomans had kept the three frontier provinces socially and commercially undeveloped, with little attention to the needs of its inhabitants. The centuries-long process of self-inflicted ruin and incessant war expenditures and reparations had wrought the expected result. By 1875, after 14 foreign loans, the Ottoman Public Debt Administration was compelled to admit it could not repay its multimillion-pound obligations and the attendant debt service. The Ottoman Empire declared bankruptcy. The empire created a Public Debt Administration in 1881, employing some 5,000 revenue agents, who forwarded Turkish tax revenues directly to European creditors.[42] Consequently, there was little development in Mesopotamia—only the continued extraction of what value existed for tribute, tax, and foreign levy.

But there was a brief three-year period when Mesopotamia appeared ready to catapult into a golden age of reform and modernization. Midhat Pasha, a charismatic, youthful Turkish reformer, was determined to bring the empire into modern times with recognition of individual rights. For six months in the late 1850s, Midhat traveled to the great capitals of Europe, studying their constitutions and judicial systems. In 1860, Midhat pushed for similar reforms and modern advances throughout the Turkish provinces, east and west. As governor of the Danube province of Nis, encompassing Bulgaria, he built some 2,000 miles of roads and 1,500 bridges within a short period of time. He erected schools and hospitals and brought that neglected territory into the nineteenth century.[43]

The palace was uncomfortable with Midhat's emphasis on service to the citizenry and emphasis on human rights. With typical Ottoman intrigue, Midhat was kicked upstairs, recalled to serve as a minister in Istanbul under the palace's close scrutiny, and then transferred to the distant Mesopotamian provinces. Midhat arrived in Baghdad as governor on April 30, 1869. He immediately permitted the establishment of *Al Zawra,* the first newspaper in Baghdad. Hence, several thousand years after Mesopotamia endowed the world with the gift of writing, its capital finally had its own newspaper. Midhat introduced land reforms that would allow peasants to register the lands they had lived on for generations, thus acquiring legal ownership. He tried to settle the traditionally nomadic tribes into villages and provide them with land rights as well. Land ownership would be inviolable and would pass from father to son as an inheritance. His efforts encouraged some tribes to abandon millennia of looting and wandering to enter a new way of life.[44]

Turning to health, Midhat insisted the Persians stop sending moist, freshly deceased corpses to Najaf for sacred Shi'a burial, this to reduce the risk of infection from decomposing bodies. He was willing to accept the bodies, but only after they had dried and reposed for a year. Determined to bring the provinces into the modern age, he built a tramway in Baghdad, plus an orphanage, factories, a hospital, a secondary school for boys, and other public institutions. Moreover, the outspoken Midhat openly criticized corrupt Ottoman administrators and successfully conspired with his fellow Young Turks to depose despotic officials—even those in the palace.[45]

Midhat was dangerous. In 1872, after only three years, his forward momentum in Baghdad was abruptly stopped. He was transferred to imperial positions in Istanbul and then moved from province to province. No matter. In 1876, he was determined to bring European democracy to the empire. Midhat was the chief architect of a revolutionary national constitution along the European model. On December 23, 1876, Sultan Abdulhamid was pushed, pressured, and cajoled into publicly accepting a sweeping, purely democratic constitution that promised to change everything Ottoman—from Basra to Bulgaria.[46] Democracy would come to the Middle East.

Midhat's constitution was a model of egalitarian democracy. Article 8: All subjects of the empire are without distinction called Ottomans no matter what religion they profess. Article 9: All Ottomans enjoy individual liberty so long as they do not attack the liberty of other people. Article 10: Individual liberty is absolutely inviolable. Article 12: The press is free. Article 17: All Ottomans are equal before the law. Article 22: The domicile is inviolable. Article 26: Torture in all its forms is completely and absolutely prohibited. In 119 terse articles, Midhat outlined complete separation of church and state and respect for all religions, while maintaining an Islamic national identity. Separation of powers between court, palace, and legislature, checks and balances, and the right of all men to live in freedom and equality were all guaranteed.[47]

Not stopping, Midhat challenged Abdul the Damned himself. Nothing less than total democracy would do—and quickly. About a month after the constitution was accepted, Midhat wrote a January 30,

1877, letter to Sultan Abdulhamid, chastising the royal reluctance to speedily inaugurate the reforms. "It is now nine days, Sire, since you have abstained from giving a favorable answer to my petition. You thereby refuse to sanction laws indispensable to the welfare of the country."[48]

Such impudence was intolerable to Abdulhamid. A few days later, the sultan exiled Midhat, and then, once again, shuffled him from one temporary appointive position to another, from one territory to another. In 1881, Midhat was tried for murder and conspiracy, but not imprisoned. The trial just gave Midhat a platform to denounce the inequities of the regime. Nothing would stop the visionary Midhat, who dreamed of an Ottoman Empire and a Middle East of freedom, enlightenment, and democracy. By 1884, Midhat had been removed to Taif, a distant province in the Arabian Peninsula. In May of that year, at age 72, Midhat suddenly died. At first, the palace declared that a terrible swift disease had struck Midhat.[49]

However, a few years later, a trusted sergeant of the Taif pashas came forward to reveal what he asserted was his eyewitness account. The sergeant confessed that he was instructed by the recently installed local governor, Mohammed Nuri Pasha, an official loyal to the sultan, to summon Midhat to the Taif governor's private room. Midhat seemed to be unnerved by the unexpected request and muttered the classic Islamic prayer of distress: "There is no help nor strength except in the Almighty God." The prayer soothed him, and Midhat calmly accompanied the sergeant into the royal chamber. When Midhat entered, Governor Nuri was there to greet him. Six other soldiers were in attendance. Governor Nuri saluted Midhat and then exited. The door was locked.[50]

Midhat turned to the squad of soldiers and spoke calmly, with dignity, "You have been ordered to kill me, my children." He commonly referred to all citizens as "my children." They replied, "Yes, your excellency." The father of Turkey's brief march toward democracy, a man who stood for everything that could cure the Sick Man of Europe, the man who crusaded for the rights of all men no matter how high or low, was profoundly pacific in his final moments. Midhat's serenity in the face of death overcame his executioners. The sergeant fought his tears, but still visibly wept. Midhat asked simply, "How am I to die?" The men replied, "The orders are by strangulation."[51]

Midhat promptly replied, "I die for my efforts to give you, my children, and all the people of the Empire, more liberty. Children, you can carry out your orders." As tears traveled down their cheeks, and after debating whether they could mutiny, the squad decided to obey the lawful order of Abdul the Damned. They carefully tied his hands and feet, and gently laid him on his back. Four men held him down. Two others then wrapped their hands around his neck, and strangled him until he breathed no more.[52] With this execution, the last chance for democracy in Mesopotamia was smothered as well.

Midhat's constitution, previously accepted, was now discarded as an inert document. Progress in Mesopotamia slowed to a crawl. Abdulhamid was now free to systematically usurp the land reform laws intended to benefit the common man. He used the registration laws to legally transfer vast oil-endowed provincial lands to the *Civile Liste*. The April 8, 1889, transfer of all of Mosul's oil rights and revenues was just the first. On September 24, 1898, Abdulhamid added all of Baghdad province.[53]

The sultan was now ready for any business Gulbenkian cared to transact.

CHAPTER SEVEN

The Race to Monopolize

No one will ever know the true legal owner of Mesopotamia's multibillion-dollar petroleum resources.

Some almost owned it. Some should have owned it. Some believed they owned it. A few just demanded it. Was the oil German? Was it British? Was it Turkish? Was it government owned, corporate owned, or privately owned? The answer is probably all of the above and none of the above. Mesopotamian oil once again proved that possession is nine-tenths of the law. Still, it is the nagging tenth that haunts the millionaires, billionaires, and corporate heirs of Mideast oil who still wonder who the rightful owner is.

To be sure, a torturous cavalcade of near misses and "almost" ownerships played out for 15 years through the corridors of European commerce, diplomacy, and government. The combative claims and disputes zigzagged through the ever-shifting dunes of Ottoman legality amid the ravages of an international bidding war, subtle deceptions, not-so-subtle blackmail, roller-coaster negotiations, moment-to-moment compromises that evaporated as soon as they were accepted, and the unpredictable and often unseen actions of one man: Mr. Five Percent.

The tangled, confusing, seemingly impossible saga began as the twentieth century neared and as Europe slowly drifted toward a great war that many expected and all feared.

The Sick Man was on his deathbed. Throughout the last decades of the nineteenth century, the Ottoman Empire and its neighbors had been fighting one bloody war and one insurrection after another, from Bulgaria and Greece to Armenia and Russia. Turkish finances were a mirage of mirrors. The Eastern Question—who would inherit, lead, profit from, or be damaged by the inevitable collapse of the Ottoman Empire—was being answered simultaneously by all the leading European powers. They all had plans—and plans to realize their plans.

Some capitals wanted to dominate the soon-to-be dismantled territories as their own spheres of interest. Some merely wanted to prevent others from doing so. A few wanted to see new, friendly nations emerge in the aftermath of Turkey's disintegration. Certainly, local populations throughout the empire were rising up angry and demanding an end to their dynastic, ecclesiastic, and purely monarchical regimes. The seams of Europe were unraveling.

To keep them stitched, endless overlapping alliances, pacts, and secret agreements were sewn among friends and enemies both, as London, Paris, Berlin, Vienna, Moscow, and Istanbul tried to maintain the so-called balance of power in Europe. War was to be avoided because the rapid mechanical, scientific, and industrial advances of recent decades had created a new style of modern warfare that could kill millions; if war could not be avoided, steeled preparation was needed.

Hence, as the nineteenth century drew to a close, Turkish Mesopotamia and indeed the entire extended Middle East suddenly catapulted in importance—especially to England. No longer were the three provinces considered mere transit corridors and stepping-stones to India and Asia. Now Mosul, Baghdad, and Basra were coveted for their legendary but unexploited oil.

Quite simply, as the twentieth century opened for business, the world needed much more oil. Petroleum was no longer just to illuminate lanterns, boil stew, and lubricate moving parts. Modern armies and navies demanded vast new supplies of fuel and petroleum by-products.

Among the first to recognize the need for fuel-burning vessels was Admiral John Fisher, a visionary British naval leader with a decidedly imperialistic outlook. He knew the future of England's navy was a fleet of swift battleships that could maneuver sharply and fire torpedoes and long-range guns from a distance. Speed required oil-burning vessels that could be refueled quickly and cleanly—even at sea. These advanced ships would make obsolete the messy coal-burning monstrosities that required throngs of sooty dockside laborers hefting coal baskets into holds and gangs of grimy engine-room stokers. Fisher's revolutionary new battleships would be called *dreadnoughts,* and they would be the anchor of a rapidly expanding, well-financed modern armada of fast and deadly vessels. Britain pursued a "two power" naval policy; that is, its fleet should be as large as the two next largest fleets combined.[1] Only an oil-powered flotilla could achieve that.

As England's fleet needed oil, the prospects for finding it were troubling. Baku's petroleum industry was certainly expanding and by century's end represented more than half the world's supply. It had already surpassed even Standard Oil, which was suffering under legal restraints and now controlled only 43 percent of the world market. Russian oil was dominant in Europe. Royal Dutch Shell—still majority Dutch-owned—was also emerging. Germany had secured control over the vast fields of Romania. But Britain's new source of supply could not be controlled by any potential adversaries, such as Russia, expanding into eastern Europe, Germany, threatening to sever the British Empire, or Holland, which even then was fighting the bloody Boer War with England in South Africa.[2]

The most logical candidate for new supply was, of course, the Persian Gulf. Britain could have chosen the United States or Mexico or Poland as a trusted new supplier. But Persia had been within the sphere of British influence since the days of the East India Company. Persia was halfway to India. Persia it was.

Clearly, Persia had promise. Continuing geological exploration, such as a two-year French government survey in the 1890s, suggested good deposits. What's more, some in Britain harbored the mistaken impression that Baku's massive deposits were soon to be depleted. A British diplomat in Teheran in 1890 was typical as he reported, "The virgin oil fields of Persia promise a good fortune as they may be made to engage the whole of western markets in a short time." Many of Russia's oil workers in Baku were actually trained Persians, so Persia possessed a ready source of semiskilled workers. Consumption of household kerosene had doubled and tripled in some Persian towns in recent years.[3]

As the new century debuted, it was time to relegate Baron de Reuter's bad oil concession experiences with Persia to the past. Representatives of the cash-strapped and high-living Persian shah, unable to secure a loan in any foreign bank, informed British diplomats that the kingdom was still interested in selling a proper oil concession. With strategic military needs pressing, Britain was eager to try anew.[4]

In 1900, Australian mining entrepreneur William D'Arcy heard of the opportunity and stepped forward to take the risk. D'Arcy's own representative had suggested to the Persians that "an industry may be developed that will compete with that of Baku." After paying several thousand pounds to all the right go-betweens, D'Arcy secured a powerful and seemingly safe concession. His concession, dated May 28, 1901, required that a functioning petroleum company be founded within two years or the deal would be rescinded. To forfend a repeat of the Reuter debacle, the Persian government openly agreed to "take all necessary measures" to facilitate D'Arcy's exploration. For this arrangement, D'Arcy would pay the monarch £20,000 and sign over £20,000 in shares, but only after successful exploration justified a proper petroleum company. In addition, the shah would receive 16 percent annually, but only from "net profits," a term which—conveniently—was never defined.[5]

The ornate concession document, replete with British consular service stamps certifying the French, English, and Persian translations, plus the shah's royal indicia and green knotted twine secured by sealing wax, granted D'Arcy the exclusive oil rights to all but the five northern provinces. To mollify Russia, these five provinces were excluded because they were too close to the neighboring Baku field. D'Arcy's concession would run 60 years—until 1961.[6]

Quickly, D'Arcy dispatched a geologist who confirmed the prior French estimates and reported "ample justification" to expect "a highly profitable industry of immense magnitude." Soon thereafter, cash-short D'Arcy made arrangements with Burmah Oil, a Scottish oil firm operating in India, to bring Polish, Canadian, Russian, and other workers to drill in the most promising Persian sectors.[7]

The work and terrain were dangerous and challenging. Since roads did not exist, D'Arcy's people built their own. Marauders were everywhere. D'Arcy paid volatile and scruffy Bahktiari tribesmen, bullet belts crisscrossing their waists and chests, to guard the riggers from attack. Sometimes their leaders failed to distribute the cash, causing more than one edgy encounter. But nothing could protect the drillers from the incessant fleas, foul water, and searing heat.[8]

Ironically, months before D'Arcy's experts began scrambling over the rough-hewn Persian valleys, Ottoman sultan Abdulhamid's own expert, Paul Ghrostopnine, was undertaking a secret survey just over the border in Mesopotamia. Ghrostopnine left Istanbul for Mesopotamia on January 4, 1901. During the next weeks, he made careful assessments of the numerous existing but completely undeveloped bitumen wells throughout the three provinces. Many in the Mosul, Kirkuk, and Baghdad areas were so well endowed, they pooled on the ground or gurgled beneath tributary creeks. "I have visited several oil wells all over the world, both before and after exploitation," Ghrostophnine reported enthusiastically, "but none of these have proved to be so rich. . . . I have never seen the like as yet." However, the existing surface-scooping operations were simply anemic. One typical well's refining output was measured in "gallons per day," another in "donkey-loads per day."[9]

Abdul the Damned well understood that his lands might hold fabulous reserves of oil. But no effort was made to organize a national drilling enterprise or a Turkish petroleum company for the good of his nation. That would have taken much investment and long-term effort. Instead, the Sublime Porte opted to extract whatever value it could for the moment, thereby forestalling total economic collapse yet another day. Mortgaging the future and selling off segments of the realm was the Ottoman way. Oil wealth was not something to develop as a national treasure, but to auction off to industrial others.

Employing the tactics of the bazaar, the sultan patiently, excruciatingly, juggled the several offers, maneuvering for the best price. Many came calling. The Germans were especially interested and stepped forward as part of an effort to create a sphere of interest in Turkey. Kaiser Wilhelm's state visit to Istanbul in 1898—his second—was a momentous occasion for the sultan. Abdulhamid staged enormous banquets wherever in the empire the kaiser traveled. The sultan even removed a section of Jerusalem's Old City wall to make way for Kaiser Wilhelm to enter on his magnificent white stallion. The cost of these festivities—a staggering 1 million Turkish pounds—prompted Ottoman government officials to protest, inasmuch as "civil and military officers are literally starving."[10]

The Ottoman Mining Law of 1882 and 1886 had undergone changes so that only narrow one-year permits of research were issued—but these were not concessions, merely the bought-and-paid-for right to survey and return in a year for another round of tedious discussions and paid permits. German interests applied for such rights. In 1888, the Deutsche Bank, working through its essentially captive Anatolia Railway Company, acquired a concession to build a short railroad line to Ankara in central Turkey. In 1902, this right was extended all the way through Mesopotamia to Baghdad and ultimately to Basra on the Persian Gulf. This railroad line was not seen by the European powers as a mere industrial improvement bettering transportation in the region, but also as a profound German military threat and oil asset—a land check to England's naval supremacy.[11]

Influential German writer Paul Rohrbach explained in his well-read pamphlet, *Bagdadbahn,* later expanded into a book of the same name, "England can be attacked and mortally wounded on land in Egypt. The loss of Egypt will mean to England not only the loss of control over the Suez Canal and its connections with India and Asia, but probably the sacrifice of its possessions in Central and Eastern Africa as well. Moreover, an Islamic power like Turkey could exercise a dangerous influence over England's 60 million Islamic subjects in India, Afghanistan and Persia, that is, if Turkey should conquer Egypt. However, Turkey can subjugate Egypt only if it possesses an extended system of railroads in Asia Minor and Syria, and if by an extension of the Anatolian Railway it is able to ward off an English attack upon Mesopotamia."[12]

With the Baghdad railroad concession came mineral and oil rights for 20 kilometers on either side of the track. About the still undeveloped Kirkuk oil fields, Rohrbach wrote: "We ought to attach the greatest importance to the circumstance that the Baghdad Railway will pass close to the petroleum districts. The only thing to be feared is . . . foreign speculators securing a preferential right in the exploitation of Mesopotamian naphtha before any effective German initiative."[13]

Britain followed every vicissitude of German and Russian expansion into the Ottoman Empire and the wider Middle East region. London undertook strategic precautions and counterchecks everywhere it could. For example, in late 1898 and early 1899, the German kaiser tried to assist Abdulhamid in reasserting control over Kuwait, a distant and only nominally Ottoman territory in the Gulf. To thwart that, on January 23, 1899, the British sealed a pact with the Kuwaiti sheikh. In exchange for a one-time British payment of 15,000 Indian rupees, the sheikh agreed not to transfer or lease any part of his territory without London's approval. As part of the pact, India would send troops should the Turks attempt to invade. Kuwait became a British protectorate, and remained one for more than 60 years.[14]

Pacts and political promises were only part of the realpolitik of the day. The beginning of the twentieth century was so serpentine a period in Europe that the great powers also found it expedient to project their power and interest via strictly commercial corporations. Hence, the Deutsche Bank's Baghdad Railway project, through the Anatolia Railway Company, was little more than a surrogate for imperial Germany. In fact, in 1903, the Anatolia Railway Company restated its rights in an actual treaty, the 1903 Baghdad Railway Convention. Article 22 specified the mineral rights. This then elevated the commercial agreement to an international covenant.[15]

The next year, in 1904, Abdulhamid's *Civile Liste* bestowed upon the Anatolia Railway far more than the original 40-kilometer corridor. It granted a one-year research permit for any oil in the provinces of Mosul and Baghdad. The railway's concession was promptly transferred to the true owner, the Deutsche Bank. If oil were to be discovered, a 40-year concession would be activated.[16] Mesopotamian oil seemed destined to be German.

However, as Germany was securing the vast oil resources of Mesopotamia, Britain's thirst for naval fuel only magnified. In 1903, Admiral Fisher, increasingly known as the "oil maniac," headed up the Admiralty's Oil Fuel Committee. That body later declared it "inexpedient to depend in peace time upon resources which would probably fail in wartime." Moreover, when Fisher became First Sea Lord, he commissioned a number of oil-only destroyers and torpedo boats, again increasing England's strategic requirement for petroleum.[17] But the source for all this needed oil was still unknown.

Meanwhile, D'Arcy's company had made little progress in Persia. He was running out of money, time, and patience in the struggle to bring in a gusher. Fisher met D'Arcy quite by accident while the two were visiting a Czech medical facility, and their oil interests naturally

blended. D'Arcy wanted cash from the Admiralty to prop up his failing enterprise. Fisher wanted the oil. But after several applications by
D'Arcy, the Admiralty declined because D'Arcy's efforts were simply
too speculative. He had not yet brought in even one well. Instead, the
Admiralty reached out to its existing contacts with Burmah Oil, a
proven oil-producing concern. Burmah was already working with
D'Arcy in Persia in the exploration effort. So the British navy in late
1905 awarded Burmah a lucrative fuel contract for its existing oil in
India, and then encouraged Burmah to take over in Persia as well.
With enough lawyers, bankers, and official sponsorship, that happened. Burmah now pursued the Persian project, with D'Arcy scheduled to receive a cash settlement should the project achieve success.[18]

In 1904, D'Arcy was fundamentally out of the Persian project and
therefore free to make new inquiries in Mesopotamia. He had tried
and failed once before. In late 1901, just after signing the Persian concession, D'Arcy's negotiator had hoped to seal a similar agreement in
Istanbul. He was unsuccessful. Now, three years later, D'Arcy received
secret Foreign Office encouragement to try again and this time to
secure for Britain a concession from the sultan calculated to undercut
the Deutsche Bank and Anatolia Railway. D'Arcy sent his trusted
agent Herbert Nichols to Istanbul.[19]

Anatolia Railway's oil concession contract was issued on July 17,
1904. Within a week, D'Arcy's chief negotiator, Nichols, petitioned
the palace in the saccharine idiom of concession seekers: "Your
Majesty's only endeavor, since His accession to the Imperial Throne,
has been the progress of trade and industry, the increase of the prosperity and richness of His vast country. Since that happy day [of the
sultan's accession], so much has been done to this effect and consequently we humbly pray you let us give our humble help to your
Imperial projects by granting us the right of working, through a new
Ottoman corporation, to be floated by us, the mines of Mosul and
Baghdad, from which up to now no benefits or profits have been
drawn."[20] Fawning was a language the palace understood.

Nichols's supplication went on to promise exploration within two
years, and if successful, a going concern shortly thereafter would
export petroleum, generating vast wealth for all. If given permission
for the privilege of exploration, the offer promised that "the sum of
three million francs would be paid to the Ministry of the *Civile Liste,*

half (say 1.5 million) in cash and half (1.5 million) in shares of the new corporation. As a guarantee, a sum of 250,000 francs will be paid the Ministry of the *Civile Liste"* immediately upon signature. Should the new company not come to pass, the sultan could keep the down payment. Once petroleum was being pumped, 15 percent of the oil or its value would be kicked back to the *Civile Liste,* that is, Abdulhamid's personal treasury. This deal would continue for 60 years, thus considerably multiplying the sultan's wealth now and for his subsequent generations.[21]

Clearly, this was a good deal.

But the Germans and their Anatolia Railway had already been granted the oil rights in Mosul and Baghdad on July 17, 1904—just days earlier. No matter. Palace officials scrutinized the language of the Anatolia agreement, taking special note of Article 1, which required drilling studies to take place within one year, and these to be forwarded to the Ministry of the *Civile Liste.* In the bazaar, all things come to he who is patient. Abdulhamid was patient.

Conditions in Mesopotamia were challenging. Communications and connections were poor. Anatolia Railway knew trains, not oil wells. Organizing industrial exploration and proper geological studies would not be easy or expeditious. As expected, Anatolia Railway was a little late. But late they were. However, the Ministry was on time. One year and a week after the July 17, 1904, agreement was signed, Minister of the *Civile Liste* Ohannès Effendi Sakisian dispatched a carefully worded letter to the Anatolia Railway Company.[22]

"Following the settlement of the Agreement concluded with your honorable management," wrote Sakisian, "you were required within one year's time to undertake the necessary studies related to the petroleum deposits in the provinces of Baghdad and Mosul, and then confirm to the Minister of the *Civile Liste* that a technical Commission has been directed to the sites for studies." That was not done. But just in case it had been done, nothing was actually submitted to the Ministry as the agreement called for. Therefore, Sakisian cleverly added, "Even if the necessary studies have been done, the set time limit has already passed—and the result has not been communicated to our Ministry as of today."[23]

True, Anatolia Railway was late. But the company had been earnestly working on the project with an international team of experts.

Mail and other communications between Europe and Mesopotamia were slow. On September 4, 1905, several days after getting the unexpected letter from the *Civile Liste,* Anatolia's assistant general manager replied with a degree of honest enthusiasm. He attached a just-received and encouraging letter from their chief geologist. "We have the honor to bring to your Excellency's attention," the railway director wrote, "a letter that we have just received from Professor Dr. Porro, chief specialist of the mission sent to Mesopotamia to evaluate the petroleum deposits and their future exploitation. Only now, after enormous difficulty and long delays, have the geologic and other samples, numerous and heavy, arrived in Europe."[24]

The railway director explained, "The original [one-year] timeframe determined at the outset was too short." He continued, "Because of its great importance . . . all samples will be analyzed with minute care, and the supplementary studies which these analyses require will be carefully assessed by the knowledgeable specialists." The railway almost routinely requested an additional "ten to twelve months."[25]

That was a mistake. Sakisian was unyielding. Where were the reports? He began papering the file to demonstrate a breach. "I request that you send me the reports concerning the petroleum deposits of the regions of Baghdad and Mosul, so that my Department can study the results of the studies . . . this based upon the written and executed terms of the Agreement relating to these deposits."[26]

Meanwhile, the British were finding more reasons to believe Mesopotamia would be their source for oil. The Persian project in 1905 was floundering beneath burning deserts, swarms of gnats, and swirling dust storms, yielding dry hole after dry hole. At the same time, esteemed Foreign Office official Mark Sykes filed a secret and very enthusiastic summary of commercial, geological, and economic forecasts, titled *The Petroliferous Districts of Mesopotamia,* in which he asked Britain's consuls in the region to preempt other European competitors.[27]

The world may have been frantically seeking oil. But negotiations in the Ottoman Empire progressed glacially. Tedious correspondence and evidentiary papers to document a breach were needed because foreign corporations in the Ottoman Empire were more than mere associations of businessmen, they were surrogates for and protectorates of their foreign offices. Moreover, the Ottomans observed a "capitulation" system that basically created detached colonies of foreign businessmen, dwelling and dealing within the empire but virtually immune from Ottoman jurisdiction. Some called these "capitulation communities" an empire within an empire. Indeed, all foreign businessmen relied on pressure tactics from their foreign offices, as well as competent attorneys who were quite capable of litigating against the Ministry for the *Civile Liste*. Upon judgment, any victorious plaintiff could join the many creditors seizing and sometimes controlling Ottoman assets, debt, taxes, and duties.[28]

Lacking the funds and the studied geologic proof of exactly where to drill, the Germans in 1906 were now biding their time. They tried not to respond to *Civile Liste* pressures to admit that the concession had been breached. But the demands kept coming.[29]

In late July 1906, the *Civile Liste* sent yet another careful, self-serving letter to the Anatolia Railway Company, this one reminding, "As stipulated in Article 1 of the preliminary agreement concluded and exchanged with your management . . . concerning the petroleum deposits in the regions of Mosul and Baghdad, the necessary studies and statements were to be completed in a timeframe of one year . . . and all the results of these studies . . . were to be made available in detail to my Department. I hereby [again] request . . . that you send me the related reports and documents." Noting Anatolia's silence and failure to respond to the previous letter, the Ottoman letter warned, "My Ministry has the power to authorize a different exploitation of the deposits in question, if your Company no longer wishes to do so. . . . Let me know, as soon as possible, and formally, if your management will or will not undertake the exploitation of the deposits in question."[30]

Several more demand letters were sent, but Anatolia remained mum until August 22, 1906. Anatolia cautiously replied that it had received a positive and promising expert analysis and was now sharing a copy of those results with the Ministry as required. But before proceeding with additional investment, new assurances were needed. "The expenses for this expedition were 340,000 francs," Anatolia advised, and test drilling based on the preliminary geologic analyses would cost much more. "Our Company can only take on this heavy job after the establishment of an equitable accord between the *Civile Liste* and our company."[31]

The *Civile Liste* seemed determined to disallow the German concession and maneuver for a better offer from the British. It rejected the German-language studies and messengered them back unread, insisting, "They must be translated into Turkish and French." At the same time, the *Civile Liste* demanded a whole new contract to replace the old concession agreement. The puzzled German group did not know what to do. Mesopotamian petroleum deposits were fabulously valuable. The reports proved that. So the German company's attorneys drew up another proposed contract, this one upping the offer by virtue of a new company worth 12.5 million francs. At incorporation, 2,100 shares would be issued and 1,400 of these would be allocated to the *Civile Liste* to extract annual profit.[32]

Not good enough. The *Civile Liste* replied in January 1907, formally notifying Anatolia that the time for talk was over. There would be no further negotiation. Their concession had been officially "abrogated." Anatolia's representatives shot back a letter reminding the palace that it had already spent 340,000 francs on a preliminary survey, moved as expeditiously as science would permit, and from the company's point of view, "Our rights . . . are still intact and we can exercise all powers in those rights."[33] The Germans were not giving up their oil without a fight.

Legally, however, Anatolia Railway was weak. *Civile Liste* officials had sufficiently papered the file to show protracted noncompliance over a period of many months. Confidently, the sultan's people sent Anatolia a curt note calling its claims "pretentious" and dismissing the 1904 concession for Baghdad and Mosul as completely "null and void."[34]

Meanwhile, D'Arcy's people, ever trying to finalize their offer, also encountered frustration after frustration. Nichols was said to be "still hammering away at the Mesopotamian oilfields, but [just] as he is on the point of closing, something [always] goes wrong and the *Civile Liste* slips out."[35]

In the wings were other, smaller venture groups from the United States and Europe. These syndicates and venture capitalists were vying for a concession as well.[36] It seems many were laying claim, or hoping to lay claim, to the same oil deposits. Yet no one was successful.

But the more suitors who came knocking, the more the sultan knew he possessed an extraordinarily valuable property, and the more the stakes were raised. Abdulhamid sensed he needed to wait out the offers, allowing the several competitors to continuously outbid each other. Moreover, the longer Mesopotamian petroleum was not extracted from the ground, the more valuable it became. Europe was edging toward war. Abdulhamid understood that he owned what the great powers needed. The longer he delayed, the more it all appreciated, and the more precious his oil became.

Following developments closely was the cleverest of them all: Gulbenkian. His family friends controlled the Ministry of the *Civile Liste*. Since the turn of the century, Gulbenkian had been working with the Royal Dutch Shell companies as they expanded into Baku and other territories. Now, in 1907, he convinced Royal Dutch Shell to enter the Mesopotamian oil fray. The bazaar always craves more bidders. Royal Dutch Shell opened an office in Istanbul as Gulbenkian suggested, and they appointed as director none other than Gulbenkian.[37]

Gulbenkian later wrote that during these years, "solid foundations were laid for keeping prices high and assuring big profits."[38] He now felt certain he could create an enormous monopoly in Mesopotamia—one step at a time.

As Gulbenkian was edging Shell in and as the exasperated Germans were trying to understand why their generous offers were being spurned, the *Civile Liste* was meeting with D'Arcy's representative Nichols to iron out the most lucrative offer yet. In previous exchanges, the escalating down-payment demands had been fixed at 50,000 Turkish pounds, and later inflated to 80,000. Now, on August 27, 1907, *Civile Liste* negotiators offered Nichols something new. Upon signature, the *Civile Liste* would receive 100,000 Turkish pounds "as an advance," but also a generous royalty per 1,000 kilos of oil, paid twice annually—regardless of profit, net or gross. Moreover, the sultan was offering only a narrow nine-month option, after which a new concession would have to be renegotiated.[39]

The latest offer was too rich for D'Arcy. For several months, the matter was discussed with no resolution. In December 1907, Nichols returned to London empty-handed, hoping to return one day soon to secure a Mesopotamian concession that was affordable and reasonable.[40]

At 4 A.M., May 26, 1908, everything changed. Exploration in Persia was about to be canceled for lack of results and the utter depletion of operating cash. But just as the enterprise was folding and staff being dismissed, Burmah Oil's drill at the Masjid-i-Suleiman site pierced beyond 1,180 feet of desert strata. The bore unleashed a monster gusher rising 75 feet toward the sky, soaking everything with black gold. D'Arcy, for years waiting to be reimbursed for his investment, declared, "If this is true, all our troubles are over." Several months later, additional wells came in, including a sudden, unexpected, and bounteous oil spout on September 18. A new corporation named the Anglo-Persian Oil Company was created. Excitement on London's financial markets could barely be contained. All available shares were purchased within 30 minutes.[41] Britain was now assured of an abundant supply of Mideast petroleum.

Throughout 1908 the dynamics of regional oil played out. Did the Persian oil strike outmode the quest for Mesopotamian oil, or merely increase the frenzy to find it? Some could have easily argued that Anglo-Persian's oil was the answer to Britain's needs. On the other hand, abundance in business rarely satiates—it only whets the appetite for more.

The promising Mosul and Baghdad fields were, after all, just miles from the lush Persian fields. If the British did not control those fields, who would? The Germans? The French? The Russians? If the British did control them, England would possess a monopoly on the enormously wealthy deposits across an entire region. Moreover, a pipeline could transit Persia directly to the Turkish ports on the Mediterranean, avoiding the perilous mountain route to the Gulf. Hence, Mesopotamia remained directly in London's sight line even as England sped toward a feared armed conflict with its rivals over the Eastern Question and any number of linked crises.

The equation was suddenly altered again that year when, in the summer of 1908, Turkish agitators in Greece rose up against the sultan. Since the days of Midhat Pasha and his visionary but stillborn constitution in 1876, the flame of reform had been kept alive in secret Ottoman societies. Most of these reformers were military men and oppressed Christians in distant provinces, or disillusioned expatriates who had settled throughout Europe. All were determined to end the generation-to-generation corruption of the sultanate and the unending decay of the empire. Various dissident groups coalesced into the Committee of Union and Progress. One of the Parisian groups published a journal that became emblematic of the movement. The journal was named *La Jeune Turquie—The Young Turk*.[42]

By the early years of the century, many of these "Young Turks," especially those in Salonica, Greece, became convinced only a coup could save Turkey. Indeed, several attempts had been aborted. But by 1908, the agitators believed they were finally ready. They focused on September 1, the anniversary of Abdulhamid's accession. But rumors and leaks again compromised their plans. Instead, a bloodless coup was staged in the summer. Reformist pashas invaded the ministries to place them on a businesslike basis. A key demand made of the sultan was to restore Midhat Pasha's 1876 constitution and parliament. Abdul the Damned told the militants he had always intended to do so—of course. Now was a perfect time. In July, he reintroduced the constitution and the parliament with great fanfare as though it were his long-delayed pet project. That only bought him some time. The sultan remained in an imperial limbo even as the entire Ottoman government was being resculpted in the image of reform, union, and progress.[43]

The Sick Man was going through a new stage. The Young Turks were eager to cement intelligent commercial and military alliances in Europe that would strengthen the empire. That meant closer strategic economic and military cooperation with Germany.

London's concerns were summarized precisely in one key dispatch from the British embassy in Istanbul to British foreign secretary Edward Grey: "During the last few years," the embassy stated, "our policy, if I may call it so, in Turkey has been, and for some time to come will be, to attempt the impossible task of furthering our commercial interests while pursuing a course . . . which the Sultan interprets as preeminently hostile in aim and tendency. These two lines are diametrically opposed and consequently incompatible with one another. In a highly centralized theocracy like the Sultanate and Caliphate combined, with its pre-economic conceptions, every big trade concession is regarded as an Imperial favor to be bestowed on the seemingly friendly, a category in which, needless to say, we are not included."[44] As the sultan was being dislodged from power, even if not from his throne, the Turkish tendency to sidestep Britain intensified.

An idea emerged at Whitehall: the National Bank of Turkey. However, in reality, this financial institution would be neither Turkish nor national. Instead it would be a commercial creature of Britain's projected foreign policy, employing British money, managed by Britons, and operating for British interests. Similar banks had been created during the previous century in Teheran, with the British-owned and -operated Imperial Bank of Persia, which was a by-product of Reuter's debacle. British financiers had also established the Egyptian National Bank in Cairo as part of its sphere of influence at the Suez Canal.[45]

Now, in November 1908, the Foreign Office brought together a number of influential British businessmen to found yet another Near East national bank, the National Bank of Turkey. Private by all its paperwork, this bank was strictly tied to official British desires. "It seems to me very desirable that there be an independent British financial interest in Constantinople [Istanbul]," wrote Foreign Secretary Grey as the bank was being established. The Foreign Office asked Henry Babington-Smith to resign from his current position with the post office to become the new bank's director. Babington-Smith carried fiscal gravitas in Istanbul, since he was formerly the British representative on the Ottoman Public Debt Administration. The internationally recognized businessman and diplomat Sir Ernest Cassel became president. Such eminent men as Lord Revelstoke and Lord Farrington joined as principal financial backers. The main office address was 50 Cornhill, in a well-known London banking district.[46]

But now Britain needed a fixer, someone with good Turkish connections. That would be Gulbenkian, now living in London and a naturalized British subject since 1902. Gulbenkian regularly circulated among a monied crowd as a result of his close associations with Shell. Moreover, Gulbenkian was at that very time serving as a financial consultant to both the Paris and London embassies of the new Ottoman government. He was placed on the bank's board. Soon, Gulbenkian became more than just a notable board member—he emerged as a central figure in the structure and operation of the bank.[47]

At first, there was much discussion about financing for many noble and profitable projects in Mesopotamia, such as irrigation canals, a tramway in Baghdad, and electrical grids, as well as municipal bonds for Istanbul and Baghdad. These loans would only enhance Britain's standing, especially in the reshaping and reform-minded empire dominated by a coterie of Young Turks and technocrat pashas. Ultimately, some of these loans were finalized, providing the bank with a profitable loan repayment stream. But quickly, Gulbenkian's attention turned to Mesopotamian oil. Gulbenkian contacted his friends at Shell and asked them to apply for the concession, since a new administration was in power. During 1908, Shell sought Foreign Office support for the move.[48]

But the Foreign Office was put off. Royal Dutch Shell, even though partly owned by Londoner Marcus Samuel and run by Dutch citizen Henri Deterding, was still considered an alien company. Only 40 percent of its stock was actually British-owned, with the 60 percent majority owned and controlled by Dutch interests represented by Deterding. An unreceptive Foreign Office dismissed Shell executives, asking them to scrap their own initiative and instead work with the Anglo-Persian Oil Company. The government explained it had been backing Anglo-Persian for years.[49]

Meanwhile, the Young Turks and their Committee of Union and Progress were rapidly reorganizing the entire Ottoman government along twentieth-century lines. By October 1908, the Committee of Union and Progress made clear its priority to deprive Abdul the Damned of the many properties transferred to his *Civile Liste*. These included the Mesopotamian oil concessions. Encouraged, D'Arcy's group elected to start all over again and negotiate with what they hoped would be level-headed bureaucrats. D'Arcy's agent contacted the Ministry of Mines.[50]

But the newly empowered pashas who had taken over the government were not certain exactly which ministry should acquire the sultan's oil concessions. Should it be the Ministry of Mines, the Ministry of Public Works, or the Ministry of Finance? Moreover, a vexed Ministry of the *Civile Liste* complained that some of its properties could not be legitimately transferred to governmental ownership for disposition because preexisting concessions, debt, and other obligations encumbered them. Perfect examples were the oil assets, which included the Anatolia agreements, that is, both the contested 1904 concession and the earlier and completely uncontested mineral rights grant within the 40-kilometer railway corridor. Indeed, those 40-kilometer rights were enshrined under international law in the Baghdad Railway Convention.[51]

With the oil properties soon to be—but not quite yet—transferred out of the sultan's hands, a new impetus for a fast deal gripped the parties. Possession was still nine-tenths of the law. In February 1909, the oil concession reclaimed from the Germans, desired by the Dutch and Americans, but still possessed by Abdulhamid was available to the British—for the right price. The new terms: 10,000 Turkish pounds up front, a so-called loan of 100,000 Turkish pounds, plus a 15 percent cut of the net profits, defined simply as revenues minus working costs, plus fixed depreciation and other itemized costs. The exploration period would be two years.[52]

D'Arcy's agents, jointly with Anglo-Persian Oil Company negotiators, moved quickly now. After some casbah haggling, a new contract was drawn up March 11 securing a four-year exploration period and dividing the demanded loan of 100,000 Turkish pounds into two phases—half now and half after oil was struck.[53]

Deal.

The grand vizier, that is, the Ottoman prime minister, approved as well, thus signifying governmental acceptance. On April 13, 1909, applications were filed for the sultan to sign the actual decree. Those were approved. Finally, after years of exasperating maneuvering, the Mesopotamian oil fields were to be Anglo-Persian's and Britain's. The next day, April 14, the minister of the *Civile Liste* and the grand vizier assembled all the paperwork and scheduled an immediate visit to Abdulhamid's office to obtain his signature.[54]

However, everything was now moment to moment. For days, Istanbul, the foreign press, and the great capitals of the world were burning with wild reports that Abdul the Damned would soon be deposed and perhaps even put to death. So many thousands of palace spies patrolled so many institutions throughout the empire that military men and government officials were afraid to smile at each other, lest they be accused of conspiracy. The nervous sultan, his dry, wrinkled, and worried face a living banner for the anxious moment, took refuge behind a corps of 16,000 ethnically diverse bodyguards stationed throughout his palace grounds. Yet undeterred rebel soldiers kept streaming into the capital pledging a bloody confrontation and a coup. Some swore to hang the tyrant from the lamppost outside his palace. Others wanted him tried for corruption. Still others were readying a pro-palace mutiny to maintain the status quo. Intrigues were everywhere, as revolution and counterrevolution edged toward an explosion.[55]

April 14: Documents were readied. The grand vizier was prepared. The sultan was ready to sign. The Foreign Office continuously monitored reports by telegraph. Anglo-Persian emissaries waited in suspense.[56]

But riots broke out in the city early in the day and could not be contained. Thousands of soldiers loyal to the sultan stormed into the main square. The counterrevolutionary mob invaded parliament and killed two deputies. Young Turks moved against them in armed conflict. The palace locked down. Nothing came in or out.[57]

Anglo-Persian's all-important oil documents were not signed.[58]

In the days that followed, Istanbul deteriorated into complete chaos as contending armies and political factions clashed, and the fate of the barricaded sultan changed hour to hour. Germany, France, and Great Britain dispatched warships to protect their interests and their citizens. Day after day dragged on, and Anglo-Persian's documents were still not signed. All parties tensely hoped to just wait out the crisis. At the time, Abdulhamid was rumored to be hiding in the British embassy— no, the Russian embassy—now it was the French embassy—no, actually on a warship steaming away from Turkey. In fact, he was cowering in the palace, where food and electrical supplies had been cut off by the plotters in an effort to starve the royal household into surrender.[59]

On April 27, after tense negotiations between the angry factions, revolutionaries finally broke into the beleaguered palace. There they found a trembling Abdul the Damned, surrounded by 20 black eunuchs, pathetically pleading for his life. It was agreed not to execute the sultan who had executed so many thousands, nor even to subject him to a divisive trial. Instead, Abdulhamid would simply be dethroned and exiled with his several wives to a small villa in Salonica. His harem would be dispersed. The chief eunuch would be hung from a local bridge for all to see. Abdul the Damned's personal fortune—some guessed it to be $25 million, others guessed $200 million—was reclaimed. "His property, acquired illegally, will be confiscated by the state," the new Turkish prime minister declared to reporters. Within days, the billion-dollar oil properties were transferred to the Ministry of Finance.[60]

Yet from the Anglo-Persian point of view, the company had a bankable deal. True, the decree had not been signed that April 14, 1909. But the lawful owner of the moment, the sultan, had come to final terms, confirmed by the prime minister, and the agreement was scheduled for execution, this only as a formality. Once the shouting subsided in Istanbul, Nichols and his group reapplied to the new possessor, the Ministry of Finance. The officials there, eager to industrialize the empire, saw the wisdom of Anglo-Persian's contract. A government analysis had confirmed that the deposits were probably superior to those in Baku and even America. In late June, ministerial officials agreed to resurrect the contract. A number of verbal assurances to finalize were exchanged in both directions, and it seemed Anglo-Persian finally had the oil.[61]

Just one thing. The newly appointed finance minister requested from among all these rivers of oil the "reservation of a few springs for government purposes." A few springs? That is not how oil exploration and geological strata work. Anglo-Persian objected and the fractious debate over terms resumed. But the contract terms were quickly tweaked until both sides accepted them. Now in July, verbal assurances were again conveyed that the matter was final once and for all and ready to be granted—this time for sure.[62]

Just one other thing. Following the avarice and corruption of the sultan, contracts would now be let on an open and progressive administrative basis. Under the new mining law, the concession would have to be advertised in the newspapers for 30 days to allow others to bid. That would necessitate a three-month procedural delay. Advertising? Anglo-Persian saw its carefully negotiated plan unraveling yet again. Company negotiators protested strenuously, but the concession opportunity was subjected to public advertising as a sign of open government. The sole redeeming advantage, by agreement, was that only sealed bids would be accepted.[63]

As feared, a flood of fresh offers and exhumed claims began pouring in: from Romania, America, England, and from within the empire. A gallery of individuals, syndicates, aristocrats, and corporations coveted the oil.[64]

Moreover, the Germans and the Anatolia Railway demanded that their original rights be recognized. The Ministry of Finance reviewed Anatolia's files and declared the demand baseless. Actually, the Germans knew their claim was flimsy because they had, in fact, exceeded the time limit. One telling letter exchanged between railway officials in Berlin and Istanbul confidentially confessed, "Legally, our rights to the petroleum wells are very weak." But Anatolia kept up its staunch argument. On August 4, 1909, Anatolia threatened legal action if the

Ottoman government did not confirm the railway's concession within 15 days.[65]

Just when it seemed the bedeviled concession competition could become no more complex, it did. Things were happening in London.

Winston Churchill's zeal for oil exceeded Admiral Fisher's.

Churchill had become intimately familiar with the commercial thickets surrounding oil during his stint from 1908 to 1910 as president of Britain's Board of Trade. In late October 1911, he became First Lord of the Admiralty, where he intensified the race to build more ships, all faster and more powerful, all of them oil guzzlers.

When Churchill arrived at the Admiralty, he discovered that some 189 vessels, from torpedo boats to dreadnoughts, had been or were being built, every one fueled by oil, not coal. Those ships—let alone the new ones envisioned—would consume more than 200,000 tons of oil annually. Yet Britain possessed a mere four-month reserve.[66]

Anglo-Persian's oil venture was making progress. But it was hardly a reliable source. True, eight wells were pumping. But a working refinery was still needed. Construction on the refinery at Abadan on the Persian coast began in 1910. But would that refinery distill kerosene for stoves, fuel oil for battle cruisers, or some of both? It all depended on the market and contracts. A gargantuan nearly 150-mile pipeline was being constructed to link the distant oil wells with that refinery. Sixty miles of 5-inch pipe and 80 miles of 8-inch pipe had been ordered, and these would be erected by backbreaking labor under heatstroke conditions, 16- and 22-foot segments at a time. Erratic personnel, periodic worker rebellions, management conflicts, engineering problems, construction mishaps, and an unexpectedly smelly and sulfurous crude oil, not to mention gnats and dysentery, plagued the entire project, from wellhead to refinery. The oil business entailed more than just bringing in a gusher. Oil: Anglo-Persian had it. But now it lacked the cash and investors to pump it, pipe it, refine it, and then ship it to market and siphon off a profit.[67]

In December 1911, Churchill summoned a departmental oil committee to forecast the navy's needs. Estimated 1912 consumption was fully 225 times that of a decade earlier. Moreover, the study committee concluded that at least a one-year reserve supply was needed to sustain fleet operations. But where was this fuel to come from? Churchill established a more sweeping Royal Commission on Fuel and Engines and appointed the recently retired oil maniac himself, Fisher, to locate that fuel.[68]

In June 1912, Churchill wrote, "My Dear Fisher. . . . You have got to find the oil: to show how it can be stored cheaply, how it can be purchased regularly and cheaply in peace; and with absolute certainty in war."[69]

But now Shell was purchasing Anglo-Persian's oil for other markets. The first 15,000 barrels had already been loaded onto a Dutch tanker in May 1912. Moreover, cash-strapped Anglo-Persian was contemplating a buyout from Shell—exactly what the Admiralty and Foreign Office did not want. Shell was not British controlled, it was Dutch controlled. A perfect example of the problem played out in front of the Royal Commission for Fuel in spring 1912 during testimony from both Shell executives, British subject Samuel and Dutch citizen Deterding. Samuel was nicely reassuring the committee that if given an extended contract, Shell would certainly promise a million tons per year. But Deterding interrupted and corrected Samuel in front of the committee saying: Make that a half a million.[70]

What was driving Deterding and Shell?

A threatened Shell takeover of Anglo-Persian was now more than dominating the stage in the unfolding oil drama. Such a takeover meant a foreign-controlled monopoly of virtually all known Mideast oil. Minority Shell owner Samuel was asked point-blank by the Royal Commission for Fuel whether foreign directors would not control the oil. His response was noted by commission members as "absolutely." Samuel carefully added, "but . . . fortunately, they are extremely pro-British."[71]

How long could that be relied upon if war broke out?

The attitude of Anglo-Persian Oil Company also turned alarming. Its executive, Charles Greenway, bluntly told the Foreign Office his company wanted more than diplomatic support and a willing customer in the Royal Navy. Unless Anglo-Persian received a large contract and cash infusion from the British government, the company would become a Royal Dutch Shell operation.[72] That sounded like blackmail.

Undersecretary of State Louis Mallet wrote bitterly, "I do not like the attitude of the Anglo-Persian Oil Company who have hitherto posed as being ultra-imperialist. Mr. Greenway first comes to me and hints that, if Shell obtains the Mesopotamian oilfields it will be difficult for the Anglo-Persian Oil Company to resist coming to an agreement with them—unless the Admiralty can give them a contract. I did not at that time understand that an agreement meant more than an understanding as to the sale price of oil. Greenway now threatens complete absorption with the Shell unless the Admiralty gives him a contract."[73]

Shortly thereafter, Foreign Secretary Grey sent a message in plain words, "The support which His Majesty's Government have given your company in the past, both in obtaining their concession in Persia, and in other ways, was given on the understanding that the enterprise would remain British and that it would be a matter of great surprise and regret if your company made any arrangement whereby a syndicate, predominantly foreign, got control of their interests in that country." If that occurred, the Foreign Office insisted, "Your company could not of course hope to get from His Majesty's Government the same support as in the past."[74]

As the British government was being squeezed, astonished officials could only wonder what had caused such a turn of events.

A Shell takeover meant a huge oil price gouging campaign against the British government. "It is clear," Undersecretary Mallet wrote, ". . . the Shell group are aiming at the extinction" of Anglo–Persian "as a competitor—one of their objects being to control the price of liquid fuel for the British Navy."[75]

Greenway audaciously admitted as much to the Royal Commission for Fuel when he testified, "We know very well that if we join hands with the Shell Company, we shall probably make very large profits, and that it will result in their securing a practical monopoly of oil in the Eastern Hemisphere if not in the whole world."[76]

The concept of price gouging by a Shell-directed monopoly clearly was fixed in Churchill's mind. The price of fuel oil was skyrocketing, having more than doubled during the previous 18 months, from 37 shillings 6 pence per ton to 77 shillings 6 pence per ton. "Daily, the prices of oil are rising," proclaimed a memo given to Churchill.[77]

A new approach would be needed to avoid what Churchill termed "being mercilessly fleeced at every purchase."[78]

Anglo-Persian had been angling for a cash infusion and a reliable contract that would not only secure their Persian petroleum, but finance the acquisition and development of the Mesopotamian lands. The many departments of the British government converging on the question—Admiralty, Foreign Office, Board of Trade, and the India Office, to name a few—were coming closer to agreeing that some special economic relationship was needed for Anglo-Persian. That would solve everything.

Not everything.

On August 6, 1912, the Foreign Ministry received a cable from its embassy in Istanbul advising there was a major new group threatening to take over the Mesopotamian oil concessions. It suddenly appeared out of nowhere. Moreover, it was a potent alliance of the Deutsche Bank—contributing their Anatolia Railway oil concession—and the National Bank of Turkey. The group seemed intent on creating a monopoly controlled by non-British interests. In truth, the syndicate had been operating for some months behind the scenes.[79]

And who was responsible for this sudden debacle?

Soon it would become clear: Mr. C. S. Gulbenkian.

TOP: Akkadian cylinder seal; when rolled upon a surface, authenticated information about ownership, circa 2254-2193 B.C.E.
Oriental Institute Museum

RIGHT: Six-sided inscribed clay prism recording eight military campaigns of King Sennacherib, circa 689 B.C.E.
Oriental Institute Museum

BOTTOM: Artist's conception of Timur.
Richard Hook

TOP: Anglo-Persian Oil Company's original 1901 oil concession.
MIDDLE: Native workman carrying cans of Anglo-Persian kerosene via mule, circa 1905-1910.
BOTTOM: Tribal horsemen hired to protect Anglo-Persian oil wells in Persia, circa 1905.

All photos: BP Archive/BP plc

TOP: Iraq's first oil gusher, Baba Gurgur, October 14, 1927.
BP Archive/BP plc

INSET: River of oil from first oil gusher, Baba Gurgur, October 14, 1927.
BP Archive/BP plc

BOTTOM: British Indian troops shell the Turks during Mesopotamia Campaign, circa 1916.
Imperial War Museum

INSET: C. S. Gulbenkian's passport picture, circa 1933.
BELOW: C. S. Gulbenkian relaxing with kitten.

C. S. Gulbenkian Foundation

Top: Detail of a Standard Oil highway map in Nazi Germany featuring a gas station attendant giving a Hitler salute.
Author's Acquisition

Below: Mufti of Jerusalem Haj Muhammed Amin al-Husseini reviews Moslem Waffen-SS troops in Bosnia, as shown on a Nazi magazine cover, 1944.
Author's Private Collection

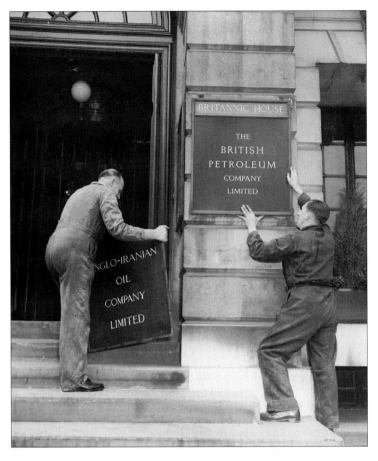

TOP: Changing of the signs, December 1954. *BP Archive/BP plc*

LEFT TO RIGHT: Winston Churchill during his Admiralty years before World War I. *Courtesy: Sir Martin Gilbert.* King Faisal in London in 1933 shortly before his death. *AP Worldwide Photos.* Saddam Hussein, 1987. *Jim Hollander, Reuters/Corbis.*

LEFT: Iraqi Jewish refugees disembarking from plane in Israel during Operation Ezra and Nehemiah. Circa 1950-1951.

BELOW: Iraqi Jewish refugees being airlifted to Israel.

Government of Israel Press Office Photo Archive

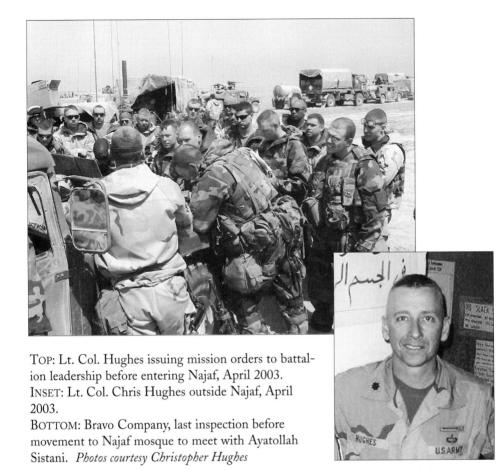

TOP: Lt. Col. Hughes issuing mission orders to battalion leadership before entering Najaf, April 2003.
INSET: Lt. Col. Chris Hughes outside Najaf, April 2003.
BOTTOM: Bravo Company, last inspection before movement to Najaf mosque to meet with Ayatollah Sistani. *Photos courtesy Christopher Hughes*

CHAPTER EIGHT

Mr. Five Percent

C. S. Gulbenkian loved to annoy people.

He was wealthy enough to get away with it. In his posh London residence, Gulbenkian regularly slammed doors and snarled at the butlers. At the theater, if Gulbenkian disapproved, he might loudly blurt, "The play is stupid!" When nearby rows would shush him, Gulbenkian would just start conversing with himself even more loudly. One time, he even purchased tickets closer to the stage, just to more audibly razz an actor whose performance he disliked.[1]

Gulbenkian was stern and unforgiving with his family. He once punished his six-year-old daughter Rita with a week's diet of bread and water for behaving badly toward another little girl he wanted her to emulate. His son, Nubar, was terrified of his father. Once, Nubar was placed on bread and water for running away from his nanny. Another time, Nubar got sick and vomited while riding in the coach in the compulsory backward position reserved for him. He was spanked for "disgracing the equipage." When the children were told to dress for dinner, they were compelled to sit motionless on a high table until summoned for display among the adults. None dared disobey the protocol.[2]

Gulbenkian fancied himself a collector of fine art. If he wanted a rare coin or a statuette, he would simply demand it—and was willing to pay any amount. In one case, he insisted on preempting a scheduled auction for a pair of miniatures. "No price is too high for me!" he chastised the owners before the auction. "I want these miniatures and I'll have them fetched this evening. Good day, sir!" He treated the art he owned as a sultan would his women. He once declined to show some favorite paintings to an intrigued guest, exclaiming, "What! Would I unveil the women of my harem to a stranger?"[3]

Gulbenkian's own harem in London, Paris, and Lisbon included dozens of young women over the years, each no older than 18 or 19. He replaced them annually until he was 80. "While it is very unkind on a young girl to have sexual relations with an old man because she loses her youth," his son recalled him bragging, "it does rejuvenate the sexual functions of the old man."[4]

Most of all, Gulbenkian was a tenacious scrapper, especially in the murky business of petroleum. He once quipped, "Oil men are like cats." Gulbenkian knew how to win a catfight. What he termed "rousing great jealousies" among contenders was a specialty of his. It "worked both ways to my advantage and to my disadvantage," he conceded. Gulbenkian happily confessed that as he maneuvered between the captains of oil, his "position . . . was delicate . . . and not in any way a pleasant one." No matter. His goal was not to be liked, but to create an enormous oil monopoly.[5]

The cantankerous Gulbenkian employed any number of high-powered attorneys ready to litigate. At the same time, he was a patient man when it came to achieving his objective—patient beyond all reason and to the point of intractable obstinance. Once the billionaire lost a tiny, almost insignificant, piece of rental property because he failed to pay local taxes. For years, Gulbenkian's enterprise continuously filed lawsuits and motions to regain the lot, and pressured any number of foreign authorities to intervene as though it were the most important matter in his life.[6] He could outlast the best of them.

Gulbenkian's effort to create an oil monopoly in Mesopotamia began long before August 6, 1912, when the Foreign Office first learned of the endeavor. In fact, the machinations began at the end of 1910 as new groups of highly nationalistic Young Turks emerged in Istanbul. Some of these new ministerial figures continued to favor

Germany and Holland over Britain. This was something Gulbenkian, an experienced oil financier, could exploit. As Britain edged ever closer to securing its concession in a company it could rely upon— Anglo-Persian—Gulbenkian brought together the key dissident parties to undermine the plan.[7]

Sir Ernest Cassel, a director of the National Bank of Turkey, was on good terms with German circles, being of dual British-German citizenship. In late 1910, amid the fluid state of Young Turk politics, as a new regime was taking hold in the empire, Gulbenkian convinced Cassel to open negotiations with the Anatolia Railway and its parent, the Deutsche Bank. Anatolia Railway, at this point, was cash-hungry for its transportation construction program. The company was more interested in securing some other entity to work the Mesopotamian oil fields, preferring to just profitably transport the products and services. Next, Gulbenkian turned to his contacts with prominent pashas in the government who, despite their reformist temperament, were not above keeping old Ottoman traditions of baksheesh alive. Naturally, Gulbenkian's good friend Deterding and Shell would also want to join in.[8]

New money and new political connections had been successfully attached to Anatolia's decade-old oil rights, real and disputed. A new oil alliance was created, albeit still unnamed and unincorporated.

Gulbenkian lost no time in inventing a legal entity for his alliance. With so many foreign syndicates competing for the concession, speed was obviously a factor. Moreover, amid the sifting, shifting dynamics of concession politics, Gulbenkian wanted to act before Anatolia changed its mind. So on January 31, 1911, one of Cassel's South African mining companies, named African and Eastern Concessions, was registered in London as a shell corporation for the new oil enterprise.[9]

Gulbenkian quietly worked throughout 1912 to lay the groundwork for the regional monopoly he envisioned. By early August 1912, the Foreign Office learned that the National Bank of Turkey— an institution the British government had helped sponsor—was intruding into the oil concession being groomed for Anglo-Persian. London immediately worried that Gulbenkian's group might genuinely pose a threat. When asked, British Embassy Counselor Charles Marling in Istanbul admitted in a September 10 message, "This finan-

cial alliance with German interests . . . [is] . . . most disquieting."
Paramount in that fear was National Bank of Turkey's "disagreeable
political favor through its relations with the Committee [of Union
and Progress]," that is, the Young Turks.[10]

The Foreign Office replied to Marling in Istanbul, "After consulting with the Admiralty, who do not at all like the idea of a foreign syndicate having control of large oil supplies in Mesopotamia,
we have . . . told the National Bank that we are unable to support
their request for a concession. Of course, our main reason is that
we have already advocated and supported the demands of the
Anglo-Persian Oil Co. . . . The reason which we have given to the
National Bank is simply that we have already pledged ourselves to
support Mr. D'Arcy and company and that it is therefore impossible
at a late hour to encourage another competitor, but we are going to
verbally tell [the bank] confidentially that after considering the
whole matter our Government do not like the idea of entrusting to
a syndicate which, though nominally British, is in reality composed
of two very powerful foreign syndicates, the control of so large a
supply of oil fuel."[11]

Rather than submitting to British desires to desist, Gulbenkian
accelerated. On September 25, 1912, Gulbenkian held an extraordinary shareholder meeting in London—really just a gathering of the
circle of personalities—to formally change the name of the paper corporation to Turkish Petroleum Company (TPC). The address of the
new entity was identical to that of the National Bank of Turkey: 50
Cornhill in London. Of course, the company engaged in no real business except to speculate in Mesopotamian oil. Gulbenkian's intent
was now perfectly clear.[12]

At that September 25 meeting, the bylaws were also changed. By
the power of the papers they drew up, the group created 80,000 shares
of value, each worth £1. The first 40,000-share block, called "Group
A," controlled four directors on the board. The next 20,000 shares
called "Group B" controlled two directors, as did the final 20,000
shares of "Group C." Clearly, Group A shares controlled the company
by virtue of its four directors.[13]

A month later, October 23, 1912, the major economic dimensions
of the TPC were formally structured in an important agreement that
permanently changed the face of petroleum in the Middle East. Meet-

ing at TPC's titular London address, 50 Cornhill, in the actual offices of the National Bank of Turkey, the representatives of Deutsche Bank, the National Bank of Turkey, and Gulbenkian signed a contract specifying TPC's value. What's more, they hammered out the ownership segments that would regulate TPC's single important asset: the oil concessions. Deutsche Bank received Group C shares, numbered 60,001 through 80,000, in exchange for transferring any and all of its oil concessions. These included both the still-valid original 40-kilometer right-of-way concession and the dismissed but disputed general provincewide concessions. Deutsche Bank's only contribution for its quarter ownership was its concession.[14]

Of the first 60,000 shares, the National Bank of Turkey corporately, and its officer Cassel individually, divided 28,000 shares. Since Cassel was president of National Bank of Turkey, he wielded a double vote. That left 32,000 shares. These went to Gulbenkian personally. *Gulbenkian initially owned 40 percent.*[15]

While Gulbenkian was quietly creating Turkish Petroleum Company as a formidable challenger to be reckoned with, the British government was more focused on the threat of the moment: that Royal Dutch Shell would absorb nearly bankrupt Anglo-Persian. "I think we should go [to] every length in supporting the independence of the Anglo-Persian Oil Company," insisted Foreign Office Assistant Undersecretary Mallet, "and subsidize them if necessary."[16]

Britain's sense of urgency only intensified when the so-called Balkans Wars erupted across Greece, Macedonia, Serbia, Thrace, Albania, and other Ottoman Christian territories in Europe. Guerrilla forces raiding Turkish installations in bayonet charges and long 40-car trains wending across the region packed to the rooftops with eager soldiers were only the latest fuses in the explosive Eastern Question. Right now, only the Balkans was aflame. But no one was certain how many other powers would be drawn into the broadening conflicts, creating a massive war.[17]

As Churchill and the Admiralty continued their public inquiries on the urgent need for new oil sources, news emerged of Gulbenkian's hitherto unknown German-dominated oil axis in Mesopotamia, which although not yet named was in fact Turkish Petroleum. Headlines in the November 14 *Financial News* were typical: "Will Germany control the oil supply for our Navy?"[18]

Now the struggle for oil became a three-way battle among Britain, Holland, and Germany—being fought in London's corridors of power. Gulbenkian stood at the hub, playing the contenders off each other.

His next move only further complicated an already complex situation. Gulbenkian secretly leveraged most of his 32,000 shares in TPC. Under the terms of original issuance as part of the National Bank of Turkey's block, Gulbenkian could distribute some of those 32,000 shares to another oil company. So he parceled off 20,000 of his 32,000 shares to yet another participant. "In view of my connection with the Royal Dutch Shell group, and the urgent necessity to have an oil organization capable of carrying out practical work . . . I therefore offered them 20,000 shares, that is to say 25 percent of the company . . . keeping for myself 12,000 shares."[19] *Gulbenkian now owned just 15 percent.*

By late 1912, TPC possessed everything it needed: Germany's oil concession; Shell's ability to explore, refine, and market; the economic wherewithal of both the National Bank of Turkey and Deutsche Bank; and the political connections of Gulbenkian. Moreover, through an exchange of binding letters of self-restriction among all the parties, TPC shareholders all agreed not to engage in petroleum exploration, refinement, or distribution anywhere in Mesopotamia except through their jointly owned Turkish Petroleum Company.[20]

Gulbenkian's Mesopotamian oil monopoly-in-waiting was now up and running.

TPC promptly began applying for research permits all over the Ottoman Empire: at the Sea of Marmora, in central Syria, and at the Dead Sea in Palestine. In Mesopotamia, its concession application covered "[any]where surface indications of petroleum exist," beginning with the Anatolia Railway's right-of-way from Mosul to Tikrit. By mid-November, the Foreign Office began seeing TPC for what it was: a viable contender for the future of all Mideast oil—before, during, and after any war.[21]

Ironically, even if Anglo-Persian were left intact in Persia and price gouging were made unlikely by competition, prices could still be unstable. If TPC and Shell succeeded in controlling Mesopotamian oil, warned the Foreign Office, "it would enable the Shell Transport Company to cut prices." What was wrong with cutting prices? Shell could then artificially push prices so radically downward via an oil price war that the loss of stable income would cripple the Anglo-Persian just the same. Then Anglo-Persian would again be ripe for takeover.[22] The British government did not want oil prices too high or too low—but "just right."

Before it could address its competitive viability, Britain was first fiercely determined that Anglo-Persian not be absorbed by Shell, either directly or through the TPC. Foreign Secretary Grey understood that "our position, both commercial and political, will be seriously jeopardized if the most important British concession in Persia, the Anglo-Persian Oil Company, is allowed to pass under foreign control by absorption in the Shell Company."[23] The question was how to prevent a commercial takeover.

Anglo-Persian continually pleaded for long-range contracts and advance payment for oil not yet delivered—or even pumped. But the government simply could not justify paying millions of pounds to a financially wracked company on the verge of being devoured by rivals. Admiralty contracts people pointedly asked "whether the money would be repaid" in the event of an oil failure, adding, the whole thing is "a business subject to much speculative risk."[24]

Instead of financial aid, the Foreign Office instructed its embassy in Istanbul to do whatever it could to prop up Anglo-Persian and D'Arcy against the TPC and the Germans. After all, in April 1909, the paperwork granting the sultan's concession to D'Arcy had been all but signed. Did that not carry weight?[25]

Ambassador Gerald Lowther sent back a disparaging rebuff: "As a matter of fact, I do not believe that D'Arcy [has] a leg to stand on." On the other hand, he added that "the Germans have their rights legally assured," based on the 1903 Baghdad Railway Convention, an international treaty that granted the oil concession for 20 kilometers on either side of the track.[26] Hence, even if the 1904 Anatolia concession for Baghdad and Mosul was voided for lateness, Anatolia's earlier concession for the 20 kilometers on either side of its railroad track was quite solid.

What about D'Arcy's so-called claim of a proper 1909 concession from the sultan that was completely written but never actually signed? That had even been tentatively endorsed later that year by the Council of Ministers, subject to as yet unresolved stipulations. Lowther deprecated the whole theory as "mere waste paper." He added, "If D'Arcy's [group] do not take the trouble to come out here and work their business, the impression is naturally created that they do not care about it." Adding that D'Arcy's agent in Istanbul was "quite useless," Lowther emphasized, if "I am only to frame my protests on 'rights,' I am afraid I shall be done for."[27]

In early January 1913, the British were so worried about the prospects for oil that Whitehall policymakers debated whether they should return to the less militarily effective but more reliable realm of coal. Speed at sea would be sacrificed, but at least Britain possessed its own coal. Budget planners even calculated the cost of coal retro-conversion: £150,000 per ship.[28]

At the end of February 1913, just before the Royal Commission on Oil Fuel concluded its second series of hearings, Deterding offered more testimony. He tried to attenuate the fear that a Dutch-controlled oil company could not be trusted by England during a war with Germany. Asked whether German money was not already in his enterprise, he parried, "Not a penny!" And if Germany tried to pressure Holland and its oil enterprise? "We could snap our fingers at Germany," Deterding wisecracked. "What can the German Government do? They can write very nasty letters and say anything they like to the Dutch Government, but that has not anything to do with us."[29] His braggadocio was not persuasive.

A few weeks later, as if to prove Churchill's point, Deterding revised his own guarantee of Shell's annual fuel capability for the navy should Shell be tapped for oil. Months earlier, when Samuels spoke, he had pledged a million tons per year, only to see that number instantly halved by Deterding during commission testimony. But now Deterding promised only a fifth of even that reduced amount, that is, 100,000 tons annually. Even that 100,000 tons included no assurances about grade or quality. Navy officials clearly saw what was happening with each passing week, writing, "In the meantime [since Deterding's last estimate], prices have risen very greatly and he has pledged all his oil supplies for years ahead." Ironically, Deterding only worsened official apprehension when he promised what he thought was a saving grace. He offered any volume of oil if the navy paid enough: "It is entirely a question of price," he declared. "If the Admiralty pays [a premium rate] . . . you will always get supplies with no difficulty."[30]

At the same time, Turkish officials in Istanbul were wondering just how much currency would salve their own palms. Those in the Sublime Porte wielding administrative powers over Mesopotamian petroleum now regularly mentioned multimillion-pound loan offers from oil speculators, plus lucrative commissions and participations—some real, some imaginary. Waters were tested and anxieties probed in search of personal reward for aiding the process. It was hard for fretful concession chasers from the United States, the United Kingdom, and other countries to determine a genuine competitor from the shades of commercial dissimulation.[31]

Ironically, TPC officials fully comprehended that much of the value they attached to Anatolia's most promising asset, the concession for the provinces of Baghdad and Mosul, was fundamentally worthless puffery. Shortly after the TPC agreement was signed, Turkish National Bank president Babington-Smith confessed to a colleague at Shell that "it is quite true . . . the Anatolia Railway Company Concession is somewhat vague, and of this we have of course been aware all along." TPC's Istanbul attorney echoed those reservations, advising in a private opinion that "the situation of the Anatolia Railway Company [concession for Mosul and Baghdad] is not what I should call a 'strong case.' The exploration work was not done and the reports not rendered within the time allowed."[32]

But in the volatile realm of Turkish concessions, appearances were as important as facts. Both changed continually and interactively. Threats, veiled and explicit, spiced every dialogue on the topic. The Turks threatened to grant the concession to TPC, or to unnamed others, and sometimes the mysterious "others" were in fact TPC under one guise or another. For their part, the British threatened to withhold approval of badly needed increases in Turkish customs and duties; Britain ironically maintained a veto over those revenues due to the capitulation system and the Ottoman debt. Hence, any Ottoman attempt to profit from any oil concession other than Anglo-Persian's would cost the regime dearly once taxes were tallied.[33]

On April 25, 1913, Ambassador Lowther grimly reported that his efforts on behalf of D'Arcy had "now reached a point not far from deadlock and I am apprehensive lest the pressure" cause the Turks to "not give the exclusive rights to either group."[34]

In spring 1913, frustrated Foreign Office officials suggested a radical solution: TPC should merge with Anglo-Persian, as long as

Anglo-Persian retained majority control. This would take TPC's concession threat off the table, shunt a share of the Mideast oil profits to TPC's corporate owners, yet maintain Anglo-Persian as a "British concern" that the government could still support financially and diplomatically. Throughout the spring, endless, unnerving negotiations roiled between Anglo-Persian executives and Babington-Smith of the Turkish National Bank and TPC. Anglo-Persian offered Babington-Smith a financial majority, but a rubber-stamp minority vote—reducing TPC to a silent partner. Rejected. By June 12, Anglo-Persian suggested a clean fifty-fifty split, but mandated a British chairman to ensure true control. Likewise, rejected.[35]

Periodic appeals by Anglo-Persian executives to the Foreign Office for intervention were fruitless. As negotiations stalled, the National Bank of Turkey was proving its potency. It became active in financing oil infrastructure, principally ports and railways, not only in Mesopotamia, but beyond. For example, the bank had already become involved in port facilities at Trabzon, Turkish gateway to the rich oil fields of Baku.[36]

By mid-June 1913, the stalemate of threat and counterthreat, offer and counteroffer, and accelerating actions by the TPC combine forced Churchill and his colleagues to revise their strategy. On June 16, Churchill filed a secret memo to the cabinet admitting that Persian oil was "more important than anticipated." He argued that Anglo-Persian must be awarded a substantial advance contract, plus some form of government financing to ensure the company's survival. "The future of the oil market is so uncertain," wrote Churchill, "and the present prices are so unfavorable. . . ." He insisted that "action is urgent as the future oil supplies are being increasingly bought up . . . and the oil market is being rapidly contracted both from natural and artificial causes." The cabinet began studying just how far Britain would go to protect its favored oil company.[37]

If Whitehall assured Anglo-Persian of lucrative long-term contracts, and even offered advance payment, what would prevent another foreign company from buying the company anyway? England would then be supplying up-front cash and contracts to the very foreign firms they hoped to resist—and still be at their mercy. The answer: On July 11, the cabinet decided that the British government "should acquire a controlling interest" in Anglo-Persian. Britain would buy the company.[38]

A few days later, Churchill explained to Parliament: "Our ultimate policy is that the Admiralty should become the independent owner and producer of its own supplies of liquid fuel . . . to make us safe in war, and able to override price fluctuations in peace. . . . We must become the owners, or at any rate the controllers at the source . . . of [the] natural oil which we require."[39]

British officials were now contemplating both long-term contracts and a £2.2 million cash infusion in exchange for 51 percent of Anglo-Persian's stock, plus two government-appointed seats on the board, an assurance that the chairman would be British, and a sure policy that Anglo-Persian would forevermore operate as a captive quasi-governmental British corporation.[40]

To certify that the government was purchasing a worthwhile company and dependable reserves, a five-man team of experts, headed by Rear Admiral Sir Edmond Slade, director of naval intelligence, embarked on a three-month expedition to Persia. Their job: Investigate and verify those fabulous Persian oil fields and APOC's ability to exploit them. Dressed in classic safari suits and stereotypical British India pith helmets, periodically stopping for a civilized spot of tea served on a portable table and chairs in the desert wilderness, the five men were dazzled by the bountiful oil deposits they surveyed. "It seems to be a thoroughly sound concession," reported Slade, "which may be developed to a gigantic extent." However, he stressed, Britain must "control the company," and warned, "it would be a national disaster if the concession were allowed to pass into foreign hands. . . . All possible steps should be taken to maintain the company as a British undertaking."[41]

Even as the Slade Commission was poking around Persia, Undersecretary Mallet received a new assignment: He was abruptly transferred to Istanbul as Britain's new ambassador. There he continued to importune the various Turkish ministers about the concession.[42]

Quickly, Mallet's high-powered diplomacy was seen in action. First, he settled a strategic border issue. For centuries, the fuzzy frontier between Mesopotamia, Persia, and Russia had been contentious and disputed—often militarily. As part of the many efforts to forestall the expected chain-reaction war in Europe, a border commission had been established during the previous year to permanently set a mutually recognized boundary. After 18 sessions, the delegates finally fixed the international border, placing some of the richest oil-producing lands of Persia into Ottoman Mesopotamia. A treaty was drawn up to delineate the so-called Transferred Territories. But once those Persian lands were incorporated into Turkey, what would become of Anglo-Persian's concession, which was legal only within Persia? Through Mallet's pressures and persuasions, the new Turco-Persian Frontier Protocol included a unique provision recognizing Anglo-Persian's still largely unexploited concession as an international geopolitical fact that transferred with the land itself.[43] Mideast oil now proved it was bigger than international borders.

Clearly, Britain expected Anglo-Persian and D'Arcy to extend their control from Persia farther into all of Mesopotamia. The Turco-Persian Frontier Protocol proved that. Discussions about amalgamating Turkish Petroleum and Anglo-Persian now resumed in earnest, this time with German and British diplomats interceding. Germany was as eager as Britain to resolve the problem in exchange for a share of the oil. A compromise emerged. The National Bank of Turkey— established as a fundamentally British financial institution—would sell its approximately 50 percent share of TPC, held by the bank and its officers individually, to Anglo-Persian. Thus, Anglo-Persian would acquire majority control of TPC—ending the controversy. Germany would then receive a sizable portion of the extracted oil by virtue of its co-ownership of the TPC. Babington-Smith, president of the National Bank of Turkey, and his counterparts in the Deutsche Bank were both amenable, if only to stay on good relations with the governments in question. Little money had changed hands. After all, the distribution of bank shares had been fundamentally a paper transaction. So the bank officials were willing to cede their stock.[44]

Both British Foreign Office and German Foreign Ministry officials were feeling relieved, as neither wanted to tangle over the issue. But then, in the last days of November 1913, just as the merger deal was to be finalized, a bank official contacted British diplomats. There was just one other thing. In point of fact, while the main bank executives were indeed willing to simply relinquish their stock, which had cost little if anything in cash, one shareholder, whose name did not appear anywhere on the corporate rolls, was not cooperating. They had tried convincing him, to no avail.[45]

Who was that one shareholder whose name did not appear on the corporation registrations? Gulbenkian—and he wasn't budging.

Hence, the National Bank of Turkey was not free to just relinquish its share in TPC—that is, not without Gulbenkian's permission, since he controlled 15 percent. As far as duty to the British or German government, Gulbenkian did not feel obligated to either. When the Foreign Office telegraphed Gulbenkian asking him to join the compromise, he sneered at the very idea. His view: "It was for *me* to decide with the Royal Dutch Shell group what we should do." He later wrote, "I was a private individual who had worked so persistently [to establish TPC] without remuneration and had invested in cash in the company." In fact, the most Gulbenkian could have paid for his 12,000 shares was £12,000, but no one could find any indication of just how that £12,000 might have been paid and to whom—if paid at all. No matter. Gulbenkian had his paper share and it was now invaluable.[46]

British officials were astonished and furious.

On December 1, 1913, the Foreign Office summoned their main Ottoman contact, former Turkish prime minister Hakki Pasha, sent by the Turkish government to London to resolve matters. During a four-and-half-hour meeting, Hakki Pasha revealed he was fully aware that the German and British settlement was blocked because Gulbenkian still held 15 percent of TPC's Group A shares from the original bank distribution. Moreover, the Group A shares Gulbenkian had proffered to Shell were just as important to him because Gulbenkian had much of his personal fortune in Shell.[47] Gulbenkian had even invested his children's allowance money in Shell stock.[48]

Moreover, if anyone tried to work around him, Gulbenkian vociferously promised a lawsuit. Hakki Pasha asked embassy officials "what was to happen if the Shell Company, or [Mr.] Gulbenkian, brought an action . . . for an illegal transfer of some of their holdings." The Foreign Office was not amused by or worried about Gulbenkian. Hakki Pasha was answered bluntly that the British government, if need be, would "[paralyze] partially, if not entirely, the operations of the Turkish Petroleum Company in Mesopotamia."[49]

By now, Whitehall riled at the very mention of Gulbenkian's name and felt the National Bank of Turkey itself could not be trusted. They saw it all as subterfuge preceding a shakedown. "The upshot of this seems to be that the National Bank is not behaving very well," wrote one Near East desk foreign officer on December 2. His colleague replied, "*That* is putting it very mildly. . . . The failure of the National Bank to disclose this important feature [Gulbenkian's 15 percent share] when entering the [merger] negotiation has made a painful impression upon [Foreign Secretary] Sir E. Grey."[50]

Shell stood equally guilty in British eyes. Foreign Office diplomats also castigated Shell for being "selfish and utterly unscrupulous." Before any more surprises emerged, the Foreign Office demanded a written statement that "no voting power attached" to those original shares "held at first by Gulbenkian and now . . . transferred to the Shell." The imperative now: "It is of importance that we know exactly where are we as regards the Gulbenkian shares."[51]

Whitehall was convinced the Turkish government was prepared to grant the concession to whomever London designated, if only to keep the tax and customs duty increase intact. Whitehall continually threatened to veto those if the concession imbroglio was not resolved in Anglo-Persian's favor. Indeed, in early January 1914, foreign officers repeatedly reassured themselves about the concession, given Istanbul's precarious financial situation. For example, January 15 handwritten minutes of the Foreign Office on the oil concession asserted the Turks "are very short of money." This was based on a telegram that same day from Ambassador Mallet in Istanbul, which used similar language: "They are very hard up for money."[52]

At the same time, British officials tried to keep Anglo-Persian executives in London from constantly trying to take advantage of and better the subsidy Britain was willing to extend. One request by Anglo-Persian managing director Charles Greenway for a special Mesopotamian exploration company funded by a million-pound government subvention was met with an irked warning from Foreign Office staffers: "Enter into an arrangement on the terms which have been communicated" or "stand out of the Mesopotamian concession altogether."[53] In other words: "Take it or leave it."

Greenway took it. In a January 31, 1914, letter, he replied, "Seeing that in the opinion of the Foreign Office no better terms are obtainable . . . my colleagues, after careful examination and discussion, are willing to accept the proposals made."[54]

Everyone could agree to everything. But not Gulbenkian. Defiant, he met with Hakki Pasha, in London, reminding him that he, Gulbenkian, owned 15 percent, or about a third of the bank's half ownership in TPC. Gulbenkian's point was that he and only he, by virtue of his powerful fraction, controlled the destiny of oil in Mesopotamia. Hakki Pasha went to the Foreign Office and related the exchange: "He [Gulbenkian] was not going to allow the National Bank of Turkey to bargain away his rights, and if they attempted to do so he would send a solicitor to see them, and they would be involved in a lawsuit, in which he was sure to win."[55]

Unfortunately, the Foreign Office was not responding to the threats. Feeling left out despite his key ownership, Gulbenkian wanted to discuss the matter in person. But alienated British officials simply refused to meet with the man. So Gulbenkian was reduced to passing messages through others, such as Hakki Pasha. Ironically, sometimes the messages were conciliatory, offering to reduce his percentage and relinquish voting rights to permit the merger. Other times, they were all threats and belligerence.[56]

Finally, after repeated urgings from Hakki Pasha, Whitehall reluctantly agreed to meet with Gulbenkian. On February 13, 1914, a nattily dressed Gulbenkian strode into the Foreign Office and met with Near East expert Sir Llewellyn Smith. Self-laudatory and alternating between a spirit of compromise and a penchant for combativeness, Gulbenkian cleared up any question that he, and he alone, was the prime "creator of Turkish Petroleum Company." It was he who had put the parties together—the National Bank of Turkey, the Deutsche Bank, and Shell. Gulbenkian stated that, of course, he enjoyed a great friendship and "intimate acquaintance" with Deterding at Shell—yet was willing to act independently of Deterding if need be. In other words, he could be either a steadfast ally of his friend Deterding or undercut him, as required. Gulbenkian indicated he was willing to be helpful to the government, but "very unwilling to be cut out of the Mesopotamian enterprise." Smith recorded, "He is evidently disposed to be very tenacious of what he regards as his rights."[57]

The next day, German delegates visited Mideast expert Alwyn Parker at the Foreign Office. They were anxious that the matter be settled, thereby amicably dividing Mesopotamian oil between the two nations. But the one obstacle remained: "the position of Mr. Gulbenkian, his desire to remain interested in the concession, and his contention that the National Bank could not legally transfer his shares without his consent." This stymied all plans to create an enlarged

Anglo-Persian Oil Company in Mesopotamia. One Deutsche Bank official, Emil Strauss, claimed, almost certainly disingenuously, "that the Deutsche Bank only learned a few weeks ago of this sub-participation of Mr. Gulbenkian." Had Deutsche Bank known of Gulbenkian's involvement, Strauss averred, "they never would have joined the Turkish Petroleum Company." Strauss was now explicit: "It is necessary, in order to clear the way, that either Mr. Gulbenkian's interest be eliminated, or that the Turkish Petroleum Company be wound up."[58]

Alwyn Parker and his colleagues at the Foreign Office agreed. They insisted the National Bank of Turkey treat the situation as an "internal matter" and simply "eliminate Mr. Gulbenkian's interest." Unknown was Shell's response, since it held stock through Gulbenkian, who remained a longtime friend and associate of Deterding. But by any measure, if Gulbenkian and his alliances with Shell presented so many obstacles to the Turkish Petroleum Company merging with Anglo-Persian, the governments concluded it was up to "that Company to remove them."[59]

So assured was the British government that it would prevail, the cabinet voted on February 18 to authorize £2.2 million to fund the acquisition of Anglo-Persian and to forward the measure to Treasury for approval.[60]

Gulbenkian undoubtedly now sensed he might have overplayed his position. Matters were moving forward without him. He urged Babington-Smith to contact Parker at the Foreign Office to arrange another meeting. On March 2, 1914, Babington-Smith telephoned and "asked me if I wanted to see Gulbenkian again. I said 'No,' " reported Parker, who took a tough stand, knowing the Germans and British were now unified against Gulbenkian. Even when Babington-Smith passed on a message that Gulbenkian was willing to reduce his percentage from 15 percent, Parker was not moved. As Babington-Smith pressed ahead with more compromise ideas, Parker bluntly threatened, "The German and British governments had it in their power to prevent the Ottoman giving the concession to anyone of whom they [the two governments] did not approve, and neither . . . [Shell] nor Mr. Gulbenkian could attach much importance to being shareholders in a paralytic company." Babington-Smith agreed on that point.[61]

A few days later, March 5, after conferring with Gulbenkian, Babington-Smith telephoned Parker again with a new proffer: Perhaps Gulbenkian could relinquish control of his 15 percent but "retain the profits." A sorely tried Parker later made a note of his reply: Once again, "I said 'NO,' " making sure he typed NO in capital letters. Babington-Smith retorted that the Gulbenkian negotiations were therefore now in deadlock. Later, Gulbenkian himself called and appealed for a meeting. Parker replied that "this was impossible, useless and undesirable," telling Gulbenkian that if he had anything to say, "he had better put in writing."[62]

The next day, a handwritten instruction from the Board of Trade was sent over to Parker: "The time has come when the F.O. should <u>formally</u> tell the Turkish Petroleum Company that this is the final decision." The word *formally* was underlined. Immediately thereafter, a curt and official letter was typed and delivered to Babington-Smith. "I am directed by the Secretary Sir E. Grey to inform you . . . the proposal that Mr. Gulbenkian should retain his interest . . . is not one which [we] can . . . accept. . . . His Majesty's Government have reached a final decision that a 50 per cent interest [by Anglo-Persian] . . . must be obtained."[63]

Europe was beset by regional military clashes at that very moment, and alliances with the greater powers were being called into play. The Continent could break into war at any time. Hence, the formal letter from the Foreign Office to Babington-Smith concluded: "The matter is one which cannot be longer delayed without grave inconvenience, and consequently, if the Turkish Petroleum Company cannot see their way to participate in such [a merger] arrangement, His Majesty's Government will feel compelled to take such steps as they may think proper to secure the interest of the D'Arcy group."[64]

As for Shell, according to Gulbenkian, the whole idea of relinquishing shares to Anglo-Persian sent Deterding "into a state of frenzy." Deterding detested Anglo-Persian and its executives. Gulbenkian related, "He became wild" at the very mention of yielding. In fact, during the back-and-forth negotiations, Deterding was difficult to gauge. He swung from offering sincere cooperation to the Admiralty to hard-nosed offers of ever-diminishing amounts of oil. Shell's position shifted at every turn. But why? "I was in daily contact with Mr. Deterding," explained Gulbenkian, "and, although I did not appear [so], I was, in fact, the pilot of his negotiations."[65]

All the self-assuredness of the Foreign Office abruptly crumbled when it received reports on March 10, 1914, that "the Germans are working with the Turks behind our backs." A syndicate of wealthy Ottoman pashas and businessmen had created an alliance of politically potent Young Turks to seize the concession as soon as the paperwork could be drawn up. More than just a paper consortium, the group was meeting frequently, making advanced plans, and was quite earnest about overpowering the entire oil business in Mesopotamia. Embassy officials warned London that this consortium seemed too powerful, moneyed, and determined to stop.[66]

The Foreign Office unsheathed its fiscal sword once more the following day. Foreign Secretary Grey dispatched a cable to Mallet in Istanbul: "You may state categorically that if concession for these fields is given to any company in which D'Arcy group does not receive 50% of the whole, I shall be compelled to break off all negotiations with Hakki Pasha and to reconsider terms on which HMG could consent to customs increase and monopolies."[67]

At the same time, the cabinet had obtained Treasury's approval for the £2.2 million investment in Anglo-Persian. The next step was parliamentary approval. Toward this end, a special cabinet committee was appointed to oversee the final acquisition of Anglo-Persian—public and private. Churchill, on March 17, went before a parliamentary naval committee to establish the core principle of the Admiralty securing its own Mideast oil supply.[68]

It was uncertain how long the rest of heavily armed and intricately allianced Europe could remain aloof from regional tensions and conflicts such as those that had recently set the Balkans ablaze. Millions of men could be thrown into a great war that would not only span the continent but also engulf colonies across the world. If the concession were not obtained immediately, no one could predict who would devour it once war commenced. Regardless of when—or where—war broke out, it would be at least a year before oil could be drilled and transported for use. But from Churchill's point of view, "A year gained over a rival might make the difference. Forward, then!"[69]

Britain's sense of urgency suddenly became a sense of immediacy on Thursday, March 19. London circles learned that Istanbul could no longer resist the powerful new Turkish syndicate that had formed to acquire the concession. Greenway sent a note to D'Arcy indicating that Turkish authorities had at first delayed, "in view of the strong representation made by the British and German Ambassadors," but no more. How much time was left? Until Monday. "The Turkish Government have agreed not to commit themselves to other parties," explained Greenway, "until after Monday next, but will consider themselves as free to dispose of the concession as they please after that date. The matter must therefore be settled, one way or the other, between us and the T.P.C. before then."[70]

Quickly, that same day, March 19, the oil concerns—TPC, Shell, and Anglo-Persian, as well as the German diplomats and Deutsche Bank, plus the National Bank of Turkey, converged on the Foreign Ministry. Gulbenkian was not invited, although he had signaled his willingness to reduce his share from 15 percent to something smaller to advance the process. The remaining contentions regarding structure and methodology were hastily debated, and finally a secret contract was propounded, titled "Arrangements for Fusion of the Interests in Turkish Petroleum Concessions of the D'Arcy Group and the Turkish Petroleum Company."[71]

The ownership of the restructured Turkish Petroleum would now be 50 percent "D'Arcy's group," a synonym for Anglo-Persian, 25 percent Shell, and 25 percent Deutsche Bank. Half of the eight-man board of directors was to be appointed by D'Arcy's group, with two by Shell and two by Deutsche Bank. The original 1912 monopoly would be retained. "The three groups participating in the Turkish Petroleum [Co.]," the document required, "shall give undertakings on their own behalf and on behalf of the companies associated with them not to be interested directly or indirectly in the production or manufacture of crude oil in the Ottoman Empire in Europe and Asia . . . otherwise than through the Turkish Petroleum [Co.]." The specified exceptions recognized prior British commitments in Egypt, Kuwait, and in the recently "Transferred Territories" on the Turco-Persian frontier.[72]

TPC's corporate restructuring process was succinctly delineated in the document. Step 1: The shares of TPC were doubled from 80,000 to 160,000, still valued at £1 each, creating an enlarged company now worth £160,000. Step 2: Those additional 80,000 shares were allocated to D'Arcy's group. Hence, D'Arcy and Anglo-Persian now each owned half of TPC. Step 3: National Bank of Turkey transferred all of its shares to Shell and the Deutsche Bank. That completely eliminated the involvement of the National Bank of Turkey, which included Gulbenkian's 15 percent. In place of Gulbenkian's prized 15 percent, D'Arcy's group and Shell each carved out 2.5 percent of their holdings to create a conjoint 5 percent beneficial share for Gulbenkian. Both 2.5 percent blocks would be registered in the names of D'Arcy's group and Shell, which would each hold and control the stock. Gulbenkian would enjoy the beneficial 5 percent interest during his entire lifetime.[73]

Signing the document were ranking diplomats of the German Embassy in London, the Foreign Office, plus the director of the Deutsche Bank, Babington-Smith for the National Bank of Turkey, Greenway for Anglo-Persian, and Deterding for Shell.[74]

What began by paper was reduced by paper. It was all the power of paper. *Now Gulbenkian owned 5 percent.*

CHAPTER NINE

Fuel and Fuse

"When I saw this document, I immediately protested to Mr. Deter-ding whom I had myself brought into the Turkish Petroleum Company—and the whole participation of this group was, in fact, due to me," wrote Gulbenkian. He bitterly damned the entire fusion agreement, cobbled together by the Foreign Office on March 19, as a "preposterous usurpation of power crushing a minority without even consulting or asking the latter's advice."

Gulbenkian later railed, "Mr. Deterding, although he was then my friend—but oil friendships are very slippery—assured me that he had done his level best but that the [two] governments and the Anglo-Persian Company had compelled him to accept it. He stated, at the same time, that as it was a preposterous arrangement as far as I was concerned, I certainly ought not to accept an illegality."[1]

Immediately, Gulbenkian did as promised. He called his lawyers—one more esteemed than the next. Sir Wilfrid Greene, later Lord Greene, was an expert in corporate liquidation law. Sir Douglas Hogg, later Lord Hailsham, was the attorney general who had championed the Trade Disputes Act through Parliament. Sir John Simon, later Vis-count Simon, had just served as solicitor general and then attorney general; the next year, in 1915, Viscount Simon became home secretary and was later tapped as foreign secretary. Greene, Hogg, and Simon were just the leading edge of a powerful legal team. There were others. They "all assured me," recalled Gulbenkian, "that this was an inconceivable decision and that I should not worry myself because, not being a party to the Foreign Office agreement, my rights could not be in any way affected and that, sooner or later, I could rely on the signatories of the Agreement making satisfactory arrangements with me."[2]

Ironically, while Gulbenkian stewed and steamed over his disenfranchisement, he openly contradicted his own grievance when he later confessed that he voluntarily allowed his share to be diminished. "In order to show my genuine desire for peace and satisfactory arrangements," he wrote later, "I placed at the disposal of Deterding two-thirds of my participation in the Turkish Petroleum Company. . . . Out of my 15%, I authorized him to dispose of 10% if a basis could be found for a general arrangement. This is how my 15% became 5%." Those sentences were written directly under an all-capitals heading: "VOLUNTARILY REDUCED MY PARTICIPATION FROM 15% TO 5%."[3]

Even as Gulbenkian fumed over his new fraction, cables and telegrams flew from London and Berlin to Istanbul instructing the British and German diplomats there, as well as the designated commercial agents, to immediately inform the Ottoman ministries. Turkish Petroleum now enjoyed the full backing of both the German and British governments, and this new, enlarged entity was officially applying for a sweeping concession for the entire Baghdad and Mosul provinces. By the deadline of Monday, March 23, the Turkish authorities were presented with all the documentation they required to issue the concession.[4]

Just one other thing. The revised Turkish Mining Law now prohibited monopolies. Hence, the requested concession was just too broad. It clearly encompassed the entire provinces of Mosul and Baghdad, and in some correspondence with TPC parties, this coverage was stretched to include Basra. Some discussion even suggested the concession might include the entire Ottoman Empire, crossing three continents. Indeed, there were so many other contenders, the matter would now have to be studied. While it was being studied, the Young Turks followed in the footsteps of some older Turks before them, constantly asking when their baksheesh would be tendered. Compulsory loans, special commissions, and consultation fees running into six digits once more were suggested, or even demanded, in order for the right papers to pass to the right places at the right velocity.[5]

Throughout April 1914, arcane historical facts of the Anatolia concession and the sultan's *Civile Liste* were debated back and forth between officials of Britain, Germany, and Turkey. Every petition from London and Berlin that invoked the *Civile Liste* was answered by the pashas with a reminder that those original early-century concessions predated the recent mining law and its antimonopoly provisions. So many different legal theories were expounded that the juridical haze seemed impenetrable. One solution suggested was to cement a secret understanding with the Turks that while a monopoly would not be ordained in law, it would be granted *in fact*. Hence, other syndicates could apply, but none would actually be approved— just endlessly delayed.[6]

Regardless of what was happening with the Mesopotamian concession and TPC, the acquisition of Anglo-Persian was proceeding. On May 11, Churchill advised officials in both Treasury and the Admiralty that the legal technicalities had been mostly worked out. An agreement was typed up.[7]

On May 20, 1914, the Treasury and the Admiralty together with Anglo-Persian signed a three-page, 14-point contract, adorned at the top with the words "An Agreement" in large gothic script. In doing so, the government essentially sealed the government's acquisition of 51 percent of the shares and hence control of the board of directors and the firm's commercial destiny in exchange for £2.2 million. That same day, a private letter from the government was issued to Anglo-Persian stating that the day-to-day commercial affairs of the company would be left to the management. No veto would be invoked unless any action affected naval contracts, sales to foreign entities, the geopolitical territories of drilling, or corporate status.[8]

While the specifics of the oil contracts with Anglo-Persian would remain secret, like any other military supply contract, the £2.2 million funding itself was a public expenditure that would need ratification by an act of Parliament. Rather than subject the measure to an elaborate and protracted parliamentary process, Churchill prepared for a single significant public presentation before legislators, with an up or down vote.

Meanwhile, in Istanbul, the Council of State reviewed TPC's Mesopotamian concession application as well as the whole question of monopoly. The pashas ruled that no monopolistic concession could be granted—regardless of London's threats of a tax increase veto.[9] This refusal opened the door for influential and cash-flush competitors to continue peddling their influence and push for petroleum. Mesopotamia's concession was again spun round within the maze.

As Churchill prepared to conclude a deal with Anglo-Persian in Persia to the exclusion of Shell, its executives went on the offensive. Shell's reluctant involvement in TPC was a project for the future. There was oil to be sold to the British navy in the here and now. Therefore, at the end of May, Shell's Samuel and Deterding circulated a series of letters attacking the plan to acquire Anglo-Persian as governmental market rigging, injecting intolerable favoritism into the oil business. Churchill denounced those criticisms as nothing more than vile efforts by unscrupulous Shell to "keep prices up to the present blackmailing levels."[10]

Indeed, pressures from Shell only reinforced Churchill's drive to acquire Anglo-Persian—and quickly. All that remained was Parliament's vote. The culminating day was June 17, 1914, when Churchill made his long, impassioned, and often sarcastic speech. His goal was to ignite the simmering animosities of the MPs against monopolies, trusts, and even Jews in defense of the navy and its quest for fuel at a fair price.

"We have experienced, in common with private consumers, a long steady squeeze by the oil trusts all over the world," declared Churchill in cynical tones, "and we have found prices and freights raised steadily against us until we have been pressed to pay more than double what a few years before we were accustomed to pay. . . . For many years it has been the policy of the Foreign Office [and] the Admiralty . . . to preserve the independent British oil interests of the Persian oil-field . . . and, above all, to prevent it being swallowed up by the Shell or by any foreign or *cosmopolitan* companies."[11]

The term *cosmopolitan* was a snide contemporary code word for manipulative immigrant Jewish businessmen, a clear reference to Marcus Samuel, 40 percent owner of Shell. This provoked a sharp response from MP Watson Rutherford: "I think it is a very great pity that the First Lord of the Admiralty . . . should have gone out of his way to attack the Shell Company, or Sir Marcus Samuel." Rutherford added that Churchill obviously knew he "would have every great difficulty with some of his own followers . . . and that the best course of action to get them to support it [the funding of Anglo-Persian] was to raise the question of monopoly and to do a little Jew-baiting." Rutherford added, "There is a world shortage . . . of an article which the world has only lately begun to see is required for certain special purposes. This is the reason why prices have gone up, and not because evilly-disposed gentlemen of the Hebraic persuasion—I mean *cosmopolitan* gentlemen—have put their heads together in order to try and force prices up."[12]

More than sarcastic appeals, Churchill unabashedly made the case for state-controlled capitalism. "We knew that by our contract we confer upon the Anglo-Persian Company an immense advantage which, added to their concession, would enormously strengthen the company and increase the value of their property. If this consequence arose from the necessary action of the State, why should not the State share in the advantage, which we created? . . . Why should we not go a step further? Was it not wiser . . . to acquire control of an enterprise . . . on which, to a large extent, we must rely? That was the process of reasoning by which the Admiralty and the Cabinet were drawn from the making of a simple supply contract to the definite acquisition and control of the company and its concessions. . . . We have to pay for the oil, but the Treasury will recover the profits."[13]

Churchill again and again slammed the ruthless oil monopolies. "Look out upon the wide expanse of the oil regions of the world! Two gigantic corporations—one in either hemisphere—stand out predominantly. In the New World there is the Standard Oil. . . . In the Old World, the great combination of the Shell and the Royal Dutch, with all their subsidiary and ancillary branches, has practically covered the whole ground. . . . Amongst British companies who have maintained an independent existence . . . the Anglo-Persian Oil Company, is almost the only noticeable feature."[14]

He concluded: "It is for Parliament to balance . . . an independent oil supply against the extortion of which the taxpayer would otherwise be the victim."[15]

Hecklers and adversaries in the House let loose. Not a few criticized the plan because oil in far-off Persia was clearly not defensible. "Nobody denies that the properties are valuable," asserted MP George Lloyd, "but . . . the whole of that country and the whole of your properties is surrounded by material which is far more flammable than the oil which you seek . . . I am absolutely in favor of our seeking an oil supply independent of all trusts, in any part of the world, outside or inside the British Empire, where it can be found and properly controlled. I say, 'properly controlled,' which this cannot be."[16]

Lloyd emphasized, "Those places [in Persia] are situated in a country which has no central control whatever . . . in a country which is surrounded by war-like tribes . . . which is in the hands of turbulent tribesmen whose influence is proportionate locally for their capacity to terrorize and raid, and whose policy is directed by no respect for foreign undertakings or treaties."[17]

Another member declared, "It is as if he had stored his gunpowder near some furnace."[18]

Some members wondered how Britain could morally meddle in another nation's territory without regard for the inhabitants. "It is almost amusing," charged MP Arthur Ponsonby, "the way the great powers, when discussing a matter of this sort, consider that they are conferring an untold benefit on the country in question, and the interests of that country, so far as its population is concerned, are entirely disregarded. I suppose the Persian Government has been consulted, although I daresay that would be considered an unnecessary formality. It has been the policy of the British Government too often to concentrate attention on the material development of a country without sufficient regard to the welfare and liberties of the inhabitants to whom that country belongs. . . . It is a matter of small moment to any honorable member in this House how the Persians will fare. We think in our arrogance that, of course, British capital and British enterprise can do nothing but confer an immediate benefit and advantage on a country in such a backward state as the Persian Empire. That may or may not be the case. Persia had a complete civilization when we were walking about in skins."[19]

At the end of the day, the tempestuous debate over the bill known as "Anglo-Persian Oil Company—Acquisition of Capital," culminated in a vote of 254 ayes against only 18 nays. When Greenway

asked, "How did you manage to carry the House with you so successfully," Churchill readily admitted that it was the "attack on monopolies and trusts that did it."[20]

The next day, the press energetically cross-examined the just-ratified
measure. "The real issue," blasted the London *Times,* "is whether the
Government have, by this new enterprise, entered upon a fresh and
dangerous policy in the Middle East, which may in the end lead them
into responsibilities of a character which Ministers still seem unable to
comprehend." The *Times* did not quibble with the need for oil. But
"we do not quite understand why he [Churchill] went to Persia for it."
The newspaper repeated MP George's question: "How are these properties to be defended?"[21]

Finally, in one editorial, the *Times* warned, "We want the Navy to
have oil. But we do not want to run the risk of fresh embroilment anywhere in the Middle East; and it is for this reason that we fear the country may come to regret an impetuous and careless undertaking."[22]

On June 18 and 19, with Parliament's vote still fresh and even as
the headlines raged, identical coordinated telegrams were sent to the
Turkish prime minister by the British and German governments
applying maximum pressure in pursuit of the long-awaited and
decade-delayed concession. These two communications only reinforced a barrage of telegrams earlier that month reminding that the
tax increases were completely contingent on the concession.[23]

On June 28, 1914, London received the requested definitive and
positive response. "The Ministry of Finance, which has taken over
from the *Civile Liste* matters concerning petroleum deposits already
discovered or to be discovered in the *villayets* [provinces] of Mosul and
Baghdad agrees to lease them to the T.P.C. and reserves the right later
on to fix its own share as well as the general terms of the agreement."[24]

There was just one other thing. Worried over claims that Gulbenkian and others might launch, the prime minister added a sentence: "It is understood that the Company must indemnify, in case of
necessity, the third parties who may be interested in the petroleum
deposits situated in those two *villayets* [provinces]."[25]

Indemnification? Once again the concession was not final—just
almost final. The Foreign Office was about to mount yet another
démarche on that June 28, when the world's attention was suddenly
riveted on Sarajevo in the tiny realm of Bosnia. Bosnia was one of

those tiny emerging post-Ottoman realms swirling at the heart of the Eastern Question and the Balkans Wars.

Archduke Francis Ferdinand, heir apparent to throne of the Austro-Hungarian Empire, and his wife were on an official state visit to mountain-cradled Sarajevo that June 28, 1914. About a month earlier, while sipping tea beneath a flickering gaslight at Belgrade's Café Zlatna Moruna, three fanatical Serbian Moslem nationalists from an organization called the "Black Hand" had read a short newspaper notice about the impending state visit. They immediately organized a conspiracy of some 22 individuals. A vanguard of three assassins slowly made their way to Sarajevo.[26]

June 28. Approximately 10 A.M. Driving in an open car as part of a six-vehicle motorcade, with a wealthy loyal supporter riding upright on the sideboard, the archduke's attention was drawn by a loud crack. It was a hand grenade, thrown by one of the conspirators. The grenade bounced off the vehicle, exploding harmlessly away from the car. Archduke Ferdinand and his wife Sofia sped off to their destination, city hall, to complain to the mayor about an assassination attempt. Believing the attack to be over, and deciding to stand up to fanatics, the archduke and his wife sat patiently through the mayor's trite speech. They were en route to their next stop when the driver took a wrong turn, accidentally cruising right into the sight lines of the second conspirator, Gavrilo Princip. Princip approached the car, aimed, and shot twice.[27]

Princip was wrestled to the ground by guards and placed in shackles. At first, it was uncertain how seriously injured the couple was. But as the vehicle drove on, blood spurted from the archduke's mouth. His pregnant wife slumped to the floor in pain. The archduke, mortally wounded himself, turned to her and pleaded: "*Sterbe nicht! Bleibe am Leben für unsere Kinder!*" (Don't die, my love! Stay alive for our children!) Shortly thereafter, she died. Then he died.[28]

Europe was thrown into chaos. Throughout a tumultuous and nerve-wracking July, Vienna charged Serbia with trying to start a war. The many alliances that had been revving darkly for decades began lining up on either side of the conflict. The Eastern Question was about to be answered on a global scale.

One month after the murders, July 28, Austria-Hungary invaded Serbia. On August 1, as the czar rushed to bolster his ally Serbia, Germany declared war on Russia, and the next day on Russia's ally, France. Britain demanded the kaiser respect Belgium's neutrality, and when he invaded Belgium on August 4, London declared war on Germany. Within days, Japan, too, declared war on Germany. The conflict deployed great new modes of warfare: submarines, airplanes, massive trenches, tanks, long-range cannons, and many more devices and methods of terrible devastation. The Great War was on.

During those fiery weeks of July, August, and October, frantic efforts were nonetheless undertaken to save the Mesopotamian oil concession, even as Istanbul and London sped toward the abyss of war. On October 29, 1914, the Ottoman Empire entered the war on Germany's side. Within a week, Britain was at war with Turkey as well.

The captains of industry and the leaders of nations had walked through the intoxicating vapors of Middle East petroleum, some for country, some for avarice, many for both. But two gunshots in Sarajevo ignited a fuse that exploded into a monstrous conflict that killed millions. Thereafter, fuel and fuse would be inseparable throughout the world. One would beget the other for decades.

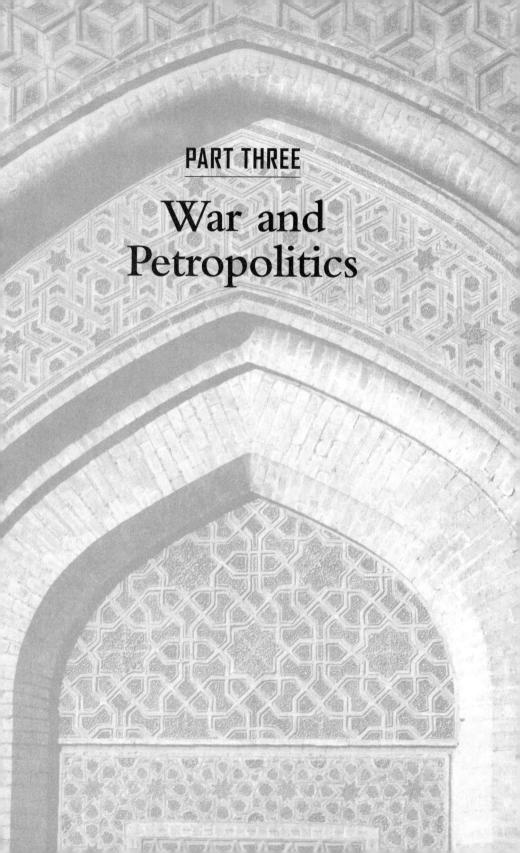

PART THREE

War and Petropolitics

CHAPTER TEN

Invasion

World War I: 8 million dead, 21 million wounded, 2 million missing in action, $180 billion spent.[1]

The Great War that many thought would be concluded within weeks dragged on mercilessly for nearly half a decade. In numbers that defy the darkest imagination, young men continually climbed out of muddy trenches to valiantly charge barbed wire, mines, and machine-gun fire. They were blown to bits, poisoned, and starved en masse in the irrepressible bloody conquest, loss, and bloody reconquest of mere meters of territory.

The disastrous 1915 Gallipoli campaign killed more than a half million men from both sides. During the Battle of the Somme in 1916, about a million men died from all countries; on the first day alone, there were 58,000 British casualties, a third of whom were killed. At Verdun in 1916, the dead and missing were generally estimated to be nearly a million. Russia lost more than any country: mobilizing 12 million, suffering 1.7 million fatalities, 5 million wounded, and 2.5 million missing or taken prisoner. Germany's numbers were almost as staggering.[2] The best explanation of why the nations of Europe went to war and sacrificed so many men was this: They just wanted to.

However, long before most of Europe's deadliest battles, the British invaded Mesopotamia with a real purpose. Britain declared war on Turkey November 5, 1914. Weeks before, sealed orders had been sent to Bombay for Indian Expeditionary Force D to sail to the Persian Gulf. Not a barrel of commercial oil had been pumped in Mesopotamia, nor had a drill been sunk or a concession even granted. But Admiral Edmond Slade had urged the government to protect Anglo-Persian's recently completed refinery at Abadan, Persia, located directly downstream from Basra on the Shatt-al Arab waterway at the head of the Persian Gulf. Admiral Slade was the man who headed Churchill's fuel expedition to Persia in advance of acquiring government control of Anglo-Persian Oil Company. Shortly thereafter, Slade was appointed as one of two ex officio government board members of the company. He was now able to call for military action in his dual role as an advocate for Anglo-Persian and the British navy.[3]

When it appeared that the transport of Anglo-Persian's oil through the Gulf would be imperiled as part of general hostilities, the British took action. On October 31, 1914, after the Ottoman Empire joined the war on Germany's side, but before war had been officially proclaimed with Turkey, the Admiralty in London dispatched a coded telegram to Indian naval forces lying in wait near Abadan: "Commence hostilities against Turkey."[4]

Pre-positioned Indian forces promptly secured Anglo-Persian's facilities on November 6, just 24 hours after Whitehall actually declared war. British and Indian forces then pressed on toward Basra, which they occupied on November 23. When the British arrived in Basra, as thousands of Turks rapidly retreated, recalled one senior officer, "We found the lower-class Arabs busily employed in looting and burning the houses and murdering the occupants." Order was restored only after several agitators were hanged. Thereafter, Basra became the center of a British occupation that steadily penetrated north.[5]

Now came a confluence of economic, political, and military invasions that established Britain as the new power in Mesopotamia. Indeed, as millions of young men hurtled back and forth across the ghastly trenches of Europe's battlefields, so did diplomats, oil executives, and occupation officials jockey across Mesopotamia's commercial landscape. Millions died in Europe. But in far-off Mesopotamia, the military-industrial oil complex survived and eventually prospered beyond anyone's dreams.

The war for Mesopotamia's strategic location and resources began in London even before the first troops landed in the Persian Gulf. The law enabling the British government to acquire Anglo-Persian Oil Company passed on June 17, 1914, but did not receive the obligatory confirming Royal Assent from King Edward until August 10. By then, England had been at war with Germany for a week.[6]

In early September, "Trading with the Enemy" proclamations made it illegal to transact business with German companies. In early November, as war was extended to the Ottoman Empire, Turkish entities were included. But the government now owned a majority of Anglo-Persian Oil Company, which on March 19, 1914, was fused with a reorganized Turkish Petroleum Company, which itself was 25 percent owned by an enemy corporation—Deutsche Bank. Hence, any and all commercial transactions, even routine business communications, with TPC were illegal.[7]

Nonetheless, on November 2, Anglo-Persian chairman Charles Greenway pleaded with the Foreign Office to permit the fusion agreement to go forward "without delay in order that the interests of the D'Arcy group (i.e., of the Anglo-Persian Oil Co. Ltd.) may be preserved, no matter how the present war may eventuate." Greenway added that failure to allow certain consummating transactions, such as the exchange of stock and resolutions necessitated by the fusion agreement, would mean that "we fail now to complete the agreement . . . [and] lose all claim to an interest in these [petroleum] rights." In such a case, "whatever the result of the war," Greenway warned, ". . . these rights between the Baghdad Railway Company and the Turkish Petroleum Company will doubtless hold good, inasmuch as it was concluded long before the war with a company of an ostensibly British character [the National Bank of Turkey]."[8] In other words, the German-Turkish group engineered by Gulbenkian would still own much of Mesopotamian oil. Britain, without a concession, would own nothing.

Several weeks of legal deliberations throughout the Foreign Ministry and other departments forced an unwanted conclusion. The government's lead petroleum official, Maurice de Bunsen, curtly informed Greenway that the government had ruled "that the agreement of March 19, 1914 has, in the circumstances, no longer any legal validity." He added that the government "will decline to take this agreement into account when the moment comes to arrange for the future of the oil areas in these [Mesopotamian] districts." De Bunsen stressed, "Take no steps to carry out the arrangements embodied in the agreement." However, in a not so subtle wink and a presage, de Bunsen appended, "but I am to add that the necessity of safeguarding . . . the interests of the British parties to that agreement will not be lost sight of."[9] Possession remained nine-tenths of the law. Britain intended to possess Mesopotamia's oil.

At the same time, the British executives of the National Bank of Turkey scrambled to resign from the bank's board because they felt their position was meaningless and, in view of Gulbenkian's deal with the Germans, probably illegal. But a government exemption permitted the institution to continue its affairs in non–Turkish-controlled territories, thus allowing it to formally divest itself of its ownership of Turkish Petroleum Company in favor of Deutsche Bank. This divestiture would later prove fateful.[10]

For his part, Gulbenkian in January 1915 resigned from the board of Turkish Petroleum as an individual in his own name. He immediately rejoined as a representative of Dutch Shell, lest he officiate as a director representing himself in his own disenfranchisement. At about that time, Gulbenkian met with Greenway and other APOC executives about Anglo-Persian contributing its share of some of TPC's minor operating expenses. After all, APOC was now half owner of TPC. The meeting was both tense and telling. As Gulbenkian asked commercial questions, Greenway, mindful of Trading with the Enemy provisions, declined to answer directly and suddenly turned the conversation to "Persian pottery." A colleague chimed in about "Persian miniatures." A riled Gulbenkian later recalled, "The whole conversation was very cute, but I felt helpless." Gulbenkian, along with Shell's chief, Deterding, then paid for various routine operational expenses out of their pockets.[11] The episode only further entrenched Shell and APOC forces as bitter adversaries in the battle for Turkish Petroleum.

As Britain prosecuted the war, Anglo-Persian's oil contributed a mere 20 percent of its fuel needs. The remainder was imported chiefly from the United States. Yet by January 1915, a full British division—some 10,000 men—had occupied Basra, and thousands of additional British, Indian, and other colonial units were stationed nearby along the Persian Gulf.[12] Thus, the massive expenditure of men, matériel, and fuel was disproportionate to protecting the Anglo-Persian refinery at Abadan. Britain was locking down not the present strategic advantage, but the future of Mesopotamian oil and Gulf commercial routes.

Charles Hardinge, the British viceroy of India, complained that the massive investment of Indian troops and military resources was completely unjustified, since most of Britain's oil was coming from sure and safe sources in America. He wrote, "How I do hate that pipeline," which had been sabotaged by local Persian tribesmen. "It is inconceivable," he added, "that the Admiralty can be in any way dependent upon the supply of oil derived from Abadan."[13]

But when Hardinge visited the Abadan refinery on February 3, 1915, and witnessed its commercial value, he changed his mind. "In the first instance," he admitted to a Foreign Office colleague, "I was strongly opposed to the acquisition by the Admiralty of so large a share in this undertaking [the Anglo-Persian Oil Company], since I realized that the responsibility for its defense would fall upon India. Now I am delighted that we have so large a stake in Abadan, since it makes it absolutely certain that we can never give up Basra, which I regard as the key of the Gulf. . . . It is therefore absolutely essential from every point of view that we should remain at Basra where we shall have complete control over the trade of Mesopotamia, and we ought to be able to make the Basra *vilayet* [province] into a second Egypt." Just weeks before, Britain had unilaterally declared Ottoman Egypt a British protectorate, assuming all civil and military authority for the region.[14]

The Foreign Office in London concurred with Hardinge's enthusiasm. On March 31, 1915, Hardinge received an assurance from a London colleague, "I quite agree with you that we should certainly possess the Basra *vilayet* [province], and have perhaps some kind of autonomous province at Baghdad more or less under our protectorate."[15]

By the fall of 1915, the road from Basra to Baghdad was clearly foreseen. Hardinge flippantly suggested to the British palace, "My little show in Mesopotamia is still going strong and I hope that Baghdad will soon be comprised within the British Empire."[16]

However, making Mesopotamia a British satellite required more than just defeating the Turks. It meant allying with the tradition-infused and insular Arabs who lived there. That brought Britain face-to-face with the rising tetrahedron of Arab nationalism—a fractious jumble of tribal rivalries and alliances, kings without constituents, and constituents without kings, all churning across obscure landscapes of impenetrable political intrigue.[17]

Arab nationalism began in earnest as an early-century surge of Arab Christian and Islamic intellectuals who envied Christian Europe's international movement to achieve self-determination, autonomy, and national independence for its ethnic and religious groups. Arab activists, however, were completely disunified on the geopolitical form for their aspirations. Some craved a network of decentralized, locally ruled Islamic states stretching across the Middle East. Others preferred a Turco-Arabian federation akin to the Austro-Hungarian Empire. Still others wanted territorial independence at home linked to economic dependence on an industrialized foreign power, such as France or Great Britain. Large tribal groups yet to be swayed could not decide which nationalist expression was best—if any. But many Arabs were quite simply loyal to Istanbul as the traditional seat of the Islamic caliphate.[18]

More important, which part of the Arab domain was to be liberated—just the Hijaz region of the coastal Arabian Peninsula, Egypt, Palestine, Syria, some of it, all of it, none of it? The struggle was contentious and competitive. But this much independence-minded Arab leaders had concluded: The long-crumbling Ottoman Empire that had ruled them for centuries was now too weak to retain domination. Soon the Sick Man would collapse. With the Great War raging, the Arab national moment had finally arrived.[19]

Nationalist yearnings, percolating for years, manifested most fiercely beginning with the newest iteration of the Ottoman Empire. True enough, Turkey's revolution, in 1908 and 1909, had brought administrative reform to the corrupt ways of the sultans. But soon thereafter, the Committee for the Union and Progress—that is, the Young Turks—had turned repressively chauvinistic. The ruling pashas decided that all the diverse ethnic groups within the empire should become one people: Turkish. They should speak one language: Turkish. They should live with one identity: Turkish. Those who would not change willingly would be changed forcibly. The much-resented Turkification campaign of Arab lands throughout the Middle East administratively and economically favored those Arabs who assimilated into the modern Turkish culture and bowed to Istanbul's authority. The campaign snubbed the Arabic language and customs.[20]

However, the whole bundle of Arab wartime resentment toward the Turks also tore at the fabric of Islamic sensibilities. To side with the British against the Turks meant siding with the Christian infidel against other Moslems, and indeed the modern center of the Islamic world, Turkey. After all, the sultans, for all their moral decay, were still the caliphs of Islam, that is, the supreme leaders of all Moslems. For better or worse, Istanbul was the seat of the caliphate.[21] Thus all Arab alliances were uneasy. Like so many mirages and dust devils in the desert, one minute an alliance with the Arab potentates was visible and furious, the next it was gone, only to reappear a moment later.

Ironically, amid all the agitation for Islamic independence burning throughout the Mideast during World War I, the one key marginalized region was Mesopotamia. Why?

Mesopotamia's peripheral place in the wartime quest for Arab nationalism was intrinsically affected by the composition of the various Arab national parties. In response to repressive and insensitive Turkification, several contending parties and secret societies emerged throughout the Middle East—but these were mainly outside Mesopotamia. These included the Literary Club in South Lebanon, comprising disaffected former Arab spies and privileged functionaries of the sultan; the Arab Association in Cairo; and the Decentralized Party, also Cairo-based, which sprang from Lebanese and Syrian immigrants favoring separate Arab states federated with the Ottoman Empire. The two enduring societies that eventually subsumed the nationalist movement were al-Fatat and al-Ahd, which mainly operated in Paris, Istanbul, and the Arab capitals beyond the Mesopotamian provinces.[22]

For a few years before the war, the three Mesopotamian provinces did host several nationalist, revolutionary, and/or reform societies, some secret, some open. Mosul's Green Flag organization, the Basra

Reform Society, and Baghdad's National Scientific Club were among them. But these groups were frequently compromised by Ottoman spies and police agents, or co-opted in the traditional Ottoman fashion by elevating their organizers to lucrative positions. The main agitation within the three provinces was left to the local chapters of al-Ahd and al-Fatat in Baghdad and Basra, which advanced pan-Arab issues. However, this agenda was necessarily focused on Syria, Lebanon, and Egypt, where those groups were headquartered, plus the holy sites of the Hijaz.[23]

Demographics played a role as well. Mosul in the north was Kurdish; Baghdad was largely Sunni; the south was overwhelmingly Shiite. Of the approximately 2.6 million people in Mesopotamia's three provinces, more than half were Shiite. The Kurds constituted about 20 percent. An additional 8 percent throughout Mesopotamia hailed from non-Arab and/or non-Islamic groups, such as the Jews, Christians, Armenians, Turkomans, and the secretive Kurdish Yazidis, a tiny sect that abhorred lettuce and dark blue clothing. Although concentrated into a dense and commanding power base in south and central Mesopotamia, the Shi'a were still considered by the larger Arab world to be Islam's outcast 10 percent.[24] In turn, the alienation Mesopotamian Shiites felt for the Sunni majority never subsided. Hence, the ancient Shi'a-Sunni rivalries and ingrained disregard for infidels held fast as nationalists considered Mesopotamia's place in their precious campaign.

Just as important, who were the movers of the nationalist movement? They were not drawn from the multitudes of Bedouin and other tribal groups who constituted much of Mesopotamian life. The foot soldiers of nationalism were just that, rebellious Arab soldiers serving in the Turkish army. As 1915 began, the million-man Ottoman army included at least 100,000 Arabs, perhaps more, including many recently conscripted in the war mobilization. Mesopotamian Arabs were mainly concentrated in four divisions, the 35th through the 38th. Yet these men were stationed not in their home provinces but in Damascus and other parts of Syria.[25]

Various pan-Arab divisions hailing from lands beyond Mesopotamia, including the 12th Corps originally headquartered in Mosul, were also transferred to Syria. In fact, the 12th Corps chief of staff was a leader of al-Ahd, one of the two main nationalistic organizations. What's more, Baghdad's brightest militants, who had attended Istanbul's War College, became officers who, like the ranks they commanded, were also assigned to Syria and other regions beyond Mesopotamia. Therefore, should masses of Arab soldiers mutiny and launch a revolt, it would not be in Mesopotamia, but where they were stationed—in Syria. By virtue of the deployments to Syria and that country's intellectual base and connections with France, Damascus had become in fact the epicenter of the Arab national movement.[26]

In truth, because of the inherent conflicts in allying with the British infidel against Moslem Turkey, Arab leaders did not care whether the facilitator of their national hopes was Istanbul or London. Arabs simultaneously offered the same fierce allegiance to both sides: the British and the Turks. For example, from the moment war broke out in August 1914, al-Fatat opposed Turkey's entanglement in a bloody Christian European conflict. Once Istanbul officially joined Germany and Austro-Hungary, al-Fatat's administrative committee declared: "The goal of the Arabs is independence . . . to guard the existence of Arab countries, and not out of hostility to the Turks. Therefore, if Arab countries will stand up to the danger of European imperialism, the Society will work alongside the Turks, together with all free Arabs to protect the Arab countries."[27]

In the first flammable months of 1914, as prewar contingencies and stratagems were being brokered with Britain, one family rose to prominence: that of Hussein ibn Ali, the sharif of Mecca. Hussein, a short but striking and bearded figure, had been appointed by the Young Turks in 1908 to be the guardian of Mecca's holy sites. Hussein's Hashemite clan traced its lineage directly to the first Quraysh chieftains of Mecca, some five centuries before the Prophet Mohammed rose against the establishment in 610. Thereafter, the Quraysh descendants of the Prophet's wife Fatima became the honored Sunni rulers of Mecca, later known as "the Hashemites." These were the ancestors of Hussein. Through the ages, the distinguished Sunni Hashemite clan became the hereditary defenders of Mecca and superintendents of the hajj pilgrimage to Mecca, mandatory for all Moslems. Therefore, Hussein's family was known throughout the entire Arab domain as a noble one. For London, despite many seething competitors and detractors, it was easy to anoint Hussein and his two sons, Abdullah and Faisal, as the chief applicants and negotiators of the Arab national movement.[28]

London's price for any Arab national reward was strategic revolt against the Turks. But could any Arab deliver? On February 5, 1914, Abdullah met with Lord Kitchener in Cairo. Kitchener was Britain's consul general in Egypt and a leading military star who would soon become Britain's war minister. Abdullah's message: The Turks were threatening to administratively terminate his father's honorary position in Mecca. In such a case, Hussein just might lead a local revolt against the Turks. Would the British support him against Istanbul?[29]

Kitchener and the Foreign Office were cool to the whole idea. They knew that fundamentally Hussein was acting less nationalistic than protective of his financial stake in guarding the holy sites. Moreover, the English knew that a planned Turkish railway extension into the Arabian Peninsula would decimate Hussein's lucrative camel trade. Kitchener literally laughed at Abdullah and explained that "the Arabs of the Hijaz could expect no encouragement from us and that our only interest in Arabia was the safety and comfort of Moslem Indian pilgrims [en route to Mecca]."[30]

Several weeks later, in late March 1914, Louis Mallet, British ambassador in Istanbul, reported to Foreign Secretary Grey, "It is still impossible to say what real prospect there may be of any united Arab movement." But Mallet added an enticing thought. "If the Arabs are eventually successful in defeating the Ottoman armies, the loss of the Caliphate would probably follow, where, shorn of a further large portion of territory and of the religious leadership, Turkish rule, as it exists today, would presumably disappear." To that, he added a caution: "[But] Europe might then be faced with the question of a partition of the Turkish Empire which might easily produce complications of a serious nature."[31]

Since war had not yet broken out, and commercial relations with the Ottomans remained vibrant, Britain was determined not be dragged into any localized revolt in Mecca or even in Baghdad. "If the plan of creating an insurrection in Mesopotamia should take shape," Mallet warned Grey, "one of the aims of its promoters would be to compel British intervention. . . . [We] have no intention of pursuing a policy of adventure, which could only compromise serious British economic interests in Mesopotamia."[32]

But by late October, with the war in Europe fully under way and the war in the Middle East just days away from ignition, Whitehall reversed itself. In July 1915, the British high commissioner in Egypt, Sir Henry McMahon, entered a back-and-forth written correspondence with Hussein that included some 10 confidential letters. The full written exchange was kept secret for 15 years until revealed by the press and parliamentary investigation.[33] Those 10 letters, later to become famous as "the Hussein-McMahon correspondence," offered ambiguous British promises of national recognition within an ambiguously defined territory in exchange for ambiguous Arab offers of revolt predicated upon calculated deceptions and implied threats by both sides.

Decades later, activists on all sides of the Arab national debate would point to the McMahon-Hussein correspondence as proof— or lack of it—of broken pledges and unfulfilled national obligations. Any arguer indeed could seize upon passages within any of the several most prominent letters to validate any argument. But embedded within the full set of 10 letters—including some of the forgotten ones—are British demands and the Arab willingness to cede control to the British over one specified region in exchange for national rights elsewhere. The region the Arabs were willing to cede: Mesopotamia.[34]

The prelude to the historic 10-letter McMahon-Hussein correspondence was Kitchener's introductory note of October 31, 1914, which stated: "If the Sharif and Arabs in general assist Great Britain in this conflict that has been forced upon us by Turkey . . . Great Britain will guarantee the independence, rights and privileges of the Sharifate against all external foreign aggressions, in particular that of the Ottomans." Referring to the notion of replacing Turkish religious supremacy with Hussein himself, Kitchener appended, "It may be that an Arab of true race will assume the Caliphate at Mecca or Medina, and so good may come by the help of God out of all the evil which is now occurring."[35]

Arab self-definition and mapping began in earnest in early 1915 in Damascus. In March and April, during a series of secret meetings, the two leading nationalist societies, al-Fatat and al-Ahd, joined forces with each other and with Emir Faisal, who was representing his father Hussein. Together they drafted "the Damascus Protocol," which created a map for the envisioned Arab state. It resembled a dented rectangle tilted left toward eleven o'clock, encompassing and extending the Arabian Peninsula to the shores of the Mediterranean. The proposed northern border coursed east from the Mersin-Adana railway in Turkey, just beyond Syria, along the railroad tracks and across the 37th parallel to the Persian frontier; the eastern border followed the Persian frontier down to the Persian Gulf, then continued to the bottom of the Arabian Peninsula; from there the outline traveled back north to the Mersin-Adana starting point in Turkey, thus completing the geopolitical box. Both Palestine and the three Mesopotamian provinces resided completely within that approximate rectangle. The Damascus Protocol specified that if Britain granted this proposed new state, the British Empire would become the new Arab nation's defense partner. In addition, the new Arab nation would extend "the grant of economic preference to Great Britain."[36]

Fearing Turkey's seemingly omnipresent spies, the Damascus Protocol was reduced to miniature script, and then sewn into the boots of a member of Faisal's party. Faisal returned to Mecca, where he unveiled the plan to enlist his father's support for a so-called Arab Revolt. The suggested insurrection would begin during the winter of 1915 in Syria, where the troops were supposedly standing by. But Ottoman commanders detected the conspiracy, and suddenly transferred most of the Arab divisions out of Syria east to the Gallipoli front. That brought certain death, and Arab soldiers were promptly cut down as part of that battle's mass carnage. The Arabs in Syria did not revolt that winter.[37]

In truth, no one knows how many hundreds or thousands of Arab troops were ever really ready to turn on their commanders. But the aborted Syrian uprising was characteristic of an Arab Revolt that was always being devised and revised, located and relocated, launched and postponed. Moreover, the Arab leaders constantly exaggerated their forces, their base of popular support, and their willingness to take action. These demerits the British understood well, which is why the British were cool and uncertain about forming reliable military alliances with Arab elements.[38]

To reassure London, Hussein on July 14, 1915, began the famous exchange with McMahon. The letter tendered the Damascus Protocol territorial outline almost word for word, asking for a straight yes or no within 30 days. "If this [30-day] period should lapse before they [the Arabs] receive an answer, they reserve to themselves complete freedom of action," the letter stated in a soon-familiar veiled threat to instead seek alliance with the Turks against Britain.[39]

Not anxious to respond to arbitrary 30-day deadlines, and disturbed over Arab contingents already fighting valiantly in Turkish units, McMahon replied a full 45 days later. Mixing overblown effusiveness with snubbing hesitation, McMahon wrote, "We rejoice . . . that your Highness and your people are of one opinion—that Arab interests are English interests and English [are] Arab. . . . With regard to the questions of limits and boundaries," he continued, "it would appear to be premature to consume our time in discussing such details in the heat of war . . . especially as we have learned, with surprise and regret, that some of the Arabs . . . far from assisting us, are neglecting this, their supreme opportunity and are lending their arms to the German and the Turk, to the new despoiler and the old oppressor."[40]

A worried Hussein replied on September 9, 1915, with obsequious fawning: "To his Excellency the Most Exalted, the Most Eminent— the British High Commissioner in Egypt; may God grant him Success. With great cheerfulness and delight I received your letter dated August 30, 1915, and have given it great consideration and regard, in spite of the impression I received from it of ambiguity and its tone of coldness and hesitation with regard to our essential point. . . . Permit me to say clearly that the coolness and hesitation which you have displayed in the question of the limits and boundaries by saying that the discussion of these at present is of no use and a waste of time . . . [and] might be taken to infer an estrangement or something of the sort."[41]

Hussein's reply continued deferentially, and at one point referred to McMahon's "perfectness." He emphasized, "In order to reassure your Excellency, I can declare that the whole [Arab] country, together with those who you say are submitting themselves to Turco-German orders, are all waiting the result of these negotiations, which are dependent only on your refusal or acceptance of the question of the limits [borders]." In the best tradition of the Turkish bazaar, Hussein's next sentence asked exactly what Great Britain wanted in return for national support. "Whatever the illustrious Government of Great Britain finds conformable to its policy on this subject, communicate it to us and specify to us the course we should follow."[42]

McMahon's reply: Britain wanted Mesopotamia.

On October 24, 1915, McMahon wrote back that the United Kingdom would "recognize and support the independence of the Arabs in all the regions within the limits demanded by the Sharif of Mecca," but minus the Turkish portion, and minus any other area in which Britain enjoyed an obligation with other chiefs, and minus any other area, namely Syria, that would conflict with the interest of France. Plus, just one other thing: "With regard to the *vilayets* [provinces] of Baghdad and Basra, the Arabs will recognize that the established position and interests of Great Britain necessitate special administrative arrangements in order to secure these territories from foreign aggression, to promote the welfare of the local populations and to safeguard our mutual economic interests."[43]

Hussein immediately replied on November 5 with a flurry of great defensive conviction on behalf of Mesopotamia. Using the region's historic cartographic name "Iraq," Hussein staunchly explained how inseparable and sacred Iraq was to all Arabs—and had been since time immemorial. "As the Iraqi *vilayets* [provinces] are parts of the pure Arab Kingdom," wrote Hussein, "and were in fact the seat of its Government in the time of Ali ibn Abu Talib, and in the time of all the Caliphs who succeeded him; and as in them began the civilization of the Arabs, and as their towns were the first towns built in Islam where the Arab power became so great; therefore they are greatly valued by all Arabs far and near, and their traditions cannot be forgotten by them. Consequently," he insisted, "we cannot satisfy the Arab nations or make them submit to give us such a title to nobility."[44]

The Arabs would not give up Mesopotamia—but Britain could rent it.

"In order to render an accord easy," continued Hussein, ". . . we might agree to leave under the British administration for a short time those districts now occupied by the British troops without the rights of either party being prejudiced thereby (especially those of the Arab nation; which interests are to it economic and vital), and against a suitable sum paid as compensation to the Arab Kingdom for the period of occupation, in order to meet the expenses which every new kingdom is bound to support; at the same time respecting your agreements with the Sheikhs of those districts, and especially those which are essential."[45]

Britain was by now persuaded by the defection of a key Arab officer in the Turkish army, Mohammed Faruki, that it was worth securing a deal with the Arabs for a revolt if the right terms could be obtained. In early November 1915, Faruki on behalf of Hussein passed a message to the British Foreign Office that the Arabs would be willing to grant Great Britain governance over Baghdad and north Mesopotamia. Faruki also assured, as a British diplomat recorded it, "Arabs would agree to Basra town and all cultivated lands to the south being British territory."[46]

But McMahon was uncertain how much financial and political consideration the Arabs would require for Mesopotamia. He was undoubtedly certain it would be complex and time-consuming. "The Government of Great Britain," he wrote on December 14, ". . . are ready to give all guarantees of assistance and support within their power to the Arab Kingdom, but their interests demand, as you yourself have recognized, a friendly and stable administration in the *vilayet* of Baghdad, and the adequate safeguarding of these interests calls for a much fuller and more detailed consideration than the present situation and the urgency of these negotiations permit."[47]

Hussein answered on New Year's Day 1916: "With regard to what had been stated in your honored communication concerning El Iraq, as to the matter of compensation for the period of occupation, we, in order to strengthen the confidence of Great Britain in our attitude and in our words and actions, really and veritably, and in order to give her evidence of our certainty and assurance in trusting her glorious Government, leave the determination of the amount to the perception of her wisdom and justice."[48] In other words, pay what you wish.

Of course, there was no real payment. Britain and Hussein simply agreed: Mesopotamia would be in British hands.

In fact, several opportunities for the Arabs to rise up against the Turks in Mesopotamia were never taken before or during the McMahon-Hussein correspondence. For example, when the suspicious Turks in 1915 transferred numerous Arab divisions from Syria to the bloody Gallipoli front, they also moved two divisions, the 35th and the 36th, to Mesopotamia. There were suggestions that two leading Arab nationalists be sent in from Syria to foment the population in Baghdad and Basra. The Foreign Office shied away, since national agitation in Mesopotamia would not only inspire rebellion against the Turks, but against the new British occupiers as well. The balking Foreign Office concluded, we cannot "let loose revolutionaries whose actions may extend beyond our control." Others in the British government concurred: "Their [the two proposed agitators] political views are much too advanced to be safe pabula [baby food] for the communities of occupied territories and their presence in any of the towns of Iraq," as the three provinces were now increasingly being called, "would be, in our opinion, undesirable and inconvenient."[49]

On March 16, 1916, just after receiving a letter laying out the attack specifics against Turkish garrisons, Hussein gave the Turks yet another chance to ally with the Arabs. Turkey had declared a jihad against Britain in every mosque across the empire. Hussein offered to send desert warriors to join the jihad if Istanbul granted amnesty to Arab activists sentenced to death in Syria, granted self-rule to Arab states, and also recognized Hussein's sharifate in Mecca. Otherwise, Hussein threatened, Hijaz volunteers would sit out the war.[50]

Turkish war minister Enver Pasha's reply telegram was fierce: "Dealing with questions of war and the Arabs is none of your business. The political criminals in Syria will receive a just sentence. If you continue to concern yourself with this, the result will be no cause for you to rejoice." Then Enver added his own threat: "You will not see your son Faisal again unless you send the volunteers to the front as you promised. If you do not do this, the result for you, as we have said, will not be good."[51]

Hussein decided to cast his lot with the British. The volunteers to fight for Turkey were indeed sent to Syria on condition Faisal lead them personally. But Faisal's forces were, in fact, mutinous, and merely awaiting instructions to rebel. On June 5, Arab fighters on camel and horse began demonstration attacks against the railways of the Hijaz. On June 9, Hussein's family sent a final telegram to the Turks offering to join the jihad against Britain if the Mecca sharifate were recognized. The Turks did not comply. The next day, June 10, the revolt began in earnest in the Arabian Peninsula and then spread elsewhere.[52]

Ironically, even as the dialogue with Hussein was fully under way, McMahon's chief advisor and director of military intelligence, Lt. Col. Gilbert Clayton, confessed to a friend: "To set up a great Arab State . . . was never my idea. . . . The conditions throughout Arabia, Syria and Mesopotamia did not allow of such a scheme being practical, even if anyone were so foolish as to attempt it . . . the object we have to aim at is, I consider, to work to preserve all the various elements in the Arab territories very much in the same position as they were before the war, but minus the Turks. In this way we shall have an open field to work in."[53] Everyone was fooling everyone, and no one was fooling anybody.

Hussein and some of his scattered Arab forces did ultimately join the military action against Turkey in the Hijaz, Palestine, Gaza, Syria, and elsewhere. A jihad was promulgated by Hussein to justify joining infidel Christians against fellow Moslems: "The defense of the Hijaz from this evil and aggression [the Turks], the observance of the Rites of Islam that Allah has commanded, and the guarding of the Arabs and the Arab countries from the danger to which the Ottoman Empire is doomed because of the misbehavior of this wicked society—all of this will be achieved only by full independence and the cutting of all ties with the bloodthirsty conquerors and robbers."[54]

But in large part, Hussein's Bedouin fighters were "show forces." Not infrequently, they were ceremoniously marched into a town for local applause after a battle was in fact hard-won from the Turks by British units from Australia, India, or elsewhere. Britain certainly provided money and rifles for a campaign of camel riders and horsemen, led by such liaison officers as T. E. Lawrence, dubbed "Lawrence of Arabia." Lawrence's exploits were later romanticized in movies and novels. In reality, as submarine wolf packs hurled torpedoes through the waves, as airplane formations dropped bombs and strafed from the air, as tanks rumbled across the battlefield, as poison gas wafted over the trenches, and as those fighting in Europe gave their lives in a cataclysmic war that swept away 15 million, the scant Arab uprisings were considered merely cosmetic by many. Lawrence himself termed the Arab raids a "sideshow to a sideshow."[55]

The Arabs were unimportant in defeating the Turks. But more important, there was no Arab uprising in Mesopotamia when the British first entered Mesopotamia. Not when they first entered.

The British drive for Baghdad really began in late November 1914 as the military occupied Basra and pointedly asked itself: What next? Everyone was optimistic. The Turks were oppressive masters. London believed its troops would be greeted as liberators.

"Arab element is already friendly and notables here volunteer opinion that we should be received in Baghdad with the same cordiality as we have been here [in Basra]," reported Britain's military's chief political officer Percy Cox. He continued, "Baghdad in all probability will fall into our hands very easily."[56]

Cox, who had served as the key political resident in Persia from the first days of Anglo-Persian's oil strike, added, "I find it difficult to see how we can well avoid taking over Baghdad . . . but once in occupation, we must remain." Oil advocates, such as Admiral Fisher, pressed Prime Minister Herbert Asquith in a letter, "I hope you are not losing any time annexing the Tigris and the Euphrates!"[57]

The politicians misjudged everything. Often, the War Office was equally misinformed and confused. In the beginning, British military men knew that the Ottoman resistance would be formidable. True, almost all of the regular Arab-heritage brigades were absent. But the Turks had deployed other staunch fighting forces, made up mainly of loyal Turkish-heritage soldiers. One fast-changing War Office estimate temporarily placed enemy forces in Baghdad at 15,000. But the Turks were constantly implementing draconian drafts that added more men in large numbers. Moreover, Turkish reinforcements could pour in from the Russian front en masse to defend Baghdad. "If this happened," warned one general, ". . . we should have to withdraw or run the risk of a considerable disaster."[58]

Another general argued against "an advance on Baghdad by land on account of the scarcity of water at camps" amid the broiling summer heat. Yet another assured that a thrust against Baghdad clearly "would be impossible to execute at present." What's more, with or without military readiness, message after message exchanged between the generals dismissed Cox's political objective of taking Baghdad as undoable and inadvisable without the local Arab population agreeing to be occupied. The locals would by necessity want to join the winning side for fear of reprisals after the battle. One general expressed the prevailing view held by many: "It would be unwise to decide on going to Baghdad . . . till we see clearer . . . the inward attitude of the Arabs."[59]

The official military history of the campaign concluded that without the friendship of the Arabs, any commander could expect "supplies and information would be cut off, and his baggage and convoys plundered."[60]

Yet the decision to take Baghdad emerged nonetheless—and for years thereafter the generals would argue about exactly who had authorized the orders. No one would take credit for the campaign. But most concluded that orders originated with British officials in Bombay, perhaps because many of the mesmerized civil administrators in colonial India considered Baghdad "the glittering prize to which all eyes turned." Certainly, Indian viceroy Hardinge energetically encouraged the campaign. In a mid-January 1915 letter to the Foreign Office, he wrote, "It is, in my opinion, a matter of cardinal importance to India that Basra should be retained and that the predominance of England in the Persian Gulf should thus be assured. We may never get the chance again." His braggadocio constantly encouraged movement north. "You will have heard of the successful attack made by our troops on the Turkish position near Basra," he wrote on April 26, 1915, adding, "We have given the Turks a real good knock."[61]

Newly installed Mesopotamian commander in chief Sir John Nixon, who led the push to Baghdad, could explain only vaguely that when he visited Bombay, "I gathered we were to advance on Baghdad." In any event, the War Office, fully apprised of the campaign once it began in September 1915, authorized its progress north.[62]

But no one was ready for what happened. The short drive up the road to Baghdad took 18 months. And it cost tens of thousands of lives.

Initial and deceptively easy victories were experienced in the first miles up the Tigris. In late September 1915, after successfully conquering the scantly defended town of Kut, suffering 4,200 dead or wounded, heat-stricken and greatly undersupplied British forces trudged farther north toward the ancient settlement of Ctesiphon. It was at Ctesiphon in 782 that the first Moslem conquerors had elected to build their new capital named Baghdad, just 16 miles north. Unbeknownst to the British, seasoned Turks were waiting in long defensive trenches. British troops were violently turned back to Kut, 100 miles south of Baghdad. Then at Kut, the British were effectively surrounded by as many as 60,000 Turks. Moreover, local hostile Arab elements energetically joined the Ottoman jihad against the invader.[63]

By mid-January 1916, beleaguered commanding general Charles Townshend wired, "I have twenty-two days food left, but by . . . eating up the horses, we can last out much longer." Townshend ordered the immediate slaughter of 1,100 animals. By February, rations, including horsemeat and mule meat, were halved. Regardless, many Indian troops refused to eat such animals, so their hunger increased more quickly.[64]

Starvation among the troops continued. Hostile Arab merchants in Kut were loath to sell British soldiers any grain. Meanwhile, British officials in India, including Viceroy Hardinge, refused to allow commanders to describe their condition as "besieged." Indeed, reports from Kut were colored rosy, and the situation characterized as a mere momentary setback.[65]

British reinforcements were en route. But they were far off. Meanwhile, the men in Kut were falling from hunger, suffering gastroenteritis from filthy river water, and slowly dying from battle wounds. Then came rains and flood. By the end of February 1916, some 3,000 had died. Disease killed off hundreds more in the following weeks.[66]

Local Turkish commanders offered to let the starving British men retreat for a £1 million bribe, but War Minister Enver Pasha in Istanbul blocked it. London doubled the offer to £2 million. This, too, was refused. Enver Pasha did not want money—he wanted British troops to surrender. Finally, on April 29, 1916, in a humiliating defeat, 13,309 British troops and noncombatant support elements destroyed their weapons and equipment, and surrendered to the Turks.[67]

When the Turks reoccupied Kut, British officers, including the sick and dying among them, were subjected to the most savage violence. The beatings were incessant. Hostile Arabs and Turkish soldiers alike looted their few possessions, boots and blankets, and pummeled those who resisted.[68]

Quickly, the Turks turned to any Arabs in the town of Kut who had cooperated with the British. These people, drawn from the Arab leadership, were tortured, mutilated, and frequently strangled. One British translator from town was seized. The Turks broke his legs, and then hung him upside down until the pain was so unbearable he desired death. That he achieved when in an unguarded moment he hurled himself off a roof.[69]

As for the British soldiers, too emaciated from disease or starvation to walk, they were nonetheless mercilessly marched almost the entire 100 miles from Kut to Baghdad. Hundreds died of thirst, starvation, or beatings. Local Arabs along the way demanded boots or clothing for mere handfuls of dates or black bread. Uniformed Arab soldiers accompanying the march forced the feeble men forward by merciless whipping and assaults with rifle butts.[70]

"We tingled with anger and shame," recalled one key British captain, "at seeing . . . a sad little column of British troops who had marched up from Kut, driven by a wild crowd of Kurdish horsemen who brandished sticks and what looked like whips. The eyes of our men stared from white faces, drawn long with the suffering of a too tardy death. . . . As they dragged one foot after another, some fell, and those with the rearguard came in for blows from cudgels and sticks. I saw one Kurd strike a British soldier who was limping along; he reeled under the blows. . . . Some have been thrashed to death, some killed, and some robbed of their kit and left to be tortured by the Arabs. I have been told by a sergeant that he saw one . . . [British naval officer] killed instantly by a blow on the head from a stirrup iron swung by a Kurdish horseman, [this] for stopping on the road for a few seconds."[71]

The captain's account continued, "Men were dying of cholera and dysentery and often fell out from sheer weakness. . . . A man turned green and foamed at the mouth. His eyes became sightless and the most terrible moans conceivable came from his inner being. . . . They died, one and all, with terrible suddenness. . . . One saw British soldiers in a similar state dying of enteritis with a green ooze issuing from their lips, their mouths fixed open, in and out of which flies walked. . . . Details of other similar cases I won't write about."[72]

The heat only worsened their desperate plight. "Seldom, if ever, have our troops been called upon to campaign in more trying heat," wrote one commander.[73]

In Baghdad, the prisoners were marched through the streets to jeering crowds. From there, they were forced farther north. At Tikrit, where some men were housed, starvation took even more souls. The men "looked ghastly," as one senior officer penned in his diary. He added, "The Arabs used to bring milk and eggs to sell and asked exorbitant prices. Consequently, they [the soldiers] would soon have no money and die of starvation or neglect. . . . Sometimes, when a sick man would crawl out of the hovel . . . Arabs would throw stones and chase him back into the yard."[74]

When the long-marched British soldiers were finally examined by English doctors and the International Red Cross as part of a prisoner exchange, the starved British and Indian captives were reduced to corpselike survivors, their pronounced ribcages hanging pitifully below skulls with eyes. "They were wasted to wreathes of skin hanging upon a bone frame," wrote one of the examiners.[75]

British reinforcements arrived. Kut was retaken. Then the advance to Baghdad was resumed. The British entered Baghdad triumphantly on March 11, 1917, in columns of weary Tommies and turbaned Indians, Lee-Enfield bolt-action rifles on their shoulders, a dust storm swirling around them.[76]

Baghdad was not taken for oil. It was not taken for commerce. It was taken for Kut and the memory of 13,000 captured, many of whom were propelled through a bleak nightmare gauntlet that one commander described as Dante's Inferno.[77] Baghdad was not taken for oil. Baghdad was taken because, while the British could swallow the horror of hundreds of thousands of their best and brightest dying courageously if naively in the slimed trenches and muddied fields of battle, they could not stomach the eye-searing images of their men being beaten, tortured, and slowly starved into shuffling skeletons yearning to go home or die. Baghdad was not taken for oil.

But Basra was.

CHAPTER ELEVEN

The Proclamation

The following proclamation was read aloud in Baghdad by General Stanley Maude on March 18, 1918, one week after occupation by the British. This is the complete proclamation.

TO THE PEOPLE OF BAGHDAD

In the name of my King, and in the name of the peoples over whom he rules, I address you as follows:

Our military operations have as their object the defeat of the enemy and the driving of him from these territories. In order to complete this task, I am charged with absolute and supreme control of all regions in which British troops operate; but our armies do not come into your cities and lands as conquerors or enemies, but as liberators.

Since the days of Hulagu your city and your lands have been subject to the tyranny of strangers, your palaces have fallen into ruins, your gardens have sunk in desolation, and your forefathers and yourselves have groaned in bondage. Your sons have been carried off to wars not of your seeking, your wealth has been stripped from you by unjust men and squandered in distant places.

Since the days of Midhat the Turks have talked of reforms, yet do not the ruins and waste of today testify to the vanity of those promises?

It is the wish not only of my King and his peoples, but it is also the wish of the great Nations with whom he is in alliance, that you should prosper even as in the past, when your lands were fertile, when your ancestors gave to the world literature, science, and art, and when Baghdad city was one of the wonders of the world.

Between your people and the dominions of my King there has been a close bond of interest. For two hundred years have the merchants of Baghdad and Great Britain traded together in mutual profit and friendship. On the other hand the Germans and Turks, who have despoiled you and yours, have for twenty years made Baghdad a centre of power from which to assail the power of the British and the Allies of the British in Persia and Arabia. Therefore the British Government cannot remain indifferent as to what takes place in your country now or in the future, for in duty to the interests of the British people and their Allies the British Government cannot risk that being done in Baghdad again which has been done by the Turks and Germans during the War.

But you, people of Baghdad, whose commercial prosperity and whose safety from oppression and invasion must ever be a matter of closest concern to the British Government are not to understand that it is the wish of the British Government to impose upon you alien institutions. It is the hope of the British Government that the aspirations of your philosophers and writers shall be realised and that once again the people of Baghdad shall flourish, enjoying their wealth and substance under institutions which are in consonance with their sacred laws and their racial ideals. In Hijaz the Arabs have expelled the Turks and Germans who oppressed them, and proclaimed the Sharif Hussein as their King, and his Lordship rules in independence and freedom, and is the Ally of the Nations who are fighting against the power of Turkey and Germany; so, indeed, are the noble Arabs, the Lords of Kuwait, Nejd, and Asir.

Many noble Arabs have perished in the cause of Arab freedom at the hands of those alien rulers, the Turks, who oppressed them. It is the determination of the Government of Great Britain and the Great Powers allied to Great Britain, that these noble Arabs shall not have suffered in vain. It is the hope of the British people and the Nations in alliance with them that the Arab race may rise once more to greatness and renown among the peoples of the Earth and that it shall bind itself together to this end in unity and concord.

O people of Baghdad, remember that for twenty-six generations you have suffered under strange tyrants who have ever endeavored to set one Arab House against another in order that they might profit by your dissensions. This policy is abhorrent to Great Britain and her Allies, for there can be neither peace nor prosperity where there is enmity and misgovernment. Therefore I am commanded to invite you, through your nobles and elders and representatives, to participate in the management of your own civil affairs in collaboration with the political representatives of Great Britain who accompany the British Army, so that you may be united with your kinsmen in North, East, South, and West in realising the aspirations of your Race.[1]

CHAPTER TWELVE

Chaos and Conquest

Chaos is probably too elevated a term to describe Allied wartime policy in the Mideast.

As men died by the thousands each week, a glissando of contradictory public declarations, private letters, formal treaties, sub-rosa agreements, and governmental pledges was enunciated to allies, neutrals, strategic corporations, nationalist organizations in Turkish provinces, and international bodies. The long list of assuring and assured parties included France, England, the United States, competing nationalist Arab factions, the Zionist Organization, and petroleum companies. Nor did any government act monolithically or even cohesively. Foreign offices, war ministries, commercial bureaus, and colonial officers often issued their promises and commitments at cross-purposes, often without checking with—or even informing—their superiors.

Promises du jour were de rigueur. Some British or French official sensed a need, perceived a valuable alliance, or sniffed an opportunity, and out went a signed pledge. Nearly all of these undertakings were completely contradictory. Not a few were disingenuous. Some were simply dishonored as needed. Many spawned their own universes of international conflicts, disputes, and lasting bitterness. Indeed, for the contracting parties of World War I, chaos was a condition to aspire to—a step up from the diplomatic bedlam that ruled.

Several small libraries would be needed to explore the evolving agreements that greatly impacted the British as they occupied Baghdad and Mesopotamia, as well as the Arabs who lived there. But among the most salient was the Sykes-Picot Agreement hammered out between senior diplomats Mark Sykes of Britain, Georges Picot of France, and Russian foreign minister Sergei Sazonov.

Sykes-Picot, negotiated in early 1916, was a secret tripartite collection of letters, complete with colored maps, agreeing to carve up the Mideast after the war. Baghdad and Basra were decreed British spheres of influence, while oil-rich Mosul and Syria would be French, with Russia exercising a privilege over its frontiers with Persia. France was virtually devoid of reliable oil fields. Controlling Kurdish Mosul would one day yield France the petroleum the Great War proved was necessary in a modern world. In return for ceding Mosul, Britain would be assured that her oil and general commerce from Persia, lower Mesopotamia, and the Gulf could transit across French-held Syria without encumbrance. Therefore, the control and extension of the Baghdad Railway into Syria was geographically split between Britain and France, with the French taking over from Mosul east. Sykes-Picot's terms would reward France for the immense losses she was suffering in the war, while preserving British and Russian interests.[1]

Relinquishing the still untested but much coveted oil deposits of Mosul was difficult for the British. But, "it is clear, that we shall have to make up our minds to the inclusion of Mosul in the French sphere," a diplomat in the India Office told the London Foreign Office on January 13, 1916, even as the agreement was being negotiated.[2]

Sykes-Picot was concluded just after the ambiguous McMahon promises to Hussein that would create an Arab national entity, but one that would exclude Mesopotamia. Under Sykes-Picot, that Arab entity would be a mere "confederation" under French and British economic and administrative control, that is, geographically and legally separated colonies but imbued with an amorphous Arab identity. The India Office in London expressed the thinking succinctly in a telegram to Charles Hardinge, the British viceroy of India: "What we want is not a United Arabia: but a weak and disunited Arabia, split up into little principalities so far as possible under our suzerainty— but incapable of coordinated action against us, forming a buffer against the Powers in the West."[3]

As the details unfolded, British diplomat George Buchanan in Petrograd, Russia, cabled Sykes a coded "urgent, private and secret message" warning that French desiderata in Syria and Mosul might incite "suicidal and foolish fanaticism" in the region. But French plans seemed to be moving toward acceptance. "I therefore suggest," stated Buchanan, "that in regard to Arabs, our policy should be let Arabs do what they can for themselves and . . . make such concessions, declarations and arrangements in Mesopotamia with regard to Arab theory of independence and participation in administration. . . . [But] keep actual terms of provisional government from knowledge [of] Arab leaders."[4] Indeed, during the give-and-take of the Sykes-Picot negotiations among the French, British, and Russians, neither the Arab residents of the territories nor their leaders were ever consulted.

Sykes-Picot was formalized by the French and British foreign ministers on May 15, 1916, and almost immediately regretted by Whitehall. Its ink had literally still not dried when oil advocates within the British government initiated a campaign to scrap the agreement. Weeks before, in early April, British government oil official Maurice de Bunsen was asked by the prime minister to establish a "Committee on Asiatic Turkey" to better assess Britain's true interests in the Middle East. The committee saw Mosul's abundance of oil as simply too precious to surrender to France. Just weeks after Sykes-Picot was framed, de Bunsen's report concluded that Turkish Mosul must remain British and that British forces ought to continue their Mesopotamian campaign northward. "Oil again makes it commercially desirable for us," de Bunsen's report concluded, "to carry our control on to Mosul, in the vicinity of which place there are valuable wells, possession of which by another power [France] would be prejudicial to our interests."[5]

The Anglo-Persian Oil Company (APOC) couldn't wait. In fact, although Anglo-Persian still possessed no petroleum concession in Mesopotamia, the company used Britain's occupation of Basra to commence oil exploration, ostensibly under the auspices of the Admiralty. In a confidential dispatch, company chairman Greenway informed the Foreign Office undersecretary, "Our geological staff has carried out extensive reconnaissance over an area 100 miles inland from the Shatt-el Arab River [in the Basra region] . . . which reconnaissance shows that there are possibilities of finding oil." Greenway explained that APOC was "not putting in [a petroleum research] application for the area" in anticipation that his company would "be given the complete oil rights over any portion of the Turkish Empire which may come under British influence."[6] This presumption might have appealed to oil allies in India, but it stunned the Foreign Office, which was mindful of other commitments.

No longer was Anglo-Persian focused solely on the realm of the Tigris and Euphrates, but on any territory awarded to Britain after the war. This new approach could stretch APOC's commercial domain all the way to Istanbul and beyond into eastern Europe. As APOC's jurisdiction expanded, so did India's commercial subcolonization of the Mideast. Unhappy, Foreign Secretary Edward Grey himself insisted Greenway's sudden expanded view be "at once controverted" by oil official de Bunsen. Recalling the fusion agreement of March 1914, which granted Shell 25 percent of the new larger Anglo-Persian entity, another Foreign Office functionary added this caution: "In case there is litigation hereafter, as I am positive there will be if we admit Greenway's claim," Shell would certainly claim it was "unfairly treated by His Majesty's Government if . . . jostled out of that 25 percent."[7]

Nonetheless, Anglo-Persian organized more pressure to keep Mosul out of French hands. The campaign intensified in the first days of April 1916, when the Sykes-Picot bargain was becoming known to inner circles. On April 1, the India Office in London sent a letter reminding the Foreign Office, "It will be borne in mind that His Majesty's Government have supported the claim of Mr. D'Arcy to a concession of all oil deposits in the vilayets [provinces] of Mosul and Baghdad," and questioning whether Anglo-Persian could still exercise its claim under French control.[8]

Other lobbying continued, including APOC playing off British fears that the Germans might seize Mesopotamia's oil fields to reassert the Deutsche Bank's Anatolia Railway claim. On April 3, Greenway sent press clips to the Foreign Office from two German-language publications, industry journal *Petroleum* and the newspaper *Frankfurter*

Zeitung. Both extolled Mesopotamian oil deposits and stressed their importance to Germany.[9]

As Anglo-Persian tried to wedge itself forward as the potentate of Mesopotamia's future oil, one insider worked behind the scenes to frustrate the company's plan. He tried to prevent any obstruction to the accord granting France primacy in Mosul. The spoiler was, of course, Gulbenkian. He had been lying in wait to reclaim what he considered rightfully his. After being expelled from the process by the British in London, Gulbenkian now sought a commercial alliance with the French in Paris.[10]

The French needed oil. Their petroleum industry was in a shambles. Gulbenkian wrote, "Having lived in France for a long time, and in view of my contacts with the French oil groups, I was fully acquainted with all the circumstances in connection with the problem. . . . The French oil groups . . . were nothing else than a monopolistic association of grocers . . . in a pitiful condition in spite of the fact that French refiners had accumulated enormous fortunes by price rigging, and dubious methods, such as bribing the press."[11]

The French government had granted refiners special economic protections and incentives to encourage development of a refinery infrastructure on French soil. But, in fact, there was no actual refining in France, according to Gulbenkian. The oil was purchased already fully refined from American firms and sometimes Royal Dutch Shell. Then, at the port, prior to shipment, French petroleum companies deliberately laced the oil tanks with a "chemical dirt" that could be easily removed. This simple removal process was passed off as genuine "refining" to maintain the charade and continue the flow of French tax exemptions.[12]

But once war was declared, imported refined oil became scarce and the French government learned its refining industry was fundamentally nonexistent. Gulbenkian saw his mission as cracking "the unwholesome, selfish and unpatriotic grip of the French refiners on their country's oil trade . . . [and therefore] increase the trade and influence of the Royal Dutch combine," while all along quietly bolstering Turkish Petroleum Company's fortunes. His motives? Gulbenkian professed that, in fact, "I was prompted by a feeling of sympathy for a country where I had been residing for many years."[13]

Working with French oil industry friends he had cultivated over time, Gulbenkian convinced French officials that France must control Mosul. When it did, Turkish Petroleum would be there to grant them the bounty of Mesopotamian northern oil fields. But while Gulbenkian in Paris was promoting French hegemony over Mosul's oil, French diplomats in London were feeling Britain's immediate change of heart. Even as the main Sykes-Picot letter was being signed on May 15, 1916, Sir Edward Grey asked the French ambassador in London for written assurances that France, when it took over Mosul, would recognize Britain's preexisting commercial rights. These commercial rights referred to the oil concessions gained from Turkish Petroleum Company and Anglo-Persian in the March 19, 1914, fusion agreement. Of course, that agreement had been deemed null and void when war broke out. But if those rights had actually been acquired, even theoretically, Britain wanted to preserve them. By May 17, France provided written assurances that it was "ready to confirm, in the regions which might be attributed to it . . . the various British concessions bearing a date prior to the war." In other words, Britain could still control TPC rights in Mosul if it chose to somehow resurrect the fusion deal.[14]

Gulbenkian was again circumvented. But not for long.

Occupation meant administration. Under the Hague Conventions of 1899 and 1907, an occupying military power was obligated to efficiently and properly administer lands under its control and safeguard the civilian populations. Within a week of overrunning Basra, the British inaugurated a civilian administration. As the British moved north, and when they eventually captured Baghdad, their occupying civil administration was extended into the new territory. Almost overnight, the occupied portion of Mesopotamia became not a national Arab state-in-waiting, not a revived version of Midhat Pasha's constitutional dream, not a prelude to any pan-Arab vision. Mesopotamia became India.[15]

Turkish paper money was banned by proclamation and replaced with Indian rupees, although valuable Turkish gold liras temporarily remained in circulation, especially in the bazaars. The Eastern Bank of

India opened branches in key centers of conquered provinces, sometimes in the very facilities of Deutsche Bank. So many rupees were needed, they were boxed and shipped from Bombay, hot off the mint. When supply for rupees was outpaced by demand, the Anglo-Persian Oil Company was asked to help through its connections at the Imperial Bank of Persia; the company was only too happy to assist. Indian Ottoman postage stamps were retained but overprinted with Indian imprimaturs for use by the troops, and these worked their way into common use. A Revenue Department was opened at Basra to accept taxes, ordinary administrative fees, and routine payments—all in rupees of course. All government funds now wove into a local civil occupation fisc controlled from Calcutta. Financial officials in India were astonished when their efficient replacement of Turkish corruption yielded a £130,000 surplus for 1915.[16]

The former Turkish territories were now increasingly called by their regional name, "Iraq," and this identity slowly came into common usage to usher in a new governmental status. Great Britain controlled the largest Islamic population in the world, some 40 million Moslems in India. Hence, London felt comfortable in morphing Mesopotamia into what was called "an Indian appendage."[17]

The Iraq Occupied Territories Code, replicating the civil and criminal laws of India, was unveiled in August 1915, complete with courts, judges, and magistrates, all from India and under the administration of the Indian political department. Section 8 of the code explicitly declared that the Iraqi territories were the equivalent of "a district . . . of Bombay." Those Indian laws were not translated into either Arabic or Turkish, and it was more than a year before any court business could be conducted in Arabic.[18]

For the tribal areas not accustomed to urbanized law, Britain imported and renamed the Indian Frontier Crimes Regulations that empowered a political officer to convene a tribal *majlis,* or arbitration of elders. The political officer could veto any *majlis* adjudication. In many cases, Iraqi tribal customs, such as token money payments to resolve feud murders and death to women who strayed from arcane Bedouin morality codes, were set aside for British traditions of punishment. Under transplanted British Indian law, murderers were now sentenced to capital execution; women accused of violating desert mores were not.[19]

Indian policemen, headed by E. G. Gregson, a senior officer of the Indian Police Service, were imported to keep order. Several hundred men in uniform patrolled, ran the jails, and superintended night watchmen. They enforced order at government offices, the Basra docks, and Baghdad facilities.[20]

A huge Indian-run bureaucracy was erected. British and Indian health officials assumed the sensitive inspection of Persian and Indian Shiite corpses for burial at Najaf, and they supervised the many pilgrims who visited Shiite shrines. Prostitutes, all 180 of them, while not officially registered, were routinely inspected by the civil medical authorities to reduce venereal disease. Passenger priorities for boatmen and carriage drivers, the sale of liquor, sanitary conditions for horse stables, the treatment of sick dogs, the rental of property, carrying of arms, and all aspects of foodstuffs were regulated by Indian bureaucrats according to an English model.[21]

Reconstruction and development plans abounded to restore the golden era of Mesopotamia and bring its long-neglected provinces into the twentieth century. British economic analysts studied all aspects of Mesopotamian commerce. Trade and traffic were to be expanded throughout the provinces and then connected to the world at large. Plans were outlined to dramatically increase the new Iraq's export of cotton and dates, as well as its imports of the manpower and machinery needed to make Iraq bloom once more.[22]

Extensive irrigation and flood control, what British trade planners called "the scientific control of the rivers," would be constructed to significantly increase food yields. Baghdad's railway chugging north and south would become a strategic commercial as well as military linchpin of this grand national design. Medical facilities, schools, public works, bridges, roads to reach the northern oil regions—so much was needed.[23]

To engineer the transformation, the heavy machines of progress were required: fleets of Ford and Peerless lorries, Caterpillar tractors, mechanized irrigation pumps, building materials, and spare everything. The primitive port at Basra, which often could not even handle conventional steamships, was completely in need of modernization. Within weeks of the 1914 invasion, three river steamers were requisitioned. Later, three dredgers were brought in from India to deepen the Shatt-el-Arab waterway leading to Basra and improve the port area generally. Lucrative and monopolistic contracts were awarded to British steamship and transport lines. Transport itself would be a fabulous economic center.[24]

There was a nation to build. But greater Basra's entire population was estimated at just 80,000. Baghdad's was approximately 230,000, split between Arabs, Jews, Persians, Syrians, and others. Many, perhaps a majority, were still living a tribal or pastoral lifestyle. More manpower was needed to implement the rapid and sweeping infrastructure improvements experts had in mind to support both the occupying army and trade expansion. "All schemes for the agricultural development and commercial exploitation of the country," declared one key trade survey, "are, however, conditioned and limited by the capacity, temperament and character of the inhabitants. The two vilayets of Baghdad and Basra are thinly populated, possessing an average of 9 inhabitants per square mile, which is inadequate."[25]

British eyes turned to India, which possessed an abundance of population and which could send in tens of thousands of laborers, who themselves would constitute a viable and economy-stimulating population in need of goods and service. "Stress must be laid upon the organic connection which already exists between Mesopotamia and India," the key trade survey concluded.[26]

Not a few who favored an industrial revolution for Iraq envisioned a new, revitalized nation that would be situated at the fulcrum of east-west trade and also to a large extent converted to an extension of India. Indeed, Sir William Willcocks, the man who a few years earlier designed the original Mesopotamian irrigation scheme for the Turkish government, admitted his ultimate plan was systematic repopulation. Willcocks wrote: "The Euphrates-Tigris delta will be reclaimed and settled by millions of natives of India, who will make it again the Garden of the East." Under this vision, Arabs would become a fringe minority in the provinces, subsumed by the biggest regional migration since the Arab conquest of Mesopotamian Eurasians more than 12 centuries before. These notions did not escape the local population. Indeed, during these years, the very concept of railroads and passenger shipping lines on both sides of the Atlantic was associated with mass international migration and settlement campaigns. From time to time, thousands in the provinces angrily rallied at their mosques to condemn the latest rumored British shipping and irrigation plans as "sinister intentions" to transfer in masses of Indian workers, some said 10,000 at a time, thus transmogrifying the nation.[27]

Hence, as the British occupation expanded the Arabs of Iraq, whom callous Ottoman Turkification had embittered, now wondered how they would resist British Indianization. To the Arabs, the threat to their identity was the same. Only the accents and garments differed.

A centerpiece of the new Mesopotamian industrial dream was petroleum. As the British military maneuvered, attacked, and fortified their positions from Basra to Baghdad, so did the combative oilmen in London.

As the Great War staggered forward, with its heavy tolls and oppressive requirements for fuel, the British government tried to balance its future oil partnerships to ensure both a British character and a guaranteed supply. Anglo-Persian continually tried to shim itself into prominence as the one company for both needs.

But Anglo-Persian simply lacked the ability to supply with certainty all the nation's needs—and the government knew it. Moreover, quality and grade issues were coming to the fore. Persian oil was constantly being denigrated in naval reports for its viscosity, which caused it to thicken at low temperatures. British officials now eyed oil fields as far-flung as Java, Mexico, Venezuela, and Romania. That meant once again scrutinizing Shell, the only company outside America already operating in all those realms. The answer seemed to be an elaborate effort, crafted over many months, to remake Shell as completely British in character, if not British in control, and somehow fuse it into Anglo-Persian. By this scenario, Shell would plunge into Mesopotamia under British aegis and finally overrun Anglo-Persian, again under British aegis.[28]

"The Royal Dutch Shell would probably consider no sacrifices too great to bring about this fusion," wrote a Treasury department official, and thereby "give them all that they have been aiming at for years past." Such a government sanction fusion would give Shell control of nearly all major oil outside the significant American and eastern European deposits and deliver much more of the growing British market, including the Royal Navy. Those "sacrifices" by Royal Dutch Shell would entail allowing the minority British side of the combine—that is, Shell—to predominate as the majority, ensuring that British subjects would function as board directors, and agreeing to grant the United Kingdom preference over its supplies.[29]

However, when Anglo-Persian realized that British officials were favoring a move toward Royal Dutch Shell, with its well-entrenched worldwide distribution system, a network that extended right across Great Britain, APOC rushed to compete. More than being a mere driller, refiner, and supplier, APOC desperately needed to be a wellhead-to-consumer oil company like Shell or Standard Oil. Such a network would take years to construct.

So Anglo-Persian purchased an existing network. The Europaische Petroleum Union (EPU) was an amalgam of continental oil distribution arms, mainly controlled by German concerns. EPU owned an operating subsidiary in Britain. This subsidiary controlled both an international oil shipping division, the Petroleum Steamship Company, and a domestic consumer sales agency, the Homelight Oil Company. Formed in London in 1906, the EPU subsidiary was profitable, reporting a 14 percent dividend in 1914. It was ripe for a takeover. The EPU subsidiary's name was British Petroleum Company, with its first name descriptive only of its operating territory, not its true ownership, which was mainly German.[30]

When World War I erupted in 1914, the British authorities seized British Petroleum Company as "enemy property." During 1915 and 1916, APOC chairman Greenway petitioned the custodian of enemy property to purchase those seized—and hence government-controlled—oil company assets. The war was not over, the seized subsidiary's disposition was not resolved, but the petition was nonetheless granted. Anglo-Persian was still short of the funds needed for any acquisition. But in late 1917, the £2.7 million "sale" was finalized by virtue of a cashless, loanless "self-financing" miracle. Payments would be made to the custodian over five years, commencing in 1918, which could easily be generated by expected revenues. The purchasing balance sheets made clear in an explanatory note: "The Anglo-Persian Company will have no difficulty in meeting the above annual payments, without raising fresh capital, as

they will be reserving [repayment funds] out of profits each year."
Indeed, both the income and transferred depreciation from British
Petroleum and its two divisions immediately began generating hun-
dreds of thousands of pounds annually to Anglo-Persian. Decades
later, Anglo-Persian Oil Company would change its name to British
Petroleum.[31]

Anglo-Persian continued to press ahead as though it actually
owned the oil rights in Mesopotamia. Even after being told by Foreign Secretary Grey that APOC did not, the company was fond of
sending confidential and carefully misleading memoranda to government and financial officials, implying that it did. For example, one
confidential memo circulated to the Treasury asserted, "The D'Arcy
Exploration Company holds a prior claim to the concession for the
petroliferous deposits in the vilayets of Baghdad, Mosul and Basra."
That assertion, the memo stated, was based on the defunct fusion deal
of March 19, 1914. APOC felt free to honor and dishonor the March
19, 1914, agreement as the need arose—always in the name of the
British government. For instance, in one case, after citing the fusion
deal, an APOC official hastened to add, "Since the outbreak of hostilities we have, at the request of the Foreign Office, taken no steps
to complete the arrangements . . . though we have been frequently
pressed to do so by Mr. Gulbenkian."[32]

In mid-1918, when the British army in Mesopotamia needed more
oil faster, Anglo-Persian was temporarily authorized to drill at Hit,
south of Baghdad, and other locations along the Euphrates. This was
an emergency war measure. The Foreign Office concurred, but specified that APOC could function only as a subcontractor to the military,
not as an independent commercial concern, this so "such action is not
subsequently advanced by them as an additional ground for claiming
preferential treatment of their interests in Mesopotamia."[33]

Anglo-Persian continued to pummel the Treasury with vexatious
entreaties to forgo any further interest in Shell and quickly grant the
company a monopoly. One such memo by Greenway, dated August 2,
1918, warned that forming a partnership with Royal Dutch Shell
would mean "the government's investment [in APOC] . . . will be
entirely lost and the Empire [will] again be at the mercy of monopo-
lists for its whole requirements of Petroleum products!"[34]

Continuing to type, but now in all capitals with generous use of
triple exclamation marks and underlining, Greenway added: "COL-

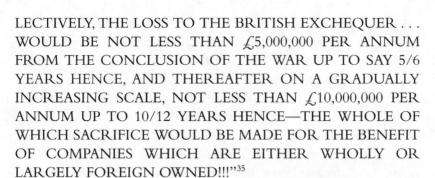
LECTIVELY, THE LOSS TO THE BRITISH EXCHEQUER . . . WOULD BE NOT LESS THAN £5,000,000 PER ANNUM FROM THE CONCLUSION OF THE WAR UP TO SAY 5/6 YEARS HENCE, AND THEREAFTER ON A GRADUALLY INCREASING SCALE, NOT LESS THAN £10,000,000 PER ANNUM UP TO 10/12 YEARS HENCE—THE WHOLE OF WHICH SACRIFICE WOULD BE MADE FOR THE BENEFIT OF COMPANIES WHICH ARE EITHER WHOLLY OR LARGELY FOREIGN OWNED!!!"[35]

In the meantime, key analysts within the military and Foreign Office continued to sound the alarm throughout the summer of 1918 that abundant oil was now a must for the United Kingdom. A key paper compiled by Admiral Slade, one of the government's Anglo-Persian board members, put it bluntly: "It is no exaggeration to say that our life as an empire is largely dependent upon our ability to maintain the control of bunker fuel." After examining oil resources worldwide, from Appalachia to Galicia, Slade stated that the United States would soon consume all the oil produced in America and Mexico, and, since the world was industrializing, the options elsewhere were meager. But, he emphasized, "in Persia and Mesopotamia lie the largest undeveloped resources at present known in the world . . . more than the whole of the Romanian and Galician fields put together."[36]

Slade's conclusion, backed by maps, tables, and studies: "The Power that controls the oil lands of Persia and Mesopotamia will control the source of supply of the majority of the liquid fuel of the future."[37]

Slade's conclusions were enthusiastically endorsed. One secret memo to the War Cabinet from the chief of the Air Staff echoed Slade's points "with all possible emphasis." The memo insisted, "It is essential . . . to monopolize all possible supplies of petroleum" in Mesopotamia and Persia. Another secret memo, this one from the Cabinet Secretariat to the Admiralty, used Slade's memo and maps to assert "the retention of the oil-bearing regions in Mesopotamia and Persia in British hands . . . would appear to be a first-class British war aim."[38]

By the fall of 1918, the exhausted armies of Europe and the Ottoman Empire were desperate to end their seemingly senseless struggle. In early October, a broken Turkey began unraveling. The cabinet resigned, leaving the empire in the hands of caretakers eager to end the war. By mid-October, British commander Charles Townshend, previously taken prisoner at Kut, was summoned to Constantinople to arrange a cessation of hostilities. At the Sublime Porte, Townshend met privately with Field Marshal and Prime Minister Izzet Pasha in one of those solemn, dignified moments when enemy generals are weary enough to admit they have killed enough. Tears welling up in his eyes, the defeated Izzet Pasha conceded his battered country was demoralized and unable to continue. "You are willing to help us?" he asked Townshend. The former prisoner, who had been well treated during captivity, replied, "with all my heart."[39]

On October 30, 1918, the Sick Man of Europe finally died. Aboard a ship at the port of Mudros in the Aegean Sea, Turkey surrendered and agreed to an armistice. Under its terms, all hostilities were to cease at noon the next day. By dawn, October 31, a riverbank of white flags began furling across Turkish entrenchments along the Tigris. The British march north was halted in place 40 miles from Mosul. But from Baghdad, the dream of a new British Iraq, enriched by the oil fields of Mosul, was too much to resist. A note marked "Very Secret—Important," sent just weeks earlier by a cabinet officer to Prime Minister Asquith, was typical in urging, "There may be reasons other than purely military for pushing on in Mesopotamia where the British have an enormous preponderance of force. Would it not be an advantage, before the end of the war, to secure the valuable oil wells in Mesopotamia?"[40]

Civil Administrator Arnold Wilson in Baghdad had regularly nagged Whitehall "as to the desirability of extending the scope of our war aims to the Mosul vilayet." Possession is nine-tenths of the law. "Whether it was ultimately to be in the French or the British 'sphere of interest' [under the Sykes-Picot Agreement]," recalled Wilson, "it was essential that it [Mosul] should be occupied by British troops before or from the moment that hostilities ceased. . . . I contended vehemently that a bird in the military hand was worth many in the thorny thickets of diplomacy, and that in dealing with Turkey, a valid post-war title could be obtained by the Allies only by securing possession."[41]

The war with Germany continued in Europe and elsewhere, but for Turkey it was over on October 31, 1918. Clause 16 of the armistice specified the surrender of all Turkish garrisons in "Syria and Meso-potamia." Civil Administrator Wilson wrote, "From our local point of view, everything turned on the meaning of the word *Mesopotamia,* which was not in current official or diplomatic use in Turkey. Was it open to us, under the Armistice, to regard Mosul . . . as forming part of Mesopotamia?" Wilson preferred it both ways: Mosul was not in Mesopotamia for purposes of seizing it, but it was in Mesopotamia for purposes of mandatory surrender.[42]

Within 48 hours of the October 31 effective date of the armistice at Mudros, Mesopotamian commander in chief William Marshall gave the order to take Mosul—cease-fire or no cease-fire. Only 1,650 outnumbered Turkish riflemen and a battery of 32 artillery pieces defended the city. General Marshall instructed the Ottoman com-mander to evacuate the town, and indeed the entire Mosul province, or be vanquished. The commander objected that moving on Mosul violated the cease-fire.[43]

Marshall refused to wait for clarification from England. Quoting Clause 7 of the armistice, Marshall directed, " 'Allies have the right to occupy any strategic points' and War Office have ordered the occupa-tion of Mosul." The full Clause 7 of course read: "The Allies to have the right to occupy any strategic points in the event of a situation aris-ing which threatens the security of the Allies." It was intended for exigent circumstances. Haggard Turkish troops at Mosul were observ-ing the cease-fire and no longer threatening British troops.[44]

For several days the two sides bickered while waiting for instruc-tions to filter back. Finally, on November 7, Marshall, willing to wait no longer, offered the local Turkish commander an ultimatum. The besieged Turks reluctantly left Mosul. The British marched in. Their occupation of Mesopotamia was now complete and included the three provinces, first Basra, then Baghdad, and now Mosul. The third province, Mosul, was home to approximately 800,000 persons, about 20 percent Arab, but more than 60 percent Kurd, with the remaining fifth split between Jews, Christians, Turks, and mystic Yazidis. An uneasy new national outline had been cobbled together that was mainly Kurdish in the north, Sunni in the midsection, and Shiite in the south.[45]

"Thanks to General Marshall," recalled Wilson, "we had estab-lished de facto, the principle that the Mosul vilayet is part of 'Iraq,' to use the geographical expression . . . and whether for the woe or weal of the inhabitants, it is too soon to say." He added that had General Marshall waited just 24 hours for the restraining instructions from London to arrive, history would be otherwise. But, Wilson continued, Marshall did not wait, and so "laid the foundation stone of the future State of Iraq."[46]

A few days later, at the eleventh hour of the eleventh day of the eleventh month, all the guns fell silent. The Germans surrendered as well. The shooting stopped. The shouting would now begin.

CHAPTER THIRTEEN

The Undeclared Country

Like most everything else in Mesopotamia, the legality of Britain's rights to Mosul and its oil fields was fuzzy and disputed. As 1918 concluded, the land inhabited by the diverse people of Mosul, nominally governed under the sovereignty of the Turks, had been promised to the French by London officials, who did not own it, and occupied mainly by a British India, which had only recently seized it. British forces were certainly the occupiers under international law, except they had occupied under a bruised—many said *violated*—proviso of the armistice. Not a few in the international community demanded an immediate withdrawal and reinstatement of the status quo ante of Turkish authority.[1]

Moreover, the ongoing scramble to control all three provinces of Mesopotamia continued to rivet the attention of France, England, and British India long before any international peace conference had even decided the ultimate disposition of the Turkish Middle East. "I must confess . . . we are rather in the position of the hunters who divided up the skin of the bear before they had killed it," quipped Brigadier General George Macdonough, even as the Sykes-Picot Agreement was being negotiated in early January 1916, nearly three years before the Turkish surrender.[2]

Nonannexation was a guiding principle of the Allies. So even though possession was nine-tenths of the law, true sovereignty over all of Mesopotamia would be decided at the 1919 Versailles Peace Conference in Paris. Strongly influencing that process would be several principles from the famous Fourteen Points enunciated in 1918 by President Woodrow Wilson after America joined the war.

> *Point Five.* "A free, open-minded, and absolutely impartial adjustment of all colonial claims, based upon a strict observance of the principle that, in determining all such questions of sovereignty, the interests of the populations concerned must have equal weight with the equitable claims of the government whose title is to be determined."[3] Translation: self-determination.
>
> *Point Twelve.* "The Turkish portion of the present Ottoman Empire should be assured a secure sovereignty, but the other nationalities which are now under Turkish rule should be assured an undoubted security of life and an absolutely unmolested opportunity of autonomous development."[4] Translation: self-determination.

Self-determination. Misguided as it was, antidemocratic as it was, the reformist compulsion to grant remedial self-determination to long-exploited nationalist movements became astral among the postwar mapmakers. But who was entitled to self-determination, and how would it be implemented? Self-determination could preferentially enfranchise one identified people over another within a region along a variety of criteria: ethnicity, religion, a common language, geographic continuity, all of it, or just some of it. The result at Paris was a patchwork of impassioned, often competing, national claims: Kurds, Armenians, Jews, and Arabs, among others, and not infrequently overlapping traditional territorial boundaries.[5] In the final analysis, the anointed legitimacy of any self-determination movement was determined not in the eyes of the beholder, but in the interest of the bestower.

Nonetheless, the provinces of Mesopotamia, by any measure, were clearly a candidate for self-determination and nationhood. The Allies understood that. But not all among the Allies wanted to admit it. Britain's numerous official agencies remained sharply divided over Mesopotamia's future. Should the new Iraq be an Indian appendage, a British protectorate, or an independent Arab nation led by Faisal, son of Hussein, or perhaps some other potentate?

Many senior ranks in the Foreign Office were steeled by an over-riding commitment to Woodrow Wilson's principles. However, not a few were still hypnotized by centuries of imperialist traditions. Adding to the debate were major personalities in the Admiralty, the War Office, and the India Office, as well as a maelstrom of voices in Parliament, the Board of Trade, and the British media.

But the life-and-breath decisions and indeed the map marks that ruled British Mesopotamia on the ground were, in fact, not decided in London, Bombay, or Paris. Those decisions were made in Baghdad by one man, waiting for no one and determined to wring history between his own two hands. That man was acting Civil Commissioner Arnold Wilson, brought in from his post in Persia to manage civilian affairs in Mesopotamia. An experienced Near East technocrat and diplomat, Wilson had just finished a stint on the Turco-Persian Frontier Commission and was in large measure responsible for transferring the oil fields of Persia into Turkish Mosul in 1913. He ensured that Anglo-Persian's oil concession transferred right along with the land, thus giving the company a gray zone of exploitation in Mesopotamia. Known for his bad manners and good organizational skills, Wilson openly proclaimed himself a "rank imperialist" and freely admitted "a strong personal leaning to radicalism."[6]

In fact, no sooner had Britain taken Basra in November 1914 than Wilson fired off a memo to his political officer proposing the repopulation of Mesopotamia with Indians for the good of imperial Britain. "I should like to see it announced," wrote Wilson, "that Mesopotamia was to be annexed to India as a colony for India and Indians, that the government of India would administer it, and gradually bring under cultivation its vast unpopulated desert plains, peopling them with martial races from the Punjab."[7]

Wilson subscribed to the wisdom of his friend and fellow theorist Arthur Hirtzel, head of the India Office political department, who at the advent of the drive to Baghdad quipped that Arabs were "no more capable of administering severally or collectively than the Red Indians [of America]." In Mesopotamia, Wilson stayed true to his self-image and his doctrine, creating a tinderbox.[8]

In theory, Britain had invaded to help the Arabs achieve national expression. In that vein, the Foreign Office regularly demanded local Arabs be employed to run their own affairs and create the infrastructure of their country's rehabilitation. For example, just days after capturing Baghdad, the War Cabinet telegraphed instructions to allow preexisting laws and customs to remain in place with subtle but de facto protectorate status afforded by England—not India. But Wilson launched a personal bureaucratic crusade to do the opposite, importing and imposing Indian law, Indian workers, Indian institutions, and broad strata of Indian officials.[9]

Wilson also abolished the elected municipal councils that even the Ottomans had permitted, replacing them with appointed Indian political officers. The provincial identities and ethnic fabrics of Mosul, Baghdad, and Basra were profoundly different, and the prevailing instruction by the Foreign Office was to administer Baghdad and Basra separately and to maintain only a defensive military presence in Mosul. But Wilson decided on his own to unify the three into an administrative whole. He even issued passports to cover all inhabitants in Mesopotamia who dwelled from the Persian Gulf north to the foothills of Kurdistan. By governing the three provinces—from Mosul to Basra—from Baghdad, Wilson in essence created a future Iraq by personal fiat.[10]

As an occupying power, Great Britain declared it had come to liberate Mesopotamia from the Turks. "Our armies do not come into your cities and lands as conquerors or enemies, but as liberators," proclaimed the generals upon entering Baghdad. Instead, Great Britain suddenly found itself almost at war with the local population. Once again, Wilson was the central character, wielding oppressive civil regulations. Under Wilson's direction, families were routinely evicted and their homes requisitioned by occupying forces and administrators, with the token rent often less than satisfying. Piped water was restricted to the burgeoning administrative and military sectors, depriving even established merchants of Basra and Baghdad of their established basics. Large numbers of ordinary residents were dragooned as minimally paid compulsory laborers for British work projects, often pulling them away from fields, flocks, or shops. Freedom of movement was greatly curtailed, purportedly to preempt Turkish spies, but this practice continued long after the Ottoman threat had been purged. The local population bitterly resented these intrusive measures, which redefined their very way of daily life.[11]

In addition, Wilson controlled the movement of all food. Some foodstuffs could not be sold unless the army's needs were filled first. More important, in some cases, he decided who could eat and who would starve. Those among the nomadic tribes who cooperated with the British were fed. Those who did not were blockaded. By this selective method, Wilson declared, he "was feeding 100,000 Bedouin," while he could "prevent hostile tribes from obtaining more than a modicum of subsistence." Recalling his activities in 1918, Wilson wrote, "The shortage of foodstuffs was so great in Iraq that without our assistance most of these [tribesmen] must have died of starvation," In justification, he wrote, "If the migrants [Bedouin nomads fleeing across borders in the wake of war movements] did not give us any material military assistance, they were at least giving none to our opponents."[12]

The British found numerous sheikhs willing to be co-opted to prop up their unpopular occupation. They were empowered to collect taxes in their area and to settle disputes with the force of law, not according to tribal traditions but based on an imported Indian code, which was itself adapted from English legal precepts. During the 12 months spanning 1916 and 1917, for instance, the local British political officer in the Suq district, H. R. P. Dickson, found one sheikh willing to be elevated in each of the 22 Suq tribes. However, in many cases, the newly elevated sheikh was not the traditional ancestral chief. Hence, the tribal hierarchies themselves, inculcated over centuries, were rewritten by Wilson's policy.[13]

Petty abuses and high-handedness by Wilson's new strongmen were common. Both the populace and the British openly considered these new boss sheikhs to be little more than stooges. One prominent reform-minded British official of the Indian government who later joined the Baghdad administration readily explained in 1916, "Once a sheik has to rely on [the] government for support, he has lost the sympathy of his tribesmen." Refeudalizing Mesopotamia effectively restored the corrupt ways of the sultan that had prevailed prior to the

Young Turk reforms. But by pointing to these new faces, the occupation could count upon approbation on cue in any controversy.[14]

Only the cash influx from the British rentals, purchases, wages, and political subsidies, plus strict noninterference with religious activities, softened the blow of the occupation. But at times, when the power of the purse retreated, seething outrage erupted. For example, on January 28, 1918, Captain W. M. Marshall was installed as the new governor of Najaf. During preceding months, the city had been mutinous. British patrols had been shot at, an airplane was almost downed by gunfire, and government offices were attacked. Intent on maintaining order, Capt. Marshall ordered all stipends and financial supports for local sheikhs terminated, demanded all rifles be turned in at once, and fired the entire Najaf police force, replacing them with hand-selected officers from Kut.[15]

Local agitators, deprived of emoluments to ease the pain of occupation, immediately decided to eliminate Capt. Marshall. On March 19, timed with the Moslem Nawruz festivities, assassins dressed as policemen entered Marshall's home and killed him. Punjabi guards were summoned to hunt down the assailants, but insurgents fought them as well. When the central killers could not be found, the British blockaded Shiite Najaf—nothing in, nothing out. Wilson and the military demanded the surrender of the murderers, plus a fine of 50,000 rupees, plus 1,000 rifles, plus deportation to India of 100 prisoners. Until those conditions were satisfied, Wilson ruled, the residents would suffer a total "food-and-water supply cut off." Any number of Shiite intermediaries from both Persia and Mesopotamia entreated Wilson's Baghdad compound offering "an amicable settlement" to help their holy city. Perhaps just the women and children could be evacuated, they pleaded.[16]

Wilson would not yield. He wanted the killers—or everyone could just starve. With food and water dwindling, many local sheikhs and ordinary citizens joined the rebellion, or strongly considered it, out of a sheer survival instinct. Wilson remained impervious to telegrams from London and Calcutta seeking moderation. After weeks of siege, Najafi food supplies held, but the water was almost gone—this approaching a summer that would reach 112 degrees. Finally, by May 4, 1918, quarter by quarter, the town had been starved into submission. Najaf surrendered the culprits.[17]

A British military tribunal at Kufa speedily convicted 11 men of murder, sentencing them to death. Nine more were sentenced to jail time for complicity. Islamic notables appealed to Wilson not to execute all the ringleaders, only the two men who actually committed the murder. Wilson refused any clemency on these—or any other— grounds. On May 25, 1918, just a few weeks after Najaf's submission, all 11 were publicly hanged in Kufa. Just hours after the execution, Wilson presumed validation when he received an invitation to a feast at the home of the caretaker of one of Najaf's shrines.[18]

In recalling the episode, Wilson wrote these words: "Najaf has never again been a source of serious anxiety to the government of the country."[19]

A chorus of hopefuls claimed Iraq's still undrilled oil. The three-way tug-of-war between Shell, Anglo-Persian, and Turkish Petroleum was itself subject to pushes and pulls by the two European Allied victors: Great Britain and France. The future oil industry of the future Iraq became the pivot among the victors competing for territorial control of the ancient Mesopotamian provinces. Once the shooting stopped, the commercial contenders and their governmental sponsors generated a long cascade of overlapping and contradictory agreements, assertions, and revocations, completely consistent with the standard of confusion that characterized everything about the promise of Mesopotamia's oil.

Within a week of the war's end on November 11, 1918, French petroleum plenipotentiary, Senator Henri Bérenger, arrived in London to meet with his counterpart, Walter Long, Britain's secretary of state for colonies and newly appointed head of the evolving committee that became known as "the Petroleum Executive." France wanted Mosul and its oil. Britain also wanted Mosul and its oil. On December 1, the British and French heads of state, Prime Minister David Lloyd George and President Georges Clemenceau met in London to discuss a broad range of issues, including petroleum. In a secret exchange that even their senior ministers did not fully understand, the two leaders adopted a hazy quid pro quo. France would relinquish its claim on Mosul on condition it retained all of Syria as promised in the Sykes-Picot Agreement. Just one other thing: France wanted a significant share in Mosul's oil. Britain agreed.[20]

Quickly, French and British negotiators began making progress on a deal. The men turned once again to Turkish Petroleum and its 25 percent ownership by Deutsche Bank, based on the Baghdad Railway's original 1898 oil concession. Capturing Deutsche Bank's stock seemed the soundest legal tactic to securing Mesopotamian oil rights. But who owned TPC's acquired Deutsche Bank concession? A nervous Anglo-Persian, apprised of renewed interest in TPC, claimed APOC did. On November 12, 1918, in a four-page brief, APOC argued that it had never finalized its half ownership in TPC afforded by the 1914 fusion agreement solely because of the war and due to explicit restraining instructions from the Foreign Office. Underlining words for emphasis in its memo, as was its custom, APOC executives pleaded for a status quo ante wherein their 50 percent ownership of TPC would be finally consummated or, in the alternative, a full, internationally binding cancellation of any Baghdad Railway rights by a formal Allied decision at the coming Paris Peace Conference.[21]

Possession is nine-tenths of the law. British government petroleum officials, aware of the coming clash over Deutsche Bank's TPC ownership, decided to preempt. In early December 1918, they began seizing Deutsche Bank's shares as enemy property, "before the Peace Conference, not only on account of the French claims . . . but in order to obviate any possibility, however remote, of the share reverting to Germany." Moreover, a Treasury official wrote on December 13, by seizing the ownership for itself, the British government ensured the shares would not "be sold to either of the rival oil groups, since this would . . . complicate the [upcoming] delicate negotiations."[22]

Treasury convinced Sir Lancelot Smith to function as what officials termed in quotes "a neutral purchaser." Smith would be asked to expend only £21,000 of his own money to acquire the liquidated Deutsche Bank holding in TPC, and even that expenditure might be backed up by a parliamentary appropriation. Officials were at first hesitant about using public money for what was ostensibly a private sell-off, but they were convinced that "the rights to oil mining in Mesopotamia remains, and will undoubtedly be, a very burning one in our negotiations with the French."[23]

Indeed, the British wanted to seize control of German ownership in TPC before the French did at the Paris Peace Conference. "The existence of shares in the Turkish Petroleum Company," explained the late December 1918 Treasury memo, "which belong to an enemy, will give the French an opportunity of putting in a claim to such a share, and we shall be in a far stronger position to resist it if in fact these enemy-owned shares have been disposed of." The strategy was to dispose of the shares through the contrived sale to "neutral purchaser" Lancelot Smith. Smith, however, was in fact a Board of Trade representative sitting on one of the interministerial oil committees. Smith would own the shares in name as a private individual, but would in fact function as a government nominee under government control.[24]

While Treasury officials were making arrangements to sell off Deutsche Bank's 25 percent of TPC to their straw man, other British and French petroleum negotiators, by mid-December, were already agreeing to sell Deutsche Bank's ownership to a Shell subsidiary, which would then discreetly transfer the stock to the French. Indeed, shortly thereafter, a rival Anglo-French agreement to sell Deutsche Bank's ownership to Shell was confirmed in a letter by the French chargé d'affaires in London to the British foreign secretary.[25] But as 1919 opened for business, the jockeying only intensified.

Paris, in January 1919, became a monumental turning point in the modern history of the world. The Paris Peace Conference brought together President Woodrow Wilson, Prime Minister David Lloyd George, and President Georges Clemenceau, with their great delegations in tow and their lofty agendas in mind. As the peacemakers bickered, postured, and rewrote maps and ethnic destinies, righted wrongs and created new ones, some empires were dismantled and some bolstered, new nations were created and old ones reincarnated. Millions was the unit of measure: millions dead, millions wounded, millions demobilized, millions massacred, millions in war cost, millions in reparations. But just behind the proprietors of peace were the captains of commerce who spoke of their own millions.

By the end of January, Clemenceau remarked, "The petroleum question seems to be one of the most important economic questions at the Peace Conference." He added, "It crucially affects the future of France's national defense and her general prosperity."[26]

Ironically, even at the Paris Peace Conference, as the world was being reshaped with pens, the legal gateway to Iraqi oil remained the Turkish Petroleum Company and Deutsche Bank's 25 percent ownership in it. The two mutually exclusive international efforts to acquire that ownership raced ahead. While one Anglo-French team of negotiators, led by Lord Long for England and Senator Bérenger for France, planned to transfer the shares to France, either directly or through Shell, the British Treasury was creating a fait accompli by preemptively seizing the company through a "sale" to their "neutral purchaser."[27]

Numerous plans and permutations unfolded between Long and Bérenger at Paris. For example, on February 3, 1919, British delegates bandied about the notion of a 20 percent interest in Turkish Petroleum in exchange for a reciprocal share in French Algerian oil, as well as transit guarantees for the planned British pipeline across Syria. That was not enough. On February 12, President Clemenceau interceded, writing Prime Minister Lloyd George to insist on "strict equality in the exploitation of petroleum in Mesopotamia," adding that London and Paris must not only enjoy parity as military victors, but also as commercial victors. "An agreement must be clearly manifested," wrote Clemenceau, "in the industrial as well as in other spheres."[28]

But so many legal vagaries attached to every aspect of the sultan's original concessions, the fusion agreement of March 19, 1914, and Turkish Petroleum Company itself. Negotiators decided that they would submit any final deal to Britain's attorney general for review. They suggested that any legally doubtful clauses could be "righted" by a subsequent friendly treaty with whatever national or administrative national entity arose in Iraq. Moreover, an idea was floated to grant the national governmental authority an unspecified interest in the oil company, perhaps as much as 20 percent. This would certainly be an incentive for any Iraqi national authority. Even still, there was no assertion whether this minority holding would be a mere token voting presence or whether it would include any genuine beneficial rights or decision-making power. Moreover, it was assumed Britain would control any such local government. Upping the ante, negotiators tacked on promises for France to approve not one but two British oil pipelines to the Mediterranean, one through Syria and a second via Haifa, in Palestine, which Britain also hoped to administer.[29]

Even as Long and Bérenger pondered the geographic and economic variables, the Foreign Office wondered just how real were
these far-reaching discussions about giving France a share of TPC. In
mid-March 1919, Mallet of the Foreign Office cautioned that talks
could continue as wholly preliminary, as long as British representatives "made it clear to M. Bérenger that we were ready to admit
French participation in the Turkish Petroleum Company" but that
nothing could be decided "until the ultimate nature of the territorial
settlement is more clearly indicated."[30]

The more detailed and advanced the conversations between Long
and Bérenger became, the more they seemed to rile the Foreign
Office, which had to deal with all the Allies about territorial matters.
In doing so, the Foreign Office would have to embrace Woodrow
Wilson's insistence on self-determined rights. This would include the
local population's right to control its own national economic
resources. At one point, Foreign Secretary George Curzon dismis-
sively remarked that TPC was being traded for "a promise of facilities
for two pipelines which we may never be in a position to construct
through a district in which the French may never be in a position to
afford us the facilities promised."[31]

But the French were tenacious. What's more, they seemed to have
a complete understanding of the ins and outs of Turkish Petroleum
and the value of Mesopotamian oil fields. Who was advising the
French? Lead French oil representative Senator Bérenger, the minister of industrial production, key personalities in the Ministry of
Finance, and the leading magnates of French oil companies all maintained a close friendship with one man. It was, of course, Gulbenkian.[32] By coaxing France into a takeover of TPC, he could
reassert from Paris the 5 percent banished in London.

Working with the French during the Paris negotiations "has been
very tedious work," bragged Gulbenkian, filled with "intrigues and
jealousies." Not a few in the French government, including the
French chargé d'affaires in London, distrusted Gulbenkian. But in the
end, key French oil diplomats concluded that his involvement was
merely to help France, where Gulbenkian had lived out the war. During those war years, Gulbenkian had been active in financing French
oil deals to compensate for the country's petroleum deficiencies. Gulbenkian recalled that despite political alarums, one key delegate "was

so convinced of my genuine collaboration that, although his hand was writing and signing the documents, it was in fact, my hand that guided his."[33]

But while Gulbenkian pushed the French forward, the British were pulling back on those confiscated Deutsche Bank shares. On February 12, 1919, the custodian of enemy property petitioned the Chancery Division of the High Court to approve selling the precious enemy property to Lancelot Smith—thus the shares would no longer exist as unclaimed enemy property. The court action set off a furious barrage of motions, arguments, and hearings from all parties, central and peripheral—including affidavits by Deterding and Gulbenkian themselves. All this occurred concomitant with the delicate negotiations in Paris.[34]

Meanwhile, Royal Dutch Shell saw its own fortunes faltering before the threats of a government takeover of TPC and from continued pressure plays by quasi-governmental Anglo-Persian. Royal Dutch Shell finally decided it was time to become a "British company" that would enjoy the benefits of official governmental favor and patronage. This corporate metamorphosis would not produce a company "controlled" by the British government, which was impossible due to its Dutch majority, but one controlled by British personalities and nominees who in turn could be controlled by British policies and preferences.[35]

On March 6 and 7, 1919, Shell and British executives finally hammered out a complex eight-point protocol referred to as "Heads of Agreement of the Royal Dutch Shell and British Government." The document focused on Royal Dutch Shell's main British subsidiary, a company known as Anglo-Saxon Petroleum. For years, Anglo-Saxon Petroleum had operated profitably within the empire and indeed was Royal Dutch Shell's official arm in its involvement with Turkish Petroleum Company. Under the agreement, "His Majesty's Government will be advised to use their best endeavors to secure, either by rearrangement of the capital in the Turkish Petroleum Company, or otherwise, that the Royal Dutch Shell by the medium of the Anglo-Saxon Persian Company . . . shall be admitted to equal participation [with Anglo-Persian Oil Company] in the exploitation of all oilfields in Asia Minor, including what is usually called Mesopotamia."[36]

Anglo-Saxon's operation would be completely reorganized and anglicized to ensure British oversight. "Certain shares," the protocol stated, "with a special majority voting power in the company operating in Mesopotamia, shall be controlled by His Majesty's Government and the management shall be permanently British." The government would receive 2 percent of Anglo-Saxon's shares. More important, however, the TPC voting percentages controlled by Royal Dutch's Anglo-Saxon, plus those of its rival Anglo-Persian, as well as the government would all be replicated and twined into a special "Voting Trust," which controlled 70 percent of the voting rights of the new Mesopotamian subsidiary.[37]

Since both Royal Dutch Shell and the British government planned to lay pipelines across the Middle East to the Mediterranean, Shell also agreed "to not oppose or obstruct directly or indirectly the laying . . . of a similar [pipe]line connecting the Anglo-Persian fields with that shore."[38]

The two parent companies comprising the Royal Dutch Shell conglomerate were Royal Dutch in the Netherlands, controlling 60 percent, and Shell Transport in the United Kingdom, controlling 40 percent. As a further protection, the board of directors of Shell Transport were now mandated to be 75 percent "British born British subjects . . . precluded from selling or disposing of their capital assets . . . outside British control." Moreover, the current approved board of directors, all British, could not change "without the consent and approval of the Governor of the Bank of England, and/or some person of similar standing nominated by His Majesty's Government."[39]

As for Henri Deterding, the Dutchman whose nationality stood at the heart of Royal Dutch's "foreign" character, he changed as well. During the war, at the beginning of these negotiations, he had become a naturalized British citizen. Shortly, he would become a knight of the British Empire, completing the transformation of his citizenship.[40]

By initialing the "Heads of Agreement" on March 7, 1919, a fiercely independent, highly competitive, unabashedly capitalist international oil combine carved out a major portion of its commercial empire to become a government-controlled enterprise, not in name but in fact—not in dollar but in deed. It was done not for love of country, but for the romance of Mesopotamia's oil fortunes.

The British now enjoyed overlapping and interlocking ownership, control, and competitive leverage in the oil of Mesopotamia, the oil that had been the subject of dreams and disputes since the previous century. Whitehall could empower or stall Shell, bury or resurrect Turkish Petroleum, favor or marginalize Anglo-Persian, govern all the oil, parcel a fraction to the French, or share a token with the local government. As the Paris negotiations proceeded, London could exercise some of those options, all of them, or none of them—as need or desire dictated.

However, regardless of what contracts or court papers were being filed in London, Anglo-Persian Oil Company was actually on the ground in Mesopotamia. With or without a concession, with or without further preferences from London, APOC was cementing a real-world monopoly, partnering with both the invasion and the civil administration. Since 1918, the company had been actively drilling in the northwestern "transferred territories," that is, the oil-rich Naft Khana region, previously Persian but moved into Turkish Mesopotamia through a frontier treaty adjustment. Most of that drilling, under the 1901 Persian concession, was proceeding under military auspices with the full endorsement of Civil Commissioner Wilson. Enthusiastically, Wilson reported, "The company takes so confident a view of the potentialities of that field, that they have dismantled a refinery in New Zealand and have had the plant shipped to Basra for the purpose of dealing with the Naft Khana output."[41]

What's more, Anglo-Persian managed and delivered all army needs through the military's Inland Water Transport, a system of pump houses and storage tank installations located in Amarah, Baghdad, Diwaniyah, Fallujah, Kut, Ur Junction, and numerous other villages, as well as "advanced bases" used by the troops. This network constituted APOC's future retail distribution arm for both kerosene and petrol after military needs were satisfied. With this in mind, APOC's chairman Greenway and Wilson worked together to change the company's relation from military vendor reporting to the army to commercial distributor authorized by the civil administration. Wilson liked the idea as long as the existing commercial middlemen were subtracted, thus moderating prices. APOC approved, as it was now ready to deal directly with consumers, and in a survey submitted to the authorities even calculated exactly how many gallons of kerosene it could store at each of 14 locations. The total was 50,401 gallons. Naturally, this would require a fleet of oil barges plying the Tigris and Euphrates. Both Wilson and APOC lobbied for these to be built and acquired.[42] The future monopoly was taking shape.

Seeing APOC's rapid entrenchment in Mesopotamia, Shell's Deterding advised his associates to enter Mesopotamia at once and get a foothold somehow. Possession is nine-tenths of the law. Recalling one frank exchange, Deterding stated, "I told [him] . . . go and get all the rights he could; as there is no government in Mesopotamia, [and] the only rights anybody can secure at present would be those of possession."[43]

Back in Paris, on April 8, Anglo-French negotiators, after numerous drafts, finally signed an oil agreement, called simply the Long-Bérenger Agreement, which in some parts read very much like the agreement signed just a month earlier with Shell. As such, it could either contradict or comply with that agreement, as desired. This latest accord created yet another iteration of Turkish Petroleum, cutting the French in for 20 percent, but cognizant that everyone was indeed carving up a nation not yet acquired under the rules of victory, and certainly not yet relinquished by the native population under the precepts of self-determination.

The Long-Bérenger Agreement declared: "In the event of His Majesty's Government receiving the mandate in Mesopotamia, they undertake to make it their duty to secure from the Mesopotamian Government for the Turkish Petroleum Company, or the Company to be formed to acquire the interests of that Company, the rights acquired by the Turkish Petroleum Company in Mesopotamia, under arrangements made with the Turkish Government. The French Government [is] to have a share in the capital in the Company. . . . The Company shall be under permanent British control."[44]

France's payment for the shares, under Long-Bérenger, would be a mere token: "that paid by the British government to the public trustee for the shares belonging to the Deutsche Bank, plus 5 percent interest." It was now clear to the French that Whitehall was seizing those shares in court. Ironically, France was agreeing to buy those shares before the court had even ruled they would be available.

Such a ruling was months away. Once the transaction was complete, however, the agreement stipulated, "The capital of the company shall be divided as follows: British interest 70 percent, French interest 20 percent, native [Mesopotamian] interest 10 percent," which would be divided between the two powers if the "native interest" declined. This last feature addressed the notion of economic self-determination, albeit the terms of inclusion for any native interest were not set forth. For its part, the French agreed to facilitate two British pipelines, plus storage depots and wharves on Syrian territory, once again emphasizing that the parties were not "implying that any territorial rights are in existence."[45]

Ten days later, the form and shape of the future Iraq and other liberated or occupied territories were becoming more apparent. In place of colonialism emerged a new concept, the "mandate." Those populations identified for self-determination but not deemed capable of forming their own government or national expression were to be mandated by the international community to "advanced nations" for "tutelage."

On April 28, 1919, the newly formed League of Nations finalized its noble covenant. Article 22 proclaimed: "To those colonies and territories which as a consequence of the late war have ceased to be under the sovereignty of the States which formerly governed them, and which are inhabited by peoples not yet able to stand by themselves under the strenuous conditions of the modern world, there should be applied the principle that the well-being and development of such peoples form a sacred trust of civilization and that securities for the performance of this trust should be embodied in this Covenant."[46]

The covenant continued, "The tutelage of such peoples should be entrusted to advanced nations who by reason of their resources, their experience or their geographical position can best undertake this responsibility . . . as Mandatories on behalf of the League." Article 22 specifically referenced "certain communities formerly belonging to the Turkish Empire [which] have reached a stage of development where their existence as independent nations can be provisionally recognized subject to the rendering of administrative advice and assistance by a Mandatory until such time as they are able to stand alone."[47]

Hence, more than 7,000 years after Mesopotamia gave the world the gift of civilization, a concept of commercial fair play, and the written word itself, the great powers were convinced the battered, exploited region could not stand with the civilized nations and peoples of the world.

It was becoming crystal clear that Britain would receive the mandate for the new Iraq, including oil-rich Mosul, which Britain and Wilson occupied. France began to fear that perhaps it had conceded the greatest known oil field in the world too easily, for a mere percentage of a British-controlled commercial company. The Long-Bérenger Agreement was signed by the two men April 8, 1919, and sent on to Paris and London for formal adoption by their governments. The British, seeing the accord as the final and much-desired demise of Sykes-Picot, notified the French ambassador in London on May 16 that they had accepted. The French, however, refused to reciprocate. After continued delays, diplomatic nerves became frayed. In the midst of a fractious dispute regarding Syria, Prime Minister Lloyd George angrily denounced the entire arrangement.[48]

On June 17, 1919, the French government introduced a bill to establish a state oil monopoly to import refined oil. About a month later, with no progress on its reinstatement, Foreign Secretary Curzon of Britain formally annulled the Long-Bérenger Agreement. In the wake of this recession, both the French and the British exchanged notes that acknowledged the protracted and bitter end of Sykes-Picot.[49]

By the end of July 1919, the High Court ruled in favor of the British government's petition to liquidate Deutsche Bank's one-quarter holding in Turkish Petroleum, thereby enabling its sale to Lancelot Smith.[50] The British government now controlled Turkish Petroleum directly through its acquisition of Deutsche Bank's 1898 oil concession and, even more substantially, albeit indirectly, through its March 1919 Heads of Agreement accord with Shell, which itself was an original 25 percent owner of TPC.

However, there was just one other thing about the High Court's order. While the High Court did confirm the government's right to liquidate the enemy property, it refused to rule on Gulbenkian's passionate objections regarding the serpentine March 1914 fusion agreement. The judge ruled: "And it is ordered that this order is not . . . a confirmation by any party of the convention dated 4th March, 1914 . . . or as a recognition that such convention is still [in force] . . . or to prejudice any question . . . in regard to the said convention or to any rights or interests . . . in regard to the shares hereinbefore mentioned."[51] Translation: It didn't matter who liquidated or acquired Deutsche Bank's stock; the true ownership and validity of Turkish Petroleum was anyone's guess.

Gulbenkian had them all guessing. The more elaborate the competing interest in Turkish Petroleum, the more the world industrialized and needed what Iraq possessed, the more valuable were his unresolved claims to the undrilled oil in the undeclared Iraqi state.

In mid-November 1919, Lancelot Smith, as chairman, imperially called a board meeting of Turkish Petroleum to undertake some clerical matters. At about this time, mindful of the court order and the legalities, Gulbenkian's name was finally added to the roster of shareholders.[52] From the day the company was registered on January 31, 1911, until that November 1919, Gulbenkian had actually preferred to keep his stock ownership verbal, unrecorded, and arguable. At least now there was a better paper—not that it would help.

Efforts to revive the Anglo-French oil negotiations continued until the end of 1919. Long-Bérenger was reformulated and revised.[53] Other ideas were floated. But all discussions about just who owned the land and the oil of the still undeclared country of Iraq would soon be subordinated to events.

The jihad was coming.

CHAPTER FOURTEEN

Jihad against Britain

In Paris, the Peace Conference began dismantling the Ottoman Empire in the Middle East. Nothing would be easier than to brand it all as a grand ploy for oil. But what empowered their avarice? What made it palatable and more than justifiable for the distinguished peace conferees to deprive Turkey of her provinces? The West's ingrained hatred of the Ottoman Empire and despotic Turkish rule played a major role.

For centuries, despite its value as the commercial nexus between East and West, the Ottomans had earned a dark place in the hearts of Europeans and Americans. The Ottomans were known to many Western minds as the "Terrible Turk" and the "Lustful Turk," caricatured as sexually perverted and bloodthirsty. Images of mass fratricides, palace murders, punishment by impalement, and severed heads presented to the sultan on silver platters all created a whirlwind of disgust within polite modern society. Going over the top, Turkish royalty was commonly depicted in Western illustrations as dripping in blood, consorting with skulls, or otherwise engaged in ghastly acts.[1]

Beyond personal misconduct, the Ottoman Empire was reviled by many twentieth-century Western leaders for creating the Eastern Question, thus inspiring wars throughout the Continent. Typical was the combined opinion of three distinguished American envoys to the Sublime Porte, Ambassadors Henry Morgenthau, Oscar Straus, and Abram Elkis. In a major *Washington Post* essay, published March 21, 1920, and headlined "Former Envoys' Remedies for Evil of Turkish Rule," the three raised the question: "What is to become of those countries which constitute the Near East is a problem, which has always been of great interest to the whole world, and now of great and immediate interest to the American people. Today the great European powers are discussing what is to become of one of the great prizes of the war—the dominion of the Ottoman Empire. . . . During the last two centuries . . . every European war has had its origin or its cause in the Ottoman Empire."[2]

Beyond blame for the wars that were endured by nations, the Turk was particularly accursed for the wholesale slaughter of innocent civilians. "They had held in bondage many races, some of them Christian," exclaimed one April 1920 *Washington Post* editorial, "and had abominably mistreated them, so atrociously, in fact, that the very word 'Turk' conjured up in the minds of scores of millions the per-sonification of all that was evil."[3] Indeed, decades before the word *genocide* was invented, the Turks systematically murdered whole pop-ulations, not once, not twice, but repeatedly. Frequently, these onslaughts were perpetrated against defenseless Christians, further inflaming Westerners.

Abdulhamid II, the sultan who reigned just before the Young Turks' revolution, himself became synonymous with the mass murder of Christians. For example, in the spring of 1876, a series of massacres collectively termed the "Bulgarian Horrors" or "Bulgarian Atroci-ties" was graphically reported by numerous eyewitnesses in the news-papers of the world, from New York and Washington to London, Paris, and St. Petersburg. In an attempt to suppress a Christian rebel-lion in the Balkans, Turkish troops and their militias raped the women and young girls in some 65 Bulgarian villages. In Kalifer, the women were herded into barns that were then set ablaze. In Karlovo, most of the homes were pillaged and then burned and many of the women ravished. In many cases, young girls were sold to other Moslems as sex slaves for five francs.[4]

In the wake of the Bulgarian outrages, former British liberal prime minister William Gladstone published his caustic pamphlet, "Bulgar-ian Horrors and the Question of the East," stigmatizing the Ottomans as bloodthirsty murderers. His tract became an immediate bestseller in London, selling 40,000 copies in a single week. A Russian-language version set a record, selling 10,000 copies in a month. In fact, it was Gladstone who coined the derogatory moniker "Abdul the Damned" that gained worldwide acceptance.[5]

Abdul the Damned, undeterred, went on to commit more atrocities against Christians. U.S. ambassador to Turkey Henry Morgenthau recorded in his diary that among the Ottomans, Christians were commonly referred to as "dogs" and ranked less valuable than a camel or a horse. Ottoman hatred of infidels played out most brutally against Armenians, who were highly nationalistic and arguably the oldest Christian community in Europe. In the mid-1890s, a series of heinous raids against Armenian villages by Ottoman Kurds led to an uprising by Armenian militias in which they took their revenge on Kurdish towns and villages. In retaliation, Abdulhamid sent in shock troops to murder, maim, and rape masses of Armenians in the Sasun highlands. For example, in the village of Semel, the local priest was encouraged by Turkish commanders to surrender the populace, which he did. But once in captivity, the priest's eyes were gouged out, he was bayoneted to death, and then all the women were raped as their husbands screamed nearby from their own tortures and execution. British and American diplomats gave ample documentation of these horrors in regular dispatches to their foreign ministries. Such organized atrocities against Armenians continued throughout the realm, not only in the far-off districts, but also on the streets of Istanbul before the eyes of ambassadors who pleaded in vain for a pause. Ghastly pictures of mass graves published in British magazines revolted London.[6]

The Young Turks deposed Abdul the Damned in 1908. With their noble ideas about human rights and a lofty constitution resurrected from the pen of Midhat Pasha, many hoped for a new Ottoman era. But as the entrenched Young Turks turned ultranationalist, demanding to turkify all the empire, the Ottomans returned to old habits. In 1909, bloody massacres were again inflicted upon the Armenian population, this in Adana. Provocative photographs published in Western capitals showed brutalized children, their skin flayed off with cotton-chopping tools.[7]

Beginning in 1915, in the midst of the war, systematic extermination on a monumental scale horrified the twentieth-century world. First, the Armenians were commercially boycotted, then identified and rounded up for destruction. They were "deported" from all over Turkey to numerous killing centers, including several in and around the Mosul province, where Kurds joined in the process. Railroad boxcars, concentration camps, and death marches through numerous Arab towns became the gruesome hallmarks of the process. Along the way, stragglers were shot, hacked to death, or hung from bridges. Newborns were ripped from their mothers' clutches and smashed to a bloody death against trees. Hundreds of thousands were sadistically murdered in a systematic state effort to exterminate once and for all the entire Armenian people.[8]

This merciless extermination continued into 1916 in full view of the world, regularly reported by diplomats and protested in Congress and Parliament. For example, on July 15, at 1 P.M., Ambassador Morgenthau sent a dispatch from the embassy in Istanbul: "Deportation of and excesses against peaceful Armenians is increasing and from harrowing reports of eyewitnesses it appears that a campaign of race extermination is in progress under a pretext of reprisal against rebellion." In England, Lord Bryce submitted an official government white paper and denunciation in October 1915, again using the term "extermination."[9]

The leading newspapers of the world headlined the inhuman campaign. In 1915 alone, the *New York Times* published approximately 145 articles detailing what was openly called "extermination." October 4, 1915: TELL OF HORRORS DONE IN ARMENIA; Report of Eminent Americans Says They Are Unequaled in a Thousand Years; TURKISH RECORD OUTDONE; A Policy of Extermination Put in Effect Against a Helpless People; ENTIRE VILLAGES SCATTERED; Men and Boys Massacred, Women and Girls Sold As Slaves and Distributed Among Moslems . . . October 7, 1915: 800,000 ARMENIANS COUNTED DESTROYED; 10,000 DROWNED AT ONCE; Peers Are Told How Entire Christian Population of Trebizond Was Wiped Out; December 15, 1915: MILLION ARMENIANS KILLED OR IN EXILE; American Committee on Relief Says Victims of Turks Are Steadily Increasing; POLICY OF EXTERMINATION; More Atrocities Detailed in Support of Charge That Turkey Is Acting Deliberately.[10]

In the United States, the Armenian extermination became a cause célèbre. Families were jingoistically exhorted to remember the starving Armenian children dying in camps and death marches. One day at the height of the killing, Talaat Pasha, one of the architects of the extermination, was so sure that all Armenians would perish, he summoned Ambassador Morgenthau to discuss their insurance policies. New York Life Insurance and Equitable Life of New York were both leading life insurers of the Armenian middle class. He bragged that 75 percent of the million or more Armenians were already dead and the Turkish government would leave none living to take revenge. "I wish," Talaat then said to Morgenthau, "that you would get the American life insurance companies to send us a complete list of their Armenian policy holders. They are practically all dead now and have left no heirs to collect the money. It of course all escheats [legally defaults] to the State. The Government is the beneficiary now. Will you do so?" Morgenthau angrily refused.[11]

Talaat had previously challenged Morgenthau's protests over the Armenian extermination. "You are a Jew, these people are Christians. . . . Why can't you let us do with these Christians as we please?" Morgenthau replied that he was speaking as an American, not a Jew, and that made his protests "97 percent Christian." Adamant, he assured Talaat that Americans "will always resent the wholesale destruction of Christians in Turkey." He also warned, "After this war is over you shall face a new situation. . . . You will have to meet public opinion everywhere, especially in the United States. Our people will never forget."[12]

In the Paris of 1919, all memories on all topics were still fresh. In fact, Armenia was one of the national groups identified for self-determination and nationhood, to be administered in mandate by the United States. The Armenian mandate was not pursued because the U.S. Congress never ratified America's entry into the League of Nations.[13]

Certainly, as the political vivisection of the Sick Man proceeded, the commercial captains circled, rubbing their hands and shifting into better positions. But the Allied leaders that tore the Ottoman Empire limb from limb, including Mesopotamia, thought of far more than oil. Allied leaders also thought of 8 million soldiers dead, 21 million wounded, 2 million missing in action, whole populations uprooted, millions of civilians east and west massacred, $180 billion spent, war reparations demanded of Germany, and an equivalent levy against Turkey in the form of oil resources. That's why Allied leaders felt completely justified in all they did in Mesopotamia. They even held the written consent of Hussein of Mecca. They just never asked the Arabs who actually lived there.

Conflicting Allied declarations in the Middle East parted the sea for some fleeing persecution and drowned the hopes and aspirations of others chasing independence.

On November 2, 1917, the British foreign secretary issued a declaration to Zionist organizations worldwide that Britain had identified the displaced and long-persecuted Jews as one of the many groups qualified for self-determination. Specifically, it committed Britain to facilitate "the establishment in Palestine of a national home for the Jewish people . . . it being clearly understood that nothing shall be done which may prejudice the civil and religious rights of existing non-Jewish communities in Palestine, or the rights and political status enjoyed by Jews in any other country."[14]

Modern Zionism had been born two decades earlier when Jewish activist Theodor Herzl proposed an ingathering of the exiled Jews back to their ancestral home as the only solution to the centuries of unstoppable civil and violent persecution. From 1903 to 1907 alone, some 284 heinous state-encouraged pogroms in czarist Russia resulted in 50,000 Jews being killed or wounded. During World War I, anti-Jewish laws throughout Europe continued to proscribe Jewish citizenship, land ownership, many professions, and even freedom of movement for millions of Jews. For example, some 4.5 million Jews in Russia were restricted to a "Pale of Settlement" and subjected to scurrilous anti-Semitic decrees.[15]

Jews had dwelled in Palestine, the seat of Judaism, for millennia. They survived the Babylonians who exiled them, the Romans who crucified them, the Crusaders who slaughtered them, and the Ottoman Turks who hanged them in the square as infidels. Throughout modern history, Jewish communities flourished in Jerusalem, where they constituted a majority—in 1864, out of 15,000 residents, some 8,000 were Jews, 4,500 Moslems, and 2,500 Christians. By the time of the Balfour Declaration in 1917, some 45,000 of Jerusalem's

65,000 inhabitants were Jewish. Additionally, Jews had always lived throughout the nearly barren land of Palestine in such cities as Gaza, Ashkelon, Jaffa, Caesarea, and Tsfat. Indeed, Jews lived in great numbers throughout the Ottoman Empire's Middle East, from Syria to the Persian Gulf.[16]

The intention of the Balfour Declaration, and its French equivalent, was to create two homelands, Arab and Jewish, living harmoniously side by side in the same fashion as other national groups. The Jews would receive a homeland carved out of the larger Palestine territory. But the Arabs despised the very idea of Zionism. Of course, Jews and many other religious groups had dwelled among the Arabs for centuries. But these Zionist Jews were seeking autonomy and self-determination. The Christians and Jews could live under Moslem authority as *dhimmis,* that is, protected second-class citizens who acknowledged the sovereignty of Islam, paid special taxes, and observed special restrictive laws. The idea of Jews establishing their own autonomous communities with international recognition was anathema.[17]

Certainly, any number of other citizens of the Ottoman Empire, or indeed from anywhere in the Eurasian region, migrated into barren and sparsely settled Palestine during the preceding decades. Local Arabs, who constituted the majority in overall Palestine, welcomed Moslem newcomers—but not the Jews. Official protests and demands by Arab committees that the sultan expel Jews trace back to the earliest Russian pre-Zionist Jewish immigrants in the late 1880s. Long before Herzl's 1896 promulgation of Zionism, Turkish laws were enacted against Jewish settling in or purchasing property in Palestine.[18]

When news of the Balfour Declaration reached the Arab masses, along with the explosive details of the Sykes-Picot Agreement, the Allies sought to reassure the restive and resentful Arabs that their national aspirations would not be supplanted. On November 7, 1918, just as the war was rapidly coming to a close, Paris and London issued the Anglo-French Declaration to the Arabs. The promulgation stressed one goal: "the complete and definite emancipation of the peoples so long oppressed by the Turks and the establishment of national governments and administrations deriving their authority from the initiative and free choice of the indigenous populations."[19]

The joint November 7 declaration guaranteed, "France and Great Britain are at one in encouraging and assisting the establishment of indigenous Governments and administrations in Syria and Mesopotamia . . . and recognizing these as soon as they are actually established." The declaration averred that these "Governments and administrations [would be] freely chosen by the populations themselves."[20]

As the Paris Peace Conference opened in January 1919, the Arabs, represented by Sharif Faisal, were snubbed by the French. Regardless of prior representations by the British, the French were uninterested in relinquishing their designs on greater Syria, especially since the Lebanon region was overwhelmingly Maronite Christian. Many French officials simply considered the Arabs a threat. Typical was a memo from the Quai d'Orsay that stated, "Damascus is a Moslem center which is very hostile to France, to tell the truth, the most hostile in all Islam. It is there that the fanatical Arabs of North Africa go who want to elude our control. It is there where all the plots against our authority in the Moslem countries are hatched, and it is there where the agitators come and preach rebellion. . . . Damascus [must] be placed under our control."[21]

Faisal, who now became the face of Arab nationalism to the Peace Conference, was busily engaged in his own declaring and maneuvering. On January 1, 1919, he submitted a formal memorandum to the Supreme Council of the Peace Conference outlining his vision for Arab nationalism throughout the Mideast. It was not monolithic or pan-Arab. The Arab national movement was headquartered in Damascus and, plainly put, they wanted Syria, along with the region of the holy cities of Medina and Mecca.[22]

"The various provinces of Arab Asia—Syria, Iraq, Jezireh, Hijaz, Nejd, Yemen—are very different economically and socially," asserted Faisal's petition, "and it is impossible to constrain them into one frame of government." Certainly, Faisal's petition was unyielding on Syria and the Hijaz, that is, the Arabian Peninsula encompassing Mecca. "Syria . . . thickly peopled with sedentary [settled] classes, is sufficiently advanced politically to manage her own internal affairs." He added proudly that while Syria would accept foreign advisors, it would do so only without paternalism. "We are willing to pay for this help in cash; [but] we cannot sacrifice for it any part of the freedom we have just won for ourselves."[23]

It was totally different for Mesopotamia. In keeping with his earlier promises in the McMahon-Hussein correspondence, Faisal reiterated that he was willing to relinquish Iraq to the British. Faisal readily acknowledged: "Jezireh [encompassing northeastern Syria and the Mosul provincial region] and Iraq are . . . made up of three civilized towns, divided by large wastes, thinly peopled by semi-nomadic tribes." He readily acknowledged Western commercial designs, continuing, "The world wishes to exploit Mesopotamia rapidly, and we therefore believe that the system of government there will have to be buttressed by the men and material resources of a great foreign Power."[24]

Rather than seeking elections in Iraq, Faisal suggested a custodial government handpicked by London and patient British tutelage to bring the population into modern times. "We ask, however, that [while] the Government be Arab, in principle and spirit, the selective rather than the elective principle being necessarily followed in the neglected districts, until time makes the broader basis possible. The main duty of the Arab Government there would be to oversee the educational processes, which are to advance the tribes to the moral level of the towns."[25]

An Arab national state in Syria was of such major importance that Faisal was even willing to endorse both an Arab and a Zionist state in Palestine, existing side by side, under a British mandate, if that would smooth the way. Therefore, while Faisal's petition stipulated that "In Palestine, the enormous majority of the people are Arabs," he added in the next sentence, "The Jews are very close to the Arabs in blood, and there is no conflict of character between the races. In principles, we are absolutely at one." That said, he acknowledged that Palestine was important to many faiths and therefore the Arab national movement "would wish for the effective super-position of a great trustee, so long as a representative local administration commended itself by actively promoting the material prosperity of the country." That welcomed a British mandate over the envisioned two-canton Palestinian entity.[26]

Continuing his own cascade of political zigs and zags, Faisal then met in Paris with Zionist Organization president Chaim Weizmann.

Following up on meetings the two leaders had held the previous year in Aqaba, Faisal signed an enlightened and tolerant nine-point agreement, endorsing the Balfour Declaration and inviting the Zionists to coexist in Palestine. "Article II: Immediately following the completion of the deliberations of the Peace Conference, the definite boundaries between the Arab State and Palestine shall be determined by a Commission to be agreed upon by the parties hereto. Article III: In the establishment of the Constitution and Administration of Palestine, all such measures shall be adopted as will afford the fullest guarantees for carrying into effect the British Government's [Balfour] Declaration of the 2nd of November 1917. . . . Article IV: All necessary measures shall be taken to encourage and stimulate immigration of Jews into Palestine on a large scale, and as quickly as possible to settle Jewish immigrants upon the land through closer settlement and intensive cultivation of the soil. In taking such measures the Arab peasant and tenant farmers shall be protected in their rights and shall be assisted in forwarding their economic development."[27]

The entire agreement was typed in English in January 1919. But at the bottom, Faisal hand-penned in Arabic this stern warning: "Provided the Arabs obtain their independence as demanded in my [forthcoming] Memorandum dated the 4th of January, 1919, to the Foreign Office of the Government of Great Britain, I shall concur in the above articles. But if the slightest modification or departure were to be made [regarding our demands], I shall not be then bound by a single word of the present Agreement which shall be deemed void and of no account or validity, and I shall not be answerable in any way whatsoever." Directly beneath that inscription were the signatures of Weizmann and Faisal duly affixed.[28]

The Allies could have Palestine and Iraq, but Faisal and the Arab national movement demanded Syria.

In mid-April 1919, Faisal met with President Georges Clemenceau and was promised total Arab independence for Syria. A declaration was typed up on April 17. But the French offer involved just one other thing: As part of that independence, the French army would occupy Damascus, and the new Arab nation would actually be a mere federation of local autonomous states in which all the government advisors, including the governors and heads of major government bureaus, as well as the judiciary, would be French and under Paris's

control as they currently were in Lebanon, plus Faisal would be compelled to publicly declare the importance of France's historic relationship with the Maronite Christians.[29] Other than that, Syria would
be completely independent.

Faisal quickly refused, encouraged by Lawrence of Arabia, who
advised him to demand total independence "without conditions or
reservations." Clemenceau, however, would not tolerate what he
considered Arab impudence. Faisal summarily left Paris for Syria to
claim his nation.[30]

Throughout later 1919, the multilateral negotiations dragged on
with the usual permutations, frustrations, reversals, and "by the ways."
Eventually, a disenchanted Faisal admitted he preferred that the Mandate be given to any nation other than France. He even suggested the
United States or Britain.[31] But France would not yield.

From the French point of view, it could not retreat from dominating Greater Syria, especially from Lebanon. French troops, religious
groups, and civilian organizations had undertaken an impressive economic and administrative reconstruction of the neglected Turkish
Lebanese provinces. Courts were overhauled, new banks were
installed with generous loans extended, emergency food was distributed, sewers laid, streets paved, and dozens of schools opened. One
leading French columnist and government advisor warned that if
forced out of Syria and Lebanon: "World opinion would consider
France 'a finished people.'" Using blunt language, an adamant
Clemenceau made it clear: If Faisal and the Arab nationalists did not
have "absolute respect . . . [and] satisfy me," the entire region would
be taken "through force."[32]

Finally, on January 6, 1920, Faisal and Clemenceau reached a provisional agreement. Syria, under a Faisal regime, would include
Lebanon and would be permitted a parliament that could enact laws
and taxes; the national language would be Arabic, not French or Turkish; and the French army would not massively occupy the country. To
help ensure that Faisal adhered to the January 6 accord, Clemenceau
had already installed in Beirut a new high commissioner for Lebanon,
General Henri Gouraud. Fiercely chauvinistic, pro-Christian and anti-
Arab, Gouraud had been the commander at the Second Battle of the
Marne and was still prepared to fight any enemy of France. Soon, Faisal
found himself teetering atop a tightrope above two constituencies:

Some virulently branded him a traitor to the infidel; others praised Faisal as the national hero who had negotiated Syria's independence.[33]

Moslem rejectionists had already been attacking the existing French troops in the region. Arab soldiers in the defeated Turkish army were now repatriated to Syria and ready to again take up arms. Rapidly, the situation deteriorated. Faisal now had to choose between the French and the possibility that their ingenuous promises might be kept, and the fervid and distrusting Arab nationalists who everywhere demanded instant independence. By late February 1920, Faisal had transformed himself again, not only insisting on total independence for Syria, but now demanding the British do the same for Palestine and Iraq.[34]

Nobody was keeping any promises. Pacts and promulgations were solemnly propounded, only to be breached, padded, and then reconstituted by all sides. Like the Great War that had just finished, political preemption led to political provocation, which led to further preemption. The vicious downward spiral was gaining velocity.

On March 7 and 8, 1920, the Second General Syrian Congress, a representative assembly of Arab nationalists from many countries, raced ahead of any League of Nations decision. It vehemently declared independence for a Greater Syria, to extend both into Lebanon and south into Palestine. The Congress elected Faisal king of Syria. Iraq was likewise declared independent and Faisal's brother, Abdullah, elected its king.[35]

The Allies were outraged. On March 11, the French premier insisted to Prime Minister Lloyd George that the Second General Syrian Congress was an illegitimate enterprise and its decisions of no value or import. The French were supporting the United Kingdom territorial desiderata on Iraq and Palestine; now Paris demanded Britain support French claims to Syria. Otherwise the hard-fought rights gained in the Middle East would be lost to all the Allies. Lord Curzon, the British foreign secretary, angrily scolded the French ambassador in London, "The future of France and Great Britain in [the seized Turkish Mideast] was imperiled because of the way in which the French Government, in pursuance of traditional or historical aspirations, had insisted on forcing themselves into areas where the French were not welcomed by the inhabitants."[36]

The British, now also defensive, demanded that Faisal engineer the nullification of the Second General Syrian Congress's declaration of

Iraqi independence. "The right of anybody at Damascus to decide the future of Mesopotamia or Mosul," insisted Lord Curzon in a letter to Faisal, "is one that cannot be admitted in any circumstances."[37]

At stake was more than geography, more than prestige. There was oil in Iraq, and it had to be transported across Syria and Palestine, as well as south through Basra. The Allies needed the Mideast.

About a month later, on April 19, 1920, the Allies, working through their League of Nations, gathered at San Remo, Italy, for a several-day conference to carve up Turkey. *Carving* was the word of the hour. Indeed, the night before the conference, the *Washington Post* article about the conference was even headlined, "The Carving of Turkey." The *Post* presaged the conference's "far reaching importance" as "the allies try to arrange for satisfactory government of many races, some of them warlike and all of them backward," who had emerged from centuries of Turkish neglect. These included national groups in the Balkans, Azerbaijan, Greece, Hungary, Georgia, and across the many provinces of the Mideast. The delegates convened against the background of numerous bloody European conflicts still flaring. The Bolshevik revolution and its consequences were burning throughout eastern Europe and Eurasia, including such countries as Latvia, Poland, and Bessarabia. Postwar Germany was in civil upheaval. Innocent civilians were being massacred regularly, as national groups contended for primacy.[38]

With the last dusk of the San Remo Conference, the conferees granted France the mandate for both Syria and Lebanon—two new nations-in-waiting were created. The British received the mandate for Iraq—one new nation-in-waiting was created. Britain also received the mandate for Palestine, under a provision to create a Jewish homeland, therefore writing the Jewish nation's establishment into international law—one nation-in-waiting was re-created.[39]

The Zionists had cooperated with the British during the negotiations, and indeed the Jewish nation's major incubating governmental institutions were almost all British corporations based in London. Zionists understood that only desperate and persecuted Jews would relocate to Palestine's inhospitable terrain and in so doing bring it to life for later generations of middle-class Jews. Palestine would become a commercial engine in the region. Moreover, once established, a Jewish state in Palestine was sure to be a reliable ally and British foothold in the heart of the Middle East. All land gained was to be legally pur-

chased under international law. The Jews were among several peoples
selected for transfer. A million Greek Moslems were slated for transfer into Turkey, and a half million Turkish Christians were to migrate
into Greece. All Jews going to Palestine were to transfer in under
international auspices, just as decided for other national groups.[40]

Many establishment Jews in the major cities of Europe and America, especially Jews of German origin, denounced the Zionist ethic as
a threat to their precarious assimilated existence. But even as San
Remo delegates met, helpless Jewish villagers were being murdered
by the thousands in Poland as a mere sidelight to a Polish-Russian
conflict. Masses of impoverished Jews, persecuted by European
regimes, as well as Jews already dwelling throughout the Ottoman
Empire, now waited to enter Palestine and escape from persecution
into a national homeland of their own.[41]

At San Remo, America did not receive the much-vaunted mandate for Armenia because Congress blocked U.S. admission into the
League of Nations. America was not even a participant in the discussions. Consequently, France and Britain were both the grantors and
the grantees of the mandates and the oil wealth that attached.[42]

On April 24, away from the main diplomacy of the San Remo
Conference, Anglo-French petroleum negotiators concluded their
own agreement. It was initialed by Frenchman M. Philippe Berthelot,
director-general of the commercial affairs section of the Foreign
Ministry, and by John Cadman, Britain's latest oil czar. In many ways,
the so-called Berthelot-Cadman agreement resembled many of the
previous accords negotiated and renegotiated by Anglo-French inter-
locutors. But Berthelot-Cadman was hardly an international treaty
sanctioned by the League of Nations and subject to the elaborate
peace process. This was a secret deal between France and Great
Britain to divide up the oil of Europe, Asia Minor, North Africa, and
Mesopotamia. The language made clear that this latest and seemingly
final agreement was essentially a resurrection of previous oil contracts
going back to prewar times.[43]

"By order of the two Governments of France and Great Britain,"
the document began, "the undersigned representatives have resumed,
by mutual consent, the consideration of an agreement regarding
petroleum. This agreement is based on the principles of cordial cooperation and reciprocity in those countries where the oil interest of

the two nations can be usefully united." The memorandum listed Romania, Asia Minor, the former czarist territories, and Galicia, as well as the French and British colonies.

Clause 7 specified the previously acceptable language about the Turkish Petroleum Company: "Mesopotamia—The British Government undertake to grant to the French Government, or its nominee, 25 per cent of the net output of crude oil at current market rates which His Majesty's Government may secure from the Mesopotamian oilfields, in the event of their being developed by Government action; or in the event of a private petroleum company being used to develop the Mesopotamian oilfields, the British Government will place at the disposal of the French Government a share of 25 per cent in such company. . . . It is also understood that the said petroleum company shall be under permanent British control."[44]

Clause 8 committed both France and England to each offer a 10 percent participation of the private company to a Mesopotamian government if such a government emerged—this as a token to American concepts of self-determination. Nothing more about local participation was specified. Clause 9 ensured that "the British Government agree to support arrangements by which the French Government may procure from the Anglo-Persian Company supplies of oil, which may be piped from Persia to the Mediterranean through any pipeline which may have been constructed within the French mandated territory and in regard to which France has given special facilities, up to the extent of 25 per cent of the oil so piped, on such terms and conditions as may be mutually agreed between the French Government and the Anglo-Persian Company."[45]

The next day, April 25, 1920, the initialed Berthelot-Cadman agreement was confirmed and signed by the two heads of state, British prime minister David Lloyd George and newly elected French president Alexandre Millerand. While the oil covenant remained secret, the League of Nations mandates soon became public.[46] News of the mandates, denying Arab sovereignty in Syria while establishing a Jewish national home, quickly burned throughout the Arab world.

On May 8, an irked Faisal sent a formal protest to the Supreme Council of the Peace Conference that he "was much surprised to learn, through public channels, the decision taken at the Conference of San Remo on the Arab countries detached from Turkey. . . . The wishes of the inhabitants have not been taken into account in the assignment of these mandates." He cautioned grimly, "The Arabs, fully conscious of their rights and their duties, did not hesitate to take up arms against their co-religionists, and to sacrifice their noblest blood in defense of the Right, thereby rendering abortive the threatened Holy War [declared by the Ottoman Empire], which the Turks and Germans wished to exploit in their struggle with the Entente [the Allies]."[47]

Faisal reminded the League of Nations that the stated intent during the Arab uprisings against Turkey was "nothing less than their complete deliverance from a foreign yoke, and the establishment of a free and independent government, which would allow them [the Arabs] to resume their place in the concert of civilized nations." Ominously, Faisal added, "The decision of San Remo puts an end to this hope. The moderate elements in the young nation, who have endeavored, and are still endeavoring, to guide it towards a policy of sincere collaboration with the Allies, are now discouraged and rendered powerless by this decision."[48]

For more than a year, Arab and Kurdish resentment of the occupation, inflamed by Bolshevik agitation in the region and resurgent postwar Turkish nationalism everywhere, had yielded Christian massacres, assassinations of political officers, ambushes of British and Indian officers, and attacks on convoys throughout the three Iraqi provinces. As the fuse of San Remo burned, Arab militancy and violence across the occupied Mideast—in Palestine, Mesopotamia, and Syria—already a problem, now ratcheted up.[49]

On May 18, 1920, Britain's foreign secretary, fed up with the violence, washed his hands of Syrian Arabs, cabling Paris, "The French authorities must be the best judges of the military measures necessary to control the local situation, and . . . they have complete authority in taking such measures." Quickly, French president Millerand confirmed to General Gouraud, "Action against Faisal is indispensable and urgent." General Gouraud immediately prepared to invade Syria with several divisions backed by tanks, airplanes, and heavy artillery.[50]

General Gouraud issued a 48-hour ultimatum to Faisal to desist and facilitate French efforts to restore order—or else. This ultimatum was calculated to be unanswerable because of the sheer difficulties of rapid communication across the region. Nonetheless, Faisal instantly agreed to General Gouraud's demands, but his reply came one day late. Therefore, General Gouraud's march on Damascus began in full force. But then British and French diplomatic sources debated whether they could move against Syrian Arabs in view of Faisal's actual acceptance of the ultimatum—even though his reply had been one day late. An irate French president Millerand saw Faisal's promises as empty, a mere ploy for time. "So as not to fall back into the previous situation," demanded Millerand, "it is now necessary to continue to take—without lending yourself to the Sherifian's [Faisal's] game to gain time—all steps necessary for your safety and for the total execution of the mandate."[51]

On July 24, 1920, French forces continued their invasion toward Damascus. The Arabs rallied to meet them at Maysalun, just west of the city. Charging with swords and bolt-action rifles, they were said to have displayed "strong resistance." But they were no match for the modern warfare that had emerged over the recent years. French tanks, airplanes, machine guns, and overwhelming infantry force slaughtered the Arabs within eight hours. The French now occupied Damascus and successfully established their mandate.[52]

That same day, July 24, 1920, after persistent fragmentary leaks, the secret San Remo oil agreement became public after being submitted to the House of Commons.[53] Clearly, the French and British had divided up the Middle East for its oil.

That same day, July 24, 1920, the Zionist Conference concluded in London with a flourish for the future. Gathering in a large hall, bedecked with Jewish-star-emblazoned flags hanging vertically from the balconies and across the stained glass windows at the front, inspired before a great Union Jack with a Jewish star inset with a portrait of Herzl, the Jewish delegates were determined to end the tragic wandering, persecution, and decimation of their people. Their solution: a legal, internationally sanctioned return to the homeland from whence they had been exiled a millennium earlier. In many ways, the Zionist Conference functioned as a counterpart to the international Arab conclave at the Second General Syrian Congress in Damascus that voted to establish an Arab nation. The Zionist Conference did the same for Jewish Palestine. Its crowning resolution created the Jewish National Fund, to be supported by cash donations from Jews worldwide, to legally purchase lands for kibbutzim and finance the formation of new Jewish villages in Palestine. Just days earlier, White-hall had appointed Sir Herbert Samuel as high commissioner of Palestine, empowered to oversee the orderly immigration of Jews into Palestine. The Jewish homeland was being sanctioned, being purchased, being peopled, and slowly brought to life.[54]

On that same day, July 24, 1920, for the Arabs, it was over. The Jews had gained Palestine. The West had gained oil. The Arabs had lost Syria. This was to be *Am al-Nakba*.

To the Arabs, it did not matter that during the war, Britain had deployed some 900,000 men against Turkey while only token platoons of Arabs had fought behind the lines; from the Arab perspective, Arabs did in fact fight and fight valiantly and upheld their end of the bargain. It did not matter that the Arabs had cruelly battled against the British in Mesopotamia alongside the Turks at Kut, at Baghdad, and elsewhere; from the Arab perspective, Mesopotamia was not part of the bargain anyway. It did not matter that within the pages of the serpentine McMahon-Hussein correspondence, nothing was firmly promised; from the Arab perspective, they sanctified the sentences most precious to them. What mattered most was that the West and the Jews had triumphed, and the domination of the Arabs would continue, but this time under a Christian mandate and now with autonomous Jews in their midst.

Three intertwined evils—the infidel European Allies, the infidel Zionists, and the black substance the West craved—became conflated in the Arab mind to create one great Satan. Indeed, these three evils would galvanize the Arab consciousness for virtually the next century. For the first time in centuries, the Arabs stopped fighting each other. Sunni and Shi'a, tribal enemies, those of the desert and those of the city, the intellectual and the peasant could all unite under one Islamic banner, because this was *Am al-Nakba*. Forevermore, 1920 would be a black year in the collective Arabic consciousness. In Arabic, *Am al-Nakba* means "The Year of the Catastrophe."[55]

Now, across the off-kilter Arab rectangle, a great jihad would be unleashed. Faisal had earlier warned the peace conference: "The unity of the Arabs in Asia has been made more easy of late years, since the development of railways, telegraphs, and air-roads. In old days the area was too huge, and in parts necessarily too thinly peopled, to communicate common ideas readily." Arab anger could now move quickly and with coordination. The Arabs would strike most fiercely where it would hurt most. They would strike in Mesopotamia, where Britain and France dreamed of the oil that had not yet been drilled and that had not yet flowed, but that the Allies could already taste. The Arabs wanted that taste to be bitter and bloody.

Ten perfect circles were drawn vertically on the paper along with the notations: "Speed = 75 MPH. Interval of Release = 2 Secs. Area: 2,000 feet long, half-mile wide, varying with wind."[56] The British had been preparing for more than a year.

War-weary and undermanned in Mesopotamia, poorly supplied and thinly deployed across the three provinces, Britain had concluded by early April 1919 that it could not police and control the Iraqi insurgency with ground troops. Air bombardment was the only answer. A November Air Ministry survey of air squadrons in the Middle East and India revealed that less than two squadrons were available to bomb positions or provide reconnaissance in Iraq.[57]

But the insurgents in Iraq were too dispersed for concentrated bombardment, air service officers believed. Moreover, in the mountainous Mosul region, Kurdish rebels often hid in caves and hard-to-identify passes. A different weapon would be needed: gas bombs.

On April 29, 1919, the Royal Air Force in Cairo advised the Air Ministry in London, "Gas bombs are required by 31st Wing for use against recalcitrant Arabs as experiment, the suggestion being concurred in by the General Staff, Baghdad."[58]

Poison gas had been a staple of the Great War. The French were the first to use nonlethal irritant gas projectiles in August 1914, the first month of the war. The Germans responded with lethal gas. Although the German use of toxic gases was roundly condemned, eventually all the Allies joined in. In the last months of the war, President Woodrow Wilson also adopted the principle of poison gas warfare. On July 18, 1918, Wilson signed General Order #62, establishing the Chemical Warfare Service. The combatants deployed chlorine, phosgene, and mustard gases, generally in artillery shells, as the preferred killing agents. When the air had cleared, more than a million casualties had fallen, some 86,000 fatally. Russia sustained the most killed, some 56,000.[59]

But gas bombs had never been successfully deployed from the air. On May 2, a handwritten note was sent to the Flying Operations Directorate at the Air Board Office in London wondering about innocent casualties and the dangers posed to the troops: "1. Could you please give the War Office view concerning the employment of gas in any form against uncivilized tribes? 2. It should be pointed out that gas is dangerous both to those who employ it and, naturally, to those against whom it may be quite unwittingly used. The great difficulty of differentiation between innocent and guilty once more presents itself and is merely accentuated by this form of warfare. 3. Gas bombs are not available at present. The question of their being produced subsequently is under discussion. 4. [Air Vice Marshal] General [Geoffrey] Salmond is against the employment of gas in any form, is of the opinion that the necessary effect is quite satisfactorily obtained with bombs of the ordinary nature."[60]

A debate ensued about the morality of gas bombs. The matter was decided several days later on May 12, when Winston Churchill, then secretary of state for War and Air, ruled in favor of tear gas and perhaps more. "I do not understand this squeamishness about the use of gas," he wrote. "We have definitely adopted the position at the Peace Conference of arguing in favor of the retention of gas as a permanent method of warfare. It is sheer affectation to lacerate a man with the poisonous fragment of a bursting shell and to boggle at making his eyes water by means of lachrymatory [tear] gas."[61]

He added with reservation, "I am strongly in favor of using poisoned gas against uncivilized tribes. The moral effect should be so good that the loss of life should be reduced to a minimum. It is not necessary to use only the most deadly gasses: gasses can be used which cause great inconvenience and would spread a lively terror and yet would leave no serious permanent effects on most of those affected."[62]

On May 19, the deputy chief of the Air Staff, R. M. Groves, confirmed in a note, "S of S [secretary of state for War and Air Churchill] approves the policy of utilizing gas bombs—please see enclosure 5A. Will you therefore please take the necessary steps with DGSR [director general of Science and Research] to obtain supplies?" Several days later, he also advised the Flying Operations Directorate, "I understand that the S of S . . . has approved the general policy of using poisonous gas against uncivilized tribes. So far, although considerable time and trouble was expended on research during the war, we have not yet evolved suitable and practicable gas bombs for use from aircraft."[63]

Shortly thereafter, the Air Ministry's director of research, Henry Robert Brooke-Popham, dashed off a handwritten note, "I think the first thing is to obtain from the gas experts of the late trench warfare department an opinion of the best gas to use. A: For incapacitating the enemy without permanently injuring him. B: For killing or permanently incapacitating him. Also an opinion on the weight of gas or gas-producing material necessary to produce an effective concentration in a given area in average atmospheric conditions."[64]

On June 16, 1919, director of research Brigadier General Brooke-Popham circulated a memo. "I sent Col. Ranken over to see the Chemical Warfare Department at the War Office to get accurate information regarding the position of gas bombs. The position is as follows—(a) the 9.45″ Trench Mortar Shell has been converted into an aerial bomb. The design of this is completed and the shell has actually been tried in the air and found satisfactory. There are shells converted for use as aerial bombs available now and only require filling and exploders provided for them. I do not know the number. They could be filled with any of the following types of gas: (1) Lachrymatory; (2) Mustard Gas; (3) Chlorine; (4) Phosgene. It is estimated that it would take at least six weeks before any filled shells complete with all their exploders would be provided. . . . The Chemical Warfare Department have made up two sample 520 lb. Bombs with a modified case but these have never been tried or put up for approval. These cannot be considered a practical proposition at the present time and it would probably be months before this type could be issued as suitable."[65]

By the end of June, Brooke-Popham concluded, "The best gas to use appears to be as follows: A) Lachrymatory; B) Phosgene." He explained, "Mustard gas is likely to make a casualty of an affected person for some six months and will foul the ground for a long period so that people stepping on rocks or stone on which the bomb has burst will become casualties. I also understand that natives of India or Africa would be liable to be killed off by Mustard gas more than Europeans would be. I attach a chart showing the approximate area affected by ten 9.45 gas bombs dropped at 2 seconds intervals. . . . The chart assumes that the first bomb is dropped in approximately the correct position with reference to the objective and that the machine keeps on a straight course for 20 seconds during which the bombs are dropped in succession. I am having a calculation made. . . . The accuracy of bombing varies so enormously with the conditions on the ground and in the air."[66]

Attached was a chart. Ten perfect circles were drawn vertically on the paper, along with explanatory notations: "Speed = 75 MPH. Interval of Release = 2 Secs. Area: 2,000 feet long, half-mile wide, varying with wind."[67] Yes, it was possible. But could it be done in time?

The jihad against Britain in Iraq did not have a precise starting date because insurgent violence, from simple sniper fire to massacres of Christians, had been ongoing in Mesopotamia since the end of World War I. But a major precursor to the full-fledged revolt erupted at 3 A.M. on December 11, 1919. Hundreds, perhaps thousands, of tribesmen stormed Dair al-Zur, a town in the no-man's-land between Syria and Mosul. Invaders, joined by local residents, set fire to the Political Office, forced open the safe and stole the money, and then attacked the hospital, a church, and even a mosque. Then they broke into the prison, freeing all prisoners. Two hours later, the marauders raided the fuel depot, but set off explosions in the process, which killed some 30 insurgents and injured dozens more. At first light, a British armored car sent out for patrol was repulsed by hostile gunfire. British machine guns, mounted on rooftops, took aim, but were also put out of commission by the rebels.[68]

British soldiers and police retreated to the barracks on the outskirts of Dair al-Zur. But by midmorning, the barracks was also under siege. Late in the morning, a momentary truce was declared, allowing the British commander to talk to the frenzied group. Just then, at 11:30 A.M., two airplanes from Mosul came into view. They carried no gas bombs, as such weapons were still months from completion.

But the airborne machine guns let loose on the town, throwing the village into panic. A frantic second truce was called as the British bargained for the safe return of their hostages and the Arabs demanded a cessation of the air strike.[69]

On December 14, 1919, three days after the assault began, Churchill announced a greatly expanded air force. Since the war, the British air fleet had dwindled from 22,000 aircraft to a mere 200 planes in 28 squadrons. Churchill asked for the equivalent of $75 million annually to fund new aircraft. This included three squadrons for Iraq. However, those planes were months away. British forces could not hold Dair al-Zur on the ground. They were forced to withdraw, and the territory was later ceded to Syria.[70] Dair al-Zur, the British thought, would now be France's problem.

But Dair al-Zur remained a British problem as well. Dair al-Zur was the closest contact point in Iraq to Damascus, and it became a new launch site for insurrection. The revolt soon spread south. On March 31, 1920, some 4,000 tribal warriors met at Kaimakamjazir to plan a general uprising. Its first glimmer occurred within 48 hours, on April 2, as a British convoy was attacked 50 miles northeast of Mosul; 10 Indian soldiers were killed.[71]

On May 1, acting Commissioner Wilson received official confirmation of the San Remo decision. Several days later, he was instructed to publish news of the mandate over Iraq bestowed by the League of Nations. The gist of London's proclamation declared, "Iraq has now been rescued from Turkey by military conquests, and armies of the British Empire are in military occupation of the country." Using visionary language and uplifting justifications, Britain promised to establish an interim civilian authority to "prepare the way for the creation of an independent Arab State of Iraq." To that end, London also pledged to form "representative divisional and municipal councils in different parts of the country." Therefore, the British mandate, the announcement declared, was "in fulfillment of promises that have been made to Arab peoples" and to Faisal.[72]

Wilson was both resentful of the "independence" being promised and extremely nervous about the restive Iraqis. He sent an urgent cable requesting permission to announce within the coming days—certainly before the onset of Ramadan—that he planned to immediately implement a constitutional process. "Once this is done," he wrote, "we shall be in a position to deal with extremists." In a separate memo, Wilson explained that in his view there were two types of extremists: "1) the sane extremists, who desire Arab independence under British control; and 2) the ultra-extremists, who desire to see the abolition of European control of all sorts throughout the East."[73]

Wilson's notion of Iraqi independence was colonial independence, or perhaps self-management. The notion of representative government for Mesopotamia's masses distressed him. The people of Iraq should be told, not asked. "I submit," he protested to London, "that it is for His Majesty's Government as Mandatory Power to prescribe what form of Government shall be set up in the immediate future. To refer the question afresh to divisional councils and to 'local opinion' can have but one result. The extremists who, following the example of their colleagues in Syria, are demanding absolute independence for Iraq—with or without [King] Abdullah [as their monarch]—will by threats and by appeals during the coming month of Ramadan to religious fanaticism win over moderate men who have hitherto looked to the Government for a scheme offering a reasonable chance of success. . . . The moderates cannot afford to oppose extremists unless they know that Government is prepared to give them active support."[74]

On May 19, the Ramadan observances that so worried Wilson began at Sunni and Shi'a mosques throughout the land. Apprehension became reality. After the religious services, combined audiences of Shi'a and Sunni gathered at the mosques to hear fiery nationalist rhetoric. In Baghdad, highly agitated throngs would emerge from the mosques, rolling through the streets, chanting and demanding independence. Moreover, some mosques featured aspects of both Sunni and Shi'a traditions, and by inviting their coreligionists as special guests projected an open show of Islamic unity.[75]

It was what Wilson feared. He recalled, "The first symptom of a rapprochement had occurred in the summer of 1919, when on two occasions Sunnis attended religious meetings which were held in memory of . . . [a revered and recently] deceased Shi'a *mujtahid* [revivalist]." Wilson continued, that it was not until Ramadan in May of 1920 "that the political significance of the reconciliation became apparent. We were well aware of the danger . . . in March and April . . . before the great fast began."[76]

Periodically, Arab deputations would try to communicate with Wilson. It was in vain. For example, when 15 delegates of the Baghdad community requested a meeting with Wilson to present their demands, he brusquely rebuffed them and denied they were genuine representatives of anyone. He instead chose to invite his own assembly of 40 handpicked representatives, all of whom he expected to support his agenda. The fact that one of these 40 was a Baghdadi Jew and two were local Christians further inflamed the populace, which only wanted a majority Islamic government.[77]

Secret meetings multiplied. A surreptitious network was established to help coordinate the coming revolt. Newly stitched national flags were quietly circulated. Leaflets printed in Najaf and Karbala rallied tribe and townsman alike for a concerted uprising. Then Imam Shirazi, a spiritual leader of Najaf, issued a pivotal fatwa that declared "none but Moslems have any right to rule over Moslems." Day and night, printing presses churned out copies of Shirazi's fatwa as activists disseminated them throughout the cities, villages, and tribal areas.[78]

The situation quickly deteriorated. In the early hours of June 4, in the village of Tel Afar, near Mosul, the commander of the gendarmes, Captain B. Stuart, was suddenly murdered in the street by his own Arab subordinate. Captain Stuart's two assistants tried to help, but a bomb killed them in their bullet-riddled bunker. Another officer was taken captive; he managed to escape, but was chased down and murdered on the outskirts of town. Convoys on the nearby road were raided. Two armored cars were dispatched, but they were surrounded and overturned; their crews, totaling 14 men, were also killed.[79]

The British retaliated. The next day, June 5, troops marched out from Mosul to Tel Afar. En route, they burned crops needed to feed the vicinity. Once at the scene of the outrages, Wilson recounts, the troops "chased the entire population of Tel Afar, innocent and guilty alike, into the desert." They destroyed suspect houses, but did not apprehend the killers.[80]

To reason with the most moderate militants, London tried to employ a more acceptable lexicon, parsing such concepts as *self-rule, autonomy, emerging democracy,* and other less-than-sovereign conditions—but all nonetheless subject to the British "tutelage" prescribed by Article 22 of the League of Nations Covenant. But words were worthless in this war. One rebellious newspaper from time to time typically verbalized the embittered feeling of the Arabs, belittling the Allied vocabulary: "We do not reject the mandate because [of] its name but because of its very meaning, which is destructive of independence . . . [Many] words . . . are used by the colonizers. But they all translate to 'mandate,' and are intended to deceive weak nations. Only the name is changed, just as when they talk of liberating humanity, [and] healing the weak."[81]

On June 6, nationalist pamphlets bearing the five-pointed emblem of resistance circulated everywhere, demanding the expulsion of the British. Ten days later, the new call to arms rallied defiance against the mandate decision at San Remo. Everywhere the movement proclaimed Faisal's brother, Abdullah, to be Iraq's king, as decided at the Second Syrian General Congress at Damascus several months earlier.[82]

On June 30, 1920, the revolt intensified dramatically. In the lower Euphrates river town of Rumaitha, an activist sheikh was gruffly rebuked for not paying his estimated agricultural tax and then arrested by the assistant political officer. Within hours, his followers descended on the local terra-cotta prison, freeing him. Emboldened, the rebels rampaged through the area, burning all the local bridges and cutting the railroad lines. Despite hard fighting and several attempts at reinforcement, the beleaguered garrison at Rumaitha was not relieved until July 20, at a cost of 35 British soldiers killed and 150 wounded. A third of the garrison they came to rescue was dead. Their surviving comrades in hand, the British civil and military authorities promptly evacuated.[83]

Even as Rumaitha was overtaken, insurgents overran the village of Samawa. By mid-July, tribesmen asserted themselves in Abu Sukhair, Kufa was blockaded, and the Bani Hasan tribe rose up defiant. Revolutionary governments were set up in Najaf, Samawa, and additional village after village as the undermanned British evacuated. Three companies of the Third Manchesters, plus cavalry, artillery, and Sikh fighters, were deployed from Hilla to restore order, but only half survived the 118-degree heat and the onslaught of some 500 attackers who suddenly appeared on their flank. The British fought at close range with bayonets, but were overwhelmed: 180 killed, 60 wounded, 160 taken captive.[84]

Following the multiple events of July 24, 1920, crowned by the French victory over Damascus, nationalist Arabs concentrated their defiance in Iraq. Insurrection became all-out jihad once formal declarations from religious leaders were promulgated during the first week of August. National zeal escalated into religious fanaticism, as everywhere the Arabs attacked everything Western.[85]

Immediately, the whole country ignited. On August 9, the village of Baquba was ransacked, the rail line cut, and the nearby Armenian refugee camp attacked. On August 10, the British vessel *Greenfly* went aground on the lower Euphrates just outside Khizr; hostile Arabs surrounded the ship, prevented it from being towed, starved the crew into surrender, and then murdered them all. On August 11, extremists tried to assassinate a political officer in the midst of a truce negotiation; the tribesmen suddenly opened fire on his military escort. On August 12, a similar ambush occurred when a political officer tried to meet with an Arab leader at Arbil.[86]

Shortly thereafter, the supply ship "S9" ran aground in the low Euphrates water; it was captured, set afire, and the crew massacred. Trains fared little better. It did not matter whether the trains were armored. Once the track was blown, belligerents attacked and killed all the passengers. So much railroad line was blown up, the British were forced to erect a series of protective blockhouses mile by mile along the track. Even constructing these was often a fatal exercise, as work crews were constantly attacked. In the Hilla area alone, six waves of attacks were repulsed, with an estimated 200 dead among the rebels and 40 British casualties.[87]

Nor did it matter whether the victim was a soldier involved in combat or reconstruction. Colonel G. E. Leachman had spent much of his time dispensing liberal subsidies to Iraqis to win their hearts and minds. He spoke fluent Arabic and was popular among local farmers. On August 12, Leachman was summoned to a meeting with Sheikh Dhari at Fallujah to discuss crops and revenue. After arriving with a military escort, Leachman was abruptly informed of a highway robbery outside of town. Intuitively, the colonel dispatched his armed escorts to assist. That left him unprotected. Sheikh Dhari then approached with two followers. Leachman knew Sheikh Dhari well, had assisted him in the past, and welcomed him. That's when Sheikh

Dhari's followers shot Leachman at close range. Sheikh Dhari approached the dying man. Leachman looked up and asked why, as he had never offended anyone in Iraq. Without hesitation, Sheikh Dhari drew his sword and mercilessly finished the job.[88]

Monstrous treatment at the hands of Arab captors was common. On occasion, British prisoners were marched from town to town in the summer heat, barefoot and nearly naked. Two captured pilots were set upon by angry crowds who murdered them, cut off their ears to deliver them as prizes to the local mullah, knocked out all their teeth and sold these as trophies, and finally further mutilated the bodies for all to see.[89]

Nor did it matter if the British were Moslem Indians or Christian. Some 85 percent of the civilian and military men were Indians—many of them Moslem; yet they were killed with equal fervor. Fallen Moslems were frequently denied an Islamic burial by the embittered religious authorities. Not infrequently, their wives were sought out and violated and their children viciously beaten in the streets for being from treasonous families.[90]

When jihadists who had been taken prisoner were interrogated, they were sometimes asked why they fought so fiercely. One report from Wilson gave this answer: "They tell me that . . . life or death is a matter of indifference."[91]

Britain was outnumbered and poorly situated. The new Meso-potamian commander, General Aylmer Haldane, semiretired and physically unfit, had arrived just a few months earlier with Victorian flourish. Haldane himself recalled that he "disliked the idea of remaining in Baghdad throughout the hot weather" because he could only exercise "an hour or two in the late afternoon." What's more, he freely admitted, "I had no conception of the system on which we governed Mesopotamia, for it had not been possible to obtain much information regarding it."[92]

How many troops could Haldane deploy? Subtracting the sick and heat-stricken, as well as artillerymen, only 29,500 cavalry and infantry, 90 percent Indian, were available to restore civil order, guard 14,000 Turkish prisoners still unrepatriated from the war, and protect the substantial civil administration.[93]

Against Haldane's 29,500 poorly supported British soldiers were multitudes of Arab tribal warriors. From Basra to Baghdad along the

Euphrates: 43,000 Muntafik, 11,500 Khazail, and 17,500 from smaller clans; and along the Tigris: 18,500 Bani Malich, 8,000 Albu Mohammed, plus 17,800 from lesser clans. From Fallujah to Ashur, some 27,000 Dulaim fighters were raiding. One military report estimated the total fighting strength in the Baghdad and Basra provinces as 160,000 warriors, plus 481,000 Kurdish fighters.[94] Everywhere and every day, the rebels sniped, murdered, pillaged, burned, kidnapped, robbed, laid siege, sabotaged, and unwove the very fabric of Britain's presence.

Only air power could save the British now, a reality that Churchill had accepted months earlier in late March 1920, when he announced to the House of Commons that the disturbances in Mesopotamia were too costly and challenging to control with ground troops. Air power would be used. The gas bombs were being rushed, but not yet ready. Trials and training were still under way.[95]

Throughout August and September 1920, the Royal Air Force strafed and bombed enemy concentrations and sympathetic towns. August 21 at Baquba, the scene of numerous outrages: "today intense bombing raid carried out on rebel villages in neighborhood"; August 23 at Baquba: "bombing raiders inflicted severe casualties on rebels— 86 known killed in Baquba and [nearby] Shiftah." Kufa was bombed heavily, especially its mosque, which had become a center for political activities. On one day alone: At Samawa, "air bombing had good effect"; outside Baghdad, "aeroplanes retaliated by bombing"; seven miles northeast of Hilla at the village Munaihillalmarjan, "aeroplane today attacked."[96]

It was never enough, and Haldane and Wilson continually asked for more airplanes to subdue the seemingly irrepressible insurrection. Additional planes did not exist. Once more, on September 28, gas was requested. London replied again that they were not ready: "We have requested Air Ministry who are now carrying on trials to push on their experiments."[97]

The purpose of the airplanes was not just military, but to shock and awe the population, what the Air Ministry called "Morale Bombing." The chief advocate and developer of Morale Bombing was Chief of Staff Hugh Trenchard, who reported directly to Churchill. One Trenchard memo to Wilson, in June 1920, set forth the new philosophy of warfare. "Aircraft depend," the memo explained, "to a great extent on the moral effect that they create; this is at present considerably owing to ignorance in the native mind. If they are constantly used for petty operations which cause no great material damage and cannot, owing to the smallness of the unit, be long sustained, *respect will change to annoyance and contempt.* If this should ever come about the reinspiring of the natives with proper respect for the air arm will be a long and expensive task. It follows, therefore, that when air operations are resorted to, they should be carried out in a strength sufficient to inflict severe punishment and in numbers adequate to sustain the attack for as long a period as may be necessary. It will be realized then that aircraft . . . by their mere presence will often induce the natives to return to peaceful ways."[98]

A keen disciple of Trenchard's philosophy was Air Marshal Chief Arthur Harris, who relentlessly bombed Iraqi civilian areas. Harris earned the nickname "Bomber Harris." During the next major war with Germany, it would be Bomber Harris who advocated and oversaw the carpet bombing of the city of Dresden.[99]

What was not achieved in Iraq by bombing from the air was accomplished by torch on the ground as Britain intensified its retaliation. Village after village was set on fire. Gertrude Bell, a staunch Arabist ally of both T. E. Lawrence and Faisal, expressed the agonizing hopelessness of the campaign, as the British found themselves in the schizophrenic position of reconstructing and democratizing the country while bombing and burning it into passivity. "We are hampered by the tribal uprising. . . . I think rightly . . . the tribes must be made to submit to force. In no other way was it possible to make them surrender their arms, or teach them that you mustn't engage lightly in revolution, even when your holy men tell you to do so. . . . Nevertheless, it's difficult to be burning villages at one end of the country by means of a British Army, and assuring people at the other end that we really have handed over responsibility to native ministers."[100]

By late October, outside funding for the fighters had dwindled to a trickle, their ammunition depleted. Karbala, a spiritual epicenter of the insurrection, was totally blockaded, and the canals cut to shut down the water supply; the village finally surrendered. Najaf notables were instructed to lay down their arms or the city would be bombed; to avoid plague and devastation to thousands of refugees, the elders complied. The submission of Karbala and Najaf was the beginning of the end of the revolution. Most of the fighters elsewhere simply retreated to their homes. Most—but not all—of the cities became quiet.[101]

Wilson was removed as acting civil commissioner. His replacement, Percy Cox, was brought in from Persia to oversee an immediate transition to a provisional government, which would include a general elective assembly and a constitutional process. Cox announced the provisional government on November 11, 1920. With that, two years after the Great War ended, the lingering conflict in Mesopotamia finally began to wind down. By spring 1921, the country was calm enough to bring in its new leader. It was not Abdullah, but Faisal. The British felt they could do business with him. The sharif of Mecca, who fought alongside Lawrence, who became the elected leader of Damascus for just a few months, was now finally anointed by the British as the "king of Iraq." Faisal officially arrived in Iraq June 23, 1921, with all pomp and circumstance, and acceded to the throne August 23. The nation of Iraq was born.[102]

The Iraq revolt of 1920 was costly: 426 British killed, 1,228 wounded, 615 missing or captured. Among the Arabs: some 8,450 casualties. British taxpayers spent some £40 million pounds. Iraq in many places was in cinders. The British public became dispirited over its losses in Mesopotamia. London's media regularly excoriated the government. One article in the *Daily Mail,* titled "The War Mongers," railed that "there is nothing in all our history to compare with our folly in Mesopotamia."[103]

Cox's replacement as high commissioner was Sir Henry Dobbs. Looking back, he wrote, "So now to raise up this Iraq we have squandered blood, treasure, and high ability. We have bound debts and taxes on the necks of generations of our descendants. . . . We have suffered the imputation that on the scene of their agony we living have betrayed the hopes of our dead. You ask: for all this shall we have our reward? I answer that I cannot say."[104]

George Buchanan, who had administered the waterways and dredging of Iraq in the Wilson administration, published his own retrospective years later. "And so the tragedy of Mesopotamia remains," Buchanan wrote, "a tragedy of heroism, suffering, wasted lives, and wasted effort, which began in 1914 when the Indian Expeditionary Force entered the Shatt-el-Arab River and which had not ended when military control ceased in 1921. The soldiers did their work, and by force of arms wrested the country from the Turks. The civilian administrators did their work and established law and order, peace and prosperity, throughout the land. The statesmen did their work and successfully annulled all that had been accomplished by the soldiers and administrators. Mesopotamia has been called the cradle of the human race, and was at one time the granary of the world. Will its former glories ever be revived and the enormous sacrifices made by Great Britain ultimately be justified by the evolution of a happy, prosperous, and free nation?"[105] Buchanan did not answer his question.

As for Wilson, the lifelong bureaucrat left government service for a new career. He went into industry. Wilson was immediately hired by Anglo-Persian Oil Company.[106]

CHAPTER FIFTEEN

The Red Line

Iraq was not quite a nation and Faisal was not quite a king when he and Great Britain signed a formal treaty of alliance on October 10, 1922. Although it was labeled a "treaty" as if between two governments and bore regal seals on its cover, the treaty was actually not with the nation of Iraq, but with the king as an individual. That's because the new Iraq was nominally an independent kingdom, yet under international law it was still a mandated territory under the control and tutelage of the British. Moreover, King Faisal, although proclaimed a monarch, was required to take counsel and instructions from Britain's appointed resident, High Commissioner Sir Percy Cox.[1]

The 1922 treaty in many ways read like the earlier protectorate contract with the sheikh of Kuwait. Except in this case, it was not the nation being protected. After all, recalcitrant villages were still regularly being bombed by the R.A.F.[2] The real protectorates were British commercial interests—shipping, railroading, oil exploitation, and pipelines, and they were being protected against Iraq itself.

Article VIII guaranteed that no Iraqi land would be ceded or leased to any power other than Britain. Article IV assured that Faisal "agrees to be guided by the advice of His Britannic Majesty tendered through the High Commissioner on all important matters affecting the international and financial obligations of His Britannic Majesty for the whole period of the treaty." Article XI included an all-important nondiscrimination clause with a vital parenthetical: "There shall be no discrimination in Iraq against the nationals of any State" with whom England maintained diplomatic relations. The parenthetical added: "(including companies incorporated under the law of such State.)"[3] This last was in effect the key to the "Open Door."

What was the Open Door? It had manifested some three years earlier when Iraq's oil was handily split between England and France. The San Remo petroleum agreement granted Paris the 25 percent of the Turkish Petroleum Company once owned by Deutsche Bank. The French government then transferred that 25 percent to what later evolved into the Compagnie Française des Pe'troles, a combine of some scores of smaller oil concerns that created a new government-controlled oil monopoly.[4] By the authority invested in San Remo, and subject to a more stabilized Iraq, France and her petroplex now gained a reliable source of crude oil. At the same time, Great Britain would be able to drill deep into Iraq, continue its exploitation of Persian oil, and transport the black treasure across Syria to the Mediterranean. But there was just one other thing. France and Britain left out one power, the newest of the great powers: the United States of America. Woodrow Wilson, the State Department, and even more important, Standard Oil of New Jersey demanded what they called "an Open Door policy" to Iraq's oil.

By way of background, the first years of the twentieth century's oil development were completely different in America than in Europe. Rockefeller's Standard Oil had accrued too much commercial power too quickly and was stopped by the U.S. government with antitrust prosecutions. But in Great Britain and Germany, the oil baronies were tools and extensions of the government itself—to a degree, even owned by the government. By the time the Great War ended in 1918, America's military-industrial self-conception had evolved and no longer felt the pangs of containment. True, the Senate had refused to ratify Wilson's League of Nations and therefore America was the only victor excluded from the spoils. But who supplied 80 percent of Britain's oil? America. Who fielded great armies on land, sea, and air, shoulder-to-shoulder with the Allies? America. Who was now being left out of the oil riches of Mesopotamia? Once again, America.

President Woodrow Wilson demanded equality in the great new world order sketched by his Fourteen Points, specifically Point III: "The removal, so far as possible, of all economic barriers and the establishment of an equality of trade conditions among all the nations consenting to the peace." This point was buttressed by the league's own principle on mandates that the Mesopotamian territory was to be administered "to assure equal treatment to the commerce and to the citizens of all nations." What's more, Britain had secured international support for its mandate by pledging "that the natural resources of Mesopotamia are to be secured to the people of Mesopotamia and to the future Arab State to be established."[5]

Activism began in earnest at the September 27, 1919, meeting of the American Petroleum Institute in Colorado Springs, where the organization's Committee on Foreign Relations launched its campaign for access to Iraqi oil. The committee, headed by Standard Oil president Walter C. Teagle, resolved to use "diplomatic channels" to press the crusade. A formal approach was made to United States secretary of state Robert Lansing.[6]

The oil industry produced a series of white papers and memoranda castigating the British and French oil monopolies as antidemocratic, anti-American, and, of course, ungrateful. Inflammatory rhetoric was borrowed from the day's preoccupation with the Red Scare and anti-Bolshevik fears of world domination. Couching the protection of American oil interests in the same phrasing as protecting the American heartland spurred the government and informed circles. One such paper, titled "The Menace of Foreign State Monopolies to the American Petroleum Industry," asserted, "During the war, the conduct of commerce and industry throughout the world was largely placed under governmental control. This was the result of the necessity under which governments labored, of devoting all their resources and all their energies to the work of the destruction then going on. . . . But it was understood to be purely temporary and was expected to come to an end with the close of the war. The fulfillment of this expectation is now gravely threatened."[7]

Another industry memo warned in early October 1919, "For a number of years, Great Britain has been slowly maturing plans . . . [for] the domination of the world's oil supplies. Great Britain needs oil for her navy, for her mercantile marine, for her industries, and the demand is that the sources of supply should be under British control." The memo recited the list of governmental oil monopolies Britain was establishing in the West Indies, Asia, and Latin America, but was especially apprehensive about Mesopotamia. "It would seem," the industry memo insisted, "that the British and the European conception of a mandate is nothing short of annexation."[8]

One policy statement, headlined "Imperative Need for Aggressive Foreign Policy as Regards the Oil Industry," bluntly proclaimed: "America produces and consumes two-thirds of the petroleum in the world, and to this extent has greater interests involved than all the rest of the world combined." Asserting that domestic use was now outpacing domestic production, the oil industry démarche again pressed the government to move decisively on Mesopotamia.[9]

Presaging a long-term struggle—twice as long as the Great War itself—the first memo prophetically concluded: "American capital, American technical knowledge, American brains and push properly organized can defeat the far reaching plans of the British. It will be a strenuous fight for a decade, but there is no reason short of sheer stupidity on the part of America, why the greater part of the oil resources of the world should not be controlled by American capital."[10]

Yet another position paper decried, "The door has already been closed to American enterprise in Persia, where the Anglo-Persian Oil Company has an exclusive concession, granted on May 28, 1901, for a term of sixty years." Hence, the name "Open Door" was affixed to America's insistence that Iraq not go the way of Persia.[11]

It was all terribly awkward. True, the United States was a principal ally in the Great War and a full-fledged party to the Paris Peace Conference, helping to establish the course of the mandate system over Mesopotamia. But the United States had never ratified the treaty creating the League of Nations and was therefore not entitled to act the role of a member. Moreover, America had only declared war against Germany, which had attacked U.S. vessels sailing for European ports. Hence, America had never been at war with the Ottoman Empire, which formerly controlled the three provinces of Mesopotamia. Still, America expected its voice to be heeded, and the European Allies indeed expected to heed it.

America's voice, of course, loudly insisted on compliance with the lofty ideals of equal treatment for all the companies of all nations and avoidance of monopolistic behavior. But these demands were in fact mere verbal levers, jingoes, and rationales coating the true driving principle: No monopoly in Iraq could be created without America. Once that was achieved, America could butt out of Britain's business.

Agitation against the unshared monopoly quickly became public. It included resolutions led by Henry Cabot Lodge in the Senate, congressional inquiries, surveys and studies of Middle East oil, as well as newspaper editorials, plus a strategic letter-writing campaign to all the right people, from Woodrow Wilson to local legislators.[12]

When in December 1919 the Civil Administration in Iraq stopped two American geologists in Baghdad from attempting to survey the land, it was nothing short of a diplomatic affront. The Civil Administration had earlier speciously assured the State Department: "No concessions in Mesopotamia for the acquisition of oil lands or oil have been granted nor has the acquisition of such concessions been permitted, and . . . no change in this policy will be effected until the future administration of this country is settled."[13]

Worried British officials from several agencies huddled at the India Office on January 2, 1920, trying to get their stories straight about what the Turkish Petroleum Company was and what it was not. "If the American Government should protest against the company being allowed to monopolize the exploitation of these wells as contrary to the principles of the Peace Conference," the officials agreed, they would simply answer that the British accepted those principles, but "were bound to recognize an agreement which [they] had made with the company before the war." This referred to the Foreign Office–engineered fusion agreement of March 19, 1914. As the January 2 strategy session progressed, the men parsed words and diced the semantics of control. One Foreign Office oil expert thought they could distract from the commercial operation if everyone would "just emphasize the military nature of the operations."[14]

Once the secret San Remo agreement dividing up Iraq's oil was initialed on April 24, 1920, the tension escalated. On May 7, 1920, a Standard Oil executive in Paris finally obtained a copy of the secret protocol. The U.S. Embassy forwarded it to recently sworn in Secretary of State Bainbridge Colby, himself a former antitrust prosecutor. Colby was furious. Within a few days, on May 12, without revealing that Washington had access to the San Remo agreement, American ambassador to Britain John Davis delivered to British foreign secretary Lord Curzon an unusually stern epistle of America's new policy. "During the Peace negotiations at Paris," the cable reminded, "leading up to the Treaty of Versailles . . . [the United States] consistently took the position that the future peace of the world required that as a general principle" any territory secured from Turkey, "must be held and governed in such a way as to assure equal treatment in law and in fact to the commerce of all nations."[15]

Blunt and incisive, the cable asserted that in the minds of most Americans, the mandate for Iraq "had given advantage to British oil interests which were not accorded to American companies and further that Great Britain had been preparing quietly for exclusive control of the oil resources in this region." Ambassador Davis demanded, "That no exclusive economic concessions covering the whole of any Mandated region, or sufficiently large to be virtually exclusive, shall be granted, and that no monopolistic concessions relating to . . . such commodity [oil] shall be granted."[16]

Outrage in official and industry circles over the San Remo accord intensified with each day. On May 13, M. L. Requa, a former director of the U.S. Fuel Administration, vigorously warned an assistant undersecretary of state that America owned 90 percent of the automobiles in the world; it was the most rapidly industrializing nation on earth. The country was already forced to import more than 60 million barrels annually from Mexico. But Mexican exports were declining due to political conditions. No matter how domestic reserves and growth were extrapolated, argued Requa, the U.S. would run out of oil in less than two decades unless it secured equal access to Iraq.[17]

Otherwise, Requa predicted, "the United States will practically pay the British war debt in the purchase of [Iraqi] petroleum, which, if things go on as they are, will within ten years amount to the purchase of 500 million barrels a year . . . [amounting to] $1.5 billion per annum." Requa ended, "Pardon this outburst; but, as an American citizen, whose ancestors came here in 1680, and as an authority on petroleum, I cannot refrain from raving at the utter indifference and incapacity of our Government toward this critical situation."[18]

On May 12, Ambassador Davis in London confronted British petroleum czar John Cadman in person. "No reference was made to the San Remo agreement . . . of which they, no doubt, believe us to be ignorant," reported Davis. First making clear that all of America would be deeply offended by any hint of monopoly, Davis demanded to know whether any oil concessions in fact had been granted in Iraq. Cadman replied that he well understood "the folly" of antagonizing America. He admitted there was some sort of company called Turkish Petroleum, which possessed some sort of concession dating back to Ottoman times. A clearly nervous Cadman lied, claiming he knew nothing of the details. Davis knew he was lying.[19]

America's petroleum industry and its friends in high places continued to foment the waters of public and governmental opinion. Newspaper articles railed against British attempts to dominate America. Restrictive legislation was proposed against British firms operating in America. Senator J. D. Phelan was prepared to draft a retaliatory bill against Shell's several subsidiaries in the United States. Washington caustically accused London of abusing its mandate in Iraq and the secretary of state issued a long condemnation in November 1920. But about then, President Wilson had become an invalid whose failed cross-country effort to rally public support for the League of Nations had broken his spirit and his health. London dispatched British petroleum official Cadman to America to begin negotiations with the American Petroleum Institute and perhaps buy time. Lord Curzon himself waited until February 1921, after newly elected American president Warren Harding assumed office, before filing a formal protest to what he called America's unfair allegations of British commercial misconduct. In a long report, Lord Curzon traced the tortuous origins of Deutsche Bank's Baghdad Railway concession from the sultan in 1898, its formalization into a treaty in 1903, its transfer to the Turkish Petroleum Company in 1912, its British-inspired fusion with Anglo-Persian just before the outbreak of war in 1914, its seizure as enemy property after the war, its route through a succession of Anglo-French postwar oil agreements, and finally its deliverance to the French as a war spoil at San Remo in April 1920. All of it was perfectly legitimate, argued Lord Curzon. With that, Lord Curzon rebuked America for promoting exclusionary monopolies in Haiti and the Philippines while decrying Britain for the same purported actions in Iraq.[20]

None of that mattered to American policymakers. The door in Iraq must open.

Negotiations moved to England in early 1922. On April 9, Cadman, along with Anglo-Persian president Charles Greenway and

Standard oil chairman A. C. Bedford, conferred at the stately Stanbridge Earls boarding school in southeast England. Stanbridge Earls
was Greenway's old boarding school. Bedford suggested that the
entire question of Iraqi oil had become too politicized, with diplomats, legislators, and regulators leading the charge. Of course, that was
the American Petroleum Institute's original strategy, to use governmental and diplomatic sources to pressure Britain. Perhaps, said Bedford, it was time to convert the crisis into a purely commercial
transaction.[21]

The impasse could disappear if America were simply allowed to
join England's Anglo-Persian, Shell's Anglo-Saxon, and France's
incubating cartel as a coequal member of Turkish Petroleum. Bedford
revealed that a consortium of American companies was ready to join
Standard to create an American oil bloc in Mesopotamia. Greenway
welcomed the opportunity. Both men agreed to lobby their respective
governments for a formula of inclusion that would dissolve all American complaints about monopoly.[22]

In other words, the door to Iraq's oil wealth would be created and
remain open just long enough for American oil to enter. That door
would then shut behind them. But how?

Nothing could be more complex. Three governments and numerous commercial concerns, all government-controlled or regulated,
were required to compromise on their portion of the billions lying
beneath the Iraqi soil. Every percent was sanctified as an indispensable national imperative. In these brittle negotiations, all who won did
so at the other's expense. But none could win unless all agreed.

In mid-July 1922, American Petroleum Institute representatives,
led by Standard Oil president Teagle, worked the government offices
and corporate boardrooms of London and Paris. The first several
meetings established the lofty Wilsonian principles of transparency,
equal trade, and a share of the wealth dedicated to the local population—this to comply with State Department expressions. The artifice
to achieve equality among all nationals was an elaborate subleasing
scheme in which numbered plots of oil-rich Iraqi fields would be
periodically advertised in certain oil publications in Holland, the
United States, England, and France—all of which were already participating with their controlled or regulated cartels. A year after the
advertising, these plots would be auctioned off to the highest bidder,

fundamentally among themselves, as decided in a special process by TPC, which they themselves would own. The "native population"—Faisal's government—would receive a royalty.[23]

Since several American petroleum companies, led by Standard Oil, were joined together in the American syndicate, the scheme did not violate antimonopoly statutes. The various oil companies, seven at first—Standard Oil of New Jersey, Standard Oil of New York, Gulf Corporation, Atlantic Refining, Sinclair Oil, and two smaller firms—would ultimately create what they called the Near East Development Company to represent their participation in the emerging captive multinational TPC enterprise. On August 22, the State Department endorsed the principles as conforming to the equal commerce tenets of the Open Door. State made clear it would continue to object to the validity and legality of the Turkish Petroleum Company and its San Remo formula until the U.S. companies joined in.[24]

Not quite three weeks later, on October 10, 1922, the treaty of alliance between Great Britain and King Faisal was signed. It carefully incorporated the Open Door policy, ensconced between parentheses wedged into Article XI. The treaty covered the three provinces of Mesopotamia.[25] But no one knew whether the questionably seized Mosul province would remain within the sovereign limits of the new Iraq. They barely knew where Mosul began and ended, since its approximate realm lay within hazy Ottoman frontiers with Syria, Persia, traditional Armenia, traditional Kurdistan, and even the new state of Turkey.

Indeed, with the war four years behind them, and riding a surge of nationalism, the Turks were demanding the return of the Mosul province—and its untapped oil billions. Yet another international conference was called, this one at Lausanne, Switzerland, in November 1923 to finally settle the numerous conflicting treaty and peace provisions between the Allies and Turkey. America could not participate because it was not a member of the League of Nations and had never been at war with the Ottoman Empire.

But America's presence was felt as an official observer. Washington's nine conditions for U.S. passivity at Lausanne required adherence to such Wilsonian goals as the protection of minorities, freedom of international navigation, and preservation of American archaeological research. Point 3, titled "Protection of American Commercial

Interests," demanded that all conferees "maintain the principle of the Open Door and equal opportunity.[26]

During the tempestuous conference, which lasted several months, the British refused to relinquish Mosul. The Turks refused to cede it, insisting the province had been illegally conquered days after the armistice of 1918. A worried American establishment wondered if the region might go back to Turkey, thus neutralizing the San Remo agreement it sought to join. Secretary of State Charles Hughes, on November 27, cabled the American Lausanne mission, "The position of the Department is in brief: 1) That the American companies would receive Department's support in their efforts to obtain adequate participation in the development of Mesopotamia, if Mesopotamia, including the Mosul vilayet, remains under British mandate. 2) That a new situation would be presented if the Mosul area reverts to Turkey. But it may be stated in general that the Department would refuse acquiescence in any monopolistic concession in the Mosul area resulting from a political trade. . . . In view of American contribution to the common victory over the Central Powers, no discrimination can rightfully be made against us in any territory won by that victory. The United States claims equality in economic rights in territories under mandate."[27]

Secretary of State Hughes carefully added, "The United States has nothing to conceal. It is not seeking any secret arrangements for itself and does not expect any on the part of other governments."[28] That said, if Mosul were restored to Turkey, America would lose mandate oil.

Britain and the Allies who controlled the League of Nations would not allow Mosul to revert to Turkey. British foreign secretary Lord Curzon himself chaired the conference. Sidestepping the issue of the illegal territorial seizure, he staunchly proclaimed that his nation entertained no oil interests in the area. In one typical defensive speech, Curzon thundered, "It is supposed and alleged that the attitude of the British Government to the vilayet of Mosul is affected by the question of oil. The question of the oil of the Mosul vilayet has nothing to do with my argument. I have presented the case on its own merits and quite independently of any natural resources that may be in the country. I do not know how much oil there may be in the neighborhood of Mosul, or whether it can be worked at a profit or whether it may turn out after all to have been a fraud."[29]

Curzon explained away the Turkish Petroleum Company by insisting, "Both the British government and the T.P.C. itself recognize that oil is a commodity in which the world is interested and . . . a great mistake to claim or exercise [as] a monopoly. Accordingly, the Company, with the full knowledge and support of the British Government, took steps . . . to associate the interests of other countries and other parties in this concern so that all those who are equally interested may have a share. If the enterprise is successful, Iraq will be the main gainer. . . . That is the substance of the oil affair which I have explained to the Conference in order that they may know the exact amount of influence, and that is *nil* . . . of oil on . . . the question of Mosul."[30]

Right through the Lausanne conference, petroleum executives and government officials continued to huddle in various capitals. The French and Shell were reluctant to reduce their participation or accept a new partner. But finally, on December 12, 1922, in London, the British and Americans both gave a little to acquire a monumental gain. Anglo-Persian, which controlled roughly half of Turkish Petroleum, agreed to transfer about half of its holdings to the American consortium. Once transferred, British Anglo-Persian, the still-evolving French corporation, British-Dutch Shell's Anglo-Saxon, and the new American consortium would each own a quarter of TPC. To compensate Anglo-Persian for cutting its ownership in half, Anglo-Persian would receive 10 percent of TPC's oil free of charge.[31] Everyone would be happy.

Not everyone. There was just one other thing: Gulbenkian. Mr. Five Percent still owned his original fraction of Turkish Petroleum. So the plan was tweaked. Each of the four giant oil combines would reduce their one-quarter holding by a single percent, to 24 percent. That totaled 96 percent. Each of the four coequal partners would then proffer 1 percent of their quarter share, to create a 4 percent nonvoting beneficial holding for Gulbenkian—yes, down from 5 percent, but then, everyone had reduced their shares for the common good.[32] That seemed fair.

Standard Oil's representative in London wired a note of success to Standard Oil president Teagle, who in turn passed the information to the secretary of state in Washington. His message included the note that TPC "does not anticipate difficulty in getting acceptance of French and Gulbenkian."[33] They were quite wrong.

TPC general manager Herbert Nichols seemed to be the only person who could communicate with the irascible Gulbenkian. Nichols began talks with Gulbenkian at once. After several meetings in Paris, Gulbenkian hemmed and hawed but finally agreed not to 4 percent of the company, which would have obligated him to contribute 4 percent of the massive capitalization, but simply 4 percent of the profits. This way Gulbenkian suffered no ongoing cash obligation and merely collected 4 percent of the profits free and clear. Nichols and the group believed this to be an extravagant concession, but agreed. With the French nearly in concert, the deal seemed on its way.[34]

But the Saturday after agreeing, Gulbenkian unexpectedly phoned Nichols and woke him from a sound sleep. There was just one other thing. Nichols was still half asleep when Gulbenkian began railing. Maybe profits were not a good thing. Gulbenkian knew, after all, that oil companies regularly manipulated their net profits to avoid taxes. Hence, 4 percent of the simple "profits" could equal simply nothing. Gulbenkian insisted on net profit, accenting *net*.[35]

A few days later, Nichols tried to reason with him in a letter filled with complex numbers, proportions, and calculations. "Let us suppose that £8,000,000 goes into the Company—if you had shares, as we propose, you would have to provide £320,000 which at 6% (a moderate figure this) is equal to £19,200 per annum. This latter sum I maintain must fall to be deducted from your suggested alternative, [that is,] 4% of the net profits. Am I not right? . . . This is a far more attractive way of dealing with the matter than the one you suggest, inasmuch as there is the risk that there will always be differences of opinion as to what constitutes 'net profits.' . . . Why not agree to shares, and the matter is settled? . . . I shall await your writing with much interest, and can only impress upon you the urgency of getting this question cleared up quickly."[36]

No. Gulbenkian held firm, he wanted 4 percent *net* profits. Fine, Nichols agreed. Plus, Gulbenkian insisted on a careful definition of exactly what constituted net profits. Fine, Nichols agreed. Plus, Gulbenkian insisted on a £10,000 reimbursement for any expenses thus far. Fine, Nichols agreed to that as well. With all points agreed upon, Nichols immediately organized a three-page agreement itemizing everything.[37]

But at the last minute, Gulbenkian just did not feel right about the arrangement. He did not sign. With billions in the balance, the oilmen and their governments were astonished. By any measure, he would be greatly enriched. But Gulbenkian just didn't like the deal. No signature.

Western oil powers held their collective breath as the Lausanne Conference dragged into early 1923, with Mosul's fate undecided. Lord Curzon continued to deny Britain was in Iraq for the petroleum. "Oil has not the remotest connection," protested Lord Curzon, "with my attitude, or with that of his Majesty's Government on the Mosul question, or the Iraq question."[38]

Since Britain would not yield to argument, demanded Turkey, would it yield to a plebiscite? If the local populations—some 800,000 over a 35,000-square-mile region—were to be consulted in their own national destiny according to Wilsonian doctrine, why not let them vote: Remain with Britain under mandate or return to Turkey. Curzon ridiculed the very notion. "Why shall a plebiscite be invoked in the province? Ankara [Turkey] demands a plebiscite. Kurds have never demanded it. This poor nation even does not know what it means. Arabs and Turks in the province have also never demanded plebiscite. The only people demanding it are the Turks of Ankara."[39]

Finally, on February 4, Lord Curzon barked at the Turkish delegate: "War may break out anew. I wish you to accept this. You have . . . half an hour in which to save your country." But the Turks did not yield. Turkey had already reconstituted its own borders with a National Pact, which included Mosul.[40]

In July 1923, after drama, oratory, and not a few corridor exchanges, Britain and Turkey finalized their peace through the Treaty of Lausanne. Final except for one item: the Mosul question. Under the rules, the Mosul dispute would be negotiated further, and then, if still unresolved, referred to the League of Nations Council for formal international arbitration. Turkey, of course, was not a member of the League of Nations. Britain was.

While oil circles nervously awaited a decision, Gulbenkian continued his campaign of obstruction. One long-winded disputation after
another flew into Nichols's hands, cleverly alternating charm and sin-
cerity with hostility or hurt feelings. As important as the details was
Gulbenkian's penchant for abstruse logomachies and endless ifs, ands,
buts, and maybes. Each time Nichols sent over a revision to satisfy
Gulbenkian's sticking point, a new one emerged.

For example, on January 11, 1923, Gulbenkian protested to obtain
the expenses not paid when he had refused to sign the December 18,
1922, document and then was asked to contribute his share of TPC's
normal minor operating costs. "You must agree," he carped, "that it
is most unfair that the other two parties . . . should vote themselves
their expenses and entirely ignore my own." In a postscript he
appended, "What is still more stupendous is that by the action you
have taken, not only am I not repaid, but you ask me, in effect to
refund some of your expenses to my detriment, as I shall have to contribute a part of what you have got the company to repay you. Then
you say that the other claims are 'years old' but you miss the point that
mine is *the origin of it all.*"[41]

His whole idea was not to negotiate in good faith to resolve the
fine points, but to wear everyone else down. Gulbenkian constantly
suggested that a final agreement might yet be just one or two more
exchanges away, and then he would abruptly dash hopes. Meetings
were a good method of wasting time and draining strength. "Sir
Henry [Deterding] suggests that it will be better that we all meet
together [in October]," Gulbenkian wrote Nichols from Paris on
September 19, 1923. "Kindly let me know the date that would be
convenient to you." Invariably the anxious oilmen seized the opportunity to make progress. Nichols eagerly replied that he and Deterding would meet "as soon as we can arrange a date."[42]

Gulbenkian continually kept negotiators off guard. Occasionally,
he would refer to a promissory letter that no one could locate. For
example, as he cajoled the oil companies to increase their offer from
4 percent back to his original 5 percent, he claimed Deterding and
TPC had jointly promised in writing that his 5 percent would never
be reduced. A letter? What letter? Nichols and staff scrambled to find
such a letter, and finally wrote to him, "As neither he nor we can trace

any such letter, will you be good enough to send me a copy?"[43] Did Gulbenkian have such a letter written as long as a decade earlier? No one knew.

Gulbenkian's 5 percent was based on an almost undocumentable marginal investment in Turkish Petroleum Company in 1912, when the entity was nothing more than a sheaf of letters. Yet a decade later, he played the victim with skill, and often as though the big companies that would spend millions drilling, erecting refineries, and constructing pipelines and shipping facilities were on an equal footing with his paper percentage. Gulbenkian understood completely that while the majority can rule, the minority can obstruct.

While Nichols fenced with Gulbenkian, oil circles in Washington, New York, Paris, and London felt certain the man would come to his senses. They forged ahead, keeping the American secretary of state informed of every step with long reports every few days. By late September 1923, Teagle and colleagues had drafted a new concession document for Faisal to grant to Turkish Petroleum. TPC, as now envisioned, would be a jointly held nonprofit entity that merely drilled for oil and sold the crude to its owners, Anglo-Persian, Anglo-Saxon, plus the French and American syndicates. It was just as Gulbenkian had suspected. TPC would be run without profits as a corporate conduit for the oil.[44]

"I see that during my absence, the matter has again been twisted," he complained to Nichols in an October 26, 1923, missive about the latest plan. In his best accusatorial tone, Gulbenkian added, "It is no use twisting the real facts. . . . I do not want you to be under any misapprehension . . . that by coercion of one kind or another, I am going to allow myself to be imposed upon with unfair and unjust conditions."[45]

For good measure he added a dollop of thinly veiled blackmail. "The document now proposed [converting TPC into a nonprofit entity] deprives His Majesty's Government of a considerable amount of income tax; it deprives the Government of Iraq of legitimate rights in the exploitation, and, above all, it is an unfair and grasping document in regard to my own rights as a private shareholder. The first two points are no concern of mine if the interested parties care to acquiesce; but as regards myself, I ask you to read this letter in a most friendly spirit, but with the deep conviction that I shall not submit to injustice."[46]

Gulbenkian's tirades were always emboldened by his adversaries' kid-gloved responses. Nichols immediately replied with caution to the October 26 harangue: "Read your letter in the most friendly spirit. You are quite wrong in assuming that things have been twisted round. You will agree with me that we can hardly hope to arrive at a speedy and amicable understanding by the constant exchange of long argumentative letters, and that consequently it is in every way preferable that we should have an early talk between the three of us in order to make a determined effort to arrive at a settlement. I should like such a meeting to take place at an early date—the sooner the better—and shall be glad to learn whether it is likely that you will be in London in the near future."[47]

Every time the oilmen rewarded Gulbenkian's abuse by continuing to chase him for a settlement, Gulbenkian was reassured that the stakes were surely worth billions and that they needed him more than he needed them. The longer Gulbenkian held out, the more intransigent he acted, the better for the deal. The men of Standard Oil, Turkish Petroleum, Shell, and French companies had never encountered anyone like Gulbenkian. They were great men of business. But he was a master of the bazaar. All good things come to those who wait. What's more, Gulbenkian enjoyed the game, making the powerful squirm and seeing his slim fraction aggrandize, all at the same time.[48]

The Open Door remained open, but no one could pass through because everything was still so uncertain. In the first weeks of 1924, Turkish Petroleum officials wondered if they should change the name of the corporation to "Iraqi Petroleum" in anticipation of Mosul remaining in mandatory Iraq. They elected to register the new name, but to continue under the old Turkish Petroleum identity in the event Mosul reverted to Turkey and they needed to work anew with officials in Istanbul.[49]

Gulbenkian's intransigence remained a fixture of the stalled Iraq oil plans. In fact, the stalemate dragged on so long, and concomitantly the stakes became so much more greatly valued, that the dispute itself became a family enterprise. Calouste Sarkis Gulbenkian's son Nubar Sarkis Gulbenkian joined his father as co-negotiator in the year-to-year bickering. The long-bearded Nubar acted just as vain, conceited, and pejorative as his father. Nubar once quipped: "The best number for a dinner party is two—myself and a damn good head waiter." In his negotiations, Nubar was pushy and condescending. He could treat his well-heeled adversaries as mere servants, inasmuch as he held a card that all the players wanted, his father's card, that is, the Five of Points.[50]

Once Nubar even snarled at one of the oil executives, "Hold your tongue!" Nonetheless, he was deferred to as the ever-important go-between to his father, much as during a bygone decade when the sultan reigned and proximity meant power. Typical was a January 25, 1924, letter from Nichols to Nubar reviewing the latest propositions from Standard Oil president Teagle: "The enclosures are sent to you in duplicate, as you will probably wish to send copies to your Father. I am not clear whether he is yet ready to take an active part in these discussions although I believe, he is back in Paris. You might let me know?"[51]

At times, some of the chief executives thought they could improve upon Nichols's tireless efforts. In late July 1924, Teagle and others traveled to London for three days of face-to-face discourse. Teagle wrested numerous concessions and compromises from Gulbenkian and agreed to some himself—progress, but nothing decisive. Nichols wistfully wrote Teagle, "Had you come to terms, you would have achieved in three days what I have failed to do in eighteen months." Of course, Gulbenkian used these meetings to launch a hitherto unvoiced claim against TPC. When Teagle asked Nichols for any information about this new claim, Nichols frankly replied, "It has only recently been put forward, and for all practical purposes it does not exist."[52]

With or without Gulbenkian, the chief executives were determined to move forward, and they used their late July meeting to develop a so-called Working Agreement, or self-denying covenant, which very much resembled the original self-denial agreements crafted by Gulbenkian when TPC was first organized in 1912, and repeated in the fusion agreement of 1914. Under this latest version, the four combines agreed not to engage in any oil business within a defined area except through Turkish Petroleum, which they would all jointly own and operate. This Working Agreement would enshrine TPC in perpetuity as the fulcrum of the entire oil industry in Iraq: drilling, refining, shipping, pipelining, and retailing—everything would be funneled through this one concentrated commercial entity.[53]

Seeing clear advancement without him, Gulbenkian's attorneys quickly fired the first shot. The prestigious firm of Freshfields, Leese and Munns, on August 12, 1924, delivered a threat: "Such an agreement," their letter warned TPC, "would be a fraud on the rights of the minority shareholders, of whom we believe Mr. Gulbenkian is the sole representative." Freshfields demanded written assurance within seven days that the Working Agreement would not be implemented. Failing that, the law firm would obtain a restraining order.[54]

Nichols sent a letter, marked "strictly Private" to the French partner, Compagnie Française des Pe'troles, "Since both Mr. Teagle and I have failed to settle with Mr. Gulbenkian, and he has seen fit to threaten legal proceedings, I have considered it best that no further meetings of principals should take place at present. No fresh proposals have therefore been made on either side, but our respective lawyers are discussing the position. My own opinion is that Mr. Gulbenkian's lawyer also considers that he is 'looking for the moon,' and that we shall in consequence shortly receive some more reasonable proposal from that quarter."[55]

Meanwhile, the outside oil syndicates deployed their own law firms, headed by attorney Harold Brown, who drafted a highly detailed, historically researched, eight-page rebuttal to Freshfields. After numerous minor changes, Brown's brief was messengered September 26, 1924. As for the Working Agreement, Brown wrote, "We have gone into this explanation of the genesis of the 'Working Agreement' as we think, although your client has been kept closely informed of the negotiations at every stage, he is inclined to lose sight of some of these facts and, without the smallest justification, to treat the document as a plan hatched with the main object of depriving him of his full rights as the holder of five percent of the shares in the Turkish Petroleum Company."[56]

Every effort had been made to find an accommodation, to no avail, said Brown. "Up to date," he argued resolutely, "your client's reply to these proposals, which seem to us very fair, has been to offer obstruction . . . [and] demand a position of preference and privilege out of all proportion to his rights. . . . [How can these demands] be justified unless he thinks that his consent must be bought by our clients at any cost."[57]

Revving up the rhetoric, Brown warned, "In a last and final effort to secure your client's adhesion and thus avoid litigation and possible disaster for the whole enterprise our clients have instructed us to make the offers set out below." Several advantageous formulae were propounded.[58] Gulbenkian did not flinch.

Teagle dispatched a memorandum to the State Department stressing that the "the American Group" did not want a percentage of a foreign company, Turkish Petroleum, but reliable access to crude oil to sell in America or anywhere in the world. Gulbenkian was now demanding an equal place on the board of directors, a deciding vote on every decision, and an exorbitant royalty on any oil produced anywhere by TPC, even outside of Iraq. "All of the partners in the Turkish Petroleum Company," Teagle informed Washington, "including the American Group, considered Mr. Gulbenkian's proposal so unreasonable and burdensome as to preclude their acceptance."[59]

Secretary of State Hughes delivered a long report to America's ambassador in London. "Gulbenkian's position is considered unreasonable by the American Group." Hughes's report itemized the minutiae of their complaints against Gulbenkian and instructed the ambassador: "You should at once bring to the attention of the Foreign Office the view set forth in the three preceding paragraphs." The gist was that this obstruction was so pronounced it was construed as "an attempt to exclude American interests from a proper participation in developing Mesopotamia resources." In other words, a slamming of the Open Door. Gulbenkian was a naturalized British national, and Washington expected the British government to do something about him. Hughes directed his ambassador to promptly telegraph the results of his protest to the Foreign Office.[60]

Gulbenkian knew the protest had reached diplomatic channels. He wrote to the Foreign Office on September 27, 1924, asking for help and a meeting to explain his side. He had resorted to such appeals in the past during the days of the fusion negotiation. But on October 10, his best contact at the Foreign Office, William Tyrrell, wrote back that the British government simply "could not usefully intervene."[61]

Delegates of the four cartels then met in London on November 11, 1924, "to consider the impasse which has arisen owing to the impossibility of coming to terms with Gulbenkian." The next day, Nichols informed the partners in Paris, "It was decided that an entirely new line of action would have to be adopted."[62]

In early 1925, the four syndicates moved swiftly to create a fait accompli, that is, to secure a new concession from Faisal in favor of the Turkish Petroleum Company. With or without Gulbenkian, and even before the Americans had joined the company, this new concession would be along the lines envisioned in the Working Agreement. Hence the Working Agreement would be, to a degree, written into law.

The oil oligarchy knew that the longer the Gulbenkian crisis continued, the more additional claimants would creep onto the stage. By early 1925, Deutsche Bank was insisting its original 1912 transfer of the Anatolia Railway concession was improper. The many heirs of Sultan Abdulhamid II hired high-powered lawyers in New York and London to press their claim that the Young Turks in 1908 and 1909 had improperly seized the oil concessions from the sultan's *Civile Liste* and that they were the rightful heirs. Plus the French were now wondering why they should relinquish even 1 percent, let alone slightly more, to create a 4 to 5 percent beneficial interest for Gulbenkian when they had received the full Deutsche Bank original 25 percent share in TPC; that share had been properly seized in London and duly transferred at San Remo. When plural billions are at stake, the values of single percents add up, and France became reluctant to part with any fractions thereof. All these emerging claimants, and several others, only added to the corporate angst. Gulbenkian demanded in a February 2, 1925, note to Nichols: "Kindly let me know how we now stand with regard to the concessions and why these are dragging so; the longer they drag, the more of these mushroom growths we shall find."[63]

On March 14, 1925, after an intense back-and-forth, Faisal issued a new 75-year oil concession covering all of Iraq. It was a problematic concession for sure. This new convention guaranteed royalties to the government based on a profit formula linked to market prices against the cost of production and transportation. But the document did not address the TPC's ability to manipulate market prices. Nor did Faisal write in any safeguards against the company threading expenses through a vast fleet of its own subsidiaries and captives to inflate the cost of drilling, refining, transporting, and pipelining. In addition, while the concession identified the territory as "the defined area of Iraq," it did not actually define what areas lay within corporate Iraq. Still, no one knew whether international arbitration would parcel Mosul to Iraq or back to Turkey. Finally, important performance benchmarks were written in to speed the pace of royalties. The concession required no less than 12,000 feet drilled before any pipelines could be laid to transport Persian oil, and in any event 36,000 feet within three years.[64]

The clock was now ticking. Backed by the new concession, the four syndicates and TPC, in March 1924, assembled an intricate and tenuous provisional agreement, termed the "Heads of Agreement," for Gulbenkian to consider anew. While the Americans believed it imperative to coax Gulbenkian to sign anything, whether the Heads of Agreement or any other instrument, Teagle and his circle were opposed to affixing their own signatures. The idea of "provisional agreements" was unbusinesslike, in their opinion. Moreover, they were rapidly approaching the point of complete fatigue over Gulbenkian's escalating demands.[65]

Nonetheless, Nichols and company pressed on. No sooner did their patience collapse than Gulbenkian renewed it with a hopeful signal. The new Heads of Agreement offered to buy out Gulbenkian at a very favorable rate yet to be established. Once more, Gulbenkian teased and annoyed the anxious oilmen with waves of seeming acceptance and then the ever-present reluctance. This latest chapter in the saga continued for months, consuming many reams of paper and causing many sleepless nights among the executives. Finally, frustrated TPC officials in London prepared a disconsolate cable for Teagle in New York. "Hopeless to expect final agreement acceptable to Gulbenkian and ourselves under several more months tedious negotiation." With a production now governed by the clock, Nichols added, "Three groups feel that if they are not to risk forfeiture of [Faisal's]

Convention they must at all costs proceed with operations in Iraq."
One TPC executive fretted about telling Teagle too much worrisome
news, and scribbled underneath those words, "Suggest leaving this
out. Don't threaten, but act—without necessarily giving Americans
notice."[66]

Just as hope was to dissipate, Gulbenkian sounded hopeful. He
asked to make a few modifications to the buyout agreement—just a
few. But by the time he was done in September 1925, one embittered
oil syndicate attorney called the revisions "a travesty."[67] Still, as the
demand for oil in the world surged, syndicate negotiators could only
again steel themselves to the onerous task of drilling until they struck
a deal.

Finally, on October 6, 1925, the American Group gathered in
New York to approve Gulbenkian's latest demands for royalties, payments, rights, and prerogatives. They even agreed to convert Gulbenkian's beneficial interest into an almost regal position, wherein he
could appoint in his place his son or son-in-law, just as the sultans
used to do. That was an improvement—but not enough. Gulbenkian
would not sign.[68]

On October 29, 1925, the top executives, including Shell's Deterding, Nichols, and Anglo-Persian chairman Greenway, as well as
attorneys, huddled. They debated one approach after another, one
contractual variance after another. Exasperated, Deterding snapped,
"If Gulbenkian dislikes that position, let him come to the TPC with
a proposition to be bought out."[69]

Matters worsened when the passage of time prompted Faisal to
balk at allowing the Americans to participate, since they had not been
part of the TPC group at the time of the March 1925 concession.
Why admit more foreigners? The Americans acted as though they
were valid partners, but in fact were not legally in TPC and would not
formally join until the Working Agreement and Gulbenkian's crisis
was finalized. The king's reluctance only trebled the oil syndicate's
worries about arranging American participation. In a December 2,
1925, review, one TPC executive, completely incensed at the whole
situation, offhandedly opined: "Has not the time come, to use such
pressure (e.g. a hint of withdrawal of military protection) as may be
necessary to bring home to the Iraq government that the British
Government, who brought them into existence, and without whose

aid they could not survive for a month, cannot allow them to obstruct indefinitely the fulfillment of promises made to the French and American Governments, and the exercise by a British Company of pre-war rights on terms pronounced by British Government experts to be eminently reasonable and fair?"[70]

If matters could not become more intense, on December 5, 1925, newly installed U.S. secretary of state Frank Kellogg sent the Foreign Office a blunt message. "The Department has been informed, by the American Group," Kellogg cabled, "that there is serious danger that their negotiations with the Turkish Petroleum Company will reach an impasse due to failure up to now of the other groups in the Turkish Petroleum Company to come to an agreement with Mr. C. S. Gulbenkian. . . . The American Group informs the Department that they would be sincerely sorry to have to withdraw from further attempts to obtain participation in the Turkish Petroleum Company on a fair basis and that they are still hopeful that an agreement will be reached which will make participation possible. . . . The Department is aware that neither our Government nor the British Government would wish to intervene in negotiations which are of a purely business nature. The British Government, however, in view of its [ownership] connection with the Anglo-Persian Oil Company, which is one of the chief parties to these business negotiations, may be able to persuade British subjects or companies not to assume an attitude which would make it impossible for American interests to participate in the Turkish Petroleum Company."[71]

Then came the threat: "Should the American Group withdraw because of failure to obtain participation in the Turkish Petroleum Company on a fair basis, the Department would reserve its entire freedom of action . . . to secure the right to a fair share in the development of the oil resources of Mesopotamia through other means than the Turkish Petroleum Company."[72]

Finally, through unending ups and downs and following the cautious intervention of Deterding, British government officials, and Gulbenkian's various contacts at TPC, a breakthrough appeared at the very end of December 1925. A new formula was finally acceptable whereby Gulbenkian would transfer his shares to Anglo-Saxon and Anglo-Persian in exchange for a diverse package of ample compensation. There was hope, and a 24-page contract between the four syndicates was drawn up finally creating a Working Agreement that could be signed. By now the TPC was operating under two names, Turkish Petroleum Company and Iraq Petroleum Company; hence the firm was ready to function with either regime once the Mosul question was decided. The intricate December 1925 agreement specified all the percentages and procedures the partners would observe, and even recited Gulbenkian's intransigence as the foundation for the accord. But it was all completely dependent upon a so-called Gulbenkian Agreement, referred to on page 5. This was the agreement for Gulbenkian to transfer his shares.[73]

The oilmen held their breath and hoped years of contractual anguish would finally come to an end that Christmas. But Christmas day, Gulbenkian sent off a note to John Cadman, one of the latest British government go-betweens. "I must say that I am disappointed," sniped Gulbenkian, ". . . chopping gradually away [at] certain rights." Gulbenkian would not sign the stock transfer agreement, but he did conclude the letter to Cadman with warm felicitations: "I send you and Lady Cadman my sincerest greetings for a happy New Year."[74]

When, on January 2, 1926, Deterding learned of Gulbenkian's latest escapade, he issued a blunt letter on behalf of Royal Dutch Shell to the entire Anglo-Persian Oil Company staff. "Dear Sirs: We have to inform you that our relations with Mr. Gulbenkian are ended," declared Deterding, "and we want to sever all connections with him. . . . Mr. Gulbenkian has . . . [been] rather successful in befogging the issue, and making it appear as if he were on the verge of being made a poor victim of the other four groups. . . . Mr. Gulbenkian is trying to exploit the other shareholders of the Turkish Petroleum Company, and has been trying to make out a pitiful tale of being squeezed by the 95%, whereas [in reality] his 5% has been trying to squeeze the 95%. . . . Finally we beg to place on record that we will have no more conversations with Mr. Gulbenkian, and that all proceedings must take place in writing through our Solicitor, Mr. Harold Brown."[75]

Deterding had been Gulbenkian's closest business ally since the earliest days of the century when Gulbenkian was financing overseas deals for Shell, and Gulbenkian was relying on Deterding to vote with him as a bloc in Turkish Petroleum. Once Deterding's support crumbled, Gulbenkian stood alone, truly alone, against all the governments and the oil companies arrayed against him.

At about that time, the League of Nations Council in Geneva had ruled and all appeals had been exhausted on the Mosul question. Citing Turkey's record of genocide, mass rape, and neglect of the Mosul province, as well as strong messages of independence from the Kurds, Mosul was to remain within the British mandate. As of March 11, 1926, the decision was final.[76]

No delay could now be justified. Mosul was open for drilling. Its oil fields were ready. Negotiations between Nichols and Gulbenkian resumed with new vigor and velocity. The Heads of Agreement— negotiated in March 1925 and almost ready in December 1925— were revisited. Finally, a year later, they were approved in principle, with some changes. On April 1, 1926, Nichols was able to notify the British government, "It gives me great pleasure to inform you that at long last we have come to a settlement with Mr. Gulbenkian." The paperwork was being readied, and with it the long-postponed entry of the American oil firms through the Open Door and into TPC. Nichols assured the government, "You may conclude that the Americans are now within the bosom of the Turkish Petroleum Company."[77]

Gulbenkian was traveling while the papers were being drawn up. But on April 12, 1926, he reassured Nichols in a warm note: "Believe me, I highly appreciate your friendly feelings, and you are aware that all along I have been animated with but one desire—to see the T.P.C. a united entity. . . . Nothing will give me more pleasure than to work cordially with all my colleagues for the end we must all have in view."[78]

On May 7, oil syndicate lawyers produced a revised version of the Heads of Agreement that incorporated Gulbenkian's demands. In a 10-page opinion, dissecting every clause, they warned TPC that there were still many vagaries and problems. But it "would be wise to accept the draft as it stands," as Gulbenkian's attorney, who had helped draft the compromise "feels fairly confident that he can get

Mr. Gulbenkian to accept it." The new agreement was printed and presented to Gulbenkian.[79]

But then Gulbenkian wanted a few changes. A month later, on June 7, syndicate attorneys found those changes to be totally astonishing. Their nine-page clause-by-clause analysis was filled with rejections: Clause 3: "The suggestion is . . . of course, utterly untenable." Clause 7: "This is an additional obligation and . . . we see no reason to agree to it." Clause 12: "The last three lines must be deleted." Clause 16: "The phraseology is utterly unacceptable. . . . The second paragraph of the clause must be deleted altogether."[80]

In the meantime, the industrialization taking place in America and Europe increased the demand for oil on an exponential basis. The Roaring Twenties gave birth to the new consumer economy. America's population center had shifted from the farm to the city. The have-nots began having. Henry Ford's new Model A, almost ready to sputter off the assembly lines, was expected to revolutionize automobile production. Movies. Dance clubs. Household appliances. Personal convenience. Gadgets. Factory mass production. Factory mass employment. The Bolshevik revolution and mass industrialization. A renewed arms race. Transatlantic shipping. Air travel. The velocity of the world had become supercharged. It all required fuel, lubricants, illuminants, petrochemicals—the stuff beneath the ground in Iraq.

After arduous weeks of agonizing over the smallest points, progress with Gulbenkian was revived during later 1926, but several salient stumbling blocks remained. The most important was how Gulbenkian was going to be paid for his 5 percent by a company ordained to never record a profit. Solution: He would be paid in oil. But at what price? The market price. But that could be manipulated; the oil monopolies were famous for manipulating market prices. Solution: global averages, calculated on separate months of the year, pegged to January, the coldest month, when prices were highest. But Gulbenkian did not want to sell oil; he possessed no retail arm. He just wanted the money. So the four cartels would purchase his oil allotment—then he would have money. But the American Group did not want to make a 75-year commitment to purchase oil from Gulbenkian. Well, then the French could step in. They needed oil, Gulbenkian was known to them, and they could buy all his oil in a special side agreement.[81]

A second major question was just what territory the Working Agreement would cover. Under the self-denying principle, none of the oil companies could function within the defined area except through TPC. But oil deposits know no borders. It would be easy for the oil companies to drill into the same subterranean layers on the Turkish side of the border or to discover oil in the Arabian Peninsula or along the Gulf. Then make it broad: Designate the whole of the Ottoman Empire. Which Ottoman Empire? The Ottoman Empire of the nineteenth century, before the Balkans War in 1912, before the onset of World War I in 1914, before the armistice of 1918, before the League of Nations adjudication of 1926?[82]

In February 1927, the British government suggested yet another face-to-face conference. This time, Gulbenkian demurred. "Many of the members who would attend such a conference," Gulbenkian wrote the Petroleum Board, "are full of suspicion and have had bitter experiences in the past."[83] Once more, negotiations for a Working Agreement and buyout underwent more iterations of burial, exhumation, reanimation, and slow death.

Then in October 1927 everything changed. Once Mosul had been adjudged Iraqi territory, TPC geologists quickly scampered all over the region to find the most likely point to sink a gusher. It did not take long. Early in the morning of October 14, 1927, at the tract known as the fiery furnace for its noxious gases and seepages, in the high foothills near the northern town of Kirkuk, the realm of Iraq finally opened its spigot: a blowout. At an estimated flow of 90,000 barrels per day, the fabulous Baba Gurgur Well #1 strike saturated everything with black gold. So fierce was the pressure, when diverted through the drilling arbor head, it created a massive horizontal jet of oil. Two American workers were overcome by deadly fumes. The effluent formed a flammable river of oil as wide as the Jordan. The seemingly unstoppable gusher did not catch fire, but continuously spewed flammable gases. It was no longer a vision. The air itself was thick with the wealth of oil.[84]

The Baba Gurgur gate valve could not be capped for three days.[85] Once capped, it stood inactive. No one could ignore the reality anymore. It was now or never. Yet another new agreement was negotiated among all the parties.

On the morning of July 31, 1928, an Imperial Airways 14-seater Handley Page charter plane flew from London to Ostend, Holland. The long-fuselaged biplane, powered by four engines and sporting a distinctive triple tail, carried Nubar Gulbenkian, an attorney for the Freshfields firm, as well as other members of the Gulbenkian family and clerical staff. Their destination was the Royal Palace Hotel. Once there, they ordered a sumptuous lunch of turbot along with a bottle of fine champagne. While the meal was being prepared, Nubar and his group stepped into one of the private rooms. There a group of oil company presidents awaited them, along with Nubar's father, Calouste Sarkis Gulbenkian himself.[86]

A 54-page document with numerous attachments, annexes, and supplements was ready. Every issue had been resolved. Each of the four partner cartels would own exactly 23.75 percent of Turkish Petroleum; each had yielded 1.25 percent to create Gulbenkian's everlasting 5 percent. A newly created family company, registered in Canada, called the Participations and Investments Company, or Partex for short, would hold the 5 percent. America's Near East Development Corporation was composed of Standard of New Jersey, Standard of New York, Atlantic Refining, Pan American Oil, and Gulf Petroleum. France's Companie Française des Pe'troles would buy Gulbenkian's oil; the complex price and procedure were arranged.[87]

Emblazoned with red foil signets, green and purple witness stamps, corporate embossments, and notary seals, the massive convention had been years in the making. Page 49 was filled with the signatures of the six major corporate participants. First, the director and secretary of D'Arcy Exploration signed for the original entity creating Anglo-Persian Oil Company, with a red foil stamp fixed to the right. Beneath that were two signatures for Shell's Anglo-Saxon Petroleum, marked to the right by an embossment. Then the two executives of Companie Française des Pe'troles signed beside the company's oval embossment. Beneath that, Teagle and another executive signed for the five companies that comprised the Near East Development Company, with the corporate seal embossed just to the right. Beneath that was affixed the seal of Partex, Nubar Gulbenkian signing for the firm. At the bottom, Turkish Petroleum's director and secretary signed with their firm's serrated red foil seal to the right. Page 51: Anglo-Persian signed for itself and all its associated companies, and a red foil seal was affixed. Page 52: Royal Dutch and Shell Transport signed for the Shell combine, and a red foil seal was affixed. Page 53: The presidents and secretaries of Standard Oil of New Jersey, Standard Oil of New York, Pan-American Petroleum, Atlantic Refining, and Gulf Oil signed, in that order, each penning his name as corporate seals were pressed over their signatures for surety.[88]

Page 54, the last page. "I, the undersigned, hereby recognize that the parties to the above written agreement have only agreed to execute the same conditionally on my entering into the underwritten Agreement, and I accordingly agree, as well on my own behalf as on behalf of my executors, administrators and estate, and on behalf of any Company which I now or may hereafter in any matter whatsoever control, to be bound by the definitions, obligations and restrictions contained in the above written Agreement, including particularly the waiver of claims contained in clause 26 in like manner as if I had been a party thereto jointly with or in place of the Participations Company." Beneath that oath were the words: "Signed Sealed and Delivered by Calouste Sarkis Gulbenkian in the presence of" the British proconsul.[89]

It was now up to Gulbenkian to place his pen upon the paper. His would be the last and most important signature. The British proconsul had flown in from Paris to witness the ratification. Billions hung upon his pen stroke, and none really knew if Gulbenkian would actually sign the agreement.

It all depended on the red line. He checked the map. During negotiations, to break the stalemate over the true borders of the Ottoman Empire, Gulbenkian had insisted not on country names and internationally set borders, which could change from time to time and war to war, but a simple red line drawn on the map. There it was on pages 21 and 22 of the agreement, faithfully reproduced per his instructions, complete with alphabetical points and a map legend. The red line circumscribed the Ottoman Empire as it existed during his lifetime, beginning with the Treaty of Berlin in 1878. Gulbenkian's line began near Baku, where an *A* was printed, and proceeded down the adjusted Turco-Persian frontier, coursing over precise zigs and zags to map points marked *B* and *C,* including all of Mesopotamia, and then down to Basra, where the red line took a pronounced detour around Kuwait, and then encircled the entire Ara-

bian Peninsula. From the tip of Yemen, it proceeded north up to the
Gulf of Aqaba, where it reached Palestine at map mark *E,* approximately at Eilat. The red line then skirted the Egyptian Sinai Desert
north to Port Said on the Mediterrean coast. From there, the line
encompassed all of Turkey, and then ended back at Baku.[90]

Names, sovereignties, nationalities, colonies, and mandates, self-
determined or undetermined—none of it mattered. Within the
bounds of that red line, none of the companies could engage in any
oil business except through their common monopoly, the Turkish
Petroleum Company, thus creating the most spectacular monopoly of
all time. Finally, a full generation after the sultan granted the Anatolia Railway an oil concession, 18 years after Turkish Petroleum was
created from paper, 16 years after the fusion deal that merged TPC
with Anglo-Persian, 8 years after San Remo divided the wealth,
nearly a decade after America demanded equal standing, Gulbenkian
finally signed, not with his usual elegant penmanship but with an
almost illegible scrawl. The British consul witnessed the signature and
quickly affixed his stamp. Two green certification stamps were pasted
down and then rubber-stamped, as six additional seals and embossments were added. Forevermore, that document would be known as
the "Red Line Agreement."[91]

The ceremony was brief. The Gulbenkian party returned to the
restaurant before their meal was served. After three decades of struggle, the matter was finished in the time in takes to cook turbot.

It was finally over. By the power of a trillion-dollar pen stroke and
the authority vested by the almighty red line, Iraq's oil would finally
flow. The country now belonged not just to Britain, but to all the
great powers.

It was finally over, but in truth it was just beginning.

PART FOUR

The Continuing Conflict

CHAPTER SIXTEEN

The Nazi Intersection

During World War II, a confusing web of complex and contradictory political and economic relationships coursed from London to Berlin to Jerusalem and back, all involving oil, the Jews, and the Mideast. In 1941, the locus shifted to Iraq, as the forces of Arab nationalism joined Nazi aggression to confront the arch-importance of oil and the question of Jewish existence. The threads of this drama came together at the height of World War II, but they had been building for years.

After the Iraq Petroleum Company's oil began flowing, the royalties—deflated or not—greatly enriched King Faisal's throne and the national treasury of Iraq. England, in 1930, renegotiated its treaty with what was now the sovereign nation of Iraq. The revised treaty guaranteed the British two air bases, along with military transit and basing rights in the event of war. By preagreement, the League of Nations ended Britain's mandate in 1932, and London sponsored Iraq's admission into the league itself as a full member.[1]

Two pipelines, as originally envisioned years earlier, were constructed to carry Iraqi and Persian oil to the Mediterranean. One, completed in mid-July 1934, traveled through Syria to meet the sea at Tripoli, Lebanon. The second, completed January 14, 1935, traveled from Kirkuk south to the Haifa coast in Palestine. The Kirkuk–Haifa line was opened to great fanfare with the king presiding, along with many government officials and Red Line consortium executives in attendance, plus some 250 invited VIPs. That year, 1935, Persia became Iran. The Anglo-Persian Oil Company changed its name to Anglo-Iranian Oil Company. By this time, the Red Line consortium of the Iraq Petroleum Company had formed hundreds of wholly owned and interlocking subsidiaries throughout the Mideast and the world to drill for, refine, transport, and sell its petroleum.[2]

Throughout the 1920s, the Zionist movement in Palestine—still under British mandate—struggled to purchase land, found kibbutzim, drain swamps, and create new Jewish towns. Immigration was unrestricted and even promoted by the British, but results were meager. Most well-established Jews were too comfortably assimilated in postwar Europe and America to emigrate to the barren and inhospitable Jewish homeland in Palestine. It was common for establishment Jews to support Zionism for others but not for themselves. They preferred to donate funds and make speeches about helping their disadvantaged coreligionists in eastern Europe. Hence, Jewish Palestine was still mainly a movement of Jewish idealists helping their eastern European brethren.[3]

The Jewish presence in Palestine grew slowly in the 1920s, but was strongly resisted at every juncture and expansion by the local Arab population. The leader of Palestine's Arabs was Haj Muhammad Amin al-Husseini. He incessantly organized fiery political resistance to the Jewish presence, and his followers frequently broke into riots and committed acts of violence and vandalism. Hardly a local rabble-rouser, Husseini would rise from an obscure figure to become the preeminent nationalist in the Arab world. His voice would be heard not only in the mosques and casbahs of Palestine, but also in the stately halls of the League of Nations and the mandatory powers, where he regularly represented the Arab cause with charisma and aplomb. Ultimately, Husseini would be a direct collaborator with Germany's chiefs of genocide, Heinrich Himmler, Adolf Eichmann, and the other henchmen of Nazi murder. Indeed, Husseini had access to Hitler personally, and for the Third Reich was the key to a calculated strategy to restage the Lawrence of Arabia saga, but in reverse—

using the Arabs to help eliminate the Jews and to help seize the oil Germany needed to dominate the world.

Who was Husseini? Muhammad Amin al-Husseini was born in 1895 in Jerusalem. The Husseini clan was one of Palestine's wealthiest and most honored. As early as the seventeenth century, the Husseini family had served as the muftis of Jerusalem. In Islamic tradition, a mufti was the respected interpreter of Koranic law, but in many ways also revered as the titular head of the community.[4]

As a young man, Amin Husseini was self-conscious, short, and frail. He spoke with a lisp. But he impressed others as highly intelligent and mature for his age. His father Tamir held the title of grand mufti until his death in 1908. Amin was too young to fill his father's shoes. Instead, the eldest brother, Kamil, assumed the important post. Kamil, meanwhile, sent 16-year-old Amin to Cairo to study at al-Azhar University. In Cairo, Husseini met prominent Islamic reformers and the earliest champions of Arab nationalism. Soon, the teenaged Husseini became his own self-styled activist, recruiting other Palestinian students to agitate against Zionism. Husseini held Zionism as the greatest threat to Arab nationalism—this, years before the Balfour Declaration was ever even framed.[5]

Once back in Jerusalem, Amin began writing mordant articles attacking Zionism. To sharpen his leadership skills, he went off to Istanbul to become an officer in the Turkish army. Harsh army training and deprivation toughened Husseini, both physically and emotionally. But the fervent Arab found he could not turkify himself into a true Ottoman. He abandoned the Turkish army, returning to Jerusalem and his beloved campaign for Arab nationalism. Quickly, he was elected president of Jerusalem's Arab Club, whereupon he assumed the leadership of the anti-Zionist movement.[6]

Husseini specialized in riling up the rumor-infused "Arab Street" with wild, often hysterical warnings of pending Jewish destruction of Islamic holy sites, Zionist conspiracy, and blood libel. He and his closest associates were instrumental in orchestrating the violence that broke out between Jews and Arabs in the April 1920 riots. Husseini escaped arrest by fleeing across the Jordan River, but was sentenced in absentia to 10 years in prison. Ironically, Palestine high commissioner Herbert Samuel, himself a Zionist, pardoned Husseini as a gesture to the seething Arab community. That brought Husseini back to Jerusalem.[7]

From that point, Husseini donned the classic rounded white-topped *imama,* or religious turban, grew a cleric's beard, and immediately launched a campaign to become the next mufti. Husseini's brother was near death, and Husseini wanted to succeed him. The position was technically not hereditary, and candidates from several rival Jerusalem families actively vied for the post. But Amin, showing his organizational prowess, began a petition drive to prove he was the choice of the Arab masses. When the votes were counted in council, Husseini ranked only fourth. But the Husseini clan attacked the legitimacy of the council itself.[8]

More petitions were presented to High Commissioner Samuels, who under British rules would make the final selection. Posters mysteriously appeared in the Old City accusing the Jews of conspiring to place a stooge in the mufti's office, someone who would then "sell" the Temple Mount to Zionists so they could rebuild the Jewish Temple. Such wild accusations became Husseini's hallmark. To keep peace on the excited Arab Street, and after Husseini declared that "his family and himself would be devoted to maintaining tranquility in Jerusalem," Samuel relented and appointed the 26-year-old Husseini. Thereafter Husseini was known as the Mufti of Jerusalem. He spent the next decade battling every increase in Jewish presence, no matter how incremental.[9]

Everything changed in Palestine when Adolf Hitler shocked the world on January 30, 1933, suddenly rising to power in Germany at the denouement of an election crisis.

Germany's relationship with Palestine was complex. The Nazis wanted to oust the Jews of Germany, and indeed of all Europe, seizing their assets in the process. While the violently anti-Semitic Nazis hated the Jews, they supported Jewish nationalism for the sole purpose of kicking Jews out of Germany and into another region—far-off Palestine. In that ironic fashion, Nazi anti-Semitism actively supported a Jewish homeland.[10]

Upon gaining power, Hitler organized Jewish expulsions from the professions, deprived German Jews of their assets, subjected them to humiliating street rampages, and began their systematic ouster. Concentration camps were opened across the Reich, their atrocities bannered in the newsreels, radio broadcasts, and headlines of the day. Nazi surrogates in Poland, Lithuania, Hungary, and elsewhere around Europe joined the fascist movement to dismantle their Jewish communities and force their Jewish neighbors out of Europe.

Suddenly, hundreds of thousands of middle-class Jewish refugees, pitiful and penniless, flooded the capitals of the world, balancing children on their hips and a few overstuffed suitcases under their arms. Many appeared with little more than books stuffed into satchels or tied with twine. Clamoring for anywhere safe—maybe New York, London, Paris, Amsterdam, or a dozen other potential sanctuaries— the refugees escaped with their lives but were now homeless.

Quickly, the fleeing multitudes became too great for a Depression-wracked world to absorb. The doors of relief were shut. One nation after another blocked the Jewish throngs at the borders they had dashed to—or been dumped at. Country after country enacted restrictive entry legislation, denied visas on flimsy grounds, and in unison declared that, somehow, another solution to the Jewish problem was needed. That solution was of course to be found somewhere beyond everybody's borders. But where? Zionist Organization president Chaim Weizmann lamented that for Europe's Jews the world was divided into two realms: "places where Jews cannot live, and where Jews cannot enter."[11]

As thousands of Jews were thrown into poverty, concentration camps, or ghettos and brutalized every day in the expanded Third Reich and elsewhere in Europe, the threat soon lurched into a race against time. The remaining destination was their ancestral home in Palestine. Jews entered the country via elaborate financial transfer and trade agreements designed to bring in the middle class, via Zionist youth programs intended to save the young, and via illegal smuggling operations determined to rescue those snatched from the very jaws of the Holocaust. All these newcomers, whether from Germany, Czechoslovakia, Poland, or elsewhere, brought into Palestine their desperation and energy, but also their European ways, from Mozart to motorcars to Linzer tortes. They also brought money, and quickly established their own European-style economy in Palestine.[12]

Between 1933 and 1941, various emergency transfer plans and corollary commercial agreements with the Third Reich enabled some $100 million in direct transfers, along with some 60,000 Jews from

Germany and elsewhere in Europe, to flow into Palestine. Many ousted Germans were able to transfer into Palestine virtual replicas of their German existence—homes, shops, and factories. The heartfelt donations of anguished Jews and Christians through religious and secular relief operations everywhere added to the effort to transplant displaced Jews of all classes into Palestine. By the outbreak of war in 1939, Jews represented roughly half of Palestine's overall population.[13]

Many Jews worked in the oil industry, processing Iraq Oil Company crude through a newly built refinery, bunkering it in towering oil tanks planted on the landscape, and loading it onto tankers for shipment overseas. Haifa, with its new, well-dredged harbor and thriving oil and shipping center, became a Jewish metropolis. So did Tel Aviv, as did a new, expanded western Jerusalem. Moreover, with poor working-class Jews pouring into kibbutzim, Jewish laborers replaced cheap Arab workers in the kibbutzim, and Jewish fruits and vegetables supplanted Arab produce in the market stalls.[14]

The Arabs saw ancient Palestine transform before their very eyes. For years, the Mufti of Jerusalem had led the local jihad against the Jews and everything Zionist. A demographic race of sorts sprang up as Arabs did all they could to encourage Moslem immigration and an Islamic renaissance to counterbalance what they called the Jewish menace. But the Arabs could not compete with the pace of Jewish expulsions from Europe and the concomitant immigration and financial transfers into Palestine.

In April 1936, Arab agitation, led by the mufti through his Arab Higher Committee, exploded into another prolonged campaign of anti-Jewish violence. This uprising, known as the Great Arab Revolt, called for all Palestinian Arabs to stop paying British taxes and to close their shops and major institutions, thus bringing their economy and British mandatory oversight to a halt. Then in May, the murders started. Jews were shot at point-blank range in the Old City, in the Edison film theater, and in other places where they traditionally felt safe. Arab extremists also killed fellow Moslems who were simply working with Jews: an Arab vegetable vendor selling his goods in the Jewish market, an Arab watchman at a Jewish company. The terror campaign touched everyone. Riots against Jews ignited all over Palestine. In Haifa, 2,000 Arabs marched until they broke into rock throwing. At Nablus, an unruly throng assembled after midday prayers and

299

promised a fight to the end. In Jaffa, protestors ran wild through the streets. Jewish buses were stoned everywhere. Bombs exploded with regularity across the country, including Jerusalem. On May 17, 1936, Jerusalem was besieged with riots. The results were disastrous. Due to the general strike, the Arab economy was almost exhausted.[15]

In 1936, yet another British fact-finding body, the Peel Commission, investigated—as had so many previous panels after surges in Arab violence. But this time, the commission's conclusions were dramatic. Peel's white paper reported, "An irrepressible conflict has arisen between two national communities within the narrow bounds of one small country. There is no common ground between them. Their national aspirations are incompatible. The Arabs desire to revive the traditions of the Arab golden age. The Jews desire to show what they can achieve when restored to the land in which the Jewish nation was born. Neither of the two national ideals permits combination in the service of a single State."[16]

Peel's white paper added, "The Arab Higher Committee was to a large extent responsible for maintaining and protecting the strike last year. The Mufti of Jerusalem as President must bear his due share of responsibility. . . . The functions, which the Mufti has collected in his person, and his use of them, have led to the development of an Arab *imperium in imperio* [an empire within an empire]."[17]

Finally, the white paper called for partition in Palestine, that is, separating the two peoples in the same fashion that had been done for the Greeks and Turks when 1.5 million Moslems and Christians were transferred across borders. In Palestine, two sovereign cantons would be created, Arab and Jewish. Rather than create the first Arab state to rule in Palestine, the mufti decreed no to all plans and propositions—not with autonomous Jews in their midst. His followers intensified the campaign of incendiary language, random violence, political assassination, and the broad incitement of interreligious strife.[18] Those who felt it possible that the two peoples in Palestine could separate peaceably were now being bullied, stabbed, shot, and dynamited by the followers of the mufti, who himself always stayed aloof from the actual terror.

London had long wanted to exile Husseini in a distant internment camp on the tiny Seychelles islands in the Indian Ocean. But indecision had delayed any move. Finally, at the end of September 1937,

British authorities shut down all the agitation committees in Palestine. They issued arrest warrants for some 200 members of the Arab Higher Committee, with the mufti at the top of the list. The first group apprehended was immediately deported to the Seychelles.[19]

The elusive mufti moved about to evade capture. He and his large traveling party slipped out of the country, driving to Damascus, where, on June 22, he checked into the Orient Palace Hotel. There he participated in numerous conferences with Palestinian agitators about merging the Syrian national bloc with the Palestinian Istiqlal resistance group. These meetings were attended not only by Syrians, but also by representatives from Saudi Arabia and Iraq.[20]

On July 3, the mufti departed for the mountain village of Sofar in Lebanon, then continued on to Beirut. Driving all day from Beirut, he suddenly reappeared in Palestine on July 4, 1937. Back in Jerusalem, the mufti hid within the protective grounds of the Dome of the Rock, where no Christian could enter. As mufti and chairman of the local Waqf religious trust, Husseini was custodian of the precious mosque complex. In fact, it was Husseini who had begun the restoration and the famous gold leafing of the Dome, which only magnified his prestige within the Arab population. Nonetheless, the British were determined and prepared to dispatch Moslem officers from the Indian army to arrest him.[21]

Husseini was one step ahead. On October 14, 1937, the mufti lowered himself down the outer wall of the Temple Mount complex to a waiting car, which drove him to the Jaffa port. There he boarded a boat for Lebanon, making good his escape. Once in Beirut, the French supposedly placed the mufti under house arrest. But his "house arrest" was a pleasure. Husseini regularly regaled fellow nationalists and other leading Syrian personalities at festive dinner parties with his talk of a pan-Arab state stretching from Damascus to Jerusalem—all to the constant chagrin of the British. For two years, the mufti was less a prisoner in Beirut than a bon vivant.[22]

At 6 A.M., September 1, 1939, Hitler launched his blitzkrieg against Poland, thus beginning World War II. This was the mufti's moment. He seized it.

The French, eager to curry favor with Palestinian Arabs during the forthcoming struggle with Germany, continued to kowtow to the mufti. When, just after war broke out, Husseini openly thanked various luminaries in the French government for gracious treatment during his visit, the highest authorities were quick to respond. For example, General Maxime Weygand, commander in chief of French forces in the eastern Mediterranean, effusively replied: "The letter in which Your Eminence has expressed to me his personal thanks, and that of the members of the Arab Higher Committee, for the hospitality extended to them by the French authorities . . . has touched me deeply. I have been particularly moved," General Weygand added, "by the allusion which Your Eminence has made to the humanitarian spirit of France, which is one of the most noble traditions of my country. Your Eminence has been good enough also to assure me of the loyalty of the Arabs in Palestine; for this I express to you all my gratitude. I beg your Eminence to accept the assurance of my highest consideration."[23]

But Husseini needed to say good-bye to his hosts in Lebanon. Hitler was fighting the two greatest nemeses of the Palestinian Arabs: the Jews and the British. The mufti bribed the French chief of police with £500 to make sure gendarmes outside his house looked the other way. The morning of either October 13 or 14, 1939, Husseini and his assistants donned the coverings of devout Moslem women and drove off unmolested. Only after Husseini failed to appear for his regular morning walk the next two days did guards admit that they saw the car depart, but presumed all within were women.[24]

The next day, the mufti appeared in Baghdad, the epicenter of Britain's Mideast strategy and the font of its oil.[25]

Hitler's plans were fueled by hate. But Hitler's tanks, trucks, automobiles, warships, submarines, and airplanes were fueled by octane. Moving parts in machinery, from locomotives to Lugers, required lubricants. Economic recovery was dependent upon great factories; military campaigns deployed great armies and defenses; and foreign domination required intrusive, far-flung administrative machinery. All of that required petroleum. Hitler needed oil. The more territory Hitler took, the more oil he needed to sustain his conquests.

In 1938, Reich consumption of petroleum products, from kerosene to aviation fuel, was estimated by some British experts at more than 6.5 million tons per year and growing exponentially as the

Reich continued to mechanize, industrialize, rearm, and make ready for the war that everyone expected. Indeed, 1938 consumption grew by 1.2 million tons over the preceding year. But through synthetic means and some local deposits, Germany produced only a few million tons of its requirements. The rest was imported. One typical top-secret analysis, titled "The Oil Supply Problem in Germany," concluded, "In spite of her efforts, Germany was still dependent on imports for over 50 percent of her requirements." An almost weekly cascade of such British estimates varied in tons and percentages. But despite Nazi industrial secrecy that fudged the numbers, British intelligence consistently concluded that Germany was overwhelmingly dependent on foreign oil. Moreover, the expanding Reich was counting every barrel, because its shortfalls were several million tons per year.[26]

In 1939, Germany's oil industry was a maze of more than 70 refiners and distributors, most of them small, dominated by a half dozen or so giant firms. Several of these dominating companies were in the forefront of importation. Chief among them was a firm named Olex.[27]

Olex had long been a household name in Germany, with thousands of convenient gas stations across the country. Its name derived from its original 1904 telegraphic address, PETROLEXPORT; the middle four letters formed OLEX. In addition to its consumer profile, Olex was also a key importer of oil. Its number one source was Romania. In 1937, Olex stocks in hand included some 6,100 metric tons of Romanian light benzine, 5,800 metric tons of Romanian middle benzine, 1,150 metric tons of Romanian heavy benzine, and 387 metric tons of Romanian white spirit, plus Romanian tractor vapor oil and kerosene, all imported through Hamburg and Regensburg. A September 3, 1936, company memo examining imports spotlighted "the Romanian market, the chief source of Olex supplies."[28]

At the end of 1937, Olex's total on hand of all petroleum products, from motor fuel to diesel oil to lubricants, equaled 88,800 metric tons valued at approximately 14 million reichsmarks. Its total 1938 sales of all products topped 475,300 metric tons.[29]

But Olex also imported gas oil, diesel oil, and kerosene from Amsterdam. The Dutch oil was brought in through a subsidiary registered in the Netherlands, the stock certificates of which were held in two locations, 995 shares in the Olex company safe in Berlin and 5 shares in its attorney's office.[30]

Iran was also an important source for Olex because the company and Nazi Germany needed foreign currency. Much of the world would not accept any of the numerous species of reichsmarks, almost all unusable outside Germany. Moreover, the international anti-Nazi boycott dramatically reduced all Nazi exports. Consequently, Germany was earning precious little foreign currency and was rationing its reserves. But through complicated barters, Olex could earn the foreign currency it needed to purchase oil, bolster Reich reserves, and earn a profit. Boycott-breaking barters were terribly complicated, generally disguised, and involved several companies in different parts of the world swapping products at a discount in exchange for some foreign currency.[31]

In a typical Olex barter, the company would import Iranian oil and sell it to the German steel company Ferrostahl, which would pay Olex in Germany with worthless reichsmarks spendable only in Germany. But how would Olex find the British pounds to pay Iran? Ferrostahl purchased 15,000 tons of inferior Iranian champa rice at an inflated price in exchange for first-class construction and railroad steel that Iran paid for in British pounds. The steel company would then turn over its British pounds to the Reichsbank, which would use it for general Nazi rearmament and other state purposes. Olex could then receive a portion of those British pounds to pay for the oil it purchased from Iran. An Olex review of the serpentine Ferrostahl barter concluded it was necessary for the Reich "because in this way Germany earns the right to some Iranian [foreign] currency." Indeed, without a cornucopia of intricate, multitransactional barters, Germany could not import the tons of British-controlled Iranian oil it craved.[32]

Iranian barter deals like the Ferrostahl swap were common for Olex. A 1938 company balance sheet included separate entries for "barter transactions," which in that reporting period totaled 150,000 reichsmarks (RM), yielding £12,000 in one category, and RM 171,000, fetching £12,457, in a second. So entrenched was Iran as a source of Olex's imports that when a German highway publication asked Olex for a pictorial, company advertising managers wrote, "Although we shall discuss in our article mainly our distribution facilities in Germany, we shall have to mention the Iranian origin of our motor fuel and give a short description of your production and refining activities in Iran and submit a few photos."[33]

Olex was a loyal vendor with the Third Reich, and highly visible. At first, Olex managers were worried about the ascent of Hitler. Depression-era sales had stagnated when they should have grown. But no sooner had der Führer assumed power than sales volume soared from slightly more than 200,000 long tons in 1932 to double that amount by the end of 1938. By 1939, Olex operated 7,000 gas stations throughout the country, sometimes adding as many as 1,000 per year as Hitler's forced economic recovery proliferated throughout the nation. During three months of 1938, Olex ran seven advertisements at one-week intervals in more than 300 German newspapers, including Nazi party newspapers. Moreover, Olex printed the newest road maps of Germany, which immediately incorporated the latest Nazi-fied street names, such as Adolf Hitlerplatz and Adolf Hitlerstrasse. In this way Olex became an important cog in the cultural apparatus of National Socialism.[34]

Who owned Olex? Olex was a wholly owned subsidiary of Britain's Anglo-Iranian Oil Company, also known as Anglo-Persian Oil Company. In 1926, Anglo-Persian acquired 40 percent of the old-line Olex, increased its ownership to 75 percent in 1929, and then in 1931 bought out the remaining 25 percent from minority owner Deutsche Petroleum. Anglo-Persian called the new entity *Deutsche Benzin- und Petroleum,* or BP. Throughout Great Britain, Anglo-Persian's green BP three-pointed shield logo stood for British Petrol. Throughout the Reich, the identical shield stood for Benzin- und Petroleum. As a wholly owned subsidiary of Anglo-Persian, all of Olex's affairs were tightly controlled out of London.[35]

Other Red Line partners were also leading purveyors of Nazi oil. Standard Oil of New Jersey operated Deutsche Amerikanische Petroleum Gesellschaft, or DAPG. As one of Germany's top six firms, DAPG operated 17,500 gas stations in Germany. Shell operated 16,500. In fact, of Germany's approximately 64,000 gas stations in 1939, Shell, Standard, and BP operated 41,000. Olex also became a key supplier of Germany's growing aircraft industry.[36]

When Olex purchased Iranian oil, it was dealing with another subsidiary of the same company, its parent Anglo-Iranian—also called Anglo-Persian. The so-called Iranian oil it purchased was often Iranian in name only, since the twin oil fields of Naft Khana and Naft i Shah straddled either side of the Iraq-Iran border, and in fact the Iraqi side was considered "transferred territory." British military planners at the time declared they could consider "the two sections of Naft Khana/Naft i Shah of the northern field as one unit." The transferred territories were, after all, Iraqi land under the original 1901 Persian concession. But Iraqi oil processed through the Iranian refinery at Abadan, across from Basra, now bore the stamp of Iran.[37] Oil deposits, and the companies that tap them, do not recognize national borders because it all runs underground.

Hence, with a clenched fist, England staunchly resisted the rise and rearmament of Hitler, while with its own imperial enterprise, Anglo-Iranian Oil Company, partially government-owned and fully government controlled when it came to international matters, contributed mightily to the recovery of the Third Reich and Hitler's preparations to wage war against nations and ethnic groups. So did the other Red Line partners—Shell, Standard, and CFP. Indeed, the massive consumption of the Third Reich allowed Red Line companies to compensate for Depression days when demand and profits stagnated.

Once war began, Anglo-Iranian Oil Company and Olex followed Nazi Germany across Europe. "It should be noted," recounted an Anglo-Iranian internal review just after the war, "that Olex took advantage of the expansion of Germany to extend their distributing network in Austria and into Poland and Czechoslovakia." For example, in Yugoslavia, the company was known as Olex Proizvodi, headquartered in Zagreb in Croatia. After Britain declared war on the Reich and its Axis partners, German "custodians" in Berlin designated Olex as enemy property, but Reich economic officials did with Olex as they did with IBM, Ford, and General Motors. The companies were seized in name only, meaning that the funds were merely sequestered in blocked accounts for collection later. Such companies were left independent, and "in the case of Olex," Anglo-Iranian's internal review recounts, "the directors and managers were reappointed by the Custodian as his advisors."[38] There was no change from one day to the next at Olex; Anglo-Iranian's executives continued to run the company—only the profits were temporarily frozen.

Ironically, the British also deemed Olex and its foreign operations as enemy activity. The Trading with the Enemy office in London sequestered what few accounts of Olex it could find in random bank accounts. For example, Olex Yugoslavia's minor assets in London were sequestered in Trading with the Enemy account Y 40720.[39]

Two other Red Line partners were also declared enemies. The first was the Compagnie Française des Pe'troles (CFP), because France had surrendered and transformed itself into a bifurcated national entity, half Nazi-occupied in the north, half Nazi collaborationist with a capital at Vichy in the south. However, by a special high-level British government decision, CFP was permitted to conduct its normal business, making investments in Iraq Petroleum Company oil ventures as called for under the Red Line Agreement. CFP would merely contribute through the British custodian, who would forward the cash to the Red Line partners of Iraq Petroleum.[40] Thus France's CFP was able to expand its Iraq-based oil empire during the war years.

The other declared enemy was C. S. Gulbenkian, because he was living in France. The Red Line Agreement called for Gulbenkian's 5 percent allotment to be purchased by Compagnie Française des Pe'troles. Naturally, Gulbenkian fiercely protested his enemy status and threatened to retaliate by rescinding a huge endowment to build a new domicile for the National Gallery and canceling what officials called "a fabulous offer of pictures [art treasures gifted to the National Gallery] . . . because he was declared an enemy." The whole idea of being declared an enemy did not please Gulbenkian. He promised to call his attorneys. He promised to sue his Red Line partners in the Iraq Petroleum Company because he held them responsible. He reminded everyone, he had rights.[41]

As the war progressed in late 1940, Hitler needed more and more oil. Reich purchases from Romania were not keeping up with the needs arising from German aggression. The Allies wanted to deny Hitler the all-important fields in Romania by any means possible. Some even suggested defensively purchasing all Romania's output, just to keep petroleum out of Reich hands. Every other day, another British intelligence estimate forecast an ever-increasing Nazi shortfall, sometimes 1 million tons, sometimes more. No one knew the exact figures, but they knew that oil was powering the Nazi onslaught. Many analysts predicted Germany would invade Romania by spring 1940 to seize the oil fields. That is what happened, although not until October 7, 1940, when Nazi troops occupied the Romanian oil fields.[42]

But even Romanian production was not enough to fuel what Hitler had in mind. At the end of 1940, der Führer issued secret Directive 21, authorizing Operation Barbarossa, the full-scale invasion of Russia, to commence in late spring 1941. The unprecedented offensive would require thousands of long-range bombers, 3 million soldiers, thousands of tanks and artillery pieces, and 600,000 motor vehicles—all in a coordinated three-pronged attack.[43] Barbarossa would drink a lot of petroleum.

The Allies were expecting the thrust into Russia because of decoded messages during the long run-up to the invasion. Given the Nazi rape of Poland, the conquest of much of western Europe, the establishment of heinous concentration camps, and horrid civilian ghettos across the Continent, the Allied leadership was convinced that only a titanic effort could stop Hitler. Debate after debate yielded a common conclusion: Only by drying up the Reich's oil supply could the Nazi war machine be halted.[44]

Typical was a mid-1940 British report by Lord Weir to Prime Minister Neville Chamberlain, which asked, "Has this formidable enemy [the Third Reich] any real weakness on which we can concentrate?" Lord Weir then answered his own question: "I believe it has such a real weakness. Germany cannot deploy her great hitting strength for any sustained effort unless she can produce, take from storage or import vast quantities of petrol, diesel oil and lubricating oil. She is so committed to the internal combustion engine in every one of its applications—military and civil—that any dislocation of supply must limit and control her effort. No transport vehicle, no tank, no aeroplane, no submarine can function without fuel and lubricating oil. No great Army, Air Force or Navy, no amount of hard work or unity can find its effective expression without immense supplies of fuel. Germany lost the last war through lack of human fuel. This time, she should be made to lose it through lack of the fuel which goes into the fuel tanks."[45]

All attention now focused on where Hitler could find the extra fuel he needed: on the gargantuan oil fields of Iraq and Iran. A 1941 War Cabinet strategy report concluded, "Oil is, of course, Germany's main economic objective both in Iraq and Iran (Persia). The oil production of Iraq (4 million tons a year) would be sufficient to solve Germany's oil problem, but there are many difficulties in the way of transporting it to Germany. The pipelines to Haifa and Tripoli must be under her control, and the sea routes in the Eastern Mediterranean must be open to her shipping."[46]

At the same time, British war planners understood that if Germany somehow did seize Iraq's oil fields, it would be cataclysmic. "The denial to us of the Iraq oil [and its pipelines]," the War Cabinet strategy report continued, "would be serious, as alternative sources of supply would involve the extra use of tankers, of which there is already a shortage." A Foreign Office report summarized the threat, "But for British control of oil production, Germany could buy all the oil which Iran could produce."[47]

Even more blunt was a focused report titled, "Note on Iraq as a Possible Source of Oil Supply to the Enemy." The report made clear that if Romanian oil was insufficient, the Nazis "must turn to the nearest source: Iraq." Focusing on the estimated billion-ton Kirkuk oil field, the report asserted that Iraq possessed enough petroleum "to supply the [British] Empire's oil requirements for half a century." Fortunately, the report explained, for 15 years "relations between the concessionaire [the Red Line group] and the Government have been smoother than the relations of any other oil concessionaire with any other Government." The report continued, "Proof . . . can be cited [by] the fact that Iraq has leased to one set of interests the whole of its oil resources, a monopoly that no other country has emulated."[48]

Despite the smooth relations, the report emphasized that if the Third Reich somehow achieved a political foothold in Iraq—now an independent country—everything would change. The Mideast, the Gulf, and then the connection to India itself would come under Nazi domination. Germany would be unstoppable west to east. The report ended, "Conclusion: The Enemy could not be denied Iraq oil if he got there. . . . Once there, the game is up, not only with Iraq oil, but with the whole of the Near East—and perhaps beyond."[49]

Enter the Mufti of Jerusalem.

Within weeks of the war's beginning, Husseini escaped his "house arrest" and dashed back to Baghdad. The Iraq he found in October 1939 had changed dramatically over recent years. In 1933, King Faisal had become ill. After tending to an outbreak of mass murder, rape, and looting by Kurdish tribesmen and Iraqi soldiers against Assyrian separatist villages, he returned to Switzerland in September for medical treatment and died within days. Faisal had, however, lived long enough to see Iraq gain its independence and enter the League of Nations as a full member.[50]

Faisal's 21-year-old son Ghazi succeeded him. Under King Ghazi, the nation quickly descended into a cavalcade of military coups, assassinations, tribal uprisings, military show trials, and political upheaval. New political parties and power bases emerged from communists, reformers, pan-Arabists, and ultranationalists. So volatile was the country that the London-based general manager of Iraq Petroleum concluded in a November 11, 1937, meeting that he was unable to visit Baghdad to negotiate for additional oil development. Meeting minutes recorded, "It was considered that the political situation in Iraq, at the moment, was unsuitable for negotiations."[51]

Seven Sunni military men, all of them conspirators in previous coups and political murders, emerged as the strongmen of Iraq. The most powerful of these seven formed their own quadrumvirate, known as the "Golden Square" for the four corners of authority they possessed. Civilians governed only with their approval—tacit or explicit.[52]

In April 1939, King Ghazi died in a car crash. The nation went into mourning as great crowds lined up to see his funeral procession. Rumors that the British were responsible burned across Iraq, fanned by anti-British elements. Ghazi was succeeded by his son, Faisal II, a three-year-old toddler. A regent was needed to act for the boy king, so yet another Hashemite scion from the Arabian Peninsula, Prince al-Ilah, was recruited to fill the post. Prince al-Ilah was selected as regent precisely because he was pro-British. He in turn, with London's approbation, established a new government led by Prime Minister Nuri al-Said, generally viewed as tolerant of the British presence in Iraq and accepting of the Peel white paper calling for partition of Palestine. In fact, Nuri, years earlier, while serving as foreign minister, had been brought in by the British in Palestine to negotiate with the mufti and the Arab Higher Committee to successfully end the paralyzing Arab revolt of 1936.[53]

The new pro-British rule of Prime Minister Nuri al-Said and the regent al-Ilah ran afoul of the fiercely nationalist and militantly anti-

British Golden Square. At the outbreak of World War II, Nuri publicly proclaimed Iraq would honor its alliance with Great Britain. The
prime minister went further and severed diplomatic relations with
Germany, expelling its diplomats and interning German nationals.
Against this fertile background of power imbalance and fast-moving
events, the mufti, in mid-October 1939, arrived in Baghdad. His entry
was especially welcomed by the Golden Square because three of the
four generals had served with Husseini years earlier in the Turkish
army. They had long ago become fast friends and comrades in the
cause of Arab nationalism.[54]

The ground had been seeded for the mufti's mission during his so-
called house arrest in Beirut. In 1938, Husseini met secretly with Wilhelm Canaris, chief of Germany's *Abwehr,* or military intelligence. The
Abwehr had sought to smuggle weapons into Palestine through Saudi
Arabia to assist the Arab revolt, but plans were aborted because Berlin
feared the British would discover the source. In another meeting, this
one in Damascus, Nazi diplomat and Arabist Fritz Grobba gave the
mufti's secretary £800 just to keep the financial connection with Berlin
alive. Grobba had been watching Iraq and had earlier reported to Berlin
that Baghdad was now the most vociferous center of defiance against
Peel's white paper. By 1939, Germany had finally concluded three
minor arms sales with Baghdad, providing Iraq with numerous machine
guns, 18 antiaircraft pieces, and other equipment. Germany was known
for pre-positioning military necessities in other countries through
seemingly routine commercial transactions. Grobba and the *Abwehr*
believed, as an intelligence colleague noted in his diary, "The Arab
movement should be activated immediately."[55]

Ironically, just as the Nazis detested the Jews and yet promoted a
Jewish homeland, they also considered the Arabs merely another version of a reviled subhuman species: the Semites. Nazi Germany
organized its ethnic relations along a pseudoscientific race science,
called *eugenics,* which created an inescapable genetic hierarchy of wor-
thy human life, with Aryan Nazis at the top. All other racial or
national groups were to be dominated, or even destroyed. As Semites,
Arabs were just a second branch of the same eugenic line that created
the hated Jews. In fact, Hitler personally named Operation Barbarossa
for King Frederick Barbarossa, who in 1190 led the German Crusade
against Islam in Palestine. However, for the sake of its goals for world

domination, the Reich was willing to promote the diametrically opposed national aspirations of both the Jews and the Arabs in Palestine. After all, even as the Nazis bolstered their condemnation of Jewish settlement in Palestine, Berlin had fostered prewar trade and transfer agreements with the Zionist Organization that brought to Palestine some 60,000 Jews, along with $100 million in goods, thus dramatically expanding the viability of the Jewish state. This rapid expansion of Jewish Palestine was in fact the very cause of the Arabs' protest.[56]

But the mufti did not care about the motivations of the Nazis, only how the Reich could advance the aspirations of Arab Palestine. Upon entering Iraq, Husseini immediately set about establishing a power base. The collaborationist Vichy police in Syria made things comfortable by hand-delivering the mufti's motorcar and household goods from Beirut. In March 1940, two police inspectors traveled to Baghdad with Husseini's personal property as a sort of moving service. Their travel expense report totaled 23,350 piastres for the 17 tins of automobile gasoline hauled along, plus food and lodging for two days in Baghdad, and an additional 100 piastres for the gasoline funnel they used to refill their vehicle from time to time.[57]

The mufti began activating his campaign. Husseini wrote passionately to the powerful All-India Moslem League in Bombay seeking support for Palestine; he hoped to open yet another political front against Britain, this time in India. The mufti also organized the Arab National Party to agitate for a Palestine without Jews. The new group included the foursome of the Golden Square, as well as leading government official Rashid Ali. Golden Square officers were only too eager to join. Their bitterness with Britain was aggravated because London, short of equipment and fearing the very agitation that was then under way, had refused to sell the Iraqi military any quantity of arms. Months earlier, when the Iraq military had requested new equipment, London replied it could spare only four small howitzers and a few radio sets. Under the close hand of the mufti, this new Arab National Party met in secret, its members used assumed names, and they swore allegiance on the Koran.[58]

As his first major plan of upheaval, the mufti tried to spark a Palestine-style violent outbreak against Britons in Iraq. Everywhere, he and his followers sowed rumors about such an uprising in the spring or summer of 1940. Nuri's government called for postal censorship. Plainclothes security police began arresting troublemakers in cafés. But the population grew more restive. Soon, with pressure mounting, Nuri resigned as prime minister, to be replaced by Rashid Ali, the mufti's comrade in the fight against Zionism. Nuri stayed on as foreign minister, but the power had suddenly shifted demonstratively toward the mufti and his cohorts in the Golden Square.[59]

Throughout May 1940, local newspapers tried to calm the populace. One typical story in *Al Istiqlal,* on May 22, excoriated a "gang of the biased and wicked . . . engaged in the promotion of false rumors."[60]

Prime Minister Rashid Ali informed British representative C. J. Edmonds in Baghdad that the entire Anglo-Iraqi relationship was now completely tied to the events in Palestine. If London solved the Jewish question in Palestine, England would not need to divert resources from the global war to defend Iraq and its oil fields against a German invasion. The men debated Palestine back and forth, but it was as though they were not speaking the same language. Edmonds used political syllogisms and diplomatic verbiage. Rashid Ali insisted that no matter what rationales were invoked, everything in Iraq now was being driven by events in Palestine.[61]

Edmonds wrote that Rashid Ali then craftily declared, "This country would easily raise 100,000 men to take its part in the common defense. But as things were, he [Rashid Ali] could not be sure that the Iraq Army would [even] march to its appointed positions." In fact, if the army did deploy, said Rashid Ali, no one could guarantee they would not fall apart due to "internal trouble." Edmonds reported that Rashid Ali was explicit: "The situation could only be rendered sound by the solution of the Palestinian problem."[62] In others words, the Iraqis would let the Germans walk in unopposed and seize the oil wells unless Zionism was promptly thwarted in Palestine.

Startled, Edmonds retorted that he was profoundly shocked "that the Iraqi Army might not cooperate in the defense of their own country." Rashid Ali replied vaguely, but returned the discussion to negotiations with the Palestinians to undo the white paper. When the meeting ended, Rashid Ali sharply reminded Edmonds "that the time was the present, and Baghdad the place; the Palestinian leaders were here and the Iraqi government, the honest broker, was willing and anxious."[63]

Soon, British diplomats in Iraq were sending home report after report warning that the mufti was orchestrating a range of anti-British plots in Iraq, and the local situation was rapidly deteriorating. Typical was one diplomatic summary that belittled the new Iraqi "instinct to indulge in blackmail over Palestine." In July 1940, Rashid Ali's justice minister met secretly in Turkey with the Reich ambassador, Franz von Papen. The mufti then sent his own secretary to talk to German foreign minister Joachim von Ribbentrop in Berlin. The mufti's condition for an Arab rebellion in Iraq: a German declaration against the Zionist homeland and in favor of a pan-Arab state.[64]

The outlines of the demanded declaration were embodied in the mufti's personal eight-point draft. It covered all the Islamic nations of the Arab realm: Syria, Lebanon, Kuwait, Egypt, Saudi Arabia, Sudan, Dubai, Oman. All these countries were to be liberated from British protectorates, reservations, and mandates. Key to the mufti's draft declaration was Point 7: "Germany and Italy recognize the illegality of the 'Jewish Home in Palestine.' They accord to Palestine and other Arab countries the right to resolve the problem of the Jewish elements in Palestine and other Arab countries in accordance with the interests of the Arabs, and by the same method that the question is now being settled in the Axis countries."[65]

To Nazi eyes the phrase was perfect: "resolve the problem of the Jewish elements in Palestine and other Arab countries . . . by the same method that the question is now being settled in the Axis countries." How was the Jewish problem being settled in the Axis countries of Greater Germany, Hungary, Romania, occupied Poland, and elsewhere? Identification, expulsion from the economy, confiscation of assets, enforced starvation, ghettoization, concentration in camps, and mass murder. The mufti's offer was to extend Hitler's merciless international campaign of Jewish destruction into the Middle East.

The mufti was not the only extremist courting the Third Reich. Other opportunist-minded Arabs beckoned as well, including Rashid Ali. Each saw Berlin replacing London as the stage manager for nationalist aspirations in Palestine and across the Arab crescent. Just as 15 years earlier, the promises and enticements only escalated as the oil and strategic location of Iraq became the prize.

The converse of the Lawrence of Arabia drama was now unfolding. The Arabs would again rise up for nationalism, but this time for German sponsors, not the British. In fact, Fritz Grobba, the central Nazi figure in rallying the Arab revolt, was openly nicknamed the "German Lawrence." Grobba was actually born Arthur Borg. For affectation, he took his name, A. Borg, reversed the letters to read "groba" and added a second B for style to create "Grobba." His mysterious exploits and evolving alliances were covered in the newspapers. One *New York Times* article, headlined " 'German Lawrence' Stirs Revolt," carried his photograph with the caption: "Dr. Fritz Grobba, whose exploits in the Arab world rival those of Britain's famous Lawrence."[66]

The *New York Times* article opened: "Behind the scenes of the war in Iraq, a German agent called Dr. Grobba has been playing an active part. Occasionally, his name has been mentioned in the dispatches, but it has never been disclosed who this man is, what he has done in the past, and what he is still doing. Officially, Dr. Grobba is the German envoy at the court of Ibn Saud, the ruler of Saudi Arabia. Previously, he was for many years German envoy to Iran. But behind this official mission something altogether different is concealed. In informed circles, in Berlin, London, Cairo, Baghdad and Mecca, this man is called 'the German Lawrence.' It is true that he does not bear the slightest outward resemblance to his famous British predecessor of the [first] World War . . . but so far as success is concerned, Grobba is not far behind the prototype."[67]

Nonetheless, der Führer still viewed Arab nationalism as a mere means to an end, that is, as a stepping-stone to the Nazi conquest and domination of the entire Middle East. Grobba himself talked to Hitler about Iraq, and recalled, "When the deep split [rivalry] emerged in Berlin between Haj Amin [Husseini] and Rashid Ali, I found myself facing a serious dilemma. Both sought from Hitler recognition as leader of the Arab world, and both put pressure on me to influence der Führer in this respect. Although Rashid Ali was the most prominent Arab politician who joined us against the democracies, we were aware that Haj Amin [Husseini] enjoyed tremendous prestige in the Arab and Moslem world, as being fearless in the revolt against the British. When I tried to raise the issue of recognition in my talks with Hitler, der Führer put me off, arguing that the time had not yet come to install an Arab leader, and that the subject would be discussed when we conquered the Arab region."[68]

The Arabs carried no illusions about their status in Western eyes. Europe cared about them only as the people who walked the ground above the oil deposits. Beginning in July, the Iraqi catchphrase of the day became "absolute neutrality," which was in fact an open code word for disavowal of the Anglo-Iraq Treaty of Alliance, which called for mutual military assistance in times of war. But more than that, "absolute neutrality" advertised an Arab allegiance purchasable by either side—British or Nazi—for satisfaction of national desires.[69] Iraqis, and indeed Arabs everywhere, called this moment a "golden opportunity."

Al Istiqlal, July 4, 1940: "Iraq's attitude of neutrality only safeguards her future and her integrity and the maintenance of her sovereignty." *Al Nasr,* August 6: "[Germany and Britain] each proclaim itself to be the sole champion of the Arabs and Arab ideals. But we may wonderingly ask whether any nation has ever served any cause but its own interests." *Al Yaum,* August 8: "The imperialistic powers are trying to make Iraq take sides, but such poisonous propaganda cannot grow in the soil of Iraq." *Al Istiqlal,* August 13: "Two peoples are fighting for world domination, each pretending to be fighting for the cause of civilization and the deliverance of small nations." *Basra Al Sijil,* September 2: "The real intentions of both sides are wellknown by weak peoples, who realize that the present struggle is inspired by greed and the desire to subjugate peoples and rob them of their wealth."[70]

Often quoted by worried British officials was *Al Istiqlal*'s August 12 editorial: "The reason for this insistence [absolute neutrality] lies in the desire, on the one hand to avoid the danger of war, and on the other to exploit all opportunities which occur." The mufti's forces in Iraq constantly preached solidarity. *Al Rai al Am,* September 28: "The Arabs cannot turn this golden opportunity to profit, nor remove the yoke of imperialism, unless they organize themselves."[71]

By early October 1940, reports from Baghdad triggered serious alarms in Whitehall. Telegraph service between Iraq and Germany had been restored. Prime Minister Rashid Ali was openly cultivating diplomatic support from the Reich. Just a few months earlier, London had believed it could safely transport Indian regiments north through

Iraq, per its treaty rights, to confront an expected Nazi advance in Syria or to secure the oil fields. This was now in doubt. Their conclusions: "A) Active hostility on the part of the Iraqis might make it impossible to use the overland route for the passage of troops from Basra to Haifa or for the maintenance of our forces in the Middle East; B) Difficulties might be expected in the use of the Empire air route from Egypt to India, the Far East and Australia, which passes through Iraq; C) The Iraqis might cut off at [the] source the oil which was piped across the desert to Haifa. The hostility of Iraq might influence Iran, and so reduce the reliance to be placed on [the] Abadan [refinery] as a source of oil; D) If Iraq and Iran become subservient to the Axis powers, our enemies would be at the gates of India."[72]

Many in Whitehall now decided to either kidnap the mufti and deport him to Cyprus or simply kill him—they weren't sure which. As for Rashid Ali, they wanted him "eliminated" as well. In a November 1, 1940, War Office review of the German push through the Balkans and into Syria, military planners wrote under Iraq "A) Removal of present Iraqi Prime Minister: *We agree.* B) The elimination of the Mufti: *We do not agree that the assassination of the Mufti is unlikely to have ill effects. We agree, however, that it is essential to put an end to his current activities.*" Fully appreciating that thinly stretched British forces could not be diverted to Iraq, other planners wondered if the Iraqis could be bought off as in prior crises. "C) Financial and Economic Aid: *Since we are unable to spare troops for Iraq, or such war materiel as anti-aircraft guns, practically the only inducement for the Iraqis to behave in accordance with our wishes lies in the financial and economic sphere.*" But militant Iraqis weren't interested in stopping Nazism—just in furthering Palestine and Arab nationalism.[73]

Nuri, now waiting in the wings as foreign minister, agreed that drastic action was needed, and "evolved scheme after scheme for his [Rashid Ali's] elimination," as one British diplomat wrote, "but none progressed beyond its initial stages." In the end, London decided to ask the regent to exercise the powers of the king and fire Rashid Ali.[74]

Meanwhile, the Arab link to the Axis was growing closer. On January 20, the mufti sent a long appeal to Adolf Hitler, using all the well-known anti-Semitic and trigger phrases of Nazi hate doctrine. "Your Excellence: England, that bitter and cunning enemy to the true freedom of the Arab nation, has never ceased to forge fetters to enslave and subjugate the Arab people, either in the name of a deceit-ful League of Nations, or by the expression of perfidious and hypo-critical humanitarian feelings but with the actual aim of effecting her imperialist machinations, which are camouflaged by principles of democracy and of deceitful internationalism." The mufti detailed the Arab plight: "By geographical coincidence, the Arab people find themselves at the center of a land and sea crossroads which, according to the English, is the major intersection of the English Empire's 'transport lines' . . . the 'holy' British transport lines!"[75]

The mufti condemned Arab monarchs for giving England oil pipelines. "King Faisal the First," he wrote, "agreed to a *modus vivendi*, and signed a treaty with England, and, despite the opposition of the majority of the Iraqi people, sold the relative independence of Iraq in return for oil concessions." Husseini's missive reviewed decades of international transgressions by the French in Syria and British in Palestine and Iraq, punctuating it with the resonant words, "This was done with the agreement of the Jews."[76]

Turning to Palestine, the mufti made his point: "His Excellence is well aware of the problem faced by this country," he wrote, "which has also suffered from the deceitful actions of the English. They attempted to place an additional obstacle before the unity and inde-pendence of the Arab states by abandoning it to world Jewry, this dangerous enemy whose secret weapons—finance, corruption and intrigue—were aligned with British daggers. . . . The Palestinian problem united all of the Arab states in a mutual hatred of the English and Jews. If mutual hatred is a prerequisite for national unity, it can be said that the problem of Palestine hastened this unity."[77]

Then came the mufti's casbah-like offer of allegiance: "Freed from certain material impediments, the Arab peoples will be ready to serve the common enemy his just deserts, and to take their place enthusias-tically alongside the Axis in order to fulfill their part in bringing about the well-deserved defeat of the Anglo-Jewish coalition. . . . Allow me to add that the Arabs are willing to put all their weight behind the campaign, and to shed their blood in the holy war for their national rights and aspirations—on condition that certain interests of a moral and material order are assured." Husseini specifically focused on the Arab ability to disrupt "the transport lines of the [British] Empire and sever the contact between India and the Mediterranean region . . . through the Persian Gulf, and thus end the exploitation of the flow of oil for the benefit of England.[78]

"I close with wishes for long life and happiness for His Excellency, and for a shining victory and prosperity for the great German people and for the Axis in the near future."[79]

In March 1941, Hitler replied through State Secretary Ernst von Weizacker. "*Der Führer* received your letter dated January 20," Weizacker's response began. "He took great interest in what you wrote him about the national struggle of the Arabs. He was pleased with the friendly words addressed to him in the name of Arab Nationalism." Now Hitler, through Weizacker, conveyed the words the Arabs wanted to hear. "Germany has never occupied any Arab countries and has no ambitions whatsoever in Arab lands. Our view is that Arabs, who possess an ancient culture and have proved their administrative, judiciary and military maturity, are capable of self-government. Germany recognizes the full independence of the Arab countries, or where this has not yet been attained, their right to it."[80]

"The Germans and the Arabs have common enemies in England and the Jews," the letter continued, "and are united in the fight against them. Germany, traditionally friendly to the Arabs . . . is ready to cooperate with you and to give you all possible military and financial help required by your preparations to fight against the British for the realization of your people's aspirations. In order to enable the Arabs to begin the necessary preparations for their future war against the British, Germany is prepared to deliver to you immediately military material, if the means for transporting this material can be found." He added, "I request you keep the contents of this communication secret."[81]

Hitler's reply, however, fell short of the unequivocal statement of national recognition the mufti was seeking, the type that der Führer had extended to other ethnic groups in Europe to cement their support.

Although the language was still evolving, the Arab-Nazi axis was moving ahead. The mufti's intrigues were not unknown to London intelligence. Whitehall most feared that Vichy Syria would allow the Germans to occupy and invade the Iraq oil fields as part of a complete push past Russia and on to the east. Britain moved quickly now. London insisted that the regent dismiss Prime Minister Rashid Ali, and in doing so stymie the Golden Square, the mufti, and the Nazi threat. The compliant regent was prepared to arrest Rashid Ali and his accomplices, but the Golden Square learned of his plans. On April 1, troops loyal to the Golden Square surrounded the palace, preparing to arrest him. The nervous regent donned a disguise, quietly slipped out to his aunt's house, and then stealthily made his way in a motorboat down the Tigris to Basra, where he rendezvoused with a British gunboat. From Basra, the gunboat steamed to safety outside of Iraq.[82]

On April 3, 1941, with the regent gone, the Golden Square launched yet another coup d'état, forming a new government under Rashid Ali and appointing trusted cronies to all the key positions, including the regency. Almost simultaneously, neighboring Syria, the anticipated gateway for the Nazi invasion, exploded with Reich propaganda, supported by Gestapo agents and specially trained Arab Nazis. The Arab Club, the National Youth Organization, and the Group of National Action all went into action. Their members all spoke fluent German. They distributed additional copies of the Arabic version of the Nazi Party's rabid newspaper, *Völkischer Beobachter,* and ensured that "the whole country is a hotbed of Nazi propaganda," as the *New York Times* reported. Soon posters were popping up in the market. One featured a large swastika surrounded by the words "In Heaven, Allah is thy ruler. On Earth, Adolf Hitler will rule us."[83]

An anxious War Office sent a general to Baghdad to analyze the British mission's defensive position. If the Iraqis moved against British interests, diplomats, staff, and civilians in the oil industry across the country, along with their wives and children, would need evacuation from Baghdad and military protection. Code words were established: *sapphire* or *emerald* meant evacuate immediately to the British base at Habbaniya by any means possible. But the small contingent of British soldiers at Habbaniya would be hopelessly outnumbered. Sending additional weapons would not help, they concluded. The situation was dire; there were no armaments to spare. Nonetheless, 25 rifles and a few other small arms were dispatched.[84]

When calls for relief troops circulated, military commanders in the region confessed they were unable to assist. The commanding general cabled, "My forces are stretched to limit everywhere and I simply cannot afford to risk part of forces . . . at Basra."[85] With the British outmanned, with German troops preparing to enter via Vichy Syria to occupy the oil fields, and with the Iraqis willing to facilitate the Nazis, there seemed to be only one option remaining.

Destroy the oil. Destroy it all.

No one was quite sure how to destroy an oil field. But the contingency had been considered as much as a year earlier. Some experts thought the fields could simply be dynamited. But they quickly concluded that an explosion would only bring more oil to the surface. Perhaps the field could be set ablaze; the fire might burn for years, they thought; but a new drill site into the vast oil layer of Kirkuk would reestablish the supply within months, even as another well burned. The wells could be plugged; but again, new borings would remedy that.[86]

Then the infrastructure would have to be blown, that is, the storage tanks, pumping stations, pipelines, and refineries. Everything: from Kirkuk to Tripoli to Haifa. That was the only way to deny Iraq's oil to the Reich just as Barbarossa was about to launch.

A memo was circulated to a trusted manager of the Iraq Petroleum Company. "It is now advisable," the memo explained, "to consider what action the IPC should take in the way of preparations for demolition or putting plant[s] out of action, and/or prevent[ing] the possibility of supplies getting into enemy hands. It is suggested . . . in the following order: 1) The destruction and elimination of stocks of Crude Oil from Tripoli. These stocks of crude oil today are approximately 113,300 tons. It is suggested that arrangements should now be made for the disposal of these stocks: by burning, or by opening the lines to allow the oil to discharge into the sea. . . . Consideration should be given to the immobilization of the field as a whole. . . . The IPC Management should now . . . draw up a line of attack . . . if, and when, it is necessary. . . . In the meantime, the IPC should give consideration to immediate action in the way of plugging up wells which are not required . . . to keep Haifa Refinery going on a one million tons per annum basis; that is, only those wells that are in production should be left open and all others plugged off and even disconnected from the pipeline system. [In addition] stocks of crude oil at K1 and

K3 [pumping facilities] should now be reduced to an absolute minimum."[87]

Some in the Ministry of Economic Warfare in London began to worry about just how many oil executives would be privy to the secret plans. On June 26, 1940, one planner wrote, "To this oil committee go quite a large number of persons, several of whom are in almost continual touch with representatives of the oil companies, many of which are international in character, and some of which must at the present time have in mind the future interest of their companies."[88]

By mid-July 1940, the War Cabinet concluded that pipelines running through Syria to Tripoli must be blown as well. "If the German war effort were to be turned eastwards," they decided, "it would be of the highest importance that the northern branch of the Iraq Pipeline should not remain intact. Even if the Kirkuk Oilfield in Iraq were put out of action, it would only be a few months before it could be brought back to production; only a relatively short part of the northern line runs through Iraq and this could be repaired by the time the field was able to produce. Destruction of the pumping stations and pipeline throughout Syria could cause a much greater delay before transport could be resumed."[89]

By November 1940, as the situation worsened, the generals wanted the demolition sequence solidified. "Plans already in preparation for the destruction of the Iraqi oil wells and the pipelines in Iraq, Syria and Palestine should be perfected," instructed one memo, "and brought to a state in which they could be operated without interference on a very short notice." The memo added, "It is important to keep these plans secret from the Iraqi Government."[90]

IPC general manager J. Skliros corrected the planners. During a December 18, 1940, conference on the question, Skliros explained that destroying Iraqi oil facilities would not be easy. In Palestine and Transjordan, he said, where British authorities reigned, the facilities could be junked at will, with troops overseeing the explosives. But in Iraq, Britain maintained a mere shadow military presence. "The Iraqi government probably suspected that such schemes were in mind," cautioned Skliros, "and, if occasion to put them into practice rose, the Iraqi Government would probably take measures to prevent the entry of British Military personnel into Iraq for the purpose, and the movements of Company personnel would probably be subject to surveillance."[91]

In the first days of April 1941, just after the Golden Square coup forced the regent to flee and then installed a tougher Rashid Ali government, Iraqi police units took up positions at Kirkuk and various pumping stations, as expected. Moreover, oil company personnel were now under suspicion and scrutiny.[92]

On April 18, Britain finally found a small contingent of troops to assist. They were suddenly airlifted and sealifted into Basra, ostensibly to transit through the country pursuant to treaty rights, but in fact to protect the oil fields and British civilians. As the naval ships approached, senior Iraqi officials were undecided whether they should challenge the landing or honor the treaty. Formal permission was granted just two hours before the seaborne troops actually arrived. The men were permitted to proceed to the British base at Habbaniya. But in view of the rapidly deteriorating position, more men would need to be mustered from Britain's overstretched forces.[93]

Ten days later, on April 28, the British Embassy advised the Iraqis that three more ships would be landing, this time carrying 2,000 men, only 400 of whom were actual combat troops. Within a few hours, the Golden Square issued a swift reply: They could not enter. The British, however, were determined, especially since an uprising against British civilians was rumored to erupt within a few days.[94]

The next day, April 29, evacuation orders were broadcast by the embassy. British women and children from all over Iraq were bused to the large base at Habbaniya. On April 30, Iraqi officials confronted the IPC's fields manager, demanding "a written guarantee that no wells or installations would be sabotaged." The statement was signed, and the installations were promptly taken over by Iraqi troops for good measure. In the meantime, a column of Iraqi troops was ordered to proceed to the British base.[95]

The Habbaniya base, located almost midway between Fallujah and Ramadi, sprawled across an eight-mile square. Within its cantonment, it housed several thousand troops, 8,000 civilians, churches, shops, and barracks. Habbaniya was extremely habitable, but quite poorly defended. One British commander fondly remarked, "It is notorious that when the Germans occupy a new station, their first task is to build defenses around it, whereas the British in similar circumstances lay out cricket and football fields." Indeed, a quaint crossroads sign out front sported arrows with two air distances: London 3,287 miles to the west, Baghdad 55 miles to the east. The base, mainly the home of a military flying school, was hardly ready for combat.[96]

On April 30, 1940, an English-speaking Iraqi messenger delivered a demand to the base commandant that all British aircraft remain grounded and all troops remain confined to base. British commanders considered the note an "impertinent gesture." Planes were demonstratively sent aloft to photograph the enemy encampments. This revealed that Iraqis and several dozen howitzers were dug in just a half mile outside the perimeter and all across the high escarpments overlooking Habbaniya. Moreover, Golden Square forces had evacuated local tribesmen in surrounding hamlets to make way for a military action against the base. One British soldier who ventured out to collect mail was arrested.[97]

During the night of May 2, Iraqi advance troops penetrated to the perimeter. At 5 A.M., the British commander opened fire. Iraqi mortar shells began raining in on the base. The flight students scrambled to become instant combat pilots to strafe and bomb Iraqi positions.[98]

One student, with only a few hours of flying experience, jumped into an Oxford trainer to ride as navigator for a sortie over Ramadi. At 2,000 feet, ground fire hit the plane, killing the pilot with a shot to the heart. The young lad pulled the pilot off the controls and attempted to land on his own. After three or four approaches, the student was finally able to put down safely.[99]

The students flew as many as 9 or 10 sorties each, round the clock, hitting every encampment and concentration of Iraqi troops. When the Iraqis tried to bring up a column from Fallujah, it became bottlenecked three miles from a bridge at a narrow bend in the road. At that choke point, the lane squeezed between palm groves elevated above irrigation ditches on either side. Hence, there was no possible way to turn around. British aircraft spotted the crawling line and attacked. First, they destroyed the lead vehicles, and then they hammered them over and over again with strafing runs and dive-bombing. Ammunition trucks exploded, a convoy of troops in an assortment of vehicles caught fire, and a battery of mobile artillery and every other type of mechanized vehicle was turned into twisted, smoldering wreckage.[100]

The German high command acted. Its chief of air staff sent one of his top aviators, Major Axel von Blomberg, along with two others, to survey available landing strips so that the Luftwaffe could fly in and assist Rashid Ali. Blomberg flew in circuitously by way of Athens and Damascus, landing in Mosul on May 11. There, he found two disused German Heinkel 111 bombers from the Iraqi air force. The next morning Blomberg flew one of the Heinkels to Baghdad to meet with Rashid Ali. Flying low, the clearly marked German craft aroused celebratory fire from tribesmen. But several bullets pierced the cockpit, killing Blomberg. He was buried the next day, with Rashid Ali offering special condolences at the funeral.[101]

Now the Germans launched missions in earnest. A heavy-fighter unit and a bomber unit dispatched 16 more Heinkels and 10 Messerschmitt heavy fighters to aid in the attack on Habbaniya. Meanwhile, some two dozen German mechanics and airmen filtered into the country, along with Grobba and other Reich diplomats. The Luftwaffe began running strafing and bombing missions of their own against Habbaniya, as well as commando formations crossing the desert to aide the besieged camp. As feared, the Germans primarily used the massive Rayak airbase in Vichy Syria. In addition, several trainloads of French arms were packed and dispatched to Mosul, where the Germans set up their local airbase.[102]

With Germans running bombing missions and Habbaniya under continuous attack, the British turned off the oil spigot at Basra. The commander in chief in India sent a coded telegram to the War Office: "Iraqi troops have also occupied pumping station K1 and K2. Iraqi police have arrested engineer in charge of plant at H3." The telegram added, "All refineries and oil installations are in Iraqi hands and demolition now possible by air action."[103]

But the students and instructors at Habbaniya were heroically flying day and night against the small Iraqi air force. Most enemy craft were destroyed on the ground, sometimes a dozen at a time. Churchill had already sent a foreboding cable to U.S. President Franklin D. Roosevelt, stating that if the Mideast fell to the Germans, victory against the Nazis would be a "hard, long and bleak proposition."[104] All understood that if Germany would secure Iraq's oil, she might proceed all the way to the East.

By May 15, 1941, urgent messages burned the telegraph wires as British commanders in the area informed London that land operations were now out of the question. One typical note declared: "In view changed situation Iraq, consider it will be impossible to destroy Kirkuk wells at short notice."[105]

Besieged and out of options, the British called in the Irgun from Palestine. The Irgun was an extremist Jewish defense organization in Palestine formed to defend kibbutzim and villages and retaliate for the constant Arab attacks. Irgun commander David Raziel, at that moment, was in a British prison in Palestine. Raziel was approached by British intelligence and asked if he would undertake a dangerous mission to destroy the oil refineries in Iraq, thereby denying the fuel to the Germans. The answer was yes, on one condition: Raziel wanted to kidnap the Mufti of Jerusalem and bring him back. Agreed.[106]

The next morning, May 17, 1941, Raziel and three comrades, along with a British officer, quietly entered the Tel Nof air base, which was located south of Tel Aviv. There they climbed into an RAF plane, which flew them to Habbaniya. While in flight, however, the British high command in London decided that the destruction of Iraq's refineries should be delayed until the very last moment in the hope it would not be necessary. Rebuilding the pipelines would take years and place an enormous strain on British fuel needs for the rest of the war. Perhaps the Germans could be stopped after all. When Raziel landed in Iraq, he was given new orders: Undertake an intelligence mission preparatory to a British sweep into Fullajah as part of the final drive to retake Baghdad from Rashid Ali and the Golden Square.[107]

As Raziel was landing, a new Zionist military organization was being formed, again with the consent of the British. They would be known as the *Palmach,* or strike forces. Even before the units were properly assembled, their first mission would be an elite commando raid, made up of 23 volunteers and commanded by Zvi Spectre. British Major Anthony Palmer accompanied them. Their objective: Blow up the refineries in Tripoli that were providing fuel to the German airplanes bombing Iraq. Very late on the evening of May 18, 1941, a small British vessel, the *Sea Lion,* equipped with three oar-driven landing boats, departed Haifa for Vichy Lebanon. By this time the British were bombing Tripoli, which placed Vichy defense forces around the Tripoli refinery on high alert. In the hours to come, the *Sea Lion* and all its men disappeared. *Palmach* commanders believed they were killed while approaching the refinery.[108]

Meanwhile, back in Iraq, on May 17, Raziel, his three comrades, along with a British officer, set out by car from the Habbaniya base toward Fallujah. At the first river, they found a boat, only big enough for two. Raziel ordered his comrades to proceed, while he went back to the car with his fellow Irgunist and the British officer. Just then, from nowhere, a German plane dived from on high, dropping a bomb. The car was destroyed and Raziel with it.[109]

That same day, RAF commanders notified the Air Ministry that the situation was becoming more precarious each day. Once German airpower had advanced from Syria into Iraq, it would constitute a major threat to the refinery at Abadan and to the Suez Canal. By May 22, the RAF cabled back to London, "I submit that the time has come for taking action against the oil refinery at Alwand (about 100 miles northeast of Baghdad)" as well as four pumping stations. "Thus, we remove his [the enemy's] main attraction in that part of the world. The cable pleaded with the high command to remember that "the history of [such] demolitions is a history of 'too late.' "[110]

A few days later, May 25, Hitler issued Order 30, redoubling support for Iraq. "The Arabian Freedom Movement in the Middle East," he wrote, "is our natural ally against England. In this connection special importance is attached to the liberation of Iraq. It strengthens beyond the Iraq borders the forces in the Middle East hostile to England, disturbs English communications, and ties down English troops as well as English shipping space, at the cost of other theaters of war. I have therefore decided to move forward in the Middle East by support of Iraq. Whether and how the English position between the Mediterranean and the Persian Gulf—in connection with an offensive against the Suez Canal—is to be later finally solved, is not up for decision until after Barbarossa."[111]

The Admiralty in London now gave the final order to destroy the refineries and pumping stations in Iraq at will. "If Germans occupy Iraq and Syria," the message read, "they cannot profit by the oil resources there for at least some time." But suddenly, the forces at Habbaniya were gaining the upper hand. Persistent bombing, Arabs abandoning their positions and equipment en masse to disappear into the populace, plus the sheer exhaustion of supplies had delivered what seemed like a victory to British forces. On May 30, the British-organized Arab Legion, led by legendary Major Henry Glubb of Britain, pushed past fatigued ground resistance and a steady barrage of German air attacks. Major Glubb reached Baghdad at about 4 A.M. to meet two Iraqi truce officers waving a white flag hanging from a pole. By now, Rashid Ali, the Golden Square, and Grobba had fled to Iran. The mayor of Baghdad was the only one left to come out and sign the cease-fire document.[112]

After the main players fled, the coup and the threat were over, at least for now. The regent returned to Iraq. Reich bomber crews flew from Mosul back to Germany. Only two of the Heinkels had escaped destruction. Grobba and his staff departed Mosul by car.[113]

London rushed new superseding instructions about destroying the oil installations. "Scheme for the denial of the Iraq oil to the enemy . . . is quite clearly out of date. If we regain control in Iraq, one of our first steps must be to secure the key points on the oil system with a view to their demolition [only] if we are compelled to withdraw subsequently." The instruction added, "Dangerous as it is to delay, I think we should not take immediate action against the Haifa pipe lines or the installations which feed it until the success or failure of 'Exporter' becomes apparent." However, the note continued, local commanders must be prepared, "to ensure the destruction of the Iraq-Haifa pipeline system in the event of the failure of 'Exporter.' "[114]

The threat to Iraqi oil was not over. The Germans were still threatening a major new advance into Vichy Syria and Lebanon. Operation Exporter, conceived almost overnight, was the only Allied hope of denying the Reich an open door in Vichy Syria. An Australian strike force, augmented by Free French Forces, assembled to launch a sneak attack.[115]

Again, the British called upon the *Palmach,* this time to cross into Syria and pave the way for Exporter. *Palmach* commanders Moshe Dayan and Yitzhak Rabin were among the men who would lead the commando missions. Dayan assembled a force of 30. The British required all of them to know Syrian territory intimately and speak perfect Arabic so they could enter disguised as Arabs. Dayan's commandos lied. None of them spoke Arabic. They didn't even have a map of Syria. But Dayan did hire a trusted Arabic guide. On the night of June 6, the *Palmach* commandos set off with a team of Australians to disrupt telegraph and telephone communications, eliminate key potential installations, and secure bridges and other strategic points. By preemptively capturing or neutralizing resistance at the major crossing points, Exporter forces could race through Vichy Syria and Lebanon to secure the oil installations and airfields.[116]

Dayan's group was operating successfully at the Litani River. Suddenly, on the morning of June 8, 1941, having secured most of their objectives, Dayan's group came under French heavy machine-gun fire. He picked up a pair of binoculars to scout out the firing positions. An incoming bullet hit the binoculars, driving steel and glass deep into Dayan's left eye. The eye could not be saved, and Dayan would later don the eyepatch that for decades became the icon of defense for the Jewish people. Rabin, the youngest member of the squad, spent most of his time cutting phone lines atop telephone poles and did not sustain any injuries.[117] Both Rabin and Dayan went on to become commanders of the Jewish state's defense forces. Rabin would go on to become the state's prime minister.

The next day, Exporter, a three-pronged assault, was launched from Iraq, from Palestine, and from the sea to seize Vichy Syria and Lebanon and thereby deny Germany the operating base it needed to dominate the Middle East. A British reporter embedded with the first troops punching in from Palestine sent back an eyewitness dispatch. Using just paper and pencil, he wrote, "I crossed from Palestine into Syria just before dawn this morning with Australian troops and am now speeding northward with our forces along the white cliffs toward Lebanon. Our advance into the French-mandated territories began under cover of darkness. Long lines of transports filled with grinning Diggers [Australians . . .] are now pushing forward at several points, accompanied by Bren gun carriers, guns and tanks. British troops, the Royal Air Force and the navy are cooperating. From dusk until midnight Sunday night our column had moved toward the frontier. While scouts crossed No-Man's Land, we waited under cover for the signal to advance. . . . French positions knew nothing."[118]

Within a matter of days, the Allied surprise attack, made up of Free French, Australian, and British forces, supported by *Palmach* scouts and commandos, overwhelmed tough Vichy forces in Syria and Lebanon.[119] The Allies became entrenched in Lebanon and Syria, stopping the Nazi advance in the Middle East. Hitler's Operation Barbarossa was launched against Russia June 22, 1941, but without Iraqi petroleum.

The oil installations were not destroyed, not in Iraq, not anywhere.

CHAPTER SEVENTEEN

The Price of Prejudice

June 1, 1941, was a turning point for Iraq. It did not matter that the Allies had stopped the German advance into Syria and prevented their occupation of Iraq's oil fields. It did not matter that the Hitler stalwarts, Rashid Ali, the Golden Square, Fritz Grobba, and the Mufti of Jerusalem, had fled to Iran. The legacy of Nazi doctrine and the mufti's hatred of the Jews had pervaded the Iraqi national psyche. Beginning June 1, the population would wage war against its own ancient Jewish community as a spearhead of its anti-Zionist and nationalist crusade.

On May 31, 1941, at 4 A.M., British forces, pushing forward after relieving Habbaniya, arrived at the gates of Baghdad, where they executed truce documents. At that moment, Regent al-Ilah was preparing to fly into Baghdad to reclaim his leadership of the country. To avoid the appearance of a London-sponsored countercoup, British troops were instructed by their commanders to remain on the outskirts of Baghdad, allowing the regent to enter unescorted.[1]

For a few hours, a power vacuum existed in Baghdad. The Golden Square and Rashid Ali had fled. The regent was en route. The British were at the city's edge. For just a few hours, Baghdad was unsupervised. But a few hours was all it took for angry masses to suddenly erupt in a maniacal pogrom against their Jewish neighbors. Within the next 48 hours, a rampage of mass murder, mutilation, rape, burning, and looting began the end of 2,600 years of Jewish life in Iraq. The carnage would be forever seared upon the collective Iraqi Jewish consciousness as the *Farhud*. In Arabic, *Farhud* means something beyond mere chaos, something more than just a riot. Perhaps *Farhud* is best translated as "violent dispossession."

The *Farhud* began at about 3 P.M. on June 1, after Regent al-Ilah's airplane landed at the Baghdad airport. That day was also the Jewish holiday of *Shavuot*, commemorating the revelation of the Torah, or Law, on Mt. Sinai. Leading members of the Iraqi Jewish community assembled to greet the returning regent, as did many other loyal citizens who welcomed his reinstallation. But the populace widely reviled the ouster of the pro-Hitler Golden Square bloc and the mufti and the repatriation of the regent as yet another British interventionist plot serving Zionist Palestine. The mufti had already publicly accused Jews of monitoring telephone conversations and telegraph transmissions and passing the information to the British Embassy during the battle to expel the Golden Square.[2] They were all considered spies. The mob wanted blood.

The sight of Jews returning from the Baghdad airport was all the excuse that antagonized bands needed to unleash vengeance. Jews were attacked as they crossed the Al Khurr Bridge, and violence quickly spread to the Al Rusafa and Abu Sifyan districts. The frenzied mob murdered Jews openly on the streets; women were raped as their horrified families looked on; infants were killed in front of their parents. Horrid torture and mutilation followed. Jewish shops were looted and torched. A synagogue was invaded, then burned, and its Torahs defiled and then destroyed in classic Nazi fashion.[3]

When wounded Jews were taken to the hospital at Baghdad Medical College, the chief surgeon rushed to the operating room. Reluctant Arab doctors and nurses in attendance declined to render aid but soon followed the doctor's adamant instruction and prepared for surgery. As the doctor scrubbed, soldiers recovering from the Habbaniya campaign rose up angry at the sight of Jewish patients. Some soldiers, although wounded, tried to rape Jewish patients right in the hospital. Suddenly, the surgeon stopped everyone in their tracks by barking into a megaphone that every soldier should return to his bed, or he would personally shoot them. Two guns clearly hung from his belt.

He meant it. Everyone backed down. The tense situation in the operating room calmed. But stories of poisoned patients elsewhere in the hospital quickly circulated. For their own protection, Jews were soon transferred to Meir Elias, a hospital with more Jewish doctors. As the pillaging continued that night, a number of Moslem Iraqis hid Jews in their homes. A few apologized to the frightened Jews for not having kosher meat to serve them.[4]

In some districts, the *Kristallnacht*-style riot quieted by 10 P.M. In others, the shooting, burning, and mayhem continued throughout the evening. Jews were dragged from their automobiles. Homes were invaded. Finally, at about dawn on January 2, the tumult quieted. But just briefly. Soon the fury resumed—now with policemen and slum dwellers joining in. Baghdad was racked with more murders, burning, looting, and home break-ins to kill the men and rape the women.[5]

At the Muallem-Cohen house, young Nezima was terrified. Her father had just returned from a brief morning foray to inspect a nearby synagogue. He was relating the terrible stories he had heard about daughters being raped and homes burned, when suddenly shouting, armed men crashed through his own front gates. Quick, Mr. Muallem-Cohen rushed his family to the stairs to escape to the roof. Up they scampered, first young Nezima, then her mother, and then her father. A shot—Mr. Muallem-Cohen was dead. Mrs. Muallem-Cohen looked back in horror. Just then a policeman appeared. "They killed my husband," she shrieked. "How do *you* want to die?" he snapped back, and then cracked her skull with his gun.[6]

As the bloody day burned on, the lord mayor of Baghdad pleaded with the director-general of the police to issue "shoot to kill" orders to stop the pogrom. The regent finally authorized the orders, but it mattered little because the police were part of the pogrom. Finally, in the afternoon, British forces punched into the city with two Iraqi brigades from Kirkuk that were loyal to the regent. They opened fire on the rampagers, dispersing them. A 5 P.M. curfew was broadcast. Scores of violators were shot on sight. The disturbances were finally quelled. The British restored the order that disintegrated during those few transitional hours.[7]

The Jewish Agency in Jerusalem cabled the Foreign Office: "Fearful picture of anti-Jewish excesses at Baghdad June 1, June 2. . . . Massacres began. . . . Jews removed from cars and brutally murdered, then mob began attack on Jewish [religious] holiday crowds walking in street. Fearful details received of ghastly tortures and murders occurred. Dead bodies defiled, children thrown into Euphrates. . . . Estimated 500 Jews killed and over 1000 wounded. Entire street full of shops ransacked and burnt. Hospitals overcrowded. Thousands homeless in streets and synagogues. Armed police . . . students, secondary schools and colleges participated. Killing and robbing continued for two days. . . . Only stopped when British troops took action. . . . Incriminated police not removed. No investigation, no punishment. Air full of poisonous incitement, renewed outbreak feared by community. Implore help and immigrant permits to Palestine."[8]

The final toll may never be known. Rabbis were forced to sign statements vastly minimizing the numbers of casualties. A commission found that at least 180 Jews were killed and 240 wounded, 586 Jewish businesses were pillaged, and 99 Jewish homes were burned, with property losses reaching $3 million.[9]

June 1, 1941, was a turning point not only for Iraq national self-definition, but for the Iraqi Jewish community as well. It was only the beginning for both.

Iraq was integral to Judaism. In about 2000 BCE, according to tradition, Abraham traveled to Palestine from the Babylonian port city of Ur on the Euphrates. About a millennium later, his Hebrew descendants established themselves in Israel. Over a period of centuries, Babylonian kings conquered the Israelites, and some 50,000, including the best artisans, were abducted into Babylon. Commencing in 721 BCE, the longest exile in history began. After Cyrus emancipated the Israelites in Babylon, many stayed on and flourished, raising a great Jewish culture, rich in learning and art. Scholars created the Babylonian Talmud, which became authoritative as Jewish law since Babylonian institutions continued to prosper and became pivotal to Judaism after the Romans destroyed Jerusalem and renamed Israel as *Syria Palestina*.[10]

In Common-Era Iraq, with its substantial Christian character, Judaism flowered for centuries. After the Moslem conquest in 637, thousands of Jews maintained their entrenched existence as *dhimmis,* that is, a subordinate non-Islamic group. Under Ottoman rule, during the eighteenth and nineteenth centuries, Jews continued to thrive, becoming part of the commercial and political ruling class. Like Armenians, the Jews could engage in necessary commercial activities, such as moneylending and banking, that were proscribed for Moslems under Islamic law. Jews functioned as state treasurers and economic advisors, in some families from generation to generation.[11]

Through the centuries, as the Arab national character dominated the Middle East, minorities became identified and hyphenated as "Arab-Christians" and "Arab-Jews," that is, Jews and Christians in Arab lands. Hence, these groups saw themselves as Arab nationals of a non-Islamic religion, just as French, Germans, and Americans saw themselves as members of the state first and adherents of a religion second.

Ottoman Jews encouraged the assimilation process and insisted on equal treatment. In that vein, in 1840, Sultan Abdulmecit I investigated the medieval blood libel against Jews and issued a royal edict against it, declaring: "An ancient prejudice prevailed against the Jews. The ignorant believed that the Jews were accustomed to sacrifice a human being to make use of the blood at their feast of the Passover. . . . For this reason . . . we cannot permit the Jewish Nation (whose innocence of the crime alleged against them is evident) to be vexed and tormented upon accusations which have not the least foundation in truth. . . . [Therefore], the Jewish Nation shall possess the same advantages and enjoy the same privileges as are granted to the numerous other nations [*dhimmis* groups] that submit to our authority. . . . In all parts of our Empire, [the Jews] shall be perfectly protected as well as all other subjects of the Sublime Porte."[12]

Like many Ottoman decrees, the ruling against the blood libel did not erase the prejudice against them as infidels. Subsequent Ottoman regimes targeted them for special restrictions. Even still, the Jews of Baghdad, who had survived the Mongols and plagues, also survived the Ottoman centuries, fortified by the value of their international trade and monetary connections. When the Young Turks arose in 1908, Turkification was easy for Mesopotamia's Jews. They, of course, thought of themselves as Turkish first, second, and third, just as assimilated Jews anywhere felt about their settled homes.

In World War I, Iraqi Jews fought for the Arab nationalist cause alongside Lawrence of Arabia. Nuri Said recalled that in 1917, when he was an officer in Cairo, "My attention was attracted by the presence of one hundred volunteers of Iraqi Jews, headed by two Jewish officers. They came from the [Turkish] prisoner camps [maintained by the British] to fight under the banners of King Hussein. The British and French Commands tried to separate these volunteers from their other brethren and employ them in the Palestine front, but did not succeed, as they [the Jews] insisted on serving under the Arab flag in the Hijaz."[13]

When the Allies installed the mandate in 1920, Jews and Christians greatly expanded their middle class and establishment niches. Moreover, Jews stepped into the vacuum created by the genocide against hundreds of thousands of Armenians during the war. Because of their education, Jews were often given preference by mandatory officials. Jewish professionals and clerical workers flocked to the new Allied-run bureaucracies. Jews served as lawyers, doctors, and judges. Jews dominated the cotton trade via their connections in Manchester, and were pivotal in other imports and exports. Wealthy Jews operated nearly all the banks, continued as essential economic advisors to government, acted as money changers, and in general functioned as the bedrock of Iraq's entire financial apparatus. Independent Iraq's new monetary system was actually devised by Jewish financial experts. Jewish negotiators loyally extracted the highest possible royalties from Turkish Petroleum for Iraq's national treasury. Several distinguished members of the Jewish community served in the Iraqi Chamber of Deputies and the Senate. Jews also became well known in the arts, letters, and music of the nation.[14]

By no means were all Iraqi Jews cosmopolitan Baghdadis. For many centuries, Jews lived in the north among the Kurds, mainly as simple farmers and herders, tending flocks and orchards and rejoicing at weddings with the same abundant food, dancing, and music as their neighbors. They lived in Mosul, Kirkuk, Arbīl, and other Kurdish areas along with the other Islamic and non-Islamic ethnic groups that created the Kurdish culture. In dress and manner, Kurdish Jews resembled their neighbors, and they adopted the national identity of their fellow Kurdish peoples in their struggle for independence. In the Shiite south, Jews also blended in with their fellow citizens as simple peddlers and bazaar stall owners. They shared the same coffeehouses and were equally affected when British forces invaded in the Mesopotamian campaign.[15]

Various censuses measured the Jewish population of Iraq differently, depending on which disputed territories were included and the demographic ebb and flow of volatile Iraq. A 1906 Ottoman census counted 256,000 Jewish citizens. A Young Turk census in 1914 listed 187,000. As a result of emigration during the postwar upheaval years, Jewish numbers dropped in the third decade, with the official 1920 census counting only 87,488. Slightly more than half of those lived in Baghdad, with the remainder split between the Mosul north and the Basra south.[16]

Naturally, persecution often confronted the Iraqi Jews. This was especially so in the 1930s after Nazi propaganda had begun to infect the thinking of many nations in Europe and the Middle East. Iraqi Jews were periodically expelled from some professions under *numerus clausus* quotas, just as they were in Germany. Moreover, the Arab Revolt in Palestine had caused uncomfortable reverberations for Jews throughout the Mideast. But Iraq's Jews weathered the discrimination of the 1930s as they had for millennia. Moreover, Iraqi Jews blamed their troubles not on their domestic status as much as on the Zionist enterprise in Palestine, an enterprise they vocally rejected.[17]

Clearly, before 1941, Iraqi Jews simply did not identify with Zionism, not after 2,600 years of accepted life as Iraqis. They were in fact following the belief adopted by most assimilated Jews throughout America, England, France, and Germany. Jews in European and American centers who rejected Zionism as a threat to their assimilated existence divided themselves into two groups: so-called non-Zionists, and anti-Zionists. Non-Zionists did not oppose a Jewish homeland, but approved of it only for their dispossessed eastern European brethren. Anti-Zionists, on the other hand, fully opposed the Balfour Declaration and the whole concept of a Jewish homeland. Iraqi Jews, like most Arab Jews throughout the Middle East, were genuinely anti-Zionist. Zionists understood this rejection and did not view the abundantly populated Arab countries next door as a source of immigration. During the 1920s and 1930s, no Zionist immigration representative was posted to Baghdad, and none was welcome.[18]

One high Zionist official, Chaim Arlosoroff, ruled Iraqi emigration out in these words: "The Jews there live contented lives, they are involved in all branches of commerce and economy, and therefore have no thought of emigrating."[19]

Menahem S. Daniel, an eminent leader of the Baghdad Jewish community, summed it up when he informed the Zionist Organization in London: "Any sympathy with the Zionist Movement is [seen by our neighbors as] nothing short of a betrayal of the Arab cause." Daniel reminded them, "Jews in this country hold indeed a conspicuous position. They form one-third of the population of the capital, hold the larger part of the commerce of the country and offer a higher standard of literacy than the Moslems. . . . [The Iraqi Jew] is, moreover, beginning to give the Moslem . . . successful competition in government functions, which . . . may well risk to embitter feelings against him. In this delicate situation the Jew cannot maintain himself unless he gives proof of an unimpeachable loyalty to his country."[20]

Public denunciations by Iraqi Jews of a Jewish Palestine were common, as much to express their rejection as to preserve their status among militantly anti-Zionist neighbors. At the time of the *Kristallnacht* riots in Germany, in November 1938, a leading Jewish attorney writing in the *Baghdad Times* declared: "The problem which the Balfour Declaration purported to solve is and remains a European problem, both by origin and present incidence." As late as 1947, the chief rabbi of Iraq proclaimed, "Iraqi Jews will forever be against Zionism."[21]

But on June 1 and 2, 1941, more than two millennia of historic coexistence abruptly shattered like a fragile knee. Overnight, shocked Iraqi Jews could no longer stand on their ancient history and steadfast loyalty. Zionist visionaries had always been convinced that sooner or later anti-Jewish impulses would drive Jews from their countries, hence the need for a Jewish homeland. Iraqi Jews woke up on June 1 as staunchly anti-Zionist. By the time they fell asleep on June 2, forlorn and traumatized, Zionism and Jewish Palestine had become an option—perhaps the only option.

For years, Iraq and the Arabs had agitated for independence and self-governance. In 1932, Britain finally sponsored an independent Iraq for full membership in the League of Nations. A condition for admission to the league was acceptance by the Iraqi government of the league's Protection of Minorities Declaration. The Baghdad government signed the declaration. But no sooner was statehood granted than state-sponsored violence against its own minorities was unleashed.[22]

In 1933, Iraq's armed forces brutally reacted to a nationalist surge by Assyrian Christians. Assyrians were one of the peoples that had dwelled in the region since the earliest days of ancient Mesopotamian civilization. In the first century of the Common Era, Assyrians widely adopted Christianity, forming one of the earliest Christian churches. After the Moslem Conquest, Christian Assyrians became a persecuted minority under both the Turks and Mandatory Iraqis. They energetically, but unsuccessfully, sought self-determination from the League of Nations and rebelled against Baghdad's authority.[23]

In August 1933, while King Faisal was in London, several thousand Iraqi troops were deployed to suppress an Assyrian insurrection. Under explicit orders, the soldiers mercilessly retaliated against all civilians in about 60 Assyrian villages. The Motor Machine Gun Unit systematically drove from village to village, dragging all the men out of their homes, lining them up in groups, and mercilessly machine-gunning them—about 500 to 1,000 were murdered. The corpses were piled into heaps and then set on fire. To complete the vengeance, the army and Kurdish tribesmen thoroughly looted the villages, burned the homes, and destroyed the grain. This created hundreds of starving and homeless women and children. Some said the atrocities were too heinous for Faisal to bear and suggested that the emotional distress of the crisis actually hastened his death.[24] League declaration or not, independence in Iraq seemed a license to rise up against its minorities. Assyrians were first. Jews were next.

Shortly after Iraq signed its 1932 declaration to protect minorities, than Fritz Grobba arrived as Germany's chargé d'affaires in Baghdad. Grobba acquired the Christian Iraqi newspaper *il-Alem il Arabi*, converting it into a Nazi organ that published in installments an Arabic translation of Hitler's *Mein Kampf.* Once Hitler assumed office in 1933, Radio Berlin began beaming Arabic programs across the Middle East. The Nazi ideology of Jewish conspiracy and international manipulation were widely adopted in Iraqi society, especially within the framework of the Palestinian problem that dominated Iraqi politics.[25]

At first, Iraq's anti-Jewish actions were simple *numerus clausus* purges. In September 1934, a few dozen government clerks were ousted from their positions because they were Jewish. The next year, 1935, the Iraqi Ministry of Education adopted unwritten quotas for Jews seeking to attend institutions of higher education. In 1936, hundreds of Jews were dismissed from government service. Jews saw these measures as fallout from the Arab Revolt in Palestine, not a manifestation of growing national hatred. But over the next few years, the situation worsened as bombs and grenades were hurled at synagogues and Jewish schools. Even an appeal by King Ghazi in October 1936 did not stop the stream of murders and anti-Jewish incitement. Palestinian gangs mainly orchestrated the campaign, not infrequently buttressed by government officials such as the governor of Basra, who was himself a major fund-raiser for the anti-Zionist resistance in Palestine.[26]

In 1940, as Nazi influence infected more and more of Iraqi society, especially under Rashid Ali, some of Iraq's Jews, who had long been careful to suffer in silence, approached the Iraqi government demanding protection. London became involved in the context of the war effort itself and fears of German encroachment into Iraq. On May 27, 1940, the British Embassy in Baghdad reported, "Some of the Jews of Baghdad had recently made representations to the Iraqi government against the campaign now being waged against them under Nazi inspiration."[27]

When the *Farhud* shook Baghdad in June 1941, the demoralized Jewish community struggled for reassurance that such pogroms would not continue. A refugee exodus was in the making. By late August, the British Consulate in Baghdad had processed about 1,000 Jewish applications for visas to enter India. Some Iraqis even pleaded for permission to enter Palestine. But by October 1941, with the return of the regent and Nuri Said as prime minister, as well as a greater British military presence, the status quo ante resumed. Establishment Jews were more comfortable in their shops, banks, and government offices and wanted to believe in a promised resumption of their beloved protections as Iraqi citizens in good standing. Ringleaders of the Golden Square putsch were eventually tried and hanged, and many of their supporters were interned, this as part of the larger political crisis that restored Nuri and the regent.[28]

Still, Nazi sentiment and agitation by the followers of the deposed Rashid Ali everywhere remained palpable among average Iraqis. For example, in Mosul, pro-Nazi Arab activists continued to propagandize against Jews throughout the fall of 1941. In Baghdad, when the war film *For Freedom* showed in cinemas, audiences cheered Hitler and booed Churchill. Leaflets circulated: "Rashid Ali, the Leader of all the Arabs, is returning with ropes and gallows to hang a number of criminal Jews, Christian traitors and other enemies of Islam."[29]

But while the older Jewish generation was grateful for every moment of continuing normalcy, the younger generation saw a horrible end coming. The *Farhud* had rocked the consciousness of Jewish teenagers, who rejected the hopefulness of their parents. These newly awakened militant teenagers formed secret Zionist societies akin to the underground Jewish defense organizations in Nazi-overrun Europe. The first Baghdad group to coalesce was Youth for Salvation; a counterpart group called the Committee of Free Jews assembled in the south. Their purpose: Be ready for the moment when the exodus would be needed. These sub-rosa movements contacted Zionist emigration emissaries in Palestine. The emissaries slipped into Iraq to upgrade these ad hoc organizations into a true wartime underground, complete with weapons and self-defense training.[30]

In the background, the Mufti of Jerusalem was constantly broadcasting anti-Jewish and anti-Zionist vitriol into Iraq via Radio Berlin. As of the fall of 1941, Husseini had established a permanent base in Nazi Germany with his own Reich-designated office called the Grand Mufti's Bureau. Through constant meetings with the Reich hierarchy, public appearances throughout Nazi-overrun Europe, and strategic lobbying with Axis governments, the mufti kept the Nazi-Arab coalition of convenience viable and in the forefront.[31]

For example, on November 28, 1941, the mufti conferred with the highest echelons of Nazi leadership. He told German Foreign Minister von Ribbentrop, "The [Rashid Ali] rising in Iraq had not proved very successful, but the Arab world took the view that this was not final, but a mere start. The Iraqis at least now understood that Britain was their enemy." Von Ribbentrop apologized that in May 1941 German forces could not do more to support and resupply Rashid Ali because of "a lack of petrol and . . . transport facilities."[32]

After the conference with von Ribbentrop, the mufti was escorted into a special audience with Hitler. Grobba attended as well. Hussein again urged der Führer to issue a public Nazi declaration in favor of

Arab nationalism. Hitler replied that the time was too soon, especially in view of French colonial sensitivities in Vichy Syria. But, Hitler vowed, the day of reckoning would come. He said, "The German aim would then be the entire annihilation of the Jews living in Arab territory under the protection of British [Palestine]."[33]

For his part, the mufti wanted to accelerate Hitler's extermination campaign in Europe. Every Jew gassed or murdered in Europe meant one less refugee streaming into Palestine. Husseini conferred frequently with extermination engineer Adolf Eichmann. Moreover, from time to time, the mufti interceded with Nazi and other Axis officials to abort Red Cross plans to save Jewish children by sending them to Palestine. For example, on June 28, 1943, as human barters were increasing, the mufti wrote to the Hungarian foreign minister: "I ask your Excellency to permit me to draw your attention to the necessity of preventing the Jews from leaving your country for Palestine; and if there are reasons which make their removal necessary, it would be indispensable and infinitely preferable to send them to other countries where they would find themselves under active control, for example, in Poland, in order thereby to protect oneself from their menace and avoid the consequent damage."[34] At the time, sending a Jew to Poland, which the Allies had publicly declared filled with extermination camps, was a clear death sentence.

Eventually, the international pro-Hitler Arab movement yielded thousands of Moslems to fight in Nazi Islamic units, such as the 10,000-man, mainly Bosnian, Waffen-SS Handschar Division, under the direct supervision of Heinrich Himmler. *Handschar* is Turkish for "sword," and the division's standard emblem was a sword or Islamic crescent alongside a swastika on their fezzes and arm patches. Many of these Moslems, who vowed to defeat the "Jewish-Anglo-Bolshevik enemy," adorned their personal lockers with photos of their spiritual leader, the mufti. Himmler personally insisted that the regular Reich military corps accommodate Moslem volunteer fighters as indispensable soldiers in the struggle against the Jews. He ordered that the Moslem diet of abstaining from pork be rigidly observed. Moslem jokes were strictly banned. "I do not wish," decreed Himmler in an official order, "that through the folly and narrowness of mind of an isolated person, that a single one of the tens of thousands of these brave volunteers . . . should suffer from ill-humor. . . . I forbid the jokes and facetious remarks about the Moslem volunteers."[35]

In regular radio programs, the mufti broadcast the rallying cry to Moslem Nazi troops and to Arabs everywhere: Destroy Britain and slaughter the Jews to save Iraq. Husseini's passionate fatwa against Britain declared: "O Moslems! Proud Iraq has placed herself in the vanguard of this Holy Struggle. . . . It is the duty of all Moslems to aid Iraq in her struggle and seek every means to fight the enemy. . . . The English have committed unheard of barbarisms. . . . I invite you to bring all your weight to bear in helping Iraq that she may throw off the shame that torments her." Fighting to save Iraq was the mufti's constant refrain. When he cursed the Jews, he spoke with equal venom. "Arabs! Rise as one and fight for your sacred rights. Kill the Jews wherever you find them. This pleases Allah, history and religion. This saves your honor."[36]

So while Arab Jewish communities, such as those in Iraq, savored every additional day of seeming peace, the desire to see their destruction only ramified throughout the Arab world and particularly so in Iraq. By 1942, the chief guarantor of Jewish protection, Prime Minister Nuri Said, had joined the ranks of popular anti-Jewish resentment. His censorship office permitted rabid libels to be printed and allowed leading participants of the *Farhud* to regain key positions in the government.[37]

The Jews were a convenient scapegoat for Iraqi politicians. In the absence of any great industrial or national achievements to lift the spirits of the average Iraqi or share the oil wealth, Arab unity now coalesced around equating all Iraqi Jews with Zionists and therefore with enemies of the state.

Major John Glubb, who spent many years in the Mideast with Bedouin fighters, rallying and forging them into the British-organized Arab Legion, and eventually dubbed "Glubb Pasha," saw Iraqi democracy as a sham. He complained bitterly to his superiors in London in his after-action report on the ouster of the Golden Square.

"The whole [pro-Nazi Rashid Ali] affair," Glubb complained poignantly, "goes a long way to prove the falseness and artificiality of the present political situation in Iraq. That country received from Great Britain an exact copy of the British Constitution, down to the smallest details of an Upper and Lower house, a Speaker, and a Constitutional Monarch. We thereby doubtless imagined that we had bestowed on the Iraqis all these blessings of democracy, which the British people enjoy with such relish and to retain which they are prepared to face death and ruin. Nothing could be more undemocratic than the result.[38]

"A handful of politicians obtained possession of the machinery of government, and all the elections were rigged," continued the major. "The people at large, not greatly interested in politics anyhow, and entirely unfamiliar with the idea of elections (a purely European conception), were entirely out of touch with the politicians. Thus, a small group of politicians were able to monopolize office for the better part of fifteen years. Every cabinet contained the same old crowd who just changed round their chairs at each change of government. In this process they all became very rich."[39]

Nor did the defeat of the Third Reich in 1945 bring Iraq into the Allied fold. The Iraqis were driven more by their obsession with Jewish Palestine and perpetuating Nazi precepts and anti-Jewish programs than by a desire to rebuild their country or strengthen their democracy. At war's end in mid-1945, hundreds of thousands of dispossessed European survivors emerged from their ghettos, concentration camps, and forests, desperate to enter Jewish Palestine to restart their lives. However, rather than stirring humanitarian notes in Iraq, the European Jewish plight only heightened hatred against Arab Jews, especially in Iraq. The Arabs resented and belittled the Holocaust tragedy as nothing more than another ploy for expanding Jewish Palestine's population.

Everything escalated fiercely in February 1947, when the United Nations agreed to vote on the question of partition. The 1937 Peel Commission's recommendation for partition was now evolving from a white piece of paper into a binding international ballot. The possibility of a legitimized and recognized Jewish state on Arab lands in Palestine was more than unthinkable. The Palestine conflict still dominated and defined the Iraqi national agenda, paralyzing Iraqi action on its other vital needs, such as the economy, infrastructure, health services, and education. The country's newspapers warned that if "the Zionist entity" came into nationhood no Iraqi government could control the Arab Street in Baghdad. Uniformly, the Arab regimes, including the Baghdad government, officially threatened that if the UN dared vote yes to partition, the Arabs would exact reprisals against the 700,000 Jews who had dwelled in countries throughout the Middle East.[40]

Violence against Iraqi Jews intensified in the months leading up to the vote. On May 9, for example, a Baghdad mob killed a hapless Jewish man hysterically accused of giving poisoned candy to Arab children. In the Jewish quarter of Fallujah, homes were ransacked and local Jews were compelled to move in with friends and relatives in Baghdad. Large Jewish "donations" were regularly extorted and sent to Palestinian Arabs. The names of the "donors" were read on the radio to encourage more of the same. Yet the Jews still deluded themselves that as loyal Iraqis, they belonged. This hardship would pass, they believed. But the Jewish Agency emissary in Iraq wrote back to Jerusalem: "No attention is paid [by the Jews] to the frightful manifestations of hostility around them, which place all Jews on the verge of a volcano about to erupt."[41]

On November 29, 1947, the UN voted 33 yes, 13 no, with 10 abstentions, to create two states: one Palestinian Arab, the other Jewish.[42]

Once the UN vote registered, an anti-Jewish campaign exploded in Iraq. This time, it was not just pogroms but systematic pauperization, taking a cue from the confiscatory techniques developed by the Nazis. Jews were charged with trumped-up offenses and fined exorbitant amounts. All the while, mob chants of "death to the Jews" became ever more commonplace.[43]

Israel was set to declare its independence on May 14, 1948. In April 1948, Iraq shut down the Kirkuk-Haifa oil pipeline, thereby slashing its own oil royalties. Production at the Kirkuk field was immediately cut by 25 percent, from 4.3 million tons annually to 3.1 million tons. Moreover, the pipeline closure convulsed the delicate negotiations between the Baghdad regime and the IPC over a number of vital issues, such as calculation of royalties in gold as compared to pounds sterling—which had recently declined in value—hiring Iraqis as key company officers, and even a much-needed £3 million IPC loan to the Iraqi government.[44] In Iraq's view, business was overshadowed by the need to confront Israel.

The day after Israel declared its independence, the new nation was invaded from all sides by armies contributed by most of the Arab states. "This will be a war of extermination and a momentous massacre which will be spoken of like the Mongolian massacres," promised Azzam Pasha, secretary-general of the Arab League. Iraq's military forces saw very limited action. But martial law was imposed by Baghdad, so the dismal battle news was censored. The Arab armies, although more numerous, and rich in death rhetoric, were poorly organized, disunified, and militarily unprepared. Israel was not defeated. The UN negotiated and implemented an armistice with Egypt, Transjordan, Syria, and Lebanon. Only Iraq refused to sign, continuing its state of war and demanding what it called "a second round," or another chance to fight. In fact, as a result of the war, Israel now controlled even more of the land of Palestine.[45] It was very convenient to once again blame Iraq's Jews and Zionist gangs for this latest military disaster.

On July 19, 1948, Iraq amended penal code Law 51 against anarchy, immorality, and communism, adding the word "Zionism." Zionism itself now became a crime, punishable by up to seven years in prison. Every Jew was thought to be a Zionist, thereby criminalizing every Jew. Only two Moslem witnesses were needed to denounce a Jew, with virtually no avenue of appeal. In sweeps, thousands of Jewish homes were searched for secret caches of money thought destined for Israel. Frequently this necessitated demolishing walls as part of the search. One man was sentenced to five years' hard labor for merely possessing a scrap of paper with an Old Testament Hebrew inscription; the paper was presumed to be a Zionist instrument. Hundreds of Jews were now arrested, forced to confess under torture, financially punished, and sentenced to long jail terms.[46]

The greatest shock to the Jewish community occurred when the single wealthiest Jew in Iraq, Ford automobile importer Shafiq Ades, was accused of sending cars to Israel. Ades was tried by a military tribunal, quickly found guilty, and fined $20 million and handed a death sentence. His entire estate was liquidated. A few days later, on September 23, 1948, Ades was publicly hanged in Basra. His body was allowed to languish in the square for hours, to be abused by the celebrating crowds.[47]

Many more arrests, executions, and confiscations followed. In October, all Jews—an estimated 1,500—were summarily dismissed from their government positions. This crippled such key infrastructure departments as the Irrigation Department, the Basra port, the Telephone and Telegraph Office, and the Railways Administration. For example, about 25 percent of the Basra port staff suddenly became unavailable. Some 350 Jewish workers were dismissed from the Railway Administration alone; there was no one to replace them and no one to train replacements, so workers were imported from Pakistan. The Jewish banks, key to foreign commerce, lost their licenses to import money.[48]

Soon the familiar sequence of Nazi-style pauperization began. Once a prosperous, generously spending community, the Iraq Jews stopped purchasing and general spending, from the bazaar to the restaurant. Jewish businesses were boycotted; their owners were arrested; funds dried up. Many Jewish firms went out of business and their Arab employees soon became ex-employees, which only further punished the weakened consumer economy. Many purged Jewish government employees, highly skilled and once well paid, now destitute, were reduced to selling matches on the streets to avoid being arrested for vagrancy. Jewish home values dropped by 80 percent. What's more, the national treasury was crippled from a 50 percent drop in oil revenues due to the Haifa line being shut down, as well as the considerable military expenditures for the unproductive venture against Israel in the war.[49]

The once genteel and gracious life of Jews in Iraq was about to terminate. The Zionists had seen the process during prior years in Germany, Austria, Poland, Holland, Hungary, and elsewhere. Now it was time for the Zionist underground to step up its activities. They had been smuggling Jews out of Iraq for years, generally through Jordan and Beirut. But the war for Israeli independence had obstructed those westward routes. The refugee caravans looked east to Iran. The first 26 persons were smuggled through in November 1948, even though Islamic Iran had not recognized Israel. But now thousands would have to transit. A little bribery helped immensely; $450,000 was given, mainly to the Iranian prime minister, but some to other government officials and media sources. Iran's prime minister announced that his country would open its doors as a grand humanitarian gesture in keeping with its 6,000-year tradition of tolerance. Iraqi Jews in large numbers were now permitted to transit via Iran, eventually 1,000 per month.[50]

With the escapees went their money and some possessions; in other words, it was a flight of capital as well as people. This further battered the national economy. A debate gripped Iraq. Should the Jews be expelled? That would only provide more manpower to the Jewish state. On the other hand, every Jew was considered a spy and an enemy; why keep them in the country? Should all their economic holdings be seized? That would glut the market with cheap land, homes, and possessions, especially since Jews were already sacrificing their assets at just 5 and 10 percent of their worth—anything to extract some value and flee. One refugee recalled, "When the Jews left, they sold their possessions for pennies. A rug worth 2,000 to 3,000 dinar sold for 20 to 30 dinar."[51] Moreover, the rapid subtraction of Jews from the financial, administrative, retail, and export sectors was devastating. One day they were just gone. Unlike in Germany, a nation of 60 million where non-Jews had rushed in to fill the professional and commercial vacuum, within the small Iraqi population, in many cases, there was no one to replace the Jews—certainly not overnight.

An estimated 130,000 Jews lived in the Iraq of 1949, half of whom resided in Baghdad. The Baghdad Chamber of Commerce listed 2,430 member companies. A third were Jewish, and, in fact, a third of the chamber's board and almost all of its employees were Jewish. Jewish firms transacted 45 percent of the exports and nearly 75 percent of the imports. A quarter of all Iraqi Jews worked in transportation, such as the railways and port administration. The controller of the budget was Jewish; a director of the Iraqi National Bank was Jewish; the Currency Office board was all Jewish; the Foreign Currency Committee was about 95 percent Jewish. Over the centuries, Jews had become essential to the economy.[52]

On March 3, 1950, to halt the uncontrolled flight of assets and people, Iraq prime minister Tawfig as-Suwaydi engineered the passage of an amendment to Law 1, the Denaturalization Act. The amendment authorized revocation of citizenship to any Jew who willingly left the country. Upon exit, their assets were frozen but were still available to the emigrants for use within Iraq. Once Jews registered to emigrate, the decision was permanent, and they were required to leave within 15 days. The window would not be wide. The amendment to Law 1 would expire in one year.[53]

The doors swung open, albeit only briefly. Iraqi officials guesstimated that 7,000 to 10,000 of the most undesirable Jews, mainly those already pauperized, would be the only ones to leave. The wealthier Jews, officials were convinced, would never abandon their lives. The state thought it could declare "good riddance" to just a fraction of its Jewish citizens and maintain the remainder. They were wrong.[54]

The doors became floodgates. Thousands immediately registered to leave. Household by household, Jewish families finally—almost unanimously—realized that their precious existence in Iraq was over. In wave after wave, groups of refugees left the country via the overland route. Soon large, overcrowded refugee camps sprang up in Iran to accommodate the exodus.[55]

Quickly it became clear that the land route was now insufficient for such a volume. Israel's Mossad, the clandestine group invented during the Holocaust to smuggle Jews to safety, knew an airlift was needed to rescue as many Jews as possible before Iraq changed its mind. The Mossad called in its most reliable partner for airlifting Jews: Alaska Airlines. Its president, James Wooten, had been instrumental in rescuing the Jews of Yemen just after the state was born. El Al, Wooten, and Alaska formed a new airline with a new identity called Near East Air Transport (NEAT). Israeli ownership was hidden, so NEAT appeared to be strictly an Alaska Airlines venture.[56]

Israel's original passenger projections vastly exceeded anything stunned Iraqi government officials had contemplated. Israel envisioned flying out about half the Iraqi Jewish population—40,000 the first year, and more thereafter, for a total of 60,000. Flights would operate through Nicosia, Cyprus, or possibly direct to Tel Aviv if the fact of Israel-bound flights could be kept secret. NEAT needed an Iraqi partner to secure charter rights in Iraq. The perfect partner was the well-established Iraq Tours, based in Baghdad. Who was the chairman of Iraq Tours? It was Iraq prime minister Tawfiq as-Suwaydi, the man who had engineered Law 1, the Denaturalization Act.[57]

On May 19, 1950, the first 175 Jews were airlifted out of Iraq in two C-54 Skymasters.[58] Israel originally called the rescue Operation Ali Baba, but it later became known by the original code name, Operation Ezra and Nehemiah, for the prophets who led the Jews of Babylon out of exile back to Israel.

Within days of the airlift's inauguration, some 30,000 Jews had registered at their synagogues and were therefore required to leave within 15 days. But only 7,000 of those first registrants had completed the lengthy and redundant bureaucratic process of obtaining all the right forms, from all the right people, with all the right stamps, in all the right order. Once at the airport, departing Jews were abused and humiliated. Rings were pulled from their hands and linings were torn from their hats as officials looked for valuables during a thorough search. Their papers were slowly reregistered and restamped, and only then were they finally approved for takeoff—generally, an additional six-hour ordeal.[59] There weren't enough hours in the day, seats on the small two-engine aircraft, or planes in the tiny NEAT fleet to possibly transfer the thousands who were now stateless in their own country, penniless amid all the wealth they had left behind, and reviled in the nation they loved.

Just one other thing. The Iraqi government, furious over the mass departure, made it clear: These Jews were now stateless refugees, devoid of legal rights in Iraq, and essentially all Zionist criminals. Many were now homeless and sleeping on the streets. If they were not removed—and swiftly—the government was prepared to move them into concentration camps.[60] The very phrase "concentration camp," coming on the heels of the Holocaust, was chilling.

More planes were needed. More firms were needed. The British wanted their national airlines, BOAC and BEA, to join the lucrative airlift. The Iraqis also wanted their national airline, Iraqi Airways, to join the lucrative airlift. So Iraqi Airways was given the ground maintenance contract, 30 dinars for every flight. British planes were used, but with a 7.7 percent fee to Iraqi Airways. Who was the director-general of Iraq Airways? Sabah Said, the son of Nuri Said, who received an additional 5.5 percent "special fee."[61]

However, Israel's fragile infrastructure was now so strained, she could barely accept any more Iraqi refugees. Scores of thousands of refugees were also streaming in from war-ravaged eastern Europe, as well as other Arab nations. Tiny Israel did not know whether it had enough tents, let alone housing units. The Jewish state tried to negotiate for fewer refugees per month.[62]

Nuri Said now realized that his 120,000 captive Jews constituted more than just undesirables. These Jews could be turned into a demographic weapon against Israel. In March 1951, Nuri engineered yet another statute, this one Law 12, permanently freezing all the assets of the Jews who were denaturalized by the previous law. Technically, those seizures were deemed a mere "freezing" of accounts, not a legal confiscation, so under international law, the assets could never be claimed. Law 12 was concocted in secret; leading government officials only learned about it just before the vote. As the measure was being ratified, Baghdad's telephones went dead so desperate Jews would not learn of the new law and use precious moments to transfer or save their property. To make sure, the government ordered the banks closed for three days.[63]

Now 120,000 Jews would arrive in Israel penniless, with no hope of later calling on their former wealth. Concomitantly, Nuri demanded that Israel absorb 10,000 refugees per month every month, this to intensify the strain on Israel's resources. Exacerbating the crisis, Nuri ruled that as of May 31, 1951, no more exit visas would be issued. If Israel would not accept these stateless enemies now, the concentration camps would be readied. Indeed, the Iraqi parliament had already discussed establishing such camps. Nuri clearly expected the Jewish state to crack beneath the weight of the humanitarian effort. Numbers negotiation commenced between Iraq's and Israel's go-betweens. However, Nuri was adamant that the Jews must transfer en masse, according not to Israel's capacity to accept them but to Iraq's roiling impatience to expel them. Otherwise, camps.[64]

Jewish Agency emissaries in the field confirmed the dire conditions of refugees who would now arrive with nothing. "The number of destitute people is growing," reported one agent. "After the passing of this law we are liable to reach a situation where 80 percent are penniless and unable to [even] cover the cost of their emigration. . . . In Basra the situation is very bad. The immigrants leaving on the next three aircraft are all poor, they have sold their blankets in return for food."[65]

Israeli foreign minister Moshe Sharett vociferously condemned Iraq's extortion and state-sponsored theft. Estimates of the value of Iraqi Jewry's blocked assets ranged from 6 million to 12 million dinars, or at its highest valuation some $300 million in twenty-first-century money. Sharett swore that Israel "considers this act of robbery by force of law to be the continuation of the evil oppression which Iraq has always practiced against defenseless minorities. . . . We have a reckoning to conduct with the Arab world as to the compensation due to Arabs who left Israeli territory and abandoned their property there because of the war of the Arab world against our state. The act perpetrated by the Iraqi kingdom against the property of Jews who have not transgressed against Iraqi law, and have not undermined her status and plotted against her, forces us to combine the two accounts. Hence," Sharett declared, "the government has decided to inform the appropriate UN institution and I proclaim this publicly, that the value of the Jewish property frozen in Iraq will be taken into account by us in calculating the sum of the compensation we have agreed to pay to Arabs who abandoned property in Israel."[66]

Israel had no choice but to absorb all 120,000 Iraqi Jews. The flights increased, day and night, using twin engines, four engines, any craft available, through Nicosia or direct to Tel Aviv—as many as possible as fast as possible. In some months, as many as 15,000 people were flown. The daily spectacle in Baghdad of forlorn Jews being hustled into truck after truck clutching nothing but a bag and their clothes was a cause for great jubilation on the streets of Baghdad. The crowds gleefully stoned the trucks that delivered the refugees to the airport. The Jews were mocked every step of the way.[67]

Between January 1950 and December 1951, Israel airlifted, bussed, or otherwise smuggled out 119,788 Iraqi Jews—all but a few thousand.[68] Within those two years, Iraq—to its national detriment—had excised one of its most commercially, industrially, and intellectually viable groups, a group that for 2,600 years had loyally seen the three provinces of Mesopotamia as their chosen place on earth. This dispossessed group, who arrived in Israel with nothing but their memories, rose to became some of the Jewish state's most productive citizens.

Indeed, hundreds of thousands of Arab Jews from across the Moslem world expelled to Israel during those first years transformed the Jewish state from a European haven to a true Mideast country, now also vastly populated with Arabs—Arabs who by religion were Jewish.

CHAPTER EIGHTEEN

The Three Gulfs

The drums of war. The drums of oil. In Iraq and the Mideast, all the drums played together. The deafening tumult was heard worldwide throughout the post–World War II era.

Three themes—resentment over foreign interference, anti-Zionism, and churning nationalism—fused into a rage against the West that pulsed through the last half of Iraq's turbulent twentieth century. Those agitated decades in Iraq were punctuated by a cascade of coups, sometimes dressed up as revolutions, sometimes encased within a so-called parliamentary process. In Iraq's thin political lexicon, the words *coup* and *revolution* often became synonyms. Competing with the coups were insurrections from the north and south, putsches within putsches, religious strife between Shi'as and Sunnis and a permanently seething population that never drank from the fountain of the nation's unlimited potential.

Yet throughout those decades of upheaval, the world continued to focus its political and military attention on Iraq. Why? The world did not crave the sand of Iraq. It was the substance beneath the sand. It was never about the people; it was never about their quests and aspirations. It was always about the oil.

As far back as the 1930s, Iraq's incessant political drumbeat had driven the Red Line consortium of the Iraq Petroleum Company to seek new dunes to exploit. Gulbenkian's red line circumscribing the Arabian Peninsula and the bulk of the Ottoman Empire offered plenty of other opportunities. First, the IPC turned to the newly sovereign Saudi Arabia, but its traditional commercial formulae of pittance royalties quickly became unacceptable to the savvy Saudi mind. The Saudis demanded remittances in gold, rather than any printed paper equivalent, and required annual payments whether oil was struck or not. Thus, the concessionaire had ample incentive to quickly drill, pump, and ship, and therefore justify payments. Moreover, the Saudis refused to be pawns for any company involved in Iraq. They understood that if included in the portfolio of the Iraqi Petroleum Company, the Saudi oil concession could be used as a strategic counterweight to Iraqi national instability. Instead, King Ibn Saud turned to an American firm, Socal—Standard of California—which met Ibn Saud's terms and in July 1933 secured the bountiful and strictly American concession with liberal Saudi participation. Texaco later joined Socal and its Saudi partners, and the combined venture became known as Aramco (Arabian American Oil Company).[1]

But the Red Line group fared better with the rest of the Gulf. The IPC signed lucrative concessions with a palette of British protectorates and client states. These included Oman, Qatar, Abu Dhabi, and a series of other sparsely populated Bedouin emirates. The smaller sheikhdoms were lumped together into "the Trucial Coast States," later, the United Arab Emirates. In addition, the Iraq Petroleum Company secured exploratory concessions in mandatory Palestine, Syria, and Lebanon. These IPC concessions resembled the company's traditional royalty-based bargains, albeit more generous than the ones it had negotiated decades earlier in Iraq and Iran.[2] Hence, with the major exception of Saudi Arabia, the Iraq Petroleum Company fulfilled the dream of Gulbenkian's thick red line, creating an oil empire within its confines.

Ironically, the red line's demonstrative detour around Kuwait was a fateful cartographic boon for the United States. It opened the door for a member of the Red Line group's American contingent to seek concessions both in Kuwait and in neighboring Bahrain. America's Gulf Oil, working with an Anglo-Persian-dominated group, secured those concessions in the 1930s, although it required extensive negotiations with the British to waive the protections of the nineteenth-century "nationality clauses," which granted British citizens exclusive rights in those protectorates. Once waived, however, American companies and citizens could participate.[3]

As the postwar world reassembled itself, Iraq remained at the apex of oil promise. But now there were many other countries with promises to keep and pipeline miles to sweep, up and down the Arabian Peninsula, including next-door Kuwait. These new sources of Mideast supply played a mighty role in Iraq's own oil quandary, since its next-door neighbors were able to capitalize on their petroleum while Iraq remained mired in frustrated output and self-inflicted economic woes.

From the corporate side, the postwar IPC was also in disarray. After World War II, a liberated France deeply resented its enemy status, as did Gulbenkian. Both Compagnie Française des Petroles and Gulbenkian resumed their full participation in IPC. But both demanded compensation for the oil allotments suspended during France's Nazi collaboration and occupation years. At the same time, Standard Oil of New Jersey acquired Standard of California, which enjoyed the Saudi Arabia concession. That violated the Red Line Agreement, which obligated its signatories to never compete within the encircled area. Standard, fresh from America's triumphant victory in Europe, decided that the Red Line Agreement was no longer in force because of the enemy status assigned to CFP and Gulbenkian.[4]

It took several years of grueling negotiations, but the four oil groups and Gulbenkian eventually came to terms in a final signed document.[5]

Even if the Red Line partners briefly stopped feuding, however, it became increasingly difficult for the IPC, and Britain for that matter, to function in Iraq. Britain was more than reviled for its intervention against the pro-Hitler Rashid Ali and the mufti in 1941 as well as its seeming sponsorship of Israel. In fact, in January 1948, just after London and Baghdad renegotiated their so-called Portsmouth Treaty of military alliance, which extended the 1930 pact another 20 years,

Baghdad broke out into bloody street riots. That day 11 people were killed; in all, 70 died before calm returned. To pacify their anger, the regent denied that the agreement had actually been signed. During a funeral procession for slain protesting students, demonstrators demanded the government reclaim the British base at Habbaniya and cancel all foreign military rights. Placards urged the mob to "execute the Iraqi negotiators." Understandably, the premier who had negotiated the agreement in London fled the country on the earliest available aircraft.[6]

The antagonism only deepened in 1950 as a result of the economic dislocation of the Jewish expulsion, the disruption of the Haifa oil pipeline, and the expenses of the failed war in Palestine. It had all wrecked Iraq's national treasury. The only way the country could keep functioning was with an advance on future IPC royalties—in other words, a multimillion-pound loan. This only further salted the wounded Iraqi sense of dependence on a foreign European nation and an export industry it despised. Then on December 30, 1950, shock waves rumbled through the Mideast oil industry after the American concessionaires agreed to a fifty-fifty split of profits with Saudi Arabia. Now the IPC's negotiations with each oil-rich realm acquired a tense new dimension.[7]

In Iran, an imperialist's nightmare was being acted out. During the prior half-century, Anglo-Iranian Oil Company, which also owned about a quarter of Iraq Petroleum, had established a prodigious presence in Iran. AIOC's complex at Abadan was a sight for Middle Eastern eyes. The British enclave boasted art deco office buildings and movie theaters, Olympic-size swimming pools with triple-decked diving boards, elaborate banquet halls, large schools, vast rows of neatly arranged housing for the mostly British company workforce, and delightful bungalows for management. The company medical system, with four hospitals and 35 clinics, was deemed "a general practitioner's dream" by a British Medical Association review. AIOC's operation in Iran, once the linchpin of Britain's naval oil supply, was worth billions. Now all that was coming to an end in the face of Iran's national purge of foreign oil domination.[8]

Within days of the Saudi Arabian fifty-fifty agreement becoming known, Iran reacted. Quickly, Anglo-Iranian's problems became insurmountable. All the company's men could not negotiate or renegotiate their way back into a concession. Strongman Muhammad Mossadegh, who never stopped making new demands, headed the Teheran government. Mossadegh was partially deaf and therefore spoke to company officials at a six-inch distance. The discourse was made all the more uncomfortable, it was said, because he gave off "a slight reek of opium." Mossadegh was not interested in any elaborate explanations of international law, commercial custom, or contractual rights and obligations. He just wanted to know how soon officials could vacate. Frantic, the company begged for the chance to arbitrate and promised a £10 million advance and £3 million per month payment even as arbitration progressed. The more AIOC offered, in hopes of delaying the inevitable, the more Mossadegh was convinced the intensely valuable concession must be nationalized.[9]

On June 10, 1951, Iranian officials arrived in force at the company's facility in Khurramshahr for an official takeover ceremony. First they slaughtered a sheep, the Iranian flag was hoisted up the flagpole atop the building, and then the Navy played the national anthem. A thousand company employees stood closely packed on every surface high and low, straining to hear the historic proclamation: The newly established state-run National Iranian Oil Company had now seized the facilities. AIOC's general manager, Eric Drake, suddenly found a soldier sporting a bayonet-fixed rifle in his office. Policemen guarded all the doors. Drake was informed that he was now an employee of National Iranian Oil Company. The new supervisors demanded he turn over organizational charts and all recent financial statements. Drake refused without written authorization from London.[10]

Days later, back in Teheran, celebratory mobs stormed AIOC's office, pulled down its illuminated sign, and marched through the streets, carrying it above their heads as an exalted trophy. A few days later, Drake, who had refused to comply with Iranian orders, was accused of industrial sabotage. He fled to Basra before he could be arrested.[11]

Teheran laughed at efforts by the AIOC to submit the matter to the International Court of Justice at the Hague. Iranian officials declined to answer a summons, refused to recognize the concession clause calling for such adjudication, and rejected the court's supposed jurisdiction, since the takeover of AIOC was an exercise of national sovereignty. Shortly thereafter, all British personnel were evicted from their corporate premises. The families were evacuated from Abadan, where the "atmosphere had become one of siege." Everything was taken over by the state: refineries, pipelines, ships, repair shops, the company printing press, office furniture, paper, and pencils. With the whole world watching, Arab and European alike, Anglo-Iranian Oil Company, the company that had invented Mideast oil a half-century before as Anglo-Persian, was expelled from whence it all began.[12]

Two years later, in mid-August 1953, Mossadegh was overthrown in Operation Ajax, a joint CIA-M16 engineered coup. The shah of Iran assumed the reins of leadership. By that time, Anglo-Iranian Oil Company's position as an international oil conglomerate tethered to an oil supply it did not control became more and more untenable. In December 1954, two workmen in coveralls at Anglo-Iranian's curved and stately Britannic House headquarters in Finsbury Circus in London climbed up the two steps at the entrance. They carefully removed the large brass plaque next to the door. It read: ANGLO-IRANIAN OIL COMPANY LIMITED. In its place, they installed a new plaque. It read: THE BRITISH PETROLEUM COMPANY LIMITED. Through patient negotiation with the shah, a fifty-fifty arrangement was finalized. The company was again permitted access to its oil. Compensation for its nationalized assets was set at £25 million payable in 10 installments plus several hundred million dollars in oil and other emoluments. A British tanker resumed oil shipments out of Abadan on October 29, 1957.[13]

The summer of 1951 was not good for British oil in the Middle East. Just as the Saudis' fifty-fifty deal sparked outrage in Iran, Iraq also demanded its rightful share of the petroleum industry—and more. In March 1951, deputies in Iraq's parliament lined up support for nationalizing its oil industry—pipe, tank, and barrel. More drastic action would have been taken, but simply put, Iraq still needed the IPC. The country's oil infrastructure was still a generation behind those of its neighbors, a situation exacerbated by the Haifa pipeline closure. Diminished throughput meant depressed royalties. Baghdad called upon the IPC to lay more pipeline to the Mediterranean, circumventing Israel. The IPC complied, quickly finishing the northern branch of a 16-inch pipeline as well as additional links to Syria.[14]

The tension between the company and the government was palpable. Iraq needed the IPC for oil infrastructure improvements. At the same time, the company fully understood that every inch of pipeline laid and every pound sterling invested could be nationalized with the next breath.

During prolonged give-and-take sessions throughout 1951, the IPC finally agreed to fifty-fifty profit sharing, and in January 1952 the company signed a new agreement with Iraq. The fifty-fifty arrangement was made retroactive to January 1, 1951. This incremental financial upgrade only bought time for the company. The firm had, however, built in its own safety valve. Those profits promised to Baghdad were pegged to the "posted price," that is, the officially posted world price for petroleum. Hence, the Iraqi treasury was once again at the mercy of international oil manipulations. The IPC, and its associated company Anglo-Iranian, could create a glut or a scarcity at will by leaning or tugging on the supply and production throttle anywhere in the world. What's worse, that world oil supply now included the vast new supplies from nearby Gulf states.

In frustration, Baghdad watched Kuwait, its tiny neighbor to the south, quickly outpace the output of all three Iraqi provinces combined. Kuwait had only begun producing oil in 1946 with an 800,000-ton year, but by 1948 that number had increased nearly sevenfold, to 6.3 million tons. In 1950, Iraq's shackled production totaled approximately 650 million tons, while Kuwait's had zoomed to nearly triple that number. Iran, now a nationalized independent that set its own production levels, was still a market giant. Bahrain and Qatar added significantly to the world supply. So, in 1950, while fractious Baghdad was forced to seek an IPC loan just to make ends meet, a smooth-running Saudi operation added approximately $2 million to the Saudi treasury each week.[15] Iraq's culture of resentment continued to roil, especially over the issue of the foreign oil exploitation.

In many ways, the anger rose from the bottom up. The masses remained largely destitute, significantly unemployed, and detached en masse from their nation's oil wealth, none of which even trickled past their doors. Instead, the riches seemed to be divided among an irrelevant government establishment, the wealthy elite, and European executives. It never took much to unleash the bitter alienation of the common man who had nothing to win and little to lose.

With the rise of cold war communism in the 1950s, Britain remained as eager as ever to maintain a strong military presence in Iraq and thereby protect its oil fields. London summoned its best friends into yet another international military alliance, and this included calls to Nuri Said, who had once again assumed the role of prime minister. As concerned about the advance of communism as any capital in the West, in February 1955, Pakistan, Turkey, Iran, and Iraq joined Great Britain in creating a northern bulwark against the Soviet Union. The West saw the Baghdad Pact alliance as a reaction to the new cold war military reality, but the citizens of Iraq saw the compact as yet another surrender to Britain and Western oil interests. All this came at a time when Nuri was disbanding political parties and trying to quell the fires of pan-Arabism. The plotting began.[16]

This time, the ignition switch for Iraq's unrest did not reside in Baghdad, London, or Damascus; this time, it was Cairo. Egypt's president, ultranationalist Gamal Abdel Nasser, who had given postwar refuge to Rashid Ali and the mufti, was now energizing the Arab world with his pan-Islamic anti-Western bravado. Indeed, in February 1958, Syria and Egypt had already formed a two-state union, called the United Arab Republic (UAR). Even though the two countries were on different continents and separated by Palestine and Israel, they had merged into a single, albeit politically cumbersome, entity.[17]

To achieve his goals, Nasser courted Moscow as a counterweight to the capitalist West, just as the mufti had courted Hitler as the alternative to the Allies. Hence, the West and some oil-rich Arab states saw the UAR in the context of a destabilizing communist move. Nuri and his Baghdad government had refused to recognize the Syrian-Egyptian UAR, and in response the Baghdad regime promptly announced its own federation, a new Hashemite binary with Jordan to be called the Arab Union. Clearly, the Arab Union competed with Nasser's UAR for pan-Arab primacy, and he was infuriated.[18]

During the next several months, Nasser viciously denounced the Baghdad regime and its Arabian Peninsula Hashemite monarchy. Nasser's vituperations were more than mere words. July 14, 1958, would become the end for the Hashemites in Iraq. At 5 A.M., the 19th

Brigade of the Free Officers, followed by a frenzied mob, suddenly attacked the king's sprawling tree-lined palace with volleys from machine guns and antitank weapons. The royal family hastily mustered outside. In an exchange of gunfire, 23-year-old King Faisal II was shot, then beheaded. Abdul al-Ilah, the former regent, was also shot. Later, Abdul's hands and feet were chopped off, jammed onto pikes, and paraded through the streets like treasured icons. More protesters poured into the streets of Baghdad, as though on cue, now carrying oversized photographs of Nasser and holding dogs aloft as representations of their executed Hashemite rulers. The mutilated body of the regent was gleefully dragged through the city. Eventually, his dismembered body was hung ignominiously from a balcony.[19]

Now where was Nuri Said? The wild crowd converged on his home, chanting "Long live Nasser." Nuri could not be found. A reward of 10,000 dinars was broadcast. Nuri had escaped through an emergency tunnel beneath his home. However, he was soon discovered walking on a street, dressed in a woman's garb. The mob pounced and strung him up. But that was not enough. They dragged his dead body through the streets, along with those of other officials, flaying them with shoes in a traditional show of disrespect. As a further expression of the mob's rage, a vehicle repeatedly ran over Nuri's body—back and forth.[20]

The new strongman was Abdel Karim Kassem. Immediately, he announced recognition of Nasser's UAR. Simultaneously, Cairo radio stations celebrated the revolution in Iraq. Hashemite rule in Iraq was dead. The planned Arab Union was dead. The Baghdad Pact was dead. An effort to thrust Syrian-Egyptian pan-Arabism into Hashemite Iraq and Jordan was very much alive. Syrian forces massed on the Jordanian border, and Lebanon's leaders were told they were next. The Mideast was about to explode again.[21]

Officials in Beirut, itself nearly in a state of civil war, and Amman, which was threatened by UAR neighbors, sent out calls for help from the West. Immediately, President Dwight Eisenhower dispatched the Sixth Fleet in the Mediterranean toward Lebanon. On July 15, 1958, the day after the Iraqi coup, 1,700 amphibious Marines landed on the beach at Beirut, with more troops airlifting into the airport. Two days later, July 17, a British airborne force of 2,000 commandoes landed in

Amman, responding to King Hussein in Jordan.[22] The Nasserite advance was blunted.

For the moment, Mideast oil was stable. Not safe, but stable.

Mindful of the CIA-MI6 coup that had overthrown Iran's Mossadegh in 1953 and the Anglo-American forces that had instantly reacted after the July 14, 1958, revolution in Iraq, the IPC and Kassem's Baghdad government resumed negotiations over what was tantamount to nationalization. In 1959, the strongman, Kassem, made clear that he wanted to rescind nearly all of IPC's concession lands. The company eventually agreed to a large giveback of the concession territory, so long as it could keep the 25 percent containing the most petroliferous fields in the north. That was unacceptable to Kassem. Frustrated IPC officials in London, tiring of the whole process of serial creeping nationalization, concluded that they "must call a halt to the current process of bazaar bargaining." One wrote, "The time had come when the company must dig in their toes."[23]

At the same time, the very same northern oil regions under discussion were in deep turmoil. Kurdish nationalists had stepped up their campaign of insurrection in the Mosul province. Official Baghdad was certain that the Mosul revolt bore the earmarks of oil company sponsorship. Whoever was to blame, Kassem's forces exacted horrific punishment on the region, hanging and mutilating villagers in a broad reign of terror.[24]

Throughout 1959, Kassem continued his brutal repression of the Kurds and consolidation of power in Iraq. At the same time, he became solipsistic about his role in Iraq, seeing himself as something more than regal, and perhaps something closer to a deliverer. Moreover, Kassem conducted himself in so aloof a fashion, disassociating himself from the political parties, that he had earned the moniker "the sole leader."[25]

By now, Kassem had survived several coup attempts, including one by the dissident Ba'ath Party. The Ba'athists had dispatched two junior officers for the attempt. One was an obscure street enforcer named Saddam Hussein. But Saddam and his teammate botched the job. Saddam was wounded by one of Kassem's bodyguards and fled to Syria to convalesce. Kassem remained in power and continued to press the Red Line group to relinquish its concession. The company at some point agreed to a full 70 percent return, but they insisted on keeping the most productive tracts.[26]

Kassem would have probably taken action, but once again the Baghdad treasury went anemic. The country was still dependent on the very foreign hand it hated: the IPC. At the end of March 1961, IPC officials in London were urgently summoned back to Baghdad for consultation. Kassem's government needed an advance of IPC's quarterly tax and royalty payment due later in April. The company agreed, accelerating a £20 million payment by several weeks and thereby saving the treasury.[27]

The £20 million favor paused but did not halt the Iraqi demand to reclaim its concession. On December 12, 1959, the Iraqi Parliament passed Law 80, which rescinded 99.5 percent of IPC's concession. The Red Line group would be left with only those operating wells that were actually producing revenues. The reclaimed lands included the prized but still undeveloped North Rumaila fields.[28]

After Law 80 was passed, IPC officials messengered letters of objection. These were ignored. Several days later, formal letters of protest were sent to the Iraqi Oil Ministry, and they were not even accepted. A year of fruitless dialogue followed. In 1962, a weary IPC submitted the matter to arbitration. Baghdad ignored the arbitration request as well.[29]

Company hopes now rested on the very nature of Baghdad politics. Executives were confident that the proven Iraqi cycle of coup and countercoup would cure their problem with Kassem. At that very time, Kassem's monstrous repression of the Kurds was still under way. The plotting Iraqi military saw him as detached. In February 1963, a band of army officers rose up and killed "the sole leader." His bullet-riddled corpse was displayed on Iraqi TV.[30]

Iraq's new oil minister was a skillful petroleum engineer, Abdul Aziz al-Wattari. He had graduated from the University of Texas and spoke the same language as IPC officials. During the next two years, as government revenues dropped again, al-Wattari and Red Line negotiators hammered out an agreement. The most precious lands, seized by Law 80, were returned, including the Rumaila fields. The

Red Line companies, except for Standard Oil of New Jersey, agreed to create a partnership with a new, state-owned Iraqi National Oil Company (INOC), which would own a third of the enterprise.[31]

Red Line oil kept pumping.

An enduring legacy of "the sole leader," Kassem, was his facilitation of a new international organization that would soon prove more potent than all the armies and all the mob violence of the Middle East.

It began in 1959 when cold war petropolitics resulted in a post-Stalin Soviet attempt to reinvigorate its oil industry and recapture the market they once dominated. The communist tactic was to regain old customers with cheaper prices. Ironically, although the CIA characterized the crisis as a destabilizing "Soviet economic offensive," the communist tactic merely employed the time-honored free-market traditions of price competitiveness—something the controlled-market Western consortiums feared. The major oil companies responded by slashing their own prices, thus inaugurating a price war. In April 1959, BP sliced 18 cents off its price per barrel, a 10 percent reduction. Four months later, Standard followed with a 14-penny drop, a 7 percent reduction. Whether political push or price war, the oil states suddenly found their royalties choked by cold war economic tactics.[32]

For some time, two Texas-trained oil experts, one from Saudi Arabia and one from Venezuela, had been secretly planning a consortium of oil-exporting nations. A group of oil ministers and representatives had, in fact, already signed what they called a "Gentleman's Agreement" during a secret meeting held during the 1959 Arab Petroleum Conference in Cairo. Now in the face of the latest oil company price cuts, they were determined to create their own controlling association. Cairo was the logical choice for the next meeting because Nasser had been the chief patron of the export organizers. However, to check Nasser's further pan-Arab ascendancy and to elevate his own importance in the Arab world, Kassem, despite concerns over further coup attempts, preemptively dispatched invitations to the oil ministers to convene in Baghdad. Kassem, with his iron military grip, made certain the interministerial conclave was protected.[33]

On September 10, 1960, Baghdad streets filled with tanks and troops took up positions as oil ministers from Saudi Arabia, Venezuela, Kuwait, Iraq, and Iran huddled. During the tense proceedings, an armed bodyguard stood behind each delegate. When the ministers finally emerged, they had founded a new international body, the Organization of Petroleum Exporting Countries. Henceforth, those whose lands held the oil would control production and pricing.[34]

OPEC first flexed its muscles in 1967 after the Six Day War. Israel had preemptively devastated the combined armies and air forces of Egypt, Syria, and Jordan just before those countries could launch their loudly announced war to finally push the Jewish state into the sea. In humiliation, OPEC's Arab countries tried to coordinate an oil blockade against those countries that supported Israel. It did not work. But for its part, Iraq tore up al-Wattari's accommodation agreement that restored lands to the Red Line group. Law 97, passed in August 1967, once again revoked the old IPC concessions, except for those wells already operating and producing revenue. A month later, Law 123 completely reorganized the Iraqi National Oil Company, purging its ranks of pro-Western executives and technocrats.[35] This set the stage for not just a wounded, bandaged, and rehabilitated Iraqi oil industry, but a reinvented one.

New contracts to new countries were let, with an accent on those that had not supported Israel. In November 1967, the first such contract was announced: a 20-year concession to a French state-owned oil exploration entity. This was followed in December by a technical assistance pact with the Soviet Union.[36]

The next year, 1968, in July, yet another coup brought a new group into power. The Ba'athists now controlled Iraq. Newly empowered Ahmad Hassan al-Bakr ruled with brutality, purging his enemies, real and potential. Any thoughts that the new Ba'athist regime under al-Bakr could improve on the Iraqi human rights record were quickly dispelled.

The nation continued to define itself by deep-seated rage against the West, Jews, and Zionism and hostility toward its minorities, as well

as carefully cultivated resentment over perceived injustices perpetrated by its oil-rich neighbors.

Although nearly all of Iraq's 120,000 Jews had safely fled to Israel
years earlier, a few thousand remained behind. The founder of Zionism, Theodor Herzl said, "Old prisoners only reluctantly leave their
cells." State harassment of Jews rose and receded depending on the
mood of the country and the need to refocus attention on enemies.
In January 1969, it rose once again as the al-Bakr regime tried 16
men, 9 of them Jews, as spies and saboteurs. The accused included
family members of some of the nation's most prominent remaining
Jewish merchants and the son of Iraq's chief rabbi. The international
community immediately saw the trumped-up espionage charges for
what they were. Despite worldwide revulsion over the trial, and
despite foreign and United Nations pleas to desist, the regime went
ahead with its spectacle. On January 27, 1969, after brief proceedings,
14 of the 16, including all 9 Jews, were sentenced to public hanging.
Minutes later, in Baghdad and Basra, the men were hauled out to gallows erected in the public squares.[37]

In Baghdad, the entire city had been summoned by radio to
enjoy the "happy occasion." A wild, chanting throng estimated at
200,000, led by President al-Bakr and his defense minister, marched
to the square. The mob surged at the gallows, and police barely kept
them back. As the men were executed, the crowd erupted in a roar.
During the full day that the dead men were left dangling in the sun,
exhilarated Baghdadis continually pelted the bodies with mud,
doused them with spittle, and repeatedly jumped for joy, trying to
touch the lifeless legs. Special treatment was reserved for the condemned Jews. Affixed to their corpses were signs prepared especially
for the occasion so there was no confusion. The signs were inscribed
with only one word: "Jew."[38]

Galvanizing the nation against Jews was not the only distraction
employed by the al-Bakr regime. The seething energies of the Sunni
ruling class were also again directed against minorities. Al-Bakr brutally repressed the Shi'a minority in the south and waged a war of
atrocities against the Kurds in the north. One of his chief henchmen
during these years was Saddam Hussein.

In late 1978 and early 1979, al-Bakr's regime was in the midst of
its latest campaign against the Shiites. Attention centered on the

widely revered Iranian holy man, Grand Ayatollah Khomeini. In exile, the supreme Shiite spiritual leader had established a Shiite power base in Najaf. From the holy city, Khomeini organized an effective anti-shah propaganda and agitation machine that constantly urged Iranians to rise up against its corrupt monarch. Khomeini's venomous radio and mosque speeches electrified the Shiite masses on both sides of the border. Thousands of tape cassettes with revolutionary messages, as well as anti-shah pamphlets and newspapers, were smuggled into Iran to further foment the population there.[39]

In October 1978, al-Bakr and Saddam saw Shiite power swelling in Iraq. They moved against Khomeini, expelling him from Najaf. Months later, Khomeini, from his new headquarters in Paris, remotely led the revolution in Iran. By February 1979, Khomeini had returned to Teheran in triumph as the new absolute ruler of Iran. His followers swept in a taut and frenzied fundamentalist Islamic regime that speedily dismantled many of the artifacts of Western influence.[40]

That was enough for the Ba'athists. The Khomeini-inspired groundswell had to be stopped. Al-Bakr and Saddam stepped up their abuses of Iraq's Shiites, arresting thousands, not only in the southern cities but also in their strongholds in the teeming slums of Baghdad. Shiite clerics were placed under house arrest, brought in for gruff questioning, and subjected to extraordinary surveillance. In June 1979, Khomeini's counterpart in Baghdad, Grand Ayatollah Mohammad Baqir al-Sadr, was placed under house arrest.[41]

In mid-July 1979, the strongman al-Bakr announced his sudden resignation for unexplained "health reasons." Saddam Hussein, his right-hand man, immediately assumed the presidency, becoming the latest in a long line of Iraqi strongmen to impose his ferocious whim and will upon the nation. Within days, Saddam orchestrated a vicious purge of any potential plotters or rivals within the Ba'ath Party.

In one famous scene of terror, he summoned several hundred party members to a hall, where he staged an unforgettable purge before their very eyes. The assemblage started off in a jubilant mood, but quickly began squirming in terror as a colleague on stage unexpectedly confessed to a broad conspiracy. Saddam puffed on a very long cigar and smiled broadly from time to time as names were read from a list. As each name was uttered, guards loyal to Saddam raced to the petrified party member in the audience and led him away to a certain fate. During the weeks to come, many more throughout the country were murdered or imprisoned as Saddam's terror tactics solidified his complete control of Iraq.[42]

In many ways, Saddam had replicated the patterns established by his predecessors. But with modern media's reach and his flair for the theatrical, a better and more accessible record was kept. Hence, an indelible impression of cruelty was made upon the world. The impression would only grow.

The dictator intensified repression of Shiites and their revolutionary organizations. In turn, the Shiite protest movement called for Saddam's overthrow. Indeed, Shiite militants had already tried to assassinate Saddam's deputy, Tariq Aziz. In April 1980, Hussein shocked all Shiites worldwide by executing their highest religious authority, Grand Ayatollah al-Sadr, as well as members of al-Sadr's family. In addition, about 40,000 Shiites of Iranian origin were deported from Najaf across the border.[43]

Hussein then tightly interwove national distrust of minorities with popular animus against neighboring countries that had allegedly conspired to deprive Iraq of its access to the sea through the Shatt al-Arab estuary. It was always easier to blame successful neighbors for Iraq's dysfunction. Now the threads converged on Iraq's rival through the millennia, Iran.

On September 22, 1980, Hussein's armies massively invaded predominantly Shiite Iran, ostensibly over control of the all-important Shatt al-Arab. The Iraq-Iran War lasted eight bloody years. Both sides deemed the conflict their Holy War. Like the worst wars of the century, this one included poison gas, unrelenting bombardment, and waves of six-digit casualties in a slender battle zone. In Iran, Shiite warriors trudged to the front carrying their coffins on their back as they proudly announced their willingness to sacrifice their lives. In Iraq, the war casualties were kept secret.[44]

Over eight years, the two nations combined lost an estimated 1.5 million men. An entire generation of young men was wiped out on both sides. Each nation spent an estimated $1 billion per month on the fight.[45] As the petrodollars burned, as the young men died, the Iraqi economy continued its stagnation.

In the background, the United States saw Iraq as a stalwart against

Iran. In November 1979, Iran's out-of-control mob had invaded the American Embassy in Teheran, taking 70 hostages and holding 52 of them for 444 days. The almost 15-month-long drama crippled the Carter administration and gripped the world's attention with day and night media attention. Because Iran's Islamic revolution threatened Western political and commercial interests more than Baghdad's reign of terror, the United States quietly but actively supported Saddam with logistical and intelligence support. In fact, Hussein formally apologized when an Iraqi Mirage fighter mistakenly fired an Exocet air-to-sea missile at a U.S. Navy frigate, the USS Stark. The Iraqi-fired French-supplied Exocet missile killed 37 American sailors and wounded 21. Hussein not only apologized, he offered reparations to the families.[46]

The Iraq-Iran War ended in a gruesome stalemate. But Saddam soon returned to issuing threats against a neighbor that had access to the sea and the Shatt-al-Arab. This time it was Kuwait. Kuwait was never part of the nation of Iraq, which itself had been cobbled together by men in Paris and London. But because of Iraqi local myth and the Ottoman Empire's fuzzy jurisdiction across the Gulf, Kuwait's identity had been debated for decades.

The sparsely populated Bedouin territory known as Kuwait was one of those realms nominally claimed at the far fringes of the empire, but in large part ignored by the Ottomans of the nineteenth century. Kuwait paid no tribute to Istanbul, and no soldiers were conscripted for the sultan's army. Its political connection to the empire was tenuous at best. By the mid-1880s, the tiny Gulf land located below the province of Basra looked to Britain, not Istanbul, for protection. London gladly offered it to secure British shipping lanes. In 1899, Britain and Kuwait signed the formal protectorate agreement.[47]

The Anglo-Ottoman Convention of 1913, a wide-ranging prewar agreement with the Young Turk regime, dismissed Kuwait as a peripheral issue. For mere expediency, the territory was recategorized as a *qada,* or subprovince. But a subprovince of what? The three provinces of Mesopotamia had undefined borders: to the northwest with Syria, to the northeast with Persia, and due north with the peoples of Kurdistan, Armenia, and Assyria. In any event, as a result of World War I, the Anglo-Ottoman Convention of 1913 was never ratified and never came into force, just like so many other 1914 agreements. Therefore, although Kuwait was not part of what became Iraq, its borders were vague and undetermined, like so many others in the region.[48]

However, years later, in 1932, Iraq was required to clearly define all its borders before joining the League of Nations. At that point, a formal treaty between Kuwait and the newly independent Iraq was signed, recognizing the sheikhdom's precise borders and its mutually acknowledged independence. This treaty, published by the League of Nations and confirmed as such by both countries, also specified exactly which of the tiny, but strategic, Shatt-al-Arab islands attached to Kuwait.[49]

When he succeeded Faisal, however, King Ghazi directed the public's anger over economic stagnation toward Iraq's offending neighbors. His foreign minister asserted, "The Iraqi Government, as the successor to the Ottoman Government in the vilayets of Mosul, Baghdad and Basra, considers that Kuwait should properly be incorporated into Iraq." In the 1950s, "sole leader" Kassem perpetuated the myth, declaring, "Iraq and Kuwait remained one indivisible whole until 1913. Since then the people have been fighting imperialists. . . . There exists no boundary between Iraq and Kuwait. If anyone claims that there are boundaries then let him prove it."[50]

In 1961, after Kuwait was granted its independence from Great Britain, Iraq's UN ambassador restated its opposition, proclaiming, "Kuwait is not more than a small coastal town on the Gulf. There is not and never has been a country or a national entity called Kuwait, never in history."[51]

After Kassem was deposed in 1963, al-Bakr signed a new treaty with Kuwait reaffirming the original 1932 agreement and "the independence and complete sovereignty of the State of Kuwait with its boundaries as specified in the letter of the Prime Minister of Iraq dated July 7, 1932." However, after Saddam succeeded al-Bakr in 1979, none of that mattered. Saddam insisted that Kuwait was the so-called nineteenth province of Iraq.[52]

In the aftermath of the Iran-Iraq conflict, Saddam faced a spectacular war debt. He pressured Gulf oil states to reduce their output, hoping to raise revenues overall, including for his beleaguered oil industry. The oil sheikhs refused.[53] The spigot that Saddam could not control by agreement, he hoped to seize.

Throughout July, Saddam accused Kuwait of "oil theft" for selling petroleum that rightfully belonged to Iraq. On August 2, 1990, Iraq launched a blitzkrieg of 120,000 troops and 2,000 tanks against the virtually defenseless kingdom and then threatened Saudi Arabia as well. Kuwait was looted of its possessions, its oil seized, and its citizens tortured and brutalized. Saddam, the tyrant who had checked the Islamic fundamentalism of Iran, now threatened much of the Gulf oil flow that America depended upon. U.S. president George Herbert Walker Bush, a Texas oilman from a family of oilmen, clearly understood this. Five days after the invasion of Kuwait, Bush landed a slender troop and tank cordon at the Saudi Arabia–Iraq border, creating a line in the sand that Saddam's aggression could not pass. This was Operation Desert Shield. The military buildup continued as dozens of nations lined up to join the coalition to oust Saddam from Kuwait.[54]

"We are doing this for the people of Kuwait," stated General Colin Powell, chairman of the Joint Chiefs of Staff, "for our other friends in the region, for our own economic interest, for the safety of Americans who are in danger, and for the promise of a safer new world where disputes will not be solved by war." On January 17, 1991, Bush's deadline to Saddam to quit Kuwait passed. Operation Desert Storm was launched. After a short, ferocious air-land-sea fight, which included the bombing of Baghdad, Saddam was ejected from Kuwait and contained.[55]

As in the World War I–era Mesopotamia campaign, there was a highway of death, as vehicles were mercilessly struck from the sky, clogging the road against escape. As in previous conflicts, the oil wells were rescued first and everything else second. Making sure the world understood that this conflict was about oil, Saddam ordered retreating Iraqi forces to set fire to the Kuwaiti oil fields, thereby robbing the West of the very petroleum it had come to protect. The world rightly saw the inferno over the Kuwaiti desert as a war criminal's vandalism. It was also a potent reminder that in the Middle East, petroleum is not just a precious resource but also a weapon. Saddam knew that destroying the oil of Kuwait was more important to the coalition than destroying the people of Kuwait. It was in fact his last resort, just as it had been for the Allies when they almost did the same to block the region's oil from the Nazis.

Beginning in August 1990, a whole new generation of Americans, and many in the world, woke up to the treacherous realities of Gulf petropolitics. Few people understood anything about tiny Kuwait. Few knew that Kuwait's first real border was a thin red line drawn by Gulbenkian in 1928, redrawn later by oilmen in France and England, and then erased and reinscribed by the powers in Baghdad and Kuwait City as situations required. To the world, the war known as Gulf I was always about territorial integrity, always about defense against aggression. The world believed it was never just about oil. Gulf I was indeed about territorial integrity, defeating a monster, defending against aggression, and liberating a people. But a single issue elevated tiny Kuwait's predicament to the world's attention over all the other problems everywhere: Kuwait had the oil.

The Desert Storm coalition chose not to destroy Saddam's fleeing Republican Guard, nor to press on to Baghdad to unseat the regime. That was not in the UN resolution or the coalition's consensus policy, and the United States was careful not to overstep those bounds. Saddam's power structure and reign of terror remained intact. Instead, the United States reignited the still simmering rage among the Kurds in the north and the Shiites in the south, inciting rebellions, hoping in this way to finally topple the Saddam regime. But Saddam ratcheted up his terror machine, eliminated even potential opposition from within, and brutally retaliated against the Kurds and Shiites, crushing their insurrections. He was not deposed and in some ways was strengthened—at least in the reduced and restricted realm created by no-fly zones and protected provinces.

During the decade that followed, Saddam's Iraq was subjected to vigorous international sanctions and inspections over weapons of mass destruction that he had used against Iran and his own people, weapons he cagily refused to admit he had destroyed or dismantled. There are many techniques in the bazaar, and one of them is bluff.

But in the year 2000, a new United States administration headed by President George W. Bush, son of the hero of Desert Storm of a decade earlier, wanted to finish the job his father had begun, not because the people of Iraq were precious but because the land beneath them was. Bush elevated Saddam's bluff to gospel. In his effort, the second President Bush was buttressed by Vice President Richard Cheney, who had served as secretary of defense under the elder Bush.

In 1998, Cheney, while serving as chief executive officer of Halliburton, the world's largest oil services and military support company, articulated his view in a speech to the Cato Institute's Collateral Damage Conference. "About 70 to 75 percent of our business," explained Cheney, "is energy related, serving customers like Unocal, Exxon, Shell, Chevron, and many other major oil companies around the world. As a result, we oftentimes find ourselves operating in some very difficult places. The good Lord didn't see fit to put oil and gas only where there are democratically elected regimes friendly to the United States. Occasionally we have to operate in places where, all things considered, one would not normally choose to go. But, we go where the business is."[56]

Back in Iraq, fortified in his barricaded and blockaded nation, opulent with billions from oil that flowed in despite sanctions, Saddam continued the legacy of sadistic mass murder, torture, humiliation, repression, and exploitation so familiar to the despots and tyrants that preceded him in the land of the two rivers.

After September 11, 2001, a still shell-shocked America wanted answers and results in its war with Islamic extremism, a war that was spearheaded by the shadowy Al Qaeda network. While Iraq was not supporting Al Qaeda, President Bush nonetheless announced his determination to achieve a "regime change" in Iraq. To him and to many in the world, Saddam embodied all that was evil and threatening to civilized sensibilities. Saddam ranked with the great mass murderers of the twentieth century and indeed all the prior centuries.

But when a preemptive war against an evil regime was opposed, Bush's language and aims changed to attacking the "clear and present danger" posed by weapons of mass destruction. However, the only proof those weapons existed was clouded within Saddam's game of bluff.

On March 19, 2003, with a disputed United Nations resolution in hand, the United States shocked and awed Saddam's power base in

Baghdad. Then American military power invaded, determined to find the weapons of mass destruction and liberate the people of Iraq from their tyranny. As before, the oil wells were secured first and everything else second. American soldiers, unfamiliar with the names, the cities, the populations, and the historic continuities, now sped across the highways of Iraq accompanied by embedded reporters. Most Americans had never heard of Najaf and barely knew the difference between Shiites and Sunnis.

April 3, 2003, 6 A.M. Najaf.

In those first chaotic days of Gulf War II, the Ayatollah Sistani had, through intermediaries, requested American military protection. Sistani feared Saddam loyalists would filter back and retaliate for the Shiite holy man's tacit approval of the invasion.

Lt. Col. Chris Hughes, a plainspoken 42-year-old from Red Oak, Iowa, was dispatched. Hughes, one of the best America has to offer, was the elite battalion commander of the lethal and legendary Second Battalion, 327th Infantry of the 101st Airborne. His men had thrust through the desert to secure Najaf, spearheading away from the main columns pouring into Iraq. Hughes was in Najaf to protect the ayatollah and the mosque. But none among the agitated mob in the street understood that. They feared the worst—infidel defilement of their sacred mosque. They trusted no one but their own.

The people in the crowd menacingly pumped their right arms in defiance, with the anger of centuries in their eyes, pressing forward against a too-thin cordon of Shiite clerics, arms barely linked, trying to calm them down. Eyeball to eyeball with the throng, Hughes wanted to understand. He wanted to help.

"In city—yes. In city—okay. Mosque—*No!*" shouted an animated, bearded Shi'a Moslem at the very front of a gathering mob.

"In city—yes. In city—okay. Mosque—*No!*" From everywhere, more Moslems raced into the narrow, bannered street leading to their historic gold-domed Ali Mosque, perhaps the holiest site for all Shi'a Moslems. By now the crowd had multiplied to several hundred chanting zealots, egged on by Saddam's loyalists secreted in the crowd. "They are coming to invade the mosque!" screamed the Ba'athist instigators in the throng. "They will invade the mosque!" That was false.

Mustered behind Hughes was Bravo Company and other units amounting to about 200 men in all. American snipers peering through their high-magnification scopes searched for fedayeen snipers—rooftops, windows, rooftops, balcony, rooftops. Fired up by the Ba'athist agitators, the screaming crowd, squeezed into the width of a narrow street, began throwing rocks. Bravo Company, armed and ready, watched sharply. The tense scene was a candidate for a bloodbath.

But Hughes stayed calm. He wanted to understand. He wanted to help. In the end, he backed his heavily armed men out of Najaf. First, Bravo took a knee, then on command they all smiled, and then they just walked off and said, "Have a nice day."

On May 2, 2003, President Bush triumphantly landed on the aircraft carrier *Lincoln*. He stood in front of an immense "Mission Accomplished" banner and declared that major combat in Iraq had concluded. Gulf II had ended.

Gulf III began. During the next 18 months and continuing beyond that, Islam once again rose up against the infidel in its midst, conducting a terror war of suicide bombings, bestial beheadings, relentless sabotage, and mass riots against the men and women who came to rebuild the country, construct a framework for democracy, and keep the oil flowing. One incident was more horrendous than the next. That was the reason such incidents were staged—because they are revolting to Western sensibilities. On March 31, 2004, in Fallujah, the crowd caught one group of American contractors and in front of TV cameras repeated the well-worn scenes of gleeful mutilation and dismemberment, as well as defilement of the corpses by public dragging and hanging.

It did not matter that average Americans came to liberate Iraq. Even those Iraqis who wanted to be liberated did not want Iraq to be occupied. In the minds of Iraqis, the best liberation would have occurred on a Monday, with a joyous and celebrated exit by Tuesday—Wednesday at the latest.

Instead, the American administration chose to replicate the full civil and military occupation of the British during the Mesopotamia campaign and the years that followed. American policymakers were certain that with their triumph over Saddam's tyranny would come the commercial fruits of victory. But Gulf III made those fruits bitter. It remains to be seen whether Gulf III will be an unending chasm of violence mirroring prior centuries or a crevasse the world can cross.

Average Americans, the ones back home watching on television and the young ones in Iraq patrolling in Humvees, were confused by everything they had seen in Gulf III. U.S. forces had liberated so many other lands. But this time it was different. The average Americans who followed policymakers were visionary, looking forward to a better day. The policymakers knew that what was at stake was more than merely the freedom of a few million people in Iraq; it was the prize beneath their feet, the prize that the industrial world had deemed the oxygen and lifeblood of civilization for a hundred years through peace and war, and mainly war.

Most important, neither average Americans nor earnest Washington policymakers understood that those who are banking on Baghdad have, for multiple millennia, only reaped the dividends of grief. Why?

Perhaps it is because in the West, we will not give up the future. And in Iraq, they will not give up the past.

NOTES

Part One: From Cradle to Crossroads

CHAPTER 1: HAVE A NICE DAY

1. Author's interview and exchange of e-mails with Lt. Col. Chris Hughes, Mar 1, 2004–Mar 3, 2004. Mark Strassmann, "On the Scene: Holy City Liberated," CBS report and video, Apr 3, 2003. Ryan Chilcote, "Heroes of War, Lt. Col. Chris Hughes," CNN report and video, Apr 2, 2003. Fayaz Ahmad, "Commander Averts Catastrophe," *Sky News* report and video, Apr 3, 2003.
2. Author's interview with Hughes. Strassmann. Chilcote. Ahmad.
3. Author's interview with Hughes.
4. Author's interview with Hughes.
5. See Ahmad.
6. Author's interview with Hughes.
7. Author's interview with Hughes.
8. Author's interview with Hughes. Chilcote. "Battalion Lineage, 2nd Battalion (NO SLACK), 327th Infantry Regiment," www.campbell.army.mil. See Pfc. James Matise, "101st 'Bastogne Brigade' Claims Piece of Desert Sand at Camp Pennsylvania," Mar 10, 2003, *Third Army/USARCENT/CFLCC News,* www.arcent .army.mil.
9. Author's interview with Hughes. "Battalion Lineage." "327th Infantry, Bastogne Bulldogs," www.army.mil/cmh-pg/. Donna Everett, "101st Airborne Division Chronicle," *World War II Division Chronicles, 101st Airborne Division,* Apr 5, 2002, www.army.mil/cmh-pg/.
10. Author's interview with Hughes. "Battalion Lineage."
11. Author's interview with Hughes.
12. Author's interview with Hughes.
13. Author's interview with Hughes.
14. Author's interview with Hughes.
15. Author's interview with Hughes.
16. Author's interview with Hughes. David Zucchino, "Deft Touch Wins Religious Battle," Apr 4, 2003, *Los Angeles Times.* Jim Lacey, "Armed with Their Teeth," *Time,* www.time.com.

17. Author's interview with Hughes. Lacey. Zucchino.
18. Author's interview with Hughes.
19. Author's interview with Hughes.
20. "The Religious Authority, Grand Ayatollah Sayyid Ali Husani Sistani, His Methodology in Researching and Teaching," www.sistani.org. Author's interview with Hughes.
21. Author's interview with Hughes.
22. Author's interview with Hughes.
23. Author's interview with Hughes. Strassmann. Chilcote. Ahmad.
24. Author's interview with Hughes. Strassmann. Chilcote. Ahmad.
25. Author's interview with Hughes. Ahmad.
26. Author's interview with Hughes. Strassmann. Chilcote. Ahmad.
27. Author's interview with Hughes.
28. Author's interview with Hughes.
29. Author's interview with Hughes. Strassmann. Chilcote. Ahmad.
30. Author's interview with Hughes.
31. Author's interview with Hughes. Strassmann. Chilcote. Ahmad.
32. Author's interview with Hughes.
33. Author's interview with Hughes. Strassmann. Chilcote. Ahmad.
34. Author's interview with Hughes. Strassmann. Chilcote. Ahmad.
35. Author's interview with Hughes.

CHAPTER 2: THE CRADLE OF COMMERCE

1. Butzer, Karl W., "Environmental Change in the Near East and Human Impact on the Land," Jack M. Sasson, ed., *Civilizations of the Ancient Near East* (New York: Scribner, 1995), 123, 127. Nissen, Hans J., Peter Damerow, and Robert K. Englund, *Archaic Bookkeeping: Early Writing and Techniques of Economic Administration in the Ancient Near East,* Paul Larsen, trans. (Chicago: University of Chicago Press, 1993), 8. See also Finkelstein, J. J., "Mesopotamia," *Journal of Near Eastern Studies,* vol. 21 (1962), 73–92.
2. d'Errico, Francesco, "The Invisible Frontier: A Multiple Species Model for the Origin of Behavioral Modernity," *Evolutionary Anthropology,* vol. 12 (2003), 188–189. d'Errico, Francesco et al., "Archaeological Evidence for the Emergence of Language, Symbolism, and Music—An Alternative Multidisciplinary Perspective," *Journal of World Prehistory,* vol. 17 (2003), 3–4. "Abstract Engravings Show Modern Behavior Emerged Earlier Than Previously Thought," www.nsf.gov. See photo, "Engraved Ochre from Blombos Cave," www.nsf.gov.
3. See "Cave of Lascaux," www.culture.gouv.fr/culture/arcnat/lascaux/en/. See "The Cave of Chauvet-Pont-d'Arc," www.culture.gouv.fr/culture/arcnat/chauvet /en/. See Fagan, Brian M., *People of the Earth: An Introduction to World Prehistory* (Upper Saddle River, NJ: Prentice Hall), 2001, 134–137.
4. *Encyclopedia Judaica,* s.v., "Jericho." Bar-Yosef, O., "The Walls of Jericho: An Alternative Interpretation," *Current Anthropology,* vol. 27 (1986), 157–159. Negev, Avraham, ed., *Archaeological Encyclopedia of the Holy Land* (New York: Prentice Hall Press, 1990), 194, 195. Mazar, Amihai, *Archaeology of the Land of the Bible, 10,000–586 B.C.E.* (New York: Doubleday, 1992), 44–55, 47. See photo, "Human Skull Covered with Painted Plaster," Archaeological Studies, www.utexas.edu.
5. Nissen, "Ancient Western Asia Before the Age of Empires," Sasson, 795. See

"The Halaf Period (6500–5500 B.C.)," Metropolitan Museum of Art, www
.metmuseum.org. See "Images from World History: Archaic Mesopotamia," www
.hp.uab.edu.

6. Nissen, "Ancient Western Asia Before the Age of Empires," Sasson, 795. *Encyclopedia Judaica,* s.v., "Jericho." See Yener, K. Aslihan, "The Archaeometry of Silver in Anatolia: The Bolkardag Mining District," *American Journal of Archaeology,* vol. 90 (1986), 469–472. See "Images from World History: Archaic Mesopotamia." See "The Halaf Period (6500–5500 B.C.)." See "The Ubaid Period (5500–4000 B.C.)," www.metmuseum.org.

7. "On Part of Mesopotamia between Sheriat-el-Beytha, on the Tigris, to Tel Ibrahim," *Proceedings of the Royal Geographical Society of London,* vol. 11, no. 4 (1866–1867), 157.

8. Nissen, "Ancient Western Asia Before the Age of Empires," 795–796.

9. Postgate, J. N., *Early Mesopotamia: Society and Economy at the Dawn of History* (London: Routledge, 1994), 15–19, 157. Roux, George, *Ancient Iraq* (New York: Penguin Books, 1992), 12–13. Englund, Robert K., lecture, University of Connecticut, April 2004, 1, 9. Author's e-mail and telephone corresp. with Robert K. Englund.

10. Astour, Michael, "Overland Trade Routes in Ancient Western Asia," Sasson, 1401–1420.

11. Nissen, *Archaic Bookkeeping,* 14–15, 70–71. Schmandt-Besserat, *Before Writing,* 176–178. Sasson, "Timeline of Ancient Near Eastern Civilizations." Author's e-mail and telephone corresp. with J. N. Postgate, Englund, and Denise Schmandt-Besserat, May 2004.

12. Schmandt-Besserat, Denise, "Accounting with Tokens in the Ancient Near East," Justus, Carol F., dir., *Numerals Project,* www.utexas.edu. See Englund, Robert K., "Proto-Cuneiform Account Books and Journals," Apr 2004, 24, 25, 26. Author's e-mail and telephone corresp. with Hans J. Nissen, Englund, Schmandt-Besserat, and Avi Winitzer, May 2004.

13. Nissen, *Archaic Bookkeeping,* 116. Schmandt-Besserat, "Accounting with Tokens in the Ancient Near East." Schmandt-Besserat, *Before Writing,* 197. See Englund, "Proto-Cuneiform," 23–44.

14. Schmandt-Besserat, "Accounting with Tokens in the Ancient Near East."

15. Melville, Duncan J., "Tokens: The Origin of Mathematics," http://web.stlawu.edu. Schmandt-Besserat, *Before Writing,* 108–110, 126–127. See Englund, "Proto-Cuneiform."

16. Nissen, *Archaic Bookkeeping,* 118–119. Schmandt-Besserat, *Before Writing,* 198–199. Englund, Robert K., "Texts from the Late Uruk Period," *Mesopotamien: Späturuk- und Frühdynastische Zeit.* Waefler and Attinger, eds. (forthcoming), ii–iv. Author's e-mail and telephone corresp. with Nissen and J. N. Postgate.

17. Postgate, 135. See Postgate, 197.

18. "Laws of Hammurabi," Roth, Martha T., *Law Collections from Mesopotamia and Asia Minor* (Atlanta, GA: Scholars Press, 1997), 73, 80–81. See Roth, 71–142. See Greengus, Samuel, "Legal and Social Institutions of Ancient Mesopotamia," *Civilizations of the Ancient Near East,* 472. See also Meek, Theophile J., trans., "The Code of Hammurabi," *Ancient Near Eastern Texts Relating to the Old Testament,* James B. Pritchard, ed. (Princeton, NJ: Princeton University Press, 1950), 163–180. See also Horne, Charles F., "The Code of Hammurabi: Introduction," and "Code of Hammurabi," L. W. King, trans., *Avalon Project,* www.law.yale.edu. See photo, "Stele of

Hammurabi," Sb 8, www.louvre.fr. See "Laws of Eshnunna," Roth. See generally Yaron, Reuven, *The Laws of Eshnunna* (Jerusalem: Magnes Press, Hebrew University, 1988). Author's e-mail and telephone corresp. with Martha T. Roth, Winitzer.

19. "Laws of Hammurabi," Roth, 81–132. See also author's analysis spreadsheet of the "Laws of Hammurabi."

20. "Laws of Hammurabi," #141, #142, Roth, 107–108.

21. "Laws of Hammurabi." Roth, 81–132. See also author's analysis spreadsheet of the "Laws of Hammurabi."

22. "Laws of Hammurabi," #35, #36, #37, #38, Roth, 88.

23. See "Laws of Hammurabi," Roth, 81–132.

24. "Laws of Hammurabi," #121, #122, Roth, 104.

25. "Laws of Hammurabi," #268, #269, #270, #271, #272, Roth, 130–131.

26. Lewy, Hildegard, "Marginal Notes on a Recent Volume of Babylonian Mathematical Texts," *Journal of the American Oriental Society,* vol. 67 (1947), 306–307. Also see Muroi, K., "Interest Calculation of Babylonian Mathematics: New Interpretations of VAT 8521 and VAT 8528," *Historia Scientiarum,* vol. 39 (1990), 29–34. Author's e-mail and telephone corresp. with Englund and Winitzer.

CHAPTER 3: ROBBING THE CRADLE

1. Nissen, Hans J., "Ancient Western Asia Before the Age of Empires," Sasson, Jack M., ed., *Civilizations of the Ancient Near East* (New York: Scribner, 1995), 801. See maps, "Near and Middle East in Early Antiquity," "Southern Mesopotamia," "Northern Mesopotamia," Roux, George, *Ancient Iraq* (New York: Penguin Books, 1992), 815ff. See also Maps, "The Near East" and "South Mesopotamia," Postgate, J. N., *Early Mesopotamia: Society and Economy at the Dawn of History* (London: Routledge, 1994), 2, 27.

2. See Hitti, Phillip K., *History of the Arabs: From the Earliest Times to the Present* (Hampshire, UK: Palgrave Macmillan, 2002), 10–11. See Roux, 150–154, 156–161, 175–176, 184, 225.

3. Roux, 88, 364–365. See Ifrah, Georges, *The Universal History of Numbers: From Prehistory to the Invention of the Computer,* David Bellos et al., trans. (New York: John Wiley & Sons, 2000), 91–94.

4. Roux, 356–358, 360, 361. See Postgate, 66–67. See Allen, G. Donald, "Babylonian Mathematics," www.math.tamu.edu.

5. See Roux, 357–371.

6. See "Timeline, Prehistory," Roux, 501–502. See figure, "The Temple at Eridu," Postgate, 25. See Postgate, 110. See Nissen, Hans J., Peter Damerow, and Robert K. Englund, *Archaic Bookkeeping: Early Writing and Techniques of Economic Administration in the Ancient Near East,* Larsen, Paul, trans. (Chicago: University of Chicago Press, 1993). See Johnson, Denise, "Art 101, Ancient Near Eastern Art Part I, Lecture 5," www.msjc.edu. See Genesis 11:1–6, NIV Study Bible.

7. See Genesis, NIV Study Bible.

8. Roux, 179, 184–185, 389–396.

9. See "The Treaty Between Hattusilis and Ramesses II," www.bakeru.edu. See "Peace Treaty between Ramses II and Hattuili III, Hittite Version," http://nefertiti.iwebland.com.

10. "The Treaty Between Hattusilis and Ramesses II," Sections 6 and 8.

11. "The Treaty Between Hattusilis and Ramesses II."

12. Roux, 319–323, 325.

13. Roux, 333, 334–335.

14. II Kings 24:14–15. See Jeremiah 52:15, 27–30. See Map, "Nebuchadnezzar's Campaigns Against Judah," NIV Study Bible, 566–567. Also see Roux, 377–379.

15. Roux, 386–387. See "Cyrus Cylinder" and photo, "Cyrus Cylinder," Museum No. ANE 90920, www.thebritishmuseum.ac.uk.

16. See Weissbach, F. H., trans., "Cyrus," Pritchard, J. B., ed., *Ancient Near Eastern Texts Relating to the Old Testament* (Princeton, NJ: Princeton University, 1969), 315–316. See Lendering, Joanna, "Cyrus Takes Babylon," www.livius.org.

17. Ezra 1:1–4, NIV Study Bible.

18. See Timeline, "Achaemenian and Hellenistic Periods," Roux, 515.

19. Genesis 12:2. See Joshua 24:2. *Encyclopedia Judaica*, s.v., "Terah."

20. Genesis 15:5. Genesis 17:4–5.

21. Genesis 21:8–18.

22. See Author's interviews with rabbinical sources.

23. See Hitti, 9–13. See Genesis 21:8–20.

24. II Chronicles 17:11. See Lewis, Bernard, *The Arabs in History* (New York: Harper & Row, 1960), 11. Hitti, 37. See Astour, Michael C., "841 B.C.: The First Assyrian Invasion of Israel," *Journal of the American Oriental Society*, vol. 91 (1971), 384, 387. See Ephal, I., " 'Ishmael' and 'Arabs': A Transformation of Ethnological Terms," *Journal of Near Eastern Studies*, vol. 35 (1976), 226–228.

25. Hourani, Albert, *A History of the Arab Peoples* (Cambridge, MA: Harvard University Press, 1991), 10. Holt, P. M., Ann K. S. Lambton, and Bernard Lewis, eds., *The Cambridge History of Islam*, vol. 1 (Cambridge, UK: Cambridge University Press, 1970), 4, 5. Crone, Patricia, "The Rise of Islam in the World," Robinson, Francis, ed., *The Cambridge Illustrated History of the Islamic World* (Cambridge, UK: Cambridge University Press, 1996), 3, 4–5. See Grinitz, Joshua, "On the Original Home of the Semites," *Journal of Near Eastern Studies*, vol. 21 (1962), 191. Hitti, 25.

26. Lewis, Bernard, *The Arabs in History*, 11, 12. See Donner, Fred M., "Muhammad and the Caliphate: Political History of the Islamic Empire up to the Mongol Conquests," Esposito, John, ed., *The Oxford History of Islam* (New York: Oxford University Press, 1999), 5. See Holt, Lambton, and Lewis, 2–4.

27. Ahmed, Akbar S., *Discovering Islam: Making Sense of Muslim History and Society* (London: Routledge and Kegan Paul, 1988), 15, 17, 19. Esposito, John L., *Islam and Politics* (Syracuse, NY: Syracuse University Press, 1984), 4. Glubb, Sir John, *The Empire of the Arabs* (Englewood Cliffs, NJ: Prentice-Hall, 1963), 17, 19–21. Crone, 5–8. Bloom, Jonathan, and Sheila Blair, *Islam: A Thousand Years of Faith and Power* (New Haven: Yale University Press, 2002), 242. Esposito, John L., *Islam and Politics* (Syracuse, NY: Syracuse University Press, 1984), 4. Hitti, 104. See map, "Ancient Arabia," Hitti, 63.

28. Esposito, 4–7. Ahmed, 17, 20. See Donner, 1–10. Fernau, F. W., *Moslems on the March*, E. W. Dickes, trans. (New York: Alfred A. Knopf, 1954), 25. Lewis, *Islam: From the Prophet Muhammad*, xvii.

29. See Hamidullah, Muhammad, *Introduction to Islam* (Chicago: Kazi Publications, 1993), 9–16. Holt, Lambton, and Lewis, 49.

30. Donner, 10–14. See Esposito, *The Oxford History of Islam*. Esposito, *Islam and Politics*, 8.

31. See Mottahedeh, Roy P., "The Foundations of State and Society," *Islam: The Religious and Political Life of a World Community*, Marjorie Kelly, ed. (New York: Praeger, 1984), 55–56. Esposito, John L., *Islam and Politics*, 12. Hamidulla.

32. Lapidus, Ira M., *A History of Islamic Societies* (New York: Cambridge University Press, 1988), 38. Lewis, Bernard, *The Arabs in History*, 52. Hitti, 170, 171, 352–353.

33. Ahmed, 34, 232. Donner, 2, 12. Hourani, 23. Holt, Lambton, and Lewis, 58–63. Donner, "Muhammad and the Caliphate," 12. See Hitti, 66. See Longrigg, Stephen, *The Middle East: A Social Geography* (London: Gerald Duckworth & Co., 1963), 39.

34. Al-Tabari, *History of the World* (Albany: State University of New York Press, 1985), 2053 as quoted in Lewis, *Islam: From the Prophet Muhammad*, 228 and Ahmed, 34.

35. See Glubb, 26, 27. See Hitti, 155–159.

36. Glubb, 24–26. See map, "Operations in Syria & Palestine, 634–635," Glubb, 25.

37. Crone, 11.

38. Rosenthal, F., "Aramaic Studies During the Past Thirty Years," *Journal of Near Eastern Studies*, 81–82. Glubb, 26. See map, "Arab Invasion of Persia," Glubb, 27. See Hitti, 123, 156–157.

39. Donner, "Muhammad and the Caliphate," 10–14. Bloom and Blair, 50.

40. Lewis, *Islam: from the Prophet Muhammad*, 6–9. Hitti, 178. Glubb, 31.

41. Lapidus, 55–58. Holt, Lambton, and Lewis, 67–72. Hourani, 24–26, 60. Donner, "Muhammad and the Caliphate," 15.

42. See Rahman, Fazlur, "The Message and the Messenger," *Islam: The Religious and Political Life of a World Community* (New York: Praeger, 1984), 49. Hitti, 176. Glubb, 31, 33. See Lewis, *The Arabs in History*, 66. Donner, "Muhammad and the Caliphate," 15.

43. Holt, Lambton, and Lewis, 69.

44. Lewis, Bernard, *The Arabs in History*, 60–61. Glubb, 33–34. Hinds, Martin, "The Murder of the Caliph Uthman," *International Journal of Middle Eastern Studies*, vol. 3 (1972), 457. Hitti, 177. Glubb, 331–34. Wellhausen, J., *The Arab Kingdom and Its Fall*, Margaret Graham Weir, trans. (Beirut: Khayats, 1963), 75. See Lewis, *Arabs in History*, 60–61.

45. Holt, Lambton, and Lewis, 69–72. Donner, "Muhammad and the Caliphate," 15–18. Bloom and Blair, 51–55.

46. Lapidus, 55–58. See Esposito, *Islam and Politics*, 9. See Holt, Lambton, and Lewis, 69–70.

47. Hitti, 180. See Wellhausen, 75. See "Battle of the Camel," http://muslim–canada .org. See "Chapter 8: Caliph Ali," *Pages of Muslim History*, www.muslimhistory.info.

48. Holt, Lambton, and Lewis, 70, 71. Hourani, 60, 61. Esposito, *The Oxford History of Islam*, 112.

49. Holt, Lambton, and Lewis, 70. Lewis, *The Arabs in History*, 61. Esposito, *Islam and Politics*, 9. Wellhausen, 53. Hitti, 179–180. *Pages of Muslim History*, 27. "Battle of the Camel."

50. Holt, Lambton, and Lewis, 70. Lewis, *Arabs in History*, 60. Hitti, 180. See "Battle of the Camel." See *Pages of Muslim History*, 27.

51. See Ahmed, 35. Holt, Lambton, and Lewis, 70. Glubb, 34, 35. See "Islamic Calendar 2004 (1424–1425)," www.al-imam.net.

52. Holt, Lambton, and Lewis, 70–72. See Wellhausen, 75–103. See Ahmed, 36.

53. Holt, Lambton, and Lewis, 74–77, 78, 102. See Ahmed, 38–40. Esposito, *The Oxford History of Islam*, 20. See Hitti, 184.

54. Esposito, *The Oxford History of Islam*, 17, 509, 691. See Ahmed, 57. See Hitti, 190. Holt, Lambton, and Lewis, 81.

55. Holt, Lambton, and Lewis, 101, 102. Ahmed, 38–40. See Hitti, 184.

56. Esposito, *The Oxford History of Islam*, 522. Cockburn, Andrew, "Iraq's Oppressed Majority," *Smithsonian*, vol. 93, no. 9 (December 2003), 98–102.

57. Holt, Lambton, and Lewis, 72. Kelly, 16. Cockburn.

58. Fernau, 306. Lapidus, 67. Hourani, 32–34.

59. Esposito, *The Oxford History of Islam*, 25. Hitti, 288, 289.

60. Kazanchi, Fouad, "A History of Baghdad," www.baghdadbulletin.com. Hitti, 292, 293.

61. Hitti, 293. See Glubb, 247. Kazanchi.

62. Hitti, 292. Kazanchi.

63. Glubb, 345, 347.

64. Holt, Lambton, and Lewis, 104–114. Hourani, 34. Dale, Stephen, "The Islamic World in the Age of European Expansion," Robinson, 65–66. Cleveland, William L., *A History of the Modern Middle East* (Boulder, CO: Westview Press, 2000), 18. See "Ismail bin Jafar Sadik," http://ismaili.net.

65. Lapidus, 132. Lewis, *Arabs in History*, 144. Hourani, 85.

66. Bloom and Blair, 89–90. Holt, Lambton, and Lewis, 149–151. Esposito, *Islam and Politics*, 24.

67. Donner, *The Oxford History of Islam*, 39, 60, 155, 160, 163–64. Bloom and Blair, 121. See Sabra, A. I., "The Scientific Enterprise," Lewis, *Islam and the Arab World*, 181–200. See "Science," www.al-bab.com/arab/science.htm. See Kazanchi.

68. Bloom and Blair, 160. Esposito, *The Oxford History of Islam,* 60–61. See Crone, 29–31.

69. Robinson, xvi–xvii. See Irwin, Robert, "The Emergence of the Islamic World System, 1000–1500," Robinson, 43.

70. See Irwin, 45, 46. See Phillips, E. D., *The Mongols* (New York: Frederick A. Praeger, 1969), 58, 60. See Saunders, J. J., *The History of the Mongol Conquests* (Philadelphia: University of Pennsylvania Press, 1971), 55. See Morgan, David, *The Mongols* (Oxford: Basil Blackwell, Inc., 1986), 68.

71. See Curtin, Jeremiah, *The Mongols: A History.* (Cambridge, MA: Da Capo Press, 2003), 101. See Phillips, 60. See Saunders, 104.

72. Spuler, Bertold, *History of the Mongols, Based on Eastern and Western Accounts of the Thirteenth and Fourteenth Centuries*, Helga and Stuart Drummond, trans. (Berkeley: University of California Press), 1972, 84. Carpini, Fr. Giovanni DiPlano, *The Story of the Mongols Whom We Call the Tartars*, Erik Hildinger, trans. (Boston: Branden Publishing, 1996), 71, 75, 125. See Chambers, James, *The Devil's Horsemen: The Mongol Invasion of Europe* (New York: Atheneum, 1985), 54, 62–63. Nicolle, David, *The Mongol Warlords: Genghis Khan, Kublai Khan, Hulegu, Tamerlane* (Poole, UK: Firebird Books, 1990), 28. See Morgan, xii–xiii. See Phillips, 50–51.

73. See Chambers, 64, 65. See Nicolle, 32, 35. See Carpini, 76.

74. See Saunders, 56. See Phillips, 41. See Irwin, 47. See Ratchnevsky, Paul, *Genghis Khan: His Life and Legacy*, Thomas Nivison Haining, ed. and trans. (Oxford: Blackwell, 1991), 151, 152, 158. Saunders, 65, 216f.

75. Phillips, 60, 61.

76. Phillips, 61.

77. Ratchnevsky, 130.

78. Irwin, 47.
79. Carpini, 78. See Saunders, 56. Hitti, 414.
80. Hitti, 482. See Hitti, 482n5. See Curtin, 122, 125.
81. Curtin, 123–124.
82. See Irwin, 47–48.
83. See Schurmann, H. F., "Mongolian Tributary Practices of the Thirteenth Century," *Harvard Journal of Asiatic Studies*, vol. 19 (1956), 304–389. See Waugh, Daniel C., "The Pax Mongolica," www.silk-road.com.
84. See Curtin 184–185. See Chambers, 142, 143.
85. See Nowell, Charles E., "The Old Man of the Mountain," *Speculum: A Journal of Mediaeval Studies*, vol. 22 (1947), 497–501, 504. See Lockhart, Lawrence, "Hasan-i-Sabah and the Assassins," *Bulletin of the School of Oriental Studies, University of London*, vol. 5 (1930), 677–682, 685–688. See Irwin, 48. See Morgan, 146–148. See Saunders, 109. See Chambers, 142.
86. See Nowell, 514. Phillips, 88–89. Morgan, 148, 149.
87. See Saunders, 108. See Phillips, 88. See Allsen, Thomas T., *Mongol Imperialism: The Policies of the Grand Qan Möngke in China, Russia, and the Islamic Lands, 1251–1259* (Berkeley: University of California Press, 1987), 202, 203. See Allsen, Thomas T., *Culture and Conquest in Mongol Eurasia* (Cambridge, UK: Cambridge University Press, 2001). 19.
88. Saunders, 108. Ratchnevsky, 159. See Morgan, 158. See Phillips, 34, 35.
89. See Saunders, 107, 108, 109.
90. See Chambers, 91–93, 142–143. See Saunders, 109.
91. See Curtin, 247. See Nicolle, 109.
92. See Curtin, 247–248.
93. Curtin, 248.
94. Curtin, 249–250. Chambers, 145.
95. See Curtin, 250.
96. See Phillips, 90. See Chambers, 144.
97. See Curtin, 251.
98. See Phillips, 90.
99. See Phillips, 90. See Curtin 252–254.
100. See Nicolle, 132.
101. See Morgan, 152. See Chambers, 145. See Curtin, 254. See Phillips, 90.
102. See Curtin, 252, 253. See Saunders, 111–112.
103. See Saunders, 110, 112. See Morgan, 151.
104. Spuler, as quoted by Savory, Roger M., "Land of the Lion and the Sun," *Islam and the Arab World*, Bernard L. Lewis, ed. (London: Alfred A. Knopf, 1976), 246. See Morgan, 151. See Curtin, 253.
105. See Saunders, 113. See Curtin, 260.
106. See Saunders, 113, 115. See Curtin, 265.
107. See Morgan, 152. Saunders, 177–178.

CHAPTER 4: THE THREE OTTOMAN PROVINCES

1. See Saunders, J. J., *The History of the Mongol Conquests* (Philadelphia: University of Pennsylvania Press, 1971), 110, 112. See Nicolle, David, *The Mongol Warlords: Genghis Khan, Kublai Khan, Hulegu, Tamerlane* (Poole, UK: Firebird Books, 1990), 110.

2. Morgan, David, *The Mongols* (Oxford: Basil Blackwell, Inc., 1986), 82–83, 145, 158.

3. Irwin, Robert, "The Emergence of the Islamic World System, 1000–1500," Francis Robinson, ed., *The Cambridge Illustrated History of the Islamic World* (Cambridge, UK: Cambridge University Press, 1996), 43–44. Hitti, Phillip K., *History of the Arabs: From the Earliest Times to the Present* (Hampshire, UK: Palgrave Macmillan, 2002), 636, 637, 639.

4. Gottfried, Robert S., *The Black Death: Natural and Human Disaster in Medieval Europe* (New York: Free Press, 1953), 33–34, 37. Dols, Michael W., *The Black Death in the Middle East* (Princeton, NJ: Princeton University Press, 1977), 26–28, 45, 48–49.

5. Gottfried, 36, 41. See Dols, 55, 60–62.

6. Morgan, 18, 19, 144, 156–157, 160–161. Irwin, 48.

7. Morgan, 200–201. See photo, "Portrait Head of Timur," Nicolle, 144. Nicolle, 145, 152, 153. Hitti, 699.

8. Saunders, 173–174. Hitti, 699.

9. Nicolle, 157–158. See Morgan, 93.

10. Hookham, Hilda, *Tamburlaine the Conqueror* (London: Hodder & Stoughton, 1962), 150–151. Nicolle, 161. Hitti, 699, 701.

11. Nicolle, 166, 167, 169. Hookham, 3. Manz, Beatrice Forbes, *The Rise and Rule of Tamerlane* (Cambridge UK: Cambridge University Press, 1989), 73.

12. Hookham, 114, 115. Irwin, 56.

13. Nicolle, 168. Saunders, 177–178.

14. Savory, Roger M., "Land of the Lion and the Sun," Bernard Lewis, ed., *Islam and the Arab World* (London: Alfred A. Knopf, 1976), 254. Ravenstein, E. G., "The Voyages of Diogo Cão and Bartholomieu Dias, 1482–88," *Geographical Journal,* vol. 52 (1918), 638–641, 648. See Nowell, Charles E., "Vasco da Gama—First Count of Vidigueira," *Hispanic American Historical Review,* vol. 20 (1940), 342–358. de Figueredo, Fidelino, "The Geographical Discoveries and Conquests of the Portuguese," *Hispanic American Historical Review,* vol. 6 (1926), 58, 59.

15. Carruthers, Douglas, "The Great Desert Caravan Route, Aleppo to Basra," *Geographical Journal,* vol. 52 (1918), 157, 159. Hitti, 696–697.

16. Morgan, 142. Saunders, 158. Nicolle 173–174.

17. Savory, 253. Nicolle 168–169. Imber, Colin, *The Ottoman Empire, 1300–1650: The Structure of Power* (New York: Palgrave MacMillan, 2002), 16–17.

18. Irwin, 56. See Hitti, 702.

19. Nicolle, 170–171. Manz, 73.

20. de Figueredo, 47. Carruthers, 158–159. Imber, 57–59.

21. Barnett, Clifford R. et al., *Iran,* Herbert Harold Vreeland and Muriel B. Lechter, eds. (New Haven: Human Relations Area Files, 1957), 21, 22. Imber, 42.

22. Bosworth, Edmond, "Armies of the Prophet," Lewis, 208. Shaw, Stanford J., *The History of the Ottoman Empire and Modern Turkey, Volume 1: Empire of the Gazis—The Rise and Decline of the Ottoman Empire, 1280–1808* (Cambridge, UK: Cambridge University Press, 1976), 78. Hitti, 441, 702, 736–737. Savory, 246–247. Cole, Juan R. I., "Rival Empires of Trade and Imami Shiism in Eastern Arabia, 1300–1800," *International Journal of Middle Eastern Studies,* vol. 19 (1987), 177, 184–185.

23. Koprülü, M. Fuad, *The Origins of the Ottoman Empire,* Gary Leiser, ed. and trans. (New York: State University of New York Press, 1992), 43, 44. Imber, 5. Shaw, 4, 5.

24. Inalcik, Halil, *The Ottoman Empire: The Classical Age 1300–1600,* Norman Itzkowitz

and Colin Imber, trans. (London: Wiedenfeld and Nicolson, 1973), 4. Köprülü, 3, 43, 45–47. Shaw 9, 10–11. Imber, 120, 121. Hitti, 716.

25. Imber, 8–10. Shaw, 12–16.
26. Imber, 28–29. Shaw, 56–57. Science Daily Encyclopedia, s.v., "Constantinople."
27. Imber, 121. Inalcik, 14. Shaw, 15.
28. Imber, 178–180. Inalcik, 106.
29. Hitti, 737. Imber, 180–181.
30. Imber, 182–183. Shaw, 26–27.
31. Imber, 184, 185. Shaw, 26. Inalcik, 105, 108–109.
32. Imber, 192–199. Inalcik, 104. See Inalcik, 105–110.
33. Imber, 185, 193–199.
34. See Bent, J. Theodore, "The English in the Levant," *English Historical Review,* vol. 5 (1890), 661. Inalcik, 140–141.
35. Inalcik, 144–145, 150–151, 154–155. Shaw, 156–160.
36. Quataert, Donald, *The Ottoman Empire, 1700–1922* (Cambridge, UK: Cambridge University Press, 2000), 7. See Faroqhi, Suraiya, *Subjects of the Sultans: Culture and Daily Life in the Ottoman Empire* (London: I.B. Tauris Publishers, 2000), 216–217. See Inalcik, 142–145. See Quataert, Donald, "Introduction," Donald Quataert, ed., *Consumption Studies and the History of the Ottoman Empire, 1550–1922,* (Albany, NY: State University of New York Press, 2000), 1–7. See Artan, Tülay, "Aspects of the Ottoman Elite's Food Consumption: Looking for 'Staples,' 'Luxuries,' and 'Delicacies' in a Changing Century," Quataert, *Consumption Studies,* 107–116. See painting, "The Coffee House," Wheatcroft, Andrew, *The Ottomans* (London: Viking, 1995), plate 3. "Covered Bazaar," www.archnet.org.
37. Inalcik, 143–145.
38. Inalcik, 128. Imber, 192–193.
39. Cassels, Lavender, *The Struggle for the Ottoman Empire: 1717–1740* (New York: Thomas Y. Crowell Company, 1967), 54–55. Inalcik, 80–83. See illustrations, Inalcik, 132ff. See illustrations, "The Sultan's Gardner," and "The Grand Vizier," Wheatcroft, plates 22, 23, 98.
40. Faroqhi, 167. See Panzac, Daniel, "International and Domestic Maritime Trade in the Ottoman Empire during the 18th Century," *International Journal of Middle East Studies,* vol. 24 (1992), 189–206. Inalcik, 128–130.
41. See Sansal, Burak H., "Turkish Bath," www.allaboutturkey.com.
42. Goodwin, Jason, *Lords of the Horizons: A History of the Ottoman Empire* (New York: Picador, 1998), 214–215. Inalcik, 85–87. Imber, 145–147. Shaw, 115. See "The Topkapi Palace, Simplified Sketch," Shaw, 116. Wheatcroft, 34. See Sansal, "Harem in the Ottoman Empire," www.allaboutturkey.com.
43. Palmer, Alan, *The Decline and Fall of the Ottoman Empire* (New York: M. Evans & Co., 1992), 19. See Imber, 145. Wheatcroft, 36–37. See Sansal, "Harem." Goodwin, 211, 214. Shaw, 202–203. Lord Kinross, *The Ottoman Centuries: The Rise and Fall of the Turkish Empire* (New York: William Morrow & Co., 1977), 288.
44. Imber, 145–146, 323. Shaw, 98.
45. Palmer, 6. See Shaw, 190–191. See Wheatcroft, 38.
46. Goodwin, 214.
47. Imber, 87–89.
48. Palmer, 20. Inalcik, 59–60. Imber, 107–108. Quataert, 90.

49. Kinross, 288. Inalcik, 60. Palmer 20. Shaw, 80, 179, 184.

50. Imber, 109. Inalcik, 60, 63.

51. Inalcik, 60. Shaw, 186. Quataert, 90–91. Dale, Stephen, "The Islamic World in the Age of European Expansion," Robinson, 67–68.

52. Imber, 78, 85, 131–140, 258. Shaw, 26, 46, 70, 179, 192–193. Inalcik, 222.

53. Shaw, 174–176. Imber, 61, 66–67, 72–73, 77–79. Kinross, 284. Inalcik, 50–51.

54. Imber, 78. Shaw, 194–195, 196–198.

55. Inalcik, 105, 127–128, 146.

56. Imber, 82. Shaw, 199–200.

57. Palmer, 19–20. Shaw, 219, 222. Inalcik, 60.

58. Imber, 79. Palmer, 23.

59. Goodwin, 211. Palmer, 15.

60. Goodwin, 211, 215. See illustration, "The Sultan Ahmed Mosque, Istanbul," Faroqhi, 144. Shaw, 190. Imber, 51, 52, 54, 66–68. See Inalcik, 37–39, 42–43.

61. Inalcik, 51. Quataert, 48. Shaw, 66–67, 120–122. Faroqhi, 228–229.

62. Quataert, 46. Longrigg, Stephen H., *Four Centuries of Modern Iraq* (Oxford: Clarendon Press, 1925), 119–123. Shaw, 238–239.

63. Cole, Juan R. I. and Moojan Momen, "Mafia, Mob and Shiism in Iraq: The Rebellion of Ottoman Karbala, 1842–1843," *Past and Present,* vol. 112 (Aug 1968), 123. Nakash, Yitzhak, "The Conversion of Iraq's Tribes to Shiism," *International Journal of Mideast Studies,* vol. 26 (1994), 443, 446. Shaw, 246. Cassels, 79–80. See Nakash, Yitzhak, *The Shi'is of Iraq* (Princeton, NJ: Princeton University Press, 1994), 287.

64. Longrigg, 134–142.

65. Longrigg, 142.

66. Longrigg, 144–146.

67. See Longrigg, 166–170. Palmer, 50. Cole and Momen, "Mafia," 122.

68. Nakash, "Conversion," 448. Nakash, *The Shi'is,* 19, 30.

CHAPTER 5: THE SICK MAN

1. See Chaudhuri, K. N., "The East India Company and the Export of Treasure in the Early Seventeenth Century," *Economic History Review,* vol. 16 (1963), 23. Farrington, Anthony, "The Beginnings of the English East India Company," *Trading Places: The East India Company and Asia,* www.fathom.com. See online exhibition, "Trading Places: The British East India Company & Asia, 1600–1834," www.bl.uk. See also "Research Guide F5: The East India Company," www.port.nmm.ac.uk.

2. Farrington, "The Impact of the East India Company," *Trading Places.*

3. Farrington, "The Impact," *Trading Places.* See, Roe, Sir Thomas, *The Embassy of Sir Thomas Roe to India, 1615–1619,* William Foster, ed. (London: Bedford Press, 1899), ii–v.

4. Cole, Juan. R. I., "Rival Empires of Trade and Imami Shiism, 1300–1800," *International Journal of Middle East Studies,* vol. 19 (1987), 182–183, 187.

5. Ferrier, R. W., "The Terms and Conditions Under Which English Trade Was Transacted With Safavid Persia," *Bulletin of the School of Oriental and African Studies, University of London,* vol. 49 (1986), 53, 54–55. Awad, Abdul Aziz M., "The Gulf in the Seventeenth Century," *Bulletin (British Society for Middle Eastern Studies),* vol. 12 (1985), 125, 126, 127. Longrigg, Stephen H., *Four Centuries of Modern Iraq* (Oxford: Clarendon Press, 1925), 102.

6. Awad, 126–127. Longrigg, 102–103. Ferrier, "Terms and Conditions," 54, 56. See Cole, "Rival Empires," 182, 188. Also see Ferrier, R. W., "The Armenians and the East India Company in Persia in the Seventeenth and Early Eighteenth Centuries," *Economic History Review,* New Series, vol. 26 (1973), 40.

7. Ferrier, "Terms and Conditions," 54. See D'Avenant, Charles, "An Essay on the East-India Trade," 1697, Avalon Project, www.law.yale.edu. See Ferrier, "Armenians," 38–62.

8. Lockhart, Laurence, "Nadir Shah's Campaigns in Oman, 1737–1744," *Bulletin of the School of Oriental Studies, University of London,* vol. 8 (1935), 160, 161.

9. Panzac, Daniel, "International and Domestic Maritime Trade in the Ottoman Empire during the 18th Century," *International Journal of Middle East Studies,* vol. 24 (1992), 189–206.

10. See Higonnet, Patrice Louis-Rene, "The Origins of the Seven Years' War," *Journal of Modern History,* vol. 40 (1968), 57–90. See "The Definitive Treaty of Peace and Friendship between his Britannick Majesty, the Most Christian King, and the King of Spain," Avalon Project, www.law.yale.edu.

11. Yapp, M. E., "The Establishment of the East India Company Residency at Baghdad, 1798–1806," *Bulletin of the School of Oriental and African Studies, University of London,* vol. 30 (1967), 323–324. Carruthers, Douglas, "The Great Desert Caravan Route, Aleppo to Basra," *Geographical Journal,* vol. 52 (1918), 159. Awad, 127.

12. See Yapp, 324, 334. See Nakash, Yitzhak, "The Conversion of Iraq's Tribes to Shiism," *International Journal of Middle East Studies,* vol. 26 (1994), 443. Panzac, 190–191. Yapp, "The Establishment," 324. See Carruthers.

13. Panzac, 192, 193.

14. Yapp, "The Establishment," 324–325.

15. Yapp, "The Establishment," 324–325.

16. Yapp, "The Establishment," 325–328. Hitti, Philip K., *History of the Arabs* (New York: Palgrave Macmillan, 2002), 721–722.

17. Yapp, "The Establishment," 326–327.

18. Yapp, "The Establishment," 329–332. Yapp, M. E., *Strategies of British India: Britain, Iran and Afghanistan, 1798–1850* (Oxford: Clarendon Press, 1980), 51–71.

19. Yapp, *Strategies,* 26–27.

20. Litvak, Meir, "A Failed Manipulation: The British, The Oudh Bequest and the Shi'i Ulama of Najaf and Karbala," *British Journal of Middle Eastern Studies,* vol. 27, No. 1 (May 2000), 70, 70n. Nakash, Yitzhak, *The Shi'is of Iraq* (Princeton, NJ: Princeton University Press, 1994), 19, 30. See Cole, Juan R. I. and Moojan Momen, "Mafia, Mob and Shiism in Iraq: The Rebellion of Ottoman Karbala, 1842–1843," *Past and Present,* vol. 112 (Aug 1968), 123.

21. Yapp, "The Establishment," 330, 334.

22. Chesney, Colonel W. Ainsworth, "A General Statement of the Labours and Proceedings of the Expedition to the Euphrates, under the Command of Colonel Chesney, Royal Artillery, F.R.S.," *Journal of the Royal Geographical Society of London,* vol. 7. (1837), 411–439. Yapp, "The Establishment," 334.

23. Yapp, "The Establishment," 330.

24. Yapp, "The Establishment," 330–332.

25. Yapp, "The Establishment," 331–332.

26. Yapp, "The Establishment," 332.

27. Yapp, "The Establishment," 332. See Yapp, *Strategies,* 62–71.

28. Yapp, "The Establishment," 333. Yapp, *Strategies,* 36.

29. Quataert, Donald, *The Ottoman Empire, 1700–1922* (Cambridge, UK: Cambridge University Press, 2000), 50–51. Nakash, "Conversion," 445–447. Longrigg, 212–217. Cole and Momen, "Mafia," 122, 123. See Hitti, 740–741.

30. Naskash, "Conversion," 466. Longrigg, 212–217.

31. Longrigg, 216, 217. Cole and Momen, "Mafia," 123.

32. Longrigg, 229. Hitti, 741. Nakash, "Conversion," 446.

33. See Cole and Momen, "Mafia," 114–120.

34. See Cole and Momen, "Mafia," 114–120.

35. See Cole and Momen, "Mafia."

36. Longrigg, 250–251.

37. Longrigg, 251, 260–261.

38. Longrigg, 251, 252–253.

39. Palmer, Alan, *The Decline and Fall of the Ottoman Empire* (New York: M. Evans & Co., 1992), 96. Lord Kinross, *The Ottoman Centuries: The Rise and Fall of the Turkish Empire* (New York: William Morrow & Co., 1977), 466–467.

40. Faroqhi, Suraiya, *Subjects of the Sultans: Culture and Daily Life in the Ottoman Empire* (London: I.B. Tauris, 2000), 94–96.

41. Palmer, *Decline,* 94. Kinross, 464.

42. Palmer, *Decline,* 92–93. Kinross, 456. Longrigg, 258.

43. Dispatch, Sir Robert Gordon, Jan 29, 1831: PRO FO195/90 (Baghdad, 1831). See Longrigg, 238, 239–241.

44. Gordon, Jan 29, 1831. Dispatch, Sir Robert Gordon, Feb 26, 1831: PRO FO195/90 (Baghdad, 1831). Longrigg, 262–263.

45. Letter, Agha Catchick Mikestich to Sir Robert Gordon, Feb 9, 1831: PRO FO195/90 (Baghdad, 1831).

46. Agha Catchick Mikestich, Feb 9, 1831.

47. Gordon, Jan 29, 1831. Gordon, Feb 26, 1831.

48. Gordon, Jan 29, 1831. Gordon, Feb 26, 1831.

49. Agha Catchick Mikestich, Feb 9, 1831.

50. Dispatch, Gordon to Taylor, Apr 15, 1831: PRO FO195/90 (Baghdad, 1831).

51. Dispatch, Gordon to Palmerston, Jul 26, 1831, Longrigg, 265–266. *St Petersburg Journal,* Jun 24, 1831, 2, Col. C. *St Petersburg Journal,* Sep 13, 1831, 24, col. B.

52. Longrigg, 265–266.

53. Longrigg, 265–267. Gordon to Palmerston, Jul 26, 1831.

54. Longrigg, 266–267.

55. Longrigg, 265–267. *St Petersburg Journal,* Sep 13, 1831, 24, Col. B.

56. Dispatch, Gordon to Lord Palmerston, Aug 26, 1831: PRO FO195/90 (Baghdad, 1831). Longrigg, 267, 268–269.

57. Gordon to Palmerston, Aug 26, 1831. Longrigg, 272–273.

58. Cole and Momen, "Mafia," 125.

59. Cole and Momen, "Mafia," 125.

60. Cole and Momen, "Mafia," 122, 126–133.

61. Cole and Momen, "Mafia," 126–133.

62. Cole and Momen, "Mafia," 135–137.

63. Cole and Momen, "Mafia," 135–137.

64. Cole and Momen, "Mafia," 135–137.
65. Cole, Juan R. I., "Iranian Millenarianism and Democratic Thought in the 19th Century," *International Journal of Middle East Studies*, vol. 24, no. 1 (Feb 1992), 1–26.
66. Cole and Momen, "Mafia," 114. See Bolsover, G. H., "Palmerston and Metternich on the Eastern Question," *English Historical Review*, vol. 51 (1936), 237–256.
67. Earle, Edward Meade, *Turkey, the Great Powers, and the Baghdad Railway: A Study in Imperialism* (New York: The Macmillan Company, 1923), vii, 4–5, 6–7. See Bolsover. See Carruthers. See Chesney.
68. See Palmer, *Decline,* 97–101. See Bolsover. See Meade.
69. Clark, Edward E., "The Ottoman Industrial Revolution," *International Journal of Middle Eastern Studies,* vol. 5 (1974), 66–67.
70. Clark, 67–68, 69.
71. Clark, 73–74.
72. Clark, 73–75.
73. Livingston, A. A., "Some Early Italian Parallels to the Locution of the Sick Man of the East," *PMLA,* vol. 25 (1910), 460. Palmer, *Decline,* 118.
74. Livingston, 460. Palmer, Alan, *The Banner of Battle: The Story of the Crimean War* (London: Weidenfield and Nicolson, 1987), 14.
75. Livingston, 460.
76. Livingston, 459–460n. Palmer, *Decline,* 118.
77. Schonfield, Hugh. *The Suez Canal in Peace and War, 1869–1969* (Coral Gables, FL: University of Miami Press, 1969), 37. See "The Suez Canal, an Achievement of Enthusiasm and Diplomacy," *Bulletin of the Business Historical Society,* vol. 3, no. 4. (Jun 1929), 1–8.

Part Two: Fumes

CHAPTER 6: OIL

1. d'Errico, Francesco, "The Invisible Frontier: A Multiple Species Model for the Origin of Behavioral Modernity," *Evolutionary Anthropology,* vol. 12 (2003), 193. Longrigg, Stephen H., *Oil in the Middle East: Its Discovery and Development* (London: Oxford University Press, 1968), 10–11. Giddens, Paul H., *The Birth of the Oil Industry* (New York: Macmillan, 1938), 11. Rister, Carl Coke, "The Oilman's Frontier," *Mississippi Valley Historical Review,* vol. 37, no. 1. (Jun 1950), 4–5.
2. Roux, George, *Ancient Iraq* (New York: Penguin Books, 1992), 151–152, 163. Exodus 2:2–3, NIV Study Bible. Ellis, Edward S., and Charles F. Horne, "Biography of King Sargon of Akkad," *The Story of the Greatest Nations, and the World's Famous Events,* vol. 1 (New York: Auxiliary Educational League, 1921).
3. See Longrigg, *Oil,* 10.
4. Xenophon, *Cyropaedia,* Henry G. Dakyns, trans., F. M. Stowell, ed., (Champaign, IL: The Gutenberg Project, 2002), bk. 7, chap. 5. Hitti, Philip K., *History of the Arabs* (New York: Palgrave Macmillan, 2002), 202. Longrigg, *Oil,* 11.
5. Miller, E. Willard, "The Industrial Development of the Allegheny Valley of Western Pennsylvania," *Economic Geography,* vol. 19 (1943), 401. See Scoville, Warren C., "Growth of the American Glass Industry to 1880—Continued," *Journal of Political Economy,* vol. 52 (1944), 345. Giddens, 19–20.
6. Giddens, 2–3, 14. Longrigg, *Oil,* 11.

7. Rezneck, Samuel, "Energy: Coal and Oil in the American Economy," *Journal of Economic History,* vol. 7 suppl. (1947), 63. See Darrah, William Culp, *Pithole: The Vanished City* (Gettysburg, PA: William C. Darrah, 1972), 2. See Tarbell, Ida M., *The History of the Standard Oil Company,* vol. 1 (Gloucester, MA: Peter Smith, 1963), 5. See Giddens, 14, 58–59. Miller, 402.

8. See Darrah, 2–3. Miller, 394. Tarbell, vol. 1, 10, 12. See photo, "The Drake Oil Well in 1859—The First Oil Well," Tarbell, vol. 1, 10f.

9. Tarbell, vol. 1, 12–20, 30–34. Rezneck, 64, 65. Giddens, 30. Miller, 394–395.

10. See Tarbell, vol. 1, 30–33. Miller, 391.

11. Darrah, 3. Giddens, 83, 86, 87, 114. See "Table of Yearly and Monthly Average Price of Refined," Tarbell, vol. 2, 384–385.

12. Lloyd, H. D., "Story of a Great Monopoly," *Atlantic Monthly,* vol. 47 (Mar 1881), 317–334. Giddens, 100. Rezneck, 64. Tarbell, vol. 2, 395. See Giddens, 101–113. See report, "Yearly Production of Crude Petroleum of the Principal Oil Producing Countries Since 1900," ca. Jan 1918: PRO CAB21/119.

13. Montague, Gilbert Holland, "The Rise and Supremacy of the Standard Oil Company," *Quarterly Journal of Economics,* vol. 16 (1902), 267. Rezneck, 65. See Giddens, 101–113.

14. Darrah, 32, 38, 40–42, 60–61, 77, 231, 232. See Montague, 266. See Tarbell, vol. 1, 24–25. See photo, "Holmden Street, Pithole, August, 1895," Giddens, 136f. See Giddens, 139–140.

15. Tarbell, vol. 1, 43–44. See Montague, 265–292.

16. McKay, John P., "Baku Oil and Transcaucasian Pipelines 1883–1891: A Study in Tsarist Economic Policy," *Slavic Review,* vol. 43 (1984), 606. "Petroleum Developments in Foreign Countries," *Science,* New Series, vol. 41, no. 1050 (12 Feb 1915), 250–251. "The Oil Wells of Baku," *Science,* vol. 7, no. 158 (Feb 12, 1886), 149–150.

17. "The Oil Wells," 149–150. McKay, 606, 609. See Hewins, Ralph, *Mr. Five per cent: The Biography of Calouste Gulbenkian* (London: Hutchinson & Co. Ltd., 1957), 23–24. See Hitti, 292. See Maunsell, F. R., "The Mesopotamian Petroleum Field," *Geographical Journal,* vol. 9 (1897), 531–532.

18. "The Oil Wells," 149. Hewins, 23–24. McKay, 607. Gulbenkian, Calouste Sarkis, *La Transcaucasie et la Peninsule D'Apcheron: Souvenirs de Voyage, 1890* (Lisbon, Calouste Gulbenkian Foundation, 1989), 274.

19. Ferrier, R. W., *The History of the British Petroleum Company,* vol. 1, *The Developing Years, 1901–1932* (Cambridge, UK: Cambridge University Press, 1982), 4. Gulbenkian, *Transcaucasie,* 186, 199, 202, 203, 218. McKay, 607. Hewins, 23.

20. Gulbenkian, *Transcaucasie,* 186, 246. Hewins, 20–21, 22.

21. Gulbenkian, *Transcaucasie,* 219.

22. Gulbenkian Foundation, *Calouste Sarkis Gulbenkian: The Man and His Achievements* (Lisbon, Portugal: Calouste Gulbenkian Foundation, 1999), 5. See Hewins, xiv, 12.

23. Gulbenkian, C. S., "Memoirs of Calouste Sarkis Gulbenkian with Particular Relation to the Origins and Foundation of the Iraq Petroleum Company Limited," Sep 16, 1945: NA RG 59 890.G.6363/3-148, 3. Hewins, 7, 8.

24. Gulbenkian Foundation, 5–6. Hewins, 12.

25. Hewins, 4–5, 13.

26. Hewins, 14–15. Gulbenkian, "Memoirs," 3. Gulbenkian Foundation, 9.

27. Gulbenkian, "Memoirs," 3. Gulbenkian, *Transcaucasie,* 186, 218–219, 225, 226, 229. Hewins, 23–25.

28. Gulbenkian, *Transcaucasie,* 226.

29. Gulbenkian, *Transcaucasie,* xxxi. Hewins, 27. Gulbenkian, "Memoirs," 3.

30. Gulbenkian, "Memoirs," 3. Hewins, 29–30. Longrigg, Stephen H., *The Origins and Early History of the Iraq Petroleum Company, Known from 1912 to 1929 as the Turkish Petroleum Company* (BP Archives, 1968), 13.

31. Telegram, Ambassador Davis to Charles E. Hughes, Mar 1, 1921: NA RG 59 800.6363/229, *FRUS* 1921 vol. 2, 81. Sultan Abdulhamid II, Decree of Transfer, Apr 8, 1889 (5 Chaban 1306), BP IPC 174-530A. Longrigg, Stephen H., *Four Centuries of Modern Iraq* (Oxford: Clarendon Press, 1925), 355. Gulbenkian, "Memoirs," 3. Longrigg, *Oil,* 12–13. Hewins, 29–30.

32. See letter, John D. Archbold to John D. Rockefeller, Jul 6, 1886: RF 1, box 51, fol. 378. See Pugach, Noel H., "Standard Oil and Petroleum Development in Early Republican China," *Business History Review,* vol. 45 (1971), 452–453. See Ferrier, 1, 259–260, 548. Generally see Tarbell, vols. 1 and 2.

33. Ferrier, 1. Longrigg, *Oil,* 12. Bishop, Michele G., "History of Exploration," *Petroleum Systems of the Northwest Java Province, Java and Offshore Southeast Sumatra, Indonesia,* U.S. Geological Survey Open-File Report 99-50R, 2000, www.usgs.gov.

34. See Jones, G. Gareth, "The British Government and the Oil Companies 1912–1924: The Search for an Oil Policy," *Historical Journal,* vol. 20 (1973), 647–648. Fielden, Ralph, "The Romance of Shell," *Great Britain and the East,* Nov 1958, cxxxvii. Miles, Lebron, "A Shell's Tale," *Insight,* vol. 4, no. 2 (Q2 2003), 19–20. "History of Shell," www.shell.com. See Moody-Stuart, Mark, "A Lasting Commitment—The Royal Dutch/Shell Group in Asia," Apr 1998, and "Protect Our Marine Environment—Globally," Jan 2001, www.shell.com. Ferrier, 4–5. Longrigg, *Oil,* 16–17.

35. Jacobs, Stefan, and Mirik Kania, "The Lubricants Industry in Poland," presentation, Union Indépendante de l'Industrie Européennne des Lubrifants, European Meeting, Budapest, Oct 25, 2002, www.ueil.org. "Tale of the Family Tree," ca. 1950: BP 90030, 1. "Drohobycz: The Petroleum Industry," www.jewishgen.org.

36. Youngquist, Walter, "Survey of Energy Resources, 2001: Country Notes—Australia," World Energy Council, www.worldenergy.org. See "Petroleum Resources Exploration," www.geoscience.gov.au. Lishmund, S. R., ed., "Report No. 30: Oil Shale," Department of Mines, Geological Survey of New South Wales, 1971, 5. Stanley, David, "Oil Springs and Petrolia," www.authorsden.com. See "Drohobycz: The Petroleum Industry."

37. Bright, Arthur A., Jr., *The Electric-Lamp Industry: Technological Change and Economic Development from 1800 to 1947* (New York: Macmillan Company, 1949), 70–71, 71n3. Rezneck, 64.

38. Longrigg, *Origins,* 9. Ferrier, 18–19.

39. Ferrier, 24. Longrigg, *Oil,* 14, 17. See Tarbell, vol. 2, 210, 211.

40. Thornton, A. P., "British Policy in Persia, 1858–1890 Part I," *English Historical Review,* vol. 69 (1954), 560, 561. See Farmayan, Hafez, "Portrait of a Nineteenth-Century Iranian Statesman: The Life and Times of Grand Vizier Amin ud-Dawlah, 1844–1904," *International Journal of Middle Eastern Studies,* vol. 15 (1983), 338. Longrigg, *Oil,* 14. Ferrier, 24.

41. Letter, Lepel Griffin to Earl of Rosebery, Dec 6, 1893: PRO FO60/576 as cited by Ferrier, 26. Ferrier, 26. See Thornton, "British Policy," 561n1.

42. Palmer, Alan, *The Decline and Fall of the Ottoman Empire* (New York: M. Evans & Co., 1992), 128. Lord Kinross, *The Ottoman Centuries: The Rise and Fall of the Turkish Empire* (New York: William Morrow & Co., 1977), 509. Quataert, Donald, *The Ottoman Empire, 1700–1922* (Cambridge, UK: Cambridge University Press, 2000), 71–72. See Anderson, Olive, "II: Great Britain and the Beginnings of the Ottoman Public Debt, 1854–55," *Historical Journal,* vol. 7 (1964), 47–51. See Longrigg, *Four Centuries,* 277–278.

43. "The Life of Midhat Pasha: An Illustrious Chief of Young Turkey," *New York Times* (*NYT*), Aug 31, 1877, 2. "Death of Midhat Pasha; The Career of the Great Reformer in Turkey," *NYT,* May 12, 1884, 5. Shaw, Stanford J., and Ezel Kural Shaw, *The History of the Ottoman Empire and Modern Turkey,* vol. 2, *Reform, Revolution, and Republic: The Rise of Modern Turkey, 1808–1975* (Cambridge, UK: Cambridge University Press, 1977), 67. Saliba, Najib E., "The Achievements of Midhat Pasha as Governor of the Province of Syria, 1878–1880," *International Journal of Middle East Studies,* vol. 9, no. 3 (Oct 1978), 307, 307n3. Hitti, 738.

44. Nakash, Yitzhak, *The Shi'is of Iraq* (Princeton, NJ: Princeton University Press, 1994), 32–34. Tripp, Charles, *A History of Iraq* (Cambridge, UK: Cambridge University Press, 2000), 16–17, 18. Farouk-Sluglett, Marion and Peter Sluglett, "The Transformation of Land Tenure and Rural Social Structure in Central and Southern Iraq, c. 1870–1958," *International Journal of Middle East Studies,* vol. 15 (1983), 492–495. Longrigg, *Four Centuries,* 298–300, 306–307.

45. Longrigg, *Four Centuries,* 299, 316. Nakash, 198. See Nakash, 184–186. See Shaw and Shaw, 68.

46. Palmer, 139, 147. Hitti, 738. Kinross, 515–516. See Longrigg, *Four Centuries,* 300.

47. "The Ottoman Constitution, Promulgated the 7th Zilbrije 1923 (December 11/23, 1876)," included in Dispatch No. 113, Dec 26, 1876, MS Records, Department of State as reproduced in *American Journal of International Law,* vol. 2, no. 4, supplement: Official Documents (Oct 1908), 367–387. See Shaw and Shaw, 166, 174–175.

48. Saliba, 317–318.

49. "The Murder of Abdul Aziz; An Attempt to Arrest Midhat Pasha—Taking Refuge at a Consulate," *NYT,* May 18, 1881. 2. "Death of Midhat Pasha." Saliba, 317–318. Shaw and Shaw, 180. Kinross, 529.

50. Shaw and Shaw, 216. "He Tells of a Murder; Former Sergeant in the Turkish Army Says That Midhat Pasha Was Strangled to Death," *NYT,* Feb 14, 1897, 15.

51. "He Tells of a Murder."

52. "He Tells of a Murder." Shaw and Shaw, 216.

53. Sultan Abdulhamid II, Decree of Transfer, Apr 8, 1889 (5 Chaban 1306): BP IPC 174-530A. Sultan Abdulhamid II, Decree of Transfer, Sep 24, 1898 (5 Diamazi-ul-Ewell 1316): BP IPC 174-530A. Earle, Edward Meade, "The Turkish Petroleum Company—A Study in Oleaginous Diplomacy," *Political Science Quarterly,* vol. 39 (1924), 266. See Longrigg, *Oil,* 27, 28.

CHAPTER 7: THE RACE TO MONOPOLIZE

1. Sumida, Jon Tetsuro, "British Naval Administration and Policy in the Age of Fisher," *The Journal of Military History,* vol. 54, no. 1 (Jan 1990), 3–4. See Jones, Archer, and Andrew J. Keogh, "The Dreadnought Revolution: Another Look,"

Military Affairs, vol. 49 (1985), 124–131. Ferrier, R. W., *The History of the British Petroleum Company*, vol. 1; *The Developing Years, 1901–1932* (Cambridge, UK: Cambridge University Press, 1982), 10. See photo, "Coaling Ship, 1910," Ritchie, Berry, *Portrait in Oil: An Illustrated History of BP* (London: James & James Publishers Ltd., 1995), 28. Miller, Geoffrey, *Straits: British Policy Towards the Ottoman Empire and the Origins of the Dardanelles Campaign* (Hull, UK: University of Hull, 1997), 424.

2. See report, "Yearly Production of Crude Petroleum of the Principal Oil Producing Countries Since 1900," ca. Jan 1918: PRO CAB21/119. See letter, Francis Hopwood to W. S. Churchill, ca. Mar 1912: PRO CAB1/33. See Tarbell, Ida M., *The History of the Standard Oil Company*, vol. 2 (Gloucester, MA: Peter Smith, 1963), 270–274. Longrigg, Stephen H., *The Origins and Early History of the Iraq Petroleum Company, Known from 1912 to 1929 as the Turkish Petroleum Company* (BP Archives, 1968), 18. See Miller, 424, 426. Ferrier, 1–3. See table, "World Crude Oil Production 1900–1932," Ferrier, 638.

3. Letter, Sir H. Drummond Wolff to Lord Salisbury, Jun 30, 1890: PRO FO511. Ferrier, 24, 25, 27.

4. See confidential letter, Sir Arthur Hardinge to Lord Lansdowne, Feb 1, 1902: PRO FO60/660. See letter, Sir Arthur Hardinge to Lord Lansdowne, Feb 16, 1902: PRO FO60/660. See Ferrier, 28–29.

5. "Petroleum Concession Granted by the Persian Government to William Knox D'Arcy, May 28, 1901," as reproduced in NA RG59 891.6363/16, *FRUS* 1920, vol. 3, 347–351. Longrigg, Stephen H., *Oil in the Middle East: Its Discovery and Development* (London: Oxford University Press, 1968), 17. Ferrier, 29, 35.

6. "Petroleum Concession," 348. See photo, "Concession Agreement," Ritchie, 10. Letter, William Knox D'Arcy to Lord Lansdowne, Jun 27, 1901: PRO FO248/733. See letter, Foreign Office to W. K. D'Arcy, Jul 9, 1901: PRO FO284/733.

7. Longrigg, *Oil*, 18. See Ferrier, 3–4, 33, 57. Longrigg, *Origins*, 27. Report, Boverton Redwood, Jul 30, 1901: BP H17/96, as cited by Ferrier, 55.

8. See photo, "Bakhtiari Guards," Ritchie, 15. Longrigg, *Oil*, 18. Ferrier, 55–58, 74.

9. Paul Ghrostopnine, "Report on Oil-Wells in Mesopotamia," attachment to letter, Rear Adm. Mark Bristol, U.S. High Commissioner, to Secretary of State, Apr 27, 1920: NA RG59 800.6363/135. See Letter, Murrietta and Company to Capt. E. Atkin, Dec 4, 1911: PRO FO371/1263. Longrigg, *Origins*, 14. See Longrigg, *Oil*, 14.

10. Lord Kinross, *The Ottoman Centuries: The Rise and Fall of the Turkish Empire* (New York: William Morrow & Co., 1977), 565–566. Longrigg, *Origins*, 17. Letter, Arminius Vambery to Thomas Sanderson, Nov 28, 1898: PRO FO800/33 as cited by Miller, 8. See photo, "State Visit to Jerusalem of Wilhelm II of Germany in 1898," Matson Collection, LC-DIG-matpc-04610, www.loc.gov. See photo, "The Jaffa Gate," *Encylopaedia Judaica*, 1,427.

11. "The Baghdad Railroad Convention, 5 March 1903," Cd. 5635 (1911), 37–48 as reproduced in J. C. Hurewitz, ed., *Diplomacy in the Near and Middle East*, vol. 1, *1535–1914* (Gerrards Cross, UK: Archive Editions, 1987), 252–263. Longrigg, *Oil*, 27. Longrigg, *Origins*, 35. Kent, Marian, *Oil and Empire: British Policy and Mesopotamian Oil, 1900–1920* (London: Macmillan Press Ltd., 1976), 16.

12. Rohrbach, Paul, *Bagdadbahn* (Berlin: Wiegandt & Grieben, 1911) as quoted by Schonfield, Hugh, *The Suez Canal in Peace and War, 1869–1969* (Coral Gables, FL: University of Miami Press, 1969), 62–63.

13. Rohrbach, 43–44 as quoted by Kent, *Oil*, 16.

14. "Agreement by the Shaikh of Kuwait Regarding the Non-reception of Foreign Representatives and the Non-cession of Territory to Foreign Powers or Subjects, 23rd January 1899," *The Road to Independence*, Al-Diwan Al-Amiri, State of Kuwait web site. "Exclusive Agreement: The Kuwayti Shaykh and Britain, 23 January 1899," as reproduced in Hurewitz, vol. 1, 218–219. Tetreault, Mary Ann, "Autonomy, Necessity, and the Small State: Ruling Kuwait in the Twentieth Century," *International Organization*, vol. 45 (1991), 570–575. See Rush, Alan deLacy, ed., *Records of Kuwait, 1899–1961*, vol. 1 (London: Archive International, 1989), 149, as cited by Tetreault, 575. See Longrigg, *Oil*, 26.

15. "The Baghdad Railroad Convention, 5 March 1903." See Longrigg, *Oil*, 27. See generally Earle, Edward Mead, *Turkey, the Great Powers, and the Baghdad Railway: A Study in Imperialism* (New York: Macmillan Company, 1923).

16. "Contrat Entre le Ministère Impérial de la Liste Civile et la Société du Chemin de Fer Ottoman D'Anatolie Concernant les Oisments Pétrolifièrers en Mesopotamie," Jul 4/17, 1904: PRO FO371/344 no. 36290. See Longrigg, *Oil*, 27–28. See Kent, *Oil*, 161–162. See Longrigg, *Origins*, 240–241.

17. Jack, Marian, "The Purchase of the British Government's Shares in the British Petroleum Company 1912–1914," *Past and Present*, no. 39 (Apr 1968), 140, 140n1, 141. "Summary of Investigations of the Committee Dealing with the Supply of Oil Fuel for His Majesty's Ships with Notes on Subsequent Action," Contract Department, Admiralty, Sep 1907: May ms, NMM MAY 6, as cited by Miller, 424. Miller, 424.

18. Ferrier, 59, 68, 70–72. See Ferrier, 42–73.

19. Gulbenkian, C. S., "Memoirs of Calouste Sarkis Gulbenkian with Particular Relation to the Origins and Foundation of the Iraq Petroleum Company Limited," Sep 16, 1945: NA RG59 890.G.6363/3-148, 3–4. Longrigg, *Oil*, 28. "Statement of D'Arcy Exploration Company's Claim to Mesopotamian Oil Concession," Nov 12, 1918: BP 100687.

20. Nichols, H. E., "Demand to the Sultan, 21st July, 1904," trans., as quoted by Longrigg, *Origins*, 242–243.

21. Nichols, Longrigg, *Origins*, 242–243.

22. Letter, Ohannès Effendi Sakisan (Minister of the Civil List) to Ottoman Railway Company of Anatolia, Jul 26/Aug 8, 1905, no. 320 (letter 1), as reproduced in Kent, *Oil*, 163. "Contrat."

23. Sakisian to Ottoman Railway Company, Jul 26/Aug 8, 1905.

24. Letter, M. Huguenin to Ohannès Effendi Sakisian, Sep 4, 1905, no. 2114 (letter 2), as reproduced in Kent, *Oil*, 163–164. Earle, *Turkey*, 63.

25. Huguenin to Sakisian, Sep 4, 1905.

26. Letter, Ohannès Effendi Sakisan to Ottoman Railway Company of Anatolia, Oct 9/22, 1905, no. 442 (letter 3), as reproduced in Kent, *Oil*, 164.

27. See letter, Edward Atkin to Secretary of State, Jan 5, 1912: PRO FO371/1487. See minutes, Jan 12, 1912: PRO FO371/1487 no. 911. See Ferrier, 72–73. Miller, 425.

28. Quataert, Donald, *The Ottoman Empire, 1700–1922* (Cambridge, UK: Cambridge University Press, 2000), 76–78. Longrigg, Stephen H., *Four Centuries of Modern Iraq* (Oxford: Clarendon Press, 1925), 108, 279–280. Earle, *Turkey*, 10–11, 24n3, 25n4. See Earle, *Turkey*, 95–96. See letter, Aristarchi Bey to Hamilton Fish, no. 314, Sep 29, 1875: *FRUS* 1876, 591–592.

29. Gulbenkian, "Memoirs," 4.

30. Letter, Ohannès Effendi Sakisan to Ottoman Railway Company of Anatolia, Jul 13/26, 1906, no. 233 (letter 4), as reproduced in Kent, *Oil*, 164.
31. Letter, Ohannès Effendi Sakisan to Ottoman Railway Company of Anatolia, Jul 27/Aug 9, 1906, no. 355 (letter 5), as reproduced in Kent, *Oil*, 165. Letter, M. Huguenin to Ohannès Effendi Sakisian, Aug 22, 1906, no. 2162 (letter 6), as reproduced in Kent, *Oil*, 165.
32. Letter, Ohannès Effendi Sakisan to Ottoman Railway Company of Anatolia, Oct 11/24, 1906, no. 556 (letter 7), as reproduced in Kent, *Oil*, 166. "Draft of Contract," ca. Nov 1906, as reproduced in Longrigg, *Origins*, 244–248.
33. Letter, M. Huguenin to Ohannès Effendi Sakisian, Feb 9, 1907, no. 354 (letter 10), as reproduced in Kent, *Oil*, 167–168. Letter, Ohannès Effendi Sakisan to Board of Ottoman Railway Company of Anatolia, Feb 19/Mar 4, 1907, no. 753 (letter 11), as reproduced in Kent, *Oil*, 168–169.
34. Huguenin to Sakisian, Feb 9, 1907. Sakisian to Board of Ottoman Railway Company of Anatolia, Feb 19/Mar 4, 1907.
35. Letter, N. R. O'Conor to Arthur Hardinge, Oct 16, 1907: PRO FO371/343 no. 12713.
36. Longrigg, *Origins*, 22–23, 39. "Agreement between S. E. Hubib Effendi Melhamé and Col. Thomas English," Nov 9/27, 1901, as reproduced in Longrigg, *Origins*, 235–238.
37. Gulbenkian, "Memoirs," 6. Hewins, Ralph, *Mr. Five per cent: The Biography of Calouste Gulbenkian* (London: Hutchinson & Co. Ltd., 1957), 71. See Kent, *Oil*, 22.
38. Gulbenkian, "Memoirs," 7.
39. Letter, Gilchrist Walker & Co. to H. E. Nichols, Aug 27, 1907, as reproduced in Longrigg, *Origins*, 249–250.
40. Longrigg, *Origins*, 44.
41. "Memorandum of Association of the Anglo-Persian Oil Company, Limited," Apr 14, 1909: BP 90423. Ferrier, 67, 86–88. Miller, 425. Ritchie, 19.
42. See "The Ottoman Constitution, Promulgated the 7th Zilbridje 1293 (December 11/23, 1876)," included in Dispatch no. 113, Dec 26, 1876, MS Records, Department of State, as reproduced in *American Journal of International Law*, vol. 2, no. 4, suppl.: Official Documents (Oct 1908), 367–387. Shaw, Stanford J., and Ezel Kural Shaw, *The History of the Ottoman Empire and Modern Turkey*, vol. 2, *Reform, Revolution, and Republic: The Rise of Modern Turkey, 1808–1975* (Cambridge, UK: Cambridge University Press, 1977), 255–256, 257.
43. "The Turkish Transformation," *Washington Post (WP)*, Aug 3, 1908, 6. "New Turkish Cabinet," *NYT*, Aug 6, 1908, 3. "Young Turks in Control," *NYT*, Aug 7, 1908, 4. "Turkey in New Guise," Aug 9, 1908. *WP*, 6. "The Turkish Situation," Aug 9, 1908. *WP*, E4. Shaw and Shaw, 266–267. See Longrigg, *Origins*, 44.
44. Miller, 28–29.
45. See Hansen, Bent, "Interest Rates and Foreign Capital in Egypt Under Foreign Occupation," *Journal of Economic History*, vol. 43 (1983), 867–868. Baster, Albert, "The Origins of British Banking Expansion in the Near East," *Economic History Review*, vol. 5, no. 1 (Oct 1943), 76–86. See Longrigg, *Oil*, 14–15.
46. Kent, Marian, "Agent of Empire? The National Bank of Turkey and British Foreign Policy," *Historical Journal*, vol. 18, no. 2 (Jun 1975), 367–389. See Earle, Edward Meade, "The Turkish Petroleum Company—A Study in Oleaginous Diplomacy," *Political Science Quarterly*, vol. 39 (1924), 265–279. Longrigg, *Origins*, 28, 52. Gulbenkian, "Memoirs," 8–9.

47. See Gulbenkian Foundation, *Calouste Sarkis Gulbenkian: The Man and His Achievements* (Lisbon, Portugal: Calouste Gulbenkian Foundation, 1999), 10. See C. S. Gulbenkian's British passport, June 1902, as reproduced in Gulbenkian Foundation, 11. Gulbenkian, "Memoirs," 6, 8–9. See Kent, "Agent of Empire."

48. Correspondence, Marcus Samuel and Robert Waley-Cohen, ca. 1909: PRO FO371/777 nos. 28640, 28858, 31930, 32301, as cited by Kent, *Oil*, 24. Correspondence, Louis Mallet and William D'Arcy, Aug–Sep 1909: PRO FO371/77 no. 32838, as cited by Kent, *Oil*, 24. See Kent, *Oil*, 24. See Kent, "Agent of Empire," 379–380, 384–385.

49. Letter to Charles Marling, Sep 30, 1912, PRO FO800/358, 393–395. Note, Hardinge to Grey, Nov 20, 1908: PRO FO371/549 no. 45717. Correspondence, Samuel and Waley-Cohen. Kent, "Agent of Empire." Kent, *Oil*, 24.

50. Longrigg, *Origins*, 44–46. See "The Baghdad-Basra Concessions Limited," private and confidential memo, ca. 1908: PRO FO371/1263.

51. Longrigg, *Origins*, 44–46. See "The Baghdad Railroad Convention."

52. Longrigg, *Origins*, 45–46.

53. Longrigg, *Origins*, 45–46.

54. Longrigg, *Origins*, 46–47.

55. Marquise de Fontenoy, "Guns Trained on Sultan's Palace," *WP*, Apr 3, 1909, 6. "Sultan Has Earned Name of Assassin," *New York Times (NYT)*, Apr 20, 1909, 2. "Young Turks Decree Death to the Sultan," *NYT*, Apr 20, 1909, 1. Stephen Bonsal, "The Red Sultan," *NYT*, Apr 25, 1909, SM2. Miller, 65–66. See Shaw and Shaw, 280–282.

56. "Dispatch Escapes Censors," *NYT*, Apr 17, 1909, 1. Longrigg, *Origins*, 47. Shaw and Shaw, 280, 281–282.

57. "Sultan Must Quit," *NYT*, Apr 20, 1909, 1. "Abdul Awaits Fate; Young Turks Have Not Told What They Will Do," *NYT*, Apr 21, 1909, 1. McCullagh, Frances, "Sultan Beaten; Capital Falls; 6,000 Are Slain," *NYT*, Apr 25, 1909. Shaw and Shaw, 279–280. See Longrigg, *Origins*, 47.

58. See Longrigg, *Origins*, 47.

59. "Abdul Hamid Deposed," *NYT*, Apr 28, 1909, 8. McCullagh, Frances, "Abdul Hamid is Deposed; Mehmed V Rules," *NYT*, Apr 28, 1909, 1. "Deposition of Sultan Abdul Hamid and Accession to the Throne of Mohammed V," paraphrase of telegram, Ambassador Leishman to Secretary of State, Apr 27, 1909: File no. 10044/167, *FRUS* 1909, 581. Letter, Ambassador H. Kiazim to Secretary of State, Apr 27, 1909: File no. 10044/174, *FRUS* 1909, 581.

60. "Sultan to Pay Young Turks' Bills," *NYT*, Apr 27, 1909, 2. "Abdul Not to Be Tried," *NYT*, Apr 29, 1909, 1. "250 Mutiny Leaders Executed in Turkey," *NYT*, Apr 30, 1909, 1. "Young Turks Suspend Siege in Honor of New Sultan," *NYT*, Apr 29, 1909, 2. Longrigg, *Oil*, 28–29.

61. "The Baghdad-Basrah Concessions Limited," confidential memo, ca. Nov 1911: PRO FO371/1263 no. 48964. Longrigg, *Oil*, 29. Longrigg, *Origins*, 47.

62. Longrigg, *Oil*, 29–30. Longrigg, *Origins*, 47–48.

63. Longrigg, *Origins*, 48. Kent, *Oil*, 22–23.

64. "Oilfields in Mesopotamia," confidential summary of correspondence, Dec 1911–Jan 1912, Jan 26, 1926: PRO FO371/1487 no. 911. Memo, Apr 6, 1912: PRO FO371/1487 no. 911. Letter, Gerard Lowther to Edward Grey, Oct 13, 1912: PRO FO371/1487 no. 911. Kent, *Oil*, 22–23. See Longrigg, *Origins*, 66–67, 68–75.

65. Kent, *Oil*, 23, 24, 218n45.

66. Winston Churchill, "Oil Fuel Supply for His Majesty's Navy," report, Jun 16, 1913: PRO CAB/115/39. Adm. Fisher to Winston Churchill, Dec 10, 1911, *WSC Comp.*, vol. 2, pt. 3, *1926–1927*, as cited by Miller, 425. Ferrier, 13, 163. See letter, W. S. Churchill to Lord Fisher, Jun 11, 1912, as quoted by Randolph S. Churchill, *Winston S. Churchill*, vol. 2, *1904–1914, Young Statesman* (Boston: Houghton Mifflin, 1967), 590.

67. Ferrier, 132–134, 135, 139–140, 148–149, 162–163. See photos, "SS *Anatolia*, First Vessel Alongside Abadan, 1909," "Laying the Pipeline, 1910," Ferrier, 131, 133. Ritchie, 22–24, 25. See photo, "A Group of Bahktiari," Ritchie, 22.

68. Churchill, W., "Oil Fuel Supply for His Majesty's Navy." Ferrier, 163.

69. Letter, Winston Churchill to John Fisher, Jun 11, 1912, as reproduced in Churchill, Randolph, 590–591.

70. Ferrier, 150. Ritchie, 25. Admiralty memo on adequacy of supplies of oil, Mar 18, 1913: PRO ADM116/1209, vol. 3, 44–45.

71. Questions to Marcus Samuel, "First Report of the Royal Commission on Fuel and Engines," Adm. Fisher, Chairman, Sep 1912–Jan 1913: PRO ADM116/1208. Questions to Charles Greenway, "First Report."

72. Louis Mallet, memo, Nov 15, 1912: PRO FO371/1486 no. 48688. Questions to Greenway, "First Report."

73. Louis Mallet, minute sheet, Nov 1912: PRO FO371/1486 no. 55654, as quoted by Jack, 147.

74. Confidential letter, Louis Mallet to Charles Greenway, Feb 5, 1913: PRO FO371/1760 no. 2463. See confidential letter, Foreign Office to India Office, Feb 5, 1913: PRO FO371/1760 no. 2463.

75. Louis Mallet, memo, Nov 6, 1912: PRO FO371/1486 no. 47846. Jack, 142n9.

76. Questions to Greenway, "First Report."

77. Admiralty memo on adequacy of supplies of oil, Mar 18, 1913. See "For British Navy's Oil," *NYT*, Jun 17, 1914, 4.

78. Winston Churchill, Secret Admiralty memo, Jun 16, 1913: PRO CAB37/115.

79. Confidential letter, Charles Marling to Edward Grey, Jul 27, 1912: PRO FO371/1486 no. 637. Confidential letter, Louis Mallet to Henry Babington-Smith, Aug 12, 1912: PRO FO371/1486 no. 637.

CHAPTER 8: MR. FIVE PERCENT

1. Lodwick, John, with D. H. Young, *Gulbenkian: An Interpretation of "The Richest Man in the World"* (Garden City, NY: Doubleday & Company, 1958), 41–42.

2. Gulbenkian, Nubar, *Portrait in Oil: The Autobiography of Nubar Gulbenkian* (New York: Simon & Schuster, 1965), 17–19, 22.

3. Gulbenkian Foundation, *Calouste Sarkis Gulbenkian: The Man and His Achievements* (Lisbon, Portugal: Calouste Gulbenkian Foundation, 1999), 13–14, 17–18.

4. Gulbenkian, Nubar, 38–39.

5. Gulbenkian, Nubar, 96. Gulbenkian, C. S., "Memoirs of Calouste Sarkis Gulbenkian with Particular Relation to the Origins and Foundation of the Iraq Petroleum Company Limited," Sep 16, 1945: NA RG59 890.G.6363/3-148, 11.

6. Gulbenkian, C. S., 15. Also see letter, N. Gulbenkian to Under Secretary of State, Feb 3, 1938: PRO WO371/21855 no. 19238. Also see Williams, "Claim of Mr. N. Gulbenkian against the Iraqi Government," memorandum, Feb 4, 1938: PRO WO371/21855 no. 19238. Also see letter, Baggallay to Gulbenkian, N., Feb 10,

1938: PRO WO371/21855 no. 19238. Also see letter, Gulbenkian, N. to Under Secretary of State, Feb 15, 1938: PRO WO371/21855 no. 19238. Also see "Gulbenkian case," memorandum, Feb 15, 1938: PRO WO371/21855 no. 19238. Also see letter, Hugh Montgomery to Baggallay, Feb 23, 1938: PRO WO371/21855 no. 19238.

7. Longrigg, Stephen H., *The Origins and Early History of the Iraq Petroleum Company, Known from 1912 to 1929 as the Turkish Petroleum Company* (BP Archives, 1968), 55, 71–72. "History of the IPC and Mr. Gulbenkian's Part in Its Foundation," Apr 1944: BP 27508, 1–2. Gulbenkian, C. S., 7–11.

8. Longrigg, *Origins,* 28. Gulbenkian, C. S., 7–12.

9. "History of the IPC," 2. Gulbenkian, C. S., 9. See Longrigg, *Origins,* 252–256.

10. Gulbenkian, C. S., 8–12. Kent, Marian, *Oil and Empire: British Policy and Mesopotamian Oil, 1900–1920,* London: Macmillan Press Ltd., 1976, 36. Note from Mallet to Grey, Sep 10, 1912: Grey mss, PRO FO800/93, as cited by Kent, *Oil,* 36.

11. Nicolson to Marling (charge), private, Sep 30, 1912: Nicolson mss, PRO FO800/358, as cited by Miller, Geoffrey, *Straits: British Policy Towards the Ottoman Empire and the Origins of the Dardanelles Campaign* (Hull, UK: University of Hull, 1997), 428.

12. Longrigg, *Origins,* 59–60, 253–256.

13. Longrigg, *Origins,* 59–60, 257.

14. Longrigg, *Origins,* 60, 257–259.

15. Longrigg, *Origins,* 60. Gulbenkian, C.S., 10.

16. Kent, *Oil,* 37.

17. See Johnson, David, "Balkan Wars," essay.

18. Jack, Marian, "The Purchase of the British Government's Shares in the British Petroleum Company 1912–1914," *Past and Present,* no. 39 (Apr 1968), 149.

19. Gulbenkian, C. S., 10.

20. Longrigg, *Origins,* 60, 260.

21. Longrigg, *Origins,* 61–62.

22. Letter, Foreign Office (FO) to the Admiralty, Nov 15, 1912: PRO FO371/1486 no. 40516.

23. Immediate and confidential letter, Mallet to India Office (IO), Dec 9, 1912: FO371/1486 no. 51935.

24. Immediate and confidential letter, Admiralty to FO, Dec 28, 1912: FO371/1486 no. 55654.

25. Telegram, Sir Edward Grey to Sir G Lowther, no. 1092R, Dec 6, 1912: FO371/1486 no. 51845.

26. Private letter from Lowther to Maxwell, Dec 11, 1912: FO371/1486 no. 53729.

27. Lowther to Maxwell.

28. Dumas, diary entry, Jan 7, 1913: IWM PP/MCR/96, as cited by Miller, 428.

29. "Royal Commission on Oil Fuel, Second Report, Evidence of Mr. H. W. A. Deterding," Feb 26, 1913: PRO ADM116/1209.

30. "Admiralty memorandum as to the adequacy of supplies of oil," Mar 18, 1913: PRO ADM116/1209, vol. 3.

31. Kent, *Oil,* 50–53.

32. Shell files, MEP 102, as cited by Kent, *Oil,* 53. "Extracts from Documents Bearing on Claims by, and the Position of, the Turkish Petroleum Company": Shell files, MEP 20, as cited by Kent, *Oil,* 53.

33. Kent, *Oil,* 51, 54–57. Gulbenkian, C. S., 13. See "Extract from the Frankfurter

Zeitung," memo, Mar 5, 1914: PRO FO371/2120 no. 10028. See letter, Mallet to Grey, Mar 10, 1914: PRO FO371/2120 no. 10784. See letter, C. Greenway, to FO, Mar 10, 1914: PRO FO371/2120 no. 10880. Also see "An Agreement Made the 24th Day of June 1914," memorandum: BP 100687.

34. Sir G. Lowther to Sir Edward Grey, dispatch 349, Apr 25, 1913: FO371/1760 no. 19792.

35. Longrigg, *Origins,* 71–73.

36. Longrigg, *Origins,* 73. Kent, Marian, "Agent of Empire? The National Bank of Turkey and British Foreign Policy," *Historical Journal,* vol. 18, no. 2 (Jun 1975), 385.

37. Admiralty memo, June 16 1913: PRO Cab. 37/115. Churchill, Winston, "Oil Fuel Supply for His Majesty's Navy," Jun 16, 1913: PRO CAB37/115/39.

38. Asquith mss: Bodleian Library, Oxford vol. 7 (Cabinet Letters to the King, 1913–1914), as cited by Jack, 157.

39. Asquith mss: P.D., 5, 1913, 1v, 1474–1475, as cited by Jack, 157.

40. Kent, *Oil,* 48–49.

41. Ferrier, R.W., *The History of the British Petroleum Company,* vol. 1, *The Developing Years, 1901–1932* (Cambridge, UK: Cambridge University Press, 1982), 183. See photo, Ferrier, 194. Kent, *Oil,* 48. Slade to Churchill, Nov 8, 1913, excerpt in Admiralty memorandum for the Cabinet, Anglo-Persian Oil Company, Proposed Agreement, December 1913: PRO ADM 116/3486, as cited by Ferrier, 195. Admiralty Commission Second Interim Report, Jan 26, 1914: PRO AMD 116/3806, as cited by Ferrier, 196. See Slade, Sir J.W. et al., "Admiralty Commission on the Persian Oilfields": PRO TI/11952/20174.

42. Longrigg, *Origins,* 74, 76. Mallet to Istanbul as cited by Longrigg, *Origins,* 74.

43. "Protocol Relating to the Delimitation of the Turco-Persian Boundary Signed at Constantinople on November 4th (17th), 1913." See Barstow, "Points Discussed at the Conference," Apr 9, 1919: PRO T1/12544/18025 no. 1920.

44. Gulbenkian, C. S., 12–13. Longrigg, *Origins,* 74–75. Letter, C. Greenway to Foreign Office, Jan 31, 1914: PRO FO371/2120 no. 4452. Written minutes, "Asiatic Turkey and Arabia—Confidential," Dec 13, 1913: PRO FO321/1761 no. 54400.

45. "Asiatic Turkey and Arabia—Confidential." Ashley, minutes, "Enclosure 7 in No. 1," Nov 28, 1913: PRO FO371/1761, no. 54729.

46. Gulbenkian, C. S., 12.

47. "Asiatic Turkey and Arabia—Confidential." Parker, Alwyn, "Mesopotamian Oil Concession: Interview with Hakki Pasha Respecting Mr. Gulbenkian's Attitude in This Question," confidential minutes, Dec 10, 1913: PRO FO371/1761 no. 55859. See confidential letter and enclosure, H. Babington-Smith to Sir E. Crowe, Dec 9, 1913: PRO FO371/1761 no. 5551. Kent, *Oil,* 81–82, 85.

48. Gulbenkian, Nubar, 20.

49. "Asiatic Turkey and Arabia—Confidential."

50. Handwritten notes, "Asiatic Turkey and Arabia—Confidential," Dec 1, 1913: PRO FO321/1761 no. 54440.

51. Minutes and handwritten notes, "Asiatic Turkey and Arabia—Confidential."

52. Minutes from Sir L. Mallet to the Foreign Office, Jan 15, 1914: PRO FO371/2120 no. 2096. Confidential telegram, Sir L. Mallet to Sir Edward Grey, Jan 15, 1914: PRO FO371/2120 no. 2096.

53. Confidential letter, W. Langley to C. Greenway, Jan 16, 1914: PRO FO371/2120 no. 3468.

54. Confidential letter, C. Greenway to W. Langley, Jan 31, 1914: PRO FO371/2120 no. 4452.
55. Minutes, "Turkey—Confidential," Jan 27, 1914: PRO FO371/2120 no. 3592.
56. "Turkey—Confidential." Gulbenkian, C. S., 14.
57. Sir H. Llewellyn Smith, "Mesopotamian Oil," Feb 16, 1914: PRO FO371/2120 no. 7067.
58. Alwyn Parker, memorandum, Feb 16, 1914: PRO FO371/2120 no. 7068.
59. Parker, memo, Feb 16, 1914.
60. Admiralty memo, Churchill to Cabinet, Feb 10, 1914: PRO CAB37/119.
61. Private letter, Alwyn Parker to Percy Ashley, Mar 2, 1914: PRO FO371/2120 no. 9311.
62. Urgent and confidential letter, Alwyn Parker to Percy Ashley, Mar 5, 1914: PRO FO371/2120 no. 9869.
63. Official letter, Percy Ashley to Alwyn Parker, Mar 6, 1914: PRO FO371/2120 no. 10010. Confidential letter, FO to Sir H. Babington-Smith, Mar 6, 1914: PRO FO371/2120, no. 10010.
64. FO to Babington-Smith.
65. Gulbenkian, C. S., 13–14.
66. "Mesopotamian Oilfields," memo, March 10, 1914: PRO FO195/2456. Letter, C. Greenway to Foreign Office, March 10, 1914: PRO FO371/2120 no. 10880.
67. Letter, Grey to Mallet, March 11, 1914: PRO FO195/2456 no. 64.
68. Jack, 160–161.
69. Churchill, Winston, *The World Crisis* (New York: Scribner, 1963), 91, as cited by Miller, 462.
70. "History of the IPC," 7.
71. Gulbenkian, C. S., 14. Foreign Office, "Turkish Petroleum Concession," Mar 19, 1914: PRO FO195/2456. See Earle, Edward Mead, "The Turkish Petroleum Company—A Study in Oleaginous Diplomacy," *Political Science Quarterly,* vol. 39, no. 2 (Jun 1924), 269.
72. "Turkish Petroleum Concession."
73. "Turkish Petroleum Concession."
74. "Turkish Petroleum Concession."

CHAPTER 9: FUEL AND FUSE

1. "Turkish Petroleum Concessions: Arrangements for Fusion of the Interests in Turkish Petroleum Concessions of the D'Arcy Group and of the Turkish Petroleum Company," Mar 19, 1914: PRO TI/1195 no. 119238, and BP 174-T16A: Treaties & Agreements, pt. 1, 1917–37. Gulbenkian, C. S., "Memoirs of Calouste Sarkis Gulbenkian with Particular Relation to the Origins and Foundation of the Iraq Petroleum Company Limited," Sep 16, 1945: NA RG59 890.G.6363/3-148, 15. See Kent, Marian, *Oil and Empire: British Policy and Mesopotamian Oil, 1900–1920* (London: Macmillan Press Ltd., 1976), 59–94.
2. Gulbenkian, "Memoirs," 15.
3. Gulbenkian, "Memoirs," 14.
4. Telegram, Anglo-Persian to F. W. Stock (decrypted), Mar 20, 1914: PRO FO195/2456 no. 64. Telegram, Henry Babington-Smith to F. E. Whittall, Mar 20, 1914: PRO FO195/2456 no. 64, 281. Ernest Weakley, memo of telephone call, Mar 21, 1914: PRO FO195/2456 no. 64, 289. Telegram, H. Babington-Smith to F. E.

Whittall, Mar 23, 1914: PRO FO195/2456 no. 64, 283. "History of the IPC and Mr. Gulbenkian's Part in Its Foundation," Apr 1944: BP 27508, 8. Longrigg, Stephen H., *The Origins and Early History of the Iraq Petroleum Company, Known from 1912 to 1929 as the Turkish Petroleum Company* (BP Archives, 1968), 78–79. Telegram, Edward Grey to Louis Mallet, Mar 19, 1914: PRO FO 195/2456 no. 64.

5. Longrigg, *Origins,* 79, 81, 82, 83. Kent, *Oil,* 103–107. See "Minute re—Civil List Firmans," May 27, 1914: PRO FO195/2456 no. 64, 454. Kent, Marian, "Agent of Empire? The National Bank of Turkey and British Foreign Policy," *Historical Journal,* vol. 18, no. 2 (Jun 1975), 379–385.

6. Edward Grey, "Turkish Petroleum Concessions," memo, Apr 20, 1914: PRO FO195/2456 no. 64, 368. See "Minute re—Civil List Firmans," May 27, 1914.

7. "An Agreement, Made the Twentieth Day of May 1914," May 20, 1914: BP 99693. Winston Churchill, confidential cabinet memo, May 11, 1914: PRO CAB37/119 1914 no. 61.

8. Letter, Anglo-Persian Oil Company to the Treasury, May 20, 1914, as reproduced in Ferrier, app. 6.1, 644–645. "An Agreement," May 20, 1914. Jack, Marian, "The Purchase of the British Government's Shares in the British Petroleum Company 1912–1914," *Past and Present,* no. 39 (Apr 1968), 161–162.

9. See telegram, Eyre Crowe to Gerard Lowther, enclosure no. 1, Feb 24, 1913: PRO FO424/237 no. 237, 119, as cited by Haddad, Mahmoud, "Iraq Before World War I: A Case of Anti-European Arab Ottomanism," Rashid Khalid et al., eds., *The Origins of Arab Nationalism* (New York: Columbia University Press, 1991), 134. Longrigg, *Origins,* 82, 83. Kent, *Oil,* 109. Grey, "Turkish Petroleum Concessions."

10. Churchill, minute sheet, Jun 9, 1914: PRO CAB37/120 1914 no. 68. Miller, Geoffrey, *Straits: British Policy Towards the Ottoman Empire and the Origins of the Dardanelles Campaign* (Hull, UK: University of Hull, 1997), 460–461. "The Naval Oil Agreement; Protest by Traders," *Times,* Jun 10, 1914: PRO TI/11953 no. 119238. See "Orders of the Day: Anglo-Persian Oil Company (APOC), Acquisition of Capital," Jun 17, 1914: PRO TI/11953 no. 119238, cols. 1123–1124.

11. Churchill, "Parliamentary debate on APOC's acquisition of capital," Jun 17, 1914, *Parliamentary Debates,* vol. 63 (1914), cols. 1138, 1139.

12. Watson Rutherford, "Parliamentary debate," Jun 17, 1914, cols. 1138–1139, 1228–1229, 1232.

13. Churchill, "Parliamentary debate," Jun 17, 1914, cols. 1140, 1146.

14. Churchill, "Parliamentary debate," Jun 17, 1914, col. 1137.

15. Churchill, "Parliamentary debate," Jun 17, 1914, cols. 1152–1153.

16. George Lloyd, "Parliamentary debate," Jun 17, 1914, cols. 1156, 1159.

17. George Lloyd, "Parliamentary debate," Jun 17, 1914, col. 1155.

18. Arthur Ponsonby, "Parliamentary debate," Jun 17, 1914, col. 1174.

19. Ponsonby, "Parliamentary debate," Jun 17, 1914, col. 1178.

20. "Parliamentary debate," Jun 17, 1914, col. 1250. Letter, Charles Greenway to John Cargill, Jun 19, 1914: BP 78/63/4, as cited by Ferrier, 199.

21. "The Navy and Persian Oil," editorial, *Times,* Jun 18, 1914, 9. "Oil for British Navy; Admiralty to Contract With a Persian Company for Supply," *NYT,* May 23, 1914, C3. "For British Navy's Oil," *NYT,* Jun 17, 1914, 4. See "Producers Attack British Oil Deal," *NYT,* Jun 11, 1914. "Great Britain's Interest in Persian Oil Fields," *Wall Street Journal (WSJ),* Jun 10, 1914, 5. See also "What Fuel Oil Means to the Petroleum Industry," *WSJ,* Jun 6, 1914.

22. "The Navy and Persian Oil."
23. See Earle, Edward Meade, "The Turkish Petroleum Company—A Study in Oleaginous Diplomacy," *Political Science Quarterly,* vol. 39 (1924), 270. See Kent, 238n57.
24. Letter, Grand Vizier of Turkey to British Ambassador, Jun 28, 1914, as quoted in "History of the IPC," 8–9.
25. Grand Vizier to Ambassador, "History of the IPC," 8–9.
26. Jevtic, Borijove, "Assassination of Archduke Franz Ferdinand," ca. Jun 1914, World War I Documents Archive, www.lib.byu.edu.
27. "Memoir of Count Franz von Harrach," ca. Jun 1914, Primary Documents, First World War Online, Michael Duffy, ed., www.firstworldwar.com. Jevtic, "Assassination."
28. "Archduke Ignored Warning," Jun 28, 1914, *NYT,* 1. "Bravery of Archduke," Jun 28, 1914, *NYT,* 1. "Exchanged Dying Words," *NYT,* Jun 29, 1914, 2. Shackelford, Michael, "Assassination of Archduke Franz Ferdinand," essay, ca. Dec 2003, World War I Documents Archive.

Part Three: War and Petropolitics

CHAPTER 10: INVASION

1. "Casualty Record of Belligerents," *New York Times* (*NYT*), Jan 19, 1919, 39. "Military Casualties of World War One," Jul 2003, First World War Online, Michael Duffy, ed., www.firstworldwar.com. BBC News, "The War to End All Wars," news.bbc.co.uk. "Timeline: 1914–1918—Casualty Figures," *Trenches on the Web: An Internet History of the* Great War, The Great War Society, eds., www.worldwar1.com. See "The Cost of War," *Washington Post* (*WP*), Nov 27, 1916, 4. See "Primary Documents: D. F. Houston on U.S. War Readiness, 1917," Feb 2004, First World War Online.
2. "The Battle of the Somme, 1916," Aug 2001, First World War Online. "The Battle of Verdun, 1916," First World War Online. "The Gallipoli Front—An Overview," Aug 2002, First World War Online. BBC History, "Battle of the Somme: 1 July–13 November 1916," Mar 2002, www.bbc.co.uk. BBC History, "Daily Mirror Headlines, Published 31 July 1916," Jan 2002, www.bbc.co.uk. "At Verdun," *New York Times,* May 3, 1916, 12. See "Allied Efforts on the Somme Called 'Gallipoli on the Continent,' " *WP,* Dec 10, 1916, 5. See "How the Battle Was Won," *NYT,* Dec 17, 1916, 2. "Timeline: 1914–1918—Casualty Figures." "Military Casualties of World War One."
3. Buchanan, Sir George, *The Tragedy of Mesopotamia* (London: William Blackwood & Sons, 1938), 4–5. See map, Buchanan, 287ff. Moberly, Brigadier General F. J., *History of the Great War: The Campaign in Mesopotamia, 1914–1918,* vols. 1–3 (London: H. M. Stationery Office, 1925), 78–81. Letter, Anglo-Persian Oil Company to Sir John Bradbury, Jul 30, 1914: PRO T1/11952/20174/1916 pt 1 no. 119238. Letter, John Bradbury, Nov 27, 1914: PRO T1/11952/20174/1916 pt 1 no. 119238. H. M. Treasury resolution, Nov 27, 1914: PRO T1/11952/20174/1916 pt 1 no. 119238.
4. Moberly, vol. 1, 104. See Buchanan, 4.
5. Moberly, vol. 1, 127–128, 130–131. Buchanan, 4–5. Wilson, Sir Arnold T., *Loyalties: Mesopotamia, 1914–1917, A Personal Record* (London: Oxford University Press, 1930), 10–11.

6. "Parliamentary Debate on Anglo-Persian Oil Company's Acquisition of Capital," Jun 17, 1914, *Parliamentary Debates,* vol. 63 (1914), cols. 1131–1252. Jack, Marian, "The Purchase of the British Government's Shares in the British Petroleum Company 1912–1914," *Past and Present,* no. 39 (Apr 1968), 163. Ferrier, R. W., *The History of the British Petroleum Company,* vol. 1, *The Developing Years, 1901–1932* (Cambridge, UK: Cambridge University Press, 1982), 202.

7. See George R. I. "By the King: A Proclamation Relating to Trading with the Enemy," Jan 7, 1915: PRO T1/11730.

8. Letter, Charles Greenway to Under Secretary of State, Nov 2, 1914: PRO T1/11952/20174/1916 pt. 1 no. 119238.

9. Letter, Maurice de Bunsen to Charles Greenway, Nov 23, 1915: BP IPC 168-F4-FO Agreement Correspondence, Oct 1912–Oct 1927.

10. Letter, H. Babington-Smith to the Under Secretary of State, Oct 21 1914: PRO T1/11952/20174/1916 pt. 1 no. 119238. Letter, E. Blackwell to Secretary of the Treasury, Dec 2, 1914: PRO T1/11730. B. McKenna, letter of permission, Nov 30, 1914: PRO T1/11730.

11. Gulbenkian, C. S., "Memoirs of Calouste Sarkis Gulbenkian with Particular Relation to the Origins and Foundation of the Iraq Petroleum Company Limited," Sep 16, 1945: NA RG59 890.G.6363/3-148, 16–17. Longrigg, Stephen H., *The Origins and Early History of the Iraq Petroleum Company, Known From 1912 to 1929 as the Turkish Petroleum Company,* 90.

12. Barrow, Sir Edmund, "Military Situation in the Middle East," Jan 25, 1915: PRO CAB37/123/5. Miller, Geoffrey, *Straits: British Policy Towards the Ottoman Empire and the Origins of the Dardanelles Campaign* (Hull, UK: University of Hull, 1997), 463. See table, "World Production of Petroleum, 1913–20," Kent, Marian, *Oil and Empire: British Policy and Mesopotamian Oil, 1900–1920* (London: Macmillan Press Ltd., 1976), 202–203.

13. Letter, Hardinge to Chirol, Apr 21, 1915: Asquith ms, vol. 93, pt. 2, no. 325, as cited by Kent, *Oil,* 119.

14. Hardinge to Nicholson, Feb 4, 1915: PRO FO800/377. "Establishment of the British Protectorate Over Egypt," December 18, 1914, J. C. Hurewitz, ed., *Diplomacy in the Near and Middle East,* vol. 2 (Gerrards Cross, England: Archive Editions, 1987), 4–5. Letter, Foreign Office to Hardinge, Mar 31, 1915: PRO FO800/377. Telegram, Chargé Blake to the Secretary of State, no. 881.00/592, Dec 20, 1914: *FRUS* 1914, 923. See "Secret Notes and Private Telegram from the Viceroy regarding the Future Settlement of Eastern Turkey in Asia and Arabia," Mar 1915: FO800/377. See "Soon to Make Egypt Part of the British Empire," *NYT,* Jun 14, 1914, SM5.

15. FO to Hardinge, Mar 31, 1915.

16. Letter, Hardinge to H. M. the King-Emperor, Oct 8, 1915: Hardinge ms, vol. 105, pt. 2, as cited by Kent, 119.

17. See Dawn, C. Ernest, "The Origins of Arab Nationalism," in Rashid Khalidi et al., eds., *The Origins of Arab Nationalism* (New York: Columbia University Press, 1991), 3–23.

18. Tauber, Eliezer, *The Arab Movements in World War I* (London: Frank Cass, 1993), 1–9, 57. See Khalidi, Rashid, "Ottomanism and Arabism in Syria Before 1914: A Reassessment," Khalidi et al., eds., 50–65. See Antonius, George, *The Arab Awakening: The Story of the Arab National Movement* (New York, Capricorn Books, 1965), 35–40, 68–70. See Ernest, 8–9, 10–13, 15–16, 21–23.

19. See Tauber, 1–10, 57.

20. See Shaw, Stanford J., and Ezel Kural Shaw, *The History of the Ottoman Empire and Modern Turkey,* vol. 2, *Reform, Revolution, and Republic: The Rise of Modern Turkey, 1808–1975* (Cambridge, UK: Cambridge University Press, 1977), 302–303, 304, 309–310. Antonius, 102. 104–105, 106–107. See Tauber, 2–3.

21. Kedourie, Elie, "The End of the Ottoman Empire," *Journal of Contemporary History,* vol. 3, no. 4. 1918–19: From War to Peace (Oct 1968), 20. Wilson, *1914–1917,* 22.

22. See Tauber, 2–3, 4, 5, 7, 8–9. See "British Imperial Connexions to the Arab National Movement, 1912–1914; Lord Kitchener, the Emir Abdullah, Sir Louis Mallet—The Case of Aziz Ali, 1914," based on Gooch, G. P., and Harold Temperly, eds., *British Documents on the Origins of the War, 1898–1914,* vol. 10, pt. 2, *The Last Years of Peace* (London: H. M. Stationery Office, 1926–1938), 824–838, The World War I Documents Archive, www.lib.byu.edu.

23. Tripp, Charles, *A History of Iraq* (Cambridge, UK: Cambridge University Press, 2000), 21–22, 24, 27, 28.

24. "Report on the Conditions for Trade in Mesopotamia," ca. Aug 1919: BL L/PS/10/386. Driver, G. R., "The Religion of the Kurds," *Bulletin of the School of Oriental Studies, University of London,* vol. 2 (1922), 197, 210.

25. "Summary of a Pamphlet, 'The Turco-British Campaign in Mesopotamia and Our Mistakes,' by Staff Bimbashi Muhammad Amin," Moberly, vol. 1, 352–353. Tauber, 59. See Tripp, 21.

26. See Tauber, 25–26, 29–31, 59–60.

27. al-Fatat, "Resolution," as quoted by Tauber, 57. Tauber, 57.

28. "Introduction," "The Hashemites," "The Hashemite Family Tree," official web site of King Hussein, www.kinghussein.gov.jo. "New Caliph of Islam Is in Power," *WP,* Jun 25, 1916, ES1. See Marquise de Fontenoy, "Turks Long Hated by the Arabians," *WP,* Dec 29, 1914, 6.

29. Secret letter, Lord Kitchener to Sir Edward Grey, Feb 6, 1914: PRO FO6672/ 6672/14/44, no. 22 as quoted in "British Imperial Connexions to the Arab National Movement." See Introduction to "The Husayn-McMahon Correspondence," Hurewitz, 13. See de Fontenoy.

30. Letter, Lord Kitchener to Sir W. Tyrrell, Apr 26, 1914: Grey mss. vol. 9, as quoted in "British Imperial Connexions to the Arab National Movement." "Emir Abdullah's Account of His Conversations with Lord Kitchener, Transmitted with Notes by Mr. G. Antonius," as quoted in "British Imperial Connexions to the Arab National Movement."

31. Letter, Sir Louis Mallet to Sir Edward Grey, Mar 18, 1914: PRO FO13871/ 4688/14/44 no. 103, as quoted in "British Imperial Connexions to the Arab National Movement."

32. Letter, Sir Louis Mallet to Sir Edward Grey, Feb 24, 1914: PRO FO9033/ 7963/14/44 no. 117, as quoted in "British Imperial Connexions to the Arab National Movement."

33. See Ireland, Phillip Willard, *Iraq: A Study in Political Development* (New York: Macmillan Company, 1938), 67n5. See Friedman, Isaiah, "The McMahon-Hussein Correspondence and the Question of Palestine," *Journal of Contemporary History,* vol. 5 (1970), 83.

34. See "Correspondence between Sir Henry McMahon and the Sherif Hussein of Mecca, July 1915–March 1916 (With a Map)," Cmd. 5957, Miscellaneous No. 3 (1939) (London: H.M. Stationery Office, 1939), 2–18, esp. letters 4–8. See also Antonius, 164–183.

35. Letter, Lord Kitchener to Sherif Hussein, Oct 31, 1914: Israel State Archives 65/2847a: 1, as quoted by Tauber, 69.

36. Antonius, 157–158. See map, "The Eastern Arab World," Antonius, 160f.

37. Antonius, 159. See "Memorandum on Proposed Agreement with the French," enclosure to secret letter, Capt. W. R. Hall to Sir Arthur Nicolson, Jan 12, 1916: PRO FO 371/2767.

38. See Tauber, 71–73. See Kitchener to Grey, Feb 6, 1914. See Friedman, 84–87.

39. Letter, Sherif Hussein to Sir Henry McMahon, Jul 14, 1915 (letter 1), "Correspondence," 3–4.

40. Letter, Sir Henry McMahon to Sherif Hussein, Aug 30, 1915 (letter 2), "Correspondence," 4–5.

41. Letter, Sherif Hussein to Sir H. McMahon, Sep 9, 1915 (29th Shawal 1333) (letter 3), "Correspondence," 5–7.

42. Letter, Hussein to McMahon, Sep 9, 1915 (letter 3).

43. Letter, Sir Henry McMahon to Sherif Hussein, Oct 24, 1915 (letter 4), "Correspondence," 7–9.

44. Letter, Sherif Hussein to Sir H. McMahon, Nov 5, 1915 (27th Zil Hijja, 1333) (letter 5), "Correspondence, 9–11.

45. Letter, Hussein to McMahon, Nov 5, 1915 (letter 5).

46. See Toynbee, Arnold, "The McMahon-Hussein Correspondence: Comments and a Reply," *Journal of Contemporary History,* vol. 5 (1970), 186. Antonius, 169.

47. Letter, Sir Henry McMahon to Sherif Hussein, Dec 14, 1915 (letter 6), "Correspondence," 11–12.

48. Letter, Sherif Hussein to Sir H. McMahon, Jan 1, 1916 (25th Safar 1334) (letter 7), "Correspondence," 12–14.

49. Busch, Briton Cooper, *Britain, India, and the Arabs, 1914–1921* (Berkeley, CA: University of California Press, 1971), 60. Tauber, 65. See Tauber, 88–89, 90–91. See Moberly, vol. 1, 156.

50. Tauber, 80.

51. Tauber, 80. Abdallah ibn al-Husayn, *Mudhakkirati* (Jerusalem, 1945), 105–107, as cited by Tauber, 80. Sa'id, *al-Thawra,* vol. 1, 110–111, as cited by Tauber, 80.

52. Tauber, 80–81.

53. Private letters, Clayton to Jacob, Mar 11, 1916, and Clayton to Beach, Apr 17, 1916, Clayton papers, as cited by Friedman, 87. Friedman, 87.

54. See Tauber, 82, 251. Sa'id, *al-Thawra,* vol. 1, 156, as quoted by Tauber, 251.

55. Clark, Arthur Tillotson, *To Baghdad with the British* (New York: D. Appleton & Co., 1918), 1–2. See Liukkonnen, Petri, "Who's Who: T. E. Lawrence," Aug 2001, First World War Online.

56. Private telegram, Sir Percy Cox to the Viceroy, Nov 23, 1914, as quoted by Moberly, vol. 1, 133. Moberly, vol. 1, 133–134.

57. Private telegram, Sir Percy Cox to the Viceroy, Nov 23, 1914, as quoted by Moberly, vol. 1, 133–134. Letter, Fisher to Asquith, Nov 5, 1915, Asquith ms, 15/124, as quoted by Kent, 123.

58. Moberly, vol. 1, 133–141.

59. Moberly, vol. 1, 137–139.

60. Moberly, vol. 1, 137–139.

61. Letter, Hardinge to Nichols, private, Jan 6, 1915: PRO FO800/377. Private letter, Hardinge to Nichols, Apr 8, 1915: PRO FO800/377. Private letter, Hardinge to Nichols, Apr 26, 1915: PRO FO800/377.

62. Wilson, *1914–1917*, 80–83.
63. Moberly, vol. 2, 63–64, 64n. See "The Present and Prospective Situation in Syria and Mesopotamia," Moberly, vol. 2, 467–468, 472–474. See generally Townsend, Charles Vere Ferrers, *My Campaign*, vol. 1, (New York: James A. McCann Company, 1920), 249–276, 277–302, 303–332. See "The Battle of Ctesiphon, 1915," Feb 2002, First World War Online. See "Blunder Made in Mesopotamia Campaign Vigorously Assailed in House of Lords," *WP,* Sep 17, 1916, ES1.
64. Moberly, vol. 2, 282, 439–453, 455, 456–457. Townsend, vol. 2, 95–96, 155–157, 171–172, 203, 205–206, 208–209, 214. Wilson, *1914–1917*, 93–94. Clark, 78–79, 82.
65. Moberly, vol. 2, 282–284. See Letter, Hardinge to Nicholson, Jan 6, 1915: PRO FO800/377, 119.
66. Moberly, vol. 2, 449–450. 451, 452. See Wilson, *1914–1917*, 96, 99.
67. Townshend, vol. 2, 235–237. Moberly, vol. 2, 459, 460n. Wilson, *1914–1917*, 99.
68. Wilson, *1914–1917*, 99–100.
69. Wilson, *1914–1917*, 99–100.
70. Moberly, vol. 2, 461–463. Wilson, *1914–1917*, 130–133, 134–138.
71. Wilson, *1914–1917*, 132.
72. Wilson, *1914–1917*, 132–133.
73. Buchanan, 19.
74. Wilson, *1914–1917*, 136.
75. Wilson, *1914–1917*, 136–137. See photo, "Indian Army Soldier after Siege of Kut," ca. July 1916: PRO IWM Q 79446 (1916).
76. See photos, "British Troops Moving through a Baghdad Street," "Indian troops entering Baghdad through a Heavy Dust Storm," Clark, 200f. See "Turkish Armies May Be Surrounded," *NYT,* Mar 18, 1917, XXI. See Wilson, *1914–1917*, 231–234.
77. Moberly, vol. 2, 465.

CHAPTER 11: THE PROCLAMATION

1. Proclamation, delivered by Gen. Stanley Maude to the people of Baghdad, Mar 19, 1917, as reproduced in Moberly, Brigadier General F. J., *History of the Great War: The Campaign in Mesopotamia, 1914-1918*, vol. 3 (London: H. M. Stationery Office, 1925), 404–405, and Buchanan, Sir George, *The Tragedy of Mesopotamia* (London: William Blackwood & Sons, 1938), 169–172.

CHAPTER 12: CHAOS AND CONQUEST

1. "Tripartite (Sykes-Picot) Agreement for the Partition of the Ottoman Empire: Britain, France and Russia," J. C. Hurewitz, ed., *Diplomacy in the Near and Middle East*, vol. 2 (Gerrards Cross, UK: Archive Editions, 1987), 18–22. Ireland, Philip Willard, *Iraq: A Study in Political Development* (New York: Macmillan Company, 1938), 68–70. See letter, Sir M. Sykes to Foreign Office, Jan 16, 1916: PRO FO371/2767 no. 11844. See "Negotiations With Arabs," memorandum of Jan 21, 1916: PRO FO371/2767 no. 14106.
2. Letter, Sir T. Holderness to Sir A. Nicolson, Jan 13, 1916: PRO FO371/2767 no. 8117. Sir A. Hirtzel, "Enclosure in Note 1," Jan 13, 1916: PRO FO371/2767 no. 8117.
3. Telegram, Crewe to Hardinge, Nov 12, 1914: *India Sec. War*, May 1915, as cited by Busch, Briton Cooper, *Britain, India, and the Arabs* (Berkeley, CA: University of California Press, 1971), 63.

4. Secret telegram to Sir George Buchanan, Mar 16, 1915: PRO FO371/2627 no. 51288.

5. Kent, Marian, *Oil and Empire: British Policy and Mesopotamian Oil 1900–1920* (London: Macmillan Press Ltd., 1976), 121–122.

6. Letter, C. Greenway to Foreign Office (FO), Feb 24, 1916: PRO T1/11952/20174/1916 pt. 1 no. 119238. See confidential letter, de Bunsen to Secretary of the Treasury, March 2, 1916: PRO T1/11952/20174/1916 pt. 1 no. 119238.

7. de Bunsen to Secretary of the Treasury. Kent, 129–130.

8. Letter, A. Hirtzel to Under Secretary of State, Apr 1, 1916: PRO FO371/2768 no. 62655.

9. Letter, C. Greenway to the Under Secretary of State for Foreign Affairs, Apr 3, 1916: PRO FO371/2721 no. 63619.

10. Gulbenkian, C. S., "Memoirs of Calouste Sarkis Gulbenkian with Particular Relation to the Origins and Foundation of the Iraq Petroleum Company Limited," Sep 16, 1945: NA RG59 890.g.6363/3-148, 18–22.

11. Gulbenkian, 17.

12. Gulbenkian, 18.

13. Gulbenkian, 18–19.

14. Hurewitz, 19. Longrigg, Stephen H., *The Origins and Early History of the Iraq Petroleum Company, Known from 1912 to 1929 as the Turkish Petroleum Company*, 55, 88. Gulbenkian, 23.

15. "Laws of War: Laws and Customs of War on Land (Hague II)," Jul 29, 1899, Section III. "Laws of War: Laws and Customs of War on Land (Hague IV)," Oct 18, 1907, Section III. Ireland, 80–85.

16. Ireland, 81–82, 87–89. Wilson, Lt. Col. Sir Arnold T., *Loyalties: Mesopotamia 1914–1917* (London: Oxford University Press, 1930), 283–284, 321–322. Letter and attached note, J. S Grosland to Craig, Sep 25, 1916: PRO T1/12047/14548 no. 19238. See also Wilson, *1914–1917*, 88.

17. Ireland, 72.

18. Ireland, 81–84.

19. Ireland, 86–87.

20. Ireland, 81. Wilson, *1914–1917*, 66–67.

21. Wilson, *1914–1917*, 290. Ireland, 74–75.

22. "Note on the Future Status and Administration of Basrah," Feb 24, 1915: PRO FO800/377. "The Prospects of British Trade in Mesopotamia and the Persian Gulf," 1919: BL L/PS/RS/386, 41–44. See Buchanan, Sir George, *The Tragedy of Mesopotamia* (London: William Blackwood and Sons Ltd., 1938), 276. Wilson, *1914–1917*, 196–198.

23. "Note on the Future Status and Administration of Basrah." "The Prospects of British Trade in Mesopotamia and the Persian Gulf," 41–44.

24. Buchanan, 5–7, 134–138. Wilson, *1914–1917*, 196–198. See telegrams, Feb 1920: PRO T1/12544/18025/1920.

25. "The Prospects of British Trade in Mesopotamia and the Persian Gulf," 41–44. "Note on the Future Status and Administration of Basrah," 2, 7.

26. "The Prospects of British Trade in Mesopotamia and the Persian Gulf," 42. Buchanan, 248–250.

27. "Baghdad Trade and Politics," *Times*, Jun 11, 1910, 7–8, as cited by Haddad, Mahmoud, "Iraq Before World War I: A Case of Anti-European Arab Ottomanism," in Khalidi et al., eds., *The Origins of Arab Nationalism* (New York: Columbia Univer-

sity Press, 1991), 126. Willcocks, Sir William, *Sixty Years in the East* (London: 1935), 72, as cited by Haddad, 126.

28. Letter, W. Graham Greene to Under Secretary of State, Apr 14, 1916: PRO T1/11952/20174/1916 pt 1 no. 19238. See "H. M. Petroleum Executive," memo, Mar 18, 1918: PRO T1/12144/11109. See telegram, Walter Long to Sir Frederick Black, Mar 14, 1918: PRO T1/12144/11109. Ferrier, R. W., *The History of the British Petroleum Company*, vol. 1: *The Developing Years, 1901–1932* (Cambridge: Cambridge University Press, 1982), 214.

29. Greene to Under Secretary of State, 4. See Kent, 132–139.

30. Ferrier, 218. Letter, C. Greenway to Inchcape, Apr 11, 1917: PRO T1/12054 no. 119238.

31. Ferrier, 218–219. See "Summary of Profits for 18 Months Ended 31st March, 1918, Anglo Persian Oil Company," Dec 17, 1918: PRO T1/12342/26812. Greenway, "Memorandum re: Purchase of British Petroleum Company and Allied Concerns," May 31, 1917: PRO T1/12054 no. 119238. "Finance Arrangements for Purchase of British Petroleum Co. & O.," ca. May 1917: PRO T1/12054 no. 119238.

32. "Oil Interests in Which the Anglo Persian Oil Company Are Concerned Outside of the Area Covered by Their Persian Concern," memorandum, ca. Apr 1918: PRO T1/12366/35297/1919 no. 14799.

33. Letter, L. D. Wakely to the Under Secretary of State, Dec 18, 1919: PRO T1/12544/18025/1920 no. 55286.

34. Letter, C. Greenway to the Secretary of the Treasury, Aug 2, 1918: PRO T1/12366/35297/1919.

35. Greenway to Secretary of the Treasury.

36. Admiral Sir E. J. W. Slade, "The Petroleum Situation in the British Empire," Jul 29, 1918: PRO CAB21/119 no. 5264, 1–6.

37. Slade, 6. See letter, M. P. A. Hankey to Prime Minister Asquith, Aug 1, 1918: PRO CAB21/119.

38. Maj. Gen. F. H. Sykes, "Notes by the Chief of the Air Staff on Admiralty Memorandum No. G.T./5267 dated 30th July 1918," Aug 9, 1918: PRO CAB21/119. Letter, M. P. A. Hankey to Sir Eric Geddes, Jul 30, 1918: PRO CAB21/119.

39. Townshend, Maj. Gen. Charles Vere Ferrers, *My Campaign* (New York: James A. McCann Company, 1920), 246–275, 280–282.

40. Wilson, Lt. Col. Sir Arnold T., *Mesopotamia 1917–1920: A Clash of Loyalties* (London: Oxford University Press, 1931), 16. Hankey to Asquith, Aug 1, 1918.

41. Wilson, *1917–1920*, 18.

42. Wilson, *1917–1920*, 17–19.

43. Wilson, *1917–1920*, 16, 19–20.

44. Wilson, *1917–1920*, 17, 19–21.

45. Wilson, *1917–1920*, 18–21.

46. Wilson, *1917–1920*, 21, 22–23.

CHAPTER 13: THE UNDECLARED COUNTRY

1. See Buchanan, Sir George, *The Tragedy of Mesopotamia* (London: William Blackwood and Sons Ltd., 1938), 266–267.

2. Letter, Brig. Gen. Macdonough to Sir Arthur Nicolson, Jan 7, 1916, as cited by Karsh, Efraim, and Inari Karsh, *Empires of the Sand: The Struggle for Mastery in the Middle East, 1789–1923* (Cambridge, MA: Harvard University Press, 1999), 225.

3. Wilson, Woodrow, "Fourteen Points Speech," address to Congress, Jan 18, 1918.

4. Wilson, "Fourteen Points Speech."

5. See Tripp, Charles, *A History of Iraq* (Cambridge, UK: Cambridge University Press, 2000), 34–36. See Black, Edwin, *The Transfer Agreement* (New York: Carroll & Graf Publishers, 2001), 72–76. See Dawn, C. Ernest, "The Origins of Arab Nationalism," Rashid Khalidi et al., eds., *The Origins of Arab Nationalism* (New York: Columbia University Press, 1991), 3–23. See Sowards, Steven W., "Lecture 13: Serbian Nationalism from the 'Nacertanije' to the Yugoslav Kingdom," Michigan State University Library, www.lib.msu.edu. See "League of Nations: Armenia: Correspondence Between the President of the Armenian Delegation and the Secretary General," Aug 25, 1921: LoN Archive A. 20. 1921 VII.

6. Paris, Timothy J., "British Middle East Policy-Making After the First World War: The Lawrentian and Wilsonian Schools," *Historical Journal*, vol. 41 (1998), 773–774, 779–782. Marlowe, J., *Late Victorian: The Life of Sir Arnold Talbot Wilson* (London: Cresset Publishers, 1967), 13. Letter, A. P. Waterfield to Barstow, Apr 9, 1919: PRO T1/12544/18025/1920. Letter, Col. A. T. Wilson to Sir A. Hirtzel, Mar 5, 1920: BL Wilson papers, Add. mss 52455C, as cited by Paris, 779.

7. Private letter, Capt. A. T. Wilson to Col. C. E. Yate, Nov 28, 1914: PRO FO371/ 2482 no. 12124. See also "Govt's Future Action in Mesopotamia," minute sheet, Jan 28, 1915: PRO 371/2482 no. 12124. See also letter, Col. Yate to Edward Grey, Jan 28, 1915: PRO 371/2482 no. 12124.

8. Minutes, Nov 6, 1915: BL L/PS/10/524, as cited by Paris, 779. Paris, 779. Also see Wilson, Sir Arnold T., *A Clash of Loyalties: Mesopotamia, 1917–1920, a Personal Record* (London: Oxford University Press, 1931), v.

9. Ireland, Philip Willard, *Iraq: A Study in Political Development* (New York: Macmillan Company, 1938), 96–97. Busch, Briton Cooper, *Britain, India, and the Arabs* (Berkeley, CA: University of California Press, 1971), 22–24.

10. Tripp, 36–37. Ireland, 111–113. "Report on the Conditions for Trade in Mesopotamia Prepared in the Office of the Civil Commissioner in Baghdad," memo, ca. Aug 1919: BL L/PS/10/386. See also "Second Additional Note on the Situation in Kurdistan," memo, Jan 10, 1920: BL L/PS/10/782.

11. Ireland, 74–77.

12. Wilson, 79.

13. Ireland, 94–95. Wilson, 77–79.

14. Ireland, 94–95.

15. Ireland, 76–77. Wilson, 73, 377. Tauber, Eliezer, *The Arab Movements in World War I* (London: Frank Cass and Co., 1993), 32.

16. Tauber, 32–33. Wilson, 74–75.

17. Tauber, 33. Wilson, 75. Letter, Gertrude Bell to Lowthian Bell, May 4, 1918: Gertrude Bell Letters. Letter, Gertrude Bell to Lowthian Bell, Sep 13, 1918: Gertrude Bell Letters.

18. Wilson, 75–76.

19. Wilson, 76.

20. Letter, Lord Eustace Percy to Sir George Clerk, Jun 5, 1919: PRO FO368/2095 no. 85781. Letter, Crowe to Curzon, Oct 10, 1919: Lloyd George mss, F/33/2/66, as cited by Kent, Marian, *Oil and Empire: British Policy and Mesopotamian Oil 1900–1920* (London: Macmillan Press Ltd., 1976), 141.

21. Letter, French Minister to Secretary of State for Foreign Affairs (trans.), Jan 6, 1919: PRO FO368/2095 no. 3251. See "Agreement for Participation of French and

British Interests in World Oil Production," minute sheet, Jan 8, 1919: PRO FO368/2095 no. 3251. "Statement of D'Arcy Exploration Company's Claim to Mesopotamian Oil Concession," Nov 12, 1918: BP 100687.

22. Letter, M. Hankey to Stanley Baldwin, Dec 13, 1918: PRO T1/12442/54465/1919 no. 171.

23. Hankey to Baldwin. Stanley Baldwin to A. H. Stanley, Dec 21, 1918: PRO BT15/76 no. 119238. See handwritten notes, Dec 21, 1918: PRO T1/12442/54465/1919.

24. Hankey to Baldwin. Baldwin to Stanley. Handwritten notes of Dec 21, 1918.

25. "Agreement for Participation of French and British Interests in World Oil Production."

26. Letter, Clemenceau to President du Conseil, Ministre de la Guerre, and Commissaire General aux Essences & Combustibles, Paris, Jan 30, 1919: PRO FO368/2242 no. 21777.

27. Kent 140–144. Hankey to Baldwin. Baldwin to Stanley. Handwritten notes of Dec 21, 1918.

28. Longrigg, Stephen H., *The Origins and Early History of the Iraq Petroleum Company, Known from 1912 to 1929 as the Turkish Petroleum Company* (BP Archives, 1968), 98–99.

29. Kent, 143–146.

30. Kent, 145.

31. Curzon to Balfour, dispatch 1837, Apr 2, 1919: PRO FO608/231 no. 2642.

32. Longrigg, 97–98. See also Gulbenkian, C. S., "Memoirs of Calouste Sarkis Gulbenkian with Particular Relation to the Origins and Foundation of the Iraq Petroleum Company Limited," Sep 16, 1945: NA RG59 890.g.6363/3-148, 20–24.

33. Gulbenkian, 22.

34. Longrigg, 92, 272–274.

35. Longrigg, 94–96. See Kent, 178–181. Earle, Edward Mead, "The Turkish Petroleum Company—A Study in Oleaginous Diplomacy," *Political Science Quarterly*, vol. 39, no. 2 (Jul 1924), 273. See "The Royal Dutch Shell Groups," memo, Oct 4, 1919: PRO T1/12351/30112.

36. Kent, 178.

37. Kent, 178.

38. Kent, 179. See "The Royal Dutch Shell Groups."

39. Kent, 179–180. "The Royal Dutch Shell Groups."

40. Earle, 273.

41. "B. 322. Mesopotamia Oil Policy," memo, Apr 10, 1919: PRO T1/12544/18025/1920.

42. "B. 322. Mesopotamia Oil Policy." Waterfield to Barstow. Office of the Civil Commissioner to the Under Secretary of State for India, Apr 20, 1920: PRO T1/12544/18025/1920. "Anglo-Persian Oil Co., Ltd. Baghdad," memorandum, Jul 30, 1919: PRO T1/12544/18025/1920. "Minutes of an Inter-Departmental Meeting held at the India Office, on Monday, 27th October 1919, to consider Colonel Wilson's proposals regarding the disposal of the Fleet and Oil Barges in Mesopotamia," memorandum, Nov 1, 1919: PRO T1/12544/18025/1920. Letter, L. D. Wakely to the India Office, Nov 19, 1919: PRO T1/122544/18025/1920. See "Draft Letter to the Anglo-Persian Oil Company, Limited," ca. Apr 1919: PRO T1/12544/18025/1920.

43. Longrigg, 94. Also see Kent, 152.
44. Kent, 172.
45. Kent, 172–174. Also see Longrigg, 272–274.
46. "Covenant of the League of Nations," Article 22.
47. "Covenant of the League of Nations," Article 22.
48. Ferrier, R. W., *The History of the British Petroleum Company* (Cambridge, UK: Cambridge University Press, 1982), 357. Kent, 148.
49. "The Menace of Foreign State Monopolies to the American Petroleum Industry," memorandum ca. Sep 1919: NA RG59/250/23/25/3 box 7236. Curzon to Cambon, Jul 27, 1919: PRO FO368/2095. Letter, French Chargé d'affaires to Curzon, Aug 12/13, 1919: PRO FO368/2095 no. 115404.
50. Longrigg, 272–274.
51. Longrigg, 274.
52. Longrigg, 92. Letter, Nichols to M. Tronchiere, Nov 3, 1924: BP 840. Letter, Anglo-Saxon Petroleum Company to H. E. Nichols, Dec 18, 1924: BP 67806.
53. Kent, 149–155.

CHAPTER 14: JIHAD AGAINST BRITAIN

1. Generally see Wheatcroft, Andrew, *The Ottomans: Dissolving Images* (London: Viking, 1995), chap. 7 and 8 ("The Lustful Turk" and "The Terrible Turk").
2. Elkis, Abram, "Former Envoys' Remedies for Evil of Turkish Rule," *Washington Post* (*WP*), Mar 21, 1920, 64.
3. "Imperialism in Turkey," *WP*, Apr 1, 1920, 6.
4. "The Bulgarian Atrocities," *New York Times* (*NYT*), Jul 29, 1876, 2. "The Barbarities in Bulgaria," *NYT*, Aug 29, 1876, 1. "Despatch from Mr. Henry Wood, Correspondent of the American 'United Press' at Constantinople; Published in the American Press, 14th August 1915," Arnold, J. Toynbee, ed., *The Treatment of Armenians in the Ottoman Empire* (London: Hodder & Stoughton, 1916), 2–3.
5. Holcomb, Willard, "Abdul a Great Ruler," *WP*, Apr 28, 1909, 2. See "The War on the Danube," *NYT*, Sep 6, 1876, 1. Palmer, Alan, *The Decline and Fall of the Ottoman Empire* (New York: M. Evans & Co., 1992), 146.
6. "The Armenian Atrocities," *NYT*, Jan 2, 1895, 5. "The Worst Was Not Told," *NYT*, Jan 14, 1895, 3. Morgenthau, Henry, *Ambassador Morgenthau's Story* (Garden City, NY: Doubleday, Page & Co., 1918), 276–277. See "Tales of Horror Retold," *NYT*, May 20, 1895, 3.
7. See photo, "Adana Massacres, April 1909," Balakian, Peter, *The Burning Tigris: The Armenian Genocide and America's Response* (New York: HarperCollins Publishers, 2003), 236f. Balakian, 145–152. "Moslem Massacres Take 5,000 Lives," *NYT*, Apr 21, 1909, 2.
8. "Greatest Horrors in History Mark Massacres in Armenia, Declares an Official Report," *WP*, Oct 4, 1915, 5. "Turks Are Evicting Native Christians," *NYT*, Jul 12, 1915, 4. Telegram, Henry Morgenthau to Secretary of State, Jul 16, 1915: NA RG59 867.4016/76, as reproduced in Balakian, 236ff.
9. Telegram, Henry Morgenthau to Secretary of State. "Armenians Are Sent to Perish in Desert," *NYT*, Aug 18, 1915, 5. "Answer Morgenthau by Hanging Armenians," *NYT*, Sep 16, 1915, 1. "Bryce Asks Us to Aid Armenia," *NYT*, Sep 21, 1915, 3. "800,000 Armenians Counted Destroyed," *NYT*, Oct 7, 1915, 3.
10. "Greatest Horrors in History Mark Massacres in Armenia." See "*New York Times* headlines of 1915," Balakian, 236ff.

11. Morgenthau, 337–338, 339. See Varzhabedian, D. K., "Armenians in Turkey," *WP,* Jan 7, 1895, 2. See poster, "You Won't Let Me Starve, Will You?" Balakian, 236ff.

12. Morgenthau, 333–334.

13. Fox, Albert, "Ratification Refused; 49 To 35, Senate Vote; Pact Sent to Wilson," *WP,* Mar 20, 1920, 1. Gerard, James, "The Mandate for Armenia," *NYT,* Jun 1, 1919, 38. "Why America Should Accept Mandate for Armenia," *NYT,* Jul 6, 1919, 44.

14. "The Balfour Declaration," Nov 2, 1917, as reproduced in J. C. Hurewitz, ed., *Diplomacy in the Near And Middle East,* vol. 2 (New York: Van Nostrand Company, 1956), 26.

15. *Encyclopedia Judaica (EJ),* s.v. "Russia."

16. "Russian Harshness to Jews Increases," *NYT,* Feb 19, 1904, 2. *EJ,* s.v. "Russia." See photo, "Public Hanging in Jerusalem," *EJ,* 300. See *EJ,* 1,458.

17. "The Balfour Declaration."

18. See "Resolution of the General Syrian Congress, 2 July 1919," as reproduced in Hurewitz, vol. 2, 62–64.

19. "Anglo-French Declaration, 7 November 1918," as reproduced in Hurewitz, vol. 2, 30. See introduction, "British and Anglo-French Statements to the Arabs, January–November 1918," Hurewitz, vol. 2, 28–29.

20. "Anglo-French Declaration, 7 November 1918."

21. Tanenbaum, Jan Karl, "France and the Arab Middle East, 1914–1920," *Transactions of the American Philosophical Society,* vol. 68, pt. 7 (1978), 21, 34, 35. Quai d'Orsay memo, "Note sur la Syrie," Feb 14, 1919: Archives du Ministère des Affaires Etrangères (AAE), série: Levant S-L-C, vol. 10, fol. 46, as quoted by Tanenbaum, 27.

22. "Amir Faysal's Memorandum to the Supreme Council at the Paris Peace Conference, 1 January 1919," as reproduced in Hurewitz, vol. 2, 38–39.

23. "Amir Faysal's Memorandum to the Supreme Council."

24. "Amir Faysal's Memorandum to the Supreme Council."

25. "Amir Faysal's Memorandum to the Supreme Council."

26. "Amir Faysal's Memorandum to the Supreme Council."

27. Weizmann, Chaim, *Trial And Error: The Autobiography of Chaim Weizmann* (New York: Harper & Brothers, 1949), 234–235. "The Faisal-Weizmann Agreement, January 1919," as reproduced in Antonius, George, *The Arab Awakening: The Story of the Arab National Movement* (New York: Capricorn Books, 1965), 437–439.

28. "The Faisal-Weizmann Agreement."

29. Letter, Clemenceau to Faisal, Apr 17, 1919: AAE, série: Levant, Arabie-Hedjaz, vol. 4, fol. 85, and "Declaration," Apr 17, 1919: AAE, série: Levant, Arabie-Hedjaz, vol. 4, fols. 36–37, as cited by Tanenbaum, 30. Tanenbaum, 29, 30, 31. See letter, Phillip Hitti to the editor, *NYT,* Feb 3, 1919, 32. Generally see Longrigg, Stephen, *Syria and Lebanon Under French Mandate* (London: Oxford University Press, 1958).

30. Letter, Faisal to Clemenceau, Apr 20, 1919: AAE, série: Levant S-L-C, vol. 12, fols. 133–134, as quoted by Tanenbaum, 30.

31. "Resolution of the General Syrian Congress at Damascus, 2 July 1919." Tanenbaum, 27–31. Antonius, 297. See letter, Hitti to editor.

32. De Caix, memo, "Esquisse de l'organisation de la Syrie sous le mandat français," Jul 17, 1920: AAE série: Levant S-L-C, vol. 31, fol. 28, as quoted by Tanenbaum, 36. Tanenbaum, 31, 36. Longrigg, *Lebanon and Syria,* 75–77, 78, 79, 82.

33. "The Provisional Agreement of January 6, 1920," AAE, série: Levant: 1918–1920, Arabie, vol. 8, fols. 83–86, as quoted by Tanenbaum, 44–45. Tanenbaum, 35–36.

Longrigg, *Lebanon and Syria,* 82. "Who's Who: Henri Gouraud," Feb 2002, First World War Online, www.firstworldwar.com. "Primary Documents: General Gouraud on the Second Battle of the Marne, 16 July 1918," Apr 2004, First World War Online.

34. Tanenbaum, 37.

35. Encrypted telegram, Egyptian G.H.Q. to War Office, Mar 12, 1920: BL L/MIL/5/799. Tanenbaum, 37–38. Antonius, 304.

36. Letter, Alexandre Millerand to Paul Cambon, Mar 13, 1920: AAE, série: Levant S-L-C, vol. 25, fol. 5, as quoted by Tanenbaum, 38. Letter, Lord Curzon to General Allenby, quoted in letter, Cambon to Millerand, Mar 13, 1920: AAE, série: Levant S-L-C, vol. 24, fol. 55, as quoted by Tanenbaum, 38.

37. Letter, Curzon to Allenby, as quoted by Tanenbaum, 38. Tanenbaum, 38.

38. "San Remo Meeting to Take Up Turkey," *NYT,* Apr 3, 1920, 3. "The Carving of Turkey," *WP,* Apr 18, 1920, 24. See James, Edwin, "Asks British Denial of Turkish Treaty," *NYT,* May 8, 1920, 3. See Secretary of State for India, "Note on the Causes of the Outbreak in Mesopotamia," secret note, ca. Aug 1922: BL L/MIL/5/799. See "Chronology, 1920," League of Nations Photo Archive, www.indiana.edu.

39. "The Mandate for Syria and Lebanon, 24 July 1922," as reproduced in Longrigg, *Lebanon and Syria,* 376–380. "The Mandate for Palestine, 24 July 1922," as reproduced in Hurewitz, vol. 2, 107–111. See "Treaty of Alliance: Great Britain and Iraq, 10 October 1922," as reproduced in Hurewitz, 111–114. See letter, John Davis to Earl Curzon, May 12, 1920: PRO BT15/16/119238.

40. Wolff, Stefan, "Forced Population Transfers: Institutionalised Ethnic Cleansing as the Road to New (In-)Stablity: The European Experience," Middle East Virtual Community, www.mevic.org. See De Zayas, A., "International Law And Mass Population Transfers," *Harvard International Law Journal,* vol. 207 (1975).

41. Wolff. See De Zayas.

42. "Draft Agreement Concerning Petroleum," confidential attachment to letter, John Davis to Secretary of State, May 7, 1920: NA RG59 800.6363/113.

43. "Memorandum of Agreement between M. Phillipe Berthelot, Directeur des Affaires politiques et commerciales au Ministère des Affaires Etrangères, and Professor Sir John Cadman, KCMG, Director in Charge of His Majesty's Petroleum Department," Apr 24, 1920: BP IPC 168-F4: FO Agreement Correspondence Oct 1912–Oct 1927.

44. "Memorandum of Agreement."

45. "Memorandum of Agreement."

46. "Memorandum of Agreement." Letter, Secretary-General of the Hedjaz Delegation to Secretary-General of the Council of the League of Nations, May 8, 1920: LoN K1 1/4284/4284. Kent, Marian, *Oil and Empire: British Policy and Mesopotamian Oil 1900–1920* (London: Macmillan Press Ltd., 1976), 155. See Telegram, Department of State to American Embassy, London, May 10, 1920: NA RG59 800.6363/111a.

47. Letter, Secretary-General of the Hedjaz Delegation to Secretary-General of the Council of the League of Nations.

48. Letter, Secretary-General of the Hedjaz Delegation to Secretary-General of the Council of the League of Nations.

49. "Riots in Jerusalem," *NYT,* Apr 8, 1920, 15. See Longrigg, *Syria and Lebanon,* 96–97. See "Note on the Causes of the Outbreak in Mesopotamia." See letter,

Millerand to Gouraud, May 11, 1920: AAE, série: Levant S–L–C, vol. 27, fol. 240, as quoted by Tanenbaum, 39–40. See Lawrence, T. E., "A Report on Mesopotamia," *Sunday Times,* Aug 22, 1920. See telegram to Wilson, Apr 7, 1919: PRO AIR2/122.

50. See letter, Hardinge to Allenby, Jul 16, 1920, as quoted by Tanenbaum, 39. Letter, Curzon to Millerand, May 18, 1920: AAE, série: Levant S–L–C, vol. 28, fol. 35, as quoted by Tanenbaum, 40. "Proposition d'une reunion de conference pour redaction d'instructions au general Gouraud," May 19, 1920: AAE, série: Levant S–L–C, vol. 28 fols. 76–77, as quoted by Tanenbaum, 40. Tanenbaum, 39–40.

51. Letters, Millerand to Gouraud, July 23 and 24, 1920: AAE, série: Levant S–L–C, vol. 31, fols. 117, 164, as quoted by Tanenbaum, 41. Longrigg, *Syria and Lebanon,* 101–102.

52. "French Begin War on Feisal in Syria; Columns Moving on Aleppo and Damascus," *NYT,* Jul 17, 1920, 1. "Syria Arms For War," *WP,* Jul 19, 1920, 1. "Feisal Mobilizes Against French in Syria; Gouraud Reported Ready to Move Today," *NYT,* 12. James, Edwin, "French Rout Emir; Enter Damascus," *NYT,* Jul 26, 1920, 1. Longrigg, *Syria and Lebanon,* 102–103.

53. "Anglo-French Oil Agreement Is Out," *NYT,* Jul 24, 1920, 7.

54. "Ten Thousand Jews Thank Great Britain," *NYT,* Jul 13, 1920, 12. See "Zionists Elect Brandeis," *WP,* Jul 24, 1920, 4. See photo, "The London Zionist Conference," The Jewish Agency for Israel, www.jafi.org.il. See "The Foundation Fund," *Zionist Bulletin,* Jul 26, 1920, 8, as reproduced in "The London Zionist Conference 1920 and the Foundation of Keren Hayesod," Jewish Agency for Israel.

55. Antonius, 312.

56. "Chart Showing Approximate Area Effected by One H. P. Machine Carrying 10-9.45 Gas Bombs," attachment to memo, C. A. S to R. Brooke-Popham, Dec 13, 1919: PRO AIR2/122.

57. "Churchill Proposes to Guard Mesopotamia by Air Patrol," *NYT,* Mar 23, 1920, 1. "Report on Air Squadrons in Middle East," Nov 4, 1919: PRO AIR2/122. See memo, War Office, Apr 14, 1919: PRO AIR2/122.

58. Secret memo to Air Ministry, Apr 19, 1919: PRO AIR2/122.

59. "Weapons of War: Poison Gas," May 2002, First World War Online. War Department, "General Orders, No. 62," Jun 28, 1918: U. S. Army Center for Military History. See Black, Edwin, *War Against the Weak: Eugenics and America's Campaign to Create a Master Race* (New York: Four Walls Eight Windows, 2003), 258.

60. Note to the Flying Office Directorate, Air Board, May 2, 1919: PRO AIR2/122.

61. Churchill, minutes, May 12, 1919, as reproduced in Gilbert, Martin, *Winston S. Churchill, Companion to Vol. 4* (London: Heinemann: 1977), 649.

62. Churchill, minutes.

63. Memo, R. M. Groves, May 19, 1919: PRO AIR2/122. R. M. Groves, War Office minute sheet B9967, May 24, 1919: PRO AIR2/122.

64. Brooke-Popham, note, Jun 16, 1919: PRO AIR2/122.

65. Brooke Popham, minute sheet 16A, Jun 16, 1919: PRO AIR2/122.

66. Brooke-Popham, memo, Jun 30, 1919: PRO AIR2/122.

67. Brooke-Popham, memo, Jun 30, 1919. "Chart Showing Approximate Area Effected by One H. P. Machine Carrying 10-9.45 Gas Bombs."

68. Tauber, Eliezar, "The Struggle for Dayr al-Zur: The Determination of Borders between Syria and Iraq," *International Journal of Middle East Studies,* vol. 23, no. 3

(Aug 1991), 367. Wilson, Sir Arthur T., *A Clash of Loyalties: Mesopotamia, 1917–1920, A Personal Record* (London: Oxford University Press, 1931), 231.

69. Wilson, 232. Tauber, 367.
70. "British Air Service Plan," *WP,* Dec 15, 1919, 4. Wilson, 234. Meilinger, Philip, "Trenchard and 'Morale Bombing': The Evolution of Royal Air Force Doctrine Before World War II," *Journal of Military History,* vol. 60 (1996), 251.
71. Secret telegram to War Office, Apr 6, 1920: BL L/MIL/5/798.
72. Wilson, 249.
73. "Note on the Causes of the Outbreak in Mesopotamia." Telegram, Wilson to Secretary of State for India, May 8, 1920, as reproduced in "Note on the Causes of the Outbreak in Mesopotamia."
74. Telegram, Wilson to Secretary of State for India, May 8, 1920.
75. Vinogradov, Amal, "The 1920 Revolt in Iraq Reconsidered: The Role of Tribes in National Politics," *International Journal of Middle East Studies,* vol 3 (1972), 135. Wilson, 253–254.
76. Vinograd, 134–135. Wilson, 253.
77. Vinograd, 135. Wilson, 255.
78. Vinograd, 135–136.
79. Ireland, Phillip Willard, *Iraq: A Study in Political Development* (New York: Macmillan Company, 1938), 238–239. Wilson, 273.
80. Wilson, 274.
81. Ireland, 262.
82. Ireland, 259.
83. "Lost 161 in Mesopotamia," *NYT,* Jul 20, 1920, 9. Ireland, 266, 267. Wilson, 277, 278.
84. "Lost 161 in Mesopotamia." Wilson, 278–279, 279n. Ireland, 266, 267–268, 269.
85. Ireland, 268. "French Rout Emir; Enter Damascus."
86. Churchill, "Situation in Mesopotamia, 20th August 1920," secret Cabinet memo, Aug 20, 1920: BL L/MIL/5/799. Wilson, 272, 282, 293.
87. Churchill, "Situation in Mesopotamia, 2nd September 1920," secret Cabinet memo, Aug 2, 1920: BL L/MIL/5/800. Wilson, 294.
88. Ireland, 270–271. Wilson, 292.
89. Wilson, 298. Despatch from High Commissioner, Baghdad, Oct 4, 1920: BL L/MIL/5/800.
90. Wilson, 298. Ireland, 272n3.
91. Secret telegram from Civil Commissioner, Baghdad, Aug 6, 1920: BL L/MIL/5/799.
92. Wilson, 270–271, 277.
93. Wilson, 271.
94. Churchill, "Recent Events in Mesopotamia," secret Cabinet memo, Sep 30, 1920: BL L/MIL/5/800.
95. "Churchill Proposes to Guard Mesopotamia by Air Patrol." Secret telegram from War Office, Oct 5, 1920: BL L/MIL/5/800.
96. "Situation in Mesopotamia, 2nd September 1920." Secret telegram, General Officer Commanding (GOCM), Mesopotamia to War Office, Aug 28, 1920 as reproduced in "Situation in Mesopotamia, 2nd September 1920." Secret memo, GOCM to War Office, Sep 30, 1920: BL L/MIL/5/800. Vinogradov, 137.
97. Secret telegram, GOCM, Mesopotamia to War Office, Aug 28, 1920 as reproduced in "Situation in Mesopotamia, 2nd September 1920." See Secret telegram, GOCM

to War Office, Sep 28, 1920: BL L/MIL/5/800. Secret telegram, War Office to GOCM, Oct 5, 1920: BL L/MIL/5/800.

98. Churchill, "Air Staff Memorandum on the Air Force as an Alleged Cause of the Loss of Popularity of the Mesopotamia Civil Administration," Aug 27, 1920: BL L/MIL/5/800. Meilinger, 244.

99. Meilinger, 244. See "Sir Arthur 'Bomber' Harris (1892–1984)," BBC History, www.bbc.co.uk.

100. Vinogradov, 137, 138–139.

101. Vinogradov, 138.

102. Wilson, 321. Ireland, 277–278, 286–287, 326, 335. See "Churchill's Speech Displeases Paris," *NYT,* Jun 16, 1921, 3.

103. Fraser, Lovat, "The War-Mongers," *Daily Mail,* July 12, 1920, as quoted by Busch, Briton Cooper, *Britain, India, and the Arabs, 1914–1921* (Berkeley, CA: University of California Press, 1971), 409. Antonius, 315. Ireland, 273. See secret telegram, War Office to GHQ Mesopotamia, Sep 8, 1920: BL L/MIL/5/800.

104. Dobbs, Sir Henry, "Britain's Work in Iraq and Prospects of the New State," address to the Royal Empire Society, Feb 1933, as quoted by Buchanan, Sir George, *The Tragedy of Mesopotamia* (London: William Blackwood & Sons, 1938), 285.

105. Buchanan, 285–286.

106. Ferrier, 308–309.

CHAPTER 15: THE RED LINE

1. *Iraq: Treaty with King Feisal,* Cmd. 1757 (1922). "British Conclude Alliance with Irak," *New York Times (NYT),* Oct 12, 1922, 5.

2. Secret telegrams to War Office, Aug 22, 1920, Aug 24, 1920, Aug 26, 1920, and Aug 26, 1920, as reproduced in Churchill, "Situation in Mesopotamia," secret cabinet memo, Sep 2, 1920: BL L/MIL/5/800.

3. *Iraq: Treaty with King Feisal.* "British Conclude Alliance with Irak."

4. See letter to Mead Taylor, Apr 26, 1924: PRO BT15/27/119238.

5. Wilson, Woodrow, "Fourteen Points Speech," address to Congress, Jan 18, 1918. Letter, Bainbridge Colby to Earl Curzon, Nov 20, 1920: NA RG59 800.6363/ 196A, *FRUS* 1920, 669, 670.

6. Letter, Thomas O'Donnell to Robert Lansing, Sep 30, 1919: NA RG59 800.6363/89.

7. See American Petroleum Institute, "The Menace of Foreign State Monopolies to the American Petroleum Industry," ca. Sep 1919, enclosure to O'Donnell to Lansing, Sep 30, 1919.

8. "Memorandum Regarding British Petroleum Policy," ca. Sep 1919, enclosure to confidential memo to the Secretary of State, Oct 10, 1919: NA RG59 800.6363/87.

9. "Imperative Need for Aggressive Foreign Policy as Regards the Oil Industry," Mar 1, 1920, enclosure to letter, Alvey Adee to Bradley Stoughton, Apr 17, 1920: NA RG59 800.6363/95.

10. "The Menace of Foreign State Monopolies to the American Petroleum Industry," 6.

11. "Memorandum on Mesopotamia, and Other Oil-bearing Regions, Affected by the Peace Settlements," ca. Sep 1920: NA RG59 800.6363 S250 R23 C25 box 7236.

12. See "Statement of Mineral Oil Rights Granted in the Ottoman Empire as of January 1st, 1920," enclosure to letter, G. Bie Ravndal to the Secretary of State, Apr 27,

1920: NA RG59 800.6363.16a. *Congressional Record,* vol. 58, pt. 4, 3304–3310, as cited by Atarodi, Habibollah, *Great Powers, Oil and the Kurds in Mosul (Southern Kurdistan/Northern Iraq),* 1910–1925 (Lanham, MD: University Press of America, 2003), 89. Longrigg, Stephen, *Oil in the Middle East: Its Discovery and Development* (London: Oxford University Press, 1968), 107, 107n3.

13. Letter, Oscar Heizer to Secretary of State, Dec 9, 1919: NA RG59 800.6363/75.
14. "Minutes of the Conference Held at the India Office on Friday 2nd January 1920:" PRO T1/12544/18025/1920.
15. Draft of telegram, Ambassador Davis to Lord Curzon, May 10, 1920: NA RG59 800.6363/111a. Confidential letter, Hugh C. Wallad to Secretary of State, May 7, 1920: NA RG59 800.6363/113. "1920–1921: Secretary of State Bainbridge Colby," US State Department Youth Website, http://future.state.gov.
16. Draft of telegram, Davis to Curzon.
17. Letter, M. L. Requa to Alvey Adlee, May 13, 1920: NA RG59 800.6363/112.
18. Letter, Requa to Adlee.
19. Letter, Davis to Secretary of State, May 18, 1920: NA RG59 800.6363/126.
20. "The Royal Dutch Shell Interests in USA," ca. Oct 1921: BP 72491. See Longrigg, 107n3. See Letter, Ambassador Geddes to Secretary of State, Apr 20, 1921: NA RG59 841.6363/143, *FRUS* 1921, vol. 2, 71. Letter, Thomas O'Donnell to Secretary of State, Sep 30, 1919: NA RG59 800.6363/89. Earle, Edward Meade, "The Turkish Petroleum Company—A Study in Oleaginous Diplomacy," *Political Science Quarterly,* vol. 39 (1924), 275. Letter, Earl Curzon to Mr. Davis, Feb 28, 1921, as quoted in "Correspondence Between H.M. Government and the United States Ambassador Respecting Economic Rights in Mandated Territories," Feb 1921: BT15/76/119238.
21. John Cadman, "Memorandum of Meeting," Apr 9, 1922, attachment to Foreign Office letter, Apr 21, 1922: PRO POWE33/95.
22. "Memorandum of Meeting."
23. Telegram, Foreign Office to M. Cheetham, Jul 18, 1922: PRO POWE33/95. Letter, Turkish Petroleum Company to H.M. Petroleum Department, Jul 6, 1922: PRO POWE33/95. "Memorandum of Negotiations in London between American Oil Interests and the Turkish Petroleum Company," Jul 21, 1922: NA RG59 890g.6363 T84/48, *FRUS* 1922, vol. 2, 340–342. Letter, Secretary of State to W. C. Teagle, Aug 22, 1922: NA RG59 890g.6363 T84/41a, *FRUS* 1922, vol. 2, 342–344.
24. Telegram, Secretary of State to Ambassador Harvey, Jun 24, 1922: NA RG 59 890g.6363 T84/41, *FRUS* 1922, vol. 2, 337. Letter, A. C. Bedford to the Secretary of State, Jun 27, 1922: NA RG59 800g.6363 T84/46, *FRUS* 1922, vol. 2, 338. Telegram, A. C. Bedford to Charles Greenway, Jun 26, 1922, enclosure to NA RG59 800g.6363 T84/46. Telegram Ambassador Harvey to Secretary of State, Aug 4, 1922: NA RG59 800g.6363 T84/43, *FRUS* 1922, vol. 2, 339–340. Letter, Secretary of State to W. C. Teagle, Aug 22, 1922: NA RG59 800g.6363 T84/41a, *FRUS* 1922, vol. 2, 342–343. Telegram to Lord Hardinge, Jul 11, 1922: PRO POWE 33/95. Longrigg, 68n1, 69.
25. *Iraq: Treaty with King Feisal,* Article XI.
26. Hurewitz, J. C., introduction to "United States Interests and Conditions of Participation in the Lausanne Conference," J.C. Hurewitz, ed., *Diplomacy in the Near And Middle East,* vol. 2 (New York: Van Nostrand Company, 1956), 114. "U.S. *Aide-Memoire* to Britain, France and Italy, 30 October 1922" and "Secretary Hughes'

Instructions to U.S. Ambassadors at London, Paris and Rome, 30 October 1922," as reproduced in Hurewitz, 114–119.

27. Telegram, Secretary of State to American Mission at Lausanne, Nov 27, 1922: NA RG59 890g.6363/156, *FRUS* 1922, vol. 2, 346.

28. Telegram, Secretary of State to American Mission at Lausanne.

29. Lord Curzon, speech at Lausanne, Jan 23, 1923: PRO CO730/46/4849, as quoted by Sluglett, Peter, *Britain in Iraq, 1914–1932* (London: Ithaca Press, 1976), 110–111.

30. Lord Curzon, speech at Lausanne, Jan 23, 1923.

31. Minutes, Dec 9, 1922: PRO FO839/10. Letter, Montagau Piesse to W. C. Teagle, Dec 12, 1922, enclosure to telegram, W. C. Teagle to Secretary of State, Dec 13, 1922: NG RG59 890g.6363 T84/62. *FRUS* 1922, 348–349.

32. Letter, Piesse to Teagle.

33. Letter, Piesse to Teagle.

34. Letter, H. E. Nichols to C. S. Gulbenkian, Dec 18, 1922: BP IPC 140-Letter Book, TPC Ltd2: 1920s.

35. Nichols to Gulbenkian.

36. Nichols to Gulbenkian.

37. Draft memorandum of Dec 18, 1922: BP 68820.

38. See "At Lausanne," *WP*, Jan 25, 1923, 6. See Lord Curzon, speech at Lausanne, Jan 23, 1923.

39. Turkish Democracy Foundation, "Is Outside Powers' Interest in Kurds Mainly Because of Humanitarian Concerns?" chap. 14, *Fact Book on Turkey, Kurds and the PKK Terrorism.*

40. "Chronology of Lausanne," Turkish Ministry of Foreign Affairs, www.mfa.gov.tr.

41. Letter, C. S. Gulbenkian to H. E. Nichols, Jan 11, 1923: BP 67810.

42. Letter, C. S. Gulbenkian to H. E. Nichols, Sep 28, 1923: BP 67764. Letter, H. E. Nichols to C. S. Gulbenkian, Oct 4, 1923: BP 67764.

43. Nichols to Gulbenkian, Oct 4, 1923.

44. "Draft Convention of September 1923 between the Government of Iraq and the Turkish Petroleum Company, Limited," Sep 1923, enclosure to letter, W. C. Teagle to the Department of State, Oct 25, 1923: RG 59 890g.6363 T 84/117, *FRUS* 1923, vol. 2, 246–259.

45. Letter, C. S. Gulbenkian to H. E. Nichols, Oct 26, 1923: BP 67764.

46. Gulbenkian to Nichols, Oct 26, 1923.

47. Letter, H. E. Nichols to C. S. Gulbenkian, Oct 31, 1923: BP 67764.

48. See Lodwick, John with D. H. Young, *Gulbenkian: An Interpretation of "The Richest Man in the World,"* (Garden City, NY: Doubleday & Company, 1958), 151, 254–258.

49. Letter to Clarke, Jan 2, 1924: BP IPC 140-Letter Book, TPC Ltd 2: 1920s. Letter, Turkish Petroleum Company (TPC) to The Registrar, Jan 3, 1924: BP IPC 140-Letter Book, TPC Ltd 2: 1920s. Letter to Clarke, Jan 14, 1924: BP IPC 140-Letter Book, TPC Ltd 2: 1920s. Letter, H. E. Nichols to Sir Henri Deterding, Jan 14, 1924: BP IPC 140-Letter Book, TPC Ltd 2: 1920s. Letter, H. E. Nichols to C. S. Gulbenkian, Jan 14, 1924: BP IPC 140-Letter Book, TPC Ltd 2: 1920s.

50. Letter, H. E. Nichols to N. S. Gulbenkian, Jan 25, 1924: BP IPC 140-Letter Book, TPC Ltd 2: 1920s. *Observer* (1965).

51. Nichols to N. S. Gulbenkian, Jan 25, 1924. Gulbenkian, Nubar, *Portrait in Oil: The Autobiography of Nubar Gulbenkian* (New York: Simon & Schuster, 1965), 95.

52. Letter, H. E. Nichols to W. C. Teagle, Jul 29, 1924: BP IPC 140-Letter Book, TPC Ltd 2: 1920s.

53. See Letter, Freshfields, Leese & Munns to H.E. Nichols, Aug 12, 1924: BP 67764. See Longrigg, 115–119.

54. Freshfields, Leese & Munns to Nichols, Aug 12, 1924.

55. Letter, H. E. Nichols to M. Tronchere, Sep 9, 1924: BP IPC 140-Letter Book, TPC Ltd 2: 1920s.

56. See "Draft Letter to be written to Messrs. Freshfields," Sep 16, 1924: BP 67806. Letter, H. G. Brown to Messrs. Freshfields, Leese & Munns, Sep 26, 1924: BP 68820.

57. Brown to Freshfields, Leese, & Munns.

58. Brown to Freshfields, Leese, & Munns.

59. W. C. Teagle et al., memo, Sep 18, 1924: NA RG59 890g.6363 T84/167, *FRUS* 1924, vol. 2, 230, 231.

60. Telegram, Secretary of State to Ambassador Kellog, Sep 20, 1924: NA RG59 890g.6363 T84/162a, FRUS 1924, vol. 2, 233–235.

61. Letter, W. Tyrrell to C. S. Gulbenkian, Oct 10, 1924: BP: 27508.

62. Letter, H. E. Nichols to E. Mercier, Nov 12, 1924: BP IPC 140-Letter Book, TPC Ltd 2: 1920s.

63. See letter, Turkish Petroleum Company to C. S. Gulbenkian, Jan 13, 1925: BP IPC 140: Letters from TPC, Jan–Aug 1925. Letter, C. S. Gulbenkian to H. E. Nichols, Feb 16, 1925: BP IPC 174-530A. See letter H. E. Nichols to C. S. Gulbenkian, Jan 24, 1925: BP IPC 174-530A. "To Fight for Billion and Rich Oil Lands for Sultan's Heirs," *NYT*, Nov 22, 1924, 1. "Riches of 'Abdul the Damned,' " *Daily Express,* Feb 23, 1934: BP IPC 174-530A. See letter, C. S. Gulbenkian to H. E. Nichols and enclosed press clippings, Feb 26, 1925: BP IPC 174-530A. See *Contract Between T.T.H. Heirs of His Majesty Sultan Abdul Hamid II and Mssrs. John Godolphin Bennett & George Maitland Edwards,* ca. Feb 1924: BP IPC 174-530A.

64. Turkish Petroleum Company, *Limited Convention with the Government of Iraq,* Mar 14, 1925: PRO CO730/158/9/119238. "The Omens From Lausanne," *WP,* Jan 25, 1923, 6.

65. John Cadman, "Memorandum of Heads of Agreement Between Sir John Cadman on Behalf of the Anglo-Persian Oil Company Limited's Group and Mr. C. S. Gulbenkian, Subject to Ratification by the Anglo-Persian Co. Ltd.'s Board," Nov 29, 1925: BP 68820. "Synopsis of the Negotiations for American Participation in the Turkish Petroleum Co.," Dec 24, 1924: BP 67809.

66. Draft cable to W. C. Teagle, ca. Sep 1924: BP 68820.

67. Letter, Anglo-Saxon Petroleum Company to TPC, Sep 30, 1925: BP 67808.

68. Montagu Piesse, memorandum on behalf of American group, Oct 6, 1925: BP 67809.

69. Minutes, TPC meeting, Oct 29, 1925: BP 67809.

70. Memo, Dec 2, 1925: BP IPC 166: C2FF. See Longrigg, 114.

71. Telegram, Secretary of State to Ambassador Houghton, Dec 5, 1925: NA RG59 890g.6363 T 84/226, *FRUS* 1925, vol. 2, 239–240.

72. Telegram, Secretary of State to Houghton, Dec 5, 1925.

73. Draft of "Agreement for Payment of Royalty to the D'Arcy Exploration Company Limited and for Making Arrangements Between the Iraq Petroleum Company Limited and Others," May 7, 1925: BP 68820.

74. Letter, C. S. Gulbenkian to Sir John Cadman, Dec 25, 1925: BP 68820.

75. Letter, Henri Deterding to Anglo-Persian Oil Company, Jan 2, 1926: BP 27810.

76. Ybarra, T. R., "War Looms As Turks Raid Christians," *NYT,* Sep 16, 1925, 1. "Turks Lose First Irak Test Despite Threat to Depart," *WP,* Dec 9, 1925, 3. Atarodi, 200–202, 204.

77. Letter, H. E. Nichols to Colonial Office, Apr 1, 1926: BP 68820.

78. Letter, C. S. Gulbenkian to H. E. Nichols, Apr 12, 1926: BP 67810.

79. Letter, Linklaters & Paines to Anglo-Persian Oil Company, May 7, 1926: BP 67810. See draft of "Agreement for Payment of Royalty to the D'Arcy Exploration Company Limited and for Making Arrangements Between the Iraq Petroleum Company Limited and Others."

80. Letter and memorandum, Anglo-Persian Oil Company and Anglo-Saxon Petroleum Company to Linklaters & Paines, Jun 10, 1926: BP 68820.

81. See "An Agreement Between the Turkish Petroleum Company Limited, The D'Arcy Exploration Company Limited, The Anglo-Saxon Petroleum Company Limited, La Comapagnie Française de Petroles and Calouste Sarkis Gulbenkian," ca. Feb 1927: BP 67811. See "Sale of Oil Agreement, La Compagnie Française des Petroles and Participations and Investments Limited and Calouste Sarkis Gulbenkian, Esq," Jul 31, 1928: BP 106287.

82. See "An Agreement." See "Mr. C.S. Gulbenkian and The Turkish Petroleum Company, Ltd., Joint Opinion," Feb 2, 1927: BP IPC 168-F4 FO Agreement Corresp Oct 1912–Oct 1927.

83. Letter, C. S. Gulbenkian to Sir John Cadman, Feb 23, 1927: BP 67811.

84. F. E. Wellings, "Note on the Blow-out of Baba Gurgur No. 1 on 14th October 1927," as quoted by Longrigg, Stephen, *The Origins and Early History of the Iraq Petroleum Company, Known from 1912 to 1929 as the Turkish Petroleum Company* (BP Archives, 1968), 287. "Gas Kills Americans in Turkish Oil Field," *NYT,* Oct 21, 1927, 8. See photos, "Baba Gurgur No. 1 Well—Oil Gushing Through Side of Arbor Head," "A River of Oil Flowing from Baba Gurgur No. 1 Well," Bamberg, James, *The History of the British Petroleum Company,* vol. 2: *The Anglo-Iranian Years, 1928–1954* (Cambridge, UK: Cambridge University Press, 1994), 160. See "Turkish Petroleum Co. Made Important Find," *Wall Street Journal* (WSJ), Jun 4, 1928, 5.

85. "Note on the Blow-out of Baba Gurgur No. 1 on 14th October 1927."

86. N. Gulbenkian, 98–99.

87. Author's complete copy of the *Red Line Agreement,* Jul 31, 1927: BP IPC 354-I8.

88. *Red Line Agreement,* 49, 51, 52, 53.

89. *Red Line Agreement,* 54.

90. *Red Line Agreement,* 21–22.

91. *Red Line Agreement,* 54.

Part Four: The Continuing Conflict

CHAPTER 16: THE NAZI INTERSECTION

1. Great Britain, *Treaty of Preferential Alliance: The United Kingdom and Iraq,* Jun 30, 1930, *Parliamentary Papers 1931,* Treaty Series No. 15, Cmd. 3797, as reproduced in J. C. Hurewitz, ed., *Diplomacy in the Near And Middle East,* vol. 2 (New York: Van Nostrand Company, 1956), 178–181. Introduction to *Treaty of Preferential Alliance,*

Hurewitz, 178. Ireland, Phillip Willard, *Iraq: A Study in Political Development* (New York: Macmillan Company, 1938), 413–415, 417–418.

2. Confidential letter, Sir F. Humphreys to Sir John Simon, Jan 28, 1935: BL L/PS/12/2882 v 17. Roach, E. Keith, "Pipe Line Across a Desert Will Link East with West," *New York Times (NYT)*, Apr 15, 1934, XXVII. "First Iraq Oil at Mediterranean Port," *Wall Street Journal (WSJ)*, Jul 18, 1934, 1. See letter, Emir Abdullah to Sir John Cadman Pasha (trans.) Jan 24, 1935: BP IPC 100-P26: See letter, Sir John Cadman to Emir Abdullah, Jan 25, 1935: BP IPC 100-P26: Political, Transjordan, 1934–39. See confidential letter, High Commissioner for Palestine to H. M. Principal Secretary of State for the Colonies, Feb 15, 1935: BL L/PS/12/2882 v 17. Bamberg, James, *The History of the British Petroleum Company*, vol. 2; *The Anglo-Iranian Years, 1928–1954* (Cambridge, UK: Cambridge University Press, 1994), xxvii.

3. Wasserstein, Bernard, "Herbert Samuel and the Palestine Problem," *English Historical Review*, vol. 91, no. 361 (Oct 1976), 763–764. See Black, Edwin, *The Transfer Agreement: The Dramatic Story of the Pact Between the Third Reich and Jewish Palestine* (New York: Carroll & Graf, 2001), 91.

4. Mattar, Philip, *The Mufti of Jerusalem* (New York: Columbia University Press, 1988), 6–7. See letter, Herbert Samuel to Winston Churchill, Oct 27, 1921: PRO T1/161/146 no. 119238.

5. Mattar, 8–10. Jbarra, Taysir, *Palestinian Leader Hajj Amin Al-Husayni, Mufti of Jerusalem* (Princeton: The Kingston Press, 1985), 14.

6. Mattar, 10–13. Jbarra, 15–16. Elpeleg, Zvi, *The Grand Mufti: Haj Amin Al-Hussaini, Founder of the Palestinian National Movement*, David Harvey, trans., Shmuel Himelstein, ed. (London: Frank Cass, 1993), 3–4, 5.

7. Mattar, 16, 20. See Wasserstein, 753–754.

8. Mattar, 22–25. Elpeleg, 8. See Jbarra, 41.

9. Note by Samuel, Apr 11, 1921: Israel State Archives 2/245 as quoted by Wasserstein, 765. Mattar, 25–27. Elpeleg, 10.

10. Generally see Black, *Transfer Agreement*.

11. "Zionist Leaders: Chaim Weizmann, 1874–1952," Israel Ministry of Foreign Affairs, www.mfa.gov.il. Generally see Black, *Transfer Agreement*.

12. Generally see Black, *Transfer Agreement*. See Black, *Transfer Agreement*, 379.

13. Generally see Black, *Transfer Agreement*. See Black, *Transfer Agreement*, 379.

14. See Sachar, 200. See Black, *Transfer Agreement*, 90.

15. "Two Arabs Killed by Police in Riot," *NYT*, May 2, 1936, 5. "Arabs Reject Plea to Call Off Strike," *NYT*, May 6, 1936, 16. "Arabs Kill 2 in Old Jerusalem," *NYT*, May 14, 1936, 14. "Terror Increases in Palestine Crisis," *NYT*, May 16, 1936. Sachar, Howard M., *A History of Israel, from the Rise of Zionism to Our Time* (New York: Alfred A. Knopf, 1981), 199–201.

16. Palestine Royal Commission, "Report of the Palestine Royal Commission," chap. 20, Jul 1937, Series of League of Nations Publications, VI.A. Mandates, 1937 VI.A.5, United Nations Information System on the Question of Palestine, http://domino.un.org. "Palestine Inquiry Proves Difficult," *NYT*, Nov 15, 1936, E5. "Palestine Chary of State Domains," *NYT*, Nov 25, 1936, 7.

17. "Report of the Palestine Royal Commission," chap. 6.

18. "Report of the Palestine Royal Commission," chaps. 21, 22. Mattar, 82. Kuhn, Ferdinand, Jr., "British Mark Time on Palestine Issue," *NYT*, Jan 9, 1938, E5.

19. See letter, W. Ormsby-Gore to Anthony [Eden], Oct 1, 1936: PRO FO954/12B no. 119571. Mattar, 82–83.

20. Letter, British Consul to High Commissioner for Palestine, Jul 5, 1937: PRO CO733/326/4.

21. Donald Mallett, secret minutes, Feb 27, 1946: PRO FO 371/27078. British Consul to High Commissioner for Palestine, Jul 5, 1937. Mattar, 28–29, 82, 83. Jbarra, 61–63, 64–65.

22. Mattar, 83. See letter, General Weygand to the Mufti (trans.), Sep 25, 1939: PRO FO371/61926/119288.

23. Weygand to the Mufti, Sep 25, 1939. Mattar, 88.

24. "London Hears Arab Chief Has Escaped to Baghdad," *NYT*, Oct 18, 1939, 3. Telegram, Consul-General, Beirut to Foreign Office, Oct 18, 1939: PRO FO684/12/119288. Mattar, 88, 89.

25. Mattar, 89. "London Hears Arab Chief Has Escaped to Baghdad."

26. "Plan W.A. 6, Appendix A: The Oil Supply Problem in Germany," July 1939: PRO AIR9/122 no. 119738. See "Analysis of German Petroleum Economy," ca. 1939: PRO AIR9/122 no. 119738. "Second Report of the Sub-Committee on the German Oil Position," ca. 1941: PRO CAB77/13.

27. "Oil Allocation and Distribution for Civilian Consumption in Germany," Jul 1944: BP 16548.

28. "Oil Allocation and Distribution for Civilian Consumption in Germany." Olex, "Valuation of Stock End-In-Hand at December 31st, 1937": BP 92868. Letter, W. B. Blackwood to F. G. C. Morris, Sep 3, 1936: BP 72201.

29. British Petroleum, "Report on Germany," Jan 1, 1947: BP 69501. "Valuation of Stock End-In-Hand at December 31st, 1937."

30. Olex, "Shares in and Advances to or from Subsidiary Companies at 31st December 1936": BP 90518.

31. Letter, F. C. Starling to A. C. Hearn, Aug 5, 1936: BP 68318. Olex, "Memorandum: Proposed Barter Transaction: Germany," Feb 6, 1936: BP 68318. Blackwood to Morris, Sep 3, 1936. Generally see Black, *Transfer Agreement.*

32. See letter, R. Blackwood to F. G. C. Morris, May 12, 1936: BP 72201. Starling to Hearn. "Proposed Barter Transaction: Germany." Olex-BP, "Anglo-Iranian Oil Company Ltd, London, Claims at 31st December 1936," Mar 15, 1937: BP 90518.

33. Olex, "Anglo-Iranian Oil Company Ltd., London: Claims at 31st December 1938": BP 90492. Letter, "Olex" Deutsche Benzin- Und Petroleum Gesellschaft mit beschrankter Häftung to Anglo-Iranian Oil Co. Ltd., Continental Distribution Department, Oct 28, 1936: BP 64902.

34. See photo, "Pump Installation in Germany, 1926," Ferrier, 490. See photo, " 'Olex' BP Service Station in Germany, Mid-1930s," Bamberg, 135. Bamberg, 132–133. "Oil Allocation and Distribution for Civilian Consumption in Germany." Memo, N. B. Fuller to Capt. W. J. A. Brown, Jul 7, 1928: BP 64902. "Draft of a Letter to the Automobile Association," Jun 2, 1936: BP 64902. See Ferrier, 489.

35. Olex, "Tale of the Family Tree," ca. 1950: BP 90030. See "Trade Mark Registration Certificate No. 499538," Jan 27, 1938: BP 97583. See letter, L. Lefroy to F. Mann, Jul 26, 1937: BP 67857. See letter, M. R. Bridgeman to F. G. C. Morris, Jul 25, 1938: BP 67857. See letter, F. G. C. Morris to L. M. Lefroy, Jul 27, 1938: BP 67857.

36. "Standard Oil Co. (N.J.): II," *Fortune*, vol. 21, no. 5 (May 1940). "Oil Allocation and Distribution for Civilian Consumption in Germany." See letter, W. B. Blackwood to

F. G. C. Morris, Dec 29, 1936: BP 72201. See letter, W. B. Blackwood to F. G. C. Morris, May 31, 1937: BP 72201. See "Trade Mark Registration Certificate No. 511307," May 5, 1939: BP 97574. See "Trade Mark Registration Certificate No. 508749," Mar 13 1939: BP 97585. See "Trade Mark Registration Certificate No. 434021," Mar 10, 1930: BP 97599.

37. Bamberg, 63–64. "Secret: An Appreciation of the Oil Position in Iran and Iraq," Oct 4, 1941: PRO POWE33/1085 no. 119945.

38. "Report on Germany." Generally see Black, Edwin, *IBM and the Holocaust: The Strategic Alliance Between Nazi Germany and America's Most Powerful Corporation* (New York: Crown, 2001).

39. "Particulars from Custodian of Enemy Property Records," ca. 1941: PRO BT271/592 no. 119571.

40. "Record of a Meeting Held in the Petroleum Department on Monday 29th July 1940, at 4:30 P.M. to Consider the Position of French Interests in the Iraq Petroleum Company," Jul 19, 1940: PRO FO371/24561 no. 119238.

41. Minutes, "Mr. C. S. Gulbenkian," Feb 1, 1944: PRO FO371/40215 no. 119238. Minutes of Feb 10, 1944: PRO FO371/40215 no. 119238. "Communicated to S.o.S. by Sir Kenneth Clark," ca. Feb 1944: PRO FO371/40215 no. 119238.

42. "Report by the Petroleum Department: The Levant Plan," ca. 1940: PRO CAB77/12 no. 358. "Lord Weir's Note of 1st April, 1940": PRO PREM1/434 no. 119738. War Cabinet, "Lord Hankey's Committee on Preventing Oil From Reaching Germany," Jul 14, 1940: PRO CAB77/12 no. 310. See Pilot Officer M. A. ap Rhys Price, "Bombing the Enemy's Fuel Supplies," secret report, Jan 27, 1940: PRO AIR9/122 no. 119738. See "R.A.F. Pours Bombs on Reich to Forestall Invasion Attempt," *WP*, Jun 21, 1941, 1.

43. Bard, Mitchell G., "Operation Barbarossa," Jewish Virtual Library, www.jewishvirtuallibrary.org. See US Holocaust Memorial Museum, www.ushmm.org.

44. "Lord Weir's Note of 1st April, 1940." "Bad Faith Charged," *NYT*, Jun 22, 1941, 1.

45. "Lord Weir's Note of 1st April, 1940."

46. War Cabinet Joint Planning Staff, "Future Strategy Review," Jun 1941: PRO CAB84/31 no. 119945.

47. "Future Strategy Review." "German Activities in Oil Producing Countries of Middle East," secret minute sheet, Dec 11, 1940: PRO FO371/24549. "Extract from D.O. (41) 39th Meeting" Jun 5, 1941: PRO AIR8/497 no. 119945.

48. "Note on Iraq as a Possible Source of Oil Supply to the Enemy," ca. 1940, BP IPC 255: Protective Measures.

49. "Note on Iraq as a Possible Source of Oil Supply to the Enemy."

50. "Feisal of Iraq Dies Suddenly in Berne," *NYT*, Sep 9, 1933, 1, 3. Tripp, Charles, *A History of Iraq* (Cambridge, UK: Cambridge University Press, 2000), 80.

51. "Ghazi Is Proclaimed King," *NYT*, Sep 9, 1933, 3. See Khadduri, Majid, *Independent Iraq: A Study in Iraqi Politics Since 1932* (London: Oxford University Press, 1951), 47–53 and chaps. 4–8. "Extract from Minutes of Group Meeting Held 17/11/37," Nov 11, 1937: BP IPC 100-45: Pipeline Survey.

52. Tripp, 81, 94–98. Warner, Geoffrey, *Iraq and Syria, 1941* (Newark, DE: University of Delaware Press, 1974), 35.

53. Tripp, 98–99. Mattar, 89. Warner, 35. Khadduri, 137–139, 140–142.

54. Warner, 35. Tripp, 98–99. Air Commodore F. W. Walker, "A Review of the Battle of Habbaniya, May 1941," ca. June 1941: PRO AIR8/549 no. 119909, 1. Khadduri, 16, as compared to Tripp, 94.

55. Nicosia, Francis, "Arab Nationalism and National Socialist Germany, 1933–1939: Ideological and Strategic Incompatibility," *International Journal of Middle East Studies*, vol. 12 (1980), 363–364. Generally see Black, *IBM and the Holocaust*.

56. Generally see Black, *War Against the Weak*, 261–277, 279–318. Generally see Black, *IBM and the Holocaust*, 93–96. Generally see Black, *The Transfer Agreement*, 371–380.

57. "Vichy Police Chief Aided Mufti in Syria," ca. June 1940: PRO FO371/61926 no. 119288.

58. Letter, War Office to D. J. M. D. Scott, Nov 24, 1939: PRO FO371/23207 no. 119238. "The Mufti's Bid for Indian Moslem Aid," copy of letter, Mufti to President of All-India Muslim League, Bombay, Mar 2, 1940 (22 Moharrem 1359): PRO FO371/61926 no. 119288. Elpeleg, 58.

59. Sir Basil Newton to Lord Halifax, Jun 10, 1940: PRO FO371/24561 no. 119238. Khadduri, 154–155.

60. "Enclosure in Baghdad Despatch No. 238 of 28.5.40: Extracts from the Local Press," May 28, 1940: PRO FO371/24561 no. 119238.

61. Letter, C. J. Edmonds to Sir Basil Newton, May 19, 1940: PRO FO371/24561 no. 119238.

62. Edmonds to Newton.

63. Edmonds to Newton.

64. "A Review of the Battle of Habbaniya, May 1941." Letter, Sir Basil Newton to Viscount Halifax, May 20, 1940: PRO FO371/24561 no. 119238. Letter, C. J. Edmonds to Sir Basil Newton, Jul 1, 1920, enclosure in Baghdad Despatch No. 315: PRO FO371/24561 no. 119238. See confidential letter, Sir Basil Newton to Mr. Eden, Feb 25, 1941: PRO FO371/27100 no. 119904. Mufti al-Amin, "Proposed Draft of an Official Declaration by Germany and Italy with Respect to the Arab Countries," ca. 1940: PRO FO371/61926 no. 119288. Elpeleg, 59. Khadduri, 195.

65. "Proposed Draft of an Official Declaration by Germany and Italy with Respect to the Arab Countries."

66. Pol, Heinz, " 'German Lawrence' Stirs Revolt," *NYT*, May 18, 1941, E5.

67. " 'German Lawrence' Stirs Revolt."

68. Elpeleg, 68.

69. See letter, Sir Basil Newton to Viscount Halifax, Oct 9, 1940: PRO FO371/24561 no. 119238.

70. Newton to Halifax, Oct 9, 1940.

71. Newton to Halifax, Oct 9, 1940.

72. Newton to Eden, Feb 25, 1941. War Office, "Iraq: February 1940 to August 1941 and May 1941 to January 1942," ca. Feb 1942: PRO WO32/11437 no. 120130.

73. "Comments on Paragraphs 9–13 of Chiefs of Staff Report of November 1st on an Enemy Advance through the Balkans and Syria to the Middle East," Nov 5, 1940: PRO FO371/24549. Elpeleg, 59–60.

74. Confidential letter, Sir Basil Newton to Mr. Eden, Jan 17, 1941: PRO FO371/27100 no. 119904.

75. Letter, Mufti Hussein al-Amin to Adolf Hitler, Jan 20, 1941, as translated and reproduced in Elpeleg, 202–205 and Khadduri (1960), 378–380.

76. Mufti to Hitler.

77. Mufti to Hitler.

78. Mufti to Hitler.

79. Mufti to Hitler.

80. Secret letter, Ernst Friherr von Wiesacker to Mufti Hussein al-Amin, Mar 1941: PRO FO371/61926 no. 119288.

81. Von Wiesacker to Mufti.

82. "Pro-Axis Leader Ousts the Premier in Iraq," *NYT*, Apr 5, 1941, 2. "Iraqi Coup Denounced," *NYT*, Apr 8, 1941, 7. Khadduri, 180–183. See "Accused of Plot, Regent Quits Iraq," *NYT*, Apr 9, 1941, 12.

83. "New Regent Is Elected," *NYT*, Apr 12, 1941, 5. Khadduri, 182. Geyder, G. E. R., "Syrians Say Nazis Keep Unrest Alive," *NYT*, Apr 5, 1941, 2. Letter to Mr. J. Skliros, Apr 5, 1941 and enclosure, letter of resignation, Taha al-Hashimi to H. R. H. The Regent, Apr 1, 1941: BP IPC 99-M4C: Misc. Correspondence. See "Uprising In Levant Fought By French," *NYT*, Mar 27, 1941, 1, 2.

84. See secret telegram, Baghdad to Foreign Office, Apr 5, 1941: PRO CAB84/28 no. 119909. "Defence of British Embassy and American Legation, Baghdad," memo, Apr 11, 1941: PRO AIR23/5925 no. 119909. "Kirkuk," memo, Apr 13, 1941: PRO AIR23/5925 no. 119909.

85. Telegram, General Wavell to C. I. G. S., May 3, 1941 as quoted in "Iraq: February 1940 to August 1941 and May 1941 to January 1942."

86. See secret telegram, Baghdad to Foreign Office, Apr 5, 1941: PRO CAB84/28 no. 119909. "Defence of British Embassy and American Legation, Baghdad," memo, Apr 11, 1941: PRO AIR23/5925 no. 119909. "Kirkuk," memo, Apr 13, 1941: PRO AIR23/5925 no. 119909. War Cabinet Chiefs of Staff (COS) Committee, "Iraq Oil: Note by the Secretary," May 30, 1941: PRO AIR8/497 no. 119945. Major D. Morton, "Iraq Oil: Memorandum by Major Morton," Jun 4, 1941: PRO AIR8/497 no. 119945. See telegram, Commander in Chief, Baghdad to War Office, Apr 15, 1941: PRO CAB85/29 no. 119909.

87. Iraq Petroleum Company, memo, Jul 1, 1940.

88. Most secret and personal letter, Noel Hall to Commodore J. C. Slessor, Jun 26, 1940: PRO AIR9/122 no. 119738.

89. "Note to Petroleum Department: Syria."

90. Dudley Pound, memo, Nov 17, 1940: PRO FO371/24549.

91. "Aide Memoire on Meeting Held at the Petroleum Department on 18th December, 1940."

92. Secret letter, J. Skliros to M. R. Bridgeman, Apr 10, 1941: BP IPC 255: Protective Measures.

93. "British Army Lands in Iraq to Guard Prized Oil Fields," *NYT*, Apr 20, 1941, 1. Secret letter, British Consulate, Basra, to Sir K. Cornwallis, Jul 16, 1941: PRO FO371/27079.

94. Letter, Sir K. Cornwallis to Anthony Eden, Jun 6, 1941: PRO FO371/27077 no. 20157. "A Review of the Battle of Habbaniya, May 1941."

95. Letter, J. Skliros to M. R. Bridgeman, Mar 3, 1942. "Note, Strictly Private and Confidential," Jun 9, 1941: PRO FO371/27078.

96. Walker, 1–2. De Chair, Somerset, *The Golden Carpet* (New York: Harcourt, Brace & Co., 1945), 79. Glubb, Sir John, *The Story of the Arab Legion* (London: Hodder & Stoughton, 1948), 277–278.

97. Walker, 3.

98. Walker, 4. Glubb, 278. Letter to Anthony Eden, Jun 6, 1941: PRO FO371/27077 no. 120157.

99. Walker, 4–5.

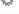
100. Walker, 5. Douglas Porch, "The Other 'Gulf War'—The British Invasion of Iraq in 1941," The Center for Contemporary Conflict, www.ccc.nps.navy.mil.

101. "Sonderkommando JUNCK," ca. Sep 8, 1952: PRO AIR20/9945 no. 119738.

102. "Sonderkommando JUNCK." Secret telegram from Sir K. Cornwallis, "List of Germans who arrived in Iraq from 2nd May, 1941," Jun 26, 1941: PRO FO371/27077 no. 120157. Secret telegram, A. H. Q. Iraq to R. A. F., May 14, 1941: PRO AIR8/549 no. 119909. Sulzberger, C. L., "Nazis At Air Bases," *NYT*, May 15, 1941, 1. Sulzberger, C. L., "Syrian Bases Bombed," *NYT*, May 18, 1941, 1.

103. Telegram, Commander in Chief, Middle East, to War Office, May 3, 1941: PRO AIR8/497.

104. Personal telegram, W. S. Churchill to F. D. Roosevelt, May 4, 1941, as quoted by Gilbert, Martin, *Winston S. Churchill, Vol. 6: Finest Hour, 1939–1941* (Boston: Houghton Mifflin, 1983), 1078–1079. Walker, 5–6. Shirer, William, *Rise and Fall of the Third Reich* (New York: Simon & Shuster, 1981), 829.

105. See Commander in Chief to War Office, May 3, 1941.

106. Lapidot, Yehuda, *The History of the Irgun*, Chaya Galai, trans., www.etzel.org.il. Elpeleg, 60. Bell, J. Bowyer, *Terror Out of Zion: The Fight for Israeli Independence* (New Brunswick, NJ: Transaction Publishers, 1996), 55.

107. Lapidot.

108. Dayan, Moshe, *Moshe Dayan: Story of My Life* (New York: William Morrow, 1976), 63–64. *Encyclopedia Judaica*, s.v. "Palmach."

109. Lapidot. Boyer, 55–56. Elpeleg, 60.

110. Telegram, Major-General Sir H. L. Ismay to War Cabinet, May 22, 1941: PRO AIR8/497.

111. Adolf Hitler, "Order No. 30: Middle East," May 23, 1941: PRO FO371/61926 no. 110288. See Shirer, 829.

112. "A Review of the Battle of Habbaniya, May 1941," 11. "Glubb's Arabs to Parade," *NYT*, Jun 4, 1941, 3. "Mosul is Occupied by British Troops," *NYT*, Jun 5, 1941, 4. "German Flight Reported," *NYT*, Jun 1, 1941, 3. Telegram, Commander in Chief, Iraq, to Foreign Office, May 31, 1941: PRO FO371/27073 no. 120157. Most secret telegram, Assistant Secretary for War to First Sea Lord, May 24, 1941: PRO AIR8/497. Secret telegram, Sir K. Cornwallis to General, Basra, May 30, 1941: PRO AIR8/549 no. 119909.

113. "Sonderkommando JUNCK." "German Flight Reported." Telegram, Sir K. Cornwallis to Foreign Office, May 31, 1941: PRO FO371/27073 no. 120157. "Armistice Ends Revolt in Iraq; Arab Chief Flees," *NYT*, Jun 1, 1941, 1. Anderson, David, "War in Iraq Ends; Regent in Baghdad," *NYT*, Jun 1, 1941, 1, 3. Telegram, D. Knabenshue to Secretary of State, Jun 1, 1941: NA RG59 740.0011 European War 1939/11558: Telegram, *FRUS*, 1941, 511.

114. "Extract from minutes of Chief of Staff Meeting held on 31st May, 1941," secret, May 31, 1941: PRO AIR8/497 no. 119945.

115. "Long Allied Columns Drive North in Syria," *NYT*, Jun 9, 1941, 4. Connell, John, *Wavell: Scholar and Soldier, to June 1941* (London: Collins, 1964), 490–492.

116. Dayan, 66–68. Teveth, Shabtai, *Moshe Dayan: The Soldier, The Man, The Legend*, Leah and David Zinder, trans (Boston: Houghton Mifflin, 1973), 116–117.

117. Slater, Robert, *Rabin of Israel* (New York: St. Martin's Press, 1993), 46. Teveth, 123–124.

118. "Long Allied Columns Drive North in Syria." "Advance Towards Capitals," *NYT*, Jun 9, 1941, 1. MacRae, James, "Airfields Blasted," *NYT*, Jun 9, 1941, 1. See Connell, 490–492.
119. "War in Iraq Ends." "Bad Faith Charged," *NYT*, Jun 22, 1941, 1.

CHAPTER 17: THE PRICE OF PREJUDICE

1. Letter, Sir K. Cornwallis to Anthony Eden, Jun 6, 1941: PRO FO371/27077 no. 20157. Telegram, D. Knabenshue to Secretary of State, Jun 1, 1941: NA RG59 740.0011 European War 1939/11558: Telegram, *FRUS* 1941, vol. 3, 511. De Chair, Somerset, *The Golden Carpet* (New York: Harcourt, Brace & Company, 1945), 127. Anderson, David, "War in Iraq Ends; Regent in Baghdad," *NYT*, Jun 1, 1941, 1, 3. "Return of the Regent," *Times*, Jun 2, 1941, 4, G.
2. Letter, Sir K. Cornwallis to Anthony Eden, Jul 11, 1941: PRO FO371/27078. Warner, Geoffrey, *Iraq and Syria, 1941* (Newark, DE: University of Delaware Press, 1974), 117. Elpeleg, Zvi, *The Grand Mufti: Haj Amin Al-Hussaini, Founder of the Palestinian National Movement*, David Harvey, trans.; Shmuel Himelstein, ed. (London: Frank Cass, 1993), 61–62. "Mosul in British Hands," *Times*, Jun 5, 1941, 4, E.
3. Cornwallis to Eden, Jul 11, 1941. Habousha, Hayim V., "The Farhud," lecture, Midrash ben Ish Hai, www.midrash.org. Levin, Itamar, *Locked Doors: The Seizure of Jewish Property in Arab Countries*, Rachel Neiman, trans. (Westport, CT: Praeger, 2001), 6. See De Chair, 127.
4. Telegram, Sir K. Cornwallis to Foreign Office, Jul 29, 1941: PRO FO371/27028. "The Farhud."
5. Cornwallis to Eden, Jul 11, 1941. "The Farhud." See Levin, 6.
6. Levin, 5–6.
7. Note, Foreign Office to Colonial Office, Jul 31, 1941: PRO FO371/27078. Cornwallis to Foreign Office, Jul 29, 1941. Cornwallis to Eden, Jul 11, 1941. "The Farhud." "Baghdad Clash Reported," *NYT*, Jun 4, 1941, 3. "Axis Intriguers Return to Syria," *Times*, Jun 5, 1941, 4, E.
8. Telegram, Jewish Agency, Jerusalem to Foreign Office, Jul 19, 1941: PRO FO371/27078. See Cornwallis to Foreign Office, Jul 29, 1941.
9. Jewish Agency to Foreign Office. Levin, 6. Elpeleg, 62. Gat, Moshe, *The Jewish Exodus from Iraq, 1948–1951* (London: Frank Cass, 1997), 21.
10. See Map, "The Near East 3200–1600 BC," Postgate, J. N., *Early Mesopotamia: Society and Economy at the Dawn of History* (London, UK: Routledge, 1994), 2.
11. "Memorandum by Mr. Kennedy on the Jews of Meshed," enclosure to confidential letter, Sir H. Drummond Wolff to Marquis of Salisbury, Apr 6, 1890: PRO FO511. Levin, 2–3.
12. Sultan Abdulmecit I, "A Firman Addressed to the Chief Judge at Constantinople," Nov 6, 1840/12 Ramadan 1256, PRO FO78/416, as quoted in Stillman, Norman, *The Jews of Arab Lands: A History and Source Book* (Philadelphia: The Jewish Publication Society of America, 1979), 401–402.
13. Nuri as-Said, "Lectures on the Arab Revolt," May 1947, as quoted by Basri, Meer, "Iraqi Jews Fought with the Arabs for Independence in the First World War," *The Scribe: Journal of Babylonian Jewry*, no. 72, 23, www.dangoor.com.
14. Sir A. Nicolson, "Note on the Future Status and Administration of Basrah," Feb 2, 1915: PRO FO800/377. Levin, 3. Gat, 12–13.
15. Gat, 10.

16. Shaw, Stanford J. and Ezel Kural Shaw, *The History of the Ottoman Empire and Modern Turkey*, vol. 2, *Reform, Revolution, and Republic: The Rise of Modern Turkey, 1808–1975* (Cambridge, UK: Cambridge University Press, 1977), 241. Levin, 7–8.
17. Gat, 18–19.
18. See Black, Edwin, *The Transfer Agreement: The Dramatic Story of the Pact Between the Third Reich and Jewish Palestine* (New York: Carroll & Graf, 2001), 71–82.
19. Gat, 16.
20. Letter, Menahem S. Daniel to Zionist Organization, Sep 8, 1922: Central Zionist Archive (CZA) Z4/2101.
21. "Rabbi Attacks Zionism," *NYT*, Apr 9, 1947, 8. Gat, 19.
22. See Ireland, Phillip Willard, *Iraq: A Study in Political Development* (New York: Macmillan, 1938), 418. See Letter, Abdullah ibn al-Hussein to Secretary of State for the British Colonies, Jul 11, 1940: PRO FO371/24549.
23. Khadduri, Majid, *Independent Iraq: A Study in Iraqi Politics Since 1932* (London: Oxford University Press, 1951), 44–46. Phares, Walid, "Middle East Christians," Malka Hillel Shulewitz, ed., *The Forgotten Millions: The Modern Jewish Exodus from Arab Lands* (London: Cassel, 1999), 20. See Stafford, R. S., "Iraq and the Problem of the Assyrians," *International Affairs*, vol. 13, no. 2 (Mar–Apr 1934), 165–166.
24. Stafford, 174–177.
25. De Luca, Anthony, " 'Der Grossmufti' in Berlin: The Politics of Collaboration," *International Journal of Middle East Studies*, vol. 10, no. 1 (Feb 1979), 127. Gat, 18.
26. "The Jews in Iraq: Government Officials Take Part in Incitements," *Jewish Telegraphic Agency (JTA)*, Oct 26, 1936: PRO FO954/12. Gat, 18.
27. "Position of Jews in Iraq," May 27, 1940: PRO FO371/24561 no. 119238.
28. Secret telegram, External Affairs Department, India to Secretary of State for India, Aug 24, 1941: PRO FO371/27116 no. 119909. Telegram, P. Crosthwaite to H. T. Peel, Sep 1, 1941: PRO FO371/27116 no. 119909. Letter, Sir K. Cornwallis to Sir Horace Seymour, Sep 25, 1941: PRO FO371/27116 no. 119909. Warner, 117–118.
29. Secret telegram, Commander in Charge, Iraq to War Office, Aug 27, 1941: PRO FO371/27079. Luks, Harold Paul, "Iraqi Jews during World War II," *Wiener Library Bulletin* no. 30, 34.
30. Gat, 25, 26, 27.
31. The Nation Associates, "The Arab Higher Committee: Its Origins, Personnel and Purposes," May 1947, 5–6: PRO FO371/61926 no. 119288. See letter, Amin al-Husseini, Grossmufti to Reichsführer Himmler, ca. Jul 1943, as reproduced in Gensicke, Klaus, *Der Mufti von Jerusalem, Amin el-Husseini, und die Nationalsozialisten* (Frankfurt am Main: Peter Lang, 1988), 185. See "Memorandum of the Conversation between the Grand Mufti and the German Foreign Minister in Berlin," Nov 28, 1941: PRO FO371/27078. Mattar, Philip, *The Mufti of Jerusalem* (New York: Columbia University Press, 1988), 103–104. Elpeleg, 66. See De Luca, 125–138.
32. "Memorandum of the Conversation between the Grand Mufti and the German Foreign Minister in Berlin."
33. "Memorandum of the Conversation between the Fuehrer and the Grand Mufti of Jerusalem in the Presence of the German Minister for Foreign Affairs and Herr Grobba, German Minister at Baghdad," Nov 28, 1941: PRO FO371/27078. Elpeleg, 66. Mattar, 102–103.
34. See "The Trial of Adolf Eichmann," transcript, District Court Session 16, pt. 3, The Holocaust Resource, www.nizkor.org. Letter, Haj Amin al-Husseini to Minister of

Foreign Affairs for Hungary, Jun 28, 1943, as quoted in "The Arab Higher Committee: Its Origins, Personnel and Purposes." Mattar, 105. De Luca, 136. Elpeleg, 69–70.

35. Lopasic, Alexander, "Bosnian Muslims: A Search for Identity," *Bulletin (British Society for Middle Eastern Studies)*, vol. 8, no. 2 (1981), 122. Bender, Roger James, and Hugh Page Taylor, "Uniforms, Organization and History of the Waffen-SS," 137–139, 144–145. Gensicke, 198.

36. Schechtman, Joseph B., *The Mufti and the Fuehrer: The Rise and Fall of Haj Amin el-Husseini* (New York: Thomas Yoseloff, 1965), 110–112, 125, 150–151.

37. Luks, 34.

38. Glubb, Major John, "A Report on the Role Played by the Arab Legion in Connection with the Recent Operations in Iraq," Jun 10, 1941, 10–11: PRO FO371/27078.

39. "A Report on the Role Played by the Arab Legion in Connection with the Recent Operations in Iraq," 10–11.

40. World Jewish Congress, "The Treatment of Jews in Egypt and Iraq," white paper, ca. 1948, 20: AJC WP1948.B140.31.

41. "The Treatment of Jews in Egypt and Iraq," 20. Gat, 29.

42. Audio recording, UN roll call vote, Nov 29, 1947, Knesset.gov.il. "United Nations General Assembly Resolution 181," Nov 29, 1947, Avalon Project, www.law.yale.edu.

43. Gat 29–30.

44. Bamberg, James, *The History of the British Petroleum Company,* vol. 2, *The Anglo-Iranian Years, 1928–1954* (Cambridge, UK: Cambridge University Press, 1994), 338–339.

45. Letter, H. Y. Orgel to the *New York Times*, Aug 28, 1958, 26. Sachar, Howard M., *A History of Israel: From the Rise of Zionism to Our Time* (New York: Alfred A. Knopf, 1981), 333. Tripp, Charles, "Iraq and the 1948 War: Mirror of Iraq's Disorder," Eugene L. Rogan and Avi Shlaim, eds., *The War for Palestine* (New York: Cambridge University Press, 2001), 125, 139.

46. "Law No. (11) of 1948, Amending Law No. (51) of 1938, Supplemental to the Baghdad Penal Code," *Iraq Government Gazette*, Nov 14, 1948: JJAC 1948/1. World Jewish Congress, "Memorandum on the Treatment of the Jewish Population in Iraq," Oct 22, 1949: AJC UNF48–49.B139.8. Gat, 36.

47. "Iraq Hangs Wealthy Jew for Arms Aid to Zionists," *NYT*, Sep 24, 1948, 8. "Wealthy Jew Hanged for Treason in Iraq," *WP*, Sep 25, 1948, 3. "Iraq Merchant to Die for Aid to Palestine," *NYT*, Sep 14, 1948, 17. "Memorandum on the Treatment of the Jewish Population in Iraq."

48. *Redifot Yehudim be-Iraq*, Nov 15, 1949: Israel State Archives (ISA) RG93, box 90, fol. 1. Mack to Bevin, "Annual Review for 1948," Jan 17, 1941: FO371/75125/E773/1011/93. Mack to Bevin, "Notes on Position of Jews in Iraq," Mar 3, 1949: PRO FO371/75182. Gat, 37. Levin, 38, Tripp, 141–142.

49. "Some Editorial Comment on the Irak Bill by the Baghdad Paper, *Al Shaab*," Mar 3, 1950: JJAC 1950/4. "Report of Interview with 'Mr. S,' Recently Come from Iraq," Jan 13, 1950: JJAC 1950/2. Baghdad to Foreign Office, Apr 1, 1950: FO371/EQ1571/17, as cited by Gat, 92. Gat, 32. Schechtman, Joseph B., "The Repatriation of Iraqi Jewry," *Jewish Social Studies*, vol. 25, no. 2 (Apr 1953), "Repatriation," 160.

50. Kadmon to Mossad, Oct 19, 1948: Hagana Archives (HA), as cited by Gat, 42–43.

"On the Immigration of the Jews from Iraq," ca. Jan 1950: ISA RG130, box 2563, fol. 8. Basra to State Department (SD), Mar 14, 1950: NA RG59 887.411/3-1450. Gat, 42–44, 71–72. Schechtman, "Repatriation," 157. See Levin, 27. See confidential memo, Basra to SD, Feb 8, 1950, Feb 15, 1950, Mar 1, 1950, Mar 8, 1950: NA RG59, S250, R41, C10, S7, Box 5488. See secret telegram, Baghdad to Secretary of State, Mar 18, 1950: NA RG59 887.411/3-1850.

51. Schechtman, "Repatriation," 159. Levin, 44.

52. "Comment on Charges of Economic Discrimination against Jewish Community in Iraq," enclosure to despatch no. 432, Baghdad to SD, Nov 28, 1949: NA RG59 890G.4016/11-2849. Gat, 74. Levin, 7.

53. Parliament of Iraq, "Iraqi Law No. 1 for 1950," Mar 9, 1950: JJAC 1950/1. See "Debate on the Jewish Emigration Bill in the Irak Chamber of Deputies," *Al-Shaab*, Mar 3, 1950. "Iraq House Adopts Bill to Permit Jews to Leave," *NYT*, Mar 4, 1950, 8. Ross, Albion, "Jews Leaving Iraq in a Steady Flow," *NYT*, Jan 24, 1950, 11. Telegram, Baghdad to Secretary of State, Mar 6, 1950: NA RG59 887.411/3-650. Confidential telegram, Baghdad to Secretary of State, Mar 11, 1950: NA RG59 887.411/3-1150.

54. Letters, Baghdad to Foreign Office, Mar 7, 1950 and Mar 21, 1950: PRO FO371/82478. Letter, Baghdad to Foreign Office, Apr 1, 1950: PRO FO371/82478.

55. Teheran to Israeli Government, Mar 19, 1950: CZA S/41/256II, as cited by Gat, 83. Yerahmiel to Zerubavel, Mar 18, 1950: CZA S/20/539II, as cited by Gat, 83. Gat, 83. See confidential despatch, Basra to SD, Mar 15, 1950: NA RG59 887.411/3-1550.

56. Michael to Kadmon, Mar 15, 1950: HA, as cited by Gat, 88. Mack to Bevin, Mar 21, 1950: FO371/EA1571/9 as cited by Gat, 88. Gat, 88. "Jewish Drive Here Brings in $5,925,000," *NYT*, Mar 8, 1950, 14. "Air-Sea Migration of 90,000 Planned," *NYT*, Mar 18, 1950, 6. Confidential telegram, Tehran to Secretary of State, Mar 23, 1950: NA RG59 887.411/3-2150.

57. "Iraqi Jews Flown by Lift to Israel," *NYT*, May 22, 1950, 5. Schechtman, "Repatriation," 161. Gat, 92. See restricted despatch, Basra to SD, Mar 28, 1950: NA RG59 887.411/3-2850. See confidential telegram, Baghdad to Secretary of State, Apr 12, 1950: NA RG59 887.411/4-1250.

58. "Iraqi Refugees Fly to Israel," *NYT*, May 20, 1950, 6. Schechtman, "Repatriation," 164. Gat, 101.

59. See Wilson, Earl, "Travel Bar by Baghdad Explained in Tel Aviv," *WP*, Aug 31, 1951, B11. See Schechtman, "Repatriation," 163. Gat, 105, 107.

60. "Iraqis Fix Deadline for Jewish Exodus," *NYT*, Jan 20, 1951, 4. Middle East Department to Evron, ca. Mar 1951: ISA Rg 136, box 2387, fol. 4. Schechtman, "Repatriation," 163.

61. Cable, Duron and Dror to Mossad, May 7, 1950: HA 14/429: May–Jun 1950. Gat, 106, 128–129, 138–139.

62. "Israel in Dilemma over Immigration," *NYT*, Mar 6, 1950, 7. "Camp Life in Israel 'Shocks' Morgenthau," *NYT*, Jan 20, 1950, 5. See "Immigrants Entering Israel From 1950 to May 1951 According to Immigration Ministry Data," Jun 20, 1951: ISA RG 130, box 2387 fol. 4.

63. Parliament of Iraq, "Law for the Control and Administration of Property of Jews Who Have Forfeited Iraqi Nationality," *Iraq Government Gazette*, Mar 10, 1951/2

Jamadi al-Akhara 1368: JJAC 1951/4. "Resumé of Iraqi Law No. 5 for 1951," Mar 10, 1951: JJAC 1950/1. "Iraq Acts against Jews," *NYT*, Mar 11, 1951, 23. Levin, 46. Note, Mar 17, 1951: HA 14/435.

64. "Israel in Dilemma Over Immigration." "Iraqis Fix Deadline for Jewish Exodus." See memo, Mar 17, 1951, HA 14/435 no. 66. Gat, 131, 152, 155. "Editorial Regarding Immigration of Jews from Iraq," despatch, Jerusalem to SD, Mar 27, 1950: NA RG59 887.411/3-2750.

65. Berman to Mossad, Mar 17, 1951: HA, as quoted by Gat, 151.

66. Sharett, Moshe, address to Knesset, Mar 19, 1951, as quoted by Schechtman, "Repatriation," 170. "Iraqi Action Brings Israeli Retaliation," *NYT*, Mar 20, 1951.

67. Levin, 46. Schechtman, "Repatriation," 164.

68. Gat, 158. See Parsons, Arch, Jr., "Israel to Restrict '52 Immigration," *WP*, Dec 23, 1951, B2.

CHAPTER 18: THE THREE GULFS

1. Abdulaziz Bin Salman, "King Abdulaziz Negotiations with Concessionaire Oil Companies in Saudi Arabia," undated, 7–8. Bamberg, James, *The History of the British Petroleum Company*, vol. 2: *The Anglo-Iranian Years, 1928–1954* (Cambridge, UK: Cambridge University Press, 1994), 171.

2. Bamberg, *The Anglo-Iranian Years,* 171–172.

3. Abdulaziz Bin Salman, 6. Bamberg, *The Anglo-Iranian Years*, 146, 147–148.

4. "Mr. C. S. Gulbenkian," minutes, Feb 8, 1944: PRO FO371/40215. Longrigg, Stephen H., *Oil in the Middle East: Its Discovery and Development* (London: Oxford University Press, 1968), 118, 174. Bamberg, *The Anglo-Iranian Years*, 335.

5. Minutes of meetings, Sep 16, 1946, Sep 23, 1946, Sep 24, 1946, Sep 27, 1946: IPC 3B 2003, as cited by Bamberg, *The Anglo-Iranian Years*, 335–336. Bamberg, *The Anglo-Iranian Years*, 335–336.

6. Khadduri, Majid, *Independent Iraq, 1932–1958: A Study in Iraqi Politics* (London: Oxford University Press, 1960), 262–269, 271. "Britain and Iraq Fix New Alliance," *NYT*, Jan 11, 1948, 2. "Baghdad Riots Threaten Britain-Iraq Pact," *WP*, Jan 23, 1948, 11. "Iraq Regent Balks At British Treaty," *NYT*, Jan 22, 1948. "Iraq Cabinet Quits as People Protest Treaty with British; 70 Killed, 300 Wounded in Riots," *WP*, Jan 28, 1948, 4. "Iraq Premier Flees to Trans-Jordan," *NYT*, Jan 29, 1948, 1.

7. Longrigg, *Oil*, 209–210. Bamberg, *The Anglo-Iranian Years*, 339.

8. Bamberg, *The Anglo-Iranian Years*, 363, 367, 375. See photos, Bamberg, *The Anglo-Iranian Years*, 368–373. Longrigg, *Oil*, 155.

9. Bamberg, *The Anglo-Iranian Years,* 413, 428.

10. Bamberg, *The Anglo-Iranian Years*, 425. See photos, "The Iranian Flag Being Raised Over the Company's Offices at Abadan" and "Husayn Makki Addressing a Crowd at Abadan," Bamberg, *The Anglo-Iranian Years*, 424, 425.

11. Bamberg, *The Anglo-Iranian Years*, 432. Longrigg, *Oil*, 164. See photos, "Iranians Removing the Illuminated Sign" and "Crowd in Teheran Carrying One of the Signs," Bamberg, *The Anglo-Iranian Years*, 432, 434.

12. Longrigg, *Oil*, 163, 165. Bamberg, *The Anglo-Iranian Years*, 438.

13. See photo, "Changing the Plaque at the Entrance to Britannic House, Finsbury Circus, London," Bamberg, *The Anglo-Iranian Years*, 522. Bamberg, *The Anglo-Iranian Years*, 508–509.

14. Bamberg, *The Anglo-Iranian Years*, 341, 342.
15. Longrigg, *Oil*, 368–369. Abdulaziz Bin Salman, 14.
16. Howard, Harry N., "The Regional Pacts and the Eisenhower Doctrine," *Annals of the American Academy of Political and Social Science*, vol. 401 (May 1972), 86–90. Khadduri, 298, 299–302. "Planned Revolt 3 Years, Iraqi Says," *WP*, Jul 28, 1958, A10. See "Britain's Palestine Policy Tied to Soviet and Arabs," *WP*, Aug 10, 1947, E5. "Iran Closes the Gap, *NYT*, Oct 13, 1955, 30.
17. "Syria: United Arab Republic," Apr 1987, Library of Congress (LoC) Country Studies, www.loc.gov. "Egypt: Egypt and the Arab World," Dec 1990, LoC Country Studies. Khadduri, 242–243. "Iraqi Premier Sensed Trouble and Appealed to Washington in Vain," *NYT*, Jul 18, 1958, 9.
18. "How Crisis Developed in Iraq," *WP*, Jul 18, 1958, A14. Khadduri, 345.
19. "How Crisis Developed in Iraq." Dispatch, "The Iraqi Revolution of July 14, 1958," Sir Michael Wright to Mr. Selwyn Lloyd, Aug 21, 1958: PRO PREM11/2368, as reproduced in de L. Rush, Alan, and Jonathan Elliman, eds., *Records of the Hashemite Dynasties: A Twentieth Century Documentary History* (Slough, UK: Archive Editions, 1995), 801–804. Letter, C. M Johnson to Foreign Office, Jul 28, 1958: PRO FO371/134201, as reproduced in de L. Rush and Elliman, 790–793. Valentine, Alex, "King Feisal Arrested, Rebels Say," *WP*, Jul 15, 1958, A1, A4.
20. "Baghdad Regains Quiet after Successful Coup," *WP*, Jul 17, 1958. Johnson to Foreign Office. See photos, "Victims of Baghdad Assassins on Public Display," *Time*, Aug 4, 1958, 20. "Iraqi Premier Sensed Trouble and Appealed to Washington in Vain."
21. "Feisal, 23, Was King 19 Years," *WP*, Jul 15, 1958, A11. "Broadcast by Three Stations," *NYT*, Jul 14, 1958, 1. "Iraq Government Reported Seized by Army Revolt," *NYT*, Jul 14, 1958, 1. "Faisal Vanishes," *NYT*, Jul 15, 1958, 1. "Kassem Tells How He Led Coup," *WP*, Aug 9, 1958, B4. "On This Day – 14 July," http://news.bbc.co.uk. "How Crisis Developed in Iraq."
22. "How Crisis Developed in Iraq." "Eisenhower Sends Marines Into Lebanon," *NYT*, Jul 16, 1958, 1. "On This Day – 14 July." See "Marines in the Mediterranean," http://hqinet001.hqmc.usmc.mil. "British Land in Jordan, Backed by U.S. Jets," *NYT*, Jul 18, 1958, 1. "British Shift Units to Back U.S. Actions," *NYT*, Jul 16, 1958, 1.
23. Bamberg, *The Challenge*, 164–166.
24. Bamberg, *The Challenge,* 166.
25. Tripp, Charles, *A History of Iraq* (Cambridge, UK: Cambridge University Press, 2000), 151, 153, 156.
26. Tripp, 158. Bamberg, *The Challenge,* 163–165.
27. Bamberg, *The Challenge,* 165.
28. Bamberg, *The Challenge,* 166.
29. Bamberg, *The Challenge,* 167.
30. Bamberg, *The Challenge,* 167. Tripp, 170.
31. Bamberg, *The Challenge,* 167. Tripp, 180–181.
32. Yergin, Daniel, *The Prize: The Epic Quest for Oil, Money & Power* (New York: Free Press, 1991), 515, 521. "Global Trade: Soviet Price Cuts Unite Oil Nations," *WP*, Sep 19, 1960, A16.
33. Yergin, 518, 522–523. "Venezuela Joins Mideast Pact on Oil Stabilization," *WP*, Sep 25, 1960, D24. "Arab Oil Congress Is Expected to Direct Fire at Price Cut-

ting," *NYT*, Oct 8, 1960, 27. "World Oil Cartel May Take Shape," *NYT*, Sep 25, 1960, F1. "Oil Price Propping," *Wall Street Journal (WSJ)*, Oct 18, 1960, 1.

34. "About OPEC – OPEC History," www.opec.org. Yergin, 522–523.

35. Bamberg, *The Challenge*, 170–171.

36. Bamberg, *The Challenge*, 171.

37. Herzl, Theodor, *Der Judenstaat* (New York: Federation of American Zionists, 1917), chap. 1. Levin, Itamar, *Locked Doors: The Seizure of Jewish Property in Arab Countries*, Rachel Neiman, trans. (Westport, CT: Praeger, 2001), 76. "Iraq Hangs Nine Jews as Spies," *WP*, Jan 27, 1969, A13. American Jewish Congress, memorandum, "The History of Jews in Iraq," Jun 16, 1969: AJC CMSS361 BH193 F13.

38. Levin, 76. "The History of Jews in Iraq." "Large Crowd at Hangings," *NYT*, Jan 28, 1969, 2.

39. "The Speeches of Ayatollah Khomeini–The Story of the Iranian Revolution," BBC World Service, www.bbc.co.uk. Viorst, Milton, "Time 100: Ayatollah Ruollah Khomeini," Apr 13, 1998, *Time*, www.time.com. "History of Iran: Ayatollah Khomeini," Iran Chamber, www.iranchamber.com.

40. Viorst. "History of Iran." Tripp, 220.

41. Tripp, 220. See "5 Killed in Shiite Clash in Lebanon," *NYT*, Apr 16, 1980, A3. See "Besides Troubles with U.S., Iran Is Embroiled in Quarrel with Iraq," *NYT*, Apr 23, 1980, A10. Aziz, T. M., "The Role of Muhammad Baqir al-Sadr in Shii Political Activism in Iraq from 1958 to 1980," *International Journal of Middle East Studies*, vol. 25, no. 2 (May 1993), 207–222.

42. "Bakr Quits in Iraq, Names Hussein," *NYT*, Jul 17, 1979, A9. "Iraqi Leader Resigns, Citing Health; Strongman Hussein Named President," *WP*, Jul 17, 1979, A7. Tripp, 222.

43. Tripp, 222. See "Purge Party," author's note.

44. Randal, Jonathan C., "Attempt to Kill Baghdad Aide Worsens Iraqi-Iranian Ties," *WP*, Apr 3, 1980, A26. Homan, Richard, "Iran, Iraq on War Footing; Khomeini Urges Coup," *WP*, Apr 9, 1980, A18. Tripp, 229–230. See "5 Killed in Shiite Clash in Lebanon." See "Besides Troubles with U.S., Iran Is Embroiled in Quarrel with Iraq," *NYT*, Apr 23, 1980, A10. "Khomeini Accuses Iraq of Killing Shiite Ayatollah," *WP*, Apr 23, 1980, A32. See "Iranian Visits Syria in Bid for Support," *NYT*, Apr 27, 1980, 16. "Iraqis and Iranians Hurl Sharp Insults," *WP*, Jun 26, 1980, A9.

45. "Iran-Iraq War (1980–1988)," www.globalsecurity.org. Robinson, Julian Perry, and Josef Goldblat, "Chemical Warfare in the Iraq-Iran War," May 1984, Stockholm International Peace Research Institute, http://projects.sipri.se. See Frank N. Schubert and Theresa L. Kraus, eds., "The Background to War," *The Whirlwind War*, U.S. Army Center for Military History, www.army.mil/cmh-pg.

46. "Operation Earnest Will," www.globalsecurity.org. See "The Background to War."

47. "Operation Earnest Will." Cushman Jr., John H., "Iraqi Missile Hits U.S. Navy Frigate in Persian Gulf," *NYT*, May 18, 1987, A1, A12. Roberts, Steven V., "Apology From Iraq," *NYT*, May 18, 1987, A1, A10. Oberdorfer, Dan, and Edward Walsh, "Iraq to Pay Damages for Attack," *WP*, May 22, 1987, A1, A30. "The Hostages and the Casualties," Jimmy Carter Library and Museum, www.jimmycarterlibrary.org.

48. Kuwait Information Office, "History of the Kuwait-Iraq Border Dispute," www.kuwait-info.org. See "Exclusive Agreement: The Kuwayti Shaykh and Britain, 23 January 1899," as reproduced in Hurewitz, vol. 1, 218–219.

49. "History of the Kuwait-Iraq Border Dispute." See "Anglo-Ottoman Draft Convention on the Persian Gulf Area," Jul 29, 1913, as reproduced in J.C. Hurewitz, ed., *Diplomacy in the Near And Middle East*, vol. 2 (Gerrards Cross, UK: Archive Editions, 1987), 269–271.

50. Letter, Sir Basil Newton to Nuri as-Said, Oct 7, 1940: BL L/PS/12/2448 v17. "Geography," 2002, Kuwait Information Office, www.kuwait-info.org.

51. Letter, British Ambassador to Viscount Halifax, Apr 19, 1938: PRO IOR R/15/5/207, as reproduced in de L. Rush and Elliman, 778–780. Tawfig as-Suwaidi, Aide-memoire, ca. Sep 1938, as reproduced in de L. Rush and Elliman, 787–789. See Khadduri, 141. See "Boundaries Between Iraq and Kuwait," (trans.) *Al Nas*, Jan 19, 1937, as reproduced in de L. Rush and Elliman, 775. "History of the Kuwait-Iraq Border Dispute."

52. "History of the Kuwait-Iraq Border Dispute."

53. "History of the Kuwait-Iraq Border Dispute."

54. Tripp, 251–252.

55. U.S. Navy, "II: 'The Gathering Storm' – The Build-up of U.S. Forces," www.history.navy.mil. Richelson, Jeffrey T., ed., "Operation Desert Storm: Ten Years After," www.gwu.edu. "The Background to War."

56. Cheney, Richard B., "Defending Liberty in a Global Economy," speech, Jan 23, 1998, Singleton, Solveig and Daniel T. Griswold, eds., *Economic Casualties: How U.S. Foreign Policy Undermines Trade, Growth, and Liberty* (Washington, DC: Cato Institute, 1999), 21.

MAJOR SOURCES

Archives

Original papers and documents were accessed at several dozen archival repositories, record collections, and unprocessed files in England, the United States, Germany, and Israel. The challenging range of repositories spanned the gamut from governmental, military, and organizational archives to corporate and private files. The Iraqi governmental records are at press time, summer 2004, fundamentally unavailable, but much of the story can be reconstructed from other sources. Most of the repositories utilized are listed below, but space precludes a complete roster.

UNITED STATES

Columbia University Library Lehman Suite	New York, NY
Iraq Foundation Archives	Washington, DC
Jacob Rader Marcus Center, American Jewish Archives	Cincinnati, OH
League of Nations Archive (LoN), Harvard University	Cambridge, MA
Museum of the Oriental Institute Photo Archive	Chicago, IL
National Archives (NA)	College Park, MD
RG 59, Department of State	
RG 242/238, Records of U.S. Army War Crimes Trials in Europe	
Rockefeller Family Archives (RF)	Sleepy Hollow, NY
RG 1, Business Correspondence	
RG 2, Business Interests	
Urman Collection, Justice for Jews from Arab Countries (JJAC)	West Orange, NJ
YIVO	New York, NY

UNITED KINGDOM

British Library (BL), Oriental and India Office Collections	London
Military (L/MIL)	
Political and Secret (L/PS)	
British Motor Industry Heritage Trust	Coventry
BP Archives	Coventry
Anglo-Iranian Oil Company (AIOC) files	

Anglo-Persian Oil Company (APOC) files	
British Petroleum Company (BP) files	
Iraq Petroleum Company (IPC) files	
Turkish Petroleum Company (TPC) files	
Modern Records Centre, Warwick University	Coventry
Public Records Office (PRO)	London
Admiralty (ADM)	
Air Ministry (AIR)	
Board of Trade (BT)	
Cabinet Office (CAB)	
Colonial Office (CO)	
Foreign Office (FO)	
GCHQ (HW)	
German Foreign Ministry (GFM)	
Ministry of Fuel and Power (POWE)	
Prime Minister's Office (PREM)	
Treasury (T)	
War Office (WO)	
Robinson Library, University of New Castle upon Tyne	New Castle upon Tyne
Gertrude Bell Papers	

GERMANY

Berlin Documentation Center	Berlin
Bundesarchiv	Berlin
Institut für Zeitgeschichte	Munich

ISRAEL

Central Zionist Archives	Jerusalem
Government Press Office Photo Archive	Jerusalem
Hagana Archives	Tel Aviv
Israel State Archives	Jerusalem

POLAND

Auschwitz Museum Archives	Oswiecim

Libraries

Libraries are crucial to research on Iraq because each library maintains its own unique and often precious collection of obscure literature and local materials, including personal memoirs of diplomats and military men. In addition, many libraries maintain manuscript collections of original papers or organizational files. Most of the libraries we accessed are listed below, but space precludes a complete roster.

UNITED STATES

Alvin Sherman Library, Nova Southeastern University	Fort Lauderdale, FL
Asher Library, Spertus Institute of Jewish Studies	Chicago, IL

Blaustein Library, American Jewish Committee	New York, NY
Columbia University Library, Columbia University	New York, NY
Columbus Metropolitan Library	Columbus, OH
Emerson Library, Webster University	St. Louis, MO
Fenwick Library, George Mason University	Fairfax, VA
Gelman Library, George Washington University	Washington, DC
Harold B. Lee Library, Brigham Young University	Provo, UT
Harold Washington Library Center, Chicago Public Library	Chicago, IL
Helen A. Ganser Library, Millersville University	Millersville, PA
Hoover Institution on War, Revolution and Peace	Stanford, CA
Johnson Center Library, George Mason University	Fairfax, VA
Klau Library, Hebrew Union College	Cincinnati, OH
Lamont (Microform Library), Harvard University	Cambridge, MA
Lauinger Memorial Library, Georgetown University	Washington, DC
Libraries of the University of Wisconsin-Madison	Madison, WI
Library, Fontbonne University	St. Louis, MO
Library, U.S. Holocaust Memorial Museum	Washington, DC
Library of Congress	Washington, DC
Library of the Simon Wiesenthal Center	Los Angeles, CA
Meriam Library, California State University	Chico, CA
Monterey Institute of International Studies Library	Monterey, CA
Monterey County Public Library	Monterey, CA
Montgomery County Public Libraries	Rockville, MD
Mullen Library, Catholic University of America	Washington, DC
New York Public Library, Main Branch	New York, NY
New York Public Library, Science, Industry and Business	New York, NY
Olin Library, Washington University of St. Louis	St. Louis, MO
Perkins Library, Duke University	Durham, NC
Pius XII Memorial Library	St Louis, MO
Rebecca Crown Library, Dominican University	River Forest, IL
Rock Hill Public Library	Rock Hill, MO
Schaumburg Township District Library	Schaumburg, IL
St. Louis City Library	St. Louis, MO
St. Louis County Library	St. Louis, MO
Washington Research Library Consortium	Upper Marlboro, MD

UNITED KINGDOM

British Library	London
Camden Libraries, Holborn and Swiss Cottage Branches	London
Charing Cross Library, Westminster	London
Robinson Library, University of New Castle upon Tyne	New Castle upon Tyne
University of Warwick Library	Coventry
Wiener Library	London

PUBLISHED DIPLOMATIC PAPERS

Documents in British Foreign Policy (DBFP)
Documents in German Foreign Policy (DGFP)
Foreign Relations of the United States (FRUS)

Blech, Edward C., and Harry I. Sherwood, eds. *British & Foreign State Papers,* vol. 105 (1912). London: H.M. Stationery Office, 1915.

de L. Rush, Alan, and Jonathan Elliman, eds. *Records of the Hashemite Dynasties: A Twentieth Century Documentary History.* Slough, UK: Archive Editions, 1995.

de L. Rush, Alan, and Jane Priestland, eds. *Records of Iraq, 1914–1966,* vols. 8, 9. Slough, UK: Archive Editions, 2001.

Gooch, G. P., and Harold Temperly, eds. *British Documents on the Origins of the War, 1898–1914,* vol. 10, pt. 2: *The Last Years of Peace.* London: H.M. Stationery Office, 1926–1938.

Hurewitz, J. C., ed. *Diplomacy in the Near and Middle East,* vols. I–III. New York: Van Nostrand, 1956; Gerrards Cross, UK: Archive Editions, 1987.

Jarman, Robert L., ed. *Political Diaries of the Arab World: Iraq,* vol. 6: *1932–1947.* Slough, UK: Archive Editions, 1998.

GOVERNMENT DOCUMENTS

Committee on Foreign Relations, U.S. Senate. *A Select Chronology and Background Documents Relating to the Middle East.* Washington, DC: U.S. Government Printing Office, 1969.

Secondary Sources

Literally hundreds of books and journal articles were consulted, from personal memoirs to scholarly works, on a range of topics. It would be impossible to list them all. However, a few hundred of the salient volumes are listed below.

UNPUBLISHED MANUSCRIPTS

Allen, G. Donald. "Babylonian Mathematics."

Church, Matthew. "The Imperial Attachment to the Suez Canal from 1914 to 1945."

Englund, Robert K. "Proto-Cuneiform Account-Books and Journals," April 2004.

Englund, Robert K. Lecture, University of Connecticut, April 2004.

Justus, Carol F., dir. Numerals Project. Austin: University of Texas–Austin, 2004.

Kanwar, Ranvir Singh. "States, Firms, and Oil: British Policy, 1939–54," PhD diss, University of Warwick, 2000.

Longrigg, Stephen H. *The Origins and Early History of the Iraq Petroleum Company, Known from 1912 to 1929 as the Turkish Petroleum Company.* BP Archives, 1968.

BOOKS

Ahmed, Akbar S. *Discovering Islam: Making Sense of Muslim History and Society.* New York: Routledge & Kegan Paul, 1988.

Ali, Abdullah Yusuf, trans. *The Meaning of the Glorious Qur'n.* Cairo: Dar Al-Kitab Al-Masri, 1934.

Al-Tabari. *History of the World.* Albany, NY: State University of New York Press, 1985.

Allsen, Thomas T. *Culture and Conquest in Mongol Eurasia.* Cambridge, UK: Cambridge University Press, 2001.

Allsen, Thomas T. *Mongol Imperialism, The Policies of the Grand Qan Möngke in China, Russia, and the Islamic Lands, 1251–1259.* Berkeley, CA: University of California Press, 1987.

Antonius, George. *The Arab Awakening: The Story of the Arab National Movement.* New York: G. P. Putnam's Sons, 1946. Reprint, New York: Capricorn Books, 1965.

Armstrong, Karen. *Islam: A Short History*. New York: Modern Library, 2000.

Ataöv, Türkkaya, ed. *The Armenians in the Late Ottoman Period*. Ankara: The Council of Culture, Arts and Publications of the Grand National Assembly of Turkey, 2002.

Atarodi, Habibollah. *Great Powers, Oil and the Kurds in Mosul (Southern Kurdistan/Northern Iraq), 1910–1925*. Lanham, MD: University Press of America, 2003.

Balakian, Peter. *The Burning Tigris: The Armenian Genocide and America's Response*. New York: HarperCollins, 2003.

Bamberg, James. *The History of the British Petroleum Company: British Petroleum and Global Oil, 1950–1975: The Challenge of Nationalism*. Cambridge, UK: Cambridge University Press, 2000.

Bamberg, James. *The History of the British Petroleum Company*, vol. 2: *The Anglo-Iranian Years, 1928–1954*. Cambridge, UK: Cambridge University Press, 1994.

Barnett, Clifford R., et al. *Iran*. Herbert Harold Vreeland and Muriel B. Lechter, eds. New Haven, CT: Human Relations Area Files, 1957.

Bauer, Josef, Robert K. Englund, and Manfred Krebernik. *Mesopotamien: Späturuk- und Frühdynastische Zeit*. Waefler & Attinger, eds. Forthcoming.

Bell, J. Bowyer. *Terror Out of Zion: Irgun Zvai Leumi, LEHI, and the Palestine Underground, 1929–1941*. New York: St. Martin's Press, 1977.

Betts, Ernest. *The Bagging of Baghdad*. New York: John Lane, 1920.

Black, Edwin. *IBM and the Holocaust: The Strategic Alliance between Nazi Germany and America's Most Powerful Corporation*. New York: Crown, 2001.

Black, Edwin. *The Transfer Agreement: The Dramatic Story of the Pact between the Third Reich and Jewish Palestine*. Washington, DC: Dialog Press, 1999. Reprint, New York: Carroll & Graf, 2001.

Black, Edwin. *War against the Weak: Eugenics and America's Campaign to Create a Master Race*. New York: Four Walls Eight Windows, 2003.

Bloom, Jonathan, and Sheila Blair. *Islam: A Thousand Years of Faith and Power*. New Haven, CT: Yale University Press, 2002.

Brent, Peter. *Genghis Khan*. New York: McGraw-Hill, 1976.

Bright Jr., Arthur A. *The Electric-Lamp Industry: Technological Change and Economic Development from 1800 to 1947*. New York: Macmillan, 1949.

Buchanan, Sir George. *The Tragedy of Mesopotamia*. London: William Blackwood & Sons, 1938. Reprint, New York: AMS Press, 1974.

Busch, Briton Cooper. *Britain, India, and the Arabs, 1914–1921*. Berkeley, CA: University of California Press, 1971.

Calouste Gulbenkian Foundation. *Calouste Sarkis Gulbenkian, The Man and His Achievements*. Lisbon, Portugal: Calouste Gulbenkian Foundation, 1999.

Carley, Patricia. *Nagorno-Karabakh: Searching for a Solution*. Washington, DC: United States Institute of Peace, 1998.

Carpini, Fr. Giovanni di Plano. *The Story of the Mongols Whom We Call the Tartars (Historia Mongalorum quos nos Tartaros appellamus)*. Erik Hildinger, trans. Rome, 1252. Boston: Branden Publishing, 1996.

Cassels, Lavender. *The Struggle for the Ottoman Empire: 1717–1740*. New York: Thomas Y. Crowell, 1967.

Chambers, James. *The Devil's Horsemen: The Mongol Invasion of Europe*. New York: Atheneum, 1985.

Churchill, Randolph S. *Winston S. Churchill*, vol. 1: *Youth, 1874–1900 and Companion*. Boston: Houghton Mifflin, 1966.

Churchill, Randolph S. *Winston S. Churchill,* vol. 2: *Young Statesman, 1900–1914* and companion volume. Boston: Houghton Mifflin, 1967.

Clark, Arthur Tillotson. *To Baghdad with the British.* New York: D. Appleton, 1918.

Cleveland, William L. *A History of the Modern Middle East.* Boulder, CO: Westview Press, 2000.

Cohen, Stuart A. *British Policy in Mesopotamia, 1903–1914.* London: Ithaca Press, 1976.

Connell, John. *Wavell: Scholar and Soldier, to June 1941.* London: Collins, 1964.

Curtin, Jeremiah. *The Mongols, A History.* Boston: Little, Brown, 1908. Reprint, Cambridge, MA: Da Capo Press, 2003.

Dadrian, Vahakn N. *The History of the Armenian Genocide: Ethnic Conflict from the Balkans to Anatolia to the Caucasus.* Providence, RI: Berghahn Books, 1995.

Darrah, William C. *Pithole, the Vanished City: A Story of the Early Days of the Petroleum Industry.* Gettysburg, PA: William C. Darrah, 1972.

Dayan, Moshe. *Moshe Dayan: Story of My Life,* New York: William Morrow, 1976.

De Chair, Somerset. *The Golden Carpet.* New York: Harcourt, Brace, 1945.

Dols, Michael W. *The Black Death in the Middle East.* Princeton, NJ: Princeton University Press, 1977.

Donner, Fred McGraw. *The Early Islamic Conquests.* Princeton, NJ: Princeton University Press, 1981.

Donohoe, M. H. *With the Persian Expedition.* London: Edward Arnold, 1919.

Earle, Edward Mead. *Turkey, the Great Powers, and the Baghdad Railway: A Study in Imperialism.* New York: Macmillan, 1923.

Ellis, Edward S. and Charles F. Horne. *The Story of the Greatest Nations and the World's Famous Events,* vol. 1. New York: Auxiliary Educational League, 1921.

Elpeleg, Zvi. *The Grand Mufti: Haj Amin Al-Hussaini, Founder of the Palestinian National Movement.* David Harvey, trans.; Shmuel Himelstein, ed. London: Frank Cass, 1993.

Esposito, John L., ed. *Islam and Politics.* Syracuse, NY: Syracuse University Press, 1984.

Esposito, John L., ed. *The Oxford History of Islam.* New York: Oxford University Press, 1999.

Fagan, Brian M. *People of the Earth: An Introduction to World Prehistory.* Upper Saddle River, NJ: Prentice-Hall, 2001.

Faroqhi, Suraiya. *Approaching Ottoman History: An Introduction to the Sources.* Cambridge, UK: Cambridge University Press, 1999.

Faroqhi, Suraiya. *Subjects of the Sultans: Culture and Daily Life in the Ottoman Empire.* London: I. B. Tauris, 2000.

Farrington, Anthony. *Trading Places: The East India Company and Asia 1600–1834.* London: British Library, 2002.

Ferrier, R. W. *The History of the British Petroleum Company,* vol. 1: *The Developing Years, 1901–1932.* Cambridge, UK: Cambridge University Press, 1982.

Feuerstein, Georg, Subhash Kak, and David Frawley. *In Search of the Cradle of Civilization: New Light on Ancient India.* Wheaton, IL: Theosophical Publishing House, 1995.

Foran, John. *Fragile Resistance: Social Transformation in Iran from 1500 to the Revolution.* Boulder, CO: Westview Press, 1993.

Frum, David, and Richard Perle. *An End to Evil: How to Win the War on Terror.* New York: Random House, 2003.

Gat, Moshe. *The Jewish Exodus from Iraq, 1948–1951.* London: Frank Cass, 1997.

Gensicke, Klaus. *Der Mufti von Jerusalem, Amin el-Husseini, und die Nationalsozialisten.* Frankfurt am Main, Germany: Peter Lang, 1988.

Giddens, Paul H. *The Birth of the Oil Industry*. New York: Macmillan, 1938.

Gilbert, Martin. *Auschwitz and the Allies*. New York: Holt, Rinehart, and Winston, 1981.

Gilbert, Martin, ed. *Britain and Germany between the Wars*. New York: Barnes & Noble, 1967.

Gilbert, Martin. *The Holocaust: A History of the Jews of Europe during the Second World War*. New York: Henry Holt, 1987.

Gilbert, Martin. *Winston S. Churchill*, vol. 3: *The Challenge of War, 1914–1916* and companion volume. London: Heinemann, 1971.

Gilbert, Martin. *Winston S. Churchill*, vol. 4: *The Stricken World, 1917–1922* and companion volume. London: Heinemann, 1977.

Gilbert, Martin. *Winston S. Churchill*, vol. 5: *Prophet of Truth, 1922–1939* and three companion volumes. Boston: Houghton Mifflin, 1977.

Gilbert, Martin. *Winston S. Churchill*, vol. 6: *Finest Hour, 1939–1941* and companion volume. Boston: Houghton Mifflin, 1983.

Glubb, Sir John. *The Empire of the Arabs*. Englewood Cliffs, NJ: Prentice-Hall, 1963.

Glubb, Sir John. *The Story of the Arab Legion*. London: Hodder & Stoughton, 1948.

Goodwin, Jason. *Lords of the Horizons: A History of the Ottoman Empire*. New York: Picador, 1998.

Gottfried, Robert S. *The Black Death: Natural and Human Disaster in Medieval Europe*. New York: Free Press, 1953.

Gulbenkian, Calouste. *La Transcaucasie et la Peninsule D'Apcheron: Souvenirs de Voyage, 1890*. Paris: Librairie Hachette, 1891. Reprint, Lisbon, Portugal: Calouste Gulbenkian Foundation, 1989.

Gulbenkian, Nubar. *Portrait in Oil: The Autobiography of Nubar Gulbenkian*. New York: Simon & Schuster, 1965.

Hamidullah, M. *Introduction to Islam*. Chicago: Kazi Publications, 1981.

Heller, Joseph. *British Policy towards the Ottoman Empire, 1908–1914*. London: Frank Cass, 1983.

Hewins, Ralph. *Mr. Five Per Cent: The Biography of Calouste Gulbenkian*. London: Hutchinson, 1957.

Hitti, Philip K. *History of the Arabs, from the Earliest Times to the Present*. London: Macmillan, 1937. Reprint, New York: Palgrave Macmillan, 2002.

Holt, P. M., Ann K. S. Lambton, and Bernard Lewis, eds. *The Cambridge History of Islam*, vol. 1. Cambridge, UK: Cambridge University Press, 1970.

Hookham, Hilda. *Tamburlaine the Conqueror*. London: Hodder & Stoughton, 1962.

Horovitz, David Phillip. *Yitzhak Rabin: Soldier of Peace*. London: Halban, 1996.

Hourani, Albert. *A History of the Arab Peoples*. Cambridge, MA: Harvard University Press, 1991.

Ifrah, Georges. *The Universal History of Numbers, from Prehistory to the Invention of the Computer*. David Bellos, E. F. Harding, Sophie Wood, and Ian Monk, trans. New York: John Wiley & Sons, 2000.

Imber, Colin. *The Ottoman Empire, 1300–1650, The Structure of Power*. New York: Palgrave MacMillan, 2002.

Inalcik, Halil. *The Ottoman Empire: The Classical Age, 1300–1600*. Norman Itzkowits and Colin Imber, trans. London: Wiedenfeld and Nicholson, 1973.

Ireland, Phillip Willard. *Iraq: A Study in Political Development*. New York: Macmillan, 1938.

James, Lawrence. *The Golden Warrior: The Life and Legend of Lawrence of Arabia*. New York: Paragon House, 1993.

Jbarra, Taysir. *Palestinian Leader Hajj Amin Al-Husayni, Mufti of Jerusalem*. Princeton, NJ: Kingston Press, 1985.

Jonnes, Jill. *Empires of Light: Edison, Tesla, Westinghouse and the Race to Electrify the World*. New York: Random House, 2003.

Kafadar, Cemal. *Between Two Worlds: The Construction of the Ottoman State*. Berkeley, CA: University of California Press, 1995.

Kafesoglu, Ibrahim. *A History of the Seljuks: Ibrahim Kafesoglu's Interpretation and the Resulting Controversy*. Gary Leiser, ed. and trans. Carbondale, IL: Southern Illinois University Press, 1988.

Karsh, Efraim, and Inari Karsh. *Empires of the Sand: The Struggle for Mastery in the Middle East, 1789–1923*. Cambridge, MA: Harvard University Press, 1999.

Kelly, Marjorie. *Islam: The Religious and Political Life of a World Community*. New York: Praeger, 1984.

Kent, Marian. *Oil and Empire: British Policy and Mesopotamian Oil 1900–1920*. London: Macmillan, 1976.

Khadduri, Majid. *Independent Iraq: A Study in Iraqi Politics Since 1932*. London: Oxford University Press, 1951.

Khadduri, Majid. *Independent Iraq, 1932-1958: A Study in Iraqi Politics*. London: Oxford University Press, 1960.

Khalid, Rashid, Lisa Anderson, Muhammed Muslih, and Reeva S. Simon, eds. *The Origins of Arab Nationalism*. New York: Columbia University Press, 1991.

Khoury, Dina. *State and Provincial Society in the Ottoman Empire: Mosul, 1540–1834*. Cambridge, UK: Cambridge University Press, 1997.

Lord Kinross. *The Ottoman Centuries: The Rise and Fall of the Turkish Empire*. New York: William Morrow, 1977.

Koprülü, M. Fuad. *The Origins of the Ottoman Empire*. Gary Leiser, ed. and trans. New York: State University of New York Press, 1992.

Landau, Jacob. *Abdul-Hamid's Palestine*. Jerusalem, Israel: Carta, 1979.

Leland, F. W. *With the M. T. in Mesopotamia*. London: Foster Groom, 1920.

Levin, Itamar. *Locked Doors: The Seizure of Jewish Property in Arab Countries*. Rachel Neiman, trans. Westport, CT: Praeger, 2001.

Lewis, Bernard. *The Assassins: A Radical Sect in Islam*. New York: Basic Books, 1968.

Lewis, Bernard. *The Crisis of Islam: Holy War and Unholy Terror*. New York: Modern Library, 2003.

Lewis, Bernard, ed. *Islam and the Arab World*. London: Alfred A. Knopf, 1976.

Lewis, Bernard, ed. and trans. *Islam, from the Prophet Mohammed to the Capture of Constantinople*, vol. I: *Politics and War*. New York: Oxford University Press, 1987.

Lodwick, John, with D. H. Young. *Gulbenkian, An Interpretation of "The Richest Man in the World."* Garden City, NY: Doubleday, 1958.

Loftus, John, and Mark Aarons, *The Secret War against the Jews: How Western Espionage Betrayed the Jewish People*. New York: St Martin's Griffin, 1994.

Longrigg, Stephen. *Four Centuries of Modern Iraq*. Oxford: Clarendon Press, 1925. Reprint, Farnborough, UK: Gregg International Publishers, 1968.

Longrigg, Stephen. *The Middle East: A Social Geography*. London: Gerald Duckworth, 1963.

Longrigg, Stephen. *Oil in the Middle East: Its Discovery and Development*. London: Oxford University Press, 1968.

Longrigg, Stephen. *Syria and Lebanon under French Mandate*. London: Oxford University Press, 1958.

MacMillan, Margaret. *Paris 1919: Six Months That Changed the World*. New York: Random House, 2001.

Macqueen, James G. *Babylon*. New York: Praeger, 1965.

Majd, Mohammad Goli. *The Great Famine and Genocide in Persia, 1917–1919*. Lanham, MD: University Press of America, 2003.

Manz, Beatrice Forbes. *The Rise and Rule of Tamerlane*. Cambridge UK: Cambridge University Press, 1989.

Marlowe, John. *Late Victorian: The Life of Sir Arnold Talbot Wilson*. London: Cresset Press, 1967.

Marr, Phebe. *Iraq: A Profile*. Boulder, CO: Perseus Books, 1986.

Marr, Phebe. *The Modern History of Iraq*. Boulder, CO: Westview Press, 2003.

Marr, Phebe. *Revolutionary Regimes in the Middle East: A Comparative Study*. Westport, CT: Greenwood Press, 1982.

Marr, Phebe, and William Lewis, eds. *Riding the Tiger: The Middle East Challenge after the Cold War*. Boulder, CO: Westview Press, 1993.

Marsden, Phillip. *The Crossing Place: A Journey among the Armenians*. New York: Kodansha International, 1995.

Mattar, Philip. *The Mufti of Jerusalem: Al-Hajj Amin al-Husayni and the Palestinian National Movement*. New York: Columbia University Press, 1988.

Mazar, Amihai. *Archaeology of the Land of the Bible, 10,000–586 B.C.E.* New York: Doubleday, 1992.

McCarthy, Justin. *The Ottoman Peoples and the End of Empire*. London: Arnold, 2001.

Miller, Donald E., and Lorna Touryan Miller. *Survivors: An Oral History of the Armenian Genocide*. Berkeley, CA: University of California Press, 1993.

Miller, Geoffrey. *The Millstone: British Naval Policy in the Mediterranean, 1900–1914, The Commitment to France and British Intervention in the War*. Hull, UK: University of Hull, 1999.

Miller, Geoffrey. *Straits: British Policy towards the Ottoman Empire and the Origins of the Dardanelles Campaign*. Hull, UK: University of Hull, 1997.

Moberly, Brigadier General F. J. *History of the Great War: The Campaign in Mesopotamia, 1914–1918*, vols. I–III. London: H. M. Stationery Office, 1925.

Morgan, David. *The Mongols*. Oxford, UK: Basil Blackwell, 1986.

Morgenthau, Henry. *Ambassador Morgenthau's Story*. Garden City, NY: Doubleday, Page, 1918.

Nakash, Yitzhak. *The Shi'is of Iraq*. Princeton, NJ: Princeton University Press, 1994.

Neff, E. Richard, ed. *Oil History: A Selected and Annotated Bibliography*. Houston, TX: International Association of Drilling Contractors, 1995.

Negev, Avraham, ed. *Archaeological Encyclopedia of the Holy Land*. Englewood Cliffs, NJ: Prentice-Hall, 1986.

Nicolle, David. *The Mongol Warlords: Genghis Khan, Kublai Khan, Hulegu, Tamerlane*. Poole, UK: Firebird Books, 1990.

Nissen, Hans J., Peter Damerow, and Robert K. Englund. *Archaic Bookkeeping: Early Writing and Techniques of Economic Administration in the Ancient Near East*. Paul A. Larsen, trans. Chicago: University of Chicago Press, 1993.

NIV Exhaustive Concordance. Grand Rapids, MI: Zondervan, 1990.

NIV Study Bible, 10th Anniversary Edition. Grand Rapids, MI: Zondervan, 1995.

Organization for Economic Cooperation and Development. *International Tax Avoidance and Evasion: Four Related Studies*. Washington, DC: OECD Publications and Information Centre, 1987.

Palmer, Alan. *The Banner of Battle: The Story of the Crimean War.* London: Weidenfeld and Nicolson, 1987.

Palmer, Alan. *The Decline and Fall of the Ottoman Empire.* New York: M. Evans, 1992.

Phillips, E. D. *The Mongols,* New York: Praeger, 1969.

Postgate, J. N. *Early Mesopotamia: Society and Economy at the Dawn of History.* London: Routledge, 1994.

Pritchard, J. B., ed. *Ancient Near Eastern Texts Relating to the Old Testament.* Princeton, NJ: Princeton University Press, 1969.

Quataert, Donald, ed. *Consumption Studies and the History of the Ottoman Empire, 1550–1922.* Albany, NY: State University of New York Press, 2000.

Quataert, Donald. *The Ottoman Empire, 1700–1922.* Cambridge, UK: Cambridge University Press, 2000.

Quataert, Donald. *Ottoman Manufacturing in the Age of the Industrial Revolution.* Cambridge, UK: Cambridge University Press, 1993.

Rashid, Ahmed. *Taliban, Militant Islam, Oil and Fundamentalism in Central Asia,* New Haven, CT: Yale University Press, 2001.

Ratchnevksy, Paul. *Genghis Khan, His Life and Legacy.* Thomas Nivison Haining, ed. and trans. Oxford, UK: Basil Blackwell, 1991.

Riley-Smith, Jonathan, ed. *The Oxford History of the Crusades.* Oxford, UK: Oxford University Press, 1999.

Ritchie, Berry. *Portrait in Oil: An Illustrated History of BP.* London: James & James, 1995.

Robinson, Francis, ed. *The Cambridge Illustrated History of the Islamic World.* Cambridge, UK: Cambridge University Press, 1996.

Rodengen, Jeffrey L. *The Legend of Halliburton.* Fort Lauderdale, FL: Write Stuff Syndicate, 1996.

Roe, Sir Thomas. *The Embassy of Sir Thomas Roe to India, 1615–1619,* vols. 1 and 2. William Foster, ed. London: Bedford Press, 1899.

Rogan, Eugene L., and Avi Shlaim, eds. *The War for Palestine.* New York: Cambridge University Press, 2001.

Roth, Martha T. *Law Collections from Mesopotamia and Asia Minor.* Atlanta, GA: Scholars Press, 1997.

Roux, Georges. *Ancient Iraq.* New York: Penguin Putnam, 1992.

Sachar, Howard M. *A History of Israel: From the Rise of Zionism to Our Time.* New York: Alfred A. Knopf, 1981.

Sasson, Jack M., ed. *Civilizations of the Ancient Near East.* New York: Scribner, 1995.

Saunders, J. J. *The History of the Mongol Conquests.* Philadelphia, PA: University of Pennsylvania Press, 1971.

Schechtman, Joseph B. *The Mufti and the Fuehrer: The Rise and Fall of Haj Amin el-Husseini.* New York: Thomas Yoseloff, 1965.

Schmandt-Besserat, Denise. *Before Writing.* Austin, TX: University of Texas Press, 1992.

Schonfield, Hugh. *The Suez Canal in Peace and War, 1869–1969.* Coral Gables, FL: University of Miami Press, 1969.

Schweitzer, Peter P., Megan Biesele, and Robert K. Hitchcock, eds. *Hunters and Gatherers in the Modern World: Conflict, Resistance, and Self-Determination.* New York: Berghahn Books, 2000.

Shaw, Stanford J. *The History of the Ottoman Empire and Modern Turkey,* vol. I: *Empire of the Gazis: The Rise and Decline of the Ottoman Empire, 1280–1808.* Cambridge, UK: Cambridge University Press, 1976.

Shaw, Stanford J. and Ezel Kural Shaw. *The History of the Ottoman Empire and Modern*

Turkey, vol. II: *Reform, Revolution, and Republic: The Rise of Modern Turkey, 1808–1975.* Cambridge, UK: Cambridge University Press, 1977.

Sheikh, M. Saeed. *Islamic Philosophy.* London: Octagon Press, 1982.

Shulewitz, Malka Hillel, ed. *The Forgotten Millions: The Modern Jewish Exodus from Arab Lands.* London: Cassel, 1999.

Sicker, Martin. *The Islamic World in Ascendancy: From the Arab Conquests to the Siege of Vienna.* Westport, CT: Praeger, 2000.

Singleton, Solveig, and Daniel T. Griswold, eds. *Economic Casualties: How U.S. Foreign Policy Undermines Trade, Growth, and Liberty.* Washington, DC: Cato Institute, 1999.

Slater, Robert. *Rabin of Israel.* New York: St. Martin's Press, 1993.

Sluglett, Peter. *Britain in Iraq, 1914–1932.* London: Ithaca Press, 1976.

Smith, Roy C., and Ingo Walter. *Global Banking.* New York: Oxford University Press, 1997.

Spandounes, Theodore. *On the Origins of the Ottoman Emperors.* Donald M. Nicol, ed. and trans. Rome, 1538. Reprint, New York: Cambridge University Press, 1997.

Spuler, Bertold. *History of the Mongols, Based on Eastern and Western Accounts of the Thirteenth and Fourteenth Centuries.* Helga and Stuart Drummond, trans. Berkeley, CA: University of California Press, 1972.

Stillman, Norman A. *The Jews of Arab Lands: A History and Source Book.* Philadelphia, PA: Jewish Publication Society of America, 1979.

Tarbell, Ida M. *The History of the Standard Oil Company.* New York: Macmillan, 1904. Reprint, Gloucester, MA: Peter Smith, 1963.

Tauber, Eliezer. *The Arab Movements in World War I.* London: Frank Cass, 1993.

Teveth, Shabtai. *Moshe Dayan: The Soldier, the Man, the Legend.* Leah and David Zinder, trans. Boston: Houghton Mifflin, 1973.

Townsend, Charles Vere Ferrers. *My Campaign,* vols. I and II. New York: James A. McCann, 1920.

Toynbee, Arnold, J., ed. *The Treatment of Armenians in the Ottoman Empire.* London: Hodder & Stoughton, 1916.

Tripp, Charles. *A History of Iraq.* Cambridge, UK: Cambridge University Press, 2000.

Von Hammer-Purgstall, Joseph, ed. *The History of the Assassins.* Oswald Charles Wood, trans. London: Smith & Elder, 1835. Reprint, New York: Burt Franklin, 1968.

Wall, Bennet H. *Growth in a Changing Environment: A History of Standard Oil Company (New Jersey) and Exxon Corporation, 1950–1975.* New York: McGraw-Hill, 1988.

Wallach, Janet. *Desert Queen.* New York: Anchor Books, 1996.

Warner, Geoffrey. *Iraq and Syria, 1941.* Newark, DE: University of Delaware Press, 1974.

Wasserstein, Bernard. *Britain and the Jews of Europe, 1939–1945.* Oxford, UK: Oxford University Press, 1979.

Weatherford, Jack. *Genghis Khan and the Making of the Modern World.* New York: Crown, 2004.

Weizmann, Chaim. *Trial and Error: The Autobiography of Chaim Weizmann.* New York: Harper & Brothers, 1949.

Wellhausen, J. *The Arab Kingdom and Its Fall.* Margaret Graham Weir, trans. Beirut, Lebanon: Khayats, 1963.

Wilson, Sir Arnold T. *A Clash of Loyalties: Mesopotamia, 1917–1920, a Personal Record.* London: Oxford University Press, 1931.

Wilson, Sir Arnold T. *Loyalties: Mesopotamia, 1914–1917, a Personal Record.* London: Oxford University Press, 1930.

Wheatcroft, Andrew. *The Ottomans: Dissolving Images.* London: Viking, 1995.

White, Gerald T. *Formative Years in the Far West: A History of Standard Oil Company of California and Predecessors through 1919.* New York: Appleton-Century-Crofts, 1962.

Yapp, M. E. *Strategies of British India: Britain, Iran and Afghanistan, 1798–1850.* Oxford, UK: Clarendon Press, 1980.

Yaron, Reuven. *The Laws of Eshnunna.* Jerusalem, Israel: Magnes Press, Hebrew University, 1969.

Yergin, Daniel. *The Prize: The Epic Quest for Oil, Money and Power.* New York: Free Press, 1991.

ELECTRONIC BOOKS

Benderly, Beryl L., et al. *Area Handbook for Iraq.* Washington, DC: U.S. Government Printing Office, 1971.

Pages of Muslim History, www.themuslimhistory.info/.

Xenophon. *Cyropaedia.* H. G. Dakyns, trans. Champaign, IL: Gutenberg Project, 2002. www.Gutenberg.net.

JOURNALS AND PERIODICALS

American Journal of Archaeology
Annals of the American Academy of Political and Social Science
The Atlantic Monthly
British Journal of Middle Eastern Studies
Bulletin (British Society for Middle Eastern Studies)
Bulletin of the Business Historical Society
Bulletin of the School of Oriental Studies, University of London
Bulletin of the School of Oriental and African Studies, University of London
Business History Review
Current Anthropology
Economic Geography
The Economic History Review
The English Historical Review
Evolutionary Anthropology
The Geographical Journal
Harvard Journal of Asiatic Studies
The Hispanic American Historical Review
Historia Scientarum
The Historical Journal
The Historical Review
The History Teacher
Insight: News & Views for the Process, Power and Offshore Industries
International Affairs
International Journal of Middle Eastern Studies
International Organization
Journal of Contemporary History
The Journal of Economic History
Journal of Field Archaeology
The Journal of Military History
The Journal of Modern History

Journal of Near Eastern Studies
The Journal of Political Economy
Journal of the American Oriental Society
Journal of World Prehistory
Military Affairs
The Mississippi Valley Historical Review
Past and Present
PMLA
Political Science Quarterly
The Quarterly Journal of Economics
The Scientific Monthly
Slavic Review
Smithsonian Magazine
Speculum: A Journal of Mediaeval Studies
Transactions of the American Philosophical Society
Wiener Library Bulletin

NEWSPAPERS, MAGAZINES, WIRE SERVICES, AND OTHER MEDIA

ABC News
British Broadcasting Corporation (BBC)
Cable News Network (CNN)
CBS News
The Guardian
Jewish Telegraphic Agency (JTA)
New York Times (NYT)
Public Broadcasting System (PBS)
Sky News
Time magazine
Times (London)
Wall Street Journal (WSJ)
Washington Post (WP)

DOCUMENTARIES

Sanders, Richard, and Jeff Goldberg, producers. Sanders, Richard, director. *Frontline,* "The Invasion of Iraq." PBS, 2003.

Electronic Sources

Electronic and digital sources were used extensively. Modern research cannot be efficiently undertaken without the use of Internet search engines as well as institutional databases. However, while Internet research is essential to historical investigation, the caveat remains high that the Web is proudly unreliable, including some web sites operated by respected academic entities. At the same time, I found certain official organizational or governmental sites important, as were a very limited number of private research sites. Hence, while I consulted and searched through hundreds, perhaps thousands, of web sites, only a precious few of the most reliable are listed below. On the other hand, the digital databases of documents and publications that I used were pivotal to my work.

DIGITAL ARCHIVES AND DATABASES

EDGAR Online Pro
Foreign Relations of the United States, Electronic Facsimile
JSTOR, The Scholarly Journal Archive
Lexis-Nexis
New York Times Historical Digital Archive
ProQuest
Questia Digital Library
Times (London) Digital Archive
Wall Street Journal Historical Digital Archive
Washington Post Historical Digital Archive
WorldCat/OCLC FirstSearch

WEB SITES

Avalon Law Project, Yale University Law School, www.yale.edu/lawweb/avalon
BBC News, news.bbc.co.uk
British Library, www.bl.uk
British Museum, www.thebritishmuseum.ac.uk
Cave of Chauvet-Pont-d'Arc, www.culture.gouv.fr/culture/arcnat/chauvet/en/
Cave of Lascaux, www.culture.gouv.fr/culture/arcnat/lascaux/en/
Fathom Archive, www.fathom.com
First World War Online, www.firstworldwar.com
Ft. Campbell, www.campbell.army.mil
The Gertrude Bell Papers, www.gerty.ncl.ac.uk
The Gutenberg Project, www.promo.net/pg/
The Holocaust Resource, www.nizkor.org
The Irgun History, http://www.etzel.org.il
The Jewish Agency for Israel, http://www.jafi.org.il
The Jewish Virtual Library, www.jewishvirtuallibrary.org
The Knesset, knesset.gov.il
The League of Nations Photo Archive, University of Indiana, www.indiana.edu/~league/
Louvre Museum, www.louvre.fr
Metropolitan Museum of Art, www.metmuseum.org
National Archives and Records Administration, www.archives.gov
National Science Foundation, www.nsf.gov
The Numerals Project, University of Texas, Austin, www.utexas.edu
PBS: *Frontline,* www.pbs.org/wgbh/pages/frontline/
The Perseus Project, Tufts University, www.perseus.tufts.edu
PORT: The Maritime Information Gateway, www.port.nmm.ac.uk
Public Records Office, www.nationalarchives.gov.uk
The Road Map Collectors Association, www.petrolmaps.co.uk.
The Silk Road Foundation, www.silk-road.com
Third U.S. Army/U.S. Armed Forces Central Command, www.arcent.army.mil
Trenches on the Web: An Internet History of the Great War, www.worldwar1.com
U.S. Army Center for Military History, www.army.mil/cmh-pg/
The U.S. Geological Survey, www.usgs.gov
The World War I Document Archive, www.lib.byu.edu/~rdh/wwi/

INDEX